Kabbalah

MOSHE IDEL

Kabbalah *New Perspectives*

YALE UNIVERSITY PRESS
NEW HAVEN AND LONDON

Designed by Nancy Ovedovitz and set in Garamond No. 3 type by The Publishing Nexus Incorporated, Guilford, Connecticut.
Printed in the United States of America by Vail-Ballou Press, Inc., Binghamton, New York.

Library of Congress Cataloging-in-Publication Data

Idel, Moshe, 1947–
Kabbalah : new perspectives.
Bibliography: p.
Includes index.
1. Cabala—History. I. Title.
BM526.I338 1988 296.1'6 87–12137
ISBN 0–300–03860–7 (alk. paper)

The paper in this book meets the guidelines for permanence and durability of the Committee on Production Guidelines for Book Longevity of the Council on Library Resources.

10 9 8 7 6 5 4 3 2 1

To Shoshanah,
Sarit, Ofrah, and Ḥemdah
with love

CONTENTS

PREFACE

Habent sua fata libelli. This work enjoyed a special fate even before it became a book. The idea of my writing a comprehensive study on Kabbalah emerged in a midnight discussion with my friends Professor Ivan Marcus of the Jewish Theological Seminary of America and Professor David Ruderman of Yale University. Since that discussion, which took place at Cambridge, Massachusetts, in 1984, the initial idea underwent several substantive changes until it took the present form. A first draft of this book was submitted at a colloquium organized by the Jewish Theological Seminary in the summer of 1986 as part of that institution's centennial events. Owing to the kind interest of Professor Gershon Cohen, the former chancellor of the seminary, and Professor Ray Scheindlin, the provost of the seminary, and Professors Marcus and Ruderman, the colloquium was designed to include about thirty American scholars of Judaica and general mysticism who discussed and argued the content of this work. Both their criticism and their encouragement contributed greatly to the final draft. The hospitality of the seminary community, the careful organization of the colloquium, and the interest of the participants came together in a way that was, at least for me, a unique experience.

Especially helpful were the remarks and suggestions I received from Professors Ewert Cousins, Louis Dupré, Michael Fishbane, Arthur Hyman, and Bernard MacGinn. Two well-known scholars were kind enough to undertake a meticulous perusal of the manuscript, suggesting important corrections and improvements of both style and the content. The late Professor Alexander Altmann devoted much energy and wisdom to proposing numerous suggestions concerning all the chapters of the book; Professor Morton Smith kindly contributed his vast knowledge regarding most of the chapters. Helpful discussions with Professor Geoffrey Hartman, Professor Yehuda Liebes, Professor Shelomo Pines, and Professor Isadore Twersky contributed to the formulations of several issues. For any mistakes still occurring in the presentation, I alone am responsible.

The writing of this book would have been impossible without the constant and generous assistance of the Institute of Microfilms of Hebrew Manuscripts, which is part of the National and University Library in Jerusalem. The institute, which became my second home and whose staff is famous for its efficiency, helped me in numerous ways, for which I would like to thank them. The National Library in Jerusalem, the Widener and Andover libraries in Cambridge, Massachusetts, and the library of the Jewish Theological Seminary in New York provided indispensable material for my researches. Part of the research was performed with the generous assistance of grants from the Memorial Foundation for Jewish Culture.

The time needed for studying and writing was diverted from the members of my family, and my dedication of this book to them is only a feeble recognition of their contribution. Jonathan Chipman kindly undertook the task of typing two drafts and improving my English; his devotion to this work contributed to its accomplishment. Finally, Yale University Press, and especially Charles Grench, changed what could have been a frustrating experience into a very pleasant cooperation whose fruit is now accessible to the reader.

INTRODUCTION

This study is based upon the assumption that there are two major trends in Kabbalah: the theosophical-theurgical and the ecstatic. This distinction is confirmed both by a phenomenological analysis of the Kabbalistic material and by the Kabbalists' own self-awareness. The first type encompasses two central subjects: theosophy—a theory of the elaborate structure of the divine world—and the ritualistic and experiential way of relating to the divinity in order to induce a state of harmony. This is a highly theocentric form of religiousness that, while not ignoring the needs of the human being, tends to conceive of religious perfection as instrumental for exerting effective influence on high. On the other hand, ecstatic Kabbalah is highly anthropocentric, envisioning the mystical experience of the individual as itself the *summum bonum*, regardless of the possible impact of this mystical status on the inner harmony of the Divine.

This distinction involves different types of religiousness, transcending the question of interest in various themes or clusters of themes. The major issues discussed in ecstatic Kabbalah—such as *devekut*, the importance of isolation, or the centrality of letter combination—are far more than themes treated in a scholastic manner. Rather, they are cardinal matters that strongly molded the *via mystica* of the ecstatic Kabbalist; he was practically oriented to mystical goals other than those of his fellow, the theosophical-theurgical Kabbalist.

I now turn to the evidence of the Kabbalistic sources. According to the characterization of the Kabbalah by an early fourteenth-century Kabbalist,[1] the topics dealt with by this lore are the nature of the ten Sefirot and the mystical meaning of the commandments, which is an excellent definition of theosophical-theurgical Kabbalah.

On the other hand, Abraham Abulafia, the main representative of ecstatic Kabbalah, described his Kabbalah as focused upon the divine names, in contradistinction to what he considered to be a lower type of Kabbalah, referred to by him as "the way of the Sefirot," evidently a reference to the theosophical Kabbalah.[2]

The differences between the two kinds, however, are not merely a matter of self-perception or a scholar imposing his own categories on the material; the historical development of the two trends itself confirms the necessity for a clear distinction between them. From the very beginning, the ecstatic Kabbalah was attacked by a major representative of theosophical-theurgical Kabbalah; the first clash between Kabbalists was a sharp criticism of Abulafia's prophetic and messianic activity, as well as of his Kabbalistic theory, issued by R. Solomon ben Abraham ibn Adret, a leading figure of theosophical Kabbalah.[3] This attack generated a sharp reaction on the part of Abulafia, who noted the theological danger inherent in the doctrine of the ten Sefirot as divine potencies and compared some Kabbalists, probably including Adret, to the Christians who believed in the Trinity.[4] The result of this controversy was the exclusion of ecstatic Kabbalah from Spain, which became from the 1280s onward the scene of the most important developments within theosophical-theurgical Kabbalah. The ecstatic trend migrated to Italy and the Orient, where it developed in a Muslim ambience,[5] strikingly different in its mystical conceptions from the Christian environment of the theosophical-theurgical Kabbalah.

Thus, the broad domain of Kabbalistic experiences comprised two major types of religiousness, each with its own particular focus. For a better understanding of the Kabbalistic phenomena, it will be helpful to deal with the two types separately before reconstructing the basic elements of each.

Rather than concentrate upon the Kabbalistic schools—or trends, as Gershom Scholem designated them—and their historical sequence, I will take a phenomenological approach that will deal primarily with the major religious foci of the Kabbalah—their nature, significance, emergence, and development. Instead of presenting a historical sequence of Kabbalists or of ideas, I adopt an essentialist attitude to the contents of Kabbalistic material that places greater emphasis upon their religious countenance than on their precise location in place and time. Such issues as esotericism versus exotericism, innovation versus conservatism, theocentrism versus anthropocentrism, the role of theurgy versus that of mystical union, philosophy versus Kabbalah, mystical salvation of the individual versus national eschatology—all are parameters as significant as the temporal and spatial data that delineate any particular Kabbalistic text. The interrelationships among these various spiritual components of Kabbalistic texts constitute the fundamental structure or texture of one Kabbalistic system as opposed to another. Therefore, it is as fruitful to discuss Kabbalistic phenomena in contradistinction to one another as to give a chronological account. The unfolding of the key concepts that characterized and directed Kabbalistic activity and thought, their exposition as atemporal modes, and the understanding of their interplay in various Kabbalistic schools is the "inner" history of Kabbalah or of Jewish mysticism, just as the temporal description can be considered the "outer" history.

As we shall see below[6] the theurgical approach was part of the classical rabbinic conception of the commandments and could justifiably be regarded as an important rationale for the *mizvot* that, inter alia, helped motivate the persistent observance of the commandments by Jews. This theocentric attitude assumed an "open" theology or theosophy, conditioned by the dynamics of human activity; centered on the halakhah, it was a strictly nomian system and, consequently, exoterically open to all Jews and therefore obligatory. The theurgical performance of *mizvot* did not include dangerous or ecstatic moments and could be regarded as part of what Max Kadushin described as "normal mysticism." Medieval Kabbalah, which elaborated this approach, had to articulate the precise correspondence of the commandments to the theosophical realm, so that a detailed theosophy became much more central for the Kabbalists than for their predecessors. I want to emphasize that theosophical motifs and structures also existed among the Jews in ancient times; the relationship between them and the commandments seems to have been implicit, as demonstrated by the correspondence between *ma'amarot* and *dibberot*.[7] These theosophical structures were effectively suppressed by the rabbinic authorities, however, who focused their literary activity on the presentation and elaboration of the halakhah rather than on its conceptual superstructure. Speculative or mystical, metahalakhic issues, as they were designated by Isadore Twersky, were regarded as esoteric. The theosophical Kabbalah, which presumably inherited these ancient traditions, structured them into complex systems by which the specific theurgical meaning of each commandment was specified.

On this ground, it is easy to understand why the emergence of more complicated theosophies was accompanied by the composition of larger commentaries on the mystical rationale of the commandments.[8] Indeed, the bulk of thirteenth-century Kabbalistic literature was dedicated to *ta'amey ha-mizvot*. *Sefer ha-Bahir* includes several important discussions on the theurgical meaning of such commandments as "sacrifice," "prayer," "priestly blessing."[9] R. Isaac the Blind had already composed a lost work dealing with this subject or, at least, transmitted mystical traditions that were cited in his name by later Kabbalists.[10] R. 'Ezra of Gerona devoted a large part of his *Commentary on the Song of Songs* to the systematic treatment of the commandments, which constituted a treatise in itself. Extensive discussions on this topic are to be found, too, in the works of R. 'Azriel, where the prayer liturgy is Kabbalistically interpreted, as are the sacrifices and the answering of "'Amen." The issue of prayer seems to have been especially important to the early Kabbalists, preceding R. 'Azriel, as indicated by short remarks of R. Abraham ben David and of R. Jacob of Lunel, and particularly by R. Yehudah ben Yakar's *Commentary on the Prayer.* The first full-fledged Kabbalistic treatment of this issue, however, seems to have been done by R. 'Azriel, who integrated within his commentary the views of R. Isaac the Blind and others, paralleling some terms and concepts recurring in the literature close in time and subject matter to the *Book of 'Iyyun.* R. 'Azriel's contemporary, R. Jacob ben Sheshet, wrote polemically on the significance of the prayer, attempting to counteract the philosophical underestimation of the ritualistic performance of this commandment.[11] Naḥmanides' Kabbalah seems to have revolved uniquely around the Kabbalistical understanding of the commandments,[12] although he only tantalizingly hinted at the existence of such a meaning, without disclosing its details.

The golden age of the Kabbalistic *ta'amey miẓvot*, however, occurred during the last two decades of the thirteenth century. A creative time also in other kinds of literary activity, this period generated an immense number of folios dealing with our topic, for this literary genre had been cultivated by most of the leading Kabbalists in Spain. An interesting commentary on the commandments spuriously attributed to R. Eliezer ben Nathan, *Ma'amar ha-Sekhel*, was composed during this period and included some important Kabbalistic discussions. Moses de Leon's *Sefer ha-Rimmon*, R. Joseph Gikatilla's *Kelaley ha-Miẓvot*,[13] and several shorter discussions of particular commandments were disseminated in printed works and manuscripts. R. Joseph of Hamadan's work, or works,[14] on *Ta'amey ha-miẓvot*; an anonymous Kabbalistical commentary on this subject; the lengthy discussions in the *Zohar*, which included not only a special treatise on the issue[15] but also numerous elaborations—all these and more unidentified manuscript materials apparently from this period are ample evidence of a renaissance of interest in the rationales of the commandments.

Nor did this phenomenon cease at the turn of the century. R. Menaḥem Recanati's commentary on *Ta'amey ha-Miẓvot* and on the prayer at the beginning of the fourteenth century and R. David ben Yehudah he-Ḥasid's *'Or Zaru'a* on the prayer and later on the *Ra'ya Meheimna* (the later zoharic stratum composed under the influence of R. Joseph of Hamadan's work mentioned above) were influential works that continued the impetus of the previous generation. In the early fifteenth century, the *Sefer ha-Kaneh*, a Kabbalistic classic written in Byzantium, dealt exclusively with the rationale of the commandments, and at the end of the century in Russia, R. Moses of Kiev compiled his *Shoshan Sodat*, which included numerous Kabbalistical treatments of the *miẓvot*. At the beginning of the sixteenth century, R. Joseph of Hamadan's work was circulated under the name of R. Isaac Farḥi,[16] and other works, such as R. Isaac Shani's *Meah She'arim*,[17] R. Meir ibn Gabbay's *Tola'at Ya'akov*, and R. David ben Zimra's *Meẓudat David*,[18] continued to reflect the impact of Spanish Kabbalah. With the emergence of the Lurianic system, a large exegetical literature of commandments and prayer was produced that reinterpreted the ritual and the significance of the *miẓvot* in terms of Lurianic theosophical concepts. Lurianic writings on this theme remained the last major Kabbalistic production in this literary genre, because Sabbatianism was not interested in commandments and because the interest in theosophy and theurgy declined in Ḥasidic mysticism. Important as they may be, such oeuvres as *Ḥemdat Yamim*, R. Menaḥem Mendel of Lubavitch's *Derekh Miẓvotekha,* and R. Isaac Yehudah Safrin of Komarno's *'Oẓar ha-Torah* generally presented Lurianic explanations, the last two on occasion incorporating Ḥasidic perspectives.

We can conclude by emphasizing that, just as each major development in the field of Kabbalistic theosophy produced its commentary on prayer,[19] so with the commandments in general. As I have already pointed out, the theurgical-theosophical Kabbalists were not interested in extreme types of *devekut*, their religious focus being the Kabbalistic performance of the *miẓvot*.

Quite different was the phenomenological structure of the other major focus in Jewish mysticism, the mystical-ecstatical trend. Its first clear state is to be found in the Heikhalot literature,[20] where the use of anomian techniques was intended to induce paranormal experiences of ascent to the realm of *Merkavah* and contemplation of the Divinity. It is worth emphasizing that this type of contemplation was not a regular response to the request of the Divine, as were the commandments, nor was God seen as the beneficiary of this kind of human activity. It was mostly a human initiative that brought the individual to undertake the perilous path of ascending to the high for the sake of attaining an extraordinary and fascinating experience. In contrast to rabbinic theurgy, Heikhalot ecstasy was fraught with dreadful dangers that threatened to annihilate the unworthy mystic. Whereas the theurgical interpretation of the commandments did not detract from their fulfillment by ordinary people, the ecstatic nature of the path of Heikhalot literature made it usually, although not always,[21] appropriate only to the elite few. Many of these features were preserved in Ashkenazic Ḥasidism, where the existence of an anomian technique was coupled with that of "prophetical" experiences that naturally were also individualistic in their exceptional nature. Like their ancient predecessors, the Ashkenazic masters employed divine names rather than halakhic precepts in order to obtain their mystical revelations or visions.

The next stage was the ecstatic Kabbalah, which was influenced by Ashkenazic mystical techniques used to attain a goal formulated by the Judeo-Arabic philosophical epistemology: the perfect act of cognition was interpreted mystically as the union of the knower with the Divine as intelligibilia.[22] Even more now than in its two preceding stages, the ecstatic Kabbalah emphasized the need for isolation for the effective performance of its anomian practices; it had also since the early fourteenth century included equanimity as a prerequisite of the mystical process. Just as in the Heikhalot literature, the ecstatic Kabbalist was embarking on a spiritual adventure that might end in death. The medieval mystic, however, was endangered not by malevolent angels but by the weakness of his own physical or psychic structure, which might be unable to resist the pressures of the Divine invading his personality so that he would die a "death by kiss"—a beatific one.[23] Now, more than earlier, mystical union was viewed as the highest religious achievement. But this school of Kabbalah paid a price for its anthropocentrical emphasis: a retreat from collective worship as the central and highest form of religious experience and concentration on an individualistic escapism. The complicated mystical techniques cultivated by the ecstatic Kabbalists were suitable to only a very few, although esotericism was not an essential feature of this type of Kabbalah.

Leading Safedian Kabbalists, such as R. Moses Cordovero and R. Ḥayyim Vital, conceived the ecstatic practices as the highest type of Kabbalah, superior to the theosophical-theurgical version.[24] They nevertheless practiced both, regarding the theosophical one as more appropriate for dissemination to a larger public and the ecstatic as suitable for more limited audiences.

This appraisement was inverted in Ḥasidism; theosophy was regarded either as a subject too difficult to be studied and practiced by the masses or as theologically suspect.[25] Although the Ḥasidic masters did not publicly expound ecstatic techniques in the same manner as did Abraham Abulafia and his followers, they were probably acquainted with them, either directly, through the study of their writings,[26] or indirectly, by means of Cordovero's presentation of them in *Pardes Rimmonim*. The founders of Ḥasidism, however, did emphasize some of the mystical values that characterized ecstatic Kabbalah; *devekut* understood as *unio mystica*, inspiration and revelation, the need for seclusion and equanimity for concentration, the psychological understanding of theosophy, and a unique interest in linguistic mysticism formed the basic structure of Ḥasidic mysticism. Notwithstanding these affinities, Ḥasidism also emphasized the importance of the mystical performance of the commandments—a nomian technique—as a vital key to mystical life. Therefore, we may consider the emergence of Ḥasidism not so much as a reaction toward Sabbatianism or Frankism but as a restructuring of Jewish mysticism already initiated by the Safedian Kabbalists. With them, as with the Ḥasidim, one major interest was the achievement of a certain balance, previously peripheral, between the theurgical-theosophical and the ecstatic elements in the Kabbalah. Although such an attempt to integrate these different and even conflicting religious values had already been adumbrated in R. Isaac of Acre's works *Me'irat 'Eynaim* and *'Oẓar Ḥayyim*,[27] which were studied in Safed, it would appear that Spanish Kabbalah itself rejected this syncretistic approach and had to await the disintegration of the stronghold of Kabbalah in the Iberian Peninsula in order to soften its resistance to ecstatic Kabbalah. Phenomenologically, we indeed can see R. Isaac of Acre a precursor of the Safedian and Ḥasidic synthesis, although the major impact of this novel approach was felt only after its "canonization" by Cordovero and Vital.

A proper understanding of the last major Jewish school of mysticism, Ḥasidism, must take into consideration the merging of these two mainstreams, which had competed with each other for more than a millennium and a half: ecstasy and theurgy, or anthropocentrism and theocentrism. The result was a synthesis that, on the one hand, attenuated the theurgical-theosophical elements and, on the other, propagated ecstatic values even more than previously. Or, as we shall see in a passage from R. Meshullam Phoebus, classical Spanish and Lurianic Kabbalah were reinterpreted ecstatically.[28] This emphasis on individual mystical experience may be one of the major explanations for the neutralization[29] of nationalistic messianism in Ḥasidism.[30] Although the aftermath of Sabbatianism could also have prompted interest in a more individualistic type of mysticism and redemption, we can envision the emergence of the Ḥasidic type of mysticism as part of the dissemination of religious values crucial for the ecstatic Kabbalistic model. From this perspective Mendel Piekarz's emphasis on the importance of Mussar literature for the understanding of Kabbalah can be understood within the larger context of the prevalence of Cordoverian thought long after the emergence of Lurianism.

Let me dwell briefly upon the manner in which I understand the term *mysticism* and its derivatives in the context of the following discussions. I consider a phenomenon to be of a mystical nature when there is achieved a contact with the Divine, differing from the common religious experiences cultivated in a certain religion both in its intensity and in its spiritual impact. Accordingly, the interest in ecstatic and unitive experiences as they occur in Kabbalistic literature are conspicuously mystical.

I also, however, consider certain types of experiences as mystical even when they differ substantially from the previous type of mysticism: I refer to the theurgical performance of the commandments as this appears in certain texts. As I shall argue below, Kabbalistic intention or *kavvanah* implied a cleaving to the Divine that preceded the theurgical operation.[31] According to other texts—and these are the great majority—the theurgical action involved a specific contact with the Divine in order to influence it (according to the moderate Kabbalistic theurgy) or even to sustain it or to "make" it, in still other texts.[32]

Moreover, the performance of the commandments in a Kabbalistic manner not only entailed the capacity to influence the supernatural world; it consisted of an initiation of the Jew into the secrets of the *miẓvot*, that is, into their rationale, including the theosophical systems that facilitated their Kabbalistic performance. The transition from the self-perception of the Jews as observant of the *miẓvot* with no particular mystical implication to that of the theurgist whose religious activity was fraught with cosmic and theosophical implications and repercussions must have had a profound impact upon the initiated. Although I assume that such a passage was different in nature from the more well-known rites of passage, it seems likely that a change of weltanschauung was indispensable for the new attitude to the idea of God and religion in general. Even if this change was a gradual one, sometimes even a matter of years, its profound impact was indispensable for the formation of a Kabbalistic type of personality. Therefore, whereas the ecstatic Kabbalah strove mainly toward a drastic change of personality that brought the Kabbalist into a direct relationship to god, in theurgical Kabbalah the change sought was in the sefirotic pleroma.

The main approach in this book is phenomenological: my assumption is that the two main foci of Kabbalistic mysticism were the ecstatic-unitive and the theosophical-theurgical. While focusing primarily upon the descriptions of these two cores of Kabbalah, I shall also take into consideration the historical development of these two themes recurring in Kabbalistic literature. Thus, my approach uses phenomenology in order to isolate significant phenomena and only thereafter to elaborate upon the possible historical relationships between them. In other words my starting point is the unfolding of the phenomenological affinity between two mystical patterns of experience, preceding their historical analysis per se. Hence, the phenomenological approach also serves historical aims, although not exclusively. In this sense, history plays a significant, but not central, role in the discussions included in this work.

For example, among the significant issues discussed in this book is the question of the antiquity of Kabbalah—a clearly historical question. My principal interest is not, however, to prove the antiquity thesis—an issue to be dealt with in detail elsewhere—but to allow for the comparison between ancient Jewish sources and the medieval mystical literature that derived from them. The detailed elaboration of the antiquity thesis is therefore secondary to my interest here. The historical dimension is nevertheless important for the conception of Kabbalah as a Jewish mystical phenomenon, one deriving from Gershom Scholem's descriptions of Kabbalah as basically a Gnostic phenomenon.

My approach therefore combines phenomenology with history, thereby avoiding "pure" phenomenological descriptions. The juxtaposition of these two methods does not lie in their unique "deviation" from adherence to a single approach; by and large, I have tried to solve problems emerging from the texts, while using various approaches that may propose solutions. From this point of view, I am rather a pragmatist, allowing myself to be directed by the problems generated by the texts rather than attempting to superimpose one method upon all analyses. I hope that this methodological "inconsistency" will avoid the reductionist attitudes that characterize those scholars who subscribe to "pure" methodologies. Phenomenology, textology, history, and psychology must in principle be used intermittently and combined in order to do justice to all the various aspects of Kabbalistic texts and ideas.

The structure of this work consists of the exposition of the two mystical concerns of the Kabbalists. Following the first two chapters, which deal with the state of research and some methodological observations, are three chapters devoted to the subject of mystical experience and some of the mystical techniques of the Kabbalists; theurgical and theosophical aspects of the Kabbalah are the subjects of the next three chapters. In two of these chapters, I focus upon issues representing the extremes of the ecstatic and theurgical trends of Kabbalah: chapter 4 treats of written evidence of extreme descriptions of unitive experiences, which, although relatively rare in Jewish mysticism, are nevertheless an interesting component of this type of mystical lore; chapter 8 discusses some rather daring views of theurgy that surpass the more common views of this type of Kabbalistic activity. These two extreme phenomena have been neglected by modern scholarship, and I hope that an elaborate exposition of them will contribute to a more variegated picture of Kabbalah. I should like to emphasize that the phenomena treated in chapters 4 and 8 are not merely marginal or bizarre but part of an inner development of the particular Kabbalistic trends they represent, albeit in a more accentuated way. Finally, the last two chapters deal with more general issues shared by the two main Kabbalistic lines referred to above: an interest in hermeneutics and symbolism crosses these lines, while some features of Kabbalistic anthropology are a common denominator of Kabbalah in general.

CHAPTER 1

Remarks on Kabbalah Scholarship

Our little systems have their days, or their hour; as knowledge advances they pass into the history of the efforts of pioneers.—Andrew Lang to Georgina Max Müller, *Life and Letters*, 2:452

The aim of this short survey of Jewish Kabbalah scholarship is to point out the main trends in the critical approaches to this mystical lore.[1] Accordingly, it is neither an attempt to summarize the achievement of the scholars nor a criticism of their findings. The focus is upon noting the development of the first historical observations on the Kabbalah written by non-Kabbalists and concisely tracing their impact on later scholarly treatments of Kabbalah. A full account of the evolution of scholarship regarding this lore is still a desideratum, without which an accurate understanding of the achievements made in modern times in the portrayal of Kabbalah is impossible. For the time being, only a few limited surveys of this subject are available, primarily in the works of Gershom Scholem.[2]

I. SCHOLARSHIP OF KABBALAH FROM THE RENAISSANCE ON

The earliest critical discussions of the phenomenon of Kabbalah are found in Provençal literature produced shortly after the appearance of the first Kabbalistic documents. R. Meir ben Simeon of Narbonne sharply criticized both the polytheistic implications of the Kabbalistic doctrine of prayers to varied divine manifestations and specific books containing Kabbalistic ideas. Strangely enough, despite the gradual broadening of Kabbalah as a religious movement, the critique against it became silenced, although it does seem that once there was more anti-Kabbalistic material than is extant in the surviving documents.[3] Some critical remarks may also be found in the works of Kabbalists who criticized different Kabbalistic approaches, although they attacked not Kabbalah itself but its misunderstandings.[4] No elaborate and detailed survey of the nature and history of this religious movement is known, however, until the period of the Renaissance. The independent events that took place in the circle of Christian scholars connected to the family of the Medicis in Florence contributed to the emergence of a critical attitude to Kabbalah, and thus to the attempts to understand it with the help of philological-historical tools.

The first event was Marsilio Ficino's translation of a large corpus of Platonic and Neoplatonic writings from Greek into Latin; for the first time, the Western intellectual world had the opportunity to study Platonic thought in its various Neoplatonic or Hermetic versions. Two leading figures in the intellectual life of the Jews, and even in that of the Christians, in northern Italy—R. Elijah del Medigo and R. Yehudah Messer Leon—were Aristotelian philosophers;[5] their acquaintance with Platonic views enabled them to perceive the affinities between Platonism, which they rejected as a philosophy, and Kabbalah, with which they were already acquainted. R. Yehudah accused the Kabbalists of attributing corporeality, change, and plurality to God;[6] in the same context, he indicated that their concepts were close to Platonic ones, a fact that could not pass unnoticed by these philosophers.[7] More elaborate, though less acid, was the critique of R. Elijah del Medigo. He described the views of the Kabbalists in the following words: "They are in line with what was said by the ancient philosophers, who have been totally rejected by those who know. Whoever has seen what the ancient philosophers and some of the Platonists said, as well as what these ⟨Kabbalists⟩ said, know that this is the truth."[8]

As del Medigo pointed out, following a lengthy comparison of Kabbalistic and Platonic views, "These statements are very far removed from the words of the Peripatetics and their principles."[9] The "philosophers" cited by Messer Leon and the "learned people" of del Medigo were the philosophical establishment of the Jews, who continued to adhere to medieval Aristotelian thought. The recent access to Platonic views in their Latin versions facilitated their articulation of Kabbalah as cognate to Platonism, and thus as a negligible way of thinking. Until the period of the Renaissance, references to the affinity of Kabbalah to Plato's corpus had invariably carried a positive significance, mainly among the Kabbalists.[10]

From an Aristotelian viewpoint, this affinity had a derogatory overtone.

Messer Leon drew no historical conclusions from his remarking of the resemblance of Platonism and Kabbalah; del Medigo, however, did. Although he did not explicitly mention any linkage between the nexus of Platonism-Kabbalah and his assertion that the book of the *Zohar* is a late forgery, it seems to me that such a linkage was implicit; del Medigo openly distinguished between "ancient philosophers"—the *prisci theologi* of the Renaissance syncretistic theory—and some "Platonics," which apparently referred to later authors, that is, in our terminology, Neoplatonic philosophers. If del Medigo had some knowledge of the history of later Platonism,[11] he must have been aware of the fact that most of them lived after the time of R. Simeon bar Yoḥai, to whom the authorship of the *Zohar* had been ascribed. As del Medigo stated that the affinities of Kabbalah to the "ancient philosophers" and "Platonists" were the result of the elaboration by the Kabbalists of Platonic and ancient philosophic themes,[12] then Kabbalah's development must have been seen as occurring after the emergence of Neoplatonism. According to del Medigo, or his anonymous sources—if he indeed had such[13]—the *Zohar* had been known for only about three hundred years, that is, since the end of the twelfth century. Del Medigo might have been aware of the existence of a Jewish Neoplatonic school that flowered in the eleventh and twelfth centuries, as evidenced by the works of R. Solomon Gabirol, Baḥya ibn Pakuda, or Joseph ibn Ẓaddik;[14] such an awareness could explain why he located the appearance of the *Zohar* shortly after the expansion of Jewish Neoplatonism.

An interesting parallel to this use of a comparative approach in order to demonstrate the forgery and, implicitly, the lateness of an allegedly ancient mystical classic is found in Lorenso Valla's assertion that Dionysius Areopagita's works were spuriously attributed to a contemporary of Paul, as they were influenced by Neoplatonism.[15] No doubt the critical acumen of the humanists with whom del Medigo might have come into contact during the years of his teaching in Padua and his presence in Florence contributed, in one way or another, to his discovery of correlations between Platonism and Kabbalah, and his dating of the *Zohar* as a late work. Finally, before leaving this issue, it should be added that this recognition of the Platonic bent of Kabbalistic thought must be seen against the background of the growing trend to interpret Kabbalah Platonically, a direction shared by Pico della Mirandola, Yoḥanan Alemanno, and later on, R. Isaac and Yehudah Abravanel. Those same resemblances that helped del Medigo to postdate Kabbalah helped his contemporaries to regard it as a source of Platonism, and hence as of greater antiquity.[16]

The second reason for the criticism of Kabbalah, particularly on the part of del Medigo, was apparently its diffusion in Christian circles and its use as an important tool in the missionary efforts of Pico della Mirandola. This explanation has already been advanced by scholars and needs no elaboration;[17] it is, however, worth emphasizing—a point to which we shall return at greater length later—that the Kabbalah's becoming a sociointellectual problem for the Jews contributed to its closer examination and, indirectly, to a more critical approach to this sacrosanct lore.

Del Medigo's work was written in 1491, but remained in manuscript until 1629. For the entire sixteenth century, no detailed criticism of Kabbalah is extant; although the antiquity of the *Zohar* was queried in a veiled manner by R. Elijah (Baḥur) Levita and R. 'Azariah de Rossi, no systematic criticism was addressed to the Kabbalah as the result of the infiltration of alien concepts.[18] But under the impact of the publication in 1629 of *Beḥinat ha-Dat*, del Medigo's critique became influential in the first work devoted to a sharp and extensive attack on Kabbalah: in his *Ari Nohem*, R. Yehudah Aryeh of Modena (Leone da Modena) expanded upon some ideas of del Medigo, especially upon the assumption that Platonic motifs penetrated into Kabbalah and thus can be dated as medieval. Modena indeed considered Kabbalah a definite distortion of Greek thought.[19]

Interestingly, he did not accept del Medigo's dating of the *Zohar* in the late twelfth century, but regarded the entire Kabbalah as a post-Maimonidean phenomenon that emerged in Spain.[20] This diagnosis of Kabbalah as a post-Maimonidean and Neoplatonic development was, for Modena, also connected with its anti-Maimonidean way of thought. One of his reasons for writing this critique of Kabbalah was to counteract the sharp criticism of Maimonides characterizing such Kabbalistic writings as R. Shem Tov ibn Shem Tov's *Sefer ha-'Emunot* and R. Meir ibn Gabbay's *Tola'at Ya'akov* and *'Avodat ha-Kodesh*.[21] Strangely, Modena does not elaborate on his opinion that Kabbalah originated in Spain at the beginning of the thirteenth century in the tense atmosphere of the anti-Maimonidean controversy.[22]

As in the case of del Medigo, Modena also had another motivation for composing his work, apart from a certain anti-Platonic bent in his thought.[23] Kabbalah, far more than in the times of del Medigo, had become a leading force in the intellectual milieu of northern Italy, and Modena had gradually become isolated in his anti-Kabbalistic attitude. His relative R. Aaron Berakhiah of Modena was an accomplished Kabbalist;[24] his son-in-law, R. Jacob ben Kalominus Segal, whom he highly esteemed, and his most brilliant student, R. Joseph Ḥamiẓ, turned before his eyes into fervent Kabbalists.[25] This lore, an "innovation" of Diaspora life, became more and more pernicious through its missionary use by Christians. Modena, therefore, fought against the intrusion of alien Greek thought into Jewish religion in general and at the same time against the use of Kabbalah in Christian propaganda. The latter was effective enough to convince Jews to convert, and he finally attempted to induce two persons who were dear to him to abandon their interest in Kabbalah.[26] The core of *Ari Nohem*, however, is his criticism of the *Zohar;* he introduces an important document to strengthen del Medigo's view of the *Zohar* as a medieval forgery.[27] Modena quotes in extenso and elaborates upon R. Isaac of Acre's story of his inquiries into the relationship between R. Moses de Leon and the *Zohar*.[28] Since then, all scholarly discussions on the history of Kabbalah have reiterated this testimony of R. Isaac.[29]

Modena's compatriot and contemporary Simone Luzzatto elaborated upon the resemblance between Kabbalah and Platonism in his presentation of Judaism.[30] In his famous *Discorso circo il stato de l'Hebrei*, he compared the Kabbalistic view of the Sefirot with the Platonic and Philonic parallels,[31] mentioning also later Neoplatonic authors, the "Syrians," such as Plotinus, Iamblicus, and Porphyrius.[32] Luzzatto noted what seemed to him a major difference between Platonic and Neoplatonic ideas and the Kabbalistic "ideas": that the Kabbalistic Sefirot formed a hierarchy that bridged the gap between the spiritual and the material, thereby constituting an important ring in the "great chain of being."[33] Another subject whose affinity to Platonism was emphasized was the Kabbalistic theory of intermediary "spirit," which links the intellectual faculty to the corporeal function;[34] this theory is reminiscent of the Neoplatonic astral body.[35] Judging from the manner in which Luzzatto formulated his view on Kabbalah, it appears that he believed in its antiquity, although he himself is not to be considered either as a Kabbalist or as an opponent of this lore.

The affinity of Kabbalah to Platonic thought was, as seen above, recognized by both the medieval and the Renaissance authors interested in Kabbalah or in its critique; modern scholarship has only elaborated, deepened, or explicated their findings. This also seems to have been the case regarding another major ancient school thought to have been influential on the Kabbalah; therefore, a short survey of the origin of the assessment of Gnosticism as a source of Kabbalistic ideas is pertinent.

The first author to note a specific resemblance between Kabbalah and Gnostic views seems to have been Cornelius Agrippa of Nettesheim.[36] In his *De Incertitudine Scientiarum*, this author suggests that the Jewish Kabbalistic superstitions had influenced Gnostics as the "Ophitae, Gnostici, et Valentiniani haeretici," and he hints at usages of "numbers and letters."[37] Agrippa's allusion is very vague, and it is rather difficult to fathom the precise significance of his assumption of pernicious Kabbalistic influence on the various Gnostic schools; however, it seems that he might have had in mind the affinity between such works as *Shi'ur Komah* and the related Heikhalot literature, which he had already mentioned in his earlier De Occulta Philosophia,[38] as well as the Gnostic theory of Marcos, as cited by Irenaeus, concerning the great size of the divine figures, whose descriptions are combined with numbers and letters.[39] This interpretation of Agrippa's view places him at the beginning of a series of scholars who maintained the view that Marcos's theory was influenced by ancient Jewish mystical views related to the *Shi'ur Komah*. They include E. Ben Amozegh,[40] M. Gaster,[41] Scholem,[42] Gedaliahu G. Stroumsa,[43] and myself.[44] For Agrippa, the similarity between Kabbalistic and Gnostic motifs showed the heretical potential of Jewish mysticism; like his older Jewish contemporary, del Medigo, he thought that the discovery of a resemblance between Kabbalah and another body of thought evinced the heretical nature of the former. Agrippa's finding was repeated by some sixteenth-century Christian sources and was adopted even by Simone Luzzatto.[45] After dealing with Kabbalistic theosophy, Luzzatto wrote that, from its ideas, "the Valentinians, Gnostics and other ancient heretics have deviated like bastards, as it can be seen from Epiphanius, the Greek doctor, or from Irenaeus, the Roman."[46] Agrippa's emphasis on the pernicious quality of Kabbalah is replaced here by the consideration of Gnosticism as a deviation from Jewish ancient lore. It remained for modern scholarship of Gnosticism gradually to recognize the importance of ancient Jewish mysticism for a better understanding of the emergence of Gnostic thought[47] without, however, paying due attention to Agrippa's remark.[48] It was Adolphe Franck alone who wrote: "We are, therefore, forced to admit that Gnosticism borrowed a great deal, if not precisely from the *Zohar* as we know it today, at least from the traditions and from the theories contained therein."[49] The main thrust of modern Kabbalah scholarship, however, followed the opposite direction; time and again, Kabbalah was presented as a mystical movement influenced in crucial issues by Gnostic thought.

Two outstanding figures of eighteenth-century Judaism, R. Jacob Emden and Solomon Maimon, contributed in various ways to scholarship concerning Jewish mysticism. As part of his anti-Sabbatian struggle, Emden incisively analyzed the zoharic corpus, demonstrating the existence of medieval material that was included in the ancient book of the *Zohar* authored by R. Simeon bar Yoḥai; this analysis is primarily philological, and his insights are still valuable.[50] Maimon, an enthusiast of Kabbalah in his youth and a philosopher in his mature years, was more interested in Kabbalah as a religious phenomenon than in its history.[51] Viewing it as a kind of Jewish science that symbolically comprised insights into psychology, physics, morals, and politics, he wrote that it had, however, degenerated as a result of the tendency to discover analogies everywhere into "an art of madness according to method" or a "systematic science resting on conceits."[52] Basically, Maimon assumed, Kabbalah was indeed a science, and he presumably attempted to decipher it accordingly, using philosophical terms—an approach reminiscent of the Renaissance understanding of Kabbalah.[53] Important also are his remarks on Ḥasidism, his penetrating observations serving as starting points for modern research into this school of mysticism.[54]

II. NINETEENTH-CENTURY JEWISH SCHOLARSHIP IN WESTERN EUROPE

The emergence of academic interest in Judaism generally since the beginning of the nineteenth century also produced a revival of scholarly research of Kabbalah. One of the earliest representatives of the school of *Wissenschaft des Judentums*, Nachman Krochmal,[55] had a sympathetic attitude toward Kabbalah, whose antiquity was, in his eyes, obvious. This ancient lore, he suggested, had reached Europe from the Orient and had proliferated in the West, this process being, however, part of its degeneration and the *Zohar* part of its decline.[56] Like his Renaissance predecessors, Krochmal pointed out the resemblances between Neoplatonism and Gnosticism, on the one hand, and Kabbalah, on the other.[57]

One of his younger contemporaries, M. Landauer, was interested in both the historical and the bibliographical aspects of Kabbalah, producing several essays on these subjects.[58] Notwithstanding many historical mistakes that spoil his surveys of the early Kabbalah, Landauer inaugurated serious study of this subject in the nineteenth century with extensive use of manuscript materials; he accepted the view of the *Zohar* as a medieval composition, adding to it the fantastic assumption that its author was Abraham Abulafia. Under the influence of German idealistic philosophy, he attempted a symbolic interpretation of the Bible using Kabbalistic categories.[59] His premature death ended a promising contribution to the integration of Kabbalah as part of the Jewish religious phenomena. We can conclude, then, that the first two scholars to be interested in the world of Kabbalah in the early nineteenth century became so under the aegis of German idealism, which, as we now know, was sometimes influenced by Kabbalistic thought via the Swabian Pietists (led by F. C.

Oetinger) who, in turn, absorbed Kabbalistic concepts from the *Kabbalah Denudata*. If the Renaissance contribution to Kabbalah research was mostly historical and provided the Neoplatonic corpus as an indispensable point of comparison to the Kabbalah (although commonly with negative overtones), the idealistic philosophy encouraged phenomenological Kabbalistic approaches, mostly sympathetic to this lore, whose repercussions are felt even in contemporary scholarship.

The first major work devoted to a detailed description of mainly zoharic Kabbalah and making use of historical, philological, comparative, and conceptual perspectives was Adolphe Franck's *La Kabbale ou la philosophie religieuse des Hebreux* printed in 1843 in Paris. This work was highly influential, enjoying two French editions (the second one in 1892), a German translation by Adolph Jellinek (1844), who added some important remarks, a Hebrew version dated 1909, and an English translation of the German version (1926), printed several times also in shorter forms. Franck's presentation contributed more to the knowledge of Kabbalah in modern Europe than did any other work prior to the studies of Scholem. Franck suggested that the *Zohar*, and Kabbalistic ideas in general, are of a hoary antiquity predating the Alexandrian philosophical school and Christianity.[60] The sources of important concepts of Kabbalah, according to Franck, were Chaldean and Persian, that is, Zoroastrian.[61] Notwithstanding this basic assumption on Franck's part—which was rejected by subsequent research—he regarded Kabbalah as a uniquely important Jewish phenomenon, and his characterization of it is worth quoting in extenso:

> We cannot possibly consider the Kabbalah as an isolated fact, accidental in Judaism; on the contrary, it is its heart and soul. For, while the Talmud took over all that relates to the outward practice and performance of the Law, the Kabbalah reserved for itself the domain of speculation and the most formidable problems of natural and revealed theology. It was able, besides, to arouse the veneration of the people by showing inviolate respect for their crude beliefs and teaching them to understand that their entire faith and religion rested upon a sublime mystery.[62]

Thus, already in 1843, Kabbalah was considered, in a well-known work, not only an important religious phenomenon in Judaism but its "life and heart." This diagnosis of the role of Kabbalah is strikingly similar to Scholem's famous perception of the role of Kabbalah as a vital component of Judaism, which enabled the latter to continue its organic life for many generations.[63] I wish to highlight this point, which was self-evident to the Eastern European contemporaries of Franck, in order to demonstrate that there was, as early as the mid-nineteenth century, clear precedent for the modern positive evaluation of Kabbalah by a Western-born scholar such as Scholem.[64]

A contemporary and compatriot of Franck, Salomon Munk, was also interested in and sympathetic to Kabbalah. A great expert in Jewish and Arab philosophy, he included within his survey of "philosophie chez les juifs" some remarkable observations on Kabbalah that are deserving of emphasis.[65] In his view, Jewish thinkers in Alexandria and Palestine influenced both Neoplatonism and Gnosticism by their combination of Oriental and Occidental doctrines. Although their emphasis upon pantheistic tendencies was not cognate to Judaism, Kabbalah and Alexandrian Jews were to be treated as important intermediaries between East and West.[66] The emphasis Munk placed on the influence upon Gnosticism of doctrines that were later to become part of Kabbalah is notable.[67] Munk considered Kabbalah as a ramification of Alexandrian thought;[68] furthermore, there were striking affinities between the Gnostic doctrines of Basilides and Valentinus and the Kabbalistic Sefirot.[69] Munk pointed out the influence of ibn Gabirol, as well as other Jewish Neoplatonic thinkers, on the Kabbalah,[70] and believed that the *Zohar* was composed in the thirteenth century,[71] on the basis of earlier lost traditions and Midrashim.[72]

Franck's evaluation of Kabbalah as the "life" of Judaism was, however, rejected by his contemporaries. Jellinek, his German translator and a scholar sympathetic to Kabbalah, reacted promptly, remarking in a footnote to Franck's passage: "The author should have added: 'Judaism after the return from the Babylonian exile until the conclusion of the Talmud.' For present-day Judaism, the Kabbalah is an entirely alien element."[73]

It must be noted that Jellinek does not here contradict Franck; he merely qualifies his assessment as applicable only to an early period of Jewish religion, whereas in the present Kabbalah is "an entirely strange element." This sense of alienation from the Kabbalah is also evident in the *Dialogue sur la Kabbale et le Zohar* by S. D. Luzzatto, who took full advantage of de Rossi's and Modena's critiques, as well as of a work by Jellinek, in order to rid the Mishnaic and talmudic masters of the spurious attribution of views contrary to their authentic thought. Luzzatto was sharply critical of Franck, writing: "les Textes de ce mysticisme que l'ignorance a appelé la *Philosophie religieuse des Hebreux*, n'appartiennent point aux auteurs de la Mishna et du Talmud et ne sont que des pseudonymes."[74] As Luzzatto frankly acknowledged, this reaction was stimulated not only by Franck's work but also by "les dangereux effets que la fanatisme Kabbalistique, sous le nom de Khassidisme ennemis de toute culture."[75] This remark is highly interesting; as Luzzatto admits, he had not only an academic aim for his *Dialogue*—which is actually an attack on Kabbalah—but also religious and cultural motivations. The disastrous results of a recent development in Jewish mysticism (Sabbatianism) prompted a sharp reaction, as it had for Emden before him. It may indeed be that later negative attitudes of Heinrich Graetz, Moritz Steinschneider, and Solomon Rubin toward Kabbalah were also based upon their reaction toward Eastern European Ḥasidism. Moreover, the relatively positive attitude toward Kabbalah expressed in the writings of Krochmal, Franck, Munk, and ben Amozegh predated most of the anti-Kabbalistic critiques launched by Jewish scholars in the second half of the nineteenth century. Some of those critical scholars, however, contributed a great deal to Kabbalah research.

Scholem's critique of the negative evaluation of Kabbalah in the writings of such representatives of the *Wissenschaft des Judentums*[76] as Steinschneider and Graetz, although justified, is nevertheless partial. These two giants of Jewish scholarship must be seen not only as critics of Kabbalah but also as two of the founders of its academic study. Graetz performed the first major historical survey of Kabbalistic literature, larger than that of Landauer, and Steinschneider's articles dealing with such Kabbalistic personalities as R. Asher ben David and R. Jacob ha-Cohen and with Kabbalistic works such as those of Abraham Abulafia are pioneering discussions, although they are colored with partiality. In general, however, the attitude toward Kabbalah on the part of some of the nineteenth-century Jewish scholars is much more sympathetic than one might deduce from the way Scholem presents them. Nachman Krochmal, ben Amozegh, Franck, Munk, and Jellinek are some examples of Jewish scholars who held what seems to me the more common positive attitude to Kabbalah. Far from being negatively biased against Kabbalah, some of the pioneers of Jewish studies in the nineteenth and early twentieth centuries not only were interested in this lore but also made several original contributions that were to lay the foundation for the later study of Kabbalah. It is regrettable that their achievements are at times ignored by contemporary scholars.

III. TWENTIETH-CENTURY KABBALAH SCHOLARSHIP

At the turn of the century, the feeling that Kabbalah had much more to reveal than scholars had previously understood emerged in Western Europe.[77] Several studies of Kabbalistic topics were written, and I consider the assessment of S. A. Hirsch as representative of this mood. He wrote: "I am strongly of the opinion that our Cabbalists have not always been fairly treated by Jewish writers of the present time. The whole subject requires an entire overhauling—but about this we need not be concerned. Jewish historiography is a comparatively recent growth. Time will assuredly show where the truth lies."[78]

This passage, which was written in 1908 as part of an essay entitled "Jewish Mystics: An Appreciation," foreshadowed the great achievements of Hirsch's younger contemporary Gershom Scholem. As Scholem's contribution is already well known and has been extensively discussed in a number of recent essays, I shall touch upon it only briefly.[79]

Scholem's tremendous achievements in the study of Jewish mysticism concern four major issues:

1. He surveyed all the major trends of Jewish mysticism on the basis of perusal of the basic documents extant in print and manuscripts. His writings therefore contain the first authoritative presentation of the history of Jewish mysticism in its entirety.
2. In a long series of bibliographical studies, Scholem laid the basis for the modern bibliography of Kabbalah, building the structure for further descriptions of Kabbalistic literature. To a far greater extent than did Landauer, Steinschneider, and Jellinek, Scholem inspected an immense amount of manuscript material, enabling him to establish the authorship of a great number of Kabbalistic works.
3. Scholem approached Kabbalah as a religious phenomenon, more than either his predecessors or his successors did, and he attempted to describe it historically as well as phenomenologically. Therefore, he can be considered the founder of the phenomenology of Kabbalah. It is, however, significant that most of Scholem's discussions on phenomenological aspects of Kabbalah were written at a relatively later stage of his scholarly activity, many of them having been presented at the Ascona annual conferences. I suppose that this late turn toward a more phenomenological understanding of Kabbalah was the result of the need to present it to the particular type of audience that was characteristic of these symposia.
4. Last, Scholem, like Franck, regarded Kabbalah as a vital part of the Jewish religion, emphasizing its centrality for a proper understanding of its evolution. His emphasis upon the pluralism of Jewish thought enabled him to integrate within it Kabbalah and its offshoot, Sabbatianism. In his view, Judaism is whatever a given generation of Jews evolves as its expression.

Scholem began his scholarly activity by attempting to disclose the metaphysical substratum of Kabbalistic thought.[80] Although he never explicitly acknowledged it, he assumed that, on a deeper level, Kabbalah expresses a metaphysical reality that can be grasped by a proper hermeneutics, using historical, philological, and philosophical tools.[81] By decoding the symbols and discerning the lines of historical development of key concepts together with minute biobibliographical work, he attempted to approach the "mountain," namely, the core of that reality. He waited, as he himself confessed, to receive a hint coming from that core.[82] I have no idea if he indeed received an intimation of this kind, for he did not commit to writing the presence or absence of such a call. What seems undeniable, however, is his conviction that Kabbalah may be a discipline that encompasses the quest of Kabbalists for the Divine and, seemingly, also their response to what they considered to be their contact with it. It is hard to describe Scholem's precise view on the relationship between these two subjects: the metaphysical core of Kabbalah and the "mountain," the core of reality. At least as far as the latter is concerned, however, he was apparently certain that academic research falls short of clarifying it. Was he of the same opinion regarding the inadequacy of these approaches to attain the metaphysical core of the Kabbalah? Scholem seems to have left no decisive answer. However, he gave explicit expression to his fear of death—that is, spiritual death—as the result of academic preoccupations.[83] Early in his life, he engaged in practical exercises based upon Abraham Abulafia's mystical techniques, as he told me in conversation and as he recorded shortly before his death in the Hebrew version of his autobiography.[84] Taken together, these personal confessions may reveal his recognition that the scholarly approach has its limits; by transcending it through spiritual orientations, the scholar can be saved from the aridity of the academic, presumably by practicing some mode of spiritual experience.

This inference from Scholem's various statements must, however, be regarded more as a timid prescription than as a descriptive confession. If one wishes, Scholem may be considered as a theoretical mystic or a mystic in theory, as well as a theorist of Kabbalah.[85] I use the term *theoretical mystic* not intending either a pejorative or a positive reflection upon his stand as a theorist. The common perceptions of his personality either solely as a historian or as a historiosopher unnecessarily reduce his spiritual physiognomy to his obvious and manifest activity, blatantly ignoring his own statements. Extraordinarily successful as Scholem was as a historian of mystical texts and ideas, he was, in his own eyes, rather a failure qua mystic, yet one who longed for mystical experience.[86]

Important contributions to the bibliography of Kabbalah and the analysis of its doctrines have been made by Alexander Altmann and Georges Vajda.

Although their intellectual formation was independent of Scholem's, they accepted most of his historical and conceptual views on Kabbalah, contributing mainly to the study of the syntheses between philosophy and Kabbalah.[87] Characteristic of their writings is the integration of Kabbalistic themes within their comprehensive studies along the line of the history of ideas, which included treatments of themes and motifs current in the Judeo-Arabic thought.[88] Altmann has also contributed to research into the relationship between ancient Jewish material and Gnosticism, as well as the relationship between Kabbalah and postmedieval thought, both Renaissance and modern.[89] The study of the philosophical-Kabbalistic synthesis was continued by younger scholars, such as Sarah Heller-Wilensky and David Blumenthal.[90]

The importance of Platonism for Jewish thought in general was stressed in Yiẓḥak Baer's studies on Second Commonwealth Judaism. Baer traced a significant number of ancient Jewish notions to the influence of Plato's thought either on the philosophy of Philo in Alexandria or on that of the Palestinian rabbis.[91] Thus, a Platonic substratum was laid for Jewish mysticism; Baer refers in some footnotes to Kabbalistic formulations that reflect these older Jewish motifs.[92] For the present, however, Baer's proposals have not been accepted by scholars; a deliberate ignoring of his assumptions can be seen in those works of Scholem and E. E. Urbach referring to issues he dealt with. Baer, however, has the merit of having offered an implicit alternative vision of the development of Jewish mysticism as a phenomenon growing organically from ancient to medieval times; notwithstanding certain shortcomings, such as his overemphasis of the importance of alien elements—mostly Greek—on the emergence of Jewish thought in general, and mysticism in particular, his approach is the only post-Scholem endeavor to proceed along lines different from Scholem's. This fact, which deserves to be highlighted, stands in contrast to the basically conformist tendency characteristic of the academic study of Kabbalah following the crystallization of Scholem's theories on the evolution of Jewish mysticism.

This brief survey of Western European Jewish scholarship of Kabbalah shows a constancy of interest in the relationship of Kabbalah and philosophy. For Franck, Kabbalah was the "philosophie religieuse" of the Jews; for Munk, it was a ramification of Alexandrian speculations; for Krochmal, Kabbalah was appreciated as connected to the imaginative faculty, which is inferior to the intellectual one—again, an implicit comparison to philosophy; even Amozegh, the nineteenth-century thinker most sympathetic to Kabbalah, repeatedly compared it to Neoplatonic views. In the approaches of these scholars one hears, mutatis mutandis, echoes of the Renaissance philosophization of Kabbalah and its critique as influenced by Neoplatonism; just as the Renaissance authors preferred the speculative aspects of this type of mysticism, neglecting its more practical and experiential sides, so did these nineteenth-century scholars. Kabbalah was envisaged as a peculiar type of esoteric knowledge, a Jewish "gnosis," rather than as a full-fledged mystical body of literature. This bias was partially accepted by modern scholars, including Scholem, who overstressed the importance of the speculative over the mystical; Kabbalistic symbolism is envisaged as a way to penetrate the texts and to understand the divine structure, rather than as a path to experiencing the divinely revealed texts. According to these scholars, Kabbalah is less a religious phenomenon using philosophical terminology in order to express idiosyncratic views than a philosophy reminiscent of other brands of speculations, albeit expressed in strange terms. Finally, the centrality of the discussions of the commandments and the particular manner of their performance were attenuated, if not completely eliminated—a tendency that can easily be understood against the background of the religious changes that had been taking place since nineteenth-century Western Judaism.[93]

In my description of the scholarly views of Kabbalah as they evolved from the Renaissance period, the affinity and resemblance of philosophy and Kabbalah, and of Gnosticism and Kabbalah, were the main foci of discussion. At this stage of our survey, some brief remarks on the relationship between Kabbalah and two other Jewish mystical movements that emerged at the same time it did would be pertinent.

Roughly speaking, the history of Kabbalah has been regarded as including two main stages: the Spanish one, from the beginning of the thirteenth century until 1492 when the Jews were expelled from Spain, and the Safedian one, which flourished during the second and third quarters of the sixteenth century. The most important Kabbalistic systems were composed in one or another of these centers, and from there they radiated throughout the entire Jewish world. But at least two additional centers have contributed certain esoteric traditions and concepts and the authority of their spiritual masters to the larger river of Kabbalistic lore. I refer to Ashkenazic Ḥasidism of the Franco-German provinces during the twelfth and thirteenth centuries and the Ḥasidism that flourished in the East—Egypt, the Land of Israel, and their environs—from the beginning of the thirteenth century. Although the mystical literature written in these centers has been studied per se, the impact for the history of Kabbalah of the ideas that were transmitted or emerged there has not been sufficiently evaluated.

A relatively long series of studies has been devoted to the subject of Ashkenazic Ḥasidism over the last century; several papers and books of Abraham Epstein,[94] Jekutiel Kamelhar,[95] Yiẓḥak Baer,[96] Gershom Scholem,[97] Joseph Dan,[98] Georges Vajda,[99] E. E. Urbach,[100] Ḥaym Soloveitchik,[101] Ivan Marcus,[102] and Abraham Grossman[103] have succeeded in elucidating several bibliographical, conceptual, and social questions related to this body of mystical literature. The publication of some important texts by Dan[104] and Vajda[105] has contributed to a better acquaintance by modern scholars with this domain of Jewish mysticism. The problematics of the relationship between Kabbalah and Ashkenazic Ḥasidism, however, have been dealt with only peripherally, most such discussions dealing with the influence of Kabbalah on the Ḥasidic masters.[106] Scholem noted the arrival of *Sefer ha-Bahir* from Ashkenaz to Provence[107] and the occurrence of theosophical motifs in a work of R. Eleazar of Worms;[108] Dan elaborated upon the details related to these motifs,[109] and his final conclusion is: "It seems that we may say that the Ashkenazi Ḥasidim did not know the Kabbalah as it was known to the sages of Provence, and even in those instances when quasi-Kabbalistic or proto-Kabbalistic sources were available to them, the Kabbalist-Gnostic element was unknown to them."[110] Therefore, he concludes, it seems that we must regard "Ashkenazic Ḥasidism as a speculative movement, totally separated from the Kabbalah, at least until the middle of the thirteenth century."[111] These clear-cut assessments issued by the most important authority on the thought of Ashkenazic Ḥasidism remain, for the time being, *le dernier cri* on the question of the influence of Ḥasidic thought upon the early Kabbalah. It seems to me that the entire question must be reopened on the ground of the existence of additional "Gnostic" motifs in Ḥasidic texts. Moreover, quotations by R. Jacob ben Sheshet and Naḥmanides of ideas from Ashkenazic Ḥasidism seem to be symptomatic of the greater influence exercised by Ashkenazic theology on the early Kabbalists.[112] As we shall see later, in the second half of the thirteenth century mystical techniques penetrated Spanish Kabbalah in various ways.[113]

The emergence in the East of a center of Jewish mysticism based upon Sufic elements remained, until the end of the thirteenth century, without influence on the European Kabbalah.[114] Such Ḥasidic-Sufic masters as R. Abraham ben Moses (Maimonides) and his followers did not make use of either theosophical or ecstatic Kabbalistic elements; but as late as the last two decades of the thirteenth century, an encounter took place between the ecstatic Kabbalah of Abraham Abulafia and Sufic elements, apparently in the Galilee.[115] This synthesis may have been eased by the previous existence of Sufic motifs in

Eastern Jewish Ḥasidism of the thirteenth century, although there is no solid evidence of the intermediary role played by this Jewish Arabic-language mystical literature in the infiltration of Sufism into Kabbalah. It may well be that some Jewish scholars in Galilee introduced Sufic concepts and practices directly from Muslim Sufism, then flowering in Damascus. The possible later influence of Sufic Ḥasidism on Kabbalah is still a matter for analysis in further studies.[116] S. Pines has recently traced the impact of some Ismaili doctrines on Kabbalah, opening an avenue that seems promising for further research.[117]

Finally, the relationship between Kabbalah and such classical Jewish literary genres as Midrash and Halakhah has been largely neglected by modern scholarship, an outstanding exception being Jacob Katz's recent pioneering treatment of the relationship between Kabbalah and Halakhah.[118]

CHAPTER 2

Methodological Observations

Gershom Scholem's works and the significant contributions of his contemporaries have served to gain considerable respectability for the academic study of Kabbalah. Nevertheless, Kabbalah does not yet enjoy the same degree of honor as Islamic, Hindu, and Buddhist mysticism. Only rarely are Kabbalistic concepts or ideas mentioned in comparative studies, and even then discussions are based almost invariably upon secondhand material; the works of Scholem or, in some rare cases, translations of the texts.[1] What is troubling about this state of affairs is not, however, the paucity of references to Jewish mysticism per se but the manner in which it is referred to even by serious scholars. On more than one occasion, some of these scholars, working in the field of Judaica or in comparative religion, have tended to the notion that his views on Kabbalah are tantamount to Kabbalah itself. The usual caution associated with scholarly research seems to be absent here; there is a widespread failure to distinguish between the authentic material and the opinions of scholars on the content of this material. Far more than in other fields, we encounter references to the view of the Kabbalah that are based solely upon Scholem's own assertions. This identification is problematic in several respects, and it may be helpful to elaborate upon the reasons for it.

I. QUANTITATIVE QUANDARIES

First, one generally unnoticed fact is the huge quantity of Kabbalistic works. At present, there is no comprehensive bibliographical survey of this body of literature in its entirety. We are in complete darkness as to the number of the thousands of Kabbalistic works and fragments, most of which are still in manuscripts and a great number of which are anonymous or unidentified; furthermore, even a list of the names of the Kabbalists is still unavailable. Great efforts to peruse this literature were made by Scholem, who, from the 1930s, roamed tirelessly through the libraries of Europe to this end. On the basis of these efforts, he produced some important bibliographic studies; one of them, written in 1933, which deals with the genre of treatises devoted to the explanation of the scheme of ten Sefirot, alone comprised at the time 130 entries, most of them extant solely in manuscripts and most of them anonymous.[2]

Second, the difficulties involved in mastering this enormous body of writings are numerous; I shall dwell at present only on the most important ones. First, the selection of books chosen to be described bibliographically and to be used in phenomenological analyses itself had a decisive impact upon the picture offered of the field. The concentration of efforts on a particular field immediately gave an unexpected importance to that figure or school. A balanced approach is, in this incipient stage of research in Kabbalah, utopian. To illustrate: Scholem spent years collecting every piece of evidence concerning the various stages of the Sabbatian movement, focusing on every historical detail regarding the lives of Sabbatai Ṣevi and Nathan of Gaza, whereas, in contrast, influential works of such central mystical figures as R. Moses Ḥayyim Luzzato or R. Naḥman of Bratslav were only rarely mentioned by Scholem. Another example: Scholem was deeply interested in Abraham Abulafia and his works, devoting an entire chapter in his *Major Trends* to him, as well as some lectures published in mimeograph form in Hebrew. But in a series of studies on Kabbalistic subjects to which Abulafia's thought is pertinent, he is not mentioned at all. Thus, Scholem's discusssion of the meaning of the Torah and Kabbalistic hermeneutics omits certain ideas found in Abulafia's works that are indispensable to a full description of the subject.[3] The same is true of Scholem's treatment of *devekut*, as we shall see in chapter 4. When the quantity of material is overwhelming and a scholar is nevertheless interested in providing a comprehensive survey, such an effort is likely to be biased either by technical factors—for example, the greater availability of works in print over those in manuscript—or by conceptual presuppositions on the centrality or importance of a given figure, school, or work. I should like to stress that, in the present state of research, an adequate and balanced description of Kabbalistic lore is impossible, a fault that lies in the very nature of the material.

The fact that Scholem did not write a comprehensive history of Jewish mysticism, but confined his scholarly activity to descriptions of major trends and schools, testifies to his awareness that it would have been improper to attempt such a grandiose project, given the sheer quantity of Kabbalistic treatises that have never been analyzed by any scholar and the continued obscurity of the material in manuscripts. It goes without saying that my attempt here to survey central Kabbalistic concepts suffers from the same deficiencies. It has nevertheless been undertaken in order to supply insights resulting either from my perusal of Kabbalistic material unavailable to Scholem (some has been unearthed only since the late sixties) or from my focusing on portions of the material that were dealt with by Scholem only in passing. The very fact that a substantial number of the quotations cited in the following discussions stem from manuscript sources illustrates the need to return to the path opened by Scholem and explore available manuscripts before attempting more general discussions of the nature of Kabbalah. The need to broaden the range of Kabbalistic literature serving as the raw material for integrative approaches would seem to be an imperative that has often been neglected since Scholem's basic studies were published.

But the exploration of new material is not the only, or even the most important, object of this proposed return to neglected manuscripts. Even a rereading of texts studied by Scholem may yield interesting new findings; newly discovered manuscripts may offer better readings that will alter conclusions based upon inferior versions, and the study of the *context* of some quotations cited by Scholem may at times foster different interpretations.

II. LOST MATERIAL

The problems posed by Kabbalistic literature, however, transcend the quantitative quandaries. Even the totality of the printed works and manuscripts, notwithstanding their huge number, hardly encompasses the whole of Kabbalistic lore, for at least two reasons. The more obvious, although less important, reason is the loss of several interesting books written by central Kabbalistic figures, the loss having been caused in part by the vicissitudes of Jewish history; pogroms and expulsions are not conducive to the preservation of unique manuscripts. This seems to be the reason, for example, for the loss of some of the writings of R. Moses of Burgos, R. Moses de Leon,[4] R. Isaac of Acre[5] and R. Abraham ben Eliezer ha-Levi.[6]

Another important reason for the disappearance of Kabbalistic works was the self-censorship imposed by the Kabbalists themselves. The loss of Abraham Abulafia's prophetic works,[7] the fragmentary nature of the extant portions of *Sefer ha-Meshiv,*[8] and the reduction of R. Joseph Karo's maggidic revelations to one-fiftieth of the original,[9] are sufficient examples of the tendency to suppress certain extreme aspects of Jewish mysticism. The survival of certain unique manuscripts in remote corners of the Jewish universe, such as Dublin, Palo Alto, and Melbourne, is evidence of the uncertain fate of these works.

III. THE PROBLEM OF ORAL TRANSMISSION

Yet in comparison to the corpus of Kabbalistic writings in our possession today, the total loss is not so great. Even during the period of the expulsion from Spain and Portugal, when the most important center of Kabbalah was destroyed, a list of the books lost would include hardly more than ten items. More important is the loss of Kabbalistic material that was never written down because it was in principle not intended to be committed to writing. When we attempt to reconstruct the various concepts of the different Kabbalistic schools, we must remind ourselves that these ideas were meant, from the beginning, to be limited to a small intellectual elite. The main medium of transmission of these traditions was, as the Kabbalists themselves indicate time and again, oral teaching. Although this fact is clear from a variety of Kabbalistic sources, modern research has failed to draw the implications from this major characteristic of Jewish mysticism.

There seem to be at least two main conclusions to be drawn from the perception of Kabbalah as an oral teaching during its formative period. The first, and more important, one is the necessity to presume the existence of oral stages preceding the earliest written documents of Kabbalah. The explicit statements of some important early figures are irrefutable evidence for the existence of esoteric traditions several generations before they were first committed to writing. In a document discovered and published by Scholem, R. Isaac the Blind, the teacher of several early Kabbalists, indicates that his father as well as his ancestors were unwilling to commit Kabbalistic matters to writing.[10] Naḥmanides, another teacher of Kabbalah and an outstanding figure in the Jewish world generally, likewise warns those interested in Jewish esotericism to study it solely from authoritative masters, as this lore could be revealed only orally.[11] Moreover, such masters of Ashkenazic esotericism as R. Eleazar of Worms refer to a long genealogy of ancestors who handed down the secrets of prayer that were finally committed to writing only by them under very peculiar historical circumstances.[12] The people I just mentioned—R. Abraham ben David, father of R. Isaac the Blind; Naḥmanides; and the Ashkenazic Ḥasidim—exemplify what I suppose to be the conservative mind of medieval rabbinism. It hardly seems likely that these persons would formulate new ideas that they would later present as the esoteric meaning of Judaism. Moreover, the manner in which some of them wrote down the earliest esoteric traditions, whether Provençal or Ashkenazic, attests to the fact that these texts reflect prior stages. We must particularly consider the fact that both the remnants of the works of R. Isaac the Blind and those of his contemporaries, such as R. Eleazar of Worms, are elaborate bodies of mystical thought that, although they may be difficult to understand, nevertheless reflect comprehensive approaches rather than brief insights or remarks. The fullness of these first mystical documents thus reflects earlier stages of development that have eluded historical documentation.[13]

I must note that this remark is not to be understood as an assertion of the antiquity of the Kabbalah. Without here entering into this highly complicated question, I would like to stress that Kabbalah may well be the result of certain religious developments without, however, stemming in its entirety from such earlier periods.

The importance of oral transmission was not drastically attenuated by the appearance of the Kabbala in the historical arena. Evidence of oral transmission can be easily adduced from a multitude of texts, even following the composition of the first Kabbalistic documents. I shall refer to only a few examples. The earliest statements on this subject by R. Isaac the Blind and Naḥmanides have already been mentioned. It should be noted, too, that certain Kabbalistic ideas were transmitted orally even to Kabbalists, and only after they attained the age of forty. As late as the early fourteenth century, a Kabbalist such R. Shem Tov ibn Gaon was ready to compose a supercommentary to Naḥmanides' hints of Kabbalistic secrets, but repeatedly mentioned that there were also matters that could not be revealed. Replying to a letter from one of his students who asked him to explain a certain Kabbalistic matter, R. Shem Tov wrote that he had not revealed it when he was teaching him because the student was then younger than forty; now that he had reached this age, he was far away, and such an issue could not be committed to writing.[14] Thus, we can readily see that, more than 150 years following the emergence of historical Kabbalah, some of its tenets were withheld even from relatively mature Kabbalists.

This example illustrates the need to distinguish carefully between what was understood as Kabbalah according to Kabbalistic masters, who revealed it only fragmentarily, and what contemporary scholars, who assumed that the discipline was disclosed in written documents, believed to be Kabbalah. It is reasonable to suppose that those Kabbalistic matters that were kept secret even from younger Kabbalists concerned sensitive pivotal subjects. Hence, if we do not attempt to uncover the hidden problems of the Kabbalists and to decode them, our view of Kabbalah may be, at least to a certain extent, misleading. As far as I know, consciousness of this methodological question is absent in modern research of Kabbalah; rather, this lore is described and analyzed on the implicit assumption that all major Kabbalistic views are presented as such in documents in an articulate manner.

Another important indicator of the crucial role of oral traditions can be found in Kabbalistic epistles and responsa, which afford a better understanding of Kabbalah. The short discussions contained in the epistles of R. Isaac the Blind addressed to R. Jonah Gerondi and Naḥmanides, in the letters of R. Abraham Abulafia, and especially in the responsa of R. David ben Yehudah he-Ḥasid to his students contain a variety of major subjects, some of which are unknown from other sources. At least in the case of R. David, in responsa intended for his students rather than for the public, certain issues are discussed in such a way as to provide clues to his esoteric doctrines. Other Kabbalistic masters who did not write down their views, such as R. Solomon ibn Adret, were frequently quoted by their students, providing conclusive evidence for the oral transmission of Kabbalistic tradition.

At this stage in the research of Kabbalah, it is difficult to evaluate the depth of the changes in our view of Kabbalah that could be brought about by a decoding of some esoteric layers of Kabbalah. It may be possible, through an analysis of R. David ben Yehudah's responsa, to fathom a level of theosophical and mystical doctrines hitherto unnoticed by modern research.[15] The existence of advanced states of ecstatic Kabbalah, taught orally, is suggested by the question the anonymous Kabbalist who authored the book *Sha'arey Ẓedek* asked his master: "In heaven's name, can you perhaps impart to me some power to enable me to bear this force emerging from my heart and receive influx from it?"[16] I would suppose that further discoveries of Kabbalists' epistles and responsa will entail major corrections in the academic understanding of Kabbalah. So much for the problems posed by the texts and their transmission.

IV. AN APPRAISAL OF A PHENOMENOLOGICAL APPROACH

Concentration on the philological-historical approach has resulted in the nearly complete rejection of the comparative study of Jewish mysticism. This concentration on texts and Kabbalistic figures, rather than on concepts and systems, was from the outset Scholem's approach. Despite his vast erudition in a large variety of religious cultures, he apparently chose textology over the comparative approach—a decision easily understood against the background of the need to carry on the hard work of preparing the first detailed inquiries into the entire Jewish mystical tradition. Bibliographical, historical, and textual research demanded a deliberate postponement of more elaborate comparisons of Kabbalah to other religious structures of thought, which would have had to be speculative, hence premature. We find no more than passing remarks on Gnostic, Catharic, or Christian sources in Scholem's works. Despite his recurrent insistence upon the influence of Gnosticism upon Kabbalah, he never presented in his published works a thorough treatment of the relationship of the two.

What I perceive as a conscious refrain in the founder of modern Kabbalah research, however, became in time a tacit ideology. For most of his students and followers, Scholem's initial commitment to the centrality of text study became an inert ideology of textology.[17] Even when the first stages of historical-textual studies were far in the past, the approach was not enriched by additional perspectives.[18] Despite the great number of studies on Kabbalah published since the late 1940s, mostly in Hebrew, the names of Mircea Eliade or R. C. Zaehner, not to mention Claude Lévi-Strauss, Gerardus Van der Leeuw, Victor Turner, and Paul Ricoeur, have been almost totally ignored. Only such "stars" of research of mystical thought as Ernst Cassirer or Evelyn Underhill occasionally shine in the firmament of these studies. These remarks, it should be noted, refer to the one-sided approach to texts based upon mythical and mystical concepts without taking into account the major developments in recent research of myth, symbolism, and mysticism. A striking lack of novel theories of the nature of Jewish mysticism that differ from those of Scholem is the result of this limited scope. His views have been repeated time and again with no proper attempt to add new theoretical perspectives influenced by modern research in comparative religion.[19]

I would like to be properly understood: I prefer a solid textological study to a bad comparative one. But the narrowness of textology when it alone is applied to mystical literature ought to be self-evident. On the other hand, I consider the simplistic addition of some comparative type of studies to textology to be equally pernicious. Let us take, for example, Mircea Eliade's booklets on comparative issues. The generalizations so characteristic of his later stage of research are only rarely sustained by textual evidence. The hybristic endeavors of Eliade to discover the "patterns" of religions can be compared only to the attempts of Jungian psychoanalysis to unfold the archetypes of the human psyche; their Platonic perspectives are highly reductionist and hermeneutical approaches to the variety of religious experiences and concepts. The mechanical application of the results of such types of research to Kabbalistic materials can only obfuscate an appropriate understanding of them. A strenuous effort to become aware of the possibilities inherent in various fields of modern religious research can, one hopes, fertilize the aridity of the conceptual approach to Kabbalah in the last decades. Only a balanced combination of textual and comparative approaches to Kabbalistic material will contribute to a better formulation of the unique nature of certain Kabbalistic views. The comparative approach, at least as practiced by Eliade, tends to ignore the unique features of any given religious structure; through sound textological examination the characteristics of a given mystical phenomenon can be retained, while its uniqueness, if and where it exists, can be placed in proper relief by its comparison to related phenomena.

Because of scholars' restraint in regard to utilizing current concepts and notions of comparative and phenomenological studies of religion, they have rarely succeeded in integrating the study of Kabbalah into the larger discussion of mysticism. Kabbalah has seldom merited mention in the studies of Joachim Wach, R. C. Zaehner, W. T. Stace, and Frits Staal. Moreover, the structure of Kabbalistic thought has been only poorly elucidated in a conceptual manner, which could fructify the modern research of religion in general and mysticism in particular. More than any other statements of Scholem, his assertion that *unio mystica* is absent in Jewish mysticism has been repeated by scholars of general mysticism.[20]

This last observation expresses the possibility or probability that Kabbalah was actually a practical-experiential type of mysticism more than a speculative theory. It was comprehensive, as it commonly included both mystical perceptions of being and attempts to modify it. A scholar who approaches Kabbalistic literature only textologically (almost the single main perspective in present research) is unable to be sensitive to vital aspects of Kabbalistic phenomena. I have already discussed the possible contributions of comparative study to a more precise understanding of this lore. But there is no reason to refrain from careful use of other branches of humanistic studies—for example, psychology. This field has provided a great variety of theories concerning the human psyche and its processes. As some Kabbalists refer covertly or overtly to spiritual experiences, we cannot neglect the contribution of one or another psychological theory to the fathoming of certain Kabbalistic phenomena. Again, Scholem avoided the use of psychological theories or concepts. Indeed, the quotations from Kabbalistic literature and their analysis by one of Scholem's great contemporaries, Carl Jung, are problematic.

Jung's interest in Kabbalah was great, and he even dreamed "Kabbalistic" dreams. But this interest in and even identification with Kabbalistic conceptions cannot mitigate his sheer misunderstanding of his sources and his reductionist approach to these texts. Although the same criticism can hold regarding Jung's analysis of other types of literature, such as alchemic, Gnostic, or Hindu texts, I am doubtful, at least insofar as Kabbalah is concerned, whether anything substantial can be learned from Jung's discussion of the particular passages he quotes in his works. I would like to stress, however, that more careful attempts to use Jungian conceptions may nevertheless be useful for certain aspects of Kabbalistic mysticism, such as, for example, the understanding of the Kabbalistic circle that appeared during revelatory experiences.[21] Furthermore, analysis of the psychological implications of using Kabbalistic techniques to attain paranormal experiences cannot be avoided. If the approach proposed here to see Kabbalah far more in terms of experiential phenomena than has been previously done is correct, then psychology, as an invaluable tool, must gradually be integrated into future study of this kind of mysticism.

V. BETWEEN SCHOLARS AND MYSTICS

It has been suggested that practical involvement of the scholar of mysticism in the mystical experience itself can contribute to his better understanding of the mystical phenomena. This assertion seems to me problematic, albeit not devoid of some truth. An experience undergone by a given individual may be highly idiosyncratic, so that any use of his own impressions and feelings in order to better understand and express those of another person may be misleading to the same extent that they are helpful. But contact with Kabbalists who both study and conduct their lives in accordance with the requirements of the Kabbalah can enrich the academic vision of what Kabbalah is. Direct contact with the manner in which Kabbalists approach mystical texts during their studies, the sight of Kabbalists praying, and especially, discussions with them regarding mystical issues can substantially contribute to the crystallization of the scholar's perception of Kabbalah. Strangely enough, despite the close proximity of Kabbalistic circles in Jerusalem and Benai Barak to the academic centers for the study of Kabbalah, such contacts are not regarded by the academic establishment as productive, all research in Kabbalah instead being focused exclusively on written texts. For this reason, no up-to-date picture is available on current Kabbalistic thought. More than one hundred years after ethnologists came to regard the collection of data and contact with remote tribes as essential for their descriptive work, and two decades after the introduction of the psychophysiological study of mystical experiences, researchers in Jewish mysticism work exclusively in relation to texts, without even an awareness of the necessity of making the acquaintance of their close neighbors, the Kabbalists.

The establishment of contacts between academicians and Kabbalists involves certain difficulties in comparison with the ethnologists' need to meet members of primitive cultures, but, obviously, it also has its own facilities. The latter are numerous: the scholar and the Kabbalist share a considerable body of knowledge of exoteric religious issues from the outset; they speak the same language (or languages—to the extent that knowledge of Yiddish is widespread among scholars of Ḥasidism); they have both already studied a certain amount of esoteric literature. But the stumbling blocks are great, although not insurmountable. The Kabbalist is, at the outset, suspicious of the strange "monstrosity" he is going to meet: a nonreligious person—such are most of the scholars of Kabbalah—who is involved in the study of the Holy of Holies of Judaism, a realm reserved, according to the Kabbalists, for the very few and even saintly persons who are already accomplished students of halakhah. But notwithstanding any initial reticence, a dialogue is not impossible, even for women scholars, who are—from the traditional Jewish perspective—not supposed to study Kabbalah at all. More problematic is the great difference in their respective perceptions of texts and concepts, inherent in the difference between the academic attitude and the traditional one. The historicist bias of the academic perspective, if not coupled with the sensibility that grows out of the phenomenological effort to understand a mystical phenomenon as an entity in itself, may cut the dialogue short at the beginning. For example, modern research is notorious in religious circles for its denial of R. Simeon bar Yoḥai's authorship of the *Zohar,* a very important issue for the Kabbalists. Thus concentration on historical problems may constitute a minefield in the way of further discussion.

One may ask why a Kabbalist would wish to embark on such a suspicious dialogue. The reasons on the part of the academician are obvious. He may enrich himself both as a person and as a scholar through his direct contact with a mentality he attempts to penetrate; moreover, he may learn of traditions that are circulating only orally or of the existence of manuscripts otherwise unknown. On the other hand, the Kabbalists today are in a strange situation: at times they are isolated individuals in their own milieu, even when they are leading figures. Interested in a more nuanced self-definition, they may endeavor to stand face to face even with the "heretical" academy. In addition, the great achievements of academic studies in the fields of bibliography and history of Kabbalah turn the scholar into a potential source of information regarding certain technical details, even for the most erudite among the

Kabbalists. The systematic classification of biobibliographical knowledge of Kabbalah in the academic world far outstrips the poor acquaintance of the Kabbalists with this particular area. Now, for the first time, academicians can not only learn from the Kabbalists and their works but also help them by providing information on manuscripts or biographical data on Kabbalists that would otherwise be inaccessible to them.

VI. JEWISH MYSTICISM AS AN EXPERIENTIAL LORE

The impression received from a perusal of the scholarly descriptions of Kabbalah is that of a system of theosophical conceptions, various beliefs, and hermeneutical devices. Kabbalah is often presented as a body of theoretical lore, more a gnosis than a practical or experiential attitude to reality. Before we discuss the problems entailed in this theoretical perception of Kabbalah, it would be helpful to consider the manner in which modern scholars view the earlier, preceding stages of Jewish mysticism.

Scholem repeatedly presented the literature of the Heikhalot or the Merkavah as a body of mystical teachings also embodying descriptions of mystical experiences. Since the beginning of the present decade, however, some scholars have insisted upon the nonexperiential nature of the various works forming this literature. Some, such as E. E. Urbach, have depicted some of the mystical descriptions belonging to the Heikhalot literature as elaborations upon prior discussions in the Talmud and Midrash concerning the experience of revelation at Sinai.[22] According to this view, the proper approach to these texts is literary: the uncovering of their written source transforms these seemingly mystical texts into literary elaborations of earlier material, a perspective adopted as well by David Halperin.[23] Minute inspection of the manuscripts of the Heikhalot texts led Peter Schäfer to the conclusion that these works are redactions of earlier traditions, implicitly reducing the possibility of regarding them as descriptions of authentic mystical experiences.[24] For the time being, this "literary" approach is the dominant one.

The next step in the development of Jewish mysticism, Ashkenazic Ḥasidism, has been described as an "esoteric theology" rather than a properly mystical movement.[25] There is sufficient evidence, however, to justify the attempt to present the experiential facets of this theology. Various references to figures from the Rhineland and northern France as "prophets" and the existence of techniques implying a deep interest in experimental mysticism are solid proof for the occurrence of mystical experiences also among the Franco-German authors; but again, no one has initiated such a project.[26]

Scholars have analyzed the literary structures of some Kabbalistic treatises and engaged in lengthy discussions on the nature of the Sefirot, of the source of evil, of the feminine aspects in the divine realm, and so on. To understand Kabbalah is, accordingly, seen as tantamount to understanding its tenets. This approach is not new; it has been in use since the Renaissance, when Christian authors interested in occult lores involved themselves in the study of the Kabbalah. For them, Kabbalah was primarily a concealed philosophy whose inner message had to be decoded, owing to the obscurity of its terminology and symbolism.[27] This attitude was also embraced by various thinkers of the Enlightenment period and ultimately adopted by modern researchers of Kabbalah.[28]

But the evaluation of Kabbalah as predominantly theoretical rather than practical is misleading. Although the large body of printed Kabbalistical literature indeed deals with theoretical issues, an understanding of Kabbalah based primarily upon this material is highly problematic, as it cannot be aptly appreciated without taking into consideration what seems to me to be the ultimate goals of Kabbalah. According to the perceptions of the Kabbalists themselves, this lore is primarily practical and experiential, and only secondarily theoretical. The practical and experiential aspects, however, are found mainly in manuscript treatises, which were intentionally preserved for the use of the few. It is sufficient to mention here the scores of R. Abraham Abulafia's works, including several handbooks of mystical techniques that were never printed. The many books written by Kabbalists belonging to the school of ecstatic Kabbalah likewise remained in manuscript, including the fourth gate of R. Ḥayyim Vital's *Sha'arey Kedushah,* which is heavily influenced by this branch of Kabbalah. Another major example of suppression is the voluminous *Sefer ha-Meshiv,* a text that originally consisted, as I understand it, of several hundred folios. Despite its influence on Safedian Kabbalah as well as on Sabbatian thought, substantial parts were never published, and others were apparently lost. This work includes divine and angelic revelations, as well as instructions on how to attain them. The Kabbalists considered both the content of the revelations and the techniques—which shall be discussed below—too sensitive to be published for a large audience. Yet the academic study of Kabbalah has neglected even this masterwork of Kabbalistic mysticism.

Another major genre of Kabbalistic literature that has passed nearly unnoticed by scholars is the extensive literature concerning the rationales for the commandments. As I have already remarked, since Kabbalah's beginnings as a historical phenomenon, Kabbalists produced an impressive number of theosophico-theurgical commentaries on the commandments—several thousand folios. Only a small part of these were published, the other, greater portion remaining in manuscript form. The contents of this field of Kabbalah have been neglected by scholarly research. The publication and detailed analysis of this material, which is of great importance for a more profound understanding of the spiritual aspect of Kabbalah, may contribute to a change in our perception of this lore from a theoretical to a more practical and experiential emphasis. Through performing the commandments with Kabbalistic intentions, a Kabbalist not only was acting according to a prescribed and fixed ritual but also was entering into a particular experience of participating in, and influencing, the divine life. This statement can easily be exemplified through a specific, though common, commandment: prayer. Although this particular commandment was analyzed more than any other, some of the Kabbalistic commentaries on prayer are still in manuscript, ignored by those scholars who have surveyed mystical prayer in Judaism. Even the scores of commentaries on the prayerbook—some of which are highly interesting, such as those of Moses Cordovero or Naftali Hirtz Treves—remained beyond the scope of various studies on prayer. This neglect has affected a large portion of Kabbalistic literature and contributed to the formation of a one-sided image of the nature of Kabbalah. Furthermore, appropriate analyses of these types of literature could catalyze an interesting transformation in our understanding of the role played by the theoretical element in Kabbalistic literature in the Kabbalists' mystical life.

Being for the most part a topography of the divine realm, this theoretical literature served more as a map than as speculative description. Maps, as we know, are intended to enable a person to fulfill a journey; for the Kabbalists, the mystical experience was such a journey. Though I cannot assert that every "theoretical" work indeed served such a use, this seems to have been the main purpose of the greatest part of this literature. I likewise presume that there were Kabbalists who never undertook mystical journeys, but were content to collect, classify, and afterward describe the material stemming from the labors of their predecessors or colleagues, just as one can sketch a map without ever having actually seen the territory involved. This reservation notwithstanding, however, an organic conception of the various bodies of Kabbalistic literature may reveal unexpected affinities among seemingly disparate literary genres; thus, for example, commentaries on the ten Sefirot may serve as aids for the performance of commandments, or for praying, with Kabbalistic intention.

VII. KABBALAH: A GNOSTIC REPERCUSSION?

Finally, some historical remarks may be in order here. Scholem's theory of the emergence of Kabbalah in Provence was based on the assumption that this religious phenomenon was the result of the merger of older Gnostic motifs or traditions with Neoplatonic philosophy.[29] This assumption was never substantiated by a separate study of the topic as such, although Scholem did eventually refer to what he considered to be parallels between early Kabbalistic material, mostly in *Sefer ha-Bahir,* and Gnostic motifs. The latter, however, were only rarely discussed in detail,[30] and the impression left is that Scholem considered the "novel" elements in the Kabbalistic version of Judaism as ancient traditions that infiltrated Jewish circles, were esoterically passed down within these closed circles, and eventually surfaced in late twelfth-century Provence, where they were combined with Neoplatonic concepts. This notion of the emergence of the theories of the Kabbalah theoretically allows for the contributions of the earlier strata of Jewish thought: Talmud and Midrash, Heikhalot literature, *piyyut* and Jewish philosophy, and, finally, Ashkenazic Ḥasidism. Practically none of these, however, was envisaged as a major source of those elements that constitute the peculiar physiognomy of the Kabbalistic phenomenon; basically, Kabbalah was seen as the result of an outbreak of new ideas that reinterpreted rabbinic Judaism according to religious categories comparatively alien in the literature of classical Judaism. Scholem's efforts were thus directed toward the uncovering of the Gnostic and Neoplatonic concepts that underlay early Kabbalah; although he considered it a Jewish phenomenon, he endeavored to explain its roots as belonging to non-Jewish intellectual universes.[31] This is, mutatis mutandis, a much more elaborated, detailed, and documented version of the perspective of Adolphe Franck and Heinrich Graetz.

This vision of Kabbalah as Jewish Gnosticism is an organic sequel to Scholem's understanding of Heikhalot literature as a "Gnostic" phenomenon. This "Gnostification" of Jewish mysticism—which was later continued in Scholem's view of Sabbatianism—took place in a particular intellectual atmosphere, in which Hans Jonas's works had begun to be influential. It is worthwhile examining the relationship between Gnosticism and Jewish mysticism against the background of modern studies on Gnosticism. Research undertaken in recent decades seems to have contributed a novel approach to the long-debated problem of the origins of Gnostic thought. Far more than did scholars in the first half of the twentieth century, contemporary scholars of Gnosticism refer to Jewish influence on the emerging Gnostic literature; the studies of Gilles Quispel,[32] George MacRae,[33] B. Pearson,[34] Gedaliahu Stroumsa,[35] and Jarl Fossum[36] have altered the earlier Iranian-Egyptian-Greek explanations of Gnosticism.[37] The potentially far-reaching significance of these modern studies for the history of Jewish mysticism has not yet been noticed. The assumption that Jewish mythologoumena were influential on ancient Gnostic literature, but not the other way around, allows for a completely different hypothesis for the sources of Kabbalah.

If the parallels noted by Scholem are indeed more than accidental resemblances, but reflect historical affinities, then I would propose another explanation: ancient Jewish motifs that penetrated Gnostic texts remained at the same time the patrimony of Jewish thought and continued to be transmitted in Jewish circles, ultimately providing the conceptual framework of Kabbalah. This theory postulates a long series of links that cannot be proven by the extant Jewish texts; however, this difficulty also holds if we accept Scholem's theory that the earliest Kabbalistic documents derived from ancient Gnostic traditions. Furthermore, the assumption that the so-called Gnostic elements that were formative factors in early Kabbalah were originally non-Jewish cannot explain why Jews were interested in absorbing them in general and how they came to be understood as the esoteric interpretation of Judaism. Furthermore, if such a metamorphosis indeed took place in antiquity and remained subterranean, it is hardly reasonable to assume that the first Kabbalists, some of whom were members of the rabbinic establishment, would be prepared to accept these traditions as constituting an authoritative understanding of Jewish texts. Such experts in texts as R. Abraham ben David, Naḥmanides, or R. Solomon ben Abraham ibn Adret can hardly be described as naive thinkers who would accept, as the mystical core of Judaism, traditions that were in principle unrelated to it. Because such a stance would have been highly uncharacteristic of these men, the misreading is a strange one.

It is, however, possible to assume that, if the motifs transmitted in those unknown circles formed part of an ancient weltanschauung, their affinities to the rabbinic mentality would be more organic and easily absorbed into the mystical cast of Judaism. According to this hypothesis, we do not need to account for why ancient Jews took over Gnostic doctrines, why they transmitted them, and, finally, how this "Gnostic" Judaism was revived in the Middle Ages by conservative Jewish authorities. Furthermore, an attempt to study Jewish mysticism along the lines I have proposed has a manifest methodological advantage: it postulates a relatively organic evolution of Jewish mysticism that can be demonstrated by using Hebrew material found in the various layers of Jewish literature and that, consequently, can also be rejected by philological or historical analysis of the texts. It is obvious that my proposal is consonant with some of the assertions of the Kabbalists themselves, who repeatedly asserted that the Kabbalah is a genuine ancient tradition which is an esoteric interpretation of Judaism. This self-perception has been systematically disregarded by modern research of Kabbalah, with no detailed analysis. The traditional understanding of Kabbalah needs, therefore, to be carefully re-evaluated and checked against findings in the related fields of Gnosticism, Midrash, and Talmud. All these types of literature could provide relevant material for what I assume was a silent growth of ancient Jewish esotericism. I do not propose to neglect Gnostic material but rather to examine it in order to extract evidence for the existence of Jewish views that were partially or totally neglected by ancient Jewish texts. The most serious work, however, must be invested in Jewish texts, which need to be meticulously inspected as relevant sources for later mystical or mythical motifs.

VIII. AN APPRAISAL FOR RECONSTRUCTION

The affinities between Kabbalistic concepts, mainly theosophical ones, and the earlier Jewish material are important for more than one reason. Not only can they provide evidence for the antiquity of some of the Kabbalistic views, as I have pointed out; these medieval mystical treatises elaborate upon seemingly ancient concepts that can eventually provide important clues for the better understanding of their meaning or of the structures in which they were incorporated. Theosophical Kabbalah is, as a whole, a systematic exposition of a worldview, which surpasses the fragmentary treatment of theological topics either in the Talmud and Midrash or in Gnostic literature. If Kabbalah preserved some material historically linked with ancient Jewish concepts that can still be detected in ancient literature, it is also plausible that early Kabbalistic literature preserved other ancient material no longer extant in other bodies of literature. This is a highly hypothetical assumption, but one that cannot be rejected without more profound examination.

On the basis of a series of studies published in recent years, I should like to propose what I call the reconstructionalist approach, which may be described as an attempt to use the more elaborate conceptual structures of the Kabbalah in order to examine various ancient motifs and to organize them in coherent structures.[38] This approach is based on the assumption that not only unrelated motifs of ancient extraction reached medieval Kabbalah but also more complex structures, no longer extant in other texts. The use of Kabbalistic literature both as a source of material that may contribute to better understanding of individual motifs and as a source of inspiration for constructing larger structures to permit a broader understanding of ancient mysticism is certainly complicated and must be attempted only with great caution. A prudent and meticulous examination of both the Kabbalistic material and the pre-Kabbalistic traditions may yield significant results. But if one assumes that ancient Jewish mystics, who exerted some influence on Gnosticism, were in the possession of a more complex notion of divine reality and of Jewish tradition, one will only rarely find more elaborate discussions on these issues in ancient texts. I assume that Kabbalah has probably preserved some ancient conceptual structures that supply a more unified view of the otherwise unrelated and sometimes unintelligible motifs and texts. This reconstructionalist approach mostly concerns the pre-Kabbalistic texts, the understanding of which can be improved by applying a previously unexpected conceptual structure to an ancient text. The adequacy of this method, however, is indirectly important for the question of the antiquity of the Kabbalah; the possibility of approaching some ancient material with the help of modes of thinking preserved in Kabbalah may demonstrate that this lore not only makes use of older motifs but also continues more comprehensive intellectual patterns.

I cannot exemplify this methodological approach here, but I have made use of it in several articles in which I have attempted to show that anthropomorphic perceptions of the angelic world[39] and of the Torah[40] preserved in an explicit and elaborated way only in Kabbalah can illuminate our understanding of earlier midrashic, talmudic, and Gnostic texts, as well as certain remarks found in the Heikhalot literature. Similarly, the Kabbalistic equation of Metatron with the "supernal anthropos" is corroborated by several ancient texts, which reflect the existence of a notion of Enoch's ascent as a return to the lost state of Adam, viewed as a cosmic anthropos.[41]

The treatment of the topics that follow is conducted in accordance with the above-described approach.[42] I shall check the earlier Jewish sources for both the conceptual attitudes of Kabbalah and the mystical techniques it employed. This task is by no means an easy one; the potentially relevant material is spread over hundreds of treatises, including talmudic, midrashic, and poetic literature in Hebrew, and apocryphal works in a variety of languages. The main stumbling block, however, is not the huge quantity of material but the fact that it has been treated to date in a peculiar way; the mythical elements inherent in its conceptual structure were neglected by scholarly analyses that commonly preferred a nonmythical reconstruction consonant with the theological inclinations prevalent in the rationalistic approaches to Judaism of the Wissenschaft des Judentums. Without a new understanding of the mystical, mythical, and theurgic motifs and concepts or the broader intellectual structures found in the ancient and early medieval Jewish literatures, Kabbalah is doomed to remain a medieval revolution that enigmatically exploded in the bosom of "nonmythical" rabbinic centers.[43] Romantic and charming as such an explanation may be, it does not take into serious consideration the conservative trend of the rabbinic mind or its critical acumen toward texts; nor can the scholarly evaluation of Kabbalah as a novelty explain how it came to be accepted—first in a few elite circles and later on by a wider public—without significant opposition during the first hundred years of its appearance as a historical phenomenon, and with only limited and ineffective protests after the late fifteenth century.[44] There seems to be a great gap in the estimation of the Kabbalah between its popular understanding as an ancient authentic esoteric Jewish lore and the scholarly disenchantment with this phenomenon as an intrusion of Gnosticism and Neoplatonism under the misleading guise of esoteric Judaism.

CHAPTER 3

Varieties of Devekut in Jewish Mysticism

If mysticism is the quintessence of religion, the quintessence of mysticism is the sense of union with God. The intensification of religious life that characterizes most forms of mysticism culminates at times in paranormal experiences, whose literary expression appears in descriptions of unitive relations with supermundane beings and sometimes ultimately with God himself. Without taking a stand in the dispute over the ultimate nature of mystical experience as such, a scrutiny of its expression in the literary medium reveals rather limited forms of semantic articulation: erotic imagery, noetic propositions, and unitive phrases constitute most of the stuff of these descriptions.

Stemming from standard religious terminology or from philosophical texts, these statements attempt to convey an experience that surpasses ordinary states of consciousness. The assumption, implicit or explicit, that these documents describe experiences that transcend normal consciousness is generally accepted by both mystics and scholars of mysticism; however, little attention has been paid by the latter to the implications of such an assumption for the study of mystical experience. At its best, the mystic's testimony is a veil covering a psychic process that as such must remain beyond the scope of textual studies. At worst, it reflects conventions accepted in their social and religious milieu and may be helpful for the understanding of their intellectual parameters.

It is my conviction that psychological or psychoanalytical approaches to mystical texts must be employed with care, given the reductionist tendency inherent in their hermeneutical techniques. The chance of success in reconstructing the nature of a mystical experience from written texts is close to nil. As the components of this experience—the human psyche, the external and inner conditions, and the divine aspects that enter the experience—are either fluid or incomprehensible, or both, any reconstruction is mostly an approximation based more on the presuppositions and tendencies of the scholar than on recombination of the authentic components of the original experience.[1]

It follows that the psychological processes described by mystical literature as unitive experiences are beyond the scope of academic research. If so, the scholar making a serious comparison among mystics, even when they belong to the same religious group, must limit himself to an analysis of their motifs, ideas, and sources, abjuring inferences as to the similarities or differences between the actual experiences. Another important consequence is that attempts to characterize the mystical experiences in a given religion must be limited to the expressions found in its literature alone, without attempting to infer from them the typology of the experiences themselves.

Textual and comparative approaches to unitive imagery, rather than tentative discussions on the "nature" of the unitive experience, are more than a literary exercise. These approaches, although intentionally refraining from defining the psychic processes themselves, transcend mere literary interpretation by focusing attention upon the self-understanding of the mystic, on the one hand, and on the religious-sociological categories accepted by both the mystic and his intellectual milieu, on the other hand. I assume that the conscious or unconscious impact of the mystic's prior intellectual structures is discernible, more in the form of the written expression of his allegedly unitive experience than in the contents of that experience itself. Therefore, more room must be allowed for hermeneutics and history of ideas than for psychology or psychoanalysis. Again, without denying the psychological and/or ontological aspects of mystical union, the focus of study must be upon their manifestation rather than on their inner essence.

My argument against the possibility of the reconstruction of unitive experience or any experience in general does not apply to the study of mysticism as a whole; as far as the mystical path is concerned, including such subjects as mystical techniques, revelations, or theosophical systems, I believe we can benefit to a far greater extent from both psychological and theological approaches. The less the matters to be analyzed depend upon momentary experiences, idiosyncratic characteristics of the mystic, or extreme anomalous or paranormal states of consciousness, the greater the likelihood that they can be successfully articulated to persons living on relatively "normal" psychological levels. Again, the argument against projection of postexperience confessions concerning *unio mystica* onto the experience itself is in a sense related to the famous "ineffability" argument of the mystics themselves. Whether this type of experience is indescribable or not is beyond my line of argumentation, as I propose to refrain from the use of descriptions for reconstruction of the experience insofar as it is defined as a mystical union, even when the mystics maintain that these descriptions may be appropriate for their experience.

Let me briefly exemplify the complexities involved in inferences from texts on the nature of experiences. Two differing states of *unio mystica* may be expressed in the same phrase taken from the same sacred text, whereas similar experiences may be expressed in various ways because of the differences between the literary sources available to the mystic. We must, therefore, be aware that similar shells may cover different cores, just as the same core may eventually hide under various shells. For more than one reason, the study of mysticism is similar to the attempt to imagine the content of a shell whose core has never been seen by the scholar.

This skeptical attitude toward the possibility of fully reconstructing the meaning of mystical experiences also implies a hesitant attitude toward the approach that overstresses the importance of traditional elements for the emergence of these experiences.[2] Without denying the probability that the mystic is sometimes conditioned by images, concepts, and various *realia* that may indeed mold his experience, whereas other times it is amorphous,[3] I think that their impact is on the manner of expression rather than on the mode of the experience itself. Emphasizing the pre-experiential elements as molding the experience itself is basically an implicit attempt to demystify it, and as Eliade succinctly put it,[4] "demystification does not serve hermeneutics."[5] To put it in Paul Ricoeur's terms: "Another reason for having recourse to exegesis rather than theology is that it invites us not to separate the figures of God from the form of discourse in which these figures occur. . . . Because the designation of God is in each case different."[6]

An important issue to be addressed in the context of the discussion of mystical techniques is the close affinity between the pre-experiential elements and the contents of the experience itself. As I have proposed above, there is a good chance that theological and sociological factors enter into the experience. I have tended, however, to emphasize the centrality of text over the variety of possible theological issues that may be relevant for an understanding of a given mystical phenomenon. Nevertheless, the cautious attitude toward granting a central role to pre-experiential elements is superfluous in the specific case of mystical techniques. In those instances in which we know for certain that a certain mystic used specific practices in order to induce his mystical experience, it would be methodologically advisable to employ the components of the techniques in order better to understand the contents of the text. I propose this approach because of the immediate proximity of the particular practice to the experience itself, a fact that renders it a potential factor molding the consciousness of the mystic in the crucial moment of the experience.

I shall open our discussion on Kabbalistic views of the mystical experience with a short terminological survey.

I. DEVEKUT: A HISTORICAL SURVEY

Cleaving to God is an explicit biblical imperative; its multiple recurrence in the Pentateuch strongly points to the importance attached to this commandment.[7] Less clear, however, is the peculiar meaning of this cleaving; given the numinous nature of the Divine in the eyes of biblical Jews, an understanding of the verb *dbk* as referring to union or to "mere" communion between the human and the divine essence is improbable. We can assume that this imperative must be regarded as a demand for devotion to the divine will or to the way promulgated in the divine revelation. Understood in this manner, *devekut* indicates a rather active attitude, a call upon the Jew to strengthen the bond between himself and God. The elite was supposed to cleave to God's ways or attributes by various versions of *imitatio dei*,[8] whereas the vulgus could participate in this cleaving only indirectly.

A certain holding back from the mystical implications of this term is evident in some talmudic-midrashic passages that, according to A. J. Heschel, stem from the school of R. Ishmael, in which *devekut* is interpreted in terms of one performing pious deeds, such as marrying one's daughter to a scholar. On the other hand, R. 'Akiva, a contemporary of R. Ishmael, is regarded as the author of a mystical perception of cleaving that maintains: "'But ye that did cleave unto the Lord your God'—literally cleaving."[9] The use of the word *mamash* (literally) in this context is intriguing; it suggests a distinctly mystical understanding that is corroborated, according to Heschel, by another passage found in the same talmudic source.[10] Rav, a mystically oriented *amora* who tended to follow R. 'Akiva's views, indicated that the same verse in Deuteronomy points to the cleaving together of "two [palm] dates."[11] From the context, we may conclude that cleaving is a closer kind of contact than "attaching," as exemplified by the contact of a bracelet with a woman's arm. Though *devekut* apparently cannot be regarded here as mystical union in the extreme sense, it nevertheless seems to imply real contact between two entities, more than mere attachment of the devotee to God. According to R. Eleazar, "Whoever cleaves to the divine presence, the divine spirit will surely dwell upon him."[12] This text presupposes the possibility of cleaving to the *Shekhinah*; from the context, it is not clear whether this entity is identical with God or is to be understood as a manifestation of him. Even if the latter alternative is the more congenial interpretation, assuming a certain independence of the *Shekhinah* from God, it is nevertheless considered to be a divine entity, cleaving to which was negated in other classical rabbinic texts.

R. 'Akiva's younger contemporary, Numenius of Apamea (in Syria), is regarded as one of the two sources of Plotinus' conception of mystical union;[13] the other is, directly or indirectly, Jewish, as E. R. Dodds has proposed.[14] As is well known, Numenius was acquainted with Jewish conceptions; it stands to reason that not only might Philo's mystical thought[15] have been the source of Numenius' view, but also concepts related to R. 'Akiva, who was close to Numenius in both space and time.[16] The fact that a certain mystical view of *devekut* occurs in both rabbinic and Philonic[17] texts would seem to point to a common source. This ancient, presumably Jewish, conception might have influenced Numenius and Plotinus.

Explicitly mystical interpretations of *devekut* occur in Jewish medieval and postmedieval texts. Some of them may convey real mystical, possibly unitive, experiences; others may represent exegetical attempts to interpret sacred texts. There is no way to either confirm or negate the possibility that such types of experience existed among Jews, even before the written evidence on unitive experiences emerged. The fact that this happened, however, only after the appearance of philosophical terminology demonstrates that philosophical concepts were a garb used by mystics in order to articulate their experiences. I should like to propose a typology of concepts and images used to communicate the unitive perception of a mystical experience that will show the gamut of divine nomenclature in this domain. One can distinguish three main types of *devekut* terminology: Aristotelian, Neoplatonic, and Hermetic, according to the specific bodies of speculative literatures that generated the various themes.

1. Aristotelian terminology primarily provided concepts for what was called intellectual union. According to Aristotelian epistemology, during the act of cognition the knower and the known, or the intellect and the intelligible, are one; this is true of both human and divine acts of intellection. It is only logical to suppose that the act of intellection wherein God is the object of the human intellect amounts to what is known as mystical union.

This conception of intellection permeated all Aristotelian schools—Greek, Arabic, Jewish, and Christian.[18] Of primary importance for the development of Kabbalah were the unitive notions of intellection (union with the Active Intellect or with God) discussed by such Jewish and Arabic thinkers as Maimonides, Samuel ibn Tibbon, Avicenna, Abubaker ibn Bajja, and Averroës.[19] It should be noted, however, that the possibility of union ("conjunction" with immaterial entities ("separate intellects"), let alone with God, was a problematic issue in these sources. The pertinent texts of these philosophers were translated into Hebrew and represent milestones of Jewish thought: some of the Kabbalists who studied them or were in personal contact with one of these thinkers, ibn Tibbon, absorbed and adopted the Aristotelian philosophical jargon. As we shall see later, an entire tradition of intellectual union can be traced from the earliest Kabbalistic documents in Gerona down to Ḥasidism. The impact of Aristotelian terminology, however, is more evident in the ecstatic Kabbalah than in any other branches of this lore. This terminology likewise occurs in instances where descriptions of extreme types of union are intended, far more than in those cases in which mere communion or attachment is meant. Therefore, at least in the case of Jewish mysticism, Aristotelian thought contributed a major share to the emergence of mystical terminology, a contribution tantamount to the Platonic one, and perhaps even greater. A general comparison of Jewish mysticism to that of Islam and Christianity would seem to support the assertion that, in the former, the role played by "intellectual" terminology transcends the importance of such terminology in the latter two.

2. Another important source of motifs, concepts, and terms supplying significant material to Jewish medieval mysticism was Neoplatonism, which was mainly interested in the union of the human soul with its root, the universal soul or, at times, God. Typical signs of the penetration of Neoplatonic thought are mention of the transformation of the particular soul into the universal soul or of the ascent of the soul or her return as central to the mystical experience. Again, as in the case of Aristotelian terminology, Neoplatonism reached the Jewish mystics via the intermediacy of philosophers—Arab, Jewish, and only rarely Christian; its influence is easily discerned as beginning with Geronese Kabbalah and continuing into Ḥasidism. The deep religious significance of this form of philosophy for mysticism has already been recognized in the cases of Islamic and Christian mysticism, and Kabbalah fully shares with these mystical systems a deep interest in Neoplatonism.

3. The last major source of terminology for the description of mystical experiences is an undefined corpus of speculative writings, including Neoplatonic and Hermetic treatises, with strong magical interests, widely known also as theurgy. According to several ancient works, which include part of the

Hermetic corpus and Iamblicus and Proclus, we are able to draw the spirits of the gods downward into humanly prepared statues, which thereby enter into communication with men. Sometimes, according to these magical views, these spirits can enter the magician himself and take possession of him.[20] These experiences were attained by the use of certain technical devices: incantations, fumigations, and so on. The contact between the magician and the higher beings was therefore achieved not by his ascent to them but by drawing them down into a lower realm. This "descent" magic gradually changed into a mysticism of descent, in which supernal spirits—commonly designated as *ruḥaniut,* spiritual beings—were drawn by the mystics upon themselves, the latter thereby attaining a mystical union.[21] The descent of these spiritual beings was accomplished by detailed practices, mainly by the combination of letters and their recitation, as in the ecstatic Kabbalah, or by the concentration of mind and direction of the heart while performing the commandments, as in Ḥasidism.

Although the various types of terminology referred to above reflect different metaphysical assumptions and entered Jewish texts from varied sources, in more than one instance their influences merged. Abraham Abulafia, who was mainly interested in the Aristotelian and Hermetic views, was also influenced by the Neoplatonic one, as was the case with R. Moses Cordovero and Ḥasidic mysticism. We cannot, therefore, speak of three separate interpretations of *devekut* presented in distinct texts of mystics, but of the interplay of three major terminologies throughout Jewish mystical material. The experiences referred to by these terminologies were held to enable one to bridge the gap between man—mainly his spiritual faculties—and God in rather radical ways.

The centrality of philosophical terminology for Kabbalistic expressions of mystical experience is a significant indicator of the fertilization of Jewish mysticism by alien views; a major segment of medieval mysticism was heavily influenced by philosophical motifs and concepts that substantially changed Jewish language expressive of human relationship to divinity. Notwithstanding the philosophical sources of that terminology, however, it underwent an important change when it was absorbed in Kabbalistic circles. Philosophical literature is poor in descriptions of personal experiences that are interpreted by speculative terminology; although there are a few examples—such as Plotinus or Porphyry—they are exceptions that confirm the rule. In Kabbalah we find not only theoretical discussions on the possibility of union with God, the Sefirot, or the active intellect but also descriptions of spiritual experiences that were occasionally interpreted by using philosophical terms. Thus, Kabbalah attempted to spiritualize philosophical thought by decoding personal mystical experiences according to speculative concepts that were rendered in terms of Aristotelian or Neoplatonic thought. For some Kabbalists, Maimonides' definition of prophecy was more than a philosophical statement about the prophetic process; it was the description of a mystical contact with a higher entity. Philosophy not only served as a discipline based upon physics and psychology but also offered the ecstatic Kabbalist a better understanding of his own experiences; instead of dealing with "objective" issues, the philosophical terms were sometimes applied by Kabbalists to "subjective" processes. One result of this metamorphosis was the attenuation of the "rational" burden attached to these terms; as we shall later see, the "cleaving of thought" possesses in early Kabbalistic texts emotional overtones that increase in the later Ḥasidic ones.

We shall analyze two major examples of philosophical terminology that had already infiltrated the earliest Kabbalistic documents: Neoplatonic terminology and "cleaving of thought."

II. DEVEKUT: NEOPLATONIC INFLUENCES

Early Kabbalistic material concerning the relationship between the human soul and higher entities reflects the obvious influence of Neoplatonic thought. R. 'Ezra of Gerona's description of such a process well illustrates this tendency:[22]

> The righteous causes his unblemished and pure soul to ascend [until she reaches] the supernal holy soul[23] [and] she [that is, the human soul] unites with her [the supernal soul] and knows future things.[24] And this is the manner [in which] the prophet acted, as the evil inclination did not have any dominion over him, to separate him from the supernal soul. Thus, the soul of the prophet is united with the supernal soul in a complete union.

The terms used here to denote the unitive experience are worthy of closer scrutiny: the Kabbalist uses the verbs *hityaḥed* and *hitaḥed,* and the noun *yiḥud,* which are best translated as "unite" and "union." The use of the adjective *complete* qualifying *union* bears evidence of the author's intention to convey the state of total fusion attained by the soul of the righteous or the prophet. More so than the more usual usage of *devekut,* which is ambiguous and lends itself to various interpretations, the occurrence of *hitaḥed/hityaḥed* would seemingly demonstrate that the experiences of these ancient figures were perceived as having been close to mystical union. Indeed, we can consider this passage as an interesting example of the overlapping of two types of union: the ontic one, explicitly referred to as "complete union," and "epistemic union," implicit in the conveyance of knowledge from the supernal to the human soul.[25] Ontic union is in turn a prerequisite for epistemic union. The same problematics appear also in R. 'Ezra's younger contemporary Naḥmanides; he indicates that the human soul, "by her sharpness[26] will cleave to the separated intellect, and will direct [her intention] to it; and this person will be called a prophet, since he is prophesying."[27]

Prophecy is here explicitly related to the state of cleaving to the higher intellect.[28] It would seem possible to trace the specific type of Neoplatonism represented in this text. Shortly before the text cited above, R. 'Ezra writes,[29] "For man is comprised of all things,[30] and his soul is linked to the supernal soul." The Kabbalist regards the conjunction between the two souls as a natural state, facilitating the union between them after the ascent of the human soul. This conception of a basic link even after the separation of the individual from the supernal soul apparently reflects Plotinus' theory on the presence of the universal soul also in individual ones. Given this natural affinity, there is nothing exceptional about the achievement of a complete fusion.

R. 'Ezra's description contains explicit Neoplatonic overtones; the "supernal soul" stands for the Neoplatonic "universal soul" to which the human soul cleaves by an act of ascent. Let us turn to another example that partly reiterates motifs already found in the previous quotation. R. Menaḥem Recanati, an important Kabbalist at the turn of the thirteenth century, wrote as follows, apparently under the influence of Geronese Kabbalah:[31]

> When the pious and the men of deeds [engaged in a state of mental] concentration,[32] and were involved in supernal mysteries, they imagined, by the power of their thought, as if these things were engraved before them,[33] and when they linked their soul to the supernal soul, these things increased and expanded and revealed themselves. . . . as when he cleaved his soul to the supernal soul, these awesome things were engraved in his heart.

This passage is evidently based upon the perception of the soul as a mirror in which higher matters are reflected when she ascends to and cleaves with the supernal soul. The nature of this experience is described by Recanati in terms that had far-reaching influence on European thought. The Kabbalist elaborated upon the talmudic dictum stating that the ancestor died by the divine kiss of divinity; originally pointing toward a blessed death, a death without pain, in the Kabbalistic-Neoplatonic interpretation, this dictum was seen as referring to an ecstatic experience:[34]

> Know that, just as the ripe fruit[35] falls from the tree, it no longer needing its connection [to the tree], so is the link between the soul and the body. When the soul

> has attained whatever she is able to attain,[36] she cleaves to the supernal soul, and will remove its raiment of dust and sever [itself] from its place [that is, the body] and will cleave to the *Shekhinah*; and this is [the meaning of] death by the kiss.

Thus, the ultimate experience of cleaving to the supernal soul enables her to attain the final union, namely, the cleaving to the divine presence; the preceding experiences are implicitly regarded as lower and intermediate states, culminating in this, a beatific union. Again, the Neoplatonic scheme seems to be transpiring in Kabbalistic garb; in both ontological schemes, the supernal soul is only an intermediary entity that must be transcended in the final return of the soul to her origin. The union with the universal soul is therefore a preparatory stage on the natural journey of the worthy soul toward her source;[37] until then, the experience of union can be regarded as a series of intermittent acts that, as we shall see below, enable the person to remain alive and active in this world. Again, Recanati seems to have used R. 'Ezra's views. In one of the latter's works, we are told:[38] "The kiss is a metaphor for the cleaving of the soul[39] . . . but since he allegorized the cleaving of the soul to the kiss of mouth, he had to employ the phrase 'his mouth,' in order to link the allegory to it, as one of the sages of [our] generation has already written in his book."

Thus, the use of the kiss as an allegory for the cleaving of the soul is presented by the first Kabbalists, who referred to it as influenced by a sage who was a contemporary of R. 'Ezra. No Kabbalistic master would have been designated by R. 'Ezra simply as a sage without further qualification. It is reasonable, therefore, to suppose that R. 'Ezra refers here to a contemporary philosopher, perhaps R. Samuel ibn Tibbon.[40] We can assume, then, that one of the earliest Kabbalistic understandings of cleaving stemmed from philosophical circles. This obviously contributed to Recanati's interpretation of the "death by kiss" as an unitive experience.

At the beginning of the fourteenth century the death by kiss was understood as a metaphor for the cataleptic state of the righteous immersed in ecstasy.[41] The anonymous author of *Ma'arekhet ha-'Elohut* explained the significance of the death by kiss in the following words:[42] "The soul of the righteous one will ascend—while he is yet alive—higher and higher, to the place where the souls of the righteous [enjoy their] delight, which is 'the cleaving of the mind.' The body will remain motionless, as it is said: 'But you that cleave unto the Lord your God are alive every one of you this day.' "[43] The cleaving of the soul is presented here as a state wherein the body undergoes a temporary death that is in reality a symptom of "real" life. It is worth emphasizing that this Kabbalist refers to two distinct events: the spiritual one, which takes place between the human soul and a higher entity, one of the divine Sefirot, and the corporeal one, which is an anesthetic experience. The soul herself does not even metaphorically undergo a mortal experience; to the contrary, she attains true life. Interestingly, death concerns only the body, whereas the soul enhances its spiritual life without an intermediary stage of "death." The Neoplatonic and Christian mystical views on the necessity of a preliminary "death" of the old man—that is, the death of his spirit—for the spiritual rebirth are not emphasized by these Kabbalists.[44]

Most of the above-mentioned citations are taken from a highly influential work, Recanati's *Commentary on the Pentateuch,* which served as a source for the later Kabbalist, R. Yehudah Ḥayyat;[45] from these authors, the theme of Neoplatonic union found its way to other Jewish Kabbalists. Moreover, Recanati was one of the sources upon which Pico della Mirandola drew for his concept of death by kiss, which reverberated throughout Renaissance literature as "morte di bacio."[46] Interestingly, Pico already recognized the affinity between Recanati's Kabbalistic views and those of Plato regarding the ecstatic death by the kiss.[47] Both medieval and Renaissance Neoplatonism met through the intermediacy of the Kabbalistic concept of *devekut*; no wonder the later Neoplatonists were so fond of Kabbalistic doctrines—they fit their unique form of philosophical thought.

The concept of the miraculous powers of the perfect soul is an issue pervading Neoplatonic literature.[48] In Jewish thought, this was adopted and discussed several times by R. Abraham ibn 'Ezra,[49] who was one of the most important channels through which the perception of soul infiltrated into early Kabbalah. His description of the cleaving of the individual soul to her supernal source, the universal soul, as the cause of the human soul's ability to change the mundane world was especially influential in Jewish philosophy,[50] as well as in Kabbalistic literature, reverberating both in theosophical and ecstatic Kabbalah.[51] Some few examples will suffice to illustrate the echoes of this view in Jewish mysticism. The anonymous Kabbalist who wrote an epistle on sexual union indicated: "When the pious make their thought cleave to the higher [entities], whatever they were contemplating and intending came immediately into existence, whether for good or for bad. . . . And from this matter, [you can learn] the matter of prayer and sacrifices, which is the secret of cleaving to the higher [entities]."[52] For this Kabbalist, the union of human thought with the supernal beings facilitates the descent of the higher powers downward upon the object envisioned by the pious, thereby fulfilling his intention.[53]

Less explicit, but still evident, is Naḥmanides' view of the relationship between *devekut* and wondrous acts.[54] Speaking of the cleaving to the Tetragrammaton, he refers to the Ḥasidim, who benefit from the "manifest miracles."[55] This cleaving seems to have the Sefirah of *Tiferet* as its object; though Naḥmanides does not specifically attribute the performance of miracles to the pious as an active deed, this is apparently the implication of his consequent use of the term *Ḥasid,* whether referring to an individual who cleaves to God[56] or to the Tetragrammaton[57] in some texts or to the magical use of the divine name of seventy-two letters in another text.[58]

III. CLEAVING OF THOUGHT

Closely related to the texts cited above are the discussions concerning "cleaving of thought." This subject relates to a distinct set of motifs, while nevertheless at times equating "union of the soul" with "cleaving of thought." We may easily see, in some of the examples to be given below, the emergence of Neoplatonic and Aristotelian terminologies. Again, we shall start with the view of R. 'Ezra of Gerona,[59] who probably inherited an already existing view:[60] "The ancient pious men caused their thought to ascend to the place of its source, and they would recite the *miẓot* and the [Ten] Commandments[61] and through this recitation and this cleaving of thought, the things were blessed and increased, and they received a [divine] influx from the annihilation of thought."[62] As in the previous discussions, the ascent of thought now precedes the act of cleaving; the object of this cleaving is, however, different. It seems that the pious have to return human thought to its supernal source in the divine world and, therefore, cleave it to the Sefirah of *Ḥokhmah*, whence it was generated. As R. 'Ezra explicitly indicates, human thought cannot rise beyond its source, analogous to water, which cannot reach a higher level than that from which it descends. Thought therefore "stands below" the Sefirah of *Keter*, or "the annihilation of thought," and receives its influx.

Another text of Geronese provenance supplies a complementary description of thought with the second Sefirah. R. 'Azriel, apparently under the influence of R. 'Ezra, wrote: " 'Say to Wisdom, you are my sister'; namely, to cleave [human] thought to *Ḥokhmah*, so that she and it [become] one entity."[63] We may assume that when thought arrives at its source it becomes totally identical with it, just as water does when it returns to its source. Here, we again witness the ascent that precedes total union, this time in relation to human thought: however, unlike the cleaving of the soul to the supernal soul, and only finally to the *Shekhinah*—the lowest divine manifestation—thought reaches the highest divine power—*Ḥokhmah*. This difference is worthy of elaboration: the union of the soul with a divine Sefirah is possible only when she is permanently separated from the body, whereas thought, a faculty of the soul, can ascend beyond the sphere the soul is able to mount. According to R. 'Ezra, an attempt to pass beyond the Sefirah of *Ḥokhmah* will end not only in confusion of thought but in the return of the soul to her source.[64] This time, the Kabbalist is dealing with a "negative" kind of death, in comparison to the ecstatic one that may occur during the union of the soul to the universal soul. In other words, ontological union may culminate in an ecstatic death, whereas epistemic union, when forced, tends to end in dreadful and mortal experience.

Extremely important in our context are Abraham Abulafia's explanations of the mystical experience as cleaving or union of the human intellect to its source in the active intellect or even in God, described as the supreme intellect. This union is the result of the epistemic act that, according to Aristotelian psychology, involves the complete identification of the intellect and its intelligibles—in this case, the active intellect or God. I shall not dwell on this issue, which has been elaborated elsewhere, but shall cite one outstanding example from a younger contemporary of Abulafia.[65] Following a short presentation of Aristotelian epistemology, he affirms:[66] "Man does not intellectualize by means of his matter, but by means of his intellect. Thus, when the righteous man intellectualizes his Creator by means of his *kavvanah* and his performance of commandments of God, he cleaves to God, as it is said: 'But you that did cleave of the Lord your God are alive every one of you this day.' "[67] What is highly interesting in this passage is the interiorization of Aristotelian psychology by an antiphilosophical Kabbalist, who applied it to the mystical performance of the commandments as a way of attaining *devekut*. As we shall see below, this avenue was later cultivated by Ḥasidic masters in similar contexts.[68]

One of Abulafia's disciples, the anonymous author of *Sefer ha-Ẓeruf*,[69] interestingly indicates the possibility of cleaving to God: "When your intellect becomes pure, though it is still in matter, in that same [material] substratum, it indeed attains a high degree, to cleave to *causa causarum* after the separation of the soul from the matter." This Kabbalist seemingly discusses the union with God that takes place after death, but the main organ of this experience is the purified intellect.

Let us turn now to an example of "return" and "cleaving" mysticism, taken from the mystical diary of R. Isaac ben Samuel of Acre, which evinces a clear echo of the Neoplatonic movement of the soul back to her source:[70]

I have seen the secret of [the verse], "But in the fourth year all its fruit shall be holy

> for praisegiving to the Lord."[71] Namely, that God has comanded us to increase the power of our rational soul over that of our appetitive soul [during] three years, which allude to the three worlds. [This is to be done] in order to cleave our soul to the secret of the fourth year, which reflects the secret of the Godhead which transcends the three worlds. "And in the fifth year," which refers to the *'Eiyn Sof*[72] which surrounds everything,[73] this [rational] soul will cleave to the *'Eiyn Sof* and will become total and universal, after she had been individual,[74] due to her palace, while she was yet imprisoned in it, and she will become universal, because of the nature of her real source.

Returning to her source, the soul regains her primordial plenitude, which is symbolized by the *'Eiyn Sof*. It is important to emphasize that the organ of the mystical union is the human intellect or rational soul, a fact demonstrating the philosophical influence upon R. Isaac of Acre.

I shall close this discussion on "cleaving of thought" with a Ḥasidic example. The Great Maggid interpreted a talmudic homily concerning phylacteries in a remarkable manner:[75]

> "What is written in the phylacteries of the Master of the world?[76] [It is written][77] 'And who is like the people of Israel, a singular[78] nation on the earth.' " It is written in the works of Isaac Luria[79] that the phylacteries are called brains—that is, brains, called pleasure and enthusiasm—by which we are united to him, be he blessed and praised.[80] "And all the peoples of the earth shall see that you are called by the name of the Lord," as if you are called by the name of the Lord, blessed be he, since you become one unity with him, and this pleasure is called our phylacteries. And his pleasure,[81] be he blessed, in which he delights because we are united to him, be he blessed, is called his phylacteries. "And who is like the people of Israel, a singular nation"—as they reach a state of unity which transcends number, but the number is under their control . . . for time is under their control to do whatever they want, as they transcend time. And he, blessed be he, is united to us, the only obstacle being our capacity, as it is written: "Turn to me, [says the Lord of hosts], and I will return to you,"[82] as he, blessed be he, dwells in the thought. And when a person thinks futile things, he pushes him away [as it is written], "And Moses was not able to enter the tent of meeting."[83] As the cloud was dwelling on him, the Mind cannot dwell on man, since darkness dwells in him.

The Mind is but a veiled reference to God, who is alluded to earlier in this passage in the following way: "as if when we perform worthy acts the world of the mind, blessed be he, is broadening. Therefore, the divine mind dwells in our thought, this state being regarded as one of union."[84] The concepts used by the Great Maggid forcefully point to a description of an experience that may be designated as *unio mystica*; the type of cleaving described in this passage transcends the mere connection between two unities since, in the end, they achieve a union passing beyond unity, an attribute reserved in medieval sources for God alone.[85] Even the atemporal nature of Israel at the moment of the cleaving is appropriate to the Neoplatonic view of the world of the intellect, here identified with Deity as surpassing time.[86] The divine phylacteries include the statement of the unique—literally, one—nation, whereas the human phylacteries, in which Israel is designated as if it is called by the divine name, hint at the state of union; it is the union of two thoughts that is performed out of enthusiasm and causes delight to God.[87] We have here an interesting example of what Scholem designated as the transformation of thought into emotion during the *devekut* process.[88] Nevertheless, we perceive the continuation of philosophical terminology—which flourished in thirteenth-century Kabbalah in order to express unitive experience—into early Ḥasidic thought. More than any other set of concepts, the philosophical framework provided a relevant terminology to the Ḥasidic masters in matters of *unio mystica*.[89]

IV. DEVEKUT: IN KABBALAH AND IN ḤASIDISM

As we shall see below, Ḥasidism preserved and continued earlier Kabbalistic terminology interpreting *devekut*. One could easily add to the list of affinities between the two mystical movements.[90] The question, even when discussing a foremost Ḥasidic concept such as *devekut*, is to what extent Ḥasidism was a novel mystical phenomenon. According to Scholem, the novelty to be found in the Ḥasidic "popularization" of the Kabbalistic view of *devekut* was the latter's presentation thereof as the starting point of the mystical path:

> The novel element is the radical character given to *devekut* by this change. Ḥasidic *devekut* is no longer an extreme ideal, to be realized by some rare and sublime spirits at the end of the path. It is no longer the last rung in the ladder of ascent, as in Kabbalism, but the first. Everything begins with man's decision to cleave to God. *Devekut* is a starting point and not the end.[91]

Since the Ḥasidic self-perception of its approach to *devekut* is that it is a novelty, no one has attempted to discover the sources of this particular interpretation of *devekut*. It seems, however, that the sources for *devekut* as the starting point of the mystical path are to be found already in R. Isaac of Acre's *Me'irat 'Eynaim:* "Whoever reaches the secret of cleaving, will reach the secret of equanimity; and if he will reach the secret of equanimity he will reach the secret of concentration, and since he has reached the secret of concentration, he will reach the divine spirit, and from it {he will attain} prophecy, and he will prophesy and foretell the future."[92] The same mystical ladder occurs again, when R. Isaac states: "The reason for equanimity is the cleaving of the thought to God, may he be blessed, since the cleaving and connection of thought with God, may he be blessed, causes that man not to be sensitive either to the honor or to the contempt people show toward him."[93]

R. Isaac of Acre's book was a classic of early Kabbalistic literature, whose influence may be discerned in Safedian Kabbalah.[94] The second passage quoted above is adduced by R. Ḥayyim Vital in the unpublished part of his *Sha'arey Kedushah*. R. Isaac's placing of cleaving of thought at the beginning of a series of mystical states, and not at its apex, could easily have been known to the first Ḥasidic masters and molded their appreciation of *devekut*.[95] Furthermore, the concepts of *devekut* in R. Isaac and the first Ḥasidim share a highly significant common characteristic—it was a value that had to be cultivated even by common Jews: "I, R. Isaac of Acre . . . say to the elite as well as to the vulgus, that whoever wishes to know the secret of the connection of his soul to the supernal {world} and the cleaving of his thought to the high God . . . must set before his spiritual eyes the letters of the divine name."[96] Hence, not only was *devekut* considered to be an initial step of a spiritual progress; it was, according to R. Isaac, recommended to the masses as well as to the elite. The connection between *devekut* and meditation upon the letters of the Tetragrammaton has a long and fruitful history, the most important stage of which was the Ḥasidic practice. I should like to discuss here some important passages, in print already in the sixteenth century, that influenced the Ḥasidic literature.[97]

Another most interesting discussion, however, that includes the elements of the Ḥasidic view is to be found in R. Elijah de Vidas's *Reshit Ḥokhmah:*

> Whoever wishes to rejoice his soul must seclude himself for a part of the day and meditate upon the grandeur of the letters of the Tetragrammaton . . . . as it is said by King David, "I set the Tetragrammaton before me always." . . . Therefore, by his meditation upon the Tetragrammaton, the soul is enlightened . . . and rejoices . . . and this is the degree of the *Ẓaddikim* who cleave to the Tetragrammaton, so that even after their death they are considered to be alive, because of their cleaving to the Tetragrammaton.[98]

This cleaving is achieved by the *Ẓaddikim*, although it is recommended to everyone, as de Vidas maintains. Indeed, it seems that the way to attain the spiritual enjoyment is simple enough and does not include any complicated exercises; the main element is the contemplation of the Tetragrammaton.

Immediately afterward, the author refers to another element, the singing of the divine name:[99]

> "Sing, O ye righteous, to the Tetragrammaton"[100] . . . so that this name be before you, in order that you unify it in such a way that this song is the complete cleaving. And it is possible that the meaning of "song" is that its mere performance causes the cleaving . . . . R. Yehudah ha-Levi, the pious, has composed several laudatory poems to God, and whoever recites them causes the cleaving of his soul to God.

The singing of the Kabbalist before the Tetragrammaton seems to be connected to Abraham Abulafia's use of music during his recitation of the combination of letters of various divine names.[101] Like de Vidas, Abulafia viewed music as part of a process the final aim of which was mystical union and prophecy. Moreover, an interesting passage on music quoted by R. Ḥayyim Vital states that its final result is "supreme union and prophecy."[102] Thus, even singing is sufficient to attain cleavage to God via contemplation of the Tetragrammaton; this contemplation is also intended, as seen above, to reach a spiritual enjoyment.[103] No ascetic element is mentioned by de Vidas in this context, and we find here a mystical technique that can be accepted even by the common Jew. It seems, therefore, that long before the emergence of Ḥasidism *devekut* was considered by Kabbalists to be a mystical status easily attainable by everybody; two of the components of the technique for attaining *devekut*—music and contemplation of the divine name—are common both to Kabbalah and Ḥasidism.[104]

At least one of the elements mentioned above was widespread at the time Ḥasidism first appeared; as evinced by the testimony of R. Pinḥas Elijah Horowitz, the contemplation of the Tetragrammaton was a famous practice.[105] The practice of *devekut* by simple Jews was also related by a contemporary of the first Ḥasidim—R. Moshe of Satanov.[106] It may well be that he hinted not at a "new" Ḥasidic practice—that is, one introduced by the Ba'al Shem Tov—but at a popular practice with a long history that was adopted by the new mystical masters who gave it a central place in their religious way of life.[107] De Vidas's recommendation that one contemplate the Tetragrammaton in isolation seemingly influenced a passage in R. Jacob Joseph of Polonnoye's *Toldot Ya'akov Yoseph:* "When he is still isolated, let the letter of Tetragrammaton be before him."[108]

V. DEVEKUT QUA MEDIATION

Devekut, in a previous text, already was regarded as an elevated state preceding such experiences as the acquisition of knowledge of the future or the reception of supernal influx or impressions. Indeed, only rarely was the aim the mystical union itself; rather, the goal was close encounters with higher entities that enabled the human soul, or thought, to act in an exceptional way. In several early texts, however, Kabbalists indicated that *devekut* of the soul, or thought, seemed to be a prerequisite for performing certain commandments. R. 'Azriel, for example, asserted:[109]

> When the priest offers the sacrifice, he attaches his soul to the altar, and his [higher] soul mounts above. . . . therefore, by the cleaving of the soul above, first the spirit of man mounts [above] . . . and returns to its source, whence it was taken . . . and afterwards it mounts even higher to the place of it source[110] . . . like the water which mounts until the level from which it came. And this is the priestly blessing. . . . they [the priests] attach their souls above and bless the people [of Israel].

The connection between *devekut* and sacrifice can be conceived as part of the integration of the psychological process into ritualistic practices: sacrifice and priestly blessing. In comparison to the previous quotations, *devekut* no longer was related solely to exceptional psychic experiences, such as prophecy, but also to two important practices of ancient Jewish service in the Temple. The transition between R. 'Ezra's discussion of *devekut* and "prophecy," on the one hand, and R. 'Azriel's connection of *devekut* and priestly worship, on the other, represented a turn in the direction of integration of mystical experience into "normal" religious values. Priests, unlike prophets, continued to bless the people of Israel also in R. 'Azriel's times. A further step in this direction was the role attributed to *devekut* in the anonymous epistle on sexual union:[111]

> It is well known to the masters of Kabbalah that human thought stems from the intellectual soul, which descends from above. And human thought has the ability to strip itself [of alien things] and to ascend and arrive at the place of its source. Then it unites with the supernal entity, whence it comes and it [the thought] and it [its source] become one entity.[112] . . . Our ancient sages stated that when the husband copulates with his wife, and his thought unites with the supernal entities, that very thought draws the supernal light downward, and it [the light] dwells upon that very drop [of semen] upon which he directs his intention and thinks upon . . . that this very drop is permanently linked with the brilliant light . . . as the thought on it [the drop] was linked to the supernal entities, and it draws the brilliant light downward.

Here, the union of human thought to its source is a prerequisite for a common act: procreation. More so than in the passages of R. 'Ezra and R. 'Azriel, the mystical union is represented as a means to ensure an ideal behavior; common people—not only priests—can and even must combine *devekut* with impregnation.

As in the previous examples, the emphasis here is obviously upon the act that follows the mystical experience—prophecy, blessing, impregnation being the ultimate goals of the union, rather than the other way around.[113] Furthermore, although *devekut* is a preeminently personal experience, it serves here as an opening toward an other-oriented action. Mystical union, or communion, thus serves as a vehicle used by the individual in order to better serve the community; personal perfection is transformed into a means of contributing to the welfare of others. A closer perusal of these sources, especially the last one, will reveal that the attainment of mystical union is tantamount to the change of the worshiper into a channel by which the supramundane influx reaches the terrestrial world.[114] The above-mentioned forms of *unio mystica* can consequently be considered as attempts undertaken by *perfecti* to reestablish a broken link between the divine and the lower worlds by the mediation of their spiritual faculties. This stand was concisely formulated in the *Zohar,* where the connoisseur of theosophic lore "who cleaves to his Lord" is portrayed as the *Ẓaddik*, the pillar of the universe, since "he draws blessings onto the [lower] world."[115] Here, *devekut* assumes an even cosmic function. Elsewhere, the *Zohar* describes "the virtuous man who with his soul and his spirit cleaves to the Holy King above with fitting love, has power over the earth below, and whatever he decrees for the world is fulfilled," as it was for Elijah in the matter of the rain.[116]

VI. DEVEKUT AND THEURGY

As seen above, the personal experience of contact with divine manifestations is sometimes envisioned as instrumental to an other-oriented goal, mainly other men. This goal may be achieved by virtue of the creation of a pathway between the divine world and the lower one. Let us now turn to the theurgical impact of *devekut* on the divine structure itself. In an early Kabbalistic text, seemingly belonging to the Geronese school, we learn:[117]

> Even if the facilities [of the Temple] have been destroyed, there remained for Israel the great name in lieu of the sacrifices, to cleave to it in holy places,[118] and the righteous and pious men, and those who practice mental concentration and unify the great name, they also stir the fire on the altar of their hearts.[119] [Thereby] all the Sefirot will then be unified in its [Israel's] pure thought and will be linked to each other until they are drawn [up] to the source of the endlessly sublime flame. And this is the secret that all Israel is cleaving to God, blessed be he[120]—"But ye that

> did cleave unto the Lord." And this is the secret of the morning and evening unification—"To show thy loving kindness in the morning, and thy faithfulness every night."[121] And this is the secret of the unification [done] by a man in the morning and evening prayer, causing the elevation of all the Sefirot into one bundle and their union[122]—and then he cleaves to the great name.

"Cleaving to the great name" is mentioned twice in this passage, at the beginning and at its end. In between, the unification of the Sefirot to one another, and all of them to their source, is presented as occurring through the activity of man's pure thought. Thought is obviously the organ of influence upon this theosophical structure; the main instrument at man's disposal is the great name,[123] which is a substitute for the sacrifice service in the Temple.[124] I assume that the theurgical operation of sacrifice was transferred to the letters of the great name;[125] I also assume that the Kabbalist conceived the role of the sacrifice as causing a unification of the Sefirot, an interpretation almost unanimously accepted by the early Kabbalists.[126]

On the basis of these assumptions, it seems reasonable to regard the role of the letters of the great name as inducing a state of union amid the divine manifestations. This activity is achieved by a preliminary cleaving of human thought to the letters of the name, meditating upon their nature and unifying them. After the unification of the letters and of the Sefirot, the cleaving to the name—presumably its unified letters—is again mentioned. We must thus consider that this text refers to two types of cleaving—the preliminary one, which serves as a starting point for theurgical activity,[127] and, at the end, the cleaving to a unified entity, as the culmination of the mystical process.

This analysis is roughly corroborated by the interpretation offered by R. Meir ibn Gabbay to a text authored by R. Isaac the Blind, as quoted by his student, R. ʼEzra:[128]

> The quintessence of the worship of the Kabbalists[129] and those who contemplate his name is "and to him shall you cleave"[130] . . . and the intent of [the verse] "and those who contemplate his name," is to hint to the appropriate [mystical] intention of the worship, and it [the intention] is that the worshiper ought to contemplate and intend during his worship to unify the great name and join it by its letters and include in it all the [supernal] degrees[131] and unify them in his thought, up to *ʼEyin Sof*. And the reason that it is said: "and to him shall you cleave" is to hint to thought, which must be free and pure of everything and subdued,[132] cleaving above in an everlasting and forceful cleaving, in order to unify the branches to [their] root without any separation.[133] And thereby will the person who unifies cleave to the great name.[134]

What is the exact nature of the "worship" mentioned in the first quotation as the substitution of cleaving to the great name in lieu of the sacrifices? A plausible answer seems to be prayer, which was considered as the counterpart of the sacrifices after the destruction of the Temple, on one hand, and "worship," on the other. Indeed, an early Kabbalistic view of the spiritual intention connected with the prayer *Shema' Yisrael* explicitly refers to the unification of the ten Sefirot.[135] One version of this view asserts:[136]

> Since you know that the Sefirot are designated as *middot* [that is, attributes], and they are not [limited][137] in attribute by their nature, but from our perspective, you ought to unify all of them twice during the day.[138] . . . As the *'Aleph*[139] in the word *'EḤaD* stands for [the Sefirah of] *Keter*, and the *ḥet*[140] stands for [the Sefirah of] *Ḥokhmah*, with the other seven Sefirot . . . and the *dalet* . . . stands for [the Sefirah of] *Malkhut*, and all the ten Sefirot are hinted at in the [word] *'EḤaD* . . . let [him] direct [the thought] as if he will cause all of them to enter the [Sefirah of] *Keter*, from whence they were emanated.

The unification of the Sefirot during the recitation of *Shema'* is also connected with the names that occur in the same context. I would therefore consider this tradition as one component within the view represented by the first two passages on the unification of ten Sefirot, the other being of the type found in R. Abraham ibn 'Ezra, who refers to cleaving to the Tetragrammaton.[141] In the first component, the motif of cleaving is absent; in the latter, that of unification of Sefirot.[142]

The implications of the previous texts for the Kabbalistic conception of *devekut* are important for more than one reason. First of all, according to some Kabbalists, the object of cleaving is a dynamic system of divine manifestations, which must be unified before the higher cleaving can be attained. This process of unification is the subject of a continuous effort to be accomplished, as these texts reveal, twice a day. The theurgical act is therefore an ongoing experience the Kabbalist must contribute toward the unification of God's powers. More than a self-oriented act, it is a theocentric operation, albeit the locus of this happening is the thought of the Kabbalist, who must integrate the ten Sefirot, as manifested in the letters of the Tetragrammaton or of the word *'EḤaD,* into their source.[143] This *restitutio rerum ad integrum* on the human spiritual level is considered to have sympathetic influence above, causing the return of the Sefirot to their source on the divine level. I would assume that human pure thought parallels supernal pure thought, the Sefirah of *Keter*. Thus, by the very act of contemplation of the most powerful symbol of the ten Sefirot, the divine name, human thought is "filled" with these contents and, presumably, becomes identical with them. This psychological interpretation seems to be corroborated by the fact that no mention of the ascent of the human soul or thought to the higher world is made in these texts. As far as human thought is described as cleaving to God, it seems that this state is achieved by the meditation on the great name. My analysis is based on the assumption that inner mental processes are able to activate the divine powers by means of their reflections in human thought, an interiorization of the Divine that could have been perceived by the Kabbalist as a real mystical union with an *imago dei*. We can therefore describe the stages of Kabbalistic worship, as presented in the above passages, as follows: (1) the primary cleaving of thought to the letters of the divine name; (2) the activation of these letters as symbols of higher entities so as to constitute a unified totality; and (3) cleaving to this unified divine totality.

Most of the previous examples stemmed from early Provençal and Catalan Kabbalah or from that of R. Isaac of Acre; after the second half of the thirteenth century, Spanish Kabbalah became progressively indifferent to *devekut* as the highest ideal. This is the case in the *Zohar,* and in the works of R. Moses de Leon, R. Joseph Gikatilla, R. Joseph of Hamadan, R. Joseph Angelino, and R. David ben Yehudah he-Ḥasid. To the extent that *devekut* is mentioned, it is by those Kabbalists who echo the earlier Geronese texts, as does the Italian Kabbalist R. Menaḥem Recanati. The focus of religious activity is now theurgic; the biblical commandment to cleave to God is reinterpreted in a manner similar to that done by R. Ishmael's school in the Talmud. In one example of this demystification of *devekut*, it is given mythical perspective. According to R. Moses de Leon:[144] "It is incumbent upon man to be in the supernal image, as it is said, 'to Him you shall cleave'[145] and it is written, 'and walk in his ways'[146]—[namely] according to this very image." Here, imitatio dei is referred to both as an accomplished fact and as an ideal to be achieved by proper acts. Cleaving turns out to be an assimilation by operation.[147] The emphasis is conspicuously on the structural relation of the human body to the supernal image—namely, the Sefirot—and on the resemblance of the activity of the human and divine entities.

Following the view of Geronese Kabbalah, the *Zohar* presents the state of *devekut* as a precondition for theurgic influence on the *Shekhinah*; this state is, however, achieved at the moment of death, thereby attenuating the mystical nature of the act.[148] This nexus thereafter reverberates in theurgic Kabbalah, and it represents the main way in which mystical experience was absorbed in religious systems that focus upon actions and their impact above.[149]

According to R. David ben Zimra, writing in the middle of the sixteenth century:[150]

> When a person unifies [the Sefirot] with a whole heart and wholehearted intention, then his soul is linked with and made to cleave to the love of God,[151] as it is written, "I have set the Lord before me always, surely he is at my right hand. . . ."[152] Just as I do not forget my right hand, so I do not forget his love, as he is always before me. Know that whoever loves God with a wholehearted love causes love above, and the [divine] attributes [turn] their faces to each other with great passion and love.[153]

This passage must be understood—in light of a statement preceding it—as pointing to the theurgical implications of love of and cleaving to God.[154] As evinced by the use of the verse from Psalms, R. David does not emphasize the unitive nature of this cleaving, as the awareness of the presence of God, rather than union with him, is the major feature of his sort of mysticism; setting God "before" one highlights the distance from him rather than its reduction. As in the preceding examples, the goal of the act of cleaving to a divine manifestation is the theurgical effect.

In Lurianic Kabbalah, for example, *devekut* was mobilized for the achievement of the main goal of Kabbalistic activity: the restoration, or *tikkun* of the supernal anthropos:

> Concerning the study of Torah . . . all his intention must be to link his soul and bind her to her supernal source by the means of Torah. And his intention must be to achieve thereby the restoration of the supernal *anthropos*, which is the ultimate intention of the creation of man and the goal of the commandment to study Torah. . . . As when studying Torah man must intend to link his soul and to unite her and make her cleave to her source above . . . and he must intend thereby to perfect the supernal tree [of Sefirot] and holy *anthropos*.[155]

It is evident that the mystical aspect of union with the supernal source—which was central in some earlier Kabbalistic sources in Gerona as well as later Ḥasidic ones—is here only a means of attaining a higher objective: theosophical restoration.

Following the Lurianic pattern, the Sabbatian theosophy portrays the Messiah as cleaving to the divine power in order to restore the divine system to its harmonious status:[156] "The soul of the King Messiah cleaves to the tree of life[157] [and] he is the master of all the treasures of his Father[158] and he performs restorations [*tikkunim*] in all aspects [of the divine powers] and [all levels of] existence. . . . by virtue of his adherence to the tree of life everything he does is a restoration." Cleaving and adhering are strikingly presented as enabling the Messiah to play a restorative role on all levels of reality, the theurgical goal being achieved only after the accomplishment of the mystical experience.

Safedian Kabbalah, however, absorbed not only the zoharic attitude to *devekut* as instrumental for theurgical purposes but also the perception of *devekut* in ecstatic Kabbalah, in which the ultimate goals are the achievement and revelation of *unio mystica*.[159] The last phase of Jewish mysticism, Ḥasidism, not only continued the perception of *devekut* as *unio* but also interpreted, or factually misinterpreted, the major interest of the basic works of theurgical Kabbalah. Thus, according to R. Menaḥem Mendel of Premyshlyany:[160]

> *Nistar*[161] is the name given to a matter which one cannot transmit to another person; just as the taste of [a particular] food cannot be described to a person who has never tasted this taste,[162] [so] is it impossible to explain in words how it is and what it is; such a thing is called *seter* [hidden]. Thus is the love and fear of God, blessed be he—it is impossible to explain to another person the love [of God] in one's heart; [therefore], it is called *nistar*. But the attribution of the term *nistar* to the lore of the Kabbalah is strange, as whoever wishes to study [Kabbalah], the book is available to him, and if he does not understand he is an ignoramus, as [indeed] for such a person, the *Gemara* and *Tosafot* are also *nistar*. But the concealed matters in the *Zohar* and the writings of R. Isaac Luria are those based upon the cleaving to God,[163] for those who are worthy to cleave and to see the supernal *Merkavah*, like R. Isaac Luria, to whom[164] the paths of the firmament were clear and he walked on them [seeing his way] with his mental eyes,[165] like the four sages who entered *Pardes*.

The significance of this passage lies not only in the characterization of Kabbalah as a mystical experience but also in the reinterpretation of the entire Kabbalistic heritage as a quest for mystical experience rather than as a theosophical gnosis.[166] Thus, the gamut of conceptions of *devekut* in Ḥasidism is an intermingling of theurgic interpretations, in the vein of the zoharic-Lurianic tradition, and mystical interpretations, stemming from Geronese, Abulafian, and Safedian texts.

Let us now turn to some expressions of extreme forms of *devekut*, which can reasonably be classified as *unio mystica*.

CHAPTER 4

Unio Mystica in Jewish Mysticism

I. UNIO MYSTICA: METHODOLOGICAL OBSERVATIONS

One of the most widely accepted theses regarding Jewish mysticism asserts the reticence of Kabbalists to express their experiences in terms that could be understood as pointing to a total union of the mystic with God. Edward Caird has formulated this preconception in a lucid manner: "The Jew was always defended against the extreme of Mysticism by his strong sense of the separate personality of God and man, and, as a consequence, his vivid consciousness of moral obligation as involved in the worship of God."[1] Caird's stand was expressed in contrast with Plotinus' opposite perception of the relationship between the human and the Divine, which can reach a stage wherein "the barrier between the infinite and the finite is thrown down, and the former is brought into immediate contact with the latter, so that every distinction and relation of the finite vanishes away."[2]

Apparently independently of Caird's diagnosis, Gershom Scholem stressed, time and again, that a total union with the Divine is absent in Jewish texts: "It is only in extremely rare cases that ecstasy signifies actual union with God in which the human individuality abandons itself to the rapture of complete submersion in the divine stream. Even in this ecstatic frame of mind, the Jewish mystic almost invariably retains a sense of the distance between the Creator and his creature."[3] This assessment offered by such a fine scholar of Jewish mysticism has reverberated in a long series of studies and has been endorsed by most of Scholem's followers,[4] as well as by scholars of general mysticism.[5] Scholem's diagnosis was accepted with such certainty that such a fine scholar as Stace could regard *unio mystica* as "an aberration from standard Jewish types [of mysticism]."[6] A leading scholar of Judaica, Salo Baron, went so far as to affirm that exclamations of identity with God, such as are found in the Islamic mystic Hallaj, "would have sounded as execrable blasphemies in the ears of the most confirmed Jewish followers of Sufism. . . . they never forgot the chasm which separated the Infinite from all his creatures. . . . Individually, too, they sought mere communion not actual union, with the Deity."[7] Obviously, Scholem's view has been accepted without qualification.

Some scholars did attempt to qualify this generalization, but even they regarded the Kabbalists who expressed "audacious" stands on *unio mystica* as exceptions that might slightly modify Scholem's view without, however, necessitating an overall reassessment of its validity.[8] Scholem himself was not convinced by these exceptions and tended to interpret them in a less radical manner.[9] To my knowledge, no attempts at revising Scholem's thesis as such have been undertaken by scholars of Kabbalah, and notwithstanding certain minor reservations, it has remained the regnant view in Kabbalah research. In the following pages, I shall propose an alternative view on expressions of *unio mystica* in Kabbalah: far from being absent, unitive descriptions recur in Kabbalistic literature no less frequently than in non-Jewish mystical writings, and the images used by the Kabbalists do not fall short of the most extreme forms of other types of mysticism.

I shall begin with the implicit assumption underlying both Caird's and Scholem's negation of extreme mysticism in Judaism. It presupposes that the transcendence of God as affirmed in an exoteric religion does not allow *unio mystica* even on the esoteric level.[10] Such an assumption, however, is unfounded on both theoretical and factual grounds. As we have seen above, the Kabbalists employed unitive philosophical terminology that had been in existence long before the composition of their works and that was recognized as acceptable in Jewish circles.[11] Concepts regarding union with supernal entities, such as R. Abraham ibn 'Ezra's view of *devekut* or Averroës's notion of intellectual union, were well known and recurred frequently in Kabbalistic treatises.

Moreover, the transmutation of Enoch into the angel Metatron, an important motif in some ancient Jewish texts, could be understood in some instances as the fusion between the human patriarch and the angel that predated this experience. According to the ancient Jewish texts, Enoch was invested not only with garments of glory and a huge size but also with all-comprehensive knowledge. No wonder that his example was considered a mystical ideal among ecstatic Kabbalists.[12] Therefore, we cannot attribute the "reticence" concerning the use of unitive imagery to inhibitions caused by external conceptual factors, such as the lack of unitive motifs in Jewish theologies. To the contrary, philosophical terminology, for example, could and did serve as a conceptual frame that could at the same time facilitate communication with certain intellectual groups.[13] The fact that a religion that gives rise to a certain mystical movement subscribes to a transcendental theology cannot be adduced as decisive proof for the suppression of unitive imagery. For example, Islam, whose transcendental character is undisputed, gave birth to extreme types of mysticism.[14] Islamic rationalistic theology, in its unsuccessful attempts to suppress mystical groups, was backed by strong sociopolitical forces that were absent in Judaism. The same was also the case in Christianity; despite the powerful domination of the intellectual arena by the church, which had condemned spiritual dissenters and sometimes even executed them, one finds from the end of the thirteenth century on an abundance of assertions of the possibility of union with God. Against this background, the existence of a plethora of unitive expressions in Jewish mysticism is neither problematic sociologically nor curious from the religious point of view.

II. UNION IN ECSTATIC KABBALAH

So much for the theoretical aspect of the problem. The textual evidence also points to a direction other than that indicated by Scholem. Part of the material to be discussed below was, to be sure, known to Scholem and used by him; he interpreted it in a way different from the one I shall follow. Another part was not used by him at all, although we can reasonably assume that he was well acquainted with it; still another part may not have been known by him. I shall first outline the historical context of the usage of unitive descriptions and then discuss some important examples.

As noted above, Geronese Kabbalah was interested in *devekut* as a central mystical value, and in some instances, the unitive interpretation of this term is more appropriate than a communitive understanding. Yet from the second half of the thirteenth century onward, Spanish Kabbalists tended to deemphasize *devekut*, giving primary emphasis to the theurgical significance of performing commandments with Kabbalistic intention. Such is the case in the *Zohar* and in the works of R. Moses de Leon, R. Joseph Gikatilla, R. David ben Yehudah he-Ḥasid, and R. Joseph of Hamadan. Notwithstanding the vivid Geronese interest in *devekut* as one of the highest religious values, the late thirteenth-century Kabbalists overemphasized the centrality of theurgical practice for

Jewish life. Although these Kabbalists eventually mentioned *devekut* with respect, it never became the center of their religious outlook. Spanish Kabbalah followed this type of theurgical religion until the Expulsion in 1492, and continued doing so in northern Africa, Italy, and the Ottoman Empire.

Outside thirteenth-century Spain, the ecstatic Kabbalah of Abraham Abulafia regarded the attainment of ecstatic experiences as the summum bonum of human spirituality and at times described these experiences in unitive terms. I have devoted a detailed study to Abulafia's views concerning mystical union, in an attempt to show that several passages in his works can be understood only as indicative of unitive tendencies. I shall restrict myself here to some representative examples. In one of his commentaries on the *Guide,* Abulafia asserts that the Kabbalist "prophesies, according to the entity which causes him to pass from potentiality into the final and perfect actuality, and he and He become one entity, inseparable during this act."[15]

The "inseparableness" of the factors that enter the ecstatic experience is here explicitly referred to in the classical formula "he and He become one entity."[16] The philosophical gist of this passage is unmistakable: the transition from potentiality into the perfect actuality is tantamount to the transformation of the individual human intellect into the active intellect, which is achieved by an act of union. Elsewhere in the same work, Abulafia indicates that the human faculties gradually ascend to the active intellect[17] "and will unite with it after many hard, strong, and mighty exercises, until the particular and personal prophetic [faculty] will turn universal,[18] permanent and everlasting[19] similar to the essence of its cause, and he and He will become one entity."

This kind of unitive expression abounds in Abulafia's works, many of which are extant in manuscript form and some of which are influential treatises. The total absence of Abulafia in Scholem's most elaborate analysis of the phenomenon of *devekut* is hard to explain.[20] Only by neglecting such a major Kabbalistic figure in a study devoted to *devekut* or by misinterpreting his views in others could a totally nonunitive picture of Jewish mysticism be constructed.[21] Moreover, Abulafia was not merely a major exception; he opened an avenue that was followed by several interesting Kabbalists, some of whom were themselves as highly influential in the spiritual physiognomy of Jewish mysticism as he was.

III. MYSTICAL UNION: RECONSTRUCTION OF A BROKEN UNITY

Let me illustrate the affinity among the perceptions of *devekut* in three mystical schools, which may be seen as constituting a continuum of interest in this matter—the ecstatic Kabbalah, Safedian Kabbalah, and Ḥasidism. All these schools envisioned *devekut* as a reintegration of the human into the primordial unity, whose other half is the Divine.

According to one of Abulafia's disciples, the anonymous author of *Sha'arey Ẓedek,* man is the last of the compound entities (as Maimonides[22] and Abulafia[23] already maintained) and is therefore represented by the letter *yod,* that is, the number ten, which is considered the last primary number. He then continues:

> He is the *yod* in this world, who has received the power from the all, and he comprises the all, like the *yod* in [the realm of] the Sefirot. Understand, therefore, that there is no discernible difference between this *yod* and that *yod* but a very fine one, from the aspect of spirituality, and that it [the letter *yod*] is the *milluy* [plene spelling] of the other *yod* . . . . And this is the secret [of the verse] "and cleave unto Him"—the cleaving of *yod* to *yod*, in order to complete the circle.[24]

Each of the two *yod*s are explicitly defined as halves of the circle, which is completed by the ascension of the lower man and his turning into "the higher man, the man who [sits] on the throne and[25] shall be called: 'The Lord our righteousness.' "[26]

Man, then, is but half of a greater unit, the circle, and by his ascent he can reconstruct it. Against this background, we may understand the elaboration of the two *yod*s; in Hebrew, the word *yod* stands for ten, and in the plene spelling (*YWD*) the letters *WD* also bear the numerical value of ten. Hence, the form *yod* itself comprises two *yod*s: one symbolizing the human, the other the divine part. Each of these is represented graphically by a semicircle, the shape of the *yod* in the Hebrew alphabet.[27] The cleaving together of these semicircles results in the formation of the complete circle.[28]

The shared metaphor of the circle as a symbol of the union of the human and the Divine is deserving of closer examination; its occurrence as part of the description of human perfection recalls the Jungian conception of the mandala as a symbol of individualization. Abraham Abulafia indeed visualized a circle as part of his ecstatic experiences. The recurrence of the metaphor here allows us to understand that these two references to the circle are not only a literary description; they also point to a vision of a circle during an experience interpreted as unitive. Moreover, the explicit formulation of *unio mystica* in the Bodleian manuscript to be quoted below helps us understand the significance of these passages, including the circle metaphor that occurs in *Sha'arey Ẓedek*; I assume that the anonymous Kabbalist who wrote this book understood the mystical experiences recorded in his work as unitive experiences.

In another work closely related to Abulafia and preserved in the Bodleian Library, we read:[29] "He told me: 'Thou art my son, this day I have begotten thee,'[30] and also: 'See now that I, even I, am He.'[31] And the secret [of these verses] is the cleaving of the power—that is, the supernal divine power called the circle of prophecy—with the human power; and it is also said: 'I, I.' "[32] The phrases "I, I" and "I even I, am He," stand for the union of the Divine with the human; according to the plain reading of the texts, the "circle of prophecy" is tantamount to the divine power. A closer reading, however, reveals another sense: the numerical value of the Hebrew phrase *galgal ha-nevu'ah* is 132; the same holds true of the phrase *'Aniy 'Aniy hu'*, this *gematria* being a decisive indication that the circle includes two I's—both human and the Divine.

In both sources from the ecstatic Kabbalah, mystical union is presented as a process of assimilation to the Divine. In *Sha'arey Ẓedek,* man ascends to the status of an entity sitting on the divine throne. The second passage uses three verses that forcefully point to a union of man with the Divine to the extent that the former is referred to by the same phrase as the Divinity: *'Aniy.* Before I leave the anonymous author of *Sha'arey Ẓedek,* it is pertinent to quote his view of the soul:[33] "The universal soul is one, and she was divided into two [parts] because of the division of matter."[34] These two parts are the soul of the "sphere of *'Aravot*"—seemingly the highest sphere, the most spiritual of the souls existing in the entire world—and "the natural soul" derived from the first one.[35] This affinity enables the human soul to ascend to the soul of *'Aravot* and change its nature. This description of the soul parallels the description above of the two semicircles, although this point cannot be proven definitively. In both cases, an ascent that precedes the attainment of human perfection is mentioned.

Some possible sources of the view of man as a semicircle, and of his soul as part of the universal soul may be the following: (1) Plato's description of the division of the primeval androgynous spherical being into two halves, male and female,[36] and (2) the medieval versions of this myth, both Arabic[37] and Jewish,[38] which transferred the division from the body to the soul. Our anonymous Kabbalist seems to have drawn upon both versions, albeit introducing a substantial change: the whole is no longer the primordial man or his soul but the universal man and the universal soul; the division is no longer "vertical," resulting in two sexually differentiated and "equal" beings, but rather "horizontal," creating an asexual polarity of supernal man or higher soul, versus lower man or human soul.

Phenomenologically, and perhaps also historically, the conceptions of *Sefer Sha'arey Ẓedek,* are close to those of R. Elijah de Vidas, an important Safedian

Kabbalist and moralist.[39] Dealing with the significance of the term *part* (*ḥelek*), he wrote: "It indicates that the souls are hewn from him, and he and they are two parts, like the matter of 'half-bodies' . . . and when the part of the lower soul unites with him, the two parts become united and one."[40]

The view of the union of the two semicircles as a metaphor for *unio mystica* has its closest counterpart in the famous interpretation by the Great Maggid R. Dov Baer of Mezherich[41] of the meaning of the verse: "Make thee two trumpets."[42]

> Two halves of forms, as it is written "on the throne, a likeness in the appearance of a man above upon it,"[43] as man ['*ADaM*] is but *D* and *M*,[44] and the speech[45] dwells upon him. And when he unites with God, who is the Alpha[46] of the world, he becomes '*ADaM* . . . . and man must separate himself from any corporeal things, to such an extent that he will ascend through all the worlds[47] and be in union with God, until [his] existence will be annihilated, and then he will be called '*ADaM*.

The Maggid bases his homily on the verse: "Make thee two trumpets of silver, of a whole piece shall thou make them." The Hebrew word for *trumpets, Ḥaẓoẓerot,* is interpreted as *Ḥaẓi-ẓurot,* that is, "[two] half-forms." This phrase occurs already in one of R. Joseph Gikatilla's short treatises, in which he refers to the two halves of the original soul, which is divided into male and female souls.[48]

In Gikatilla, this partition of the soul reflects a higher one: that between the Sefirot of *Yesod* and *Malkhut*. The earthly intercourse between male and female, who derived their souls from an original unity, is conducive to the attainment of the harmony on high. This theurgical perception of the two halves of souls was presumably known to the Great Maggid. R. Moses Ḥayyim Ephraim of Sudylkow reported an interesting version of R. Dov Baer's interpretation of the trumpets, according to which they correspond to the name[49] and heaven, who long to be united with each other;[50] our duty is to facilitate this union.[51] The mystical conception of the two half-forms may thus represent a neutralization of an earlier theurgical view existing in thirteenth-century Kabbalah.[52]

Let us return to the passage from R. Dov Baer. According to Scholem, his unitive terminology must be considered in the "context of his thought," which points to a state wherein "man finds himself by losing himself in God," a view consonant with "the eminently Jewish and personalistic conception of man"; thus, the Great Maggid does not intend a "pantheistic obliteration of the self within the divine mind."[53] This view, however, is far from being a definitive interpretation: the Great Maggid's terminology—"union with God" and the annihilation of individual existence—support a rather more radical interpretation, which is corroborated, as we shall see below, by the existence of extreme unitive conceptions in the circle of R. Dov Baer.[54] Scholem's reading of "Adam" in the last sentence of the quotation as the new spiritual identity of the mystic following the unitive experience is no more than one of the many possibilities inherent in the Ḥasidic text. It is equally valid to assume that "Adam" refers not to the mystic who has returned from the annihilative experience but to what remained absorbed in the depth of the Godhead. The reference to union as a step preceding annihilation is evidence that the unitive experience culminates with the total loss of individuality.[55] A similar sequence is found in another text of R. Dov Baer. Describing the state of the world designated by a talmudic dictum[56] as *ḥaruv* (destroyed), he wrote: " 'and one [thousand years the world] is destroyed'—when all arrives at union, the world is destroyed and annihilated."[57] Annihilation is, again, preceded by union. The unqualified reference to the annihilation of existence leaves no room for the assumption that the term *Adam* persists beyond the state of annihilation. According to one version of this passage, the "complete form" is attained only when God and man are together, without any hint of the possibility that the phrase is applicable to either of these entities when separated.[58]

The same verse from Ezekiel was employed both by the author of *Sha'arey Ẓedek* and by the Great Maggid in order to refer to the new stage achieved by the mystic. These authors likewise share similar linguistic techniques to demonstrate their view: *Y* plus *WD*,[59] or *A* plus *DM*. Moreover, they use the term *half* to describe each of the entities involved in the mystical union. These affinities, however, important as they may be, are insufficient as conclusive proofs of a direct influence of *Sha'arey Ẓedek* on the Great Maggid; but they clearly establish the similarity between an important aspect of ecstatic Kabbalah and mystical Ḥasidism.

In all three mystical schools mentioned above, the Neoplatonic motif of the cleaving of the human soul to its source is prominent. This was combined with the Platonic theory of "halves," and the synthesis functioned as a powerful expression to convey the state of mystical union. Let me conclude this point with a quotation from the work of one of the first masters of Ḥasidism, R. Menaḥem Naḥum of Chernobyl:[60] " . . . to bring himself closer to the divine part which dwells in him, closer to the root of all, to him, blessed be he; and he becomes attached to the divine unity by means of the union of the part to the all,[61] which is *'Eiyn Sof*. Consequently, the light of the holiness of *'Eiyn Sof* shines in him, as the part cleaves to its root."[62] The Neoplatonic terminology of "the part" (individual) cleaving to "its root" (all) is obvious. The fusion of the particular with the general, as presented here by a member of R. Dov Baer's circle, has, in my opinion, nothing personalistic about it; what remains is the divine light that invades the individual in a unitive experience.

IV. THE DROP AND THE OCEAN

At this stage in our analysis of *devekut*, it would be worthwhile to survey the recurrence of another classical metaphor of *unio mystica* in Kabbalistic texts—namely, the dissolution of the drop of water within the sea. This metaphor is an ancient one that had already appeared in the *Katha Upanishad* IV:15; in Zaehner's rendering, it reads: "As pure water poured into pure becomes like unto it—so does the soul of the discerning sage become [like unto Brahman]."[63] Both Muslim and Christian mysticism have employed this image as well.[64] In Kabbalistic sources, it apparently appears for the first time in R. Isaac of Acre:[65] "She [the soul][66] will cleave to the divine intellect, and it will cleave to her . . . . and she and the intellect become one entity, as if somebody pours out a jug of water into a running well, that all becomes one. And this is the secret meaning of the saying of our sages: 'Enoch is Metatron.'[67] And this is the secret meaning of [the phrase] 'a fire devouring fire.' "

For R. Isaac, the dissolution or absorption of the human soul into the supernal entity is total and presumably final. No wonder that he warns against the dangers of sinking[68] into the ultimate experience of union:[69]

> When Moses our master said: "show me thy glory,"[70] he sought his death in order that his soul should obliterate the barrier of her palace[71] which separates her and the wondrous divine light, which she was eager to contemplate. But because Israel still needed Moses, God did not wish that Moses' soul would leave her palace in order to apprehend this light of his. . . . Now you, my son, strive to contemplate the supernal light since I have certainly introduced you into "the sea of the ocean"[72] which surrounds the [whole] world.[73] But be careful and guard your soul from gazing and your heart from pondering [upon the light], lest you sink; and the effort shall be to contemplate but [at the same time] to escape from sinking. . . . Let your soul contemplate the divine light and certainly cleave to it, as long as she dwells in her palace.

In principle, the great endeavor of the mystic is to attain the state of union without, nevertheless, being absorbed and lost in the divine abyss. Sinking is envisioned here as a perilous possibility inherent in the unitive experience.[74] However, at least in the case of Moses, death—which I suppose is parallel to sinking[75]—is portrayed as a higher mystical step that Moses attempted to achieve; it was denied him only because he was needed to lead the people of

Israel, an activity consisting of corporeal acts.[76] Cleaving—and in R. Isaac's texts we can use the term *union*—is not the terminal point of the mystical path. Beyond that lies the "ocean," tempting the mystic to accomplish his spiritual adventure by an ecstatic sinking.[77] It is worth emphasizing that, in fact, R. Isaac of Acre assumes that a total fusion with the Divine is possible and that Moses, the paragon of Jewish mystics, indeed strove to attain such an experience. Therefore, from the theological point of view, the abyss that separates the human and the Divine is not unbridgeable.

One of R. Isaac's contemporaries and probably also a compatriot, the anonymous author of *Sha'arey Ẓedek,* explicitly expresses his overwhelming experience in oceanic terminology. He requested of his master:[78]

> "In heaven's name, can you perhaps impart to me some power to enable me to bear this force emerging from my heart and to receive influx from it?" For I wanted to draw this force toward me and receive influx from it, for it much resembles a spring filling a great basin with water. If a man [not being properly prepared for it] should open the dam, he would be drowned in its waters and his soul would desert him.[79]

These texts all strongly illustrate that images of the ocean are to be found in Kabbalah as in other types of mystical literature.[80] Moreover, some of the earliest Christian mystics who used this simile in its most extreme mode—that of the absorption of a drop of water into the sea[81]—were condemned as heretics; one of them, Marguerite Porete, was even burned for heresy.[82] This happened at roughly the same time when the Kabbalistic sources above were being written, with no condemnation or even protest uttered by Jewish theologians or halakhists. Even stronger examples can be adduced from Ḥasidic literature.

The "drop" imagery is found in early Ḥasidism. R. Yeḥiel Mikhael of Zloczow,[83] one of the Besht's important disciples and a companion of the Great Maggid, indicates that the Jews[84]

> made all their powers cleave to their thought [and] to the Creator, blessed be he, as they were wont to do in the past. Therefore, they are very great, for the branch arrives at its root,[85] this [arrival] being a union with the root, and the root is the *'Eiyn Sof*; thence the branch is also *'Eiyn Sof*, as its existence was annihilated[86] as in the simile of the single drop[87] which has fallen into the great sea, and arrived at its root, and hence is one with the water of the sea, so that it is totally impossible to recognize[88] it per se.

The soul is therefore dissolved into *'Eiyn Sof*, so that she can no longer be distinguished as a separate entity; she is completely obliterated in the ocean from which she emerged. This passage seems to be more than just a random uncharacteristic utterance. It accurately expresses the view of the Great Maggid, with whose works it shares terminological and conceptual views. R. Yeḥiel Mikhael's far-reaching perception illuminates the Great Maggid's concepts, bringing into sharper relief his more radical, impersonal stand.[89]

The relationship between *devekut* and "death"—which has Kabbalistic precedents, some of which have been mentioned previously—is also found in the circle of R. Dov Baer. R. Jacob Isaac ha-Levi Horowitz, the Seer of Lublin, reports in the name of the Rabbi of Pinsk, R. Levi Isaac of Berdichev, a fascinating interpretation of the talmudic dictum "One who is poor is considered as if he is dead,"[90] presented in the context of another talmudic statement "One who wishes to live should mortify himself."[91] R. Levi Isaac asserts:[92]

> One who wishes to live should disregard the concerns of his body, and let his thought cleave to God, blessed be he. He will mortify himself and will depart[93] from himself; but he is nevertheless alive, as he cleaves to the life of {all} lives.[94] . . . whoever is impoverished by his cleaving to God, blessed be he, is certainly considered . . . as if dead,[95] as freed from {actual} death, but {nevertheless} lives by them {the commandments}.

Devekut is here closely related to the state of poverty or "death"; indeed, cleaving leads to the emergence of the next mystical stage of total disengagement from the world. We can formulate a three-stage mystical path hinted at by R. Levi Isaac: (1) detachment from one's corporeal needs,[96] (2) attaching of one's thought to God, and (3) spiritual "poverty," or "death" at the culmination of the mystical path. Like the annihilation that comes after union in the text of the Great Maggid, his disciple assumes a spiritual death that crowns one's experience of union.[97] There is nothing new in the argumentation about the true life that succeeds one's dying to this world; it is a reverberation of a Neoplatonic motif[98] already recorded in the Babylonian Talmud.[99] The Ḥasidic text locates *devekut* as an initial step on the mystical path; only after cleaving does one "die," and this "dying" ensures everlasting life.[100] In the last passage the term *poor* (*'aniy*) bears an overt mystical overtone, implying the natural result of cleaving rather than a self-induced awareness of *pauperitas sancta* vis-à-vis God. This perception of "poverty" is to be compared to R. Dov Baer's "self-annihilation" that follows cleaving.[101] Again a mystical state emerges without any initiative on the part of the mystic; no self-abasement is referred to by the Great Maggid, or at least not such a state alone, but a passive experience of annihilation that seems closely related to "death"[102] or "poverty."[103]

The very end of R. Levi Isaac's passage, *ve-ḥay bahem* (Lev. 18:5), is an obvious reference to the performance of commandments. Cleaving and total detachment cannot release one from the yoke of the commandments. Such a reference is indispensable since, according to a talmudic view, only the dead are free from the commandments. Furthermore, according to the well-known perception of *devekut*—which was described above—cleaving is sometimes regarded as a prerequisite for the spiritual performance of the commandments. But this point was not elaborated by R. Levi Isaac in our passage; by comparing it to conceptions of prayer during unitive experiences in the Great Maggid's circle, we may perceive that this performance has lost its activistic, intentional characteristics, being replaced by quietistic acts. The very occurrence of the phrase *ve-ḥay bahem* evinces a sensibility toward the possibility that someone might understand *devekut* and "spiritual death" as states of consciousness that keep one from the performance of commandments, rendering them superfluous. Rather, the mystic reaches a state in which the *mizvot* are performed as if God himself performed them through him, the mystic having attained a state of *Gelassenheit,* to use Meister Eckhart's term. "Death" in the metaphorical sense is here applied exclusively to the soul with no reference to the body, a fact that strengthens our observation that the performance of commandments is still going on.[104] Again, as in the case of the earlier Kabbalists, no protests were raised, as far as I know, against these extreme statements and expressions, despite the fact that Ḥasidism was, in the very years these texts were written, under heavy attack from its opponents.

V. THE SWALLOWING METAPHOR

Another interesting image for mystical union can be found in the writings of the fourteenth-century Flemish mystic, John Ruysbroeck. According to him, "To eat and to be eaten? This is union. . . . since his desire is without measure, to be devoured of him does not greatly amaze me."[105] This text is considered an example of extreme unitive metaphor and is indeed a fascinating expression.[106] Judged by the criterion of the presence or absence of the "devouring" type of imagery, Jewish mysticism also presents extreme tendencies.[107] Thus, for example, we learn from R. Isaac of Acre that the mystical significance of the biblical phrase describing God as "a devouring fire" is the "eating,"[108] referring to[109]

> that thing which is swallowed by another. "And he cleaves to his wife [and they become] one flesh."[110] When the pious mystic causes his soul to ascend [in order] to cleave in an appropriate cleaving to the divine mystery to which she [the soul]

> cleaves, [the Divinity][111] swallows her.[112] And this is the secret meaning of [the verse],[113] "but they shall not come to see when the holy things are covered [literally, swallowed][114] lest they die."

There can be no doubt that the cleaving referred to here, portrayed as a state of being swallowed up, takes place between the human soul and the Divine.[115] Not only does this passage precede the discussion of the jug of water and the running well, in which the divine intellect is mentioned; both images, those of fire and water, are supposed to reveal the significance of a phrase explicitly referring to divinity.

Another pertinent discussion is to be found in the *Commentary to the Prayer Book* by R. Shneur Zalman of Lyady, the founder of Ḥabad Ḥasidism. According to him, the ritual of *Nefilat Appayim* (prayers recited in a semiprone posture) symbolizes the union of two different entities that become like one inseparable body.[116] Even when a man continues his regular activity after prayer, he does not fall from this state of union. Commenting upon his own remarks on mystical union, R. Shneur Zalman asserts:[117]

> As we see that when man cleaves to God, it is extremely delightful for Him, and very sweet,[118] so much so that he will swallow it into his heart,[119] and so on, as the bodily throat swallows. And this is the true cleaving, as he becomes one substance with God into whom he was swallowed, without being separate [from him] to be considered as a distinct entity[120] at all. That is the meaning [of the verse], "and you shall cleave to him"[121]—[to cleave], literally.

Some comments on this passage are in order. This is more than a mere metaphorical usage; the beginning of the quotation expresses, through the simile of devouring, common experience. As I remarked above, from the methodological point of view we are not in a position to compare the contents of R. Shneur Zalman's experience either with that of R. Isaac of Acre or with that of Ruysbroeck. At least on the literary level, however, the similarity between their images is surprising.

The sequence "cleaving—swallowing," obvious in R. Shneur Zalman, is presumably parallel to that of "cleaving—annihilation" occurring in some Ḥasidic texts, including some of those discussed above. Accordingly, "swallowing" is similar to the annihilation of the human soul after the act of union. If this understanding is correct, then a major disciple of the Great Maggid envisioned mystical annihilation as the highest step on the mystical ladder, an interpretation confirming our previous allegedly radical understanding of the two-trumpets simile.

Two final remarks concerning the Ḥasidic usage of the "devouring" simile.

First, R. Shneur Zalman's view can be better understood against the background of the widespread Kabbalistic concept of elevation by ritualistic eating; as the vegetable and animal entities are elevated through their consumption by a human being, so is the latter elevated through being swallowed by the Divine.[122] In all these cases, the spiritual cores or the holy particles are liberated and thereby achieve their return to a pristine status. And second, from both the R. Isaac of Acre and Shneur Zalman passages, we can gather that, in spite of the imagery used, the experience it reflects does not seem to be considered a final one. Neither of these authors is searching for a mystical death as an aim in itself, although the nature of this experience may indeed be attractive.

The possibility of total assimilation of the human to the Divine is also conspicuous in *Kedushat ha-Levi,* written by another disciple of the Great Maggid, R. Levi Isaac of Berdichev:

> When the *Ẓaddik* cleaves to the nought, and is [then] annihilated, then [alone] he worships the Creator from the aspect of all the *Ẓaddikim*, since no division of the attributes is discernible there at all . . . . There is a *Ẓaddik* who cleaves to the nought and nevertheless returns afterward to his essence. But Moses our master, blessed be his memory, was annihilated all the time since he was constantly contemplating the grandeur of the Creator, blessed be he, and did not return to his essence at all, as it is well known, since Moses our master, blessed be his memory, was constantly cleaving to the nought, and from this aspect he was annihilated. . . . Since when he contemplates the Creator, blessed be he, then there is no essence in him, since he is annihilated . . . he contemplated the nought and was annihilated . . . . and Moses was constantly cleaving to the nought.[123]

The distinction between Moses' constant contemplation, which caused an annihilative state from which he did not return, and that of the *Ẓaddikim*, who return from their unitive experiences, is highly significant. What is at stake is not the possibility of assimilation by or in God from the divine perspective—or, in other words, the possibility of bridging the distance between man and God—but the problem of human nature, which can hardly sustain a state of continuous immersion in a contemplative/annihilative experience. Moses was seen as a mystic who was capable of maintaining this supreme state of union and hence served as an ideal for the *Ẓaddikim*; he was seen similarly by R. Isaac of Acre.

Let us now return to the "swallowing" image, which is alluded to again in a later Ḥasidic text by R. Eliezer Ẓevi Safrin. God here expresses the relationship to the *Ẓaddikim* in these terms: "In the entire exile I have only 'a little [literally, "few"; *me'at*} food'; namely, at certain [rare] times a union with a *Ẓaddik*, designated as 'few,' occurs. And eating is the holy union, as is known [in the phrase] 'a little food.' "[124]

We may compare the "swallowing" imagery as reflective of mystical experiences to the type of imagery occurring in the initiatory ordeals of tribal rites.[125] In the mystical type of imagery, there is a clear fascination with being swallowed as the culmination of a long process of approaching the Divine. In the mythical worldview of the archaic mentality, the initiate is involved in a dreadful experience of meeting with "the monster," which, by "devouring" the initiate, enables him to attain a more mature level of behavior as well as a new social status.[126] In both types of experience, the person is elevated to a higher level: the primitive approach uses the technique of presenting to the youth the *mysterium tremendum*,[127] and the mystical approach, that of seeking a meeting with the *mysterium fascinans*.[128] In the former case, the personality is supposed to develop into a mature mode of perceiving reality; in the latter, we can assume that the encounter with the Divine brings about a disintegration of the "old man," but without substituting a higher structure of social personality. In the tribal initiation, a person enters a new society; in extreme mysticism, man leaves society and enters God. The initiation ordeal is a rite of passage; the mystical experience is mostly an exit into God. The ordeal is primarily physical; the mystical experience is essentially psychical.

Given the material we have examined in this chapter, it is apparent that the rarity of the existence of mystical union in its extreme form in Jewish sources should be reconsidered; both the Kabbalistic theory and praxis call for such a revision. Let us turn now to the ways in which Jewish mystics attained their mystical experiences—their mystical techniques.

CHAPTER 5
Mystical Techniques

I. NOMIAN AND ANOMIAN MYSTICAL TECHNIQUES

Like mystics of other faiths, Kabbalists used certain techniques in order to induce paranormal states of consciousness. But despite the great importance of these practices, their history and description have received only scant attention in the modern study of Jewish mysticism.[1] The very existence of elaborate systems of mystical practices constitutes significant evidence for the reliability of the confessions of Jewish mystics. The fact that those Kabbalists who related their mystical experiences are the same Kabbalists who described mystical techniques enhances their credibility as to the practical use of the techniques and the experiential nature of their mystical life.[2]

Unlike unitive terminology, which is heavily influenced by external sources, the descriptions of mystical techniques combine ancient and presumably authentically Jewish elements with practices that were absorbed from alien sources. One can distinguish between two main types of Kabbalistic techniques, which I will designate nomian and anomian. *Nomian* refers to the internalized halakhic practices that were performed by the Kabbalists with "intention" or *kavvanah*, one of the important goals of which was *devekut*. Thus, *nomian* stands for the spiritualization of the halakhic *dromenon,* which is thereby transformed into a mystical technique. *Anomian* refers to those forms of mystical activity that did not involve halakhic practice. I should like to stress from the outset that *anomian* is far from synonymous with alien practices. Although some anomian techniques may indeed have stemmed from non-Jewish sources, others were practiced by ancient

Jewish mystics but did not become a part of the halakhic way of life. It was precisely the anomian practices that, during the later stages of development of Jewish mysticism, became the most esoteric part of Kabbalistic techniques. Before I enter into detailed discussion, it should be remarked that part of the material to follow stems from anonymous treatises or from literary genres such as hagiographical and pseudepigraphic works. I decided to include such material when there was sufficient reason to suppose that, even if it did not reflect the actual practices of the persons to whom it was attributed, the details provided in these texts can nevertheless be useful for a better understanding of certain techniques. Actual or spuriously attributed practices may have been imitated by the mystics.

I shall present below four main mystical techniques. The first two—weeping and the ascent of the soul—exemplify the continuity of Jewish mysticism throughout the centuries, notwithstanding the changes in theological conceptions that occurred; the last two—combination of letters and visualization of colors—are representative of the more intensive types of techniques characteristic of the medieval period. I deliberately ignored a long series of other devices for attaining paranormal states of consciousness, such as oneiric techniques,[3] isolation,[4] or mental concentration,[5] which I have described elsewhere. Of the four techniques dealt with here, the first two are analyzed extensively, whereas the third and fourth ones are, for various reasons, only generally surveyed.[6]

II. WEEPING AS MYSTICAL PRACTICE

I shall begin my description of the techniques by focusing on a practice—unnoticed before—that can be traced back through all the major stages of Jewish mysticism over a period of more than two millennia. I refer to the recommendation of the use of weeping as a means for attaining revelations—mostly of a visual character—and/or a disclosure of secrets.[7] Before introducing the relevant material, I will review the role played by weeping in Judaism. Within the nomian framework, weeping was incumbent for a limited time within the period of mourning for either a member of one's family or an outstanding sage. It is obvious from the halakhic regulations that, although weeping was obligatory during the period of mourning, it was not viewed as appropriate common behavior. Weeping was likewise recommended in connection with mourning for the Destruction of the Temple, either as part of the rite of *Tikkun Ḥaẓẓot* or as an integral component of the observance of the Ninth of *Av*. The shedding of tears on the latter occasion was indeed highly appreciated, God himself being portrayed as weeping for the Destruction of the Temple.[8] In addition to these instances of bewailing a personal or national loss, weeping was seen as part of the process of repentance.

All these occurrences of weeping were past-oriented, being directed toward an event or events that had already taken place. The future-oriented uses of weeping were more limited; repentance and weeping could contribute to the coming of the Messiah, and groups of mourners were established to hasten this event. According to another version, weeping was part of the effort toward repentance that aimed at safeguarding the Jews from the dreadful events anticipated in the period immediately preceding the arrival of the Messiah. These past- and future-oriented types of weeping were connected with value concepts that were themselves an integral part of the midrashic-talmudic view of life and history. Although participation in these future-oriented practices was not seen as obligatory, they were intended to achieve goals of national importance.

I shall discuss here two present-oriented uses of weeping elaborated upon in Jewish mystical texts. The first was mystical weeping: that is, the effort to receive visions and information about secrets as the direct result of self-induced weeping.[9] The second type, the theurgical one, was intended to induce "weeping" above—internal processes within the Divine triggered by the shedding of human tears. This present-oriented theurgic activity will be analyzed in the chapter on Kabbalistic theurgy, but the main differences between these two kinds of present-oriented weeping ought to be noted here. The latter activity was essentially a theurgic reinterpretation of the nomian recommendations to weep; the focus of this technique was the supernal processes, the Kabbalist being the instrument and not the goal of this activity. Mystical weeping, by contrast, posited as the ultimate goal of weeping the acquisition of paranormal consciousness by the Kabbalist. Although it can be viewed as a spiritual interpretation of nomian practices, it can just as easily be defined as an anomian activity, as nowhere was disclosure of secrets, or even study of esoteric topics, let alone visions of God, part of the midrashic-talmudic conception of things. Moreover, the occurrence of the earliest evidence for this practice in pre-talmudic or midrashic texts is an important proof of its independence from classical halakhic regulations. On the other hand, there are only scanty references to this perception of weeping in classical rabbinic sources, an issue to which I shall return at the conclusion of this discussion.

The earliest evidence for mystical weeping is found in the apocalyptic literature. One version of II Enoch states that this patriarch was "weeping and grieving with [my] eyes. When I lay down on my bed, I fell asleep; and two huge men appeared to me."[10] An interesting parallel occurs in IV Ezra; the angel who has previously revealed some secrets to the prophet ends his speech by saying, "and if you pray again, and weep as you do now, and fast for seven days, you shall hear yet greater things than these."[11] Later, 'Ezra indicates, "I fasted seven days, mourning and weeping, as Ariel the angel has commanded me," and he received a second vision.[12] The third one is also preceded by a similar process: "I wept again and fasted seven days as before."[13] Similar statements occur in the Apocalypse of Baruch. Baruch and Jeremiah had repeated the same practice: "we rent our garments and wept and mourned and fasted for seven days, and it happened after seven days that the Word of God came to me."[14] A common feature of "apocalyptic" weeping was a state of desolation, associated with the Destruction of the Temple or other signs of religious decline; the feeling of despair was expressed in weeping, followed by comforting revelations.

The connection between weeping and paranormal perceptions taking place in dreams is also evident in a midrashic story:[15]

> One of the students of R. Simeon bar Yoḥai had forgotten what he learned. In tears he went to the cemetery. Because of his great weeping, he [R. Simeon] came to him in a dream and told him: "When you wail, throw three bundles,[16] and I shall come." The student went to a dream interpreter and told him what had happened. The latter said to him: "Repeat your chapter [that is, whatever you learn] three times, and it will come back to you." The student did so and so indeed it happened.

The correlation between weeping and visiting a grave seems to point to a practice intended to induce a vision. This was, to be sure, part of a larger context in which graveyards were sites where one might receive a vision.[17] Falling asleep weeping, which is mentioned here, also seems part of the sequence: visiting a cemetery—weeping—falling asleep weeping—revelatory dream. As we shall see later, this sequence, with the exception of the use of graves, repeats itself in R. Ḥayyim Vital's experience. It is evident that this story was preserved in the Midrash because it was focused upon obtaining a remedy—the mnemonic technique of repetition—for the forgetting of the Torah. Again, the connection between weeping and improving one's knowledge of Torah will recur.

Against this background, I shall analyze a passage from *Midrash Hallel,* a late Midrash, elaborating upon a theme[18] that had already been discussed in the earlier *'Avot de-Rabbi Nathan:*[19]

> "Who turned the rock into a pool of water, the flint into a fountain[20] of water."[21] We have taught that R. 'Akiva and ben 'Azzai were as arid as this rock, but because they

> were anguished for the sake of the study of Torah, God opened for them an opening to [understand] the Torah, to those matters which the School of Shammai and the School of Hillel were unable to understand. . . . and matters which were closed to the world were interpreted by R. 'Akiva, as it is said: "He binds the floods that they trickle not; and the thing that is hidden, he brings forth to light."[22] This demonstrates that R. 'Akiva's eye[23] had seen the *Merkavah*, in the same manner that Ezekiel the prophet had seen it; thus it is said: "Who turned the rock into a pool of water."

The metamorphosis from a rock into a fountain of water is a metaphor for R. 'Akiva's transformation from an ignoramus into the source of both halakhic and esoteric knowledge—a metamorphosis that was the result of his anguish, accompanied by weeping. Job 28:11 contains the Hebrew word *bekhi* ("weeping"), usually translated here as "trickle." The anonymous interpreter evidently understood the verse as indicating that through "weeping" God caused the hidden things to surface;[24] decisive proof for the role of weeping in bringing about R. 'Akiva's new status is the emphatic mention of his "eye." The entire passage may be interpreted on two levels: weeping transformed R. 'Akiva from a rock into a fountain; his eye, which caused it, received a vision of the divine chariot. Following the two verses in the Book of Job, we may summarize the subjects hinted at in *Midrash Hallel;* suffering and weeping open the way to (1) revelation, that is, vision: "his eye sees every precious thing," or the vision of the *Merkavah*; and (2) understanding of esoteric matters: "he brings forth the things which are hidden."[25] These two effects of suffering and weeping occur in some Kabbalistic texts that will be analyzed below. It ought to be emphasized that the combination of vision and of the secrets of the Torah indicates that these secrets are more than unknown information hidden from the eyes of preceding generations; I assume that their understanding has some transformative value for "R. 'Akiva," who is presented here as a "fountain," presumably of the teachings of the Torah.

Before proceeding with our discussion, however, it would be worthwhile to analyze briefly the combination of weeping with placing one's head between one's knees. This posture is mentioned in connection with Elijah on Mount Carmel, probably as part of his prayer;[26] it recurs in the Talmud as part of R. Ḥanina ben Dosa's prayer for the life of R. Yoḥanan ben Zakkai's son.[27] In yet another passage, the Talmud mentions R. Eleazar ben Dordia's attempt to repent, in which he places his head between his knees and weeps.[28] The outcome of R. Eleazar's sorrow and weeping is death, envisaged by a talmudic authority as the acquisition in a moment of the bliss of the world to come.[29] This story cannot in itself serve as decisive evidence for the technical status of weeping; however, its association with the posture of Elijah is highly suggestive, as in both the Heikhalot literature and in a later description of its practices[30] the mystical vision of the supernal palaces is attained by using Elijah's posture.[31] As we have already seen, R. 'Akiva attained his vision of the *Merkavah* through means of weeping. Nowhere in the texts related to the Heikhalot literature, however, are these two practices combined.

The single exception of which I am aware, probably conveying a certain casual affinity between a pattern of acts and a revelatory experience, states as follows:

> R. Ishmael said: I devoted myself to the pursuit of wisdom and the calculation of the holidays and moments and of the [eschatological] dates and times and periods [of times], and I turned my face to the Supreme Holy One through prayer and supplications, fasting and weeping. And I said: "God, Lord of Ẓevaot, Lord of Israel, until when shall we be neglected."[32]

R. Ishmael's prayer had an overt messianic goal: to know the date of the redemption, that is, to receive a revelation whereby he might receive occult information thereof. It seems that the more "mathematical" methods for achieving knowledge of the secret date of the end of the suffering of Israel either were inappropriate or had to be attained by a mystical technique, which included weeping, together with other types of ascetic practices.

Nevertheless, we may assume that such a combined practice existed in ancient Jewish mysticism, and not only on the evidence of the talmudic story about R. Eleazar. The *Zohar* describes R. Simeon bar Yoḥai as both practicing Elijah's posture and weeping in connection with a mystical experience.[33] The mystic asked who could disclose to him the secrets of the Torah and then "wept and placed his head between his knees and kissed the dust." His friends encouraged him, saying, "be happy in the happiness of your Lord." He then wrote down all he had heard that night and learned it without forgetting anything. R. Simeon remained in this posture the entire night and in the morning lifted his eyes and saw a vision of light representing the Temple. Thus, for R. Simeon, as for R. 'Akiva in *Midrash Hallel,* weeping is connected both with the disclosure of secrets of the Torah and with a vision; although the *Merkavah* is not identical with the Temple, the similarity between *Midrash Hallel* and the *Zohar* passage is striking.[34] Can we perhaps infer from this that the author of the *Zohar* had available to him a source in which weeping and Elijah's posture were already combined in the talmudic text?

An important instance in which weeping was part of a larger pattern culminating in a mystical experience is found in a thirteenth-century Judeo-

Arabic treatise, *Perakim be-Haẓlaḥah,* spuriously attributed to Maimonides. The Oriental author describes the act of prayer in these words:

> The one praying shall turn to God, blessed be he, standing on his feet and delighting in his heart and lips [!]. His hands shall be stretched and his vocal organs shall murmur and speak [while] the other limbs tremble and shake; he shall not cease singing sweet melodies, humbling himself, imploring, bowing and prostrating himself [and] weeping, since he is in the presence of the Great and Majestic King, and [then] he will experience an ecstatic experience and stupefaction, insofar as he will find his soul in the world of the intellects.[35]

No doubt the anonymous author presents here an intentional device for an ideal prayer ending in a mystical experience.

The weeping technique is powerfully expounded by R. Abraham ha-Levi Berukhim, one of Isaac Luria's disciples. In one of his programs for attaining "wisdom," after specifying "silence" as the first condition, he names

> the second condition: in all your prayers, and in every hour of study, in a place which one finds difficult, in which you cannot understand and comprehend the propaedeutic sciences or some secret, stir yourself to bitter weeping until your eyes shed tears, and the more you can weep—do so. And increase your weeping, as the gates of tears were not closed and the supernal gates will be opened to you.[36]

It is obvious that, for Luria and Berukhim, weeping is an aid to overcoming intellectual difficulties and receiving secrets.[37] It is plausible to interpret the final sentence as referring to a revelatory experience, in which the supernal gates are opened. This text is recommended for a practical purpose; it appears that R. Abraham Berukhim indeed had the opportunity to apply this recommendation, as it is reported that Luria had revealed to him that he would die unless he prayed before the Wailing Wall and saw the *Shekhinah*. It is then reported:[38]

> When that pious man heard the words of Isaac Luria, he isolated himself for three days and nights in a fast, and [clothed himself] in a sack, and nightly wept. Afterward he went before the Wailing Wall and prayed there and wept a mighty weeping. Suddenly, he raised his eyes and saw on the Wailing Wall the image of a woman, from behind,[39] in clothes which it is better not to describe, that we have mercy on the divine glory. When he had seen her, he immediately fell on his face and cried and wept and said:[40] "Zion,[41] Zion, woe to me that I have seen you in such a plight." And he was bitterly complaining and weeping and beating his face and plucking his beard and the hair of his head, until he fainted and lay down and fell asleep on his face. Then he saw in a dream the image of a woman who came and put her hands on his face and wiped the tears of his eyes. . . . and when Isaac Luria saw him, he said: "I see that you have deserved to see the face of the *Shekhinah*."

It is clear that the two visions of the woman—that is, of the *Shekhinah*—are the result of R. Abraham's bitter weeping: the former a waking vision of the back of the *Shekhinah*, the latter a vision of her face, which occurs only in a dream. The first one provokes anxiety; the second, comfort.

Akin to the story of R. Abraham Berukhim is the autobiographical confession of his friend, R. Ḥayyim Vital:[42]

> In 1566, on the Sabbath eve, the eighth of *Tevet*, I said *Kiddush* and sat down to eat; and my eyes were shedding tears, and I was sighing and grieving since . . . I was bound by witchcraft[43] . . . and I likewise wept for [my] neglect of the study of Torah during the last two years. . . . and because of my worry I did not eat at all, and I lay on my bed on my face, weeping, and I fell asleep out of much weeping, and I dreamed a wondrous dream.

As in the ancient apocalyptic texts and in R. Abraham Berukhim's story, Vital seems to have combined here weeping, sorrow, and—to a certain extent—even fasting. The last is indeed curious, as the entire incident took place on the eve of the Sabbath, a time when the consumption of a ritual meal is incumbent upon all Jews. The content of the dream that followed is intricate, and this is not the place to deal with it. It is sufficient to note that Vital had a highly elaborate revelation, paralleled by revelations already found in other Kabbalistic works: it is reported as a revelation rather than as a dream.[44] What is certainly novel in Vital's relating of the revelatory dream is his vision of a beautiful woman whom he thought to be his mother, who in the dream asked him:[45] " 'Why are you weeping, Ḥayyim, my son? I have heard your tears and I have come to help you.' . . . and I called to the woman: 'Mother,[46] Mother, help me, so that I[47] may see the Lord sitting upon a throne, the[48] Ancient of Days, his beard white as snow, infinitely splendid.' "

The references to biblical prophetic visions, found only in Safrin's quotation, are extremely relevant to our discussion. In the first stage, Vital apparently wept in order to receive an answer to two problems that were troubling him: his sexual impotence and his interruption of the study of the Torah. In the revelatory dream, he saw himself as weeping in order to obtain a vision of God. Vital's request to see God, formulated in prophetic verses, reminds one of the end of the passage in *Midrash Hallel,* in which R. 'Akiva's vision of the *Merkavah* is compared to that of Ezekiel.

Also relevant to our subject is Nathan of Gaza's description of his own vision. After a complacent description of his religious perfection, the Sabbatian prophet indicates:[49]

> When I attained the age of twenty, I began to study the *Zohar* and some of the

> Lurianic writings. [According to the Talmud], he who wishes to purify himself receives the aid of heaven; thus, he sent to me some of his holy angels and blessed spirits, who revealed to me many of the mysteries of the Torah. In the same year, my force having been stimulated by the visions of the angels and the blessed souls, I was undergoing a prolonged fast during the week before the feast of Purim. Having locked myself in a separate room in holiness and purity, and reciting the penitential prayers of the morning service with many tears, the spirit came over me, my hair stood on end and my knees shook, and I beheld the *Merkavah*.[50] And I saw visions of God all day long and all night, and I was vouchsafed true prophecy like any other prophet, as the voice spoke to me, beginning with the words "Thus speaks the Lord." . . . The angel that revealed himself to me in a waking vision was also a true one, and he revealed to me awesome mysteries.

The vision of the *Merkavah*, quite unusual in the medieval period, is depicted here as following a protracted fast that culminated in the shedding of tears. Interestingly, Nathan was vouchsafed not only a visual experience but also "awesome mysteries." Thus, the two topics mentioned in the early Middle Ages *Midrash Hallel* recur in the experience of the seventeenth-century Kabbalist. Again, as in the midrashic source, the vision of the *Merkavah* is apparently related to the "awesome mysteries"—the latter concerning Sabbatai Ṣevi's messianism, Nathan having envisioned Ṣevi's image engraved on the *Merkavah*.[51]

Mystical weeping also seems to have been cultivated in certain Ḥasidic circles. Before discussing in detail the evidence for this practice, I shall cite a highly interesting dream of R. Joseph Falk, the cantor of the Besht:[52]

> In his dream he saw an image of an altar to which the dead man ascended, and he saw him put his head between his knees and begin to cry the *Seliḥah*: "Answer us, O god, answer us. Answer us, our father," and so on throughout the alphabet. After that he said: "Answer us, O God of our fathers, answer us. Answer us, O God of Abraham, answer us. Answer us, O revered of Isaac, answer us. Answer us, O mighty one of Jacob, answer us. Answer us, O compassionate one, answer us. Answer us, O king of the chariots, answer us." Then he ascended to heaven.

This technique of entreaty—Elijah's posture and crying—seems to reflect the older motif of weeping while sitting in Elijah's posture. R. Israel Ba'al Shem Tov interpreted it as an attempt to ascend to a higher level by the recitation of the "answer us" formula. Therefore, according to the earliest Ḥasidim, crying and, I assume also tears, seem already to have been part of a mystical technique.

A younger contemporary of Ba'al Shem Tov, R. Elijah, the gaon of Vilna, also presumably cultivated the device of weeping. His main disciple, R. Ḥayyim of Volozhin, reported to R. Elijah's grandson that his grandfather had several times been very pained and had fasted and avoided sleeping for one or two days and wept copiously because God had withheld from him a certain secret of the Torah.[53] But, he continued, when the secret was revealed to R. Elijah, his face became joyful and his eyes lighted up. R. Ḥayyim's report points to a certain pattern of behavior intended to attain knowledge of hidden secrets of the Law. The fact that it was used several times points to the apparently technical nature of the pattern. We can see that in early Ḥasidism and in the practice of their opponents, the *Mitnaggedim,* weeping was employed as a component of mystical technique.

An interesting example of the relationship between weeping and revelation is reported by R. Isaac Yehudah Yeḥiel Safrin, in his *Megillat Setarim* and *Netiv Miẓvotekha,* in which he relates an experience of his own.[54] I shall present here a combined version of this mystical confession, based on the author's account in these two books:

> In 1845, on the twenty-first day of the *'Omer*, I was in the town of Dukla.[55] I arrived there late at night, and it was dark and there was no one to take me home, except for a tanner who came and took me into his house. I wanted to pray *Ma'ariv* and to count the *'Omer*, but I was unable to do it there, so I went to the Beit Midrash alone, and there I prayed until midnight had passed. And I understood from this situation the plight of the *Shekhinah* in exile,[56] and her suffering when she is standing in the market of tanners.[57] And I wept many times before the Lord of the world, out of the depth of my heart, for the suffering of the *Shekhinah.* And through my suffering and weeping, I fainted and I fell asleep for a while, and I saw a vision of light,[58] splendor and great brightness, in the image of a young woman[59] adorned with twenty-four ornaments.[60] . . . And she said: "Be strong, my son," and so on. And I was suffering that I could not see but the vision of her back[61] and I was not worthy to receive her face. And I was told that [this was because] I am alive, and it is written, "for no man shall see me, and live."[62]

The vision of the feminine apparition possessing maternal features—she calls R. Isaac "my son"—is characteristic of the Kabbalistic image of weeping, and is shared by the visions of R. Abraham Berukhim and R. Ḥayyim Vital. R. Levi Isaac of Berdichev must also have experienced such a vision. In *Netiv Miẓvotekha,* prior to the passage cited above, after quoting R. Ḥayyim Vital's account from *Sefer ha-Ḥezyonot,* R. Isaac wrote:

> "And it happened to the holy R. Levi Isaac, that on the evening of *Shavu'ot* he achieved the vision of the *Shekhinah* in the image of . . . and she said to him: 'My

son, Levi Isaac, be strong, for many troubles will befall you, but be strong, my son, for I shall be with you.' "[63]

R. Levi Isaac therefore also experienced a vision of *Shekhinah*, who appeared to him as a young woman, although R. Isaac Safrin censored this word, just as he did when he related his own vision shortly thereafter. Moreover, the time when the well-known master of Ḥasidism attained this vision is also significant for two reasons; the eve of *Shavu'ot* is close in time to the period when Safrin experienced his own vision, on the twenty-first day of the *'Omer*; in addition, the night of *Shavu'ot* was the precise time when two noted Kabbalists received their revalation of *Shekhinah*. I refer to the vigil of R. Joseph Karo and R. Solomon ha-Levi Alkabeẓ.[64] Therefore, R. Levi Isaac attempted to imitate the experience of his Kabbalist predecessors. Safrin, however, does not even hint at the experience of these two sixteenth-century figures, although it is impossible to assume that he was unaware of it, as it was printed in the famous *Sheney Luḥot ha-Berit*.[65] His failure to mention it is all the more inexplicable since he alludes to the less well-known cases of R. Abraham Berukhim and R. Ḥayyim Vital. But the answer to the quandary is simple and highly relevant to the understanding of Safrin's view. In the heading to the discussions we quoted above, he writes, "The revelation of the *Shekhinah* [happens] by means of and following the suffering that one is caused to suffer, by means of which he feels the suffering of the *Shekhinah*, and the fact that this relevation has a form and an image is on account of his being corporeal."[66] This title postulates a visual relevation of the *Shekhinah* as a female image resulting from suffering —two elements that are absent in the vigil of Karo and Alkabeẓ. In their session, the *Shekhinah* was audible through the lips of Karo, but invisible. Safrin and the examples he adduces deal exclusively with the visible revelations of the *Shekhinah*. Furthermore, in the *Shavu'ot* vigil the technique used by the Kabbalists entailed study of various passages excerpted from Jewish classical sources. If participation in and affliction for the fate of the *Shekhinah* occurred, these were the result of the revelation, not its cause. In the cases of Abraham Berukhim, Ḥayyim Vital, Levi Isaac, and Safrin, weeping preceded the appearance of the *Shekhinah*. In other words, Safrin viewed self-induced suffering culminating in weeping as a technique for contemplating the image of the *Shekhinah*.[67] He seems to have striven for the vision of the face of the *Shekhinah*, a quest similiar to Vital's desire, but he was prevented from doing so because of his human condition.[68]

The activation of the eye ends in a visual experience. In the case of Karo and Alkabeẓ, the organ activated was the lips; indeed, the *Shekhinah* spoke from the throat of Karo. The correlation between the technique and the nature of the revelation is striking; Safrin regarded weeping as a trigger for the mystical experience. We can propose an even more elaborate explanation: his presence at night in a small town was a premeditated device intended to induce a state of deep melancholy culminating in weeping. His journey to Dukla can be seen as part of a self-imposed exile, a *Galut* imitating the self-exile of the *Shekhinah*; the reward for this "participation mystique" was the revelation of the *Shekhinah*.[69] As it took place during the period between Passover and *Shavu'ot*, we can suppose that the journey was a preparatory exercise in suffering and weeping whose goal was the revelation on the eve of *Shavu'ot*; the *Shekhinah*, however, made its appearance sooner than expected.

According to another passage from Safrin, penitential prayer performed with weeping and a broken heart may bring about the appearance of divine light and a "second birth."[70] But the most important case in which weeping is used in order to induce an experience of the *Shekhinah* is absent from Safrin's collection of examples in *Netiv Miẓvotekha*. I refer to the custom Of R. Ẓevi Hirsch of Zhidachov, R. Isaac Safrin's main teacher in Kabbalah matters; in his commentary on the *Zohar,* Safrin relates an event pertinent to our discussion:[71]

> It was his [R. Ẓevi Hirsch's] custom regarding the matter of holiness to pray in order to bring upon himself a state of suffering, uneasiness and affliction on every eve of Sabbath. This was done in order ro efface himself completely before the Sabbath, so as to be able to receive his light,[72] blessed be he, during the prayer and the meal of the Sabbath [eve] with a pure, holy, and clear heart. This was his custom regarding the matter of holiness, owing to his constant fear lest arrogant and alien thoughts would enter his heart. Once, on the feast of *Shavu'ot,* hundreds of people crowded around him. Before the [morning] prayer, with the [first] light of dawn, I entered one of his rooms, but he did not see me, for he was pacing about the room to and fro, weeping and causing heaven and earth to weep with him before God.[73] And it is impossible to write it down. And he humbled himself before God with a mighty weeping, supplicating that he not be rejected from the light of his face.[74] . . . then I was overcome by a great trembling, because of the awe of the *Shekhinah*, and I opened the door and ran away.

According to this report of R. Isaac Safrin, R. Ẓevi Hirsch's self-afflictions were a means of preparing himself to receive the divine light on the Sabbath eve, as well as on at least some feasts; weeping, however, is related only in connection with the *Shavu'ot* account. Moreover, Safrin witnessed an overwhelming feeling of the presence of the divine countenance, seemingly induced by the self-abasement and weeping of his uncle. Although an experience of the *Shekhinah* is not directly mentioned, the fact that Safrin attests such an experience is clear evidence that R. Ẓevi Hirsch himself intended to induce such an experience; that the occasion of this event is *Shavu'ot* is evidence, too, that the master from Zhidachov is continuing an already existing tradition concerning the possibility of experiencing the presence of the *Shekhinah* on *Shavu'ot*. I have already mentioned the major predecessors—Karo, Alkabeẓ, and Levi Isaac of Beridichev—but here we learn for the first time of the occurrence of weeping as part of an actual practice. Safrin's vision of the *Shekhinah* can now be seen in the context of a broader mystical endeavor, cultivated in Ḥasidic circles, to attain experiences of the *Shekhinah*, and we can well assume that this was a continuation of earlier Kabbalistic practices.

I shall now turn to the relationship between weeping and secrets. At the end of Safrin's *Commentary* to the first volume of the *Zohar*, he confesses:[75]

> By much weeping, like a well, and suffering I became worthy to be transformed into "a flowing stream, a fountain of wisdom";[76] no secret was revealed to me, nor a wondrous apprehension, but afterward I became like dust and wept before the Creator of the universe like a spring, lest I should be rejected from the light of his face, and for the sake of gaining apprehensions out of the source of wisdom, and I became as a flowing well, weeping.

This voluminous commentary on the *Zohar,* one of the most comprehensive of its kind, was composed, according to the author's confession, with the help of revelations triggered by, among other things, weeping.

As late as the second half of the nineteenth century, the old mystical technique of weeping was still being practiced in order to attain the same goals alluded to in *Midrash Hallel*: visual revelation and disclosure of secrets. Following in the footsteps of his father, R. Eliezer Ẓevi Safrin confesses in the introduction of his own commentary on the *Zohar* that when he was mature,[77]

> I once woke in [the middle] of the night and wept greatly with a broken heart before God, for the exile of the *Shekhinah* and of the community of Israel, the holy ones who are suffering . . . and I woke up after the middle of the night on the second day as well, and I wept even more than the previous day for the same things. And before daybreak I went to sleep for half an hour, so that my mind would be calm and tranquil for the [morning] prayer. And during my sleep I saw in a dream that I was standing in the Land of Israel.[78] . . . and it is possible that because of this dream which I was worthy to see, that Old Holy Man[79] gave me the strength to interpret the holy book of the *Zohar.*

Before concluding our discussion of this mystical practice, some general observations on the nature of the material above are in order.

1. In all the cases analyzed, the practice of weeping was attributed to, or practiced by, figures who were part of the Jewish elite; in other words, it was nowhere recommended that weeping be popularly used as a means of inducing the vision of the *Shekhinah*. It was intended for, and indeed practiced by, the very few who were interested in experiencing such a vision.
2. The passages quoted above are excerpted from texts that did not belong to the mainstreams of talmudic-midrashic literature. The absence of halakhic treatment of mystical weeping is no mere matter of chance; rabbinic thought proposed alternative means to attain the goals of mystical weeping. According to one dictum, the study of the Torah for its own sake is rewarded by the disclosure of its secrets to the student;[80] a midrashic statement recommends the study of the Torah in the Land of Israel for whoever wishes to contemplate the *Shekhinah*.[81] Thus, the nomian way of receiving secrets or visions of the *Shekhinah* did not include weeping but provided an avenue not only for the elite but for all Jews.[82]
3. Again, the aforementioned revelations were described as attained in a state of desolation and mourning for the sake of the *Shekhinah* and participation in her suffering because of an incapacity to learn Torah. A talmudic-midrashic view concerning the indwelling of the *Shekhinah*, however, affirms that "the *Shekhinah* does not dwell [on one] either through sadness, or laziness, or frivolity of mind, but through the joy of performing a commandment."[83] Thus, there is an overt contradiction between the talmudic requirements and the mystical weeping triggered by an initial state of desolation.

These remarks heighten the anomian character of the weeping technique; whatever it promises can be attained as well within the framework of classical halakhic activities, such as the study of Torah or the performance of commandments. As the earliest evidence of the existence of this technique is ancient, it seems to me that the practice must have been suppressed in rabbinic sources for a long period but was revived upon the emergence of Kabbalah, which was interested in attaining mystical experiences far beyond the "normal mysticism" inherent in the rabbinic system. A closer inspection of the ancient materials in the above discussions seems to deny the likelihood that the medieval practices were propagated through the perusal of ancient literary evidence alone. It is hardly reasonable to assume that *Midrash Hallel,* for example, is the source of the later practices. Therefore, assuming that there are no crucial texts that have escaped my examination of the pertinent literature, we can presume the oral transmission of this ancient mystical technique, probably among the elite.

I should like to note that early Christian ascetic traditions may have been influenced[84] by ancient Jewish traditions concerning the mystical possibilities inherent in weeping and, directly or indirectly, Sufi asceticism as well.[85] These kinds of ascetic practices have been presented in unrestrained ways, as neither Christianity nor Islam was interested in obliterating extreme types of asceticism. This proposal is, for the time being, a hypothesis, as no significant research has been conducted in this direction. But the very fact that such an ascetic practice existed in ancient Jewish texts, as well as later on, may foster a novel approach to this issue.[86]

Finally, a brief remark on the psychological mechanism triggering these experiences: weeping is never described as a discrete practice; it is always part of a more elaborate sequence of ascetic exercises—fasting, mourning, self-induced suffering—and is commonly their last step. In some instances, the mystic is actually exhausted by the time he begins weeping; a state of falling asleep or sometimes previous fainting gives concrete evidence of this exhaustion.

On the other hand, the hyperactivation of the ocular system represents a concentration on one mode of perception at the very moment when all other doors of perception are progressively being repressed. This new balance of stimuli prepares the way for paranormal states of consciousness focused upon visual experiences. In such cases, the ideas or concepts upon which one has focused his intellectual and emotional activity tend to reveal themselves through the hyperexcited medium. From a more strictly psychological point of view, the visions that follow a painful and sorrowful state of mind can be related to what Marganita Laski designated as "desolation ecstasies."[87]

III. ASCENT OF THE SOUL

The next type of mystical technique I wish to present is the ascent of the soul in order to perceive the supermundane entities—the *Merkavah*, the seat of glory, the angelic company, or God himself—as well as to receive sublime secrets. The following presentation will exclude discussion of bodily journeys to heaven, on the one hand, and the mental ascent from the material to the spiritual, on the other.[88] My focus will be, rather, on the celestial ascent of the soul, in which the body is left below, commonly in a cataleptic situation or during the night's sleep, in order to undergo a paranormal experience and return to the body thereafter.[89]

This device is part of a more complex technique, including reciting divine names, chanting hymns, fasting, and assuming special bodily postures. These components, as well as the act of ascent, have nothing to do with halakhic prescriptions and may therefore be classified as an anomian type of mystical technique.

The ascent of the soul has been repeatedly discussed by scholars of ancient religions; the long sequence of studies dedicated to this topic renders superfluous any further presentation of the basic facts concerning this matter.[90] I should like to dwell, however, upon the recent discussions of Morton Smith, who has emphasized the importance of the ascent experience for a better understanding of certain passages concerning Jesus himself in early Christian literature.[91] According to this scholar, "We can fairly conclude that one or more techniques for ascent into heaven were being used in Palestine in Jesus' day, and that Jesus himself may well have used one."[92] As Smith indicates, Paul attributed an ascent to Jesus,[93] saying that he was caught up to the third heaven "whether in the body or out of the body."[94] Therefore, the conception of the soul ascending to Paradise—"out of the body"—for the sake of an ineffable experience, even before death, was current among Jews of the first century.[95] This obviously represents a concept different from the more widespread belief in the possibility of bodily ascent to heaven, which seems to have prevailed much earlier. This mystical perception of celestial ascent is a remarkable parallel to the frequent ascent of the soul to heaven in order "to draw life" for her body during the night.[96]

According to some discussions in Heikhalot literature, it is obvious that, alongside what was seemingly conceived as bodily ascent, the ancient Jewish mystics also practiced ascent of the soul. In *Heikhalot Rabbati,* R. Neḥuniya ben ha-Kaneh is described as sitting in the Temple, apparently in Elijah's posture, while contemplating the divine chariot and the wondrous glory.[97] As it is evident that R. Neḥuniya was in the world and at the same time also contemplating on high, it must be assumed that it was his soul that ascended above. The same conclusion applies to the passage that immediately follows the discussion on R. Neḥuniya's recall by his students. There, the "descenders to the chariot" were requested to employ worthy amanuenses, whose role was to record the revelations of the mystics. Thus, those who did not ascend (or descend) to the *Merkavah* heard what was revealed to those who did, from the latter's mouths.[98] I presume that the mystics, whose bodies remained in this world while their souls wandered in the higher realms, functioned as transmitters of supernal secrets through the collection of their speeches by their amanuenses.[99]

Related to this perception of the *Merkavah* experience is the report of R. Hai Gaon, who elaborated on our topic in a singular way. In one of his responsa, he indicates:[100]

> Many scholars thought that one who is distinguished by many qualities described in the books, when he seeks to behold the *Merkavah* and the palaces of the angels on high, he must follow a certain procedure. He must fast a number of days and place his head between his knees and whisper[101] many hymns and songs whose texts are known from tradition. Then he perceives within himself and in the chambers[102] [of his heart] as if he saw the seven palaces with his own eyes, and it is as though he entered one palace after another and saw what is there. And there are two *mishnayot* which the *tannaim* taught[103] regarding this topic, called the *Greater Heikhalot* and the *Lesser Heikhalot,* and this matter is well known and widespread. Regarding these contemplations, the *tanna* taught: "Four entered Pardes"—those palaces were alluded to by the term *Pardes*, and they were designated by this name. . . . For God . . . shows to the righteous, in their interior, the visions of his palaces and the position of his angels.

The contemplation of the *Merkavah* is here compared to the entrance into *Pardes*, both of which activities are, according to R. Hai Gaon, allegories for the inner experience attained by the mystics.[104] I believe that the mystical flight of the soul to the *Merkavah* has here been interpreted allegorically; the supernal palaces can be gazed at and contemplated not by referring to an external event but by concentrating upon one's own "chambers." The scene of revelation is thus no longer the supermundane hierarchy of palaces, but the human consciousness.

According to a younger contemporary of R. Hai Gaon, R. Nathan of Rome, the gaon's intention was that the ancient mystics[105] "do not ascend on high, but that they see and envision in the chambers of their heart like a man who sees and envisions something clearly with his eyes, and they hear and tell and speak by means of a seeing eye,[106] by the divine spirit." Therefore, the earliest interpretation of R. Hai's view emphasizes inner vision rather than mystical ascent. This type of mystical epistemology is congruent with Hai's view concerning the revelation of the glory of God to the prophets through the "understanding of the heart"—*'ovanta' de-libba'*. Therefore, far from expounding a mystical ascent of the soul, the gaon offers a radical reinterpretation of ancient Jewish mysticism. In the vein of more rationalistic approaches, he effaces the ecstatic or shamanic aspects of the Heikhalot experiences in favor of their psychological interpretation. Although I imagine that this recasting of an earlier religious mentality was motivated by R. Hai's adherence to rationalist thinking,[107] I cannot ignore the possibility that his psychological perception may bear some affinities to much earlier views of the *Merkavah*.[108] But even if such early understandings of *Merkavah* mysticism indeed existed, they were seemingly marginal in comparison to the bodily and spiritual ascent cultivated by the Heikhalot mystics. This kind of rationalization consistently reveals a reserved attitude toward the object of interpretation;[109] therefore, R. Hai Gaon seems to have been reacting against a relatively common practice, as we may infer from his remark "and this is a widespread and well-known matter." Even the opening statement of the quotation, although formulated in the past tense, bears evidence of the recognition of the technique by "many scholars."[110] On the ground of R. Hai's passage we can therefore conclude that the use of Elijah's posture in order to attain paranormal states of consciousness perceived as visions of the *Merkavah* was still on the agenda of Jewish mystics, notwithstanding R. Hai Gaon's attempt to attenuate some of its "uncanny" facets.[111]

The main heirs of Heikhalot mysticism were the Ashkenazic Ḥasidic masters of the twelfth and thirteenth centuries, who preserved the ancient texts, probably redacted parts of them, and, I assume, also continued the practice of their mystical techniques. Some of the figures related to Franco-Ashkenazic Jewish culture were regarded as "prophets"[112] or as having various types of intercourse with the higher worlds.[113] I should like to give here two significant examples of the acknowledgment of the existence of an ascent of the soul. It is reported of R. Mikhael the Angel, a middle-thirteenth century French figure, that

> [he] asked questions, and his soul ascended to heaven in order to seek [answers to] his doubts. He shut himself in a room for three days and ordered that it not be opened. But the men of his house peered between the gates [!], and they saw that his body was flung down like a stone. And so he laid for three days, shut in and motionless on his bed like a dead man. After three days he came to life and rose to his feet, and from thence on he was called R. Mikhael the Angel.[114]

Thus, the ascent heavenward was a technique to solve problems. The nature of the questions is not specified in this passage, but on the basis of the range of questions asked of heavenly instances, they may include both halakhic and theological issues. Even more interesting is the report regarding R. Mikhael's compatriot and older contemporary, R. ʼEzra of Moncontour. R. Moses Botarel mentions a tradition received from his father, R. Isaac, asserting: "The soul of the prophet from the city of Moncontour ascended to heaven and heard the living creatures singing before God a certain song;[115] and when he awoke he remembered this song and told his experience as it was, and they wrote down the song."[116]

This particular technique of composing verses is not, however, unique. The prominent early medieval *paytan* R. Eleazar ha-Kallir is described as having ascended to heaven and asked the Archangel Michael the manner in which the angels sing and how their songs are composed. Afterward he descended and composed a poem according to the same alphabetical order.[117] Interestingly, R. Eleazar ascended to heaven by the use of the divine name, an ascent technique attributed by Rashi to the four who entered *Pardes*[118]—no doubt an affinity expressing an attempt to include this famous poet among the *Merkavah* mystics. This also seems to be the tendency of another report concerning this poet; R. Ẓedakiah ben Abraham[119] states in the name of his father, who heard it from his masters, the Ashkenazic sages, that while R. Eleazar was composing his well-known poem, *The Fourfold Living Creatures*, "fire surrounded him."[120] This phrase has an obvious connection with the mystical study of sacred texts or discussions of *Merkavah* topics, particularly in the *Merkavah* tradition.[121] Again, in a third description of R. Eleazar, likewise of Ashkenazic origin, he is referred to as "the angel of God,"[122] an epithet reminiscent of R. Mikhael mentioned above. Thus, R. 'Ezra of Moncontour's study in the celestial academy via the ascent of his soul, and his transmission of a poem he heard there, find close parallels in the tradition regarding a much earlier person, portrayed with the help of motifs connected with the *Merkavah* traditions.

The ascent of the soul gained a certain impetus from the Safedian Kabbalah onward. Its main hero, R. Isaac Luria, is reported as one

> whose soul ascended nightly to the heavens, and whom the attending angels came to accompany to the celestial academy. They asked him: "To what academy do you wish to go?" Sometimes he said that he wished to visit the academy of R. Simeon bar Yoḥai, or the academy of R. 'Akiva or that of R. Eliezer the Great or those of other *tannaim* and *amoraim*, or of the prophets. And to whichever of those academies he wished to go, the angels would take him. The next day, he would disclose to the sages what he received in that academy.[123]

This quote reveals one of two ways by means of which the mystic may acquire supernal secrets of the Kabbalah: he may either ascend to study Torah together with ancient figures, as above, or else be taught by Elijah or others who descend in order to reveal Kabbalistic secrets, as we read in other texts concerning Luria.[124]

The frequency of heavenly ascent is indeed remarkable: every night Luria visited one of the celestial academies and thereafter transmitted the teachings to his students. This perception of Luria is no doubt closely connected to the huge amount of Kabbalistic material he communicated that produced the extensive Lurianic literature. Nor is the description of the celestial academies as the mystical source of this esoteric lore any novelty in Kabbalah. According to R. Shem Tov ibn Gaon, the mystic who sees divine visions is like one who dreams with eyes shut; once he opens his eyes, he forgets those visions and prefers death to life, as the ideal is[125] "to ascend from the lower academy to the supernal academy and to subsist from the splendor of the *Shekhinah*[126] and not worry about his sons or the members of his family, because of his great cleaving."

Significantly, immediately prior to this passage, R. Shem Tov mentions the need to fathom intellectually the secrets of the *Merkavah* and the structures of the Creation. The result is not only beatific or divine visions but also an impressive explosion of literary creativity, consisting in "copying" the contents revealed in his mind as if from a book.[127] The affinity of this description to Luria's own creativity is startling; we must remember that R. Shem Tov's work quoted above was partially composed in Safed, where he lived during his last years.

Such perceptions of the celestial academy as a source of mystical revelations recur in the visions of Solomon Molkho, at least one of which appears shortly after a reference to dream revelations.[128] Although these texts make no explicit mention of the ascent of the soul, I assume, from the fact that these were events connected to dreams, that we can infer in Molkho as well the existence of a visionary technique perceived as a spiritual ascent to a higher academy. Thus, Luria's portrayal as a mystic adept in these celestial universes is not an invention of Kabbalistic thought.

We find several discussions of spiritual ascent in the writings of Luria's main disciple, R. Ḥayyim Vital. In his mystical diary, he reported a dream of one of his acquaintances, R. Isaac Alatif, concerning himself, which Vital described as follows:[129]

> Once I fainted deeply for an hour, and a huge number of old men and many women came to watch me, and the house was completely full of them, and they all were worried for me. Afterwards the swoon passed and I opened my eyes and said, "Know that just now my soul ascended to the seat of glory, and they sent my soul back to this world in order to preach before you and lead you in the way of repentance[130] and in matters of charity."

Although the dream itself concerns Vital, one cannot infer from it his own stand regarding this technique. Nevertheless, we can assume that the ascent to the seat of glory has a certain mystical implication, perhaps an effort to contemplate God, such as Vital attempted according to one of his dreams.[131] The cataleptic state here reminds one of the earlier description of R. Mikhael the Angel.

R. Israel Ba'al Shem Tov was well known for his practice of soul ascent. In the famous epistle to his brother-in-law, he relates:[132]

> On *Rosh ha-Shanah* of the year 5507 [1746], I performed an incantation for the ascent of the soul, known to you. And in that vision I saw wondrous things, which I had never seen until then from the day that I became spiritually aware. And it is impossible to relate and to tell what I saw and learned in that ascent hither, even in private. But when I returned to the lower Paradise, I saw the souls of living and of dead persons, both of those with whom I was acquainted and of those with whom I was not acquainted . . . numberless, in a to-and-fro movement, ascending from one world to the other through the column[133] known to adepts in esoteric matters. . . . And I asked my teacher and master[134] that he come with me, and it is a great danger to go and ascend to the supernal worlds, whence I had never ascended since I acquired awareness, and these were mighty ascents. So I ascended degree after degree, until I entered the palace of the Messiah.

Thus, in 1746, R. Israel was already familiar with the practice of ascending heavenward. In order to attain this experience, which surpassed all his previous ascents, he made use of a device known also to his brother-in-law, R. Gershon of Kutow. The mystical nature of the revelations received by R. Israel is obvious, concerning as they did the eschatological meaning of the dissemination of his mystical teachings.[135] One of the anticipated results of the spread of Ḥasidic lore would be, the Messiah told R. Israel, that all Jews would become able to "perform *yiḥudim* and ascensions" as he did.[136] This inclusion of the ascent as a common ideal is highly significant; until then a privilege for a small elite, it was included in the Ḥasidic program to be diffused to a larger public.[137]

Another known ascent is that of 1750, introduced by the phrase "and on *Rosh ha-Shanah* 1750 I performed an ascent of soul, as is known."[138] From this epistle it seems obvious that the practice of spiritual ascent was a common experience for the founder of Ḥasidism. Indeed, he is described as disclosing to one of his followers that each night, when he ascended above, he was preceded by R. Ḥayyim ben 'Atar, his older contemporary and a paragon of Eastern Jewish mysticism. According to R. Israel, ben 'Atar was more rapid in his ascent, although he considered himself superior to the Moroccan sage.[139]

As we have seen above, in his own opinion at least two of R. Israel's contemporaries either practiced this mystical technique or—as in the case of R. Gershon—were aware of its details. Moreover, this list can easily be expanded to include at least one leading figure of R. Israel's entourage. R. Yeḥiel Mikhael of Zloczow, a student of the Besht and of the Great Maggid, was portrayed by R. Abraham Joshua Heschel of Apt as sleeping for only two reasons, one of them being his wish to ascend to heaven.[140] In the generations immediately following the death of the Besht, the importance of such spiritual ascents of the soul was manifestly attenuated. In lieu of this mystical technique, commonly connected with the state of sleep or of dreaming, the major students of the Great Maggid preferred mystical activities performed in a waking state.

During the mid-nineteenth century, however, there was a revival of interest in spiritual ascent. In some of R. Isaac Yehudah Yeḥiel Safrin's writings, R. Israel's ascents are mentioned and elaborated upon far more than in Ḥasidic writings of the preceding hundred years. R. Israel is portrayed as attaining spiritual perfections, and he mentions, inter alia, "the ascents of the soul and ascents to *Pardes*" and "the apprehensions of R. 'Akiva and his companions."[141] The affinity between ascent of the soul and ascent to the *Merkavah* or to *Pardes* is self-evident. We can easily perceive the connection between the two also in Safrin's *Heikal ha-Berakhah,* in which the journey of the four who entered *Pardes* is described as a celestial ascent, taking place after one had stripped himself of corporeality and uncleanness.[142] In contrast to the ancient discussion of the *Pardes* journey in which the ascent seems to have taken place *in corpore,* for Safrin it is a spiritual experience. Moreover, according to this Ḥasidic master, even Moses' ascent to receive the Torah was an ascent of the soul. In his commentary on the *Zohar,* he interprets Moses' abstention from eating and drinking for forty days in a way reminiscent of the description of R. Mikhael the Angel. The body of Moses, he states:[143]

> was thrown in the cloud with but little vitality,[144] as it is for all those who practice ascents of the soul, such as our master R. Israel the Besht, and others like him. [But] their body is thrown down like a stone for only a short hour or two, no more; however, Moses' body was thrown down for forty days and [the vitality] returned to it after forty days, and he was [again] alive.

Moses was thus the incomparable master of ascent of the soul, as he sustained his mystical experience for an uncommonly long period and nevertheless returned to life.[145] Thus, even the receiving of the Torah is seen as accomplished by the help of this mystical technique. No wonder that R. Isaac Safrin himself practiced it. In his mystical diary, he confessed:[146]

> I performed a *yiḥud* and linked myself with the soul of our divine master, Isaac Luria. And from this union I was overcome by sleep, and I saw several souls until I was overwhelmed by awe and fear and trembling, as was my custom. And from this it seemed that I shall rise to greatness.[147] And I ascended further and I saw R. [Abraham] Joshua Heschel . . . and I awakened.

This experience was doubtless closely related to that of R. Israel Ba'al Shem Tov. It is rare, however, for a later mystic to confess that he seemingly employed this technique in order to communicate with the souls of the dead. In any event, as late as 1845,[148] this ancient practice remained viable enough to be used.

Even a superficial examination of the above material will yield the impression that nearly all of the medieval authors mentioned above in connection with heavenly journeys were of Franco-Ashkenazic extraction. I know of no Sephardic mystic involved in this type of mystical technique: Vital's report might have been the result of Luria's influence, while R. Ḥayyim ben 'Atar's practice of this technique, as attested by the Besht, is uncorroborated by authentic evidence from his writings or other independent testimonies.[149] It is difficult to determine if this is a mere coincidence or whether this sequence of Ashkenazic authors who reported on ascent of the soul can be described as a continuous tradition. I tend to accept the second possibility, notwithstanding the serious gap between the evidence for the twelfth and thirteenth centuries and Luria. Interestingly, the extant material concerning the technique of weeping would seem to suggest a pattern similar to that of the ascent technique. In that case, the only exception seems to be in my proposed understanding of the *Zohar* passage; otherwise, we find only persons who were Ashkenazic by origin or under obvious Ashkenazic influence, such as Berukhim or Vital. This conclusion holds true also in the case of a practice of oneiric divination: the majority of earliest European evidences for the usages of *She'elat Ḥalom* are of Ashkenazic origin. As we shall see in the following section, Abraham Abulafia's mystical technique also derives from Ashkenazic sources. We may therefore infer that the Ashkenazic provinces were an important source of older esoteric traditions—in our case, mystical techniques[150]—which were at times accepted and adopted by Spanish Kabbalah, whereas others remained the patrimony of Ashkenazic culture alone. This conclusion holds true not only for the movement of these techniques from the Rhineland to Provence and Spain but also for the transmission of important segments of Kabbalah in general, a point to be elaborated elsewhere.

IV. COMBINATION OF LETTERS OF THE DIVINE NAME

Ongoing recitations of letters and divine names are well-known techniques for the attainment of paranormal states of consciousness; they are used alike by Christian,[151] Muslim,[152] Hindu,[153] and Japanese[154] mystics. Most, if not all, of these techniques seem to operate upon the consciousness of the mystic by enabling him to focus his attention upon a short phrase or sentence—"There is no God but Allah," "Jesus Christ," "*Namou Amida Boutso*"—or even a few letters, as in the Hindu *Aum*. This relatively simple device is comparable to fixing one's vision upon a point;[155] the mystic must escape the impact of external factors, and in this respect his activity is similar to that of someone undergoing sensory deprivation.

Ancient Jewish sources, primarily those of Heikhalot literature, present a technique closely parallel to those found in non-Jewish forms of mysticism.[156] These affinities become evident when one compares some of the details shared by the Jewish and non-Jewish techniques. In another type of Jewish technique, however, the psychological result is different, given the discrepancy between this technique and its parallels on one important issue—namely, the use by Jewish mystics of a complex and intricate system of letters to be pronounced or meditated upon. Instead of the simple formulas of non-Jewish techniques, the Jewish texts evince elaborate combinations of letters with hundreds of components. Moreover, as we shall see, according to Jewish practice the mystic had not only to pronounce them according to strict, fixed patterns but had also actively to construct these combinations as part of the mystical practice. The effect of combinatory techniques was the result both of the process of their utterance and of the hyperactivation of the mind required to produce the contents that were pronounced. These monotonous repetitions of well-known phrases or divine names thus achieved not a calmness or stillness of the mind but rather a high excitation of the mental processes, triggered by the unceasing need to combine letters, their vocalizations, and various bodily acts—movements of the head or hands or respiratory devices.[157] Although superficially similar to a variety of mystical techniques based upon language, the Kabbalistic practice possessed an idiosyncratic psychological mechanism, only rarely occurring in such techniques. I shall briefly discuss here some sources concerning the pronunciation or repetition of divine names—a practice paralleled in non-Jewish techniques; I shall then discuss the medieval use of combinations of letters, which differs significantly from the more ancient technique.

It is a striking fact that a detailed and systematic technique of letter combination forming the divine name appears for the first time in a work of R. Eleazar of Worms and, under his influence, among Spanish Kabbalists. More than in the other examples of mystical techniques attested by Franco-German sources prior to their appearance in Spanish Kabbalah, in this case there are reliable indications that the repercussions of this technique in Spain were directly connected to the Ashkenazic culture.[158] Abraham Abulafia explicitly mentions R. Eleazar's works as books he had studied; thus, the transition can easily be proven.[159] The other two Kabbalists of the late thirteenth and fourteenth centuries acquainted with combination techniques—R. Joseph ben Shalom Ashkenazi and R. David ben Yehudah he-Ḥasid—were either Ashkenazic by origin (the former) or had visited Germany (the latter).[160] We can reasonably conclude, then, that the mystical techniques surveyed below passed from Germany to Spain. According to the historical evidence, this movement took place only from the middle of the thirteenth century, thereby excluding Provençal and most Catalan theosophical Kabbalah from its influence. Thus, in contrast to the Ashkenazic influence on the emergence of the Kabbalah in those centers with regard to theosophical issues, this mystical technique was cultivated in Spanish circles relatively late. The delay can be understood in terms of the topic's esoteric nature, a feature that seems to be corroborated by the fact that, even centuries after R. Eleazar of Worms had recorded some details of this technique, they remained in manuscript, as did the mystical handbooks of Abulafia and his disciples.[161]

Several indications of recitations of names—either angelic or divine—are extant in Heikhalot literature.[162] These reservations, as we have seen above, were still practiced during the Gaonic period.[163] There is conclusive evidence that the pronunciation of mystical names was known and cultivated in Germany, at least during the lifetime of R. Eleazar of Worms. The anonymous author of *Sefer ha-Ḥayyim*[164] indicates: "He pronounces the holy names or names of the angels in order to be shown [whatever] he wishes, or to inform him of a hidden matter, and then the Holy Spirit reveals itself to him, and his flesh . . . trembles . . . because of the strength of the Holy Spirit."[165]

The fiery attack by R. Moshe of Taku, written shortly after the *floruit* of R. Eleazar, is highly instructive. He speaks of persons "void of understanding" and "heretics who pose as[166] prophets and are accustomed to pronouncing the holy names; and sometimes, they direct [their heart] when they read them [pronounce the names] and their soul is terrified. . . . But when the power of the pronounced name leaves him, he returns to his initial state of confused reason."

These statements provide appropriate background to understand R. Eleazar's statement that neither the divine names nor their vocalizations ought to be written down, lest those "devoid of understanding" use them.[167] R. Eleazar's fears can easily be understood in light of the criticism of a more conservative figure such as Taku; significantly, both use the same phrase, *ḥaserey da'at,* in order to describe those who make use of the divine names. R. Eleazar, however, confesses that[168] "some future things and spirits were revealed to us by means of the [divine?] attributes[169] through the pronunciations of the depths of the names[170] in order to know the spirit of the wisdoms."

The use of the phrase "revealed to us" clearly shows that this refers to a practical technique, not a repetition of no longer active formulas;[171] therefore, the three above-mentioned statements, like the analogous evidence in the preceding section concerning the ascent of soul, are conclusive proof of the experiential use of the pronunciation of divine names. The names cited by R. Eleazar shortly before the above text are mystical names already occurring in Jewish texts related to Heikhalot literature, such as *Adiriron, Bihriron,* and so on.[172] Moreover, the assertion of this Ashkenazic Ḥasidic master that each of the forty-two letters of the divine name is a divine name in itself obviously reflects an ancient Jewish conception.[173] It is therefore reasonable to assume that R. Eleazar preserved ancient mystical material and techniques that had been passed down to Spanish Kabbalists via the intermediacy of Ashkenazic masters, the most important of whom, Abraham Abulafia, elaborated upon the received traditions in a relatively detailed fashion.[174] Abulafia also explicitly refers to Heikhalot literature as an important source of his use of divine names.[175] Before entering into a brief presentation of Abulafia, however, I should like to discuss the influence on two important Kabbalists who flourished in Spain of a peculiar pattern of combination of divine letters occurring in R. Eleazar.

In his *Sefer ha-Shem*,[176] R. Eleazar discusses the combination of the letters of the Tetragrammaton with each of the letters of the alphabet.[177] Moreover, these combinations are in turn combined with their vocalizations by two of the six vowels. Thus, the combination of *'aleph* with *yod*, vocalized according to these six vowels, is expressed by this sample:

אְיֻ	אֶיֻ	אֵיֻ	אִיֻ	אַיֻ	אֻיֻ
אְיַ	אֶיַ	אֵיַ	אִיַ	אַיַ	אֻיַ
אְיִ	אֶיִ	אֵיִ	אִיִ	אַיִ	אֻיִ
אְיֵ	אֶיֵ	אֵיֵ	אִיֵ	אַיֵ	אֻיֵ
אְיֶ	אֶיֶ	אֵיֶ	אִיֶ	אַיֶ	אֻיֶ
אְיְ	אֶיְ	אֵיְ	אִיְ	אַיְ	אֻיְ

R. Eleazar explains the combinations of these letters only on the cosmological and theological levels, with no reference to their possible use as a mystical technique. However, the fact that not only letters but also vowels are included in this table points to a praxis of pronunciation. Against the background of the earlier evidence concerning R. Eleazar's revelation using divine names, and the fact that he perceived their vocalization as connected with the use of these names, we can infer that, notwithstanding his silence, the author conceived these combinations as a mystical practice. This assumption is corroborated by a description of the creation of a *golem* (the vivification of a humanlike form made out of clay) by R. Eleazar, in which he wrote that we must pronounce all the letters of the alphabet over every limb of the *golem*, combined with one of the letters of the Tetragrammaton and vocalized according to the six vowels mentioned above.[178] Thus, despite the author's silence, the table found in *Sefer ha-Shem* was meant to be pronounced as part of a magical praxis for the creation of a *golem* by a certain incantation of combinations of letters. According to Scholem, this technique can culminate in ecstasy.[179] This assumption seems to be corroborated by R. Eleazar's confession that he received a revelation by means of the divine names.

The table above was copied in its entirety by R. David ben Yehudah he-Ḥasid, who presumably learned it during his visit in Regensburg.[180] He, however, considered the thirty-six combinations and vocalizations to be paralleled by the thirty-six movements of the *lulav,* an issue I was unable to locate in Ashkenazic texts. R. David's contemporary, R. Joseph Ashkenazi, an important source for some of his Kabbalistic ideas, elaborated upon R. Eleazar's table in his *Commentary on Genesis Rabbah*[181] and in an unidentified discussion of the creation of a *golem.*[182] These two Kabbalists do not, strictly speaking, belong to the ecstatic Kabbalah; however, both of them were interested in combinatory techniques, as indicated in their works. R. Joseph quoted Abraham Abulafia's *Commentary on Sefer Yeẓirah* and, as we shall see in the next section, preserved an important text on ecstasy and visualization of the divine names;[183] R. David apparently received revelations of Elijah.[184] Although I cannot conclusively describe these Kabbalists as following the mystical technique of R. Eleazar, the supposition that they were more than mere repositories of the Ashkenazic master's views seems a reasonable one.

There is little room for doubt as to the use of R. Eleazar's technique of combination for mystical purposes by his older contemporary, R. Abraham Abulafia. In his mystical handbook, *'Or ha-Sekhel,* one finds a similar table, albeit in slightly changed form: instead of six basic vowels, Abulafia prefers only five; thus, his tables consist of twenty-five basic combinations of letters and vowels.[185] As in R. Eleazar, Abulafia's table is no more than a sample for the recitation of the combinations of all twenty-two letters, combined with the four letters of the Tetragrammaton. According to this table, the pronunciation of the divine name involves many sublime matters, and whoever does not take care when performing it endangers himself. For this reason, asserts Abulafia, the ancient masters concealed it. But the time has now come to reveal it, since, as he says, the messianic eon has begun.[186] Abulafia's assessment is indeed interesting: he argues that he merely reveals a hidden technique that has been in existence for a long time. This assertion strengthens the earlier assumption that R. Eleazar's table was intended to serve mystical, and not only magical, purposes.

Abulafia was more than a Kabbalist who disclosed esoteric techniques; his *'Or he-Sekhel* was an attempt to integrate this technique into a speculative system including a philosophy of language and a definition of the ultimate goal of the technique—the attainment of *unio mystica*.[187] Thus, he succeeded in imposing an elaborate mystical technique on a larger public, as convincingly indicated by the relatively large number of manuscripts of *'Or ha-Sekhel*.[188] In early sixteenth-century Jerusalem, R. Yehudah Albotini composed a mystical handbook, *Sullam ha-'Aliyah,* based upon Abulafia's techniques, including among other things the tables found in *'Or ha-Sekhel*.[189] Moreover, Abulafia's tables, accompanied by some of his explanations, were quoted in one of the classics of Kabbalistic literature, Cordovero's *Pardes Rimmonim*.[190] Significantly, this Safedian Kabbalist begins his extensive discussion of pronunciation of the divine name with Abulafia's system,[191] afterward mentioning that of R. Eleazar of Worms, copied from a secondary source.[192] As we learn from the testimony of R. Mordecai Dato, a disciple of Cordovero, his master, influenced by Abulafia's works beyond their quotation, practiced Abulafian techniques and taught them to his students.[193] Furthermore, he regarded Abulafia's technique as a "Kabbalistic tradition transmitted orally, or the words of a *Maggid* [celestial messenger]."[194] It is no wonder, then, that he considered Abulafia's type of Kabbalah as superior even to that of the *Zohar*.[195] Cordovero, however, not only contributed to the dissemination of Abulafia's tables, as he did with those of R. Eleazar; quoting Abulafia's explanations, he also propagated the view that the union of the human and divine minds was to be achieved through this technique,[196] which, as Abulafia put it, "draws down the supernal force in order to cause it to be united with you."[197] This Hermetical understanding of Abulafia's technique[198] had an important influence on the Ḥasidic perception of *devekut* as attained by causing divine spiritual force to descend upon the mystic.[199] Strangely, the old Ashkenazic mystical technique had to travel throughout Spain and Italy, as well as Safed, before it eventually returned to Ashkenazic mysticism.

I have surveyed the history of one combinatory technique. A few others, connected with the recitation of the alphabet according to the permutations of letters given in *Sefer Yeẓirah,* were used both by R. Eleazar of Worms and by Abulafia.[200] The latter presented several elaborate techniques in his other handbooks: *Sefer Ḥayye ha-'Olam ha-Ba, Sefer ha-Ḥeshek* and *Sefer 'Imrei Shefer.* This willingness to propose more than one technique as a suitable path for attaining a mystical experience is decisive proof that Abulafia transcended the magical perception shared by the mystics that there was one and only one way to attain the supreme experience. Although his various techniques shared some elements in common, such as the need for isolation, breathing exercises, bodily movements, and the wearing of clean garments, they differed in many basic details. Abulafia also cultivated the pronunciation of letters of the divine names inscribed variously in different kinds of circles, a technique having nothing to do with the table technique mentioned above. These circles consisted of permutations of some of the biblical and later divine names according to different combinatory techniques; the use of circles is also conspicuous in *Ḥayye ha-'Olam ha-Ba,* which was aptly designated *The Book of Circles.*[201] No wonder, then, that one of the most elaborate visions reported by Abulafia is that of a circle, a Kabbalistic mandala including both cosmic and psychological structures.[202] Interestingly, the vision of circles recurs in the works of other ecstatic Kabbalists, who used Abulafian or similar techniques of combinations of letters, such as R. Isaac of Acre, R. Shem Tov ibn Gaon, and R. Elnathan ben Moses Kalkis.[203]

In *'Or ha-Sekhel* Abulafia emphasizes, more than does R. Eleazar in his works, that his tables, as well as his circles, are methods for facilitating all possible combinations of the letters of the divine names. These letters are sometimes permutated without adding other letters; at other times—as in the table—the entire alphabet is used in order to pronounce the letters of divine names. Although the pronunciation of the Tetragrammaton was conceived as a transgression of both biblical and rabbinic interdictions, there was no attack on Abulafia's technique on this ground in the Kabbalistic material with which I am acquainted. Although it is a conspicuously anomian technique, the recitation of letters as described by Abulafia managed to escape the fierce criticism to which his prophetic and messianic activities were subjected.

We can summarize this short survey of one of Abulafia's techniques by stating that the incorporation of R. Eleazar's method of combination of letters into the Spanish Kabbalah fertilized it by allowing for the construction of a more elaborate technical path intended to attain mystical goals such as revelations and union with supernal beings. This technique remained the patrimony of a few, albeit important, Kabbalists, contributing to the emergence of extreme types of mystical experiences.

V. VISUALIZATION OF COLORS AND KABBALISTIC PRAYER

The final type of mystical technique to be surveyed here is a nomian one relating to a particular understanding of the Kabbalistic meaning of *kavvanah*—that is, that intention which, according to the Talmud, should accompany the performance of the commandments. In Provence and Catalonia, the Kabbalists had already emphasized the mystical significance of such intention; it was no doubt connected to the theosophical system of Sefirot, toward which the Kabbalist was to direct his thought throughtout prayer.[204] The basic assumption of earlier Kabbalah, which remained unchanged for centuries, was that the words of prayer were symbols of the supernal divine potencies and hence could serve either as starting points for the contemplation of higher entities or as ways of influencing them, or as both together.

According to this understanding, *kavvanah* effects an elevation of human thought from the words of prayer to the sefirotic realm, apparently achieved without any intermediary mental operation or external factor. The intrinsic affinity of language to its sources in the divine realm enables human thought to ascend to the Sefirot and to act upon them.[205] Externally, the Kabbalist is supposed to recite the standard prayer text; the mystical *kavvanah* is an additional activity, in no way intended to change the halakhic regulations of prayer.[206] Mystical *kavvanah* can therefore be defined as a nomian technique, using as it does the common prayers as a vehicle for accomplishing mystical and theurgical aims.

But this presentation of mystical prayer fails to answer certain basic questions concerning the psychological processes enabling the shift from language to Sefirot. Is concentration on the symbolic connotations of a given word the only mental operation that ensures the mystical elevation of thought? How does the linguistic medium, corporeal in both its written and its oral forms, enable human thought or soul to penetrate utterly spiritual dimensions of reality? Can *kavvanah* be regarded as an attempt to interiorize the supernal pattern of Sefirot in some unknown way in order to cleave to and be capable of influencing it?[207] No answers to these and similar questions regarding the psychological aspects of *kavvanah* have been proposed, since they were evidently never asked by academic research. I cannot propose an answer or even a range of alternative answers, as the material involving the technical part of *kavvanah* is very scanty. No descriptions of the stages of *kavvanah* are extant, nor are confessions concerning the inner changes in one's consciousness provided by early Kabbalists. I suppose that we can view this technique as involving an extensive process of deautomatization, every word being pronounced not as part of an automatically performed prayer but in a meticulous way.[208] The Kabbalist would direct his attention toward both the precise pronunciation of the sounds and their symbolic significance.

I should like to elaborate here upon a far more complex technique that was part of Kabbalistic prayer—namely, the enactment of *kavvanah* through the visualization of colors as part of traditional prayer. What follows is a sampling of some significant texts treating these issues out of several score that I have identified, almost all in manuscripts, and that I hope will be printed and analyzed in detail elsewhere. Let me start with a brief historical survey of the emergence of the technique.[209] Early Kabbalistic discussion of prayer never mentioned the visualization of colors in general nor in connection with prayer in particular.[210] With the exception of a single text attributed (in my opinion spuriously)[211] to an eary Kabbalist—R. 'Azriel of Gerona[212]—even the question of the experience of light or lights in prayer is absent in texts composed in the first three quarters of the thirteenth century.[213] The earliest texts explicitly referring to this technique are those connected to the name of R. David ben Yehudah he-Ḥasid, a Spanish Kabbalist of the late thirteenth and early fourteenth centuries:[214]

> R. David[215] said: We are not allowed to visualize the ten Sefirot, except in accordance with the *rashey perakim* which reach you, such as *Magen David* to *Ḥesed* and *Ḥonen ha-Da'at*[216] to *Tiferet*. Therefore, you should always visualize that color which is [attributed to the Sefirah according to] the *rashey perakim,* that color being the *ḥashmal* of the Sefirah, the *ḥashmal* being the covering[217] [or dress] of that very Sefirah around [it]. Afterward you shall draw [downward] by your visualization the efflux from "the depth of the river" to the worlds down to us—and this is the true [way], received [in an esoteric manner] by oral tradition.

According to R. David, any attempt to visualize the Sefirot themselves is forbidden; instead, we must visualize their colors. For this reason, the focus of human activity during Kabbalistic prayer was not upon the sefirotic domain but rather upon the realm of colors produced by the creative imagination of the Kabbalists. These imaginary colors, being the "covering" of the Sefirot, formed a lower ontological level open to human contemplation and manipulation. The exact relationship between the fact that the colors were humanly created and their ontic status as surrounding the Sefirot is not altogether clear; it may have related to the world of lights emanating from the Sefirot according to the theosophy of the anonymous author of *Tikkuney Zohar* and *Ra'ya Meheimna*.[218] The peculiar correspondences between the Sefirot and their parallels in the imaginative world of colors appear in a highly esoteric tradition that was transmitted orally, and even then only in an abbreviated form or in notes—*rashey perakim*. The aim of this type of prayer was obviously theurgic; by means of the process of visualization, the Kabbalist drew the efflux from the supernal realm to the world under it and finally into our world. We can therefore surmise that the process of visualization enabled the ascent of the Kabbalist's imaginative faculty to a higher ontological level, and only afterward could he attract the divine efflux downward.[219]

Before proceeding to the description of this technique of prayer, I should like to discuss briefly two texts that seem to me to be highly significant for understanding the mystical nature of visualization of colors. From the conceptual point of view, the closest Kabbalistic system of thought to this appears in the writings of R. Joseph ben Shalom Ashkenazi, also called R. Joseph ha-'Arokh, a late-thirteenth-century Kabbalist who emigrated from Germany to Barcelona.[220] The affinities are unmistakable, some already having been noted by Scholem.[221] This Kabbalist affirmed:[222]

> The philosophers have already written on the issue of prophecy, saying that it is not improbable that there will be a person to whom matters will appear in his imaginative faculty, comparable to that which appears to the imaginative faculty in a dream. All this [could take place] while someone is awake, and all his senses are obliterated, as the letters of the divine name [stand] in front of his eyes,[223] in the gathered colors.[224] Sometimes, he will hear a voice,[225] a wind, a speech, a thunder, and a noise with all the organs of his hearing sense, and he will see with his imaginative faculty with all the organs of sight, and he will smell with all the organs of smell, and he will taste with all the organs of taste, and he will touch with all the organs of touch, and he will walk and levitate.[226] All this while the holy letters are in front of his eyes, and its colors are covering[227] it; this is the sleep[228] of prophecy.

The problems posed by this text are numerous and complex. From our perspective, it is important only to stress the occurrence of colors in close connection with the divine name and the fact that an altered state of consciousness is induced by the appearance of these colored letters. Although it is not obvious from a first reading of the passage, it seems plausible to surmise that the letters and their colors emerge as the result of the activation of the imagination—that is, that their appearance is the result of an effort of visualization. The difference between the occurrence of the Sefirot in R. David and of the divine name in R. Joseph is obvious, although not as significant. For the Kabbalist, the divine name and its letters are among the most common symbols of the ten Sefirot; moreover—and this is a decisive proof of the affinity between these two Kabbalists on the issue of colors—R. Joseph repeatedly refers to the symbolism of color for Sefirot in his writings, far more than did any of the preceding Kabbalists.[229] Highly interesting is his description of the contemplation of the "prophet" or "unifier" (*meyaḥed*), who looks to the "holy lights" that, however, appear and disappear intermittently. According to this passage, the colors are by-products of the increasing inner movement of the Sefirot and therefore are constantly changing.[230] They seem to be entities "standing" in front of the prophet's eyes in a relatively steady manner. The psychological state described is very close to one of anesthesia, allowing for the arousal of the faculty—imagination—which can now mold the sense perceptions by their activation from within; for the Kabbalist—who bases himself on philosophers—this state is tantamount to prophecy. For the time being, we can conclude that, in the view of R. Joseph Ashkenazi, the visualization of letters and colors is a technique for achieving the prophetic state.

Let us turn now to another Kabbalist, otherwise unknown, who indicates that[231] "when you vocalize *Devarekha*,[232] you shall visualize[233] in your thought, the letter of the Tetragrammaton before your eyes, in a circle [or sphere] with a color red as the fire, and your thought is performing many things." This passage constitutes solid evidence that the Kabbalists practiced visualization of the Tetragrammaton in colors. Hence, our understanding of R. Joseph Ashkenazi's first text quoted above is corroborated by this additional source. R. Tanḥum describes a circle, including a visualized Tetragrammaton, vocalized with the vowels of the word *Devarekha* and the color "red as the fire." This circle, or at least a similar one to that described by Tanḥum, is evidently extant in a manuscript.[234] As I have shown elsewhere, just before and after this circle, this manuscript includes Kabbalistic material stemming from the writings of R. Joseph Ashkenazi and R. David ben Yehudah he-Ḥasid.[235] The circle consists of a diagram containing ten concentric circles, each one representing a Sefirah whose name is inscribed on it and beside which is the name of the color corresponding to the Sefirah and a vocalized Tetragrammaton. Thus, next to the Sefirah *Gevurah* we read the phrase "red as the fire" and a vocalization of the Tetragrammaton identical with that of *Devarekha*. We can therefore assume that the list of colors and the vocalization of the Tetragrammaton in the concentric circles constitute detailed instructions for visualizing the Tetragrammaton in various colors corresponding to the Sefirot. We can furthermore assume that this list is at least some part of the "notes" mentioned by R. David when he wrote, "you shall always visualize according to that color which is [attributed to] the Sefirah [according to] the *rashey perakim*.

On the basis of this material, as well as of other material there is not room for here, I consider the existence of traditions dealing with visualization of colors, as well as their actual practice, an established fact. But before returning to the subject of mystical prayer, I should like to discuss the significance of the circle. In the Kabbalistic material accompanying this figure, there are no instructions regarding either the role it may fulfill or the meaning of the various details inscribed within the circles. The way in which R. Tanḥum refers to the circle, however, opens the possibility that we can envision not only the details as instructions for visualization but also the circle itself as part of this process. R. Tanḥum states, "You shall visualize the letter of the Tetragrammaton before your eyes in a circle in your thought," and so on. I see no reasonable argument against interpreting his words as a recommendation for visualizing the divine name along with the color and the circle. If this understanding is correct, then the circle can be regarded as a Kabbalistic mandala incorporating the colors corresponding to the ten divine powers, the Sefirot, and their names. Interestingly, this diagram draws a distinction between the first Sefirah, *Keter*, and the other nine, designated as *Ze'ir 'Anpin*—the lower divine configuration according to zoharic symbolism. The latter is an obvious anthropomorphic symbol, which in the *Zohar* refers to the second and lower divine head, that consisting of the Sefirah of *Tiferet* alone or of the Sefirot between *Ḥokhmah* and *Yesod*, whereas in the works of R. David it includes ten Sefirot or, as in the diagram, nine.[236] In other contexts of R. David's thought, this configuration is manifestly anthropomorphic; the fact that the concept appearing in the diagram differs from that of the *Zohar* does not obliterate its anthropomorphic character. If the understanding proposed above is correct, then the process of visualization includes not only divine names, colors, and a circle or circles but also an anthropomorphic configuration symbolizing an aspect of the divine realm. The outer circle is the well-known list of thirty-two mystical paths by means of which the world was created, and the second circle contains the names of all the realms of reality—for example, stones, planets, spheres, angels, and various kinds of living creatures, such as fish, animals, and man. It is obvious that the compiler wished to express the idea of the macrocosmos that stands beside the divine macranthropos.

The phenomenological affinity between this diagram and the Hindu mandala is interesting. The two practices share the process of visualization and of imaginary representation of divine forces and colors; in both cases the circle also has a macrocosmic aspect.[237] There are also clear differences, however: the Kabbalistic diagram is graphically different from those forms of mandala that I could see, their details are conspicuously unrelated, and the construction of a mandala is accompanied by a special liturgy, whereas I would suppose that the visualization of the Kabbalistic diagram accompanies Jewish ritualistic prayer. These differences notwithstanding, one cannot underrate the possibility that Hindu traditions infiltrated into Kabbalah, perhaps via the intermediacy of Sufi material. As I hope to show elsewhere, R. David lived for a time in Acre, a fact that may be a clue to the penetration of an alien mystical technique into a Jewish milieu.

Let us return now to colors and prayer; the previous assumption that the diagram contained the "notes" mentioned in R. David's text can be substantiated by the comparison of the details about Sefirot and colors with a short anonymous commentary on the prayer *Shema' Yisrael*. This highly interesting document is based upon the visualization of the divine names included in this prayer in various colors, most of which correspond to the list of colors and Sefirot in the diagram. Since the similarity between the colors and Sefirot in the diagram and the commentary is astonishing, including the peculiar ways used for denoting the colors, the conclusion that the diagram list was intended to supply instructions for visualization of divine names in prayer is inescapable. I shall give here only one sentence to exemplify this conclusion: "Don't pronounce the word *Israel* until one visualizes the divine name, which is *YHWH*, with its vowels and its color, and one visualizes it as if the last letter of the [divine] name, namely *H*, surrounds the entire world, from above and below."[238]

We learn that the visualization of the letters and colors is accompanied by the vision of the letters as circles that bear explicit macrocosmic overtones. The vision of the letters as circles is probably not identical with the diagram; this difference notwithstanding, this is incontrovertible evidence that, during prayer, not only were colors visualized but also circles. Our previous understanding of the diagram as a mandala is thus partially confirmed by the anonymous commentary on the *Shema' Yisrael*. Moreover, the pronunciation of the first Tetragrammaton in this prayer ought to be directed[239] "to *Binah* in the color of green, like the color of the rainbow, the entire [divine] name." Compare this to the diagram in which the third Sefirah corresponds to the color "green as the rainbow."[240] Finally, the following passage from a Kabbalistic responsum[241] dealing with prayer illuminates the purpose of visualization as perceived by the Kabbalists themselves:[242]

> When you shall think upon something which points to the *Keter* and pronounce it with your mouth, you shall direct [your thought] to and visualize the name *YHWH* between your eyes with this vocalization, which is the *Kammaẓ* under all the consonants, its visualization being white as snow.[243] And he will direct [your thought] so that the letters will move and fly in the air, and the whole secret is hinted at in the verse, "I have set the divine name always before me."[244]

According to this passage, the visualized colored letters are meant to ascend.[245] Thus, human imagination is ontologically creative, its products being able to ascend to the supernal *Merkavah*. This peculiar ascent may elucidate the allusion of R. Tanḥum that, by the means of visualized divine names, "your thought is performing many things"; this performance is accomplished by drawing the influx downward into the lower worlds and finally into our world, as stated at the end of R. David's passage.

The two different results of visualization of colored divine names can be summarized as follows: according to R. Joseph Ashkenazi, it induces a paranormal state of consciousness, and hence this technique can be appropriately regarded as a mystical practice. The second result is a theurgic one: if my reconstruction of the process of causing the letters to ascend and enabling the descent of the divine influx is correct according to this Kabbalistic school, then imagination is fraught with theurgic powers.

This Kabbalistic technique has passed unnoticed by modern scholarship. One of the major reasons for this is the fact that none of the texts dealing with the details of visualization is extant; they are available only in manuscripts that are, at the present time, generally ignored by scholars. This situation is not a matter of mere chance but rather a result of the technique's highly esoteric nature. A few statements will demonstrate this esotericism.

Underneath the diagram, we read: "All these allusions must be transmitted orally"—a wording virtually identical with that found at the end of R. David's passage quoted earlier.[246] Even more impressive are the statements of the anonymous author of the Kabbalistic responsum; I shall quote here only a part of his elaborations on the esoteric nature of the visualization:[247] "Know that this is a Kabbalistic tradition which was handed down to you, and we are writing it down, [but] it is forbidden to disclose it or to pass it down to everyone, but [only] to 'those who fear the divine name and take heed of his name,'[248] blessed be he, 'who tremble at his word.' "[249]

Owing to this atmosphere of mystery, the details of the technique of visualization remained hidden in fragments of various manuscripts; nevertheless, it was hardly neglected by the Kabbalists. My brief exposition of some of its texts, which represent only the initial stage of its crystallization, can be complemented by a longer historical survey, which is not possible here. I shall refer now only to some milestones of its evolution.

As I have attempted to show elsewhere, R. David ben Yehudah he-Ḥasid's extensive commentary on prayer, *'Or Zaru'a,* was composed as an exoteric Kabbalistic commentary, esoterically alluding to the performance of prayer with the help of visualization technique.[250] On the ground of several fragments elaborating on prayer and visualization, I conjecture that its practice was cultivated in the Kabbalistic school of R. David ben Yehudah he-Ḥasid, which is characterized by the transmission of additional esoteric issues.[251] This technique was well known to the generation of Kabbalists who were exiled from the Iberian Peninsula and came to Jerusalem and Safed, as we learn from the existence of a handbook for visualization known in these cities.[252] R. Moses Cordovero was well acquainted with this technique, as we learn from his *Pardes Rimmonim:*

> It is good and fitting if he wishes to visualize these *havvayot* [that is, the different vocalizations of the Tetragrammaton] according to their color, as then his prayer will be very effective, on the condition that his [mystical] intention is that there is no other possible way to represent the activity of a certain attribute [but] the certain [corresponding] color. And as the colors in the gate of colors are many, we shall not discuss here the colors. But when he is interested to direct [his prayer], behold that gate which is before [the eyes] of the disciple.[253]

The effectiveness of visualized colors is here, for the first time, hinted at in a Kabbalistic treatise that was intended to be studied by a larger public; the details, however, were not delivered. The last major Kabbalistic figure to mention the technique of visualization is R. Ḥayyim Vital. In the unprinted part of his *Sha'arey Kedushah,* he gives a text, which was partly discussed above, ending with the ascent of thought to the highest firmament, the *'Aravot,* where[254] "he shall visualize that above the firmament of *'Aravot* there is a very great white curtain, upon which the Tetragrammaton is inscribed in [color] white as snow,[255] in Assyrian writing in a certain color." I cannot explain how one can visualize white letters on a white curtain, nor why a "certain color" is mentioned in addition to the white one. Whatever the explanation, it is clear from this that Vital was interested in color visualization, as is evident also from the fact that he twice copied the aforementioned passage of R. Joseph Ashkenazi.[256]

At this point, it would be pertinent to compare the technique of visualization with that of letter combination. In both, the letters of the divine names are crucial; the letters visualized, however, are always those of the Tetragrammaton, which maintain their regular order—a significant difference from the continuous changes in the positions of the letters in Abulafia's technique. The fluctuating element in the visualization technique is that of the vowels, which change together with the colors, according to most of the passages referring to visualization. Moreover, the visualizer is not supposed to write down the divine names nor to pronounce them, as Abulafia would recommend. Visualization is a process to be accomplished in addition to regular prayer and concomitant with it, whereas Abulafia's practices are independent of the Jewish rites.

Notwithstanding its novelty in the field of Kabbalah, then, the mystical interpretation of *kavvanah* became a sacrosanct technique that was absent from the early Kabbalah insofar as we know. Although the early Kabbalists discussed the problem of *kavvanah* in principle, nowhere did they propose a detailed sequence for the enactment of mystical prayer. The fact that an alien technique, and this is presently my evaluation of the origin of color visualization, was adopted by Kabbalists only demonstrates the readiness, at the end of the thirteenth century, to expand Kabbalah in various ways. It was exactly at this period that we can also detect other influences of Sufic views among the Kabbalists, as is attested by the appearance of the concepts of "world of imagination"[257] and "equanimity."[258]

Let me now summarize the above discussion. In all known periods of the development of this mystical tradition, Jewish mystics were in possession of, and apparently practiced, a wide variety of mystical techniques. Some of these bore obvious magical color, whereas in a few this aspect was overcome; all of them included a deep involvement of the mystic, who was expected to invest considerable effort in order to attain his religious goal. The understanding of Jewish mysticism must, therefore, take into consideration the practical and experiential facets of this phenomenon to a far greater extent than has been done up to now. The integration of the analyses of those mystical techniques that produced the experiential aspects of Jewish mysticism in the academic study of Kabbalah will presumably reinforce the more extreme interpretation of Jewish mysticism proposed above. It can also contribute to a more balanced view of Jewish mysticism as not only a system of theosophical symbolism, abstract speculations, and "moderate" "communion" but as a full-fledged mystical phenomenon including a variety of speculations, experiences, and techniques.

CHAPTER 6

Kabbalistic Theosophy

The mainstream in Kabbalistic thought undoubtedly is the theosophical Kabbalah, whose dominant conception is that of a complex and dynamic structure of divine powers commonly known as Sefirot. This term, first occurring in *Sefer Yeẓirah,* has been interpreted since the late twelfth century as designating manifestations that are either part of the divine structure or directly related to the divine essence, serving as its vessels or instruments; almost universally, these powers number ten. Classical Kabbalistic theosophy includes both an elaborate anthropomorphical hierarchy and dynamic interrelationships among the components of this hierarchy. In the following discussion, I present the thesis that the motif of a divine anthropomorphical decad, instrumental in the creational process, was part of ancient Jewish thought; this decad was presumably the source of the ten Sefirot of *Sefer Yeẓirah.* I shall then analyze the affinities between certain ancient Jewish terminology—*forms* and *du-parẓufim*—and Kabbalistic theosophy; finally, I shall survey the medieval conceptions of the Sefirot. I want to emphasize that this chapter is not meant to serve as an exposition of Kabbalistic theosophy; rather, I deal primarily with several points from new perspectives and refer the reader seeking more general information to the scholarly literature cited in my notes.

I. MONAD, DECAD, AND ANTHROPOS

The Bible opens the account of the Creation without any indication of the existence of precosmogonic processes. From the outset, this account departs from the pattern—

widespread in ancient cultures—of mythical theogonies that were always preceded by precosmogonic myths. The first phrase of the Bible, "in the beginning," was evidently intended to counter polytheistic theogony; the implication is that no event occurred prior to the Creation. Even the remnants of ancient mythologies, such as the struggle with Behemoth or Leviathan, that are alluded to in various biblical passages apparently relate tensions generated by the Creation process itself rather than precosmogonic conflicts.[1]

Moreover, the mode of Creation by divine fiat established an abyss between the Creator and his Creation; the latter was no longer derived from the body of a defeated and dismembered divinity nor had it been directly constructed or begotten by one of the gods.[2] Material contacts between God and the Creation were severed insofar as possible. In the Bible, God stands *beyond* the universe. Mythical descriptions in ancient sources, however, regarded the gods as standing *within* the cosmos;[3] hence, there was an organic link between theogony and cosmogony, a link eliminated in the biblical account. Discussions concerning divine nature or precosmogonic action therefore were irrelevant for earlier layers of Jewish cosmogony.

This reticence was evidently motivated by antipolytheistic tendencies that were crucial for the religious physiognomy of biblical Judaism. This unwavering attitude toward polytheism, however, cannot always be considered as an opposition to myth per se. As has been recently noticed, "Monotheism of itself does not imply that the myth could not have been taken literally. . . . for some in ancient Israel the mythology was living and for others it was not, and even for some of those for whom it was living, Israelite monotheism has transformed it out of all recognition."[4]

We find explicit warnings in rabbinic texts against any speculation regarding what preceded the Creation of the world; the Mishnah states:[5] "Whosoever speculates upon four things, a pity for him! He is as though he had not come into the world:[6] what is above, what is beneath, what is before, what is after." Nevertheless, in both rabbinic and ancient Jewish mystical literature, speculations concerning precosmogonical matters began to emerge. We find various lists of things that were in existence before the world: the Temple, the Torah, the divine name, the Messiah, and so on.[7] None of these, however, seems to reflect a domesticated divinity; most of them overtly serve as ideal values of the future Jewish religion, only the Torah being partially instrumental in the very act of Creation.[8]

In *Masekhet Ḥagigah,* however, we learn in the name of Rav that "by ten things was the world created: by wisdom, by understanding, by reason, by strength, by rebuke, by might, by righteousness, by judgment, by lovingkindness, and by compassion."[9] We learn from this passage not only the way in which the world was created but also the attributes or agencies of God that were instrumental in the cosmogonical act. The ontological status of these "ten things" is not elucidated in the talmudic discussions that follow this list.[10] The recurrence of the figure ten in other contexts dealing with God's Creation of the world hints at the existence of a certain pattern of divine cosmogonical activity. The picture derived from such a description suggests a certain development in Jewish theology: the ten agencies of God are no longer the ten creative words but semipersonalized characteristics of him. Moreover, in the list of biblical verses adduced to support the assertion of the creative role of the ten things, an implicit connection is manifested between each of these things and a given domain of the universe created by a particular thing. The correlations are far from systematic; nevertheless, we witness an important step toward a more complex perception of Creation. The multiplicity of divine attributes involved in the cosmogony, already in the talmudic text, opens the door for the construction of an elaborate theosophy. But we must also consider the possibility that the form in which the statements on the ten things are cast in Talmud reflects a relatively later stage of Jewish thought. We know that the figure ten within the context of Creation occurs in such early Jewish sources as the tractates *'Avot* and *'Avot de-Rabbi Nathan,* where they refer to ten creative *logoi* that were instrumental in the various acts of Creation. Early undated Gnostic sources—seemingly no later than the middle of the second century—that refer to ten *logoi* seem to represent formulations, or reformulations, of Jewish speculations on the process of Creation.

According to an obscure Gnostic author, quoted by Hippolytus, the son of man is both a monad—the "tittle of the iota"—and a decad. As we shall see below, the notion that an anthropomorphical figure is composed of a decad is crucial for medieval Kabbalah: "that one indivisible tittle—as Monoimos indicates[11]—is . . . one tittle of the [letter] iota,[12] with many faces, and innumerable eyes,[13] and countless names, and this [tittle] is an image of that perfect invisible man." There are astonishingly precise parallels to this comparison of "a perfect invisible man" to a "tittle of iota" in the Kabbalah. According to one such, formulated by R. Menaḥem 'Azariah da Fano: "this primeval anthropos is alluded by the tittle of the yod of the Tetragrammaton, which functions as the aspect of Keter of the wholeness of all the worlds."[14]

It is clear that some motifs included in this statement precede R. Menaḥem 'Azariah: the tittle of iota as a symbol of Keter is widespread in Kabbalistic literature;[15] the identification of the Sefirah with an "anthropos" is rare but nevertheless did exist long before the Italian Kabbalists.[16] Moreover, just as the "invisible man" of the Gnostics constituted a decad,[17] "the primeval anthropos" is formed of ten supernal Sefirot.[18] Monoimos links his anthropos speculations with biblical motifs:

> This [tittle] constitutes a perfect son of a perfect man. When, therefore, he says, Moses mentions that the rod was changeably brandished for the [introduction of the] plagues throughout Egypt—now the plagues, he says, are allegorically expressed symbols of Creation—he did not [as a symbol] for more plagues than ten shape the rod. Now, this [rod] constitutes one tittle of the iota, and is [both] twofold [and] various. This successison of ten plagues is, he says, the mundane Creation.[19]

It is obvious that Monoimos, an Arab, was acquainted with Jewish motifs and traditions. Moreover, his notion of the decad qua "perfect son" is seen as symbolically hinted at in certain biblical themes; therefore, this Gnostic presented his view as a symbolic interpretation of biblical themes. The decad represented by Moses' rod is explicitly connected to the Creation of the world and to the ten plagues. Monoimos continues by saying: "With that one tittle, the law constitutes the series of the Ten Commandments which expresses allegorically the divine mysteries of [those] precepts. For, he says, all knowledge of the universe is contained in what relates to the succession of the ten plagues and the series of the Ten Commandments."[20]

The correspondence between the Ten Commandments, the ten plagues, the decad related to the rod, and the Creation of the world is echoed in a similar correspondence in Jewish sources between the ten creative words (*ma'amarot*), the Ten Commandments, and the ten plagues.[21] I would assume that the decad connected with the Creation is parallel to the ten *ma'amarot*. Moreover, the ten plagues symbolize the Creation—that is, presumably the *ma'amarot*; the son of the perfect man, qua "tittle of iota"—namely, as the decad—"is an image of that perfect invisible man." I conjecture that the son reflects the nature of the father, just as the ten plagues symbolically reflect the "symbols of Creation."[22] It therefore seems that there were two decads in Monoimos—the ten plagues and commandments—and that the "symbols of Creation" and "divine mysteries" respectively reflect the decad of the son and that of the perfect man. This theory is corroborated by the existence of two decads, each described by an anthropomorphic term, in a Coptic Gnostic text. In a fragmentary description of the Creation of man, the anonymous author states: "He made the twenty digits after the likeness of the two decads: the decad that is hidden and the manifested decad."[23]

According to the editor, the hidden decad is known as the "first man," and the "anthropos" probably represents the manifested decad.[24] This double decad can be meaningfully compared to those cited above from the texts of Monoimos. As in his case, the anonymous author of the Coptic treatise was also acquainted with Jewish material.[25] Another, less significant, shared feature is the absence of anti-Jewish views.

To summarize: two anthropomorphically portrayed decads are mentioned, explicitly and implicitly, by two Gnostics—apparently independent of each other—who likewise share a certain knowledge of Jewish traditions. Their views are only tangentially paralleled by ancient Jewish texts but are reflected by extensive and elaborate Kabbalistic material. The existence of two anthropomorphic decads is evidenced by a long series of Kabbalists, from the beginnings of the Kabbalah until R. Isaac Luria and his followers. How are we to understand this similarity between ancient Gnostic texts and Kabbalistic ones composed in the high Middle Ages? The commonly accepted explanation, following Scholem's view, is that the Jews of antiquity accepted Gnostic notions and preserved them for a millennium or more in closed circles, the Kabbalists only gradually disclosing them afterward. The question remains, however, as to why these traditions are found specifically among Gnostics acquainted with Jewish texts. Moreover, what ground is there for the supposition that these were originally Gnostic views that afterward were considered Jewish esoteric teachings? An alternative view would be that these views on the two decads were originally Jewish ones that afterward infiltrated Gnostic circles and were simultaneously passed down among the Jews until the emergence of the historical Kabbalah.

An important point common to the Gnostic texts of Monoimos, to the Midrash, and to the Kabbalah is the cosmogonic role of the decads. The Jewish *ma'amarot* number ten, as do the Gnostic plagues; in the Gnostic texts, they constitute the image of the perfect man and the archetype of the universe. We can thus formulate the role of the perfect son or anthropos as both the image—*ikon*—of the perfect man and the archetype of the world. This peculiar perception is reminiscent of a well-known portrayal of Jesus Christ in the New Testament,

> who is the image of the invisible God, the firstborn of every creature. For by him were all things created that are in heaven, and that are in the earth, visible and invisible, whether they be thrones, or dominions, or principalities, or powers: all things were created by him, and for him. And he is before all things, and by him all things consist . . . . For it pleased the Father that in him should all fullness dwell.[26]

Traces of this passage may be found both in Monoimos' text, where only verse 19 is quoted,[27] and in the anonymous treatise, where, as C. A. Baynes has already noticed, it seems to be implicitly referred to.[28] The background of these verses in Judaism, especially in Jewish mystical thought, has recently been pointed out in a detailed article by G. Stroumsa.[29] He analyzed the peculiar meaning of Christ qua Ikon by way of comparison with Metatron traditions and *Shi'ur Komah* texts, concluding that a Jewish pre-Christian macranthropos notion underlies the Christian text.[30] I should like to discuss here a conception that has not been sufficiently dealt with—the expression "in him should all fullness dwell." The Christ there is not only instrumental in the act of Creation, the image of the Creator, and the purpose of creation—that is, "for him"; he apparently comprises both the image of the Creator and the Creation. Being the form of God, "his cosmic body filled the whole world and was identical to the pleroma"—as Stroumsa put it.[31] Thus, the "form of God" is regarded as an all-comprehensive being. This view is repeated in the *Coptic Gnostic Treatise,* where the father is described as follows: "In [comprehensible] is he in his un[attainable] unapproachable image [ikon]; by this the universes are enclosed; thus within it ⟨they move to and fro⟩ . . . . Within his own self did he represent himself to the mass of those [things] that were in him."[32] Elsewhere in this same treatise, we learn that the father made a city and a man.[33] "In him he portrayed the universes[34] . . . Each one in the city knew him, each one gave myriads of praises to the man or the city of the father, who is in all things."

Monoimos likewise regards the "son of man" as a monad, "as it were, a certain musical harmony which comprises all things in itself . . . and it manifests all things, and generates all things."[35] The precise meaning of "comprises all things in itself" is unclear, but this phrase may be an explanation of another sentence in Monoimos, "man is the universe," although he seems to distinguish between "man" and "son of man."[36]

Although the Christian text was influential on the Gnostics, I assume that it was not the unique source of their elaborate creationist anthropomorphism: first, because, as Stroumsa has pointed out, there were Jewish sources that influenced the passage from Paul, and second, because there are two additonal motifs, found in Jewish texts, relevant to the Gnostic, one of which apparently also influenced Paul's verses. Let me quote a striking passage, originally stemming from *Midrash 'Avkir:*[37]

> Rabbi Berakhya said:[38] When God wished to create the world, he began his Creation with nothing other than man and made him as a golem. When he prepared to cast a soul into him, he said: If I set him down now, it will be said that he was my companion in the work of Creation;[39] so I will leave him as a golem [in a crude, unfinished state], until I have created everything else. When he had created

> everything, the angels said to him: Aren't you going to make the man you spoke of? He replied: I made him long ago, only the soul is missing. Then he cast the soul in him and set him down and concentrated the whole world in him. With him he began, with him he concluded, as it is written: "Thou hast formed me before and behind."[40] God said: "Behold, man is become like one of us."[41]

Several striking points of this passage are pertinent to our discussion: (1) as in the Gnostic and Christian texts, unlike the biblical and classical rabbinic sources, man is presented here as the first creature;[42] (2) similar to the Coptic treatise and to Paul's epistle, the world is concentrated in this first creature; and (3) all these texts explicitly express a resemblance between God and his first creature; man is thereby given cosmic dimensions, a common view in Jewish classical texts.[43] Since the Jewish origins of certain aspects of the Christian text have already been recognized by Stroumsa, the first two points seem to reinforce his argument. Again, as I have suggested above, the assumption of Gnostic influence on *Midrash 'Avkir* seems to me to complicate the situation rather than to explain how the affinities between Jewish and non-Jewish sources came about. I assume that the reaction in *Midrash 'Avkir* against the view that primeval man was already a living creature prior to the end of the Creation of the world is to be understood as directed against mythical traditions existing in the Jewish religious milieu. The assumption that we must regard any critique against a conception found in a Gnostic text as a reaction against extraneous concepts seems to me to be only one possible explanation.[44] One can equally well argue the hypothesis that certain Midrashim were formulated as part of an inner controversy within Jewish thought. The conception that the world was concentrated into an anthropomorphic structure—Adam in *Midrash 'Avkir,* Christ in Paul's epistle, "man" in the Coptic treatise—points, I would assume, toward a different version of the well-known macranthropic view: that the anthropos is not identical with the cosmic structure but is the vessel which, although it may in part correspond to this or that part of the universe, also surpasses them not only in eminence but also in its particular fashion.

This view of Adam as comprising the entire creation in himself can be easily traced to the Kabbalah. According to R. 'Ezra, one of the early Kabbalists, "Man is composed of all the spiritual entities."[45] According to another passage, "Man is composed of all things and his soul is linked to the supernal soul."[46] Thus, "man" stands for the body, which resembles and comprises the ten Sefirot; R. 'Ezra uses the same verb, *kll,* to describe the constitution of man. This formula recurs verbatim in R. Moses de Leon's *Sefer ha-Rimmon,*[47] the "spiritual entities" again referring to the Sefirot.[48] Particularly interesting is the occurrence of this view in R. Menaḥem Recanati, who integrates the formula used by the previous Kabbalists in order to explain the power of man to modify or influence the sefirotic structure: "Since man is composed of all the essences, his power is great and so is his perfection when he directs his intention and knowledge to draw downward, and cause the emanation out of the 'nought of thought.' "[49] Let us compare this to the zoharic description of man:[50] "Since the image of man is the image of the higher and lower [entities][51] which were concentrated in him, and since the structure of this image comprises higher and lower [entities], *'Attika Kaddisha* has prepared this form and the form of *Ze'ir 'Anpin* in this image and form."[52]

The *Zohar* views the structure of man in a manner similar to, though not identical with, that of R. Moses de Leon. Whereas the latter's formulations are identical with those of R. 'Ezra, those of the *Zohar* differ from both of these: man is portrayed as comprising the higher and lower entities.[53] It is worth noting that the *Zohar* deals here with the human body, not with the human soul, as comprising the divine and lower entities, whereas in the writings of de Leon the soul is described as comprising the higher and the lower entities, and the body is viewed as a microcosmos.[54]

For seemingly the first time in medieval Kabbalah, the *Zohar* implies that divine structures in human shape compose the higher and lower entities, in a way similar to the ancient texts, where not the lower but the divine anthropoi are regarded as comprising everything. According to Cordovero,[55] "man comprises in his composition all the creatures, from the first point until the very end of [the world of] Creation, [the world of] Formation, and [the world of] Making, as it is written:[56] 'I have created him, formed him and even made him.' " Thus, even before the Lurianic view that *'Adam Kadmon* comprises the four worlds, there were hints of this in connection with man, as, for example, in this passage of Cordovero's.[57]

According to Lurianic Kabbalah,[58] "all the worlds are concentrated in this *'Adam [Kadmon]*."[59] Let us elaborate upon this statement. It sounds similar to the midrashic text; however, the shift from "world" to "worlds" is reminiscent of the Coptic Gnostic treatise, in which "universes," not a single universe, are mentioned; and one of the zoharic descriptions of *Ze'ir 'Anpin*.[60] The similarity between the Gnostic view and that of Luria—who adduced neither the midrashic text nor the *Zohar* as a *locus probans*—may betray a common source or tradition that is, I assume, of Jewish origin. This hypothesis, which prima facie seems far-reaching, is corroborated by the affinity between the other Lurianic definition of *'Adam Kadmon* and the Gnostic text. Both views regard this anthropos as also constituted of ten forces—the decad previously mentioned in the Coptic text, and the supernal Sefirot named *Ẓaḥ-ẓahot* in pre-Lurianic and Lurianic texts.[61] The fact that two specific concepts of man are found in one Gnostic treatise and, later on, in Kabbalistic theosophy is strongly suggestive of the historical affinity between ancient and medieval notions, for which the Gnostic texts serve not as sources for later mystical literature but as evidence of the existence of some of these notions in ancient times in Jewish milieus as well.[62]

As we have seen above, the relationship among the three elements—anthropos, decad, and Creation within the anthropos—is shared by Monoimos, by the anonymous author of the Coptic treatise, and by the Kabbalah. There is also a fourth element explicitly or implicitly present in these sources. Despite the obvious references to the decad, the same anthropomorphic entity is described also as a monad. Let us start with Monoimos:

> The monad, [that is] the one tittle, is, therefore, he says, also a decad. For by the actual power of this one tittle are produced duad, and triad, and tetrad, and pentad, and hexad, and heptad, and ogdoad, and ennead, up to ten. For these numbers, he says, are capable of many divisions, and they reside in that simple and uncompounded single tittle of the iota. And this is what has been declared: "It pleased [God] that all fullness should dwell in the son of man bodily."[63]

Unlike this text, which explicitly discusses the relationship monad-decad, the Coptic treatise applies the terms *monad*[64] and *decad*[65] to the identical entity in separate discussions. Nevertheless, the editor has perceived this relationship, and after adducing additional material from a related text, the *Apocryphon of John,* he concludes: "the term man was first predicated of the divine image, viewed both as a monad and as the male-female pentad of members = the decad."[66] Knowledge of the decad is therefore tantamount to knowledge of the monad and of the anthropos. In early Kabbalah, we find a recurrent interpretation of the meaning of the word *'Eḥad*—one—as alluding, by its linguistic structure, to ten Sefirot.[67] According to R. Isaac the Blind,[68] the letter *ḥ* of the word *'Eḥad* symbolizes the eight Sefirot from *Ḥokhmah* to Yesod, concluding that "everything is comprised[69] in the word *'Eḥad.*" These hints were further elaborated by his disciple, R. 'Ezra of Gerona:"We ought . . . to unify everything in one word, since the *'aleph* of *'Eḥad* alludes to [that entity] wherein thought cannot expand. The [letter] *ḥet* [of *'Eḥad*] hints of eight Sefirot, and the [letter] *dalet,* which is [written] as a majuscule, hints of the tenth Sefirah."[70]

The need to unify the ten divine powers is a commonplace one in Kabbalah; however, the union of these powers is not only *'Eḥad,* a monad comprising ten other entities, but also the divine anthropos. The same R. 'Ezra indicates that the human body comprises the supernal entities, namely the ten Sefirot.[71] From the early Kabbalah, the human structure reflects the supernal one; we may therefore conclude that the unification of the decad of the Sefirot into the monad is related to their anthropomorphic structure. The unity that goes beyond the ten Sefirot is a basic tenet of Kabbalah, which was time and again attacked on this ground; according to Abraham Abulafia, the theosophical Kabbalists who follow "the way of the Sefirot" say that "divinity is ten Sefirot, and these ten are one."[72]

At this point, we can summarize the relevance of the ancient material to our understanding of the emergence of Kabbalistic theosophy. In the second century A.D., explicit discussions concerning the Creation of the world by the intermediacy of an anthropos, described as both monad and decad, appeared in texts with some affinities to Jewish traditions. The later Jewish theosophical understanding of the ten Sefirot as continuing an anthropomorphic structure that in its ideal state is to be regarded as a unity presents striking parallels to ancient traditions extant in Gnostic texts. The Kabbalists who presented this type of theosophy claimed a hoary antiquity for their system; it would seem that this claim can be corroborated on the basis of the previous analysis. Their other claim, however—that this theosophy is an esoteric interpretation of Jewish thought—is far more difficult to demonstrate. Essentially, the Gnostic ideas of Creation by means of a decad recur in rabbinic sources that do not, however, explicitly mention the anthropomorphic nature of the ten creative *logoi*. We can nevertheless attempt to reconstruct such a presumably ancient Jewish perception from oblique references. According to *'Avot de-R. Nathan,* "One who saves one person is worthy to be regarded as if he has saved the entire world, which was created by ten *logoi* . . . . And someone who causes one person to perish is to be regarded as if he caused the destruction of the entire world, which was created by ten *logoi*."[73] This source explicitly compares man to the world created by these ten *logoi*; moreover, according to the same source, man is defined as a microcosmos,[74] or according to a gloss on the passage quoted previously, "one man is tantamount to the entire act of creation."[75] The passage from *Midrash 'Avkir* may also be reevaluated in this perspective; as the whole world was concentrated in the body of Adam, he is implicitly tantamount to the world created by ten *logoi*. Moreover, according to a twelfth-century Yemenite Jewish author who could not have been known to the early European Kabbalists,[76] there are ten limbs in man, who is a microcosmos corresponding to the ten *ma'amarot*.[77] We can thus conclude that, although there is no conclusive evidence of an anthropomorphic view of the ten *ma'amarot* or ten Sefirot in pre-Kabbalistic Jewish material, there are nevertheless statements regarding the human body as reflecting the ten *ma'amarot* in a certain way.

I would interpret the above findings as follows: a hypothetical Jewish account of Creation consisted of a description of the first creature as man, who at one and the same time includes the ten things, or *logoi*, and is at the same time the monad. This creature is intermediary in the Creation of the world, which is sometimes envisaged as existing within him. This pre-Christian, pre-Gnostic view presumably underwent several metamorphoses in the various types of literature in which it was absorbed: (1) the Christian texts, such as Paul's epistle, identified it with Christ, thereby eliminating the motif of the decad; (2) Gnostic texts, which also showed their authors' awareness of the Christian versions of the Jewish idea, sometimes identified the man as the son of man, but *mutatis mutandis* reflected the original view; (3) rabbinic sources obliterated the anthropomorphic nature of the creating anthropos but preserved the innocuous term *logoi* as the principal means of creation; and (4) medieval Kabbalah, inheriting these presumably ancient Jewish traditions, developed them in an elaborate form that is closest to the Gnostic accounts, albeit using rabbinic terminology: *ma'amarot,* or such terms as *Sefirot.*

II. DIVINE FORMS AND POWERS

The existence of Jewish description of intermediary beings as "forms of God" has recently been analyzed in a study by G. Stroumsa.[78] According to its findings, ancient authors showed Jewish theological discussions as employing the idea of form: *morphé,* or *forma.* The occurrence of this term in Gnostic literature and its coherence with the anthropomorphic conception of ancient Jewish mysticism likewise tend to corroborate the conclusion that such an ancient Jewish view existed and was thereafter adopted in non-Jewish circles.[79] Furthermore, Stroumsa noted the resemblance between certain terms attributed by non-Jewish authors to ancient Jews—but not extant in ancient Jewish texts—and the phrase *ẓurot kedoshot,* which occurs in one of the earliest Kabbalistic works, *Sefer ha-Bahir.*[80] Thus, we witness the same situation as that described above in connection with the anthropomorphic image of the monad and the decad—that is, that concepts considered to be of Jewish extraction are found in ancient non-Jewish sources and medieval Kabbalistic material. We can, however, add two observations to the interesting picture presented by Stroumsa. He mentioned the occurrence of the seventy-two forms of the divine chariot in a text of Nag Hammadi,[81] and a parallel in another

Gnostic treatise in which "seventy-two dynameis" are mentioned.[82] Stroumsa was not particularly interested in the figure seventy-two; therefore, I should like to elaborate upon this issue here.

The text of *Eugnostos* states:

> The twelve powers which I have already mentioned agreed with one another. There were manifested thirty-six male and thirty-six female [beings], so that they make up seventy-two powers. The seventy-two, each one of them, showed forth five spiritual [beings], which are the three hundred sixty powers.[83]

Compare this passage with the following from the *Bahir*:[84]

> These twelve stones are seventy-two, which correspond to the seventy-two names of God. What is the reason? [The biblical text] opened with twelve to teach you that God has twelve leaders,[85] and each and every one of them has six powers.[86] . . . And what are these? The seventy-two languages.

The similarity between the two texts is manifested in the way in which the number seventy-two is derived; moreover, the Hebrew text uses the term *koḥot,* assuming the existence of seventy-two divine powers, corresponding to the Gnostic concept. Let us quote another highly significant Gnostic text dealing with this figure that is apparently a remnant of an ancient Jewish description of the *Merkavah*. Sabaoth is described as creating[87]

> a dwelling place for himself. It is a large place which is very excellent, sevenfold [greater] than all those which exist [in the] seven heavens. Then in front of his dwelling place, he created a great throne on a four-faced chariot[88] called "cherubin." And the cherubin has eight forms for each of the four corners—lion forms, and bull forms and human forms and eagle forms—so that all of the forms total sixty-four forms. And seven archangels stand before him.[89] He is the eighth, having authority. All of the forms total seventy-two. For from this chariot the seventy-two gods receive a pattern; and they receive a pattern so that they may rule over the seventy-two languages of the nations.[90] And on that throne he created some other dragon-shaped angels called "seraphin" who glorify[91] him continually.

The affinity between the "seventy-two languages" mentioned here and in the *Bahir* is obvious; so is the description in both texts of the "powers" connected to these languages as rulers or leaders. According to another passage in the *Bahir,* "all the holy forms are appointed over all the nations."[92] Moreover, the entire Gnostic passage dealing with a chariot is an explicit elaboration upon the throne mentioned in Ezekiel 1, as can be seen by a superficial comparison. But in this Gnostic text the figure seventy-two is derived in a way different from that found in *Eugnostos,* to which there is a surprising parallel elsewhere in the *Bahir*:[93]

> All of them are no more than thirty-six forms, and all of them are perfected in thirty-two [forms]; thirty-two are given[94] to thirty-two, and there remained [out of thirty-six] four; and they are sixty-four forms. Whence do we know that thirty-two were given to thirty-two? From the verse: "for he that is higher than the highest watcheth"[95]—thus, there are sixty-four. But eight is [yet] lacking from the seventy-two names of God, and this is [alluded] in the phrase, "and there be higher than they"[96]—these are the seven days of the week.[97] And one is [yet] lacking, and that which is [alluded] in the verse: "Moreover the profit of the earth is for all."[98]

The figure seventy-two here emerges from the sum $64 + 7 + 1$, exactly as in the Gnostic text. The number sixty-four occurs explicitly in connection with the divine chariot in the Targum to Ezekiel and thus reflects a Jewish tradition.[99] Moreover, in both texts, the seventy-two forms are the result of the combination of $64 + 8$. The relationship between the seventy-two powers and the divine chariot would seem to have been present in a Kabbalistic text; a thirteenth-century text close to the above passage from *Bahir,* presumably authored by R. Moses de Leon,[100] indicates that the cosmic tree described in bahiric terminology[101] "has[102] its roots in the Lebanon,[103] which are [!] the seat of glory, blessed be he, and the Lebanon corresponds to the supernal Lebanon, and its roots are seventy-two roots." An interesting parallel appears in a text composed a century earlier. In Maimonides' *Mishneh Torah,* the intellect of the contemplative who freed his thought of the vanities of this world "is linked under the seat [of glory] to understand those holy and pure forms."[104] Here, as in de Leon's text, the forms are associated with the seat of glory. Interestingly, the contemplation of the forms is equated by Maimonides with "entering Pardes."[105] This connection of the throne with the forms is at least implicit in the *Bahir,* since the land mentioned in connection with the forms is identical with the seat of glory.[106]

The term *form* for *angel* had already appeared in R. Yehudah ha-Levi's *Kuzari*. According to this theologian, there are two kinds of angels: those that are eternal and those created for a specific purpose. The former are described as "the lasting spiritual forms" and are identical with "the glory of God which is the wholeness of the angels and the spiritual vessels; the seat [of glory], the chariot, and firmament, the Ophanim and the wheels, and everything which is lasting."[107]

Not only does the author consider the eternal angels to be forms but, as in the Gnostic and bahiric texts, the term *form* qua angels is connected with the seat of glory. Furthermore, the distinction between "the seat [of glory]" and "the chariot" is reminiscent of the throne that is found on a chariot, mentioned in the Gnostic treatise *On the Origin of the World,* quoted above.[108] It must be mentioned that the term *forms—ṣurah* or *ṣurot*—recurs several times in the *Kuzari* in contexts concerning the question of revelation.[109]

We can thus assume that there was a Jewish tradition extant in the twelfth century connecting the number seventy-two with the divine throne, as in the Gnostic text. To return to two subjects mentioned in the Gnostic text—the term *cherubin* and the location of the throne of Sabaoth—we again find in *Sefer ha-Bahir,* that the thirty-two forms correspond to thirty-two wondrous paths mentioned in *Sefer Yeẓirah.*[110] In the latter it says: "On each of these paths a form guards, as it is written: 'to guard the way to the tree of life.'[111] What is the meaning of 'forms'? As it is written: 'And he placed the cherubim east of the Garden of Eden and the bright blade of a revolving sword to guard the way to the tree of life.' "[112]

Thus, in at least one case *forms* is tantamount to *cherubim,* just as the seventy-two forms are designated by the name cherubim in the Gnostic text. Moreover, in both texts, these cherubim are located at a place that must be guarded: in the Gnostic text, in the eighth heaven; in the *Bahir*, in the Garden of Eden. According to Maimonides, the "holy and pure forms" are to be found underneath the seat by those who enter the *Pardes*.

It is worthwhile elaborating upon the structure of seven archangels plus Sabaoth as the eighth, which form part of the seventy-two forms. We can assume that, besides the forms that constitute the cherubim, there is a special pattern of eight forms. I propose comparing this view of the treatise *On the Origin of the World* with a passage from the *Hypostasis of the Archons*:[113] "This ruler, by being androgynous, made himself a vast realm, an extent without limit. And he contemplated creating offspring[114] for himself, and created for himself seven offspring, androgynous just like their parent. And he said to his offspring: 'It is I who am the god of the entirety.' " In this passage, the creator or ruler is Sakla, alias Yaldabaoth, and not Sabaoth, as in *Origin of the World.* Nevertheless, it seems to me that we find here a similar pattern of seven plus one who is the leader; moreover, in both these Gnostic treatises the appearance of seven occurs immediately following the mention of the realm belonging to the ruler. We can therefore reasonably assume that a pattern of ruler plus seven powers is shared by both these texts. In the *Hypostasis,* the seven are known not as forms, but as offspring.

Let us now compare these two related Gnostic texts with some passages from *Sefer ha-Bahir.* In a parable intended to illustrate the relationship between the seven lower divine powers and the *Shekhinah*, we read: "A king had seven sons, and he gave each one of them his place; he said to them: sit one above the other."[115] The author explains the significance of these sons: "I have already told you that God has seven holy forms."[116] The peculiar arrangement of the sons, one above the other, is paralleled by another bahiric text: "What is the [significance of the] tree you mentioned? He replied to him: these are the powers of God, one above another, and they are similar to a tree."[117]

We can assume from these statements that God's forms were conceived both as powers and as sons; the latter term is, in other passages, connected to the seven weekly days:[118] "What is the significance of [the verse]: 'and the sons take to yourself'?[119] R. Reḥumai said: 'those sons whom she raised.' What are they? The seven days of Creation." Or, in another text: ". . . as the number of the days of the week, to teach that each day has a power [which is appointed upon it]."[120]

Thus, the sons or powers are appointed over the seven days. In the passage from the *Bahir* mentioned earlier, however, these seven days were enumerated among the seventy-two forms.[121] If the equation of the seven forms and powers holds true for the sons, we can assume that the seven offspring and the forms in the Gnostic texts are interrelated. Moreover, the bahiric tradition on the interconnection between the seven days of the week and the powers or sons has implicit astrological characteristics, as does the Gnostic view of the seven powers that are related to the seven heavens.[122] In both cases, the ruler, or the eighth, populates the lower heavens with his progeny; in the texts from the *Bahir,* the coordination is suggested by the phrase "each one above the other," in which a vertical hierarchy is formed, paralleling the seven days and, implicitly, the seven corresponding planets.

Another interesting affinity between the *Bahir* and the above-mentioned texts pertains to the name Sabaoth. In a Gnostic text, it is used to designate the power that created the throne and apparently also the forms connected to this, including the seven archangels. In the *Bahir* we read:[123]

> What is [the significance of]: "Holy, Holy, Holy,"[124] and then "the Lord of Ẓevaot fills the whole earth with his glory"? "Holy"—is the supernal crown; "Holy"—the root of the tree; "Holy"—adhering to and united with all of them,[125] [namely], "the Lord of Ẓevaot, who fills the whole earth with his glory." And what is the significance of " 'Holy'—adhering to and united with"? It is comparable to[126] a king who had sons and grandsons; when the sons do his will, he enters among them and sustains everything.

When the author goes on to explain the nature of "glory," he states, "Is not the glory of the Lord one of his hosts? No, the [verse] does not eliminate it [from the hosts]."[127]

The divine glory is thus one of the powers that form the hosts of God—his Ẓevaot. These hosts, regarded here as sons and grandsons, are also implicitly the forms or powers; the Lord is viewed here as a being who fills all his powers with his presence, thereby sustaining them. Simultaneously, he is conceived of as their father, according to the parable. Scholem explains the meaning of "Yaldabaoth" as "the begetter of Sabaoth," in terms of this conception of the Lord as the father or begetter of the seven forms of Sabaoth.[128] This strange denomination was, as Scholem pointed out,[129] connected to the phrase "Lord of forces."[130] If our analysis is correct, then we find the term *Ẓevaot* used in the *Bahir* to refer to a complex of forms or powers, conspicuously parallel to Gnostic texts, a point not noticed in Scholem's article.[131]

From the previous discussions, we have learned that the forms—as they appear in Jewish sources—are conceived of as powers or angels; elsewhere in *Sefer ha-Bahir,* however, they are explicitly described as divine powers. In one paragraph, the anonymous author asserts that[132] "there are seven holy forms which are God's, and all of them have their counterparts in man, as it is said,[133] 'for in the image of God made he man.' " These angelic powers are therefore also regarded as divine forms, a view that can be understood against the background of an ancient Jewish conception of the angels as corresponding to the divine limbs, thereby forming an anthropomorphic structure.[134]

Let us now consider a final point concerning the antiquity of the Hebrew terminology related to *form.* As Stroumsa pointed out, ancient authors—both Christian and pagan—attributed the use of the term *form* to the Jews; however, no instance of occurrence of the term *Ẓurah* has been found in Jewish sources. Nevertheless, such a usage is attested by a short passage found in Qumran. In a recent thesis, C. A. Newsom deciphered two lines, one of which includes the phrase "צ]ורות אלהים חיים"—"the forms of the living God," and immediately thereafter the phrase "צורות אלוהים מחוקקו"—presumably "[he?] engraves the forms of God."[135] This last phrase may reflect a sentence found in a passage from the *Bahir:* "God hewed out the letters of the Torah, and engraved them in the spirit, and made his forms in it."[136] The occurrence of the verb *ḥkk* together with "divine forms" is curious and points to the fact that the *Bahir* inherited here an older tradition. The existence of the phrase "forms of God" in a Qumran text demonstrates that at least one important term of Jewish theosophy presented in the *Bahir* has a long prehistory. Moreover, an important parallel to the concurrence of letters and forms is manifest in the Gnostic presentation of letters qua angels. According to Marcos,[137] the thirty letters[138] that form the "insubstantial eon" or *du-parẓufim* and their sounds are the "morphé" and the "angels" that incessantly see the face of the Father. An interesting passage from R. Eleazar ha-Kallir seems to illustrate the association of the number thirty in connection with the angels:[139]

> and under them thirty degrees[140] . . .
> ascending upon one another
> unto the seat of glory they fly and ascend
> in their singing: "the song of the degrees."[141]

It is obvious that these "degrees," which are underneath the seat of glory, are angels, or at least angel-like creatures. As we have seen above, the angels beneath this throne are viewed as forms.

R. Barzilai,[142] an early Geronese Kabbalist, describes the Sefirah of Gevurah as "the beginning of the awesome forms, apprehended in the prophetic visions.[143] From them the seat of glory,[144] and Ophanim, seraphim, holy creatures and servant angels are created." Not identical with the angelic realm, but rather its source, the awesome forms are the object of prophetic vision, sharing this essential quality with R. Yehudah ha-Levi's forms. R. Barzilai and ha-Levi likewise present the forms as connected with the seat of glory and with certain types of angels. R. Abraham ibn 'Ezra and, under his influence, the anonymous Ashkenazic author of *Sefer ha-Ḥayyim,* spuriously attributed to ibn 'Ezra, mention the "forms of truth"—*Ẓurot 'Emet*—that signify a higher class of angels.[145] Interestingly, in Marcos's system the *Aletheia* is formed of letters that, as we have seen above, are also angels and forms.

III. DU-PARẒUFIM

One of the striking characteristics of Kabbalistic theosophy is the strong role played by erotic and sexual motifs; they recur repeatedly in Kabbalistic works and have been explained by some in terms of R. Moses de Leon's personality.[146] As far as I know, no detailed analysis of the history of Jewish conceptions of eroticism and sexuality exists.[147] The discussion that follows deals with some aspects of a significant motif of Kabbalistic theosophy related to this issue, namely, the evolution of the concept of *du-parẓufim*—the double-faceted nature of primeval man—and its interpretation in Kabbalistic texts. I shall begin with an analysis of one of the earliest texts including theosophical elements: *The Secret of Du-parẓufim* by R. Abraham ben David of Posquieres (Rabad):[148]

Adam[149] and Eve were created *du-parẓufim*,[150] so that the woman would be obedient to her husband, her life depending upon him, lest he go his [own] way, while she go her [own] way; rather, affinity and friendship will exist between them, and they shall not separate from one another, and peace will rest upon them and calmness in their houses. Likewise is it as concerns "the doers of truth,"[151] whose actions are truth. The secret of *du-parẓufim* refers to two matters: first, it is well-known that two opposites were emanated, one of them stern judgment, and its counterpart, complete mercy. And were they not emanated [as] *du-parẓufim*, and [if] each were to work out its actions [separately] according to its characteristic, it would be possible to see [them] as if they are two powers acting [separately], without any connection with its partner and without its assistance. But now, since they were created *du-parẓufim*, their actions are performed in cooperation and equality and in a total union, without any separation. Furthermore, unless they had been created *du-parẓufim*, no union would emerge from them and the attribute of judgment would not converge with [that of] mercy, nor would the attribute of mercy converge with [that of] judgment. But now, since they were created *du-parẓufim*, each of them may approach his partner and unite with it, and its desire is willingly to unite with its partner, that the Tabernacle may be one.[152] A proof for this [view] is found in the [divine] names which refer to each other, since *Yod He* refers to the attribute of judgment and *Elohim* to the attribute of mercy, as in "Then YHWH rained upon Sodom and upon Gomorrah."[153] "YHWH rained" [means that] he passed from one attribute to another attribute.

It seems that the two divine attributes are regarded as corresponding to the bisexual nature of primordial man, who was later divided into masculine and feminine entities. Thus, implicitly we find a three-stage process taking place concomitantly within the emanational system and on the historical plane. The first androgynous stage is obvious in the biblical story; these two attributes seem to have existed on a higher level or on the divine level prior to their separation.[154] In this initial stage, the two opposing attributes are prepared for a certain kind of cooperation that would be impossible had these attributes emerged separately or from different sources. Second, these divine attributes were separated, as Eve was from Adam, according to this midrashic view. Third, the activities both of the attributes and of human beings thereafter reflect an essential cooperation of opposite factors. This is evident from the biblical text insofar as the human couple is concerned, but is also evident from the midrashic texts with regard to the relation between the two attributes.

Although Rabad does not state this explicitly, the sexually conceived attributes are related to the divine names: the Tetragrammaton, which commonly symbolizes the attribute of mercy, symbolizes judgment in this verse in Genesis in order to indicate that the actions of the two attributes are not separate. May we then conclude that the parallel polarity of divine attributes, divine names, and sexes indicates that the two divine attributes and the two names are considered as masculine and feminine?

The relationship between the two divine names and their corresponding attributes, defined as masculine and feminine, implicitly existed in a midrashic text. According to *Midrash Tadshe,*[155] "the two cherubim on the ark of testimony correspond to the two holy names: the Tetragrammaton and Elohim." As is well known, the talmudic tradition quoted in the name of R. Katina envisaged these cherubim as male and female,[156] sometimes found in sexual embrace, at other times separated from each other.[157] I assume that the distinction between the divine names corresponds to the sexual differentiation between the cherubim. What is implicit in this Midrash is stated explicitly by the younger contemporary of Rabad, R. Eleazar of Worms. He quotes *Midrash Tadshe* without elaborating upon the sexual matter,[158] and in a longer discussion an additional correspondence is mentioned:[159] "The Tetragrammaton on the seat of judgment is inscribed, and likewise on the seat of mercy and on the foreheads of the cherubim as it is written:[160] '. . . whose name is called by the name of the Lord of hosts who dwells upon the cherubim,' and corresponding to it are the two [divine] names." Thus, in addition to the correspondence of divine names and the cherubim already elucidated in the Midrash, we also find here an allusion to the two divine attributes in the two seats of judgment and mercy. This is made explicit in R. Isaac ben Yehudah ha-Levi's *Pa'aneaḥ Raza.*[161]

The talmudic sexual perception of the cherubim is stated emphatically in R. Eleazar's *Commentary on Sefer Yeẓirah*[162] . . . "as the sexual union of man and [his] partner, which were in the Temple, in order to increase fruitfulness in Israel."[163] The verse in Kings explicitly mentions the cherubim, portrayed here as images that function as catalyzer of human intercourse.[164]

Before proceeding further, let me summarize those ideas common to Rabad and R. Eleazar of Worms. Both assume a threefold set of correspondences beyond those found in the Midrash: in Rabad's text, these pertain to the two divine names, to two divine attributes, and to Adam and Eve; thus, the sexual overtone is explicit. R. Eleazar relates to two divine names, two divine attributes—referred to as seats—and two cherubim, so that the sexual motif is thereby muted. Rabad, however, articulates an interesting principle, absent in the Ashkenazic writer: the divine attributes were primarily one before they were separated, in order to ensure cooperation between them in the future. It seems to me that each of these two authors, in his own way, reflects a previous larger conception that presumably contained motifs found in their discussions.

That is, Rabad's principle of original union prior to division for the sake of cooperation might have been in existence also in connection with the two cherubim, even though the passage from Rabad does not mention the cherubim.

Before examining the discussion of these topics in antiquity, I would like to quote a short statement of R. Shem Tov ibn Gaon, written later on, in 1325: "Adam and Eve were created—equally, *du-parẓufim*—intertwined in one another—as symbolized by the form of the cherubim."[165] Such an androgynous description of the cherubim is otherwise unknown to me; if this Kabbalist reflects an older tradition, this strengthens my supposition as to the existence of a discussion following Rabad's line incorporating the cherubim.[166] It should, however, be noted that in Rabad's text Adam and Eve stand respectively for the attributes of judgment and mercy, which are supposed to cooperate. These attributes reflect what was later designated in classical Kabbalah as the Sefirot of *Ḥesed* and *Gevurah*. These two divine powers were, however, symbolized by the cherubim, at least since the time of R. ʿEzra of Gerona, the student of R. Isaac the Blind, the son of Rabad.[167] Again, according to R. ʿEzra, these two Sefirot were conceived as masculine and feminine.[168] I therefore submit a hypothesis as to the existence of a mystical tradition preceding both Rabad and R. Eleazar of Worms, in which the two divine attributes, the two divine names, and the cherubim were envisioned as syzygies. The correspondence between attributes and divine names was well known in rabbinic literature, as was the sexual quality of the cherubim. We require—in order to substantiate this assumption that a more comprehensive sexual polarity of divine qualities existed prior to the first Kabbalistic documents—an ancient nexus among cherubim, divine names, and attributes. In the citation above from *Midrash Tadshe,* we adduced a partial nexus in which divine names correspond to the cherubim, but a more ancient text of Jewish provenance may serve to corroborate our hypothesis.

Particularly close to Rabad's text is a highly interesting passage from Philo, discussed in some detail by Erwin Goodenough. Describing the peculiar nature of the cherubim, Philo asserts that they represent the divine attributes:[169]

> For it is necessary that the powers, the creative and royal, should look toward each other in contemplation of each other's beauty, and at the same time in conspiracy for the benefit of things that have come into existence. In the second place, since God, who is one, is both the Creator and King, naturally the powers, though divided, are again united. For it was advantageous that they be divided in order that the one might function as creator, the other as ruler. For the functions differ. And the

> powers were brought together in another way by the eternal juxtaposition of the names[170] in order that the creative power might share in the royal and the royal in the creative. Both incline toward the mercy seat. For if God had not been merciful to the things which now exist, nothing would have been created through the creative power nor be given legal regimentation by the royal power.

Goodenough, who discussed this passage in his earlier work, *By Light, Light,* without recognizing its affinities to rabbinic legends concerning the cherubim, later came to the conclusion that Philo's hints were "made explicit in the Talmud itself,"[171] in the passage of R. Katina referred to above.[172] But according to this scholar, the talmudic passages include conceptions "completely foreign to the traditions of Judaism as the rabbis ordinarily presented them."[173] Goodenough therefore assumes that the idea of union of the divine powers "reflects the sort of thinking which lies at the very heart of gnostic speculation"! Finally, he regarded the rabbinic perception of the cherubim as stemming from Philo's thought! It seems to me unnecessary to refute these three highly speculative assertions; a fourth one, however, deserves closer examination.

Goodenough states that the Philonic passage "is quite in harmony with later cabbalistic speculation, by which the divine power in its descent is at once divided between the right and the left, which are the male and the female."[174] Although he does not refer to any specific Kabbalistic source, it seems to me that the above passage from Rabad corroborates Goodenough's remark.[175] This Kabbalist shared with Philo the assumption that the divine powers had been divided, presumably after originally existing as a unity in God. Again, both theologians discuss the need for common operation of the attributes; Philo furthermore hints at the fact that each of the two divine names points to the two attributes. On his part, Rabad asserts, along with the Midrash, that the Tetragrammaton stands for the attributes both of mercy and judgment.[176] But a crucial point sharply distinguishes this Kabbalistic passage from all preceding material: Rabad asserts that the relationship between the two attributes or the two divine names corresponds to that of male and female; such a relationship never occurs explicitly in the talmudic, midrashic, or Philonic texts. Nevertheless, I imagine that Rabad reflects an ancient tradition that can be corroborated by the findings of a recent article concerning the existence in ancient Judaism of a pair of angels, male and female, symbolized by the two cherubim.[177] Only in this specific view—adduced by Origen in the name of a Jewish scholar, significantly—do we find an important hint of the symbolic value of the Jewish perception of the cherubim as male and female. According to the tradition reported by Origen, their sexual relationship is projected onto a higher metaphysical level: that of a pair of angels. This tradition can suggest to us that the other topics relating to the cherubim may also reflect their sexual nature. In other words, the sexualization of the relationship between the two divine names or two attributes found in Rabad without referring to the cherubim can be implicitly assumed, in such texts as *Midrash Tadshe* and R. Eleazar of Worms, to be phenomenologically related to the tradition reported by Origen.[178]

Is it a mere coincidence that one of the first Kabbalistic texts reflects a concept parallel to that found in Philo? I tend to answer no. There seems to be extant evidence for the existence of Hebrew traditions that may mediate between Philo's views, or other ancient Jewish traditions parallel to Philo, and the emergent Kabbalah. According to a midrashic text, the activity of God or his revelation is twofold: benevolent for Israel but pernicious for the Gentiles. This view is conveyed in the following terms: "R. Hoshaya said; *du-parẓufim* they [the divine actions] were: a *parẓuf* of light for Israel, and a *parẓuf* of darkness for the Egyptians."[179] Thus, the term *du-parẓufim*, which ordinarily describes the bisexual nature of man, stands here for a kind of *coincidentia oppositorum* in relation to God. A brief analysis of the context of this passage[180] will reveal that the term refers to terms of action rather than to physical features[181]—an understanding corroborated by parallel midrashic texts.[182] This quality of divine action is particularly close to Rabad's description of the divine attributes as *du-parẓufim*; although the sexual nature of the divine actions cannot be determined for the midrashic texts, the very use of the term in connection with divine attributes may be considered an important step toward the Kabbalistic conception.

There is no historical difficulty in assuming that this midrashic material and *Midrash Tadshe* were known to Rabad. According to Abraham Epstein,[183] *Midrash Tadshe* was known to R. Moses ha-Darshan, an eleventh-century scholar who flourished in Narbonne—the same place where Rabad was active for a certain period in his life.[184] As these considerations are, for the time being, partly speculative, it would be prudent to wait for additional material to confirm them; but even given the present state of research, the hypothesis of an ancient Jewish tradition containing a sexual conception of these two divine attributes that influenced early Kabbalah is deserving of serious consideration.[185]

Let us turn now to a specific detail included in Rabad's text. According to him, "*Yod He* refers to the attribute of judgment and *'Elohim* to the attribute of mercy." In context, the meaning of the passage is that each of the two divine names can refer to either of the two attributes; the Kabbalist thereby asserts that the correlation between divine names and attributes is changeable. Seen against the background of classical rabbinic sources, where such flexibility was unknown, this attitude is peculiar. The change could be attributed to Rabad's having introduced an innovation, but this explanation is neither the only possible solution nor the most convincing one. Another plausible explanation is that this Kabbalist, or his sources, held two traditions concerning the relation between names and attributes: (1) the standard rabbinic tradition, which related the Tetragrammaton to the attribute of mercy and 'Elohim to the attribute of judgment; and (2) another tradition, expressed in ancient sources and in Philo, in which the previous set of identifications is reversed. Rabad, or his sources, might have created a synthesis of both traditions. The view that the Tetragrammaton can stand for two attributes, at least, seems to have been taken over from a very ancient midrashic tradition. R. Meir asserted:[186] "For behold the Tetragrammaton comes out of his place.[187] He comes out from one attribute to another attribute, from the attribute of judgment to the attribute of mercy."

To conclude this excursus, I cite a view given by R. Menaḥem Recanati: "There are exegetes who view the cherubim as alluding to *dio-parẓufin*, and such seems to be the view of Naḥmanides. The opinion of our sages, who said that the two cherubim correspond to the Tetragrammaton and the Lord, also inclines to this [view].[188] It is noteworthy that, for Recanati, cherubim, dio-parẓufin, and the two divine names all refer to the same two divine manifestations: *Tiferet* and *Malkhut*. These two attributes, like the two higher ones, *Ḥesed* and *Gevurah*, were invariably conceived as a pair consisting, respectively, of the merciful and judgment aspects of divinity.

Comparing this symbolic scheme with another one already known at the end of the thirteenth century, we find that according to R. Joseph of Hamadan, the two cherubim symbolize the Sefirot *Yesod* and *Malkhut*, which are manifestly viewed as bridegroom and bride.[189] The same two Sefirot, however, like their human symbols, are consistently referred to by this Kabbalist as, respectively, *'Arikh 'Anpin* and *Ze'ir 'Anpin*.[190] I assume that this type of symbolism must be understood as an integration of the talmudic portrayal of the cherubim as "great face" and "little face"[191] within a context mentioning the face or faces of God and the supernal faces.[192] Therefore, the use of the pair of epithets *'Arikh* and *Ze'ir* in connection with faces of the cherubim and at the same time of two divine attributes is not a significant departure from the concepts related to these subjects in ancient and early Kabbalistic texts. Nevertheless, the peculiar usage of *'Arikh 'Anpin* and *Ze'ir 'Anpin* as symbols for two lower Sefirot is, as Scholem pointed out,[193] a considerable departure from the zoharic understanding of these two terms, in which they refer, respectively, to the complex of *'Eiyn Sof* and *Keter* and either to the Sefirot from *Ḥokhmah* to *Yesod*[194] or, according to other zoharic texts and to R. Joseph Gikatilla, to the Sefirah of *Tiferet*.[195] The question arises as to whether R. Joseph of Hamadan introduced a new understanding of the symbolic value of these two symbols, departing from the already existing symbolism found in the *Zohar,* or whether he is perhaps continuing an ancient esoteric tradition interpreted by the *Zohar* in a new way.[196]

Let us examine a passage in the *Idra Rabba* concerning these two countenances:[197] " 'And [the Lord God] formed [man].'[198] Why are there two yods [in the word *va-yeẓer*—formed]? [They point to] the secret of *'Attika Kadisha* and the secret of *Ze'ir 'Anpin*." According to this text, the peculiar way in which the Bible describes the creation of man alludes to the creation of two supernal anthropomorphical structures: *'Arikh 'Anpin* or *'Attika Kadisha*, and *Ze'ir 'Anpin*, who are here symbolized by two yods.[199] Moreover, the occurrence of two divine names in the biblical verse was understood as referring to the nature of these countenances: the Lord—the Tetragrammaton—refers to *'Attika Kadisha* as the countenance of mercy, and 'Elohim refers to *Ze'ir 'Anpin*, the countenance of judgment. A partial parallel to this text is found in *The Alphabet of R. 'Akiva,* in which the same verse is interpreted as follows: "One [yod] corresponds to the countenance of his front, [and] one corresponds to the countenance of his back."[200]

Again, a Midrash on *du-parẓufim* seems to preserve, at least in part, a mythic tradition that later recurs in the Kabbalah. My inference from this is that the theory of two countenances in the *Zohar* is an elaboration of the view of *du-parẓufim*, which was already connected to the two divine names in the passage from Rabad, in which the two divine attributes were mentioned as well. The transition from the views expressed by the Midrash concerning the *du-parẓufim* and opposite divine actions, to the passage from Rabad where the meaning of *du-parẓufim* is explained in terms of two divine names and attributes, to the terminology of R. Joseph of Hamadan where the sexual differentiation is obvious—as in the text of Rabad—seems far more reasonable than that of the *Zohar*, where the emphasis is laid upon the anthropomorphic presentation of the two countenances. It seems to me that traces of the view expressed in Rabad's text are still visible in a sentence found some lines before the statement of the *Zohar* cited above. Dealing with the two countenances formed in the image of man, which constitute the higher and lower entities, the *Zohar* states, "They were in one pattern, but afterward their ways separated from each other, mercy on one side and judgment on the other."[201]

The assumption that the two countenances were originally one and were afterward divided into two attributes—of mercy and judgment—corresponds to Rabad's view on *du-parẓufim*. Moreover, immediately following this, the *Zohar* again discusses the two countenances, using the verse from Genesis 2:7 in which the two divine names occur, as we have seen before. According to a classical commentator of the *Zohar,* this primeval unity of the *du-parẓufim* existed in the "depths of the nothingness," and was only afterward split into two attributes.[202]

IV. VARIOUS CONCEPTIONS OF THE SEFIROT

Among all topics within the Kabbalah, the doctrine of the Sefirot enjoyed the greatest popularity in its presentations. Time and again, the list of names of the Sefirot, with the anthropomorphic pattern, is repeated as the core of this lore. The same is true of scholarly research: the various conceptions of the Sefirot have been analyzed far more extensively than any other Kabbalistic topic.[203] But notwithstanding this wealth of interest, there is as yet no comprehensive study of the history of the Kabbalistic doctrines of the Sefirot. The emergence of the specific names of the Sefirot and the structure and functions of the sefirotic pleroma are all crucial matters for a precise understanding of theosophical Kabbalah; their study is urgent. In the following pages, a short survey of this subject is presented, taking into consideration some detailed studies devoted to specific authors or periods.

The earliest theosophical perceptions of the Sefirot occur concomitantly in Provençal Kabbalah, in *Sefer ha-Bahir,* and in the esoteric materials preserved in R. Eleazar of Worms's *Sefer ha-Ḥokhmah.* Conspicuous in their elaboration of the nature of the Sefirot are certain passages of the *Bahir* (although the term itself is only rarely mentioned) and the *Commentary of Sefer Yeẓirah* of R. Isaac the Blind. Although the names of the Sefirot there are similar, these two texts seem to originate from different theosophical traditions.[204] *Sefer ha-Bahir* presents a mythically oriented picture of the sefirotic pleroma, whereas R. Isaac the Blind gives a much more complex theory of the emergence of the Sefirot from the depths of divinity, betraying a deep speculative tendency probably influenced by Neoplatonic thought. The Geronese Kabbalists inherited both these trends; for the first time, they mention the bahiric theories of the Sefirot, sometimes as infradivine powers and at other times as extradivine forces or forms, alongside the Provençal views, in which the Sefirot are invariably depicted as constituting an infradivine structure. The central theme characterizing the history of the sefirotic concepts is the vacillation between infra-

and extradivine theories, just as the history of philosophy is marked by the philosophical theories on the existence of ideas within or outside the divine mind.

The Geronese theories, found in the writings of R. Barzilai, R. 'Ezra of Gerona, R. Jacob ben Sheshet, and R. Asher ben David of Provence, do not present a single unified answer to the question of the ultimate essence of the Sefirot. From the early thirteenth century, three major answers were offered: (1) the theory that the Sefirot are part of the divine nature and partake in the divine essence, referred to below as "Sefirot qua essence"; (2) the theory that Sefirot are nondivine in essence, although closely related to divinity, either as its instruments in creating and governing the world or as vessels for the divine influx by which it is transmitted to the lower worlds; and (3) the theory that the Sefirot are the divine emanation within created reality, constituting, as it were, the immanent element of divinity.[205] I shall briefly describe the expressions used in order to convey the emphases at the earlier stages of Kabbalah; interestingly, only later, at the end of the fifteenth and the early sixteenth centuries, were these earlier positions presented as conflicting stands and thereby crystallized as independent perceptions. Still later, these opposing views were unified in the theosophy of R. Moses Cordovero, and since then the coexistence of the Sefirot qua essences of the divinity and as its vessels and instruments became a dominant factor in Kabbalistic theosophy. Finally, I will survey a fourth interpretation, the human or psychological understanding of the Sefirot.

I. Sefirot qua Essence of Divinity

The assumption that the divine anthropos comprises a plurality of forces, ten in number, already existed in antiquity, as we have seen above. This stance generated the perception of the ten Sefirot as part of the divine structure, but it is absent in *Sefer ha-Bahir,* where the anthropomorphic structure comprises eight powers, which can hardly be viewed as part of the essence of divinity. The earliest comprehension of the ten Sefirot as being divine entities and forming the divine structure seems to be found in the texts of R. Isaac the Blind and, under his influence, in the writings of other Kabbalists. R. Isaac stressed the perfect unity of the sefirotic pleroma:

> "Their end is [found] in their beginning": just as many threads come out of the burning coal, which is one, since the flame cannot stand by itself but only by means of one thing; for all the things [that is, the Sefirot], and all the attributes, which seem as if they are separate, are not separated [at all] since all [of them] are one, as the[ir] beginning is, which unites everything "in one word."[206]

The world of separation exists only below this united world of Sefirot.[207] This passage permits us to infer that R. Isaac's theological position approximated what was later called the view of the Sefirot as divine essence; he himself did not make use of the later terminology that explicitly affirmed the identity of the sefirotic pleroma with the Godhead. As we shall see below, R. Isaac's closest disciples—his nephew, R. Asher ben David, and R. 'Ezra of Gerona—all accepted the bahiric view of the Sefirot as instruments and vessels, thereby establishing this view in Geronese Kabbalah. The classical version of Sefirot as divine essence seems to have been elaborated by the Kabbalistic school of Naḥmanides. According to an heir of Naḥmanides' esotericism, R. Shem Tov ibn Gaon:[208]

> First of all, my masters warned me to keep apart from three things: namely, corporeality, division, and plurality, either in speech or in thought. For in spite of the fact that we make mention of attributes and names of the Sefirot, this is done in order to refer to them, not to divide between them. But he is one, united with them all, as the intellect [to its] intelligible,[209] like the burning coal which is linked to the flame.

This discussion was further elaborated in the second chapter of *Ma'arekhet ha-'Elohut,* the classical work expressing the view that the Sefirot are identical with Godhead.[210] Its author repeatedly insists that the Sefirot "are Godhead."[211] According to the anonymous Kabbalist, whatever differences there may be between the divine attributes, these must be understood from our perspective or, as he puts it, "from the perspective of the recipients,"[212] a well-known Neoplatonic formula.[213]

Notwithstanding this obvious perception of the Sefirot as an organic part of divine essence, the particular term that was later accepted as encapsulating this view, *'aẓmut,* apparently does not occur in Naḥmanides' school. However, in an epistle copied by R. Shem Tov ibn Gaon and, according to his manuscript, sent to Naḥmanides by a student of an obscure Kabbalist, R. Joseph ben Mazaḥ, we learn:

> Just as the essence of God is unknown, so is his counsel not [known]; but from the Kabbalah we have learned that his name and his image and himself are all him, as his name is a great sign [enabling us] to comprehend the greatness of his excellency and beauty, and his image and his essence [which are] the ten Sefirot. . . . The ten Sefirot *Belimah* are the essence of the Creator and his image.[214]

As Scholem has already noted, the terminology of this epistle is close to that of the *'Iyyun* circle.[215] As far as we are concerned, the definition of the ten Sefirot as the essence of God is here evident; the term used is *'aẓmo,* which also occurs in an instructive description of the Sefirot as divine essence to be found in a *Commentary on Ten Sefirot,* which is a treatise close to the concepts of the *'Iyyun* circle:[216]

> . . . the Sefirot, which are so to speak the essence of God, like the elements of man are within man. Understand this, for to this Ezekiel referred in saying, "as the appearance of a man above upon it,[217] the image of all the glory. . . . For all these Sefirot are separated forces, of an utmost simplicity, and they are all one glory, without any division or separation, save through the actions that reach us from them.[218] All these Sefirot were created by god, blessed be his name, for his glory, and one harmonious union is formed from them, and all are called "Soul," and God—"the Soul of all Souls."

The Hebrew form translated here as "the essence" is again *'aẓmo,* which is the closest approximation to the classical form, *'aẓmut*.[219] At present, it appears that its earliest usage appears in the writings of R. Menaḥem Recanati, the first overt opponent of the essentialist perception of the Sefirot. He criticizes the view that "the ten Sefirot are the very essence of the Creator."[220] Even the possibility that there is no real differentiation in the supernal realms, but only from "the perspective of the recipients," is rejected as meaningless nominalism.[221] Recanati was well acquainted with both the Kabbalah originating from Naḥmanides' students and that represented by those texts conceptually close to the *'Iyyun* terminology.[222] We can see in Recanati's formulation of the nature of the Sefirot as the essence of the divinity, the crystallization of the earlier terminology into what was to become the classical formula: Sefirot are *'aẓmut*. Interestingly, from the late fifteenth century those Kabbalists who adopted the essentialist stand not only used Recanati's term, referring explicitly to his arguments against this theory, but also sometimes reinterpreted it in order to strengthen their argument.[223]

Before concluding this short survey of the essentialist views of the Sefirot, I will present a specific and central version belonging to this category, that of the *Zohar* and of R. Moses de Leon. Although the essentialist conception presumes a more dynamic nature of the Sefirot than does that which grants them an instrumental role, there are also static or more paradigmatic essentialist views, such as those that identify the Sefirot with the Platonic ideas in the divine mind.[224] The theosophy of *Ma'arekhet ha-'Elohut,* following the formulations of R. Shem Tov ibn Gaon, also explicitly denies any changes in the Godhead,[225] including the Sefirot.[226] This categorical rejection of intradeical dynamism is one extreme stand within the essentialist view; the other is found in the *Zohar* and the writings of de Leon. Although the essentialist perception is crucial for their theosophy, these texts nevertheless emphasize the constant dynamism of the Sefirot. A few examples will suffice to illustrate this point; in de Leon's *Shekel ha-Kodesh,* we learn:[227]

> The secret of the hidden world and all of its entities hidden and concealed is [alluded in the verse]: "the creatures run and return."[228] . . . And if you will take a dish with water to the "eye" of the sun, and you will shake it, you will see on the wall the splendor of the mirrors which are shining; they run and return and no one is able to fix them, because of the speed of their movement to and fro.

In de Leon's works, the hidden world is a recurring symbol for the Sefirot of *Binah*. In order to understand the nature of this universe, we create an unceasing movement of water that, reflecting the light of the sun, symbolizes the ongoing dynamism in the higher world.[229] According to an untitled work of de Leon:

> Contemplation is not perfect but by [a process of] understanding and stopping [it] . . . like the light emerging from the shaking of the water in a dish, since that light shines in one place and immediately leaves it and it returns and shines in another place. When man thinks that he has already grasped this light, it immediately flees from this place and returns to appear again in another place. And man runs after it, in order to comprehend it, but he does not comprehend. . . . so is it in this place, which is the beginning of the emanation.[230]

I wish to emphasize that de Leon refers to two levels: that of the *Merkavah*, in which the dynamic entities are Ezekiel's "living creature," namely angelic powers; and those processes taking place in the sefirotic realm, mostly in the Sefirot of Binah and its entities, which is referred to not only by the phrase "the hidden world" but probably also by the term "beginning of the emanation." This metaphor of shifting light reflected within the moving water recurs twice in Aramaic versions in the *Zohar*[231] and is corroborated by de Leon's discussions of the motion of the shut eyes generating inner light and color that, according to both de Leon[232] and the *Zohar*,[233] reflect the sefirotic dynamism. A comparison of the manner in which de Leon and the *Zohar* make use of the contemplation of lights in the water, with the very similar usages of Ashkenazic Ḥasidism and of R. Joseph Gikatilla, conclusively shows that the prescription to shake the water in order to obtain a dynamic process of reflection is unique in the sources referred to above. The theosophy reflected by this technique of contemplation is dynamic par excellence; the difficulty in contemplating the lights reflected on the wall must be precisely defined. At stake in de Leon's or the *Zohar's* texts is not their essential hiddenness but the human inability to grasp a dynamic, visible, but ever-changing process.[234] This peculiar quality of zoharic theosophy has important repercussions on the centrality of the symbolism related to these dynamic processes; the focus of the symbolism moves, as we shall see below, from symbolic reflection of Sefirot to the reflection of processes—hence, the dynamic quality of zoharic symbolism. As this type of symbolism was influential, it contributed a unique feature to Kabbalistic symbolism in general.[235]

2. The Sefirot qua Instruments or Vessels

Although the concept of the Sefirot as instruments of divine activity has been examined several times, the origins of this instrumental terminology have not been discussed.[236] I will elaborate upon this issue and then briefly survey its evolution.

According to *Sefer ha-Bahir,* a presumably esoteric tradition indicates that[237] "I received the verse 'for the six days the Lord made,'[238] as one says, 'God made six fitting vessels.'[239] And what are they? 'The Heavens and the earth.' " The Hebrew phrase, "six fitting vessels"—*Shishah kelim na'im*—presumably refers both to the "six days of creation" and to "the heavens and the earth." The same verse is again discussed by the *Bahir*,[240] which states that "each and every day has its [own] *ma'amar*,[241] over which it is master, not because it [the *ma'amar*] was created on it, but because it performs the specific operation upon which it [the *ma'amar*] is appointed." Thus, the seven days reflect particular operations rather than periods of time; if the six vessels mentioned above in connection with the six days also each performs particular operations, then the term *kelim* denotes those instruments by means of which certain things are accomplished.

This interpretation, which is admittedly tentative as far as texts of *Bahir* are concerned, was expanded by the subsequent Kabbalists. According to R. 'Ezra of Gerona, the emergence of the Sefirot into existence from their hiddenness in the "darkness" or "nought" is tantamount to the formation of "attributes and instruments which are finite and can be apprehended."[242] His contemporary, R. Asher ben David,[243] envisions the "six extremities"—the six Sefirot—as "instruments of the inner spirit,[244] which are its branches, its attributes, and it operates by them." This statement is similar to another statement of R. 'Ezra:[245] " 'And the heavens and the earth were finished'[246]—they became instruments[247] . . . and these are the six extremities . . . which God wished[248] to create." The identification of the Sefirot with six[249] extremities indicates that both these Kabbalists inherited a common tradition, the *Bahir.*[250]

In addition to this instrumental understanding, however, the *Bahir* alludes to a significant alternative approach; immediately following paragraph 158, this book adduces the following parable, which apparently elaborates upon the meaning of the seven days of the week:[251] "There was a king who had seven gardens, and in the middle garden a spring which wells up[252] from the source of life:[253] three [gardens] to its right, three to its left; and immediately when it performs an act or it fills up, all [the seven] are delighted, as they say, 'for our needs is it filled.' " Here, the instrumental value of the days recurs; however, the seven days are also, implicitly, envisioned as vessels that are to receive the influx of the spring.

This perception was expanded on by R. Asher ben David; in a lengthy elaboration of the preceding views of the *Bahir,* without alluding to his source, he wrote:

> Every operation performed by the median line, which is the attribute of mercy, operates by the inner force which acts in it . . . and it is as a vessel to the spirit . . . and the prophet is in its image, a vessel to the divine spirit which is in him when the speech is with him, even despite his will. . . . The spirit speaks in him and the prophet is as its vessel, how much more so that this median line which is a vessel to the inner spirit which breaks out in it.[254]

The divinely inspired prophet, as one who is both a vessel and an instrument for the divine, thus becomes an interesting metaphor for the operation of the spirit or force in the seven Sefirot.[255] He not only contains the divine spirit but acts through its influence. Thus, we see that the two meanings of *keli* converge: a Sefirah of the lower seven Sefirot receives the divine influx as a vessel but thereby also becomes an instrument. According to R. 'Ezra,[256] again following bahiric motifs,[257] the human body reveals the activity of the soul, thereby serving as its instrument;[258] the body itself is seen as a reflection of the supernal seven extremities through which the soul, presumably the higher Sefirot, operates.

The bahiric fluctuation between the views of Sefirot as vessels and as instruments was thus accepted and elaborated by R. 'Ezra and R. Asher ben David. The latter also made use of the metaphor of the lower Sefirot as a cluster of fruit that contains the juice—that is, the higher influx—in order to clarify his view on the nature of the Sefirot;[259] interestingly, the identical metaphor is used also by R. 'Ezra.[260]

From the above discussions, we learn that the realm of instrumentality is limited to the lower seven Sefirot,[261] a limitation probably connected to the role played by these Sefirot in the Creation of the world,[262] with which the highest three Sefirot were not generally associated.[263] This restriction holds true only for the inceptive stage of Kabbalah;[264] later on, the instrumental nature of the seven Sefirot was expanded to include the entire sefirotic pleroma, as we see in the works of R. Menaḥem Recanati or the anonymous author of *Tikkuney Zohar* and *Ra'ya Meheimna*.

At this point in my survey of the earlier stages of the concepts of Sefirot, I would like to discuss briefly the Kabbalistic circles that adopted the various concepts. The essentialist view was the dominant one in Naḥmanides' Kabbalistic school and, later on, in the *'Iyyun* circle; the instrumental one prevailed in Geronese Kabbalah as represented by R. 'Ezra and in that of Provence as reflected in the writings of R. Asher ben David. We can therefore understand the emergence of these theosophical understandings of the Sefirot as representing two Kabbalistic traditions, one continued by Naḥmanides, the other stemming from the *Bahir*, by R. 'Ezra and R. Asher. Such a picture of the situation in the theosophy of early Kabbalah demonstrates the existence of diverging traditions concerning such basic issues as the nature of the Sefirot. Of particular importance is the conclusion that there could be such significant conceptual differences among the Catalan Kabbalists, who are usually considered to be one group.[265]

An interesting counterpart to these two understandings of the Sefirot appears in the philosophical discussions on the nature of divine attributes. This similarity had been noticed by R. Elijah ben Eliezer of Candia, who notes in his commentary on the *Bahir*: "those who say that the Sefirot are attributes of God follow the path of the Muslim thinkers believing in attributes; however, while the Muslims content themselves with three [attributes]—wisdom, power, and will—these [the Kabbalists] do with more than that."[266] According to Profiat Duran, "the intention of the Kabbalists in this matter is the same as that of the philosophers concerning the attributes."[267] Duran says that the Kabbalists view the Sefirot as relational attributes, revealing our understanding of God's activities in the world, rather than as essential attributes, that is, actual differentiation in Godhead, reminiscent of the erroneous Christian view of the Trinity.[268] These perceptive remarks by Jewish philosophers were, however, preceded by R. Menaḥem Recanati's critique of the essentialist conception of the Sefirot as corresponding to Maimonides' view of the attributes.[269]

The interrelationship between the differing philosophical views on the attributes and the Kabbalistic perceptions of the Sefirot is only one aspect of the possible influence of philosophy on Kabbalah. The medieval theory of "separate intellects," widespread in Arabic and Jewish neo-Aristotelianism, finds its counterpart in the conception of the Sefirot as separate intellects found in the writings of R. Abraham Abulafia,[270] R. Moses Narboni,[271] R. Joseph Albo,[272] and R. Abraham Shalom,[273] to mention only a few famous names.

The Neoplatonic conception of intradeical ideas likewise had repercussions on a long series of Jewish thinkers, mostly Italian or living in Italy.[274] The earliest evidence for this is apparently R. Yehudah Romano's statement that according to some Jewish scholars the *idei* are alluded to by the term *Sefirot*.[275] R. Isaac Abravanel maintains that the Kabbalists "said that the Sefirot are not created but are emanated, and that all of them unite together in him, blessed be his name, for they are the figurations of his lovingkindness and his willing what he created. In truth, Plato set down the knowledge of the separate general forms."[276] This view was later shared by R. David Messer Leon,[277] R. Yeḥiel Nissim of Pisa,[278] R. 'Azariah de Rossi,[279] and especially R. Abraham Yagel.[280]

These two philosophical interpretations of the Sefirot represent a more speculative formulation of the already existing distinction of the Kabbalists themselves between the instrumental and essentialist functions of the Sefirot; by accepting philosophical terms and concepts, these authors considerably attenuated the dynamic nature of these entities, a matter facilitating the acceptance of Kabbalah among both Jewish thinkers and Christian intellectuals.

3. Sefirot qua Modes of Divine Immanence

In *Sefer Yeẓirah,* the Sefirot are already related, inter alia, to the world; for an Ashkenazic Ḥasidic figure, R. Eleazar of Worms, the Sefirot, referred to as *havvayot*—"essences"—are the infinite presence of God in the world:[281]

> When you think in your heart on the creator of the world, how his presence is[282] above in an infinite way and so also front and back, east and west, north and south, up and down, [he is present] in an infinite way in every place. . . . and be aware that he created everything, and there is nothing outside him, and he is in everything and rules over everything.

Although R. Eleazar does not explicitly mention here the Sefirot, a comparison of the description of the *havvayot* to that of the Sefirot in *Sefer Yeẓirah* conclusively demonstrates that this author is dealing with an "immanentistic" perception of the Sefirot;[283] far from being a "merely" theological conception, R. Eleazar's view of the Sefirot is integrated in his perception of prayer. During the recitation of the *Shema' Yisrael*, the Ḥasid is to contemplate the infinities of the ten Sefirot in the world and thence the unity of God.[284]

This conception of the Sefirot, differing from both the conceptions of them as essence and as instruments, remained at the periphery of theosophical Kabbalah, although it influenced some texts of ecstatic Kabbalah. According to an early Kabbalist, R. Barzilai:[285] "The world and all the creatures were created by means of the ten *ma'amarot*, and they are [immanent] in everything like the juice in the bundle of grapes,[286] and they are the ten Sefirot, linked to each other." According to R. Isaac ibn Latif, the verbs *hayah, hoveh ve-yihyeh* are alluded to in the Tetragrammaton and "they depict the structure of the world and its existence and its size and its ten Sefirot."[287] In another passage, ibn Latif affirms that "the ten Sefirot . . . are the size of the world"[288] and that "the ten Sefirot comprise the ten degrees which are the constitution of the world and its form and its size."[289] And according to an anonymous commentator, "the universal powers which are [immanent] in the entire reality are the ten Sefirot."[290]

This commentary, written under the influence of Abraham Abulafia, should be compared with another Abulafian work, the anonymous *Sefer Ner 'Elohim*,[291] which presents a rather pantheistic theory combined with an immanentistic perception of the Sefirot: "God is in the entire world and within the world and outside the world in an infinite mode, and he rules the whole [world] and in him is it maintained."[292] This immanence is to be understood as the result of the identity of the emanations, or Sefirot, and their source: "God is [identical to] them, and they are he, but God emanated their forces on the created things and put them within."[293]

In contrast to the theosophical speculations on the preexistence of the roots of the Sefirot, this Kabbalist explicitly indicates:[294]

> His attributes are influxes and emanations and spiritual entities which arose with the existence of the world, and they emerged. That is to say, not that they were qualities inherent in him *in potentia* and [then] passed *in actu* when the world appeared *in actu;* but he himself emanated them with the world, since they are things necessary for the world. . . . And they are ten attributes and they are divided in space, time, and soul [literally, "world, year, and soul"].[295]

I would like to emphasize the significance of the pantheistic formulations accompanying the concept of Sefirot qua immanent powers. In both ibn Latif and ecstatic Kabbalah, the formula "he is in all, and all is in him" recurs several times; in ibn Latif, it occurs in relation to the divine will,[296] whereas in

Abulafia,[297] early Gikatilla,[298] and the author of *Ner 'Elohim,*[299] it refers to God himself.

The paucity of discussions on the immanent nature of the Sefirot is to be understood against the background of a major development in Kabbalistic theosophy: whereas the earlier Kabbalists construed relatively simple hierarchies that included one or two layers of ten Sefirot, a more elaborate structure of Sefirot became dominant in the second half of the the thirteenth century. In the writings of R. Isaac ben Jacob ha-Cohen, we learn of a system of thirty Sefirot, and his brother even alludes to forty "emanations"; in the writings of R. Isaac of Acre, a system of four worlds—each incorporating ten Sefirot—was well established. Thus, the idea of the immanence of the Sefirot was transmuted through the concept of the existence of a lower set of ten Sefirot, forming the "world of making"—*'Olam ha-'Asiyah*—which is either identical with or directly connected with our world.

4. Sefirot in Man

As we have seen, Ashkenazic theologians elaborated upon the divine immanence in the world through the ten Sefirot or *havvayot*; the *Bahir* and later theosophical systems emphasized the relationship between the Sefirot as essence or instruments and the Sefirot as the higher level of divinity. Modern scholarship seems to have neglected another, ancient view, claiming the presence of ten things in man. As we have seen, this may relate to a Jewish tradition, evidenced by Gnostic sources, in which the cosmic anthropos is also a decad. At the beginning of Spanish Kabbalah, R. 'Ezra was already referring to the ten Sefirot within lower man; however, this reference is no more than a reflection of the higher decad, whose divine or cosmic character is obvious. Thus, I will discuss briefly the understanding of the Sefirot as psychological processes or human qualities.

The psychological understanding of the Sefirot occurs in an explicit way in ecstatic Kabbalah[300] and, later on, in Ḥasidism; this phenomenon is probably related to their shared intense interest in extreme forms of *devekut*. When a certain mystical system focuses on inner experiences more than on theurgical activity, the entities to be activated are no longer the objectively existing divine Sefirot but rather the human spiritual Sefirot.

A distinction is drawn in Abulafia's *Sitrey Torah*[301] between the "ten matters" that are the "existence of his body taken from the lower [entities]" and the "ten entities belonging to his soul, [taken] from the higher [entities]," since "by means of ten *ma'amarot* was the world created, and see [how] the body and the soul were engraved by yod."[302] Furthermore, Abulafia also mentions the secret of "the soul which comprises ten supernal *havvayot* from the celestial ones."[303] The precise significance of the ten *havvayot* in this work is not clear; they are apparently uncreated suprasefirotic concepts.[304] Several years after the composition of *Sitrey Torah,* Abulafia wrote in his epistle "Ve-Zot li-Yihudah,"[305] that man is "the last compound[306] which comprises all the Sefirot, and whose intellect is the active intellect,[307] and when you shall unknot its knots,[308] you will find a unique union with it [that is, the active intellect] and even the first emanation, which is the thought." Thus, the fact that man comprises ten Sefirot is understood as related to the possibility of reaching mystical union, by liberating the spiritual Sefirot or powers from their material links, enabling them to ascend to the spiritual and receive a spiritual blessing from there.[309] The mention of the "first emanation, which is the thought" is to be understood allegorically, not theosophically, as we learn from another important discussion occurring in the same epistle:[310]

> The masters of the Sefirot call them by names and say that the name of the first Sefirah is "thought," and they add another name, in order to explain its meaning, which they call *Keter 'Eliyon*, since the crown is something lying on the heads of kings. . . . and the [master of Sefirot] will add another name and will call it "primeval air"[311] . . . and so will he do to each and every Sefirah of the ten Sefirot *Belimah*.[312] But the masters of the [divine] names have [quite] another intention, completely superior to that;[313] this path of names is of such a profundity[314] that in the profundities of human thought there is no one more profound and more excellent than it, and it alone unites human thought with the divine [thought][315] to the extent of the human capability and according to human nature. And it is known that human thought is the cause of his wisdom, and his wisdom is the cause of his understanding, and his understanding is the cause of his mercy, and his mercy is the cause of his reverence of his Creator; and his fear[316] is the cause of his beauty, and his beauty is the cause of his victory,[317] and his victory is the reason for his splendor, and his splendor is the cause of his essence,[318] which is named bridegroom,[319] and his essence is the cause of his kingship, named his[320] bride.

Abulafia therefore reinterprets the theosophical hierarchy, which is basically hypostatic, to refer to a hierarchy of human actions, partly psychological, partly corporeal. I wish to emphasize that this scheme is proposed as a superior understanding of the Sefirot, and Abulafia sees as its aim a mystical union rather than theurgical operation or even theosophical gnosis. In Abulafia's text, it is depicted as a translation of the divine thought—which comes into contact with human thought—into physical and external activity into which the recondite human thought "descends," on into wisdom and understanding, then to a rather external quality—mercy—and thence gradually to more corporeal aspects of man. The last two Sefirot, which have obvious sexual valences, are to be understood not on the theosophical level, on which they point to intradivine relations, but as alluding to the relationship between man and God, or between bride and bridegroom.[321]

In his *Mafteaḥ ha-Sefirot,* Abulafia again interprets the entire sefirotic realm as referring to human activities:[322]

> The influx expanding from the one who counts[323] is comprised in and passes through *'a*[leph] to *y*[od], from the first sefirot to the tenth, that is, from "thought" to "justice," and [only] through them will human thought be right.[324] That is, wisdom will emerge from thought, and understanding will emerge from the wise thought; and from the thought of wisdom and understanding, greatness,[325] which is the attribute of *Ḥesed*, [will emerge], and those who think on them will become great; and out of all of them *Gevurah* [will emerge], and the power of the thinker will increase, since he thinks that he is the counter of the Sefirot.[326] And from them truth will emerge, and immediately beauty[327] forcefully reveals[328] itself and causes the person attaining it to be proud of it and of prophecy, according to truth. However, prophecy [comprises] degrees of comprehension, and thus, whoever comprehends the truth is similar to Jacob, our ancestor, as it is written: "thou wilt show truth to Jacob."[329] . . . And the nature of victory necessarily emerges from truth, and whoever knows the truth, can subdue even the structure of planets and stars,[330] and then he will be blessed through the name *'El Shaddai,* and victory will produce from itself splendor, as in the verse: "And thou shalt put some of thy splendor upon him"[331] . . . and the ninth Sefirah . . . is called by the name *kol neshamah yesod be-Yah*[332] . . . and it is the source of influx and blessing . . . and the tenth Sefirah which is the *Shekhinah*, whose name is justice . . . . and from this issue hinted in the Sefirot—according to [someone's] comprehension of them, and according to the force someone received from them, which depends upon the knowledge of the true names—the power of one prophet will surpass and become greater than the power of another prophet.

The understanding of the true divine names is the source of higher experiences, conceived of as degrees of prophecy. Nevertheless, the Sefirot themselves are interpreted as human processes.

According to another passage from Abulafia, the interest in the Sefirot is viewed as aiming the *devekut* toward them, the Sefirot. In an epistle, he asserts:[333]

> Man can cleave to each and every Sefirah by the essence[334] of the influx expanding from its emanation on his Sefirot,[335] which are his attributes.[336] . . . And it is necessary to mentally concentrate[337] [in order to attain] an apprehension, until the expert Kabbalist will attain from them an influx of which he is aware.[338] This is so,

given the fact that the written letters are like bodies, and the pronounced letters are spiritual [by nature] and the mental [letters] are intellectual[339] and the emanated [letters] are divine.[340] . . . and out of [his] concentration[341] [intended] to prepare the power of the bride to receive the influx from the power of the bridegroom, the divine [letters] will move the intellectual ones—because of the sustained concentration and its greatness and power, and the great desire [of the Kabbalist] and his forcible longing and his mighty infatuation to attain the *devekut* and the kiss[342]—as well as the power of the bride;[343] and her name and her essence,[344] will be positively known[345] and preserved for eternity, since they were found righteous, and the separated [entities] were united[346] and the united ones were separated[347] and the reality is transformed,[348] and as a consequence, every branch will return to its root and will be united with it[349] and all spiritual [entities] [will return] to [their] essence[350] and will be linked to it, "and the Tabernacle will become one,"[351] "and[352] the Tetragrammaton[353] will be the king of the entire world, and in that day, the Tetragrammaton will be one and his name one," . . . if he will do so to the order of the Sefirot and the structure of twenty-two letters, "and join them one to the other to make one stick, and they shall become one in thy hand."[354]

For Abulafia, mystical union is to be attained by the ten Sefirot or attributes intrinsic in human nature, whereby he is able to collect or to capture the emanation flowing from the supernal Sefirot. Abulafia does not elaborate on the nature of these Sefirot, but only on the means or technique by which the Kabbalists, using combinations, pronunciations, and meditations on letters, can capture the emanations or divine letters. The above passage is an illuminating example of the Hermetic conception whereby union is attained by causing spirituality to descend upon the mystic, rather than his ascending to the divine.[355] Before leaving Abulafia's reinterpretation of the theosophical scheme, it is pertinent to take note of a similar phenomenon relating to his understanding of the two angels Metatron and Samael as two drives or inclinations inherent in human nature.[356]

This shift in focus from the theosophical to the human experience, from the Sefirot as divine to the Sefirot in man, had important implications for the subsequent evolution of Jewish mysticism. What is novel and important in Abulafia is not his assumption of the existence of ten Sefirot in the human soul but his understanding of the names of the Sefirot, according to theosophical nomenclature, as processes taking place within man.[357] This dehypostatization of the theosophical hierarchy was achieved by the emphasis upon the superiority of the human interpretation of the nature of the Sefirot.

Abulafia's emphasis upon the importance of the ten Sefirot in the soul influenced Spanish Kabbalah only slightly; his student, the anonymous author of *Sefer Ner 'Elohim* reflects some psychological views of the higher Sefirot as found in Abulafia.[358] But more important than the short reference in *Ner 'Elohim* are certain passages in R. Joseph ben Shalom Ashkenazi's *Commentary on Sefer Yeẓirah,* a widely read classic of Kabbalistic literature. He compares the soul and her spiritual faculties to the ten Sefirot without, however, stressing the centrality of spiritual powers for the attainment of mystical experiences.[359] In contrast to Abulafia, who was not interested in the theosophical conception of the Sefirot, R. Joseph elaborated upon this issue more than did any preceding Kabbalist. Similar comparisons of the Sefirot and the process of emanations to the soul and her powers appeared in the Renaissance period, again without the ecstatic or unitive implications so characteristic of Abulafia.[360] The ascent of Lurianic Kabbalah, with its emphasis on theosophy, only contributed to the suppression of the psychologistic understanding of the Sefirot or divine configurations (*parẓufim*); the same seems to have been true also of Sabbatian theosophy.[361]

It remained for Ḥasidic mysticism to reinterpret the zoharic and Lurianic theosophical systems as referring to psychological processes. This reinterpretation is part of a more comprehensive change of attitude to Lurianism, parts of which, like Lurianic *kavvanot*, became problematic and were sometimes even explicitly rejected.[362] Like Abulafia, the early Ḥasidic masters emphasized the importance of unitive and ecstatic phenomena and also envisaged the previous theosophies as allegories of human spiritual powers and processes.[363] Two changes Ḥasidism made from the dominant Lurianic theosophy—the emphasis on *devekut* and a different view of the Sefirot and *parẓufim*—parallel Abulafia's mysticism, as described above. On this basis, we can assume, directly or indirectly,[364] the influence of his Kabbalah on this turn within Jewish mysticism.[365]

The details of Ḥasidic reinterpretation appear in two types of sources: those of the Ḥasidim themselves and the critiques of their opponents. Let us begin with the former. R. Jacob Joseph of Polonnoye reports in the name of R. Israel Ba'al Shem Tov:[366] "There are ten Sefirot in man, who is called microcosmos, since the thought is named *Abba*,[367] and after the *Ẓimzum* [contraction] was named *Imma,* and so on, down to faith, which is called 'two loins of truth'[368] and delight[369] in worship of God is named *Yesod*, *Ẓaddik*, and Sign of the Covenant, and so on." Although this quotation is fragmentary, it is nevertheless obvious that the founder of Ḥasidism interpreted the entire sefirotic scheme as referring to mystical states on the human level. Like the Sufic *makamat,* the sefirotic entities stood for a sequence of experiences.

It is worthwhile comparing this reinterpretation of the Sefirot *Yesod* as "delight" resulting from the mystical worship with a passage from Abulafia. In his commentary on the *Guide of the Perplexed, Ḥayye ha-Nefesh,*[370] he writes that "the *devekut* of the whole intellect, in actu, is the secret[371] of the delight of bridegroom and bride. Abulafia reinterprets the sexual connection, viewed in the theosophical Kabbalah in connection with two Sefirot, also symbolized by bride and bridegroom, as pertaining to the human-divine relationship.[372] The similarity between the views of the medieval Kabbalist and the eighteenth-century Ḥasidic master is interesting from the phenomenological point of view: precisely the same term, *ta'anug,* is used to reinterpret mystically the theosophical conception of sexual intercourse in the sefirotic pleroma.

The most important follower of the Besht, the Great Maggid, continued his views:

> Once the rabbi admonished someone because he was discussing Kabbalah in public. That person answered him: "Why do you discuss Kabbalah in public, too?" He [the Great Maggid] answered him: "I teach the world to understand that everything written in *Sefer 'Eẓ Ḥayyim* also exists in this world and in man. However, I do not explain the spiritual matters of *Sefer 'Eẓ Ḥayyim;* but you discuss everything which is written in *'Eẓ Ḥayyim* literally, and thus you transform the spiritual into corporeal; but the sublime spiritual world is [indeed] ineffable.[373]

Like his master, R. Dov Baer did not deny the existence of the complex Lurianic theosophy, but was primarily interested in its immanence in this world and in man.

The Ḥasidic masters were reticent about the relationship between the supernal entities and the phenomena inherent in the human experiences or in the world. Insofar as their written works reflect their esoteric thought, none of them would deny the objective existence of a transcendental theosophical structure. At least two sources, however, independently attribute to Ḥasidism far more extreme stands in which the existence of an independent theosophy is explicitly rejected. Since these sources were written by anti-Ḥasidic authors, a certain caution is in order, although the fact that they corroborate each other seems to point to the general reliability of their testimony. The earlier and more important discussion appears in R. David of Makkov's *Shever Posh'im*:[374]

> They [the Ḥasidim] assert that, since all the worlds and whatever is [found] in them, Sefirot or *Parẓufim* are comprised in man,[375] then all the inner secrets which were orally passed down to us from our holy ancestors going back to Moses at Sinai, and their holy books which reached us, such as the book of *Zohar* and the *Tikkunim* and the *Bahir,* and others like them, the last [of them] but not least being R. Isaac Luria and his fine writings—as he explained to us all the secrets of the configura-

> tions of the supernal and holy worlds which are called *'Attik*,[376] *'Arokh*,[377] *Ze'ir 'Anpin*[378] Ya'akov[379] and Raḥel and Leah[380]—all these do not mean what they seem prima facie, but they all—God forbid—are the attribute of man and his powers,[381] inherent in him, and no more. And that it is not true that there are configurations in the supernal worlds, but the configuration of Raḥel—God forbid—is the human attribute of love, and thus Jacob loved Raḥel, and the configuration of Leah is the human attribute of fear . . . and the configuration of Jacob—God forbid—is the human attribute of Tiferet, and so on for all the other configurations. And the Sefirot mentioned in the *Zohar* do not mean what they seem to be prima facie, and according to the explanation passed down to us from the ancients, but everything is—as their hearts imagine—the attribute of man and his powers. . . . And so of every matter and secret written in a famous book,[382] they change its significance and transform into the attribute of man.

Thus, the entire zoharic and Lurianic superstructure is viewed, not only as comprised in man—as we find as far back as the ancient texts analyzed above—but, according to R. David's testimony, *only* in man. According to the Ḥasidic sources I am familiar with, Kabbalah is preeminently a paradigm of the human psyche and man's activities rather than a theosophical system.[383] Perceptively, this opponent of Ḥasidism compares it to the philosophical "heresy" in the time of R. Solomon ben Abraham ibn Adret.[384] There, as in his own time, psychological interpretations of the biblical text were the focus of a fierce controversy.[385] But whereas the thirteenth-century Jewish philosophers reinterpreted the biblical stories, their contemporary Abraham Abulafia reinterpreted both the biblical stories and the theosophical Kabbalah.[386] I do not imply that R. David had Abulafia in mind when he compared Ḥasidism to philosophical allegory; however, Abulafia's views are closer to those of the Ḥasidim, because he himself was a mystic who amply employed psychological allegories. It is pertinent to compare this reinterpretation of theosophical systems to a similar phenomenon discussed above: these systems were viewed as pointing to a mystical goal that is absent or marginal in them—*devekut*.[387] Again, a pivotal approach shared also by Abulafian Kabbalah served early Ḥasidic masters for building their own unique religious system.

Let us turn to the evidence of R. Pinḥas Elijah Horowitz, the author of *Sefer ha-Berit*:[388]

> There are [persons] who are not interested in secrets, and say that everything written in the account of Creation and in the account of *Merkavah*, in the *Zohar* and in the writings of R. Isaac Luria, and in those of the ancients, that all these are parables and metaphors for the powers found in man; the configurations of Leah and Raḥel are the power of fear and the power of love found in man, and the configuration of

> *Ze'ir 'Anpin* is the power of the attributes [!] of boasting[389] [found] in man, and so all of them. [Therefore], examine[390] them [the powers] and study them, since they are the account of Creation and the account of chariot, and everything found in the words of the ancients concerning the secrets of the chariot and the embodiment of the configurations and the secrets of letters, everything is an outer garment, and a parable and a metaphor for these matters. Hence, we are no longer dealing with parables and metaphors, but with their meaning and their inner sense, and this is the Torah of man, and therefore, everyone will deal with them according to his intellect.

Although R. Pinḥas does not explicitly mention Ḥasidim, it is obvious that it is their views being presented—and attacked—here. A comparison with the passage quoted above from R. David of Makkov does not reveal any textual affinity, so that I assume that the author of *Sefer ha-Berit* had independent sources for his exposition of the psychologization of Kabbalah. He also views the reinterpretation of the classical texts of Jewish mysticism as an allegory and, aptly enough, considers it as a free and rational understanding of these texts. Like R. David, he is insufficiently aware of the mystical mood of Ḥasidic hermeneutics.[391] Although R. Pinḥas was both a student of Abulafia's works and an admirer of Vital's *Sha'arey Kedushah*,[392] both of which are congenial to Ḥasidism, he never notes any affinities between these related phenomena.

V. THEOSOPHY AND PANTHEISM

Kabbalistic theosophy enabled Jewish mystics to envision all things in God. On the one hand seen as the archetypes of created things, the Sefirot were especially envisaged in their dynamics as the origin of significant processes taking place in the mundane world. The role of theosophical mysticism was accordingly to comprehend the higher entities and their interrelationship by performing the ritual in an intentional way, allowing the mystic to transcend the mundane and experience the Divine. The nexus between these two levels may be described as a gamut beginning with reflection of the Divine on the material level and ending with the emanational explanation, in which the material world is conceived as the lowest extension of a supermundane force. In the majority of theosophical systems, the transition from one plan to another may be expressed as a process of ascent; the Kabbalist follows the traces of the Divine and, decoding the symbolic cipher, recognizes the archetypes or the ongoing processes, and/or eventually experiences them.[393] The dominant pattern is viewed as existing not only beyond but also above the material realm. In other words, Kabbalistic theosophy emphasizes the transcendence of the main conceptual issues in which it was interested and the main way to transcend the gap between man and the Divine as the Kabbalistic ritual.[394]

The path of immanence only rarely occurred in theosophical Kabbalah; pantheistic views are indeed presented in the works of R. Moses de Leon, R. Joseph of Hamadan, R. Joseph ben Shalom Ashkenazi, and later on R. Moses Cordovero,[395] but even these Kabbalists would unequivocally acknowledge the existence of a transcendent layer of the Divine. For these and for similar authors, the pantheistic or panentheistic ideas were the ultimate consequences of their emanational systems: extreme substantialist interpretations of emanation could, and actually did, lead to a variety of pantheistic views. It must be emphasized, however, that these pantheistic ideas had only marginal repercussions on their perception of Jewish ritual. We can summarize the stand of theosophical Kabbalah as a *visio rerum omnium in Deo.* On the other hand, the ecstatic Kabbalah was interested in a *visio Dei in omnibus rebus,*[396] a tendency later shared by Ḥasidic mysticim:[397] the pantheistic trends of these Jewish mystical schools were part of their emphasis on a common goal—*devekut.*

VI. THEOSOPHY AND HISTORY

The emergence of a theosophical hierarchy and, even more, its move to the center of religious interest represent a major restructuring of Jewish thought in Kabbalistic circles. The two major axes influential in classical Jewish sources, the historical and the halakhic, were modulated so as to conform to the theosophical axis. The historical axis, dominant in biblical theology, stretches from the *Urzeit* to the *Endzeit;* the realization of the divine plan is taking place on the theater of history with the Jewish people as the main actor. In later texts, such as the Hebrew apocalypses composed after the gaonic period, the pressures of history were felt in a dramatic way, reflected in the awesome description of the catastrophic eschaton. This catastrophic element was attenuated and even effaced in the philosophical sources, which tended to emphasize the political and speculative aspect of the messianic era more than the conflagration of wars that were to precede it; it would seem that the philosophers were more interested in the processes causing individual salvation than in those taking place on the cosmic scene. In Neoplatonically oriented thinkers such as Solomon ibn Gabirol or Abraham bar Ḥiyya, the individual attained his salvation by the redemptive effect of his flight from the corporeal and his cleaving to the spiritual. The Aristotelian philosophers were more inclined to envisage redemption as the perfect noetic process, described by means of the medieval perception of human and cosmic intellects.[398]

The interest in the unfolding of history lost its primary role in those Jewish philosophical theologies that were influenced by Mutazilite theologians, Neoplatonism, or Aristotelianism. The Kabbalists were relatively more perceptive of the ancient emphasis on history, although it did not return to its previous importance. The horizontal sequel of events that constituted history was subordinated by the Kabbalists to the vertical axis of divine powers; for them, history was an aspect of the revelation of recondite divine processes on the horizontal axis. Creation corresponded to the first emanation in the sefirotic level; redemption was the enactment of the influence of the last Sefirah. The ancient phrase *'ikveta de-Meshiḥa*—the footsteps of the Messiah—was reinterpreted as meaning the heels of the Messiah, a symbol of the lowest point of the divine anthropos.[399] History, like the Bible, consisted of different manifestations of the basic hidden pattern—the theosophical one—embodied on varied levels that could be perceived by penetrating the veil of history or the plain meaning of the text. But there were few, if any, practical applications of this symbolic conception of history to a detailed interpretation of specific historical events.

Kabbalah preferred an understanding of cosmic processes to that of historical ones.[400] The theosophical axis was understood as the paradigm of the cosmic cycles of seven thousands—the *shemitah*—or forty-nine thousand years—the *yovel*.[401] Each of the seven lower Sefirot was regarded as appointed upon one *shemitah*, thereby embuing both the nature of the creation and the type of processes going on in this peculiar period with its own characteristic.[402] A survey of the human arena convinced most of the Kabbalists that the Sefirah presiding over our own historical cycle is that of *Gevurah*—strict judgment—a pessimistic assessment allowing little space for a dramatic change in the nature of the human situation.[403]

CHAPTER 7

Ancient Jewish Theurgy

I. MYTH AND RABBINISM

In his essay on Kabbalistic ritual, Gershom Scholem emphatically asserts that "the Kabbalists strove from the very first to *anchor the ritual of rabbinical Judaism in myth by means of a mystical practice.*"[1] Two implicit assumptions underlie this far-reaching statement: (1) that "the ritual of rabbinical Judaism" was free of myth and mysticism, which were infused into it by the Kabbalists; and (2) that the Kabbalah emerged from a non-rabbinical, presumably mythico-mystical Judaism that needed to come to terms with rabbinical Judaism. Kabbalah, and its understanding of the ritual, is, according to Scholem, an intrusion of alien elements into the domain of rabbinism, which had until then succeeded in liberating itself from mythical or mystical elements.[2] The assumption that the ritual, as well as the halakhah, are primarily nonmythical therefore enables Scholem to surmise that a tension exists between the mythically minded Jewish mystic and the "world with which he strives with all his zeal to be at peace."[3] Since the Kabbalists "inherited" *mythologoumena* from the Gnostics, Kabbalah represents "a revenge of the myth upon its conqueror."[4]

Scholem was correct in emphasizing the strengthening of mythical elements in Kabbalah, but his assumption that myth was conquered by rabbinic Judaism, which led to a tension between Kabbalah and rabbinism, remains to be proven. From my perspective, Scholem created a simplistic division between a defeated mythical Gnosticism and a triumphant nonmythical rabbinism. If ancient Judaism did not construe elaborate metaphysical theosophies and myths as did the Gnostics, Jews nevertheless preserved these elements in their perception of the commandments. As we have seen in the preceding chapter, traces of ancient Jewish theosophies, which presumably anticipated Gnosticism are evident even from "innocent" rabbinic statements concerning the ten *ma'amarot*.[5]

I should like to elaborate here upon the existence of some correlations between these remnants of theosophy or mythical thought and the concepts of the nature of the commandments. If this approach is correct, then there is no particular tension between Kabbalah and *halakhah* that need be emphasized; rather, one can propose an alternative picture according to which the need to understand the ultimate meaning of the central Jewish activity—the commandments—moved the Kabbalists to elaborate upon and reconstruct the implicit myths or theosophies that had once motivated and offered an organic significance to the commandments.[6] In other words, there is no need to divorce *halakhah* from myth in a fundamental way[7] nor to presuppose basic tensions between them.[8] Kabbalistic myth is the result of a tenuous endeavor to explain the rationales of the commandments in accordance with material extant in the recorded Jewish tradition—Talmud and Midrash—along with ancient, non-Gnostic speculative traditions passed down orally or in lost works. Therefore, an interdependence between theosophy and myth, on the one hand, and the theory of the commandments, on the other, are major factors in this construction or reconstruction of speculative superstructures.[9] Kabbalistic theosophy and myth are by and large patterns aimed at the explanation of the esoteric values of the commandments. In the following pages, an attempt will be made to elaborate upon this assessment.

Crucial for my point is the emphasis upon the theurgical nature of the commandments, as against other significant ancient rabbinic tendencies that were indifferent to, or even opposed, this evaluation of the performance of the commandments. The term *theurgy,* or *theurgical,* will be used below to refer to operations intended to influence the Divinity, mostly in its own inner state or dynamics, but sometimes also in its relationship to man. In contrast to the magician, the ancient and medieval Jewish theurgian focused his activity on accepted religious values.[10] My definition accordingly distinguishes between theurgy and magic far more than do the usual definitions.[11] The existence of theurgical trends in classical Jewish texts requires a considerable modification of Scholem's evaluation of rabbinism in general and of the emergence of Kabbalah in particular.

II. AUGMENTATION THEURGY

The theology of the *Shi'ur Komah* is grounded in the biblical description of God as "great"—*gadol*[12]—an attribute that often occurs together with his description as "mighty"—*gibbor* or *rav-koaḥ*.[13] The talmudic-midrashic literature adopted this *epitheton* as an essential attribute and changed it into a name for God: *Gevurah*, that is, *Dynamis*.[14] But whereas the *Heikhalot* literature emphasized his greatness, providing precise statistics concerning the size of the divine limbs, the talmudic-midrashic texts elaborated upon the conception of God as power. The former envisions an enormous, static Divinity, the knowledge and repetition of whose precise dimensions constitute a salvific gnosis—hence, the implicit static feature of this theology: were the sizes to change, the importance of this knowledge would diminish. The latter literature is primarily interested in a dynamic concept that stresses the changes occurring in the divine *Dynamis*. Thus, whereas the *Shi'ur Komah* gnosis is imposed on the mystic as a revelation from above, the talmudic-midrashic tradition is primarily interested in an active attitude of man, who is portrayed as the clue to the amount of divine energy. In the following pages, I will discuss this interrelationship between human acts and divine *Dynamis* as a key concept of rabbinic literature, and its repercussions on Kabbalistic theurgy.[15]

According to *Pesikta de-Rav Kahana:*[16]

> "Yet the righteous holds on his ways, and he that has clean hands adds strength."[17]—This [speaks of] Moses, of whom it is written: "he made the justice of the Lord."[18]—"He that . . . adds strength" is Moses, who causes increase of the power of the *Dynamis*, as it is written: "And now, I pray thee, let the power of my Lord be great."[19] . . . [20] R. 'Azariah [said] in the name of R. Yehudah bar Simon, so long as the righteous act according to the will of heaven, they add power to the *Dynamis*, as it is written: "And now, I pray thee, let the power of my Lord be great." And if they do not act [accordingly], it is as if: "you have weakened [the power of] the Rock that formed thee."[21] R. Yehudah bar Simon [said] in the name of R. Levi ben Parta: so long as Israel acts according to the will of heaven, they add power to the *Dynamis*, as it is written:[22] "In God we shall make[23] power," and if not, so to say,[24] "and they are gone without strength before the pursuer."[25]

I will discuss this passage in some detail. It includes an explicit hierarchy of subjects: Moses, the righteous, and Israel in general. This fact may reflect various approaches, beginning with a concept limiting human influence on high to an elite and ending with the assumption that the entire people of Israel is able to participate in this theurgy. The rabbinical authorities who advanced this view adduced various different *loci probantes* in proof, a fact that evinces the existence of a concept that was imposed on several biblical verses. As for the content itself: this passage assumes a direct dependence of the power of the divine *Dynamis* upon human activity; the way to increase it is to fulfill the divine will, which is presumably tantamount to performing the commandments.[26] This assumption is corroborated by a passage in *Leviticus Rabbah:*[27]

> R. Yehudah ben Simon [said] in the name of R. Levi ben Parta: It is written: "you have weakened the Rock that formed thee"[28]—you have diminished the power of the Creator. This is comparable to a potter[29] who was making the image of the king. When he had completed it, someone came and said to him: "The king was changed." Immediately the [power of the] hands of the potter diminished. He said: "Whose [image] shall I create, that of the former [king] or that of the latter?" Thus does the Holy One, blessed be he, involve himself with the formation of the embryo for forty days,[30] and at the end she [the woman] commits adultery with another [man]. Immediately, the hands of the Creator become weak and he says, "Whose [image] shall I create: that of the former [man] or of the latter?" As [it is said]: "you have weakened the Rock that formed thee"—you have diminished the power of the Creator.

The authorities mentioned here are the same as those cited in *Pesikta de-Rav Kahana;* however, this text elaborates upon a concrete act that diminishes the supernal power—adultery. It would therefore seem that the phrase attributed to R. Levi ben Parta—if Israel does not act according to the divine will—is to be understood in this case as referring to adultery—the transgression of one of the Ten Commandments. Particularly important for our discussion is the fact that, in the last quotation, the phrase "as if" or "so to say" (*kivyakhol*) does not occur, allowing a more literal interpretation of the text—sin actually diminishes the strength of the supernal *Dynamis*. Moreover, the specific way in which this happens is depicted here, so that no metaphoric interpretation will fit this passage. Sin thus counteracts divine activity, causing divine hesitation and weakness. On the other hand, the performance of the divine will is conceived of as contributing power to the *Dynamis*. In Midrash *Lamentation Rabbah,* we find:[31] "R. 'Azariah [said] in the name of R. Simeon ben Lakish: 'When [the people of] Israel[32] are worthy, it is as if they give power to the *Dynamis*, as it is said, 'In God we shall make power.'[33] But when they transgress, they, so to speak, weaken the power of the *Dynamis*, as it is written, 'and they go without strength before the pursuer.'"[34]

Again, transgression is seen as weakening the divine power, whereas worthiness, which probably derives from the performance of the commandments, adds power. The precise origin of this power is not clear in this Midrash; the verb *give* can easily be understood as putting one entity into another and not only as giving something of the giver. To formulate it otherwise: it is possible to assume that the *Dynamis* is given a power that already exists independent of the righteous or, alternatively, that this power is produced by man's actions and infused into the Divinity. The ancient Jewish sages do not elaborate upon the manner in which this augmentation of divine power takes place. Still another instance of dependence of the Divine on human acts—in this case relating to the study of Torah—is to be found in *Megillah,* where the neglect of the study of the Torah causes a weakness and "paucity" in God.[35]

Before leaving these classical Jewish sources, I will take note of the affinity between the preceding passages and the views found in the Hermetic Treatise XIII. God is labeled there as "energy of the powers" or "the power of these energies of mine." Moreover, the Gnostic text includes such sentences as: "The powers that are in me about these things, they hymn thee the universe; they perform thy will" and "For thou being willing, all things are performed." Although we do not find clear statements regarding the contribution of human energy to the divine energy in the Hermetic discussions, the nexus between the Divinity, will, and energy, on the one hand, and man, power, and performance of the divine will, on the other, is reminiscent of the Jewish theurgical views cited above. Furthermore, the end of the ascent of the human *nous* is to become one of the supernal *dynameis*, and ultimately to enter God. Implicitly, it is an addition of the human to the divine *Dynamis*.[36]

Let us analyze the repercussions of the midrashic view in R. Eleazar of Worms. In his *Commentary on Prayer,* he writes:[37] "When [the people of] Israel bless the name of his glory, his glory is augmented, as it is written: 'and thy pious ones shall bless thee. They shall speak of the glory of thy kingdom and speak of thy power.' "[38] Here the glory rather than the *Dynamis* is mentioned as the entity that is increased by human acts. As we know, in the theology of Ashkenazic Ḥasidism, the glory is usually separated from the Creator; the act of blessing therefore adds substantively to the glory, not to Divinity. The change of the *Dynamis* and glory is, however, not only part of the theology of R. Eleazar but also part of an ancient perception of *Dynamis* qua divine glory.[39] According to another text, close to that of R. Eleazar:[40]

> When [the people of] Israel bless God, then the glory becomes greater and ascends higher and higher,[41] . . . as [it is written]: "Cause the Lord to ascend."[42] Who can cause [the Lord] to ascend? The glory, that ascends according to the blessing and the praise. Therefore it is said, "and thy pious ones shall bless thee," and thereafter "they shall speak of the glory of thy kingdom and talk of thy power." . . . When they bless him, he becomes greater and larger . . . because of the blessings and praises that [the people of] Israel praise him, like as a man whose heart expands when he is praised.

These quotations indicate that the ancient theurgical conception was already alive and integrated within the peculiar theology of Ashkenazic Ḥasidic circles. At the same time, R. Abraham ben 'Azriel, another Ashkenazic author, preserved the midrashic formulation of the augmentation of the *Dynamis*, quoting versions that are not extant in the existing Midrashim.[43]

The extensive use by the Kabbalists of the theurgy of augmentation can be seen, on the basis of the above discussion, to be a continuation of authentic rabbinic traditions, well known in the circle of Ashkenazic Ḥasidim, who were in close proximity to the earliest Kabbalists. The perception of ritual as performing the details of the divine will and as aiming at a theurgical operation, is therefore organic to Jewish thought. But scholars of Kabbalah have either ignored the importance of augmentation theurgy[44] or else neglected its importance as a basic Jewish concept.[45] *Mutatis mutandis*, they have implicitly assumed the innovative nature of Kabbalistic thought, a view that was eloquently expressed by R. Yehudah Aryeh of Modena in his criticism of Kabbalah. He cited midrashic quotation, criticizing the dependence of the divinity upon human action, a dependence that was highlighted in Kabbalistic sources.[46] Louis Ginzberg, who recognized the midrashic origin of Kabbalistic theurgy, nevertheless presented Kabbalah in a moderate way.[47] According to him, pious actions influence the "course of nature" and "reinforce respectively the good or the evil powers of life" (*sic*)—life or nature, without referring to the intradivine processes. The Kabbalists themselves had no difficulty with this dependence, as it was the Archimedal point for the articulation of a full-fledged theurgical theory that interpreted the performance of the commandments as necessary for the divine welfare. I want to emphasize this point, for it is crucial for the understanding of the entire theurgico-theosophical Kabbalah: the theurgical Kabbalists did not originate the theory of augmentation but, rather, elaborated upon an already well-known conception, specifiying its details with the help of a theosophical system.

Sefer ha-Bahir had absorbed the midrashic theurgy, expressing it in a less audacious manner than did its sources. According to one parable: "A king had sons and grandsons; as long as the sons acted according to his will, he entered among them and maintained everything, sustaining all [of them] and giving them an abundance of good, that the fathers and sons might be satisfied. But when the sons do not act according to his will, he [only] sustains the needs of the 'fathers.'"[48] We find elsewhere what seems to be a complementary passage: "If the sons are not worthy, and will not do things which are just in my eyes then the channels . . . will receive water so as not to partake with their sons, since they do not act according to my will."[49]

Thus, the *Gevurah*—the *Dynamis*—is here represented collectively by the fathers, while Israel is represented by the sons. By its deeds, Israel can induce an influx in the channels that will exceed the needs of the supernal structure and will also provide the lower world with the "water." The occurrence of the phrases *'osim reẓono* or *lo 'osim reẓono* is clear evidence of the midrashic views reflected here. The *Bahir,* however, seems to represent a rather moderate type of theurgy; the parable presupposes a personalistic aspect of Divinity that "calculates" the worthiness of the sons and exacts retribution for human acts accordingly. In the Midrash, the *Dynamis* was presented as a neutral entity whose power was augmented or diminished automatically as the result of acting according to the divine will. Thus, the mechanistic system of the *Bahir,* represented by the channel motif, does not affect the possibility of interaction between human and divine personalities; it even regulates this interaction by means of the mechanistic theme. It should be stressed that the major repercussion of man's transgression does not occur in the divine realm—which receives its needs automatically—but only at the human level. Thus, the *Bahir* is less theurgic than the Midrash in the sense that it does not presuppose a diminution affecting primarily God. This "soft" theurgy, however, is surpassed by a stronger type that is far more faithful to its midrashic sources.

R. Baḥya ben Asher, in his famous *Commentary on the Torah,* writes in the vein of both the Midrash and Ashkenazic Ḥasidism:[50] "Since the Tetragrammaton is revealed by the glory, the latter receives an addition of the divine spirit.[51] . . . For this reason Israel has the capability to weaken or add strength to the supernal *Dynamis* in accordance with their deeds. As it is written: 'you have weakened [the power of] the Rock that formed thee'[52] and it is written: 'In God we shall make power.' "[53] This type of theosophy is clearly reminiscent of that of R. Eleazar of Worms: the glory is the recipient and beneficiary of the worship, whereas the higher entity remains recondite. For the Ashkenazic master, it is the Godhead, for the Kabbalist, the Tetragrammaton, that symbolizes the Sefirah of *Tiferet.* In both types of theology the locus of the change—whether augmentation or diminution—is the divine glory. Notwithstanding the extensive use by R. Baḥya of the *Bahir,* it is the midrashic formulations that emerge from his texts.

It would be worthwhile to elaborate upon the Kabbalistic use of the term *Dynamis* or *Gevurah.* In the Midrash, it stands for the Godhead or its manifestation qua glory, but in the Kabbalah the latter identity is dissolved. Glory is symbolized by the last Sefirah—Malkhut—and *Gevurah* is understood to correspond to the Sefirah of *Gevurah*—stern judgment. Thus, the Kabbalist interprets the liturgical formula, "Blessed be the glory of the Tetragrammaton for its place," as pointing to the reception of the influx by the glory, which the former pours out from the place—the *Gevurah*, which is a higher Sefirah. Again, according to R. Baḥya, the Sefirah of *Gevurah* receives its influx from *'Eiyn Sof*.[54] We can therefore describe an elaborate theosophical system that portrays the descent of the influx from *'Eiyn Sof*, through the *Gevurah*, upon the glory, *Malkhut*, which is in turn a manifestation of *Tiferet*—all as a result of the performance of the liturgy. Kabbalah can be regarded as an endeavor to explicate the midrashic theurgy by using the theosophical system of the Sefirot. More than does the Ashkenazic Ḥasid, the Kabbalist presents an articulated explanation for the meaning of the ritual.[55]

R. Baḥya again elaborates upon the theurgy of augmentation. Commenting on the verse in Numbers 14:17, he writes:[56]

> "And now, I pray thee, let the power of my Lord be great," that the inner power be emanated and drawn into the attributes lest it retreat to the highest heights. The meaning of the matter is that when [the people of] Israel observe the Torah and the commandments, God rides upon the heavens, as it is [written],[57] "Who rides upon the heaven[58] with thy help"—that is, with the help of [the people of] Israel he emanates power in his attributes, and thereby they [Israel] add power to the supernal *Dynamis*, as it is said, "In God we shall make power."[59] But when they do not observe the Torah and the commandments, he retreats[60] from his attributes, as it is said, "and in his excellency on the clouds"[61]—that is, he mounts up and retreats to the remotest heights. By [the observance] he emanates his power onto the attributes, and by [the negligence] they weaken the supernal power, as it is said, "you have weakened [the power of] the Rock that formed thee."[62] And since [the people of] Israel were deserving of destruction in this instance, and were weakening the supernal power, Moses said in his prayer, "And now, I pray thee, let the power of my Lord be great," in order to draw [downward] and emanate the inner power onto the attributes, lest he would retreat on high. . . . The Kabbalists referred to the drawing and the efflux by the term *help.*

R. Baḥya here portrays the drawing down of the divine emanation as an addition of power into the sefirotic realm in general, and not only upon the glory, as in the preceding text. Using a conspicuously instrumental conception of Sefirot, he envisions the purpose of the Jewish ritual as causing the presence of the divine power in its instruments; otherwise, its tendency will be to retreat on high, which is tantamount to weakening power within the Sefirot. Especially interesting is the discussion of R. Menaḥem Recanati, which interprets the view that the Sefirot "return to their origin in the depths of nothingness"[63] because of sins: "as if [we] weaken the supernal power, in opposition to what is written: 'and now, I pray thee, let the power of my Lord be great.' "[64] This Kabbalist seems to be even more radical than R. Baḥya; not only will the divine influx retreat from the sefirotic pleroma, but even parts of this very structure will be contracted to their sources because of the human transgression, which thereby weakens the divine system.[65]

Finally, a different version of augmentation theurgy is found in a widespread Kabbalistic text, the song for the Shabbat morning meal written by R. Isaac Luria. This Kabbalist indicates that "his hosts shall greatly multiply and ascend to the [God]head."[66] What is peculiar in this type of presentation is not only its assertion that the divine power is augmented apparently by the performance of the Shabbat ritual but also its conception of the ascent of the power. In a conspicuous divergence from the classical Kabbalah, Luria presents here an ascending movement of the *Dynamis*. Luria probably combined augmentation theurgy with the theme of the ascent of the Sefirah of Malkhut to Keter, an issue to be dealt with in detail in the next chapter.

An interesting version of the augmentation theurgy is included in *Pesikta de-Rav Kahana,* in a passage omitted in the text cited above:[67] "R. Ya'akov bar Aḥa[68] said . . . our sages said in the name of R. Yoḥanan: 'Let their power be great for [the sake of] thy mercy, let the attribute of mercy overpower the attribute of judgment, as it is said: "Let the power of my Lord be great." ' "[69] According to this view, the augmentation of power is to be channeled to the attribute of mercy, in order to help it prevail over the attribute of judgment. This interpretation is based upon the view, occurring in the biblical verse, that the Tetragrammaton refers to the attribute of mercy. The focus of interest is no longer upon the increase of power in the Godhead; human activity is now directed toward assuring the prevalence of one of the divine attributes over another.

This type of theurgy is also found in a famous passage included in *Berakhot;* R. Ishmael, the high priest, is asked by 'Akatriel YH Ẓevaot to bless him. In his blessing, he requests: "Let your mercy conquer your anger, and your mercy overflow onto your attributes, and may you behave regarding your sons according to the attribute of mercy."[70] A human activity—blessing—is here understood not only as an expression of a wish but as an actual contribution toward the achievement of this wish: blessing is able to cause the overflowing of mercy, just as the performance of the commandments augments the divine power. Since the setting of R. Ishmael ben Elisha's encounter with the divine is explicitly connected with the offering of the incense on the Day of Atonement, we can assume that this activation of mercy was included in the most sacred part of Jewish ritual as performed by the high priest.

Cognate to this understanding of worship in the Holy of Holies is the talmudic presentation of the union between the two cherubim and their separation as a function, respectively, of [the people of] Israel's acting according to the divine will and their neglecting to do so.[71] As we saw earlier, the parallelism between the cherubim, the two divine names, and the two attributes was an ancient one, and it may well be that this correspondence also served theurgic purposes. In other words, the people of Israel were able by their behavior to influence the divine attributes, whose corporeal manifestations could be envisioned as the two cherubim. Common to the two talmudic passages is the assumption that the nature of the divine activity is conditioned by human acts. The divine recompense and punishment depend upon human activities; moreover, the talmudic texts overtly assume a contribution of man's worship to the divine power. It must be stressed that, according to the text from *Berakhot,* the blessing is explicitly requested by God himself. As we shall see below, the theurgical influence of the blessing recurs in some Ashkenazic texts. We can conclude that the theurgical activity had already received a theosophical nuance in the rabbinic sources: the channeling of the power into one of the divine attributes in order to structure the divine activity has theosophical overtones. It is noteworthy that, at the end of the *Berakhot* passage, *middot*—attributes—are mentioned in addition to the attribute of mercy, implicitly assuming a plurality of attributes, apparently beyond the two regular ones.[72]

The correspondence between human deeds and the activity of the divine attributes is obvious in *Sefer ha-Bahir*.[73] Describing the twofold nature of the "north"—benevolent and pernicious—the author concludes that this paradoxical feature depends upon Israel's enactment of the divine will; that is, when this enactment is performed, the attribute of mercy is activated. It afterward became a basic feature of Kabbalistic theurgy to attenuate the attribute of sternness by joining it to that of mercy. It is interesting to note that, just as in the lower world man was supposed to preserve his two drives (*yeẓarim*)—and not destroy his evil drive—so also here; the activity of the attribute of stern judgment must be mitigated, but not destroyed, by adding power to its counterpart, the attribute of mercy. Also conceptually close to the augmentation theurgy is the midrashic view[74] that Israel maintains (*mefarnesim*) the Divinity, a view later elaborated by Kabbalists and Ḥasidim.[75]

Pertinent here is the particular type of theosophy implicit in this discussion;

its dynamism not only is a characteristic of the supernal power per se but is itself activated by human acts. Thus, man is conceived of as an active factor able to interact with the dynamic Divinity. Kabbalistic anthropology and theosophy, then, are both similar and complementary perceptions.

To summarize the myth that underlies the augmentation theurgy: divine power is dependent upon human activity, which is able to strengthen or to diminish it; alternatively, the relationship between the divine attributes is a function of human deeds. The performance of the divine will via the commandments is therefore the means by which man participates in the divine process. This talmudic-midrashic emphasis on the centrality of the divine will represented a continuation of biblical thought, which was aptly described by H. A. and H. Frankfort in these words: "Hebrew thought did not entirely overcome mythopoeic thought. It created, in fact, a new myth—the myth of the will of God."[76] The major focus of this myth was history as the revelation of the dynamic will of God. In a later layer of Jewish thought, a central issue was the view of the Torah as pointing the way to the augmentation of the divine *Dynamis*; the importance of history was substantially attenuated in favor of an atemporal conception of the role of the commandments. This tendency, which was already obvious in the midrashic literature, had major repercussions for the entire Kabbalistic mode of thought.

Put this way, there is no major difference between midrashic and Kabbalistic theurgy. We can conclude that a certain stream of thought about the significance of the commandments, rooted in midrashic and talmudic texts, was elaborated upon in the theosophical Kabbalah, which regarded theurgical activity as the main raison d'être of the commandments.

III. DRAWING-DOWN THEURGY

According to talmudic-midrashic thought, one of the basic repercussions of the fulfillment of the commandments is the indwelling of the Divine Presence amid the Jewish people. This indwelling is an essential characteristic of the *Shekhinah*, as *Genesis Rabbah* put it, and is conditioned by the religious perfection of the people of Israel.[77] The divine Presence once dwelled in Paradise, whence it was removed by the sin of Adam and continued to ascend heavenward as a consequence of the successive sins of subsequent generations. The ten upward ascents of the *Shekhinah* and its consequent retreat from the world required positive human activity to bring about its descent back into the world. The Midrash accordingly describes the ten-stage descent, which began with the deeds of Abraham and culminated with the construction of the

Temple by Solomon, whereby the *Shekhinah* finally returned to its original state of indwelling in this world.[78] This manifest correlation between human acts and the divine presence must be understood as the result of a theurgical conception of the commandments, whose performance is seen as having substantial bearing on the Divinity; the commandments not only draw it downward but also facilitate its indwelling. I want to elaborate upon this last point, which is crucial for the theurgical perception of human activity in Jewish sources.

According to the Hebrew *Enoch,* the idolatrous acts of the generation of Enosh were connected to a peculiar construction:[79]

> They went from one end of the world to the other and each one brought silver, gold, precious stones, and pearls in heaps upon mountains and hills,[80] making idols out of them throughout the world. And they erected the idols in every quarter of the world; the size of each idol was one thousand parasangs. And they brought down the sun, moon, planets, and constellations, and placed them before the idols on their right hand and on their left, to attend them even as they attended the Holy one,[81] blessed be he, as it is written, "And all the host of heaven was standing by him on his right hand and on his left."[82] What power did they have that they were able to bring them down? They would not have been able to bring them down but for 'Uzza, 'Azza, and 'Azziel, who taught them sorcery,[83] whereby they brought them down and made use of them.

Therefore, specific structures, together with "sorceries" (which I assume refer to various types of incantations), could, according to the ancient Jewish sources, bring about the descent of celestial entities and their magical use. This practice, although idolatrous, was perceived as effective and was not derided for its futility.[84] Thus, a special building and magical devices can induce the descent of the host of heaven; similarly, I would assume, the Temple and the service performed there were thought of as able to attract the *Shekhinah* to this place. Let us explore the locus of the revelation of the *Shekhinah*—between the two cherubim. Their perfect state of union—even sexual union—is a function of performing the will of God; otherwise, they will be separated.[85] I assume, however, that only when their union is induced by human activity can the *Shekhinah* descend upon the cherubim,[86] just as it does with a worthy husband and wife.[87] Accordingly, in order to restore the dwelling of the *Shekhinah*, not only is a certain structure required but also a certain kind of human act—the rituals of Judaism, which alone are able to sustain the dynamic bond between God and man. The descent of the *Shekhinah* is regarded by Naḥmanides as fulfilling a divine rather than a human need.[88]

Even closer to the *Enoch* passage is the descent of the *Sar ha-Panim,* the angel of countenance, who is brought down by means of magical devices in order "to reveal to man the secrets of supernal and lower [worlds] and the knowledge of the foundation of supernal and lower [worlds] and the mysteries of wisdom."[89] According to this source, this descent is accompanied by the *Shekhinah*.[90] This passage is an interesting parallel to another text of the *Heikhalot* literature concerning *Sar ha-Torah*[91]—the angel of the Torah—wherein we again witness the descent of the Divinity, in this instance in the Temple, which is conceived of as being in the process of building; this descent is understood as part of the revelation of the "secret of the Torah."[92] Here, the adjuration of God is conspicuous; he is compelled to appear together with the seat of glory. Therefore, the Temple was envisioned as the locus of revelation, which is induced by magical devices. This practice must be compared to the Hermetic and Neoplatonic techniques for obtaining revelations by causing the descent of gods into statues specially prepared for this purpose. Like the angel of the countenance, God in the *Sar ha-Torah* text, and the *Shekhinah* between the cherubim, the Hermetics heard the voice of their gods emerging from a special structure.[93] Save for the descent of the *Shekhinah* in the Holy of Holies, all the other texts include practices for drawing the spiritual power downward as part of the revelatory process. On the ground of these parallels, we can seriously consider the possibility that the Temple service was conceived as inducing the presence of the *Shekhinah* in the Holy of Holies; thus the service can be seen as a theurgical activity.

The magical use of the practice of descent had a long history in Judaism, which I cannot trace here,[94] but I would like to highlight a specific form of drawing down the *Shekhinah*. According to some texts, the structure is not a building, but the human body, which is the living statue on whom the indwelling of the *Shekhinah* takes place; this kind of indwelling on human beings is evidenced by ancient Jewish texts.[95] No prerequisites, however, were mentioned for this dwelling, it being presented as a necessity of the Divine rather than of man.[96] As I have suggested elsewhere, the human couple was conceived of as a potential substitute for the cherubim in the Temple.[97] The Kabbalah fully exploited the mystical possibilities inherent in this view, both the theosophical and ecstatic Kabbalah elaborating upon the preparations necessary to ensure the dwelling of the divine power or powers on the mystic. Thus, for example, R. Moses de Leon writes: [98] "For the quintessence of the *mizvot* and good deeds that a person performs in this world is to prepare his soul,[99] and to arrange the great and good things above, [so as] to draw down upon himself the influx of the light of the supernal emanation." For de Leon, man must become a seat upon whom another supernal seat will sit.[100] Therefore, beside the theurgical "reparation" of the Sefirot, man is able to cause the descent of the divine influx upon himself.

According to R. Joseph Gikatilla, man is created in the supernal image, and each of his limbs may become a "seat" for the supernal entity, to which it corresponds by its purification and performance of the commandments.[101] According to the author of *Ra'ya Meheimna*[102] and *Tikkuney Zohar,*[103] the Kabbalist must prepare his limbs so as to ensure the dwelling of the *Shekhinah* on them.[104] According to R. Abraham ben Eliezer ha-Levi, one of the important Kabbalists expelled from Spain in 1492, the catharsis of the limbs prepares the dwelling of the *Shekhinah* in man, whose body then becomes an organon of it.[105] R. Abraham ha-Levi expresses the concept, widespread in his generation, that the human flesh becomes "transparent"—*sefirim*—by the perfect religious life and so can contain the Sefirot.[106] Thus, comprehensive explanations of the drawing downward of the *Shekhinah* upon the perfect man metamorphosed the system of commandments into a mystical technique for collecting divine influences upon the human body.

In the ecstatic Kabbalah, the interest in drawing down divine powers was even more crucial, since this type of contact with the divine became one of the ways to unite with God. Let me begin with an Ashkenazic text that reflects both the theosophical Kabbalah and the ecstatic features of earlier periods.[107] R. Moses 'Azriel ben Eleazar ha-Darshan, a descendant of R. Yehudah he-Ḥasid, asserts: "Whoever knows it [the divine name] and prays using it, the *Shekhinah* dwells upon him and he prophesies like the ancient prophets."[108] Here, the ritual—prayer—is intertwined with the anomian practice of using the divine name in order to attain the indwelling of the *Shekhinah*. Both from the context here and from another discussion of this author,[109] however, this presence seems to produce a dramatic change in the nature of the person, so that he is tantamount to a limb of the *Shekhinah*.

Abraham Abulafia, who inherited Ashkenazic mystical techniques, describes the pronunciation of the combination of the divine names as drawing down the supernal power so as to unite with it.[110] Although many other examples could easily be offered,[111] it will suffice to cite an anonymous source quoted by R. Moses Cordovero, because of its rich implications:

> Some of the ancients commented that, by the combination and permutation of the name [of seventy-two letters] or other [divine] names after a great concentration [of mind], the righteous . . . will receive a revelation of an aspect of a *Bat Kol* . . . since he combines the forces and unites them . . . until a great influx will descend upon

> him, on the condition that whoever deals with this will be a well-prepared vessel to receive the spiritual force.[112]

Again, the ritual is hinted at as accomplished by the righteous, but the technique itself is anomian. Interestingly, the person is viewed as a vessel collecting the divine efflux, a formula reminiscent of the old prepared statues.[113] The distance between this and related texts written in the ecstatic vein of Kabbalah and Ḥasidism is not great; in those texts, man is regularly viewed as a Temple or a vessel receiving the *Shekhinah*. Is it mere coincidence that Cordovero mentions the mystic as Ẓaddik?

A striking view, apparently independent of both previous ones was preserved in the *Collectanaea* of Yoḥanan Alemanno:[114]

> After the external cleansing of the body, and an inner change and spiritual purification from all taint, one becomes as clear and as pure as the heavens. Once one has divested oneself of all material thoughts, let him read only the Torah and the divine names written therein, and there shall be revealed [to him] awesome secrets and such divine visions as may be emanated upon pure clear souls who are prepared to receive them. As the verse said: "Prepare yourselves for three days and wash your clothing."[115] For there are three preparations: of the exterior [the body], of the interior, and of the imagination. . . . When he immerses himself in these things, then such a great influx will come to him that he will cause the spirit of God to descend upon him and hover above him and flutter about him all the day.

These preparations by cleansing enable the body to become the substratum of the "spirit of God," which is to be drawn downward. Interestingly, this revelation is compared to that at Sinai, but in contrast to the theosophical Kabbalah, the halakhic ritual is not specified, nor is the specific technique of Abulafia. We can view this practice as theurgic, since the divine spirit is reported to be induced upon the person, the major technique being the incantational reading of the Torah.

IV. UNIVERSE-MAINTENANCE ACTIVITY

"What, in rabbinical Judaism, separated the Law from myth? The answer is clear: the dissociation of the Law from cosmic events."[116] This characterization of the Law as separate from myth emphasized, according to Scholem, the novelty of the Kabbalistic approach versus the rabbinic one: rabbinism succeeded in divorcing the Law "from its emotional roots" and was, in Scholem's opinion, "one of the great and fundamental, but also dangerous and ambivalent, achievements of the Halakhah, of normative Rabbinical Judaism."[117] Kabbalah, on the other hand, is presented as the possessor of "a new mythical consciousness, which often gives the impression of being old as the hills."[118]

It would be interesting to check the sources against the background of Scholem's view of normative Judaism; has the cosmic myth disappeared from the *halakhah* as surmised by Scholem? How do these statements corroborate Scholem's own view that Kabbalah, or mysticism, is the vital element of Judaism?[119] If rabbinical Judaism had survived for more than a millennium prior to the emergence of the historical Kabbalah, then there must have been other elements that maintained Judaism.[120] I would like to answer this question with the same clarity with which Scholem formulated his view: it was precisely the theurgic view of the commandments that was one of the factors that enforced the performance of the commandments, the lively interest in them, and the adherence of Jews to their rituals. As seen above, the execution of the divine will is necessary for the augmentation of divine power; long before the emergence of Kabbalistic theosophy, Jews envisioned their ritual as a God-maintaining activity and, as we shall soon see, as universe-maintaining acts as well.[121]

The receiving of the Torah by the people of Israel is presented by the Talmud as a prerequisite for the existence of the universe:[122] "The Holy one, blessed be he, made a condition with the Creation, saying: 'If Israel receive my Torah, good; if not, I shall return you[123] to chaos.' " Thus, the Talmud considers the Torah and, from the context here, even its performance as maintaining the universe. The difference between order and chaos is to be found in the enactment of the Torah. According to a Midrash, sacrifices have cosmic implications, their performance being tantamount to the creation of heaven and earth.[124] According to some sources, the *Ma'amadot*, the groups of Israelites who recited the account of Creation simultaneously with the performance of the sacrifices, performed a similar function. A tradition preserved by R. Ya'akov bar Aḥa, the same amora who maintained theurgical views, states that "without the *Ma'amadot* neither heaven nor earth could remain in existence."[125] In this context, we may understand the Ẓaddikim as the pillars of the world;[126] according to other texts, the righteous maintain the world, while the wicked men destroy the world.[127] Moreover, in a version of *'Avot* preserved in the Middle Ages: "By means of ten *ma'amarot* the world was created, and by the Decalogue it stands."[128] Rabbinical sources indeed note the parallelism between the *ma'amarot* and the Decalogue;[129] therefore, the view that the world is maintained by the performance of ten precepts is presented together with the description of the Creation by ten *ma'amarot*.

This relationship between the Creation of the world and its maintenance reflects the affinity between the Jewish ritual and cosmic welfare. What remained for the Kabbalah was to specify the peculiar meaning of each of the ten *ma'amarot* qua divine manifestation and the special precept connected to it. In the *Bahir,* the ten digits correspond to the *ma'amarot* and maintain them.[130] There are numerous extant discussions on the parallel between *ma'amarot* and dibberot dating from the beginning of the thirteenth century.[131] As we shall see below, some Kabbalistic texts considered the commandments as formative of the divine pleroma.[132] The Kabbalah considered the creational acts as part of the Divinity, transforming the cosmic significance of the commandments into a theurgical one. The Kabbalistic stand was felicitously articulated by R. Menaḥem Recanati: "It is incumbent upon man to contemplate the commandments of the Torah, {to see} how many worlds he maintains by their performance and how many worlds he destroys by their neglect."[133] Audacious as this statement may be, it represents only what I would call "soft theurgy," in comparison with other theurgical views that will be the subject of the next chapter.

CHAPTER 8

Kabbalistic Theurgy

It became obvious from the discussion in the preceding chapter that several major theurgical trends in medieval Kabbalah originated in classical rabbinic sources. I shall now present three other types of theurgy relating to pre-Kabbalistic material, whose *loci probantes* are mostly preserved in Kabbalistic sources. These theurgies are far more extreme in nature, which seems to be the reason for the disappearance of the pre-Kabbalistic sources that sustained them. If this assumption is correct, then our use of medieval Kabbalistic literature may assist us to understand ancient Jewish thought better.

I. "AS A SHADOW"

I would like to discuss the ramifications of a "lost" rabbinic view in a variety of conceptual contexts, the most important one being the theurgical one. Before analyzing its theurgical interpretation in Kabbalah, however, I shall survey the sources and their interpretation prior to the theurgical turn in Kabbalah.

In the remnants of *Midrash Hashkem,* we read: "God said to Moses: Go, say to Israel that my name is *'Ehyeh 'asher 'Ehyeh*—that is, just as you are present with me, so am I present with you."[1] The precise significance of this text is easily understood from its context: Israel is commanded to behave in accordance with two divine attributes—righteousness and justice—and will accordingly be rewarded by acquiring these two attributes. The behavior under discussion is conspicuously a moral one, and the midrashic passage serves to elucidate the strong affinity between punishments and retribution.

In other sources, however, this passage is cited in a different version. An anonymous Kabbalist, associated with the school of the ecstatic Kabbalah, writes, I presume in the late thirteenth or early fourteenth century, as follows:[2] "The sages thus interpreted the secret of the name *'Ehyeh 'asher 'Ehyeh*: that the Holy one, blessed be he, said to Moses: 'Moses, be with me and I shall be with you.' And they adduced as proof [for this interpretation] the verse: 'The Lord is thy shadow upon thy right hand,'[3] as it is expounded in *Midrash Hashkem*." We learn from the context that, just as man will cleave to God in an intellectual manner, so will he cleave to man.[4] In this text, the reciprocity is regarded as automatic—no longer the response of a higher personality to the deeds of man, as in the Midrash, but a spiritual mechanism, exemplified by the verse in Psalms. There is nothing personalistic about the divine response, since the divine intellect is one with the human intellect as soon as man is—mentally—with God. The occurrence of the motif of shadow puts the recurrence of the name *'Ehyeh* into sharp relief: the hand and its shadow correspond to the two occurrences of the word *'Ehyeh*, as well as to the human and the Divine. Surprisingly, in the logic of the text, the human is the hand, whose movement is automatically reflected by the shadow—the Divine.

We can now fathom the specific direction of this interpretation of *'Ehyeh*: "I shall be whatever I shall be," as, according to this version of the Midrash, the peculiar nature of the Divinity seems to be a reflection of human activity. For this ecstatic Kabbalist, there is no theological difficulty entailed in this conditioning of the divine essence, or even of divine activity, by human behavior; he accepted the Maimonidean and Abulafian view of the utter spirituality of God, according to which he cannot be changed by human activity. The perfection of human intellect is a continuous improvement of the human comprehension of God, culminating in union with him. The moral level of interpretation, so obvious in the first version, is obliterated, and the intellectualistic approach is uniquely represented by this Kabbalist. The Midrash represents the union of "the divine and supreme force" with the "human force," this being "the circle of prophecy."

This understanding of the anonymous text is corroborated by still another anonymous text, also stemming from the ecstatic Kabbalah. According to this text, there exist two attributes, one good and one bad: "Both of them are in the lower man, just as they are found in the excellent man, as it is well known that the excellent man does not act but in accordance with the deeds of the lower man, either for recompense or for punishment. Thus we learn that, if the lower man performs noble acts, the excellent man must follow his [the former's] acts."[5] The "excellent man" stands for the active intellect, whose influence may be either positive or negative, depending on the acts of the lower man. Its intellectual influx does not change but is received differently by various men.

The first quotation offers an important piece of evidence concerning the text from *Midrash Hashkem*. The verse of Psalms was cited as part of this Midrash by a Kabbalist who was not interested in exploiting the theological implications inherent in it, stressing the aspect of "reciprocal presence" rather than that of "reflection." A still lengthier version of the Midrash, albeit one that does not mention the name *Hashkem*, is extant in R. Meir ibn Gabbay's *Tola'at Ya'akov.* I shall first deal with the version of the Midrash as cited by ibn Gabbay, and afterward comment upon his interpretation of this version:[6]

> In the Midrash, [we learn] that the Holy One, blessed be he, said to Moses: "Go, tell Israel that my name is *'Ehyeh 'asher 'Ehyeh.*" What is the meaning of *'Ehyeh 'asher 'Ehyeh?* Just as you are present with me, so am I present with you. Likewise David said: "The Lord is thy shadow upon thy right hand." What does "the Lord is thy shadow" mean? Like thy shadow: just as thy shadow laughs back when you laugh to it,[7] and weeps if you weep to it,[8] and if you show it an angry face or a pleasant face, so it returns, so is the Lord, the Holy one, blessed be he, thy shadow. Just as you are present with him, so is he present with you. End of quotation.

This version incorporates motifs present in both previous quotations in such a way that it is highly unlikely that the larger version is a combination of these two versions. I therefore assume that ibn Gabbay, who explicitly quotes the whole passage from a "Midrash," had the longer and presumably original version of *Midrash Hashkem* available to him, which was quoted only in a fragmentary fashion in the previously discussed texts. What is the theological outlook of this presumably more original version? There are two differing, but nevertheless complementary conceptual components: God is envisioned as a shadow present with the human hand, the latter standing here for the substance,[9] whereas the "accident" is God or the shadow. In addition to this static ontological relationship, the substance and its accident exist in a functional dynamic relationship—the hand compels its shadow to move, or to react, in accordance with its movements. The shadow precisely reflects the changes in the shape of the hand. On the basis of the first quotation from *Midrash Hashkem,* we can assume that the original meaning of the longer version is moralistic as well: God responds to human activity in an appropriate fashion, and his nature reflects the profound interrelationship between merits and retribution. Nonetheless, the metaphor chosen to illuminate this religious truth is striking.

The conclusions drawn by ibn Gabbay, however, surpass even the amazing metaphor of the Midrash. Shortly prior to quoting the Midrash, he indicates that[10] "the supernal entities to the lower entities are comparable to the shadow [compared] to the form; just as the form stirs, thus the shadow stirs."[11] As we have seen above,[12] form stands for the supernal entities—angels, archangels, divine names—but also Sefirot in the Kabbalistic terminology that was accepted by ibn Gabbay.[13] Therefore, man, being the basic pattern of the higher structure, is able to influence its state by his activity: ontological resemblance serves the theurgical goal. This far-reaching presentation of man as the archetype of the revealed aspect of the Deity is a highly significant departure from the opposite metaphor, in which man is the shadow of the supernal. This reversal is noteworthy for more than one reason; theologically or theosophically, this projection of the human shape onto the pleromatic realm is explicitly articulated by an important Jewish theosophist. No longer is the image of God understood as the basic archetype; now, the human image is regarded as the original, reflected by the divine structure.[14] It must be emphasized that ibn Gabbay's striking metaphor reflects a basic perception, explicitly expressed in the zoharic theosophy, that the divine anthropomorphic structure was copied from the human structure.[15]

I should like to elaborate here upon the implication of this inverse metaphor for our understanding of the relationship between theurgy and symbolism. The mainstream of the symbolic process in Kabbalah, to be described below,[16] assumes the reflection of divine dynamics in the biblical text, in the human form, or in historical events. The lower entities serve as starting points for the contemplation of the hidden life of the Divinity. Accordingly, the symbolizing process is based upon the Platonic type of relationship, including, however, a major element of dynamism. The more distant the archetype, the greater is the need for a symbolic representation of the recondite entities and processes. The great problem of symbolism is an epistemologic one: how to bridge the gap between man's consciousness and the sublime object. In theurgy, the question is somewhat different: how to change the object whose structural contour is already known. The theurgical approach conceives man as the fulcrum of important characteristics: he is, at least to a certain extent, the paradigm and the source of power; the symbolic relationship must therefore be inverted if the theurgical operation is to be efficient. The symbolical process now serves not contemplation but action; it can explain why a certain type of activity is influential on a particular object, the epistemological goal of the symbols being evidently attenuated. As form, man possesses in his own being the archetypal structure of the Divine, while the importance of the shadow from the cognitive point of view is diminished. We can conclude that, in a sharply theurgical system such as ibn Gabbay's theosophy, the role of symbolism is substantially different from that found in more conventional theosophies.[17]

To return to ibn Gabbay: immediately following the quotation from the Midrash, the Kabbalist seems to attenuate somewhat the automatism inherent in the Midrash and in his own formulation quoted above. He writes:[18] "When the supernal luminary[19] watches men and sees their good and proper deeds, [then] in accordance with what they stir below, they stir above, and he opens his good storehouse and pours the fine oil upon his head[20] and from thence upon his other attributes." Thus, the sefirotic pleroma serves as an organon for transmitting the impression of human deeds to the highest instance of the divine realm; the semipersonalistic portrait of the supernal luminary does not, however, detract at all from the mechanistic nature of the Sefirot. Although this feature of the sefirotic structure is not emphasized in *Tola'at Ya'akov,* it is placed into relief in ibn Gabbay's chef d'oeuvre, *'Avodat ha-Kodesh:* there, as well, the Midrash is quoted and in its context the following discussion is to be found.[21]

Man and the "divine glory"—*ha-kavod*—share the anthropomorphic image, a fact that renders man, again envisaged as form by comparison with the shadow, capable of influencing the divine structure. In his later work, however, ibn Gabbay introduces two important additions. First, the human image is able to influence the higher image *demut 'eliyon,*[22] as there is also an intermediary image that connects them: the "Torah."[23] It is "the intermediary which stirs the supernal image toward the lower [one]"[24] or "the Torah and the commandments are the intermediary which links the lower image with the supernal one, by the affinity they have with both."[25] As a result of the Torah's double affinity—with its divine source and with the persons who perform the commandments—it is able to function as a bridge between the two realms. Its singular nature stems from its capacity to change human acts into theurgical influence.

Second, the other motif introduced in the discussion of the Midrash in *'Avodat ha-Kodesh* is highly relevant for the explanation of theurgic action. Ibn Gabbay elaborates upon the phenomenon of coustical resonance between two stringed instruments.[26] When someone plays on one string, the corresponding string of the other instrument—in ibn Gabbay's case, a violin—will resonate, even though no visible intermediary between these strings is to be found. The same occurs, continues the Kabbalist, when the human image, functioning as the played violin, activates the divine image, the second violin. In both cases, the manner of transmission is incomprehensible, even though the fact of its occurrence is palpable. Thus, the possibility of acting theurgically is proven by a concrete, well-known physical observation. The mechanistic nature of acoustical resonance is no doubt appropriate to the midrashic picture of hand and shadow; the gist of these types of descriptions of the human-divine relationship is conspicuous: the human initiative is the most important factor for this relationship, as it is the dominant element that shapes the higher structures. The rise of the mechanistic approach to theurgy is obviously facilitated by the more complex theosophy of ecstatic Kabbalah and, as we shall see shortly, of Ḥasidism, which affords a more elaborate explanation than that given in the Midrash. An elaborate hierarchy that suffers the impact of human activity provides the opportunity to reveal the comprehensive mechanism of the Divine and a more complex understanding of the significance of performance of the commandments.

A neglected, although interesting Kabbalist of the late sixteenth century, R. Yehudah ben Ya'akov Ḥunain, formulated a conception that, notwithstanding its affinity to that of ibn Gabbay, seems independent of it:[27] "As the war was below, so it was above, because of the sin of Israel; for just as the righteous add force and power in the higher assembly[28] . . . and when they act in the opposite [way], it is as if they weaken the supernal force. . . . for the lower [entities] are like the root and modus[29] of the supernal [entities]." This definition of the lower entities as root of the higher ones parallels ibn Gabbay's shade image; man, in this case Israel, is the source of power, hence the influential being. The occurrence of an additional strong theurgical theory demonstrates that ibn Gabbay was—notwithstanding his centrality since sixteenth-century Kabbalah—not an exception, nor was his shadow theory a mere curiosity; using different terminology, R. Yehudah Ḥunain reflects the same view. As soon as the importance of the intermediary hierarchy was reduced, however, Jewish mysticism, in its Ḥasidic version, largely returned to the original meaning of the Midrash.[30] R. Israel Ba'al Shem Tov is reported to have commented upon this Midrash as follows:[31]

> The Besht interpreted the verse: "the Lord is your shade [upon thy right hand]" that the Creator, blessed be he, also behaves with man as a shadow. Just as whatever man does, the shadow does, so does the Creator behave with man, doing just as he does. We find that when Israel sang the song [of the sea] at the time of the redemption from Egypt, so did God, as it were, sing this song. Now [the form] "he will sing" is rendered in the causative form,[32] and this is the meaning of the verse "then he will sing"[33]—that is, that Israel caused by their singing this song to God, that the Holy one, blessed be he, would also, as it were, sing this song.

The theurgical element has been eliminated, as the link between God and

Israel is now direct. The song of Israel causes a parallel song above; the mechanistic aspect of human influence thus has disappeared, the very character of the induced activity, singing, having an obvious personalistic character.

Despite the great difference among them—the strong theurgical understanding of ibn Gabbay and of Ḥunain, the moderate one of the Midrash and Ḥasidism, and the mystical one in ecstatic Kabbalah—all share a common feature: man is not mistaken for God, nor is the hierarchy understood as an entity in itself, which the Kabbalist, intoxicated by his powers, activates for his own sake. They—these powers—are a mechanism for reaching the ultimate instance and receiving the influx from above; affection and affinity, to the extent that they exist in the previously cited texts, are directed toward God, as an entity standing per se.

Let me compare the above Jewish discussion with some verses of Angelus Silesius: "God becomes what I am now, and took my humanity upon him; since I have my being from him, therefore he has done it."[34] The Christian mystic emphasizes the initiative of Christ, who underwent the humanizing process in order to pave the way for the Christian mystic. Man, considered a fallen creature, is in profound need of the self-sacrifice of God that his nature may be restored. Christ must descend to man in order to help him return to the paradisiacal status; for Silesius, this return is the spiritual birth of Christ in the inner man.

Jewish theurgical anthropology strikes utterly different chords; the problem is basically the need of the Divinity for human help, or human power, in order to restore the lost sefirotic harmony. The focus of the Kabbalistic theurgy is God, not man; the latter is given unimaginable powers, to be used in order to repair the divine glory or the divine image; only his initiative can improve Divinity. An archmagician, the theurgical Kabbalist does not need external help or grace; his way of operating—namely, the Torah—enables him to be independent; he looks not so much for salvation by the intervention of God as for God's redemption by human intervention. The theurgical Kabbalah articulates a basic feature of Jewish religion in general: because he concentrates more upon action than upon thought, the Jew is responsible for everything, including God, since his activity is crucial for the welfare of the cosmos in general. Accordingly, no speculation or faith can change the exterior reality, which must be rescued from its fallen state.[35] The metaphor of the shadow points to the reinforcement of the theurgical trend precisely by its strong delineation of the human and the Divine; only by retaining his own individuality can the theurgical Kabbalist retain his cosmic influence.

This extraordinary emphasis on human power can be properly illuminated by the anonymous *Sefer ha-Ne'elam*,[36] which explains the Kabbalistic significance of the interdiction against killing:[37]

> Man is composed of all the spiritual entities,[38] and he is perfect [containing] all attributes, and he was created with great wisdom . . . for he comprises all the secrets[39] of the *Merkavah*, and his soul is linked therein,[40] even though man is in this world.[41] Know that, unless man would be perfect [containing] all the forces of the Holy one, blessed be he, he would be unable to do as he does. And it is said that Rava created a man, and if the righteous wished they could create worlds.[42] [All these] demonstrate to you that there is a great supernal power in men, which cannot be described, and as man possesses such a great perfection, it is not just to destroy his form and his soul from the world. And one who kills a person, what is the loss he brings about? He sheds the blood of that [man] and diminishes the form,[43] that is, diminishes the power of the Sefirot.

Man is therefore an extension of the Divine on earth; his form and soul not only reflect the Divine but also actually are divine—hence, the interdiction against killing a person. Its real meaning is not the fact, emphasized in rabbinic sources,[44] that man is a whole world, a world in itself, but that this microcosmos is a divine monad. Destroying a person is tantamount to diminishing not only the divine form on earth but, as this text puts it, divine power itself. Man is conceived as a source of energy parallel to, or perhaps even essentially identical with, the Divine; nevertheless, the distance between the human and divine entities is not eliminated, as it is in the above-mentioned Christian mystic.

This delineation between human and Divine in connection with the shadow metaphor is a well-known one in the history of religion. I would like to recall briefly the normal use of this metaphor—man as shadow of the Divine—in order to highlight the essence of the Kabbalistic inversion. According to one perception of an Assyrian proverb: "Man is the shadow of the god and men are the shadow of man; man is the king, who is like the mirror of the god."[45] Man is, therefore, the shadow of a shadow or, interpreted otherwise, the protected of another protected.[46] An interesting parallel to this proverb appears in the Coptic *Three Steles of Seth,* a Gnostic treatise of Nag Hammadi. The aeons praising Barbelo state: "We are [each] a shadow of thee, as thou art a shadow [of that] first preexistent one."[47]

The Assyrian man-as-shadow can spend his life in a complete, but noncreative, obedience; his experience ends with "a keen realization of one's own insignificance of unbridgeable remoteness." Although, according to Thorkild Jacobsen, the ancient possessed "a strong element of sympathy," he nevertheless felt that he was confronted by a power that "commands allegiance by its very presence; the onlooker obeys freely."[48] For the Gnostic, the real surpasses this world, which is no more than a shadow of a shadow. The perfection and/or transcendence of the Supreme Being is so obvious that man can play no significant role in its further perfection. The Kabbalistic reversal of the role entails a tremendous change in religious mentality; although still obedient to the divine will, the Torah, according to the above sources the Kabbalist must invest particular energy in his performance of commandments, which alone have theurgical repercussions. A Kabbalist following the ritual becomes a cooperator not only in the maintenance of the universe but also in the maintenance or even formation of some aspects of the Deity.

II. THE THEURGY OF THE STATUS QUO

According to some early Kabbalistic texts, the process that produced the emergence of the Sefirot was not simply an emanational act or creation out of nothing by the will of the Creator; it was rather an act of uprooting these entities from their primeval preexistence in the bosom of the Godhead. R. ʹEzra of Gerona states that the gathering of roses mentioned in the Song of Songs refers to emanation and to causing the influx to descend downward.[49] The ancient sages—meaning the authors of *Genesis Rabbah*—designated the emanation of the highest entities and its revelation by the word *uprooting*:[50] "As it is written in *Genesis Rabbah*:[51] 'And the Lord God planted a garden eastward in Eden.'[52] This corresponds to the verse: 'The trees of the Lord have their fill; the cedars of Lebanon which he has planted.'[53] R. Ḥanina said: 'They were like the horns of the locusts, and the Holy one, blessed be he, uprooted them, and transplanted them into the Garden of Eden.' " The recurrence of the motif of planting in Genesis is connected by R. ʹEzra to the preexistence of mythical trees of the Lord, which, so I suppose, were planted as cedars of Lebanon, outside their natural locus. R. Ḥanina hints at these two stages when he refers to their preexistence as "horns of locusts," which were uprooted and transplanted in the Garden of Eden. The violent act of uprooting is obvious;[54] the transplantation is understood by the Kabbalist as the act of the forced emergence of the Sefirot out of their hidden preexistence.

The motif of Lebanon as part of the first emanational processes occurs in a significant text by R. ʹEzra:[55] " 'Who coverest thyself with light as with a garment,'[56] that is, with the splendor of wisdom, and for this reason wisdom is called Lebanon. The truth is that the [supernal] essences were [in existence], but [their] emanation is a novel [process], and it was naught but a revelation of [these] entities."[57] Thus, we learn that the minute "horns of the locusts" were already in existence prior to the "transplantation of the trees of the Lord into the Garden," that is, the emanational process, which takes place in "Lebanon," which is the symbol of the Sefirot Ḥokhmah.[58]

Against this background, we can better understand a third quotation from R. ʿEzra:[59] "The spiritual entities ascend and are drawn toward the place of their sucking; as it is said,[60] 'From the evil to come the righteous is taken away.'[61] And for this reason we ought to endeavor to cause the emanation and the blessing to descend upon the 'fathers,'[62] that the 'sons' may receive the influx." Or, according to another passage in the same work: "The goal of their will and intention is to cleave and ascend to the place of their sucking, and therefore our sages established the blessing, the *Kedushah* and the union, to [bring about] the emanation and to draw the 'source of life' to the other Sefirot—[namely,] the 'fathers'—to sustain their 'sons' after them."[63] The purpose of the three prayers mentioned by R. ʿEzra is to counteract the upward movement by the drawing down of emanation upon the higher and lower Sefirot.

The natural tendency of the spiritual entities to ascend to their source is a well-known concept in Neoplatonic thought; this is the *reversio,* a drive inherent in the essence of things, this Neoplatonic view being here applied to the Sefirot.[64] But the reintegration of *rerum ad integrum,* which in Neoplatonism is tantamount to their perfect state, is, however, conceived of here in a derogatory way: the righteous, a symbol of a Sefirah, is envisioned as taken away—in our context, reabsorbed into its source—because of the presence of evil. It is significant that the evil is connected to human activity, as its antidote is the endeavor to neutralize this tendency by a counteractivity drawing the supernal influx downward, presumably in order to balance the upward tendency of the Sefirot. I therefore assume that there are two forces acting in the dynamics of the Sefirot: their striving to return to the source after being torn away from there, and the human activity that, when positive, can counteract the ascending movement and, when negative, can contribute to the taking away of the Sefirot. The human interest in maintaining the status quo is easily understandable; only the sefirotic hierarchy can transmit the supernal influx to the lower worlds, and any disturbance in this chain of transmission may have pernicious repercussions on the lower world. Moreover, it was the divine will to uproot the roots of the Sefirot, to plant them—the lower Sefirot—in the Garden, and to thereby bring about the emergence of the entire sefirotic pleroma. Man and God cooperate in their efforts to sustain an intermediary world that mediates between them; God "pushes" this structure downward, while man "pulls" the influx that counteracts the upward tendency to return.

The preceding conception can be summarized as an expansion of the biblical account of Paradise: God planted it and he commanded Adam to keep it. Moreover, the ancient description of Jewish esotericism employs the term *Pardes*—a garden—as a designation for esoteric speculations, and "the cutting of the branches" as a designation for heresy. Accordingly, the preceding Kabbalistic theosophy can be conceived as an elaborate interpretation of the esoteric significance of the Paradise account and the mystical role of human activity. The perfect activity is the maintenance of the sefirotic pleroma in its state oriented toward the world, as in the talmudic-midrashic views surveyed above.[65] This activity maintains the *Ma'aseh Bereshit*—a symbol of the Sefirot—in its exteriorized state, not allowing it to be reabsorbed into the innermost part of Divinity. Kabbalah is thus conceived as the real force maintaining the divine Garden, as Adam was commanded to do by God. This cultivation of the Garden is an ongoing activity rather than a return to, or attainment of, a primordial state. The theosophical Paradise is not a sublime psychological experience, as the ecstatic Kabbalah would assume,[66] but a dynamic attempt to maintain this world in the best status quo—not a "nostalgia for Paradise," as finding "*oneself always and without effort* in the center of the world at the heart of reality"[67] is the core of the theosophical Paradise, but the effort to construct it continuously and actively.

As Kabbalistic thought developed, more elaborate discussions of theosophy and theurgy were to appear in writing. It is difficult to determine whether the later detailed views were innovative or only a transmission of oral traditions that elaborated the general lines of this theosophico-theurgic theory. Although I cannot conclusively prove it, I tend toward the second possibility, as it is hardly conceivable that R. 'Ezra was unable to account for the specific way in which the influx descends upon the Sefirot. Whatever may be the answer to this question, from the second part of the thirteenth century on, the status quo theurgy became more and more dominant. R. Joseph Gikatilla wrote in his *Sha'arey 'Orah:*

> If men defile and remove themselves from the Torah and the commandments and do wickedness, injustice, and violence, then the attribute of the righteous stands to look and watch and survey their deeds. And when he sees that they reject the Torah and the commandments and do injustice and violence, then the attribute of the righteous is removed and gathers itself [above] and ascends higher and higher. Then all the channels and influxes are interrupted.[68]

This classical Kabbalistic work articulates the way to maintain a particular attribute—Ẓaddik—in its proper place through the performance of the commandments; their neglect causes the return of this attribute to its source. For the first time, we are explicitly told that there is a certain affinity between religious behavior and the Sefirot remaining in an expanded form. It is obvious that Gikatilla elaborates upon the view of R. ʿEzra, as indicated by the use of his example of the righteous.[69] Moreover, this Kabbalist also puts the interrelation of commandments and Sefirot in a positive way:

> The attribute [named] *ʾEl Ḥai* is called righteous, and it stands to watch and see and survey [the deeds of] men; and seeing them studying the Torah and [performing] commandments, and wanting to purify themselves and to behave in a pure and whole way, the attribute of righteous expands and widens, and is filled by all kinds of influx and emanation from above.[70]

I am especially interested in the verbs *expand,* then *widen,* and finally *is filled.* This attribute can first be viewed as returning from its contraction above;[71] it then becomes wider; and finally it receives the supernal efflux.[72] Religious behavior is therefore the criterion for the expansion or contraction of this specific attribute. At the beginning of the fourteenth century, this principle was presented as a comprehensive explanation:[73] When "a person sins, he causes the attributes to return to nothingness,[74] to the primeval world, to their first existence, and [then] they do not emanate goodness downward to the lower world." The final return of all the attributes is described as follows:[75] "If all the powers[76] will be returned to nothingness, then the 'primeval one,' which is the cause of everything, will stand in its unity in the 'depth of nothingness,' in a harmonious union." Significantly, the return of the divine attributes to nothingness is tantamount to their return to their preexistent state, precisely because of sins. Here, we learn of a comprehensive process that comprises all the Sefirot, not only the righteous.

An even more complex formulation of this theurgico-theosophical principle appears in several Kabbalists at the end of the thirteenth century. According to *Sefer ha-Yiḥud:*[77]

> For when the lower man blemishes one of his limbs, as that limb is blemished below, it is as if he cuts the corresponding supernal limb. And the meaning of this cutting is that the limb is cut, and becomes more and more contracted, and is gathered to the depths of being, called nothingness, as if that limb is missing above. For when the human form is perfect below, it brings about perfection above; [in the same manner] the impurity of the limb below causes the gathering of the image of that supernal limb into the depths of nothingness, so as to blemish the

supernal form, as it is written "Because of the evil, the righteous is taken away"[78]—taken away, literally.

The correspondence between human and divine anthropos is here the clue to the mechanism of expansion and contraction in the pleromatic world. A perfect body below induces perfection above; impurity compels the ingathering of a certain divine limb. According to the anonymous Kabbalist, the higher structure is conditioned by the purity or impurity below; in his opinion, man supports this structure by his behavior:[79] "The perfect man, as referred to in the saying: 'The forefathers are the chariot'[80]—the chariot literally. Examine and you shall find that 'a limb supports a limb' . . . for the limb which is prepared supports the limb which is in its image."

The dictum, "limb supports limb," is a well-known one in Kabbalistic literature,[81] and although it was discussed in some studies, its theosophical significance has not yet been analyzed. In this passage, the meaning is clear enough: human limbs support the divine ones by their purity and so maintain the supernal entities in their proper places. It must be emphasized, however, that the focus of the Kabbalistic discussions is neither the glorification of the structure of the limbs nor even their dignity; purity or impurity, performance of the commandments or their neglect, are their main concern. The human structure is, in potentia, prone to perfect the divine structure or to cause its contraction; thus, action is the clue to the understanding of human influence. Here, limbs are no more than tools for the performance of the theurgical ritual, aimed at keeping the theosophical structure in its perfect position. This emphasis is obvious in *Sefer ha-Yiḥud*:[82]

The pious people and the men of deeds[83] know how to direct the powers.[84] And what is meant by "men of deeds"? As in the saying: "Whoever keeps my commandments, I regard as if he has made me,[85] as it is written 'It is a time to make God' "[86]—literally, [since] whoever blemishes below, blemishes above, and whoever purifies himself below, adds strength . . . above.

The performance of the commandments is conceived of here—at least indirectly—as making the Godhead. The gist of this daring statement must be comprehended against its background; the commandments are the way to cause the divine powers to expand, an action tantamount to "making" the divine pleroma. A younger contemporary of the author of *Sefer ha-Yiḥud* expresses this same theory in a more explicit manner:[87]

"For my husband is not at home, he is gone a long journey"[88]—that he will return to the depth of being,[89] "in the city of desolation and destruction."[90] For whosoever blemishes below causes thereby a real destruction—and whoever purifies [himself], builds[91]—and the Midrash [states]: "Whoever keeps my commandments, I regard him as if he made me."[92]

Notwithstanding his affinities with the views expressed in *Sefer ha-Yiḥud,* there is no reason to suppose that R. Abraham of Eskira was influenced by them. If this is so, then this theurgico-theosophical theory may be regarded as being widespread by the end of the thirteenth century, since *Sefer ha-Yiḥud* probably represents Castilian Kabbalah, whereas R. Abraham of Eskira is seemingly the representative of a combination of Catalan and Castilian Kabbalah.

Both the theosophy of "depths of nothingness," in which the Sefirot are contracted when man commits "evil," and the theurgical understanding of the dictum "a limb suports a limb" became influential in Kabbalistic literature far beyond the few examples given above.[93] Their dissemination provides substantial evidence for the increasing role theurgy played in Kabbalah in general, and for the importance of the correlation between a certain type of theosophy and the conception of commandments that occurs in the same texts in particular. This interrelationship is a fine example of the interdependence of two realms of Kabbalistic lore that were studied separately.

The link among evil, the return of the Sefirot to their source, and, at times, the disturbance of the harmony above and below that became more and more evident in the last decades of the thirteenth century surfaced in a clear way in Sabbatian theosophy. Following certain zoharic expressions and concepts, Nathan of Gaza envisioned the emergence of the emanational process as the effect of the victory of the "thought-some light" over the"thought-less light."[94] The latter is succinctly defined as "devoid of any thought or 'idea' that would be prefigurative or constitutive of a cosmos."[95] There is a natural inertia in this aspect of Godhead, which strives to restore the Creation to its initial chaotic state into the Godhead.[96] The early Kabbalah, however, seems to have regarded this tendency of the Sefirot to reabsorption into the divine nought as part of their return to the source in the Neoplatonic vein, whereas, after the integration of important views of evil as part of the Deity in later Kabbalah, this return was considered to be connected to the strife between good and evil. The *Zohar,* which introduced such concepts as "good thought" or "evil thought" into the mainstream of Kabbalistic thought,[97] contributed to this transformation of the significance of the return of the Sefirot.

As we have noted previously, the performance of the commandments holds the sefirotic structure in its position, as it was intended to serve as a bridge between the *'Eiyn Sof* and the world. This status quo was designated by the dictum "a limb holds [or strengthens] another limb." But a certain formula used by two of the above Kabbalists referring to the same concept, is deserving of more detailed elaboration: the performance of the commandments not only preserves the sefirotic pleroma in its balanced and perfect state; it even *makes* it. Let us begin with the zoharic formulation of this idea:[98]

> "And you do them":[99] Why is it written: "And you do them," after it is written "If you walk in my statutes, and keep my commandments"? . . . The answer is: whoever performs the commandments of the Torah and walks in its ways is regarded as if he makes the one above. The Holy one, blessed be he, says: "as if he had made me." And [the question] is raised: "And you do them"—the spelling is "And you do with them [*'itam*]."[100] This is certainly the correct form, and when they are stirred[101] to link to one another, so that the divine name will be in a proper state. This is certainly the meaning [of the spelling] "And you do with them."

The significance of the formula "you made me" is explained by the following phrases: the performance of the commandments causes the union between two divine forces and thus the perfection of the divine name, which is tantamount to the making of God on high. The peculiar type of activation of the divine manifestations is therefore presented as their formation: union or restructuring is regarded as formation; the commandments are instrumental in the theurgical operation.

This reinterpretation of the phrase "as if he made me" raises the question of the source of this view. According to Reuven Margaliot, the source is *Leviticus Rabbah* 35:6 where, however, the crucial form *'asa'ani* is missing.[102] Isaiah Tishby states that it is inconceivable for the sages to assume that man can "make" God, even if this activity is qualified by the phrase "as if"![103] It seems that both scholars are mistaken, however. As we have seen above, the author of the Kabbalistic *Sefer ha-Yiḥud* quotes the formula, "Whosoever keeps my commandments, I regard him as if he made me" as a "saying." Another Kabbalist refers to the identical formula as a "midrash," and R. Menaḥem Recanati quotes it as *Razal*: "our sages said."[104] In both texts, this statement is quoted in contexts different from that in the *Zohar.* Since the *Zohar* does not contain this formula, but indicates an awareness of it and apparently reinterprets its crucial word, *'asa'ani,* I assume that our formula was already in existence prior to the middle of the thirteenth century.[105]

What might the conceptual background of this formula be if we assume—in contrast to Tishby—that it was not introduced by the Kabbalists even though they were the first to quote it? One major assumption would be the identification of God and the Torah; whoever "makes," that is, performs the commandments, implicitly "makes" God. According to *Exodus Rabbah*, "God has given the Torah to Israel and he said to them: it is as if you have taken me."[106] Thus, the nexus between God and Torah had already been put into relief in the Midrash, but this point was exploited by the Kabbalists mentioned previously. According to both the *Zohar*[107] and the *Sefer ha-Yiḥud*,[108] the Torah is identical with God. According to *Sefer ha-Yiḥud*,[109] the peculiar writing of the letters of the Torah is important since they are the shapes or forms[110] of God, and any change spoils the Torah, as it is no longer "the form of God." Accordingly, "each and every one {of the people of Israel} ought to write a scroll of Torah for himself, and the occult secret {of this matter} is that he made[111] God himself." Therefore, the precise writing of the scroll of the Torah is tantamount to the making of God. Again, the form *'asa'o* is reminiscent of *'asa'ani*; therefore, both the writing of the Torah and the performance of its commandments are conceived of as the making of God.

Let us clarify the peculiar significance of this appreciation of theurgical activities. The above-mentioned texts occur in Kabbalistic treatises whose conception of the Sefirot is essentialist, or copied from essentialist texts. The sefirotic pleroma is considered part of the divine essence, and this is the peculiar domain where human activity influences the Divine. As in the status quo view, here too the deployment of the pleroma is a function of human activities, which alone are responsible for the welfare of the revealed facet of Divinity and indirectly of the entire world. By copying the Torah and performing the commandments, the Kabbalist multiplies or diminishes the divine manifestations.[112] Recanati, commenting upon the *Sefer ha-Yiḥud*'s view of making God, writes:[113] " . . . as if he made me. As is written: 'It is a time to make God,' as if to say that whoever blemishes below is as if he blemishes above; and of this it is said: 'he diminishes the image.' "[114] The diminished image refers, presumably, to the sefirotic pleroma. According to the same Kabbalist: "Whosoever performs one commandment causes that power to descend upon the same commandment above, out of the 'annihilation of thought,' and he is considered as if he maintained one part of the Holy one, blessed be he, literally."[115] Thus, the performance of the commandment below induces the influx to rest upon the corresponding commandment above; human activity is ontologized by the concept of the Sefirot as commandments.[116]

We witness here a parallel to the formula "a limb supports a limb." But even more than this formula, the ontologization of the commandments is considered by the Kabbalists to have a dynamic explanation. According to Recanati, "man was made in the supernal archetype," and it is incumbent on him to "cause the ascent and mounting of each and every commandment," until "the commandment will arrive unto God, blessed be he."[117] The performance of the commandments thereby has two theurgical aspects: man can open the supernal source and cause the descent of influx upon the commandment by the ascent on high of the energy connected to the performance of a certain commandment. More emphatic, and more important, are the discussions of R. Meir ibn Gabbay, who repeatedly uses the term *making of God*. In a lengthy elaboration upon the zoharic text quoted above, we find, inter alia:[118]

> For by the performance of the commandments here below, they will be done above, and they will stir their archetypes to complete by their deeds the supernal glory; and whoever does so, is regarded as if he made him, literally. . . . This is the way of making the name attributed to David, as it is written: "and David made a name"[119]—and that refers to the completion of the glory, the secret of the glorious name,[120] which was completed and unified by his study of the Torah and the performance of its commandments, and by his worship which he was continuously worshiping, without interruption. For all this causes the making of the name and its completion, which is the supernal will and volition and the intention of the Creation.

From this presentation, it is obvious that the pleroma, here referred to as the glory, or the name, is the subject of human activity; therefore, it is absolutely necessary continuously to perform the ritual that is intended to sustain the divine manifestations in their perfect state. We must define the making of God as the process of causing the deployment of the Sefirot and their union. By the intentional performance of the Jewish ritual, the Kabbalist directs his intention to God, causing his manifestation to man; this basic reciprocity is attained by the instrument revealed by the Divine: the Torah.

Let us turn to a passage of *Sefer ha-Yiḥud*, which I only briefly paraphrased previously:

> All the letters of the Torah by their shapes, combined and separated, swaddled letters, curved ones and crooked ones, superfluous and elliptic ones, minute and large ones, and inverted, the calligraphy of the letters, the open and the closed pericopes and the ordered ones—all of them are the shape of God, blessed be he.[121]

This passage should be compared to another one, authored by R. Joseph of Hamadan, a Kabbalist whose views were particularly close to those of *Sefer ha-Yiḥud*:[122]

> Happy is he, and blessed his lot, who knows how to direct a limb which corresponds to a limb,[123] and a form which corresponds to a form in the holy and pure chain,[124]

> blessed be his name. Since the Torah is his form, blessed be he, we were ordered to study the Torah, in order to know that archetype of the supernal form,[125] as some Kabbalists[126] have said:[127] "Cursed be he that does hold up[128] all the words of this Torah"—to the congregation—so that they will see the image of the supernal form: moreover, the person who studies the Torah . . . sees the supernal secrets and he sees the glory of God, literally.

Just as *Sefer ha-Yiḥud* mentions the forms or shapes of God in connection with the Torah, so does R. Joseph of Hamadan; he refers to forms together with limbs and, notwithstanding the fact that the precise meaning of these forms is not clear, I assume that they are the commandments that are related to the limbs. The view that the commandments had forms seems to me to have been evidenced already by Philo who, as a Platonist, asserted[129] that the Jews who take "the laws to be divinely revealed oracles[130] . . . bear the image of the commandments imprinted in their souls. Moreover, as they contemplate their clear forms and shapes,[131] their thoughts are full of amazement." We learn that Philo was already acquainted with a conception that the commandments have forms and shape that can be contemplated, just as R. Joseph's passage assumes that the vision of the Torah is a type of contemplation. For Philo, this contemplation is an inner one, whereas for R. Joseph it is external. Nevertheless, both use the term *form* in connection with the Torah, and I assume that R. Joseph hinted to the commandments; his views were adequately summarized by Recanati:[132]

> All the sciences are implicit in the Torah, since there is nothing outside it [the Torah], and the Torah and the commandments are one entity, and the commandments depend upon the supernal chariot,[133] and each and every commandment depends upon one part of the chariot. Thus, God is nothing outside from the Torah, neither is the Torah something outside God, and she is nothing outside God. This is the reason the Kabbalists asserted that God is [identical] with the Torah.[134]

This complete identification of God with the Torah, especially dominant in Kabbalah from the last third of the thirteenth century, raises the question of the peculiar meaning of the view that the shapes of the letters are the forms of God. As we have already seen,[135] "forms" stand for supernal entities such as angels—sometimes identical with letters[136]—or even divine powers, as in the *Bahir.*[137] To put it in other words, if the letters of the Torah are divine forms, will not the commandments expressed by these letters also be divine forms? Indeed, according to Recanati, who again follows earlier views,[138] "each commandment is branch and limb of the supernal form, so that by the completion of the entire Torah the supernal man is completed, as each and every Sefirah of the ten Sefirot . . . make,[139] by being linked [together], one form."

This reification of the commandments, which in our case is simultaneously their deification, presupposes a special mode of existence for them and of their performance; if they constitute a limb or a branch of the Divinity, they must also have forms. Accordingly, the performance of commandments has an ontological impact, which may be appropriately viewed as theurgy.

It is a highly significant point that two of the most important formulations, on whose ground Kabbalists elaborated and developed their theosophical views, were quoted from ancient, presumably midrashic sources, which are extant only in the works of the Kabbalists. Both the passage from *Midrash Hashkem* and the dictum concerning the making of God reached us only because of the interest paid by the Kabbalists to striking theological formulations that served as a point of departure for their Kabbalistic elaborations. These two examples are not unique,[140] although it would not be easy to expand the list greatly.[141] But they may serve as important indicators of the process undergone by the Jewish thought that gradually evolved into Kabbalistic theosophy. Far from being sheer innovations, these concepts [which appear to be so] are presented as part of a sustained effort to understand older oral or written traditions, whose significance is exposed by means of a more complex theology. Both of these texts deal with the close affinity between God and human activity, mainly in the performance of the commandments. This link reflects a phenomenon already discussed in the previous chapter and is a relevant precedent of the intertwining of theosophy and theurgy in later Kabbalah.

III. THE ASCENT OF THE 'ATARAH

The preceding discussions on the ascent of the commandments and their inclusion in Godhead, which is tantamount to the formation of the revealed facet of God, must be considered as no more than an elaboration of a process well known in connection with one specific commandment: the ascent of prayer and its transformation into the crown of God. The midrashic-talmudic texts present the angel Sandalfon as both forming crowns from the prayers of Israel[142] and binding them to God.[143] Especially important in this context is a mystical Midrash, *Midrash Konen,* which asserts:[144]

> There is one Ofan in the world,[145] whose head reaches the [holy] creatures and is the intermediary between [the people of] Israel and their father in heaven, and whose

> name is Sandalfon.[146] And it binds crowns to the master of glory[147] out of the *Kedushah, Barukh Hu'* and *'Amen, Yehey Shemey Rabba* which the children of Israel recite in the synagogues; and it adjures the crown by the ineffable [divine] name, and it [the crown] gradually ascends to the head of the master. Therefore, the sages said that whoever nullifies *Kadosh*,[148] *Barkhu,* and *'Amen, Yehey Shemey Raba* [thereby] diminishes the crown.

The conclusion of this passage is particularly interesting; whoever omits the recitation of certain details of the Jewish liturgy causes the diminution of the crown (*'Atarah*); this crown, formed of the words of prayers, must be perfect in order to ascend to the divine head. There is little doubt as to the biblical source of the Hebrew word *'Atarah.* In Song of Songs 3:11, we read, "Behold King Solomon with the crown with which his mother crowned him on the day of his wedding."

In *'Aggadath Shir ha-Shirim,* this verse was applied to the relationship between Israel and God:[149] "Nations of the world, come and see the feast made by the king[150] who possesses the peace, with the crown with which his mother crowned him: [She did so] at the [Red] Sea, when it is said: 'God will reign for ever and ever.' [Then] God said: 'It is as if you have bound a diadem of kingship on my head.' " This attribution of the crown to God and the concept of Israel as the meaning of "the mother" are major departures from the literal meaning of the biblical verse; a similar phenomenon is found, in connection with the same verse, in the anonymous Gnostic text I have cited several times before:[151] "The Father[152] of the Universes—the Endless one—sent a crown, the name[153] of these universes being in it. . . . This is the crown in relation to which it has been written, saying: 'It was given to Solomon on the day of the joy of his heart.' "

It is strange to see that the Gnostic text regards the crown as being a divine name, exactly as in the Jewish traditions. This identification is possible evidence of the infiltration of a Jewish view into this Coptic text. Again, another resemblance between this passage and the previously quoted Jewish texts is worth noticing, namely, that they share a dynamic quality: in the Jewish sources, it ascends to the Father; in the Gnostic one, it descends at the behest of the Father. Although opposite in direction, these movements demonstrate that a dynamic role was attributed to the crown, which is not commonly characteristic of this object.

Let us return to the end of the quotation from *Midrash Konen;* the motif of diminution of the *'Atarah* is of paramount importance for the understanding of this particular view of reification of prayer. The use of the verb *me'et* is reminiscent of the talmudic phrase *me'et ha-demut,*[154] which, in its context, is related to the view that the children of Israel must number at least twenty-two thousand in order to facilitate the indwelling of the *Shekhinah* on earth.[155] The theurgical perception of the *'Atarah* can be understood by comparing the above traditions to a passage of *Shi'ur Komah,* in which it is indicated that "the crown on his head is 600,000 [parasangs] corresponding to the 600,000 Israelites."[156] I assume that the correspondence between the *demut* and a certain number of Israelites, and the crown and the same number of Jews, and the existence of the phrase *gorem le-ma'et ha-'Atarah,* are part of a more comprehensive view. The *'Atarah* is presumably to be viewed as corresponding to the "[supernal] *demut*" and the *Shekhinah*; human activity is thus influential in relation to these three entities, and the neglect of procreation or multiplication or of prayer causes the diminution of divine manifestations. If this analysis is correct, the passage from *Shi'ur Komah* represents an implicitly theurgic view.[157]

Some of the above motifs converge in two interesting passages found in the writings of R. Eleazar of Worms. According to one text:[158]

> HWH[159]—in gematria [numerical value] is [like that of] BYT, and likewise 'HYH, which is the name of the *Shekhinah*, as it is said: "I will be ['EHYH] by him as a nurseling,"[160] and that is the *Ẓelota'* [that is, prayer],[161] namely, the voice of prayer which ascends above, as Rashi explained: "And there was a voice from above the firmament that was over their heads; when they stood still, they let down their wings."[162] He interpreted this: "And there was a voice"[163]—this is the prayer of Israel, for their prayer ascends to the firmament above their heads and goes to sit on the head of the Holy One, blessed be he, and becomes a crown [*'Atarah*] for him[164] . . . for the prayer sits [there] as a crown. . . . For when the *Ẓelota'* and the prayer ascend on high, then they[165] whisper, and they instigate the ḥashmal[166] against our prayer. . . . And[167] the *'Atarah* of the Holy One, blessed be he, is 600,000 parasangs [long], corresponding to the 600,000 Israelites, and the name of the *'Atarah* is *Sariel*[168] [an anagram of *Israel*] and its numerical value is "prayer one father,"[169] as one father arranges an *'Atarah* out of the prayers, and when[170] the crown [*Keter*] ascends, they[171] run and prostrate themselves and speedily go to put their crowns on [the firmament of] *'Aravot*, and they give Him kingship.[172] "And above the firmament that was over their heads was the likeness of a throne, in appearance like a sapphire stone; and upon the likeness of the throne was the likeness of the appearance of a man."[173] And so the prayers [and] the crowns [*'Atarot*] which ascend to the throne are like a throne, and the throne is made of a sapphire stone.

This passage combines nearly all the motifs discussed above. It also adds an important new aspect, however: the prayers, which change into an *'Atarah*, ascend to the divine throne and are considered to be "like the throne." Hence, the human prayers are transformed by their ascent into part of the divine entourage: *Shekhinah, 'Atarah* on the head of God, and "like the throne." Like the Kabbalists later on, this Ashkenazic author envisions religious worship as producing entities that reach the divine realm and enrich the divine pleroma. This theurgical view of prayer represents a paramount precedent of Kabbalistic theurgy and once again provides evidence that Provençal and Spanish Kabbalists did not introduce innovations by their theurgy, but rather elaborated upon an already existing conception.

The above text can be fruitfully compared to the anonymous *Sefer ha-Navon,* also stemming from an Ashkenazic milieu;[174] the latter author adds some motifs to those analyzed above, but especially significant are the interrelations among the disparate motifs present in this work. This theologian indicates that:[175] "The 'Ateret of his head, GNZ, is ten thousands of parasangs; the numerical value of GNZ is sixty, corresponding to 'And when it rested, he said, return Lord, to the myriads and thousands of Israel.'[176] The name of *'Ateret* is Israel . . . in the name Israel,[177] whose letters are Israel." The verse quoted from Numbers is the same as that used in *Tosefta Yebamot* to demonstrate that there must be a certain number of Israelites to facilitate the indwelling of the *Shekhinah*. Indeed, shortly after the above quotation the author writes:[178]

> The crown [*Keter*] . . . is brought by the spirits to Metatron,[179] and Metatron adjures it, and it goes onto the head of God.[180] This is why the crown [has] GNZ myriads of parasangs, since it is hidden[181] and concealed. And in the treatises *Baba Kamma* . . . and . . . *Sotah* . . . and *Yebamot* . . . it is said: "the *Shekhinah* does not dwell on less than twenty-two thousand Israelites, as in the verse 'And when it rested, he said, return Lord, to the myriads and thousands of Israel.' " And the *'Ateret* has the name Israel.

Therefore, the theurgical aspect of the commandment to multiply rather than diminish the *demut* was directly connected with the theurgical motif of the *'Atarah* in *Shi'ur Komah.* Indeed, the brief allusion to the theurgical nature of the recitation of certain liturgical formulas given above from *Midrash Konen* is corroborated by *Sefer ha-Navon:* "Whoever answers *'amen* to a blessing of the prayer, he [adds] a knot to the *'Atarah* of God; for if there is no knot, each and every letter, each and every word of the prayer would fall away from the *'Atarah*."[182] According to this passage, the formation of the *'Atarah* has two aspects: one is the recitation of prayers and the other their binding by such liturgical formulas as *'amen, Barukh Hu'*, and so on. The role of these formulas is reminiscent of the ancient descriptions of the divine garment as woven out of all the words *'Az* found in the Torah.[183]

Some of these matters are apparently related to a very important text, found in *Sefer ha-Ḥokhmah* of R. Eleazar of Worms.[184] Although this text has been printed and analyzed by scholars, its affinities to some ancient sources escaped them.[185] The passage preserved by this Ashkenazic master contains an obvious theosophical dimension, reminiscent of the Kabbalistic one, a fact that has drawn the attention of scholars:

> The place of the *'Atarah* is on the head of the Creator, in [or by the means of] the [divine] name of forty-two letters[186] . . . and when the *'Atarah* is on the head of the Creator, then the *'Atarah* is called *'Akatriel*, and then the crown is hidden from all the holy angels, and hidden in 500,000 parasangs.[187] . . . of it David said: "He that dwells in the secret [place] of the most high shall abide under the shadow of the Almighty"[188]—that is:[189] "in [or by means of] the prayer[190] of the Almighty we shall abide" . . . since the prayer is the *Ẓelota'* of God, and it sits on the left side of God, like a bride and [her] bridegroom. And it is called "the daughter of the king," and sometimes it is called *Bat Kol* after the name of its mission. of it Solomon said: "and 'EHYH, *Shekhinah* 'EẒLW"[191] and the name of the *Shekhinah* is 'EHYH, and the [Aramaic] translation of 'EẒLW is TRBYH,[192] derived from BRTYH [Aramaic for "his daughter"],[193] since it is called daughter of the king, for the name of the *Shekhinah* that is with him ['EẒLW] in this house. . . . has a *Ẓelota'* named 'EẒLW, that is the tenth kingship, which is the secret of all secrets.

The dynamic nature of the *'Atarah* is here obvious; it attains a special status once placed upon "the head of the Creator"—its name changes to *Keter*, hence *'Akatriel*, and is considered "hidden." These motifs are paralleled by views found in texts, some of which presumably preceded the passage preserved in *Sefer ha-Ḥokhmah* and some contemporary with it. In the anonymous Ashkenazic text discussed above we read:[194]

> The prayer of Israel . . . sits on the head of the Holy, blessed be he, and becomes an *'Atarah* for him, as it is said, "He that dwells in the secret place of the most high."[195] "In the secret" [*ba-seter*] has the same numerical value as *'Akatriel*,[196] as the prayer sits as a crown [*'Atarah*], as it is written, "and it is a crown on the head of *'Akatriel*,[197] Lord God of Israel."

This passage displays the same interrelationship between *Keter, 'Atarah, 'Akatriel*, and the motif of secrecy.[198] Here the dynamic ascent of the *'Atarah* and its transformation into a crown (*Keter*) is also evidenced. Moreover, the connection between "kingship" and *'Atarah* appears here, following an earlier tradition.[199] It seems, however, that not only the ascensional motifs are found in other texts; the descent of the prayer, that is, the crown, at the command of the king, is reminiscent of the above quotation from the Gnostic Coptic text.[200] The text from *Sefer ha-Navon* includes, however, two elements that are specifically characteristic of Kabbalah: (1) the prayer, viewed as *'Atarah*, is identical with "the tenth kingship," the emphasis being placed on the "tenth," which betrays the position of the *Malkhut*—"kingship" as the tenth Sefirah;[201] and (2) the prayer is viewed as a female entity, the bride of God. The dynamism of the *'Atarah*, which is the *Shekhinah* and appears both in the opposition of *Malkhut* and on "the head of God," is reminiscent of the dynamic of the *Shekhinah* in an ancient text in which the *Shekhinah* is described in these words: "just as the *Shekhinah* is below, she is on high."[202] In the *Bahir*, this view was applied to the presence of the *Shekhinah* in the entire pleromatic realm.[203]

Before I leave the Ashkenazic material, it should be mentioned that the theurgical conception of the ascending prayer was articulated in the famous *Shir ha-Kavod*, well known as part of the Shabbat liturgy: "Let my praise be a crown unto thy head, / and my prayer be set forth before thee as incense." The comparison of the ascending prayer to incense is seemingly an elaboration upon the conception that the prayers are a substitute for sacrifices.

The ascent of the *'Atarah* to the highest place in the divine pleroma was adopted by theosophical Kabbalah. Notwithstanding its being a classical symbol of the lowest Sefirot—*Malkhut*—*'Atarah* is at times portrayed as ascending to the *Keter*, in a way similar to that of the anonymous author whose view was preserved in the book of R. Eleazar of Worms. Already R. 'Ezra of Gerona had commented upon the verse in Song of Songs 3:11:[204] "the whole structure[205] will cleave and unite with and ascend to *'Eiyn Sof*." According to this Kabbalist, this is the reason "the blessing, the *Kedushah*, and the union, originating from the 'nought of thought,' are called *'Ateret* and *Keter*,"[206] an assessment based upon the midrashic text on the binding of the prayers of Israel and the depositing of the *'Atarah* on "the head of God."[207] R. 'Ezra quoted elsewhere the views on *'Atarah* in *Midrash Tanhuma* and *Shi'ur Komah*,[208] so that we may assume that the relevant classical literature concerning this issue was known to this early Kabbalist. Accordingly, he assumed the necessity of performing the prayers in order to draw influx downward on the Sefirot but, at the same time, to unite them to *'Eiyn Sof* by causing the ascent of the *'Atarah* together with the entire structure of lower Sefirot.[209] A later Kabbalist summarized this view in these words: "in spite of the fact that it is beneath [the other Sefirot], sometimes it ascends to *'Eiyn Sof* and becomes an *'Atarah* on their head, and for this reason it is called *'Atarah*."[210]

According to an anonymous Kabbalist of the fourteenth century,[211] the enumeration of the ten Sefirot began with:[212] "*'Atarah*, to let you know that it is also *Keter*; and if you will reverse the Sefirot, then *Malkhut* will be the first . . . as they have neither beginning nor end, 'the beginning[213] of thought being the end of the action.' "

To summarize: in a series of texts that precede the historical Kabbalah, we find theurgical elements referring to an entity that is presented as a part of the pleromatic realm—namely, the *'Atarah*. This peculiar type of theurgy is close to the Kabbalistic theurgy, previously analyzed, that dealt with the making of the pleroma rather than with its strengthening. We can perceive in an early text, quoted in R. Eleazar of Worms's work, the addition of specifically Kabbalistic theosophical motifs. I therefore assume that the later theurgic view of "making God" is essentially a continuation of older theurgic thought. The similarity between the Ashkenazic and the Kabbalistic treatment of the *'Atarah-Keter* relationship demonstrates the existence of common sources, which continue even older traditions.

The ritual of composing the *'Atarah* by prayer and its ascent and setting on the head of God is tantamount to the coronation of the king. This instauration by ritual is clearly reminiscent of the ancient interconnection between ritual and kingship. Kabbalah may therefore be viewed not only as the cultivation of the Garden but also as the cultivation of the Gardener. If the symbolism of Lebanon pertains to the lower facet of Divinity, that of the *'Atarah* belongs to its highest aspect. The human range of activity therefore expands beyond those divine manifestations that are ruling the created worlds, to the most recondite layers of the Divine. But while the lower manifestations are structured or made by the ritual, the higher ones are ornamented by the addition of the crown or crowns; again, these ornaments originate from the ascent of a lower divine power—the *'Atarah*.

IV. THEURGICAL WEEPING

As we saw above in *Midrash Hashkem*, human weeping elicits a similar divine response. In Lurianic Kabbalah, this midrashic view was elaborated into a fully theurgical activity, intended to trigger a certain process in the divine realm. In *Zohar ha-Rakia'*,[214] R. Ḥayyim Vital interprets the talmudic dictum,"the gates of tears were not locked,"[215] as follows: "For the lower man is the image of the supernal form,[216] and his mouth is as the mouth of the supernal [form] and his eyes as the eyes of the supernal [form]; [thus] when they stir below, they stir above [also]."

Moreover, this Kabbalist distinguishes between the lower status of the mouth whence prayer originates, which corresponds to the Sefirah of *Binah*, and weeping, which corresponds to the Sefirah of *Ḥokhmah*.[217] "When man weeps, he has to intend to mitigate the forces of judgment . . . and the shells."[218] This sympathetic theurgy, presented here in general terms, becomes much more concrete in a sermon of Vital's.[219] After stating the standard assessment that "everything happening between the supernal [powers] is the doing of the lower [entities], and the lower man moves by his acts all the high hosts for better or worse," he continues:[220]

> When a person weeps and sheds tears for [the death of] a righteous man, he also causes tears to be shed on high, and as we find it said, as it were, of God [himself]: "The Lord God of Hosts will call to weeping and mourning," and so on,[221] [or] "my soul shall weep in secret,"[222] and so on, or as it is written: "Oh, that my head were waters [and my eyes a fountain of tears]"[223]—namely, that I long for the act of the lower [entities], as by their weeping below, they cause "my head to be as waters and my eyes a fountain of tears." May they do so, and thereby I may also weep for my dead.

God therefore waits for human activity to activate him. Far from being part of a mechanistic theosophy dealing with intrasefirotic processes, as presented by Vital in *Zohar ha-Rakia'*, it is here presented as part of a widespread custom, or ritual, for mourning the righteous. Contrasting the former presentation of weeping, which must be directed toward a specific force in the divine pleroma—and is therefore a Kabbalistic act—in his sermon, Vital emphasizes that "there is no need that the weeper should be a righteous and honest [man], since everyone who sheds [tears] is causing this . . . even if the weeper is [part of] the vulgus."[224] Thus, the efficacy of weeping is not based on knowledge of esoteric gnosis, but on God's closeness to those of "broken hearts."[225] The focus of human activity is presented in a popular work as the emotional life rather than the complicated theosophico-theurgical activity; we thereby witness a shift from elitist theurgy, characteristic of Lurianic Kabbalah, to a popular one, characteristic afterward of Ḥasidic mysticism. For the latter, the affinity betweeen man and God is not so much one of structural resemblance—in *Zohar ha-Rakia'* the supernal form is mentioned—but the closeness between the emotional processes below and on high. By means of this change, the spread of Kabbalah among larger masses was facilitated. Anthropopathism, rather than anthropomorphism, is the clue to understanding the transformation of theosophy into a mystical theology.[226] To put it in other words: in lieu of the participation mystique of the Kabbalist in the divine life, we now witness a participation mystique of the Divine in human life. Only the attenuation of the importance of the complex hierarchy and its interrelationship with the structure of the human body opened a new avenue for Jewish mysticism, wherein the spiritual could come to the fore and be put in relief. The theurgical element, however, was not rejected as in the ecstatic Kabbalah but was transposed onto the spiritual-emotive plane.[227]

CHAPTER 9

Kabbalistic Hermeneutics

One of the more neglected areas of Kabbalistic thought is its hermeneutics. Modern research has formulated only some general concepts regarding Kabbalistic symbolism, but has neglected the problematics that arise from the emergence of Kabbalistic methods of interpretation, and has ignored the intricacies of the relationship between the Kabbalist qua interpreter and the divine text. In the first part of this chapter, I shall offer a preliminary discussion of some questions pertaining to Kabbalistic symbolism; in the second part, I will discuss the experiential nature of the Kabbalistic approach to the text interpreted. A particularly interesting related issue—the appearance of relatively elaborated hermeneutical methods in the writings of R. Abraham Abulafia, the anonymous author of *Sefer ha-Ẓeruf,* and R. Isaac of Acre, among the ecstatic Kabbalists, and in the *Zohar* and the works of R. Moses de Leon, R. Joseph Gikatilla, R. Joseph of Hamadan, and R. Baḥya ben Asher, among the theosophists—will be the subject of a separate study.

I. THE STATUS OF SYMBOL IN KABBALAH

1. The Nature of Kabbalistic Symbolism

One of the central axioms of modern Kabbalah scholarship is the paramount importance of symbolic perception for the understanding of this type of Jewish mysticism. In a short essay, Scholem affirms that "the symbolic *Weltanschauung* of the Kabbalah in all its forms" is one of its basic components.[1] This statement, formulated in 1936, was reiterated in all later discussions of the role of symbolism in Kabbalah. The single analysis devoted to this question, an essay by Tishby, only strengthens Scholem's view: "There is no topic dealt with in Kabbalistic literature which is not connected in one way or another with symbolism, and there is no Kabbalist who did not use symbols when expressing his conceptions."[2] These unqualified statements, expressed in categorical terms, betray a surprising agreement on the issue of Kabbalistic symbolism that one does not find in connection with any other major topic in Kabbalah. These affirmations, however, were not verified or proven by these scholars or their followers. I would therefore like to elaborate upon the correctness of the "findings" of these two eminent figures of modern Kabbalah scholarship.

The centrality of symbolic expression is obvious and indisputable only in the theosophical Kabbalah, whose central work was the *Zohar.* As far as other types of Kabbalah are concerned, the role of symbolism is problematic. Let us begin with the treatment of this issue in ecstatic Kabbalah. In the numerous and voluminous works of R. Abraham Abulafia, symbolism, as defined by Scholem and Tishby, is absent.[3] There are at least two reasons for this. First, Abulafia was singularly interested in attaining various states of mystical consciousness, either revelatory or unitive. The former were expressed in allegorical forms that could easily be decoded with the help of Aristotelian terminology; the latter experiences required symbolic expression, and when descriptions of such experiences appear they, again, belong to the allegorical mode. The second reason for the lack of symbolism in Abulafia's writings is his peculiar theology, which differed sharply from that of theosophical Kabbalah. Abulafia did not accept theosophy in general, or even any classical form of Kabbalistic theosophy; he likewise rejected the demonological views widely accepted by other Kabbalists. As these were the two major domains represented by Kabbalistic symbolism, the great bulk of symbols became irrelevant for his thought.

However, Abulafia's indifference to and even, as we shall see below, rejection of symbolism was part of a larger trend within Kabbalah, including the *Commentary on Sefer Yeẓirah* of R. Barukh Togarmi, the remnants of a similar work of R. Isaac Bedershi, the earlier works of R. Moses de Leon and R. Joseph Gikatilla, and some earlier parts of the *Midrash ha-Ne'elam,* to mention only a few works of this school. This linguistic Kabbalah, whose affinity to that of Abraham Abulafia is evident, did not share the theosophical outlook of contemporary Kabbalists; therefore, symbolism was in principle either marginal or, at times, irrelevant to it. The only important exceptions to this are the works of R. Isaac of Acre, who shared with the ecstatic Kabbalists a deep interest in paranormal experience and in a praxis of mystical techniques, and was at the same time profoundly interested in the entire variety of Kabbalistic symbolism flowering in his time in Spain.

A perusal of Kabbalistic treatises written under the dominant influence of Abulafia reveals the same indifference toward symbolic expression in the vein of theosophical Kabbalah; such works as *Sefer ha-Ẓeruf, Sha'arey Ẓedek, Ner 'Elohim,* and later, R. Yehudah Albotini's *Sullam ha-'Aliyah* demonstrate that Abulafia was not the only Kabbalist to compose important Kabbalistic treatises without significant use of a symbolic jargon. Moreover, it would seem that the elaborate symbolism of theosophical Kabbalah was the object of derision on the part of Abulafia. In his *'Imrey Shefer,* he indicates that the theosophists[4]

> claim that they received from the prophets and the sages that there are ten Sefirot . . . and they designated each and every Sefirah by names, some of them being homonyms,[5] others proper names. And when they were asked [to explain them], those who know them were unable to say what these Sefirot are, and to what [kind of] entity these names refer. . . . and their names [of the Sefirot] are well known from their books, but they are very perplexed concerning them.

The main target of Abulafia's criticism was Kabbalistic theosophy—the assumption that there are ten divine potencies referred to by a plethora of names, that is, symbols. But we also hear in passing his criticism of the numerous symbols for entities whose essence was not apprehended by the Kabbalists themselves. Indeed, Abulafia seems to have perceived here a central problem of theosophical Kabbalah: in sharp contrast to philosophy, this type of Kabbalah was either unable to define the precise nature of its emanational hierarchy or was indifferent toward exact definitions; thus, symbols substituted for precise definitions. For a Kabbalist whose theology was decisively influenced by Maimonides' thought, as Abulafia was, ambiguous formulations were seen as indicative not of the inexpressibility of the object but lack of clarity on the part of the thinking subject. For Abulafia, the mulitiplicity of names or symbols was a symptom of intellectual perplexity. Therefore, in at least one case, Abulafia not only refrained from using symbols but openly criticized their very use as a sign of lack of understanding. According to another important text of ecstatic Kabbalah, the very concentration upon a particular name was pernicious for the spiritual development of the mystic. The anonymous master of the author of *Sha'arey Ẓedek* taught his disciple

> to efface everything. He used to tell me: "My son, it is not the intention that you come to a stop with some finite form, even though it be of the highest order. Much

rather is this the 'path of the names.' The less understandable they are, the higher their order, until you arrive at the activity of a force which is no longer in your control, but rather your reason and your thought are in its control."[6]

As we know, symbols are intended to help one perceive that which it is difficult to comprehend. The symbol is therefore much more comprehensive than the symbolized process or entity itself. Indeed, the theosophical Kabbalah regards the nature of the symbol in precisely this way. In the ecstatic Kabbalah, no group of symbols can help achieve a better understanding of higher matters. Indeed, the effacement of any limited written or oral phrase is a necessary step toward the mystical experience, viewed here as the possession of the human intellect by the Divine, for which reason the limited form does not enable entities on a higher level to become transparent in our human sphere, but rather obfuscates the possibility of the spiritual dwelling in the finite. Theosophical Kabbalah uses symbols as a pathway toward attaining an otherwise inaccessible gnosis of higher dynamics;[7] ecstatic Kabbalah strives to attain an experience of the Divine. For the latter, symbols may easily become a hindrance to the mystical longing for contact with the Divine, or, as Nathan Rotenstreich once put it, "symbolism, on the one hand, and the denial of the *unio mystica* and pantheism on the other, seem to be the two correlated axes comprising, as it were, the epistemological and the ontological components, respectively, of Scholem's interpretative work."[8] These were indeed the main axes of Scholem's interpretation; however, they constitute a one-sided appreciation of the Kabbalistic phenomena. A more adequate formulation would insist that the two axes of Kabbalah are symbolism, which is related to nonunitive experiences, on the one hand, and unitive experiences, which coalesce with nonsymbolic language, on the other.

Thus, when the focus of Kabbalah is on psychological processes, or when its theology is philosophically rather than theosophically oriented, the role of symbol becomes radically reduced or, as in the case of Abulafia, totally effaced. Another pertinent example is Abulafia's older contemporary, R. Isaac ibn Latif; although his theology is basically Neoplatonic—in contrast to Abulafia's Aristotelian view—and more inclined to an allusive mode of expression, his static conception of the Deity holds him back from a dynamic symbolism, his language being closer to allegory than to symbolism. The same is true of the early fourteenth-century treatise *Masoret ha-Berit* by R. David ben Abraham ha-Lavan.[9] Later, when Ḥasidic mysticism emerged through the attenuation of the complex Lurianic theosophy, its concentration on psychology brought about a manifest diminution of the role of classical Kabbalistic symbolism.

These examples should suffice substantially to qualify Scholem's and Tishby's statements regarding the centrality of symbolism in Kabbalah.

As we have seen, ecstatic Kabbalah avoided symbolism in the sense in which it was used in theosophical Kabbalah, which for its particular purposes was superfluous. Theosophical symbolism was eventually interpreted anthropologically, as I have mentioned above;[10] this process can be designated as a psychologization of theosophy. At times, Abraham Abulafia would conceive the Sefirot as separate intellects, an explicitly philosophical term and a conception that effaced the dynamic of the Sefirot and substantially attenuated their divine status. The symbolic value of the referends to the Sefirot was thus almost totally deleted.

Another major trend used the classical symbols of theosophic Kabbalah in a way inconsistent with their very nature as symbols: I refer to the magical understanding of human influence on the sefirotic realm. According to R. Yoḥanan Alemanno, the Sefirot are superseparate intellects;[11] I will cite here his view of the way in which man activates this supernal sefirotic world:

> The Kabbalists believe that Moses, peace be with him, had precise knowledge of the spiritual world, which is called the world of Sefirot and the world of divine names, or the world of letters. Moses knew how to direct his thoughts and prayers so as to improve the divine influx, which the Kabbalists call "channels"; Moses' action caused the channels to emanate upon the lower world in accordance with his will. By means of that influx, he created anything he wished, just as God created the world by means of various emanations. Whenever he wished to perform signs and wonders, Moses would pray and utter divine names, words and meditations, until he had intensified those emanations. The emanations then descended into the world and created new supranatural things. With that, Moses split the sea, opened up the earth and the like.[12]

For Alemanno, the Sefirot became a more or less mechanical superstructure that could be precisely manipulated by an expert supermagician. Moses was the great expert of the intricacies of this world, who knew exactly how to address his prayer, how to invoke the divine names, and how to direct his thoughts in order to achieve his mundane goals. Although the letters, the divine names, and the prayer might be identical with the theosophical symbols, their role was drastically changed. They were no longer a modus cognescendi, a channel for fathoming the recondite processes of the intradivine structure, but vital components of a modus operandi; only because the Sefirot had ceased to be unknowable entities, transparent only through symbols, had they become instruments in the hands of Moses. It is worth noting the description here of Moses: he had "precise knowledge of the spiritual world." As part of this knowledge, he was acquainted with the singular relationship between a peculiar phrase, a divine name, or a letter and a certain Sefirah. Their relationship was not essentially symbolic, but rather a substantive one; the right words would directly manipulate the particular Sefirah, which would in turn produce the desired effect in the lower world. The phase of learning the symbolic value of words, of reflecting upon what they symbolize or upon how they reflect hidden essences, was part of the previous stages of Kabbalah. We have passed from the world of contemplators and theurgists interested in the divine harmony into that of Kabbalistic magicians, for whom knowledge of the supernal mechanism was only a means to more practical purposes. The sefirotic automaton was now efficiently operated by the accomplished technician; the symbolic cargo of language was transformed into a kind of quasi-mathematical command. Kabbalistic symbolism thus turned into—or perhaps returned to—a magical language of incantation. Therefore, we can add the "magification" of symbols to their psychologization as part of the process by which their symbolic value, as it flourished in the theosophical Kabbalah, was undermined.

I should like to propose a tentative explanation for the distribution of the interest in symbolism between the theosophical Kabbalah, on the one hand, and ecstatic and magical Kabbalah, as well as Ḥasidism, in part, on the other hand. Symbolism becomes prominent whenever an attempt is made to explain external reality: God, evil, the nature of the Torah, of history, or of the cosmos in general. The focus of religious meaning is found in relatively objective entities and processes, and this meaning as such is shared by a certain segment of a religious community. The symbolic recasting of external reality allowed the emergence of what John E. Smith has aptly called "a transindividual unity of experience."[13] No wonder that the *Zohar,* the most important source of "objective symbolism," also became a canonical work: it established an additional level of experience, shared by many individuals qua part of a religious community. This is the key for the revitalization of Jewish spirituality achieved by the dissemination of the *Zohar* in its various interpretations.

To use Smith's formulation again, ecstatic Kabbalah was mainly interested in what the individual does with his own solitariness.[14] Treatises of this branch of Kabbalah describe the techniques for the attainment of mystical experiences far more than they describe the experiences themselves. From its beginning, ecstatic Kabbalah was an elite lore and has remained so until now, pointing the way the very few may follow for their own spiritual perfection rather than the means for the restoration of divine harmony. The technique proposed does not involve symbolic expressions, nor are its works intended to provide detailed confessions of mystical experience, ineffable or difficult to convey.

Let me briefly exemplify this dichotomy in the Kabbalistic attitude to symbolism. According to Scholem, "the older Kabbalists never interpreted the 'Song of Songs' as a dialogue between God and the soul, i.e., an allegorical description of the path to the *unio mystica*."[15] In lieu of the "missing" allegorical interpretation of the Song of Songs, theosophical Kabbalah abounds in symbolical understanding of this text. In the works of R. 'Ezra of Gerona, the recurring zoharic discussions of the Song, and the commentaries of R. Isaac ibn Avi Sahulah, and others, the focus of interpretations are the theosophical processes taking place between the two lower Sefirot of *Tiferet*, symbolized by the bridegroom, and *Malkhut*, symbolized by the bride. Accordingly, both the biblical description and human love itself reflect, or symbolize, higher events within the intradivine structure. This is indeed the main thrust of Kabbalistic perception of the Song of Songs, and, roughly speaking, Scholem is right.

An allegorical interpretation of the Song is not completely absent, however; it occurs in ecstatic Kabbalah. For Abraham Abulafia, "The Song of Songs is only an allegory for *Knesset Yisrael* and God . . . and human love does not unite with the divine one, except after long study and after comprehension of wisdom and reception of prophecy."[16] In this context, *Knesset Yisrael* is not the transpersonal community of Israel, as it is used in midrashic-talmudic texts, or the symbol of the last Sefirah, *Malkhut*, as in Kabbalah, but, as Abulafia himself states,[17] "the secret of *Knesset Yisrael* is—Knesset I-SAR-EL, since the perfect man[18] is bringing everything together and is called the community [*Knesset*] of Jacob." Therefore, the Song of Songs becomes an allegory of human intellect and its union with God. The focus of ecstatic Kabbalah is the perfect man, namely the perfect intellect that undergoes a mystical union with the supernal intellect. This process is perceived directly by the individual, who needs no symbols to describe it. In the theosophical Kabbalah, the focus is on a process that cannot be precisely described, as it cannot be directly perceived; the theosophical process, objective as it may be, is beyond full human apprehension and therefore can only be reflected through symbolic language. By the intermediacy of its symbolism, theosophical Kabbalah functions as a unifying ideology; ecstatic Kabbalah, oriented to the isolated individual, does not care about the social structure, just as it is not concerned about the sacrosanct structure of the Scripture and emphasizes a relatively escapist type of mysticism.

Ḥasidism represents an interesting combination of the individualistic bias of ecstatic Kabbalah, with its stress upon *devekut*, and the theosophical Kabbalah, with its emphasis upon the importance of the commandments as a central, although not exclusive, means for attaining unitive experience. The Ḥasid shares a unifying religious ritual with the social group, which is nevertheless fraught with an element of transcendence that enables the achievement of a singularly individual experience of union. The initial stages of the mystical path in Ḥasidism at times also involved some symbolic significance. According to some Ḥasidic masters, however, the Lurianic *kavvanot*—that is, the symbolical referents of the Sefirot or of the divine configurations—must be respectfully rejected, at least in the usage among the masses of Ḥasidism.[19] As for the final stage of Ḥasidic mysticism, this is expressed by such metaphors as the drop and the ocean, swallowing,[20] and so on, with no significant use of symbolism.[21] Ḥasidism, interested mostly in the mystical encounter—the "event," in Heschel's language—diminished the symbolism so important for the Kabbalistic evaluation of the "process": namely, the elaborate awareness of the theosophic structure that must accompany the performance of the commandments, which "happens regularly, following a relatively permanent pattern."[22]

Let us elaborate upon a crucial reason for the rejection of symbolism in ecstatic Kabbalah. This form of mysticism emphasized, more than did theosophical Kabbalah, the chasm between the spiritual and the material: with the goal of attaining liberation from the bonds of corporeality, ecstatic Kabbalah worked on the means of severing the connection between the human soul and its body; as a corporeal being, the body could not serve as a point of departure for metaphysical meditations.[23] On the other hand, theosophical Kabbalah conceived the specific structure of the body as a powerful symbol of the sefirotic realm, and its contemplation as an important way of fathoming the recondite structure of Deity. Therefore, although even this type of Kabbalah would acknowledge the profound difference between the human and the Divine, these two entities shared a common structure, such that man as symbol permitted the mystic an ascent beyond the material world. In other words, in theosophical thought the antagonism between the two levels of reality was attenuated by the existence of a common structure embodied in varied fashions on these two levels.[24] This distinction between the attitudes to corporeality of ecstatic and theosophical Kabbalah is reflected in their perceptions of the relationship between the esoteric and exoteric levels of the text. According to a statement, probably written by Abraham Abulafia, "The curse of the plain [meaning] is the blessing of the hidden one, and the curse of the hidden [meaning] is the blessing of the plain [one]."[25] This antinomy between plain and hidden is aptly exemplified in an anonymous work written by someone in Abulafia's circle:[26]

> And the severe forces of the left will be diminished, which are called the evil urge,[27] and the left, and Samael, and Satan, and the angel of death, and the serpent. All of them will be cast away from you, as well as all their stony forces, as it is said: "and I will remove from your flesh the heart of stone,"[28] and their forces will submit to the intellectual divine forces, as it is said, "and I will give you a heart of flesh."[29] [Then] your eyes will be open to examine these divine matters, the inmost and intermediate, not [those forces pertaining to] the shells. And when you shall achieve [this] degree, then you will be purified of the corporeal defilement and thought of the senses, and the intellectual force will not be commingled, in either a great or a small measure, with the senses, except insofar as the senses will [serve] as a vessel which receives that which is [conceived] in it.

According to this Kabbalist, there are three levels of meaning in the Torah: the literal; the allegorical,[30] which is the intermediary; and the divine or innermost meaning. The author of *Sefer ha-Ẓeruf,* like Abulafia, regarded the literal meaning as utterly negative, or even demonic, as it is here; no wonder that Abulafia's hermeneutics culminated in a text-destroying exegesis that focused upon separate letters understood as divine names.

The hermeneutics of theosophical Kabbalah reflected a different anthropology. Just as the human body reflected the higher theosophy, so did the plain meaning of the text; neither the body nor the text needed to be destroyed in order to attain ultimate esoteric knowledge: they were the starting points for contemplation, material to be penetrated without obliterating its basic structure. For the theosophical Kabbalist, the basic unit was not the monadic letter, freed of its links to the canonic text, but the word, which remained generally intact while its esoteric meaning alluded to a divine hypostasis. While pointing to a higher entity, the discrete word still was part of the basic sentence, which was interpreted in toto as the symbol of a process. In contrast to monadization, symbolization referred more to the canonic text as received by the tradition. Ecstatic Kabbalah prescribed mystical techniques for the attainment of the perfection of the individual, to be used in total isolation; theosophical Kabbalah emphasized the role of the community as a unity able to act in an other-oriented way for the benefit of the Godhead more than for its own welfare. The *Zohar* envisaged a conventicle of Kabbalists: the Lurianic Kabbalah was taught to a group. For such social approaches, the text, despite its symbolic transfiguration, had to be preserved. The literal meaning then remained the patrimony of the vulgus; the esoteric, the privilege of the few. The *Zohar,* written in a special literary style, was intended from the outset for a double audience: the ordinary Jew, interested in a more exciting understanding of the text, and those few seeking its esoteric sense. In contrast, ecstatic Kabbalah, especially Abulafia's works, preferred a highly complicated style, almost unintelligible to the uninitiated. The differences between the two Kabbalistic schools in hermeneutics, anthropology, and literary style are highly significant and can be summarized as an attempt, in the theosophical Kabbalah, to transcend the literal meaning, the corporeal, and the social group without effacing their importance as such, whereas the ecstatic Kabbalah lived in a high tension with them, at times culminating in an attempt to disintegrate them.

As this discussion makes clear, symbolism was favored by the theosophical Kabbalah. But even this statement must be qualified by a closer analysis of symbolic expression and other types of religious interest, crucial for theosophical Kabbalah. Let us examine the relationship between theurgy and symbolism; this issue, which was already dealt with above,[31] deserves a complementary presentation.

One notable development in Jewish symbolism calls for clarification. From biblical times, the relationship between Israel and God had been described in terms of that between, respectively, a woman and her husband. As long as Israel, or *Knesset Yisrael*, was regarded as one entity in relation with another one, the mystical experience of the individual was not mentioned in Jewish sources.[32] Mystical meetings between the high priest and God in the Holy of Holies were never described in erotic or sexual terms.[33] The masculine symbolism for God and the feminine for the mystic appeared in ecstatic Kabbalah: the female represented the individual human soul or intellect in her relation to the active intellect or God, viewed as masculine.[34] Although theosophical Kabbalah also used this type of symbolism, we encounter in this form of Kabbalah besides a series of discussions wherein the symbolism is inverted. The lowest divine potency, the *Shekhinah*, plays the feminine role in relationship to the *Ẓaddik*, the righteous human being, who functions as the male. This view is repeatedly expressed in the *Zohar,* although it is not entirely novel; it was alluded to in the Midrash and by R. Moses of Burgos in connection with Moses'description in the Bible as the "man of God" ("man" in Hebrew—*'ish*—also has the meaning of "husband"). According to these texts, Moses is the "man," the husband of *Elohim*, a symbol for the *Shekhinah*. In the *Zohar,* however, these scanty allusions were expanded and extended to the righteous in general.

The two different patterns of symbolism reveal varied perceptions of the erotic relationship between man and Deity. The notion of the righteous viewed as male in his relationship to *Shekhinah* was part of an activistic approach that emphasized the theurgic operation; the perception of the mystic as the female in the ecstatic Kabbalah constituted part of the philosophical *weltanschauung*, whose goals were meditation and intellectual union with God. This theology, influenced by Maimonidean thought, allowed for no change in the Godhead and considered its representation as a passive feminine power unimaginable. Ecstasy, therefore, was the invasion of the human by the Divine, which was always present within reality, the encounter with it being conditioned only by man's preparation and openness to the Divine. Although the ecstatic Kabbalah emphasized an activistic approach to the mystical experience through its prescription of mystical techniques, at the very moment of the experience this activism was obliterated and replaced by a passive state.[35] The ascent of the activistic attitude in the theosophical Kabbalah brought in its train important repercussions for the place of symbolism in Kabbalah; the greater the role of theurgy, the more problematic became the role played by symbolism. The mythical relationship of the righteous man to the *Shekhinah* was expanded at the expense of the symbolic perception of this divine manifestation.[36] Therefore, we can conclude that the religious nuclei, like ecstasy, magic, and theurgy, mitigated the centrality of symbolism in some Kabbalistic systems.

We shall now survey the flowering of symbolism in theosophical Kabbalah in its historical context.

2. The Flowering of Kabbalistic Symbolism

The flourishing of Kabbalistic symbolism can be definitively located in the last two decades of the thirteenth century; its locus was Castile. During the preceding hundred years, however, theosophical symbols appeared in most of the Kabbalistic literature composed in Provence and Catalonia. Although it served as an important mode of expression for most of the earlier Kabbalists, symbolism was used in a particular way at that time. In the earlier documents, symbols are relatively rare, and the relationship between a symbol and the object symbolized is relatively stable. It stands to reason that this connection was part of an older tradition, transmitted in closed circles. A survey of symbolism as expressed in the Kabbalistic works written in Catalonia after the end of the thirteenth century, which incorporate some of the traditions stemming from Naḥmanides and his sources, reveals a distinct effort to elucidate the precise symbolic meaning of a certain word or phrase. At times, controversies between the students of Naḥmanides are reported, focusing on such questions as whether the word *Ẓion* refers to the Sefirah of *Malkhut*, as one authority argued,[37] or to Yesod, as his colleague claimed.[38] The fact that they could not settle the matter indicates that the polyvalence of a given symbol was still a rare notion among these Catalan Kabbalists, who faithfully continued much older Kabbalistic traditions. This description also fits, mutatis mutandis, the Kabbalists of Gerona, R. 'Ezra, R. Jacob ben Sheshet, and to a certain extent, R. 'Azriel, whose symbolism is relatively poor when compared to the later Castilian Kabbalists, but richer than that of *Sefer ha-Bahir* or R. Isaac the Blind. Likewise, the range of symbolism in the works of R. Jacob ben Jacob ha-Cohen, of his brother, R. Isaac, and of their followers is limited. Against this background, we find a surprising change in the role played by symbols after the end of the thirteenth century in Castile. For the first time, comprehensive commentaries on the ten Sefirot were composed, consisting of long lists of symbols referring to each Sefirah; such classics of Kabbalah as R. Joseph Gikatilla's *Sha'arey 'Orah* and *Sha'arey Ẓedek* are specifically devoted to the hundreds of symbols related to the Sefirot. Moreover, we have reason to think that an interesting literary phenomenon first occurred in Castile during this period: certain authors composed, during a relatively short time, several versions of their commentaries of the ten Sefirot. R. Joseph Gikatilla wrote at least four,[39] R. Moses de Leon, at least two,[40] and R. Joseph of Hamadan, at least three;[41] nothing similar is known to have occurred throughout the preceding century.[42]

Although there are no crucial conceptual differences among the various versions of each author's commentaries, they indicate an increasing interest in different types of symbolism. Only a small part of this symbolic *avalanche de richesse* can be traced to earlier Kabbalistic sources; thus this interest in symbolism can be regarded not as a mere organization or collection of already existing symbols but as a new eruption of a symbolic type of consciousness. I would like to present what seems to me to be one major cause for this intensive interest in and novel approach to the symbol.

By the 1270s, the province of Castile had become an important meeting center for Kabbalists. Besides the indigenous Jewish mystics, such as the students of R. Jacob and Isaac ha-Cohen, non-Castilian Kabbalists visited this region, the most famous of whom, R. Abraham Abulafia, was in contact with two major Castilian figures: R. Moses of Burgos and R. Joseph Gikatilla.[43] I assume that he was instrumental in fostering the interest in linguistic Kabbalah, which he initially studied in Catalonia; this kind of Kabbalah dominated the earlier treatises of R. Joseph Gikatilla and R. Moses de Leon.[44] At presumably the same time, R. Abraham of Cologne, an Ashkenazi visionary figure, made his way from Germany to Castile via Barcelona.[45] R. David ha-Cohen, an important disciple of Naḥmanides, arrived in Toledo no later than the 1280s and therefore represents a living channel for the transmission of Naḥmanides' Kabbalah, and evidently of Catalan Kabbalah in general, to Castile.[46] Moreover, the Kabbalistic concepts of the *'Iyyun* school can be found in writings of R. Isaac ha-Cohen and his followers dating from the second half of the thirteenth century.[47] And finally, at some time prior to 1298, the year of R. Todros Abulafia's death, R. Isaac ibn Latif, a philosopher with Kabbalistic inclinations, dedicated his work *Ẓeror ha-Mor* to the leader of Castilian Jewry. We can therefore regard Castile between 1270 and 1290 as a meeting point for all the major trends within Kabbalah.

Such a massive encounter was unprecedented, and I assume that it had important repercussions for the later evolution of Kabbalah. The acquaintance with varied forms of Kabbalah must have influenced these men's perception of its nature. At least two important figures underwent a drastic change of opinion: Gikatilla and de Leon rejected their earlier linguistic type of Kabbalah for a theosophical approach. But in our context we are not only interested in the shift from one school of Kabbalah to another. The meeting of differing types, each claiming to be "the Kabbalah," must have produced a relativization of the notion of Kabbalah. No longer regarded as a mystical tradition transmitted in an esoteric circle, it now encompassed linguistic, theosophical, and hermeneutical concepts previously cultivated in separate circles by Kabbalists whose masters are unknown to us. Gikatilla and de Leon, in their later works in theosophical Kabbalah, never mention the sources of their theosophy; at the same time, each in his own way integrates some of the earlier concepts occurring in Castilian and Catalan Kabbalah.

I suspect that this acquaintance with various Kabbalistic traditions induced a rather free attitude toward existing material and, what is more important, provided an impetus to create new symbols in a relatively unrestrained way. These two decades witnessed the final steps in most of the older Kabbalistic traditions and the birth of a more complex approach to Kabbalah as a discipline encompassing previously discrete trends of thought. This new approach, mostly represented by three Kabbalists—Gikatilla, de Leon, and Joseph of Hamadan—as well as by the *Zohar,* constitutes what I propose to call the "innovative Kabbalah" in Spain,[48] in contrast to the dominant conservative trends of the preceding generation.[49] For the Spanish Kabbalists, one major domain of creation was Kabbalistic symbols. Ready to accept symbols stemming from varied structures, the creative Kabbalists not only enriched the existing literature with novel combinations but also, I suppose, introduced new symbols. This would explain the revisions or redactions of the commentaries on the ten Sefirot that consist, almost exclusively, of lists of symbols.

These lists were intended to enable the Kabbalists to decode the Bible, the symbolic text through which one can discern the divine processes. This literary genre of cataloging symbols according to a certain structure can be compared to the bestiaries, lapidaries, and horaries so widespread in Western culture after the twelfth century. The Christians, interested in deciphering the biblical text and nature, composed and disseminated these types of organized information, which they thought would serve as clues for the decoding process. The Kabbalists, who focused their efforts upon the symbolic interpretation of the text, composed a rather limited kind of speculum; the pattern is that of the archetypal ten Sefirot, which serve as an organizing structure for the biblical material. Moreover, the Christian interest in such topics as the symbolic significance of beasts and stones was also motivated by the creative rather than the hermeneutical impulse. In contrast to their Jewish contemporaries, they created architectural structures adorned with ornaments that were, at least in part, intended to impress their contemplators by their symbolic content. Occurring at the same time, however, was the appearance, and seemingly also the composition, of a work intended to be read as a symbolic treatise: the *Zohar.* For the first time, Kabbalists used their lists of symbols not only to decode a book—the Bible—whose potential symbolic value differs from the Kabbalistic scheme, but also to produce a real symbolic work. The very composition of the *Zohar* as a symbolic opus is the best example of the vital role symbols began to play in Kabbalistic creation.

I want to examine further this spurt of hermeneutic freedom and creativity. As we saw earlier, those Kabbalists who followed the Catalan tradition conceived a given word as referring to a particular Sefirah, thus reflecting a stable relationship between the symbol and the symbolized, a conception that rapidly began to change in Castile. The beginning of this change can be found in Catalonia, where R. Jacob ben Sheshet indicated that the unvocalized text of the Bible could receive various significances, depending on the particular way in which a word was vocalized.[50] Ben Sheshet even indicated that "the Scroll of the Torah may not be vocalized in order to {enable us to} interpret each and every word according to every significance we can read {that is, to apply a certain vocalization to the word}."[51]

This interesting view, presented by the Catalan Kabbalist as his own innovation, remained unique in contemporary Catalan Kabbalah. Its resonance in Castile, however, was great; it recurred several times over a short period of two decades. The Kabbalists who shared this view were Gikatilla,[52]

R. Joseph of Hamadan,[53] and, under their joint impact, R. Menaḥem Recanati.[54] It thereby became a well-established Kabbalistic hermeneutic concept that was ultimately adopted by Christian Kabbalah via Pico della Mirandola's *Thesis*.[55] A passage on this topic was written in Barcelona during the early 1290s by a Kabbalist influenced by this revolutionary Castilian view of symbolism.[56] R. Baḥya ben Asher wrote:[57]

> The Scroll of the Torah is [written] without vowels, in order to enable man to interpret it however he wishes—as the consonants without the vowels bear several interpretations and [may be] divided into several sparks.[58] This is the reason why we do not write the vowels of the scroll of the Torah, for the significance of each word is in accordance with its vocalization, but when it is vocalized it has but one single significance; but without vowels man may interpret it [extrapolating from it] several [different] things, many, marvelous and sublime.

A comparison of this passage with R. Jacob ben Sheshet's discussions on this subject evinces what seems to me a major departure from older Kabbalistic views. Ben Sheshet assumed that the variation in vowels indeed enabled one to offer many interpretations of a given phrase; for him, however, Kabbalistic significance accrued to this variation only in the case of the divine name, which referred to various Sefirot according to the particular vowels by which it was vocalized; free Kabbalistic exegesis of the Bible was not implied. In contrast, R. Baḥya explicitly referred to "several things . . . marvelous and sublime" that could be derived by interpretation of the text *ad placidum*. This implied not simply a one-to-one relationship of the vocalized divine names to specific Sefirot but a new tenet of Kabbalistic hermeneutics. What is described is a novel way of exegesis rather than a magical-theurgical operation, as in ben Sheshet.[59] An anonymous Kabbalist contemporary of R. Baḥya, whose formulations were very close to those of Gikatilla, drew an interesting conclusion from the nonvocalized form of the Bible:[60] "Since it [the Scroll] includes all the facets and all the profound senses . . . and all of them interpreted in relation to each and every letter, facet within facet, secret within secrets, and there is no limit [limiting sense] known to us, as it is said: 'The depth said, It [a single definite sense] is not in me.' "[61] Thus, the various vocalizations are here explicitly connected with secrets, presumably Kabbalistic secrets. Moreover, this Kabbalist notes the unlimited nature of the unvocalized Torah. According to the same source, the relationship between vocalization and consonants is like that between, respectively, soul, or form, and matter; a certain vocalization is seen as tantamount to giving form to the *hyle*.[62] Therefore, reading the Torah is equivalent to limiting the infinity of the Torah and the embodiment of one meaning potentially inherent in the consonants of the Torah. The Kabbalistic reading is an act of cooperation with God, or a cocreation of the Torah.

It is instructive to compare this openness toward a free reading of the Torah as expounded by the Spanish Kabbalists in the 1280s and 1290s to Abraham Abulafia's view presented in the same period in Italy. Abulafia's sixth hermeneutical method consists of restoring the letters constituting a word "to their *hyle* and in giving them a form."[63] A comparison with other texts on the same subject clearly demonstrates that the mystic is the source of the form given to the letters, which have been changed into amorphous matter by the disintegration of the word. By a new combination of those letters, the mystic infuses them with a new meaning, thereby imitating the activity of the active intellect, the supernal giver of forms.[64]

Abulafia's method goes beyond that of his Spanish contemporaries. In this method, the sequence of letters in the Torah can be radically and freely changed, thereby allowing for the creation of more meanings; for the theosophical Kabbalists, the consonants maintain their traditional order, the vowels alone being allowed to vary. Their shared conception is still significant, however. No longer is Kabbalah identified with specific traditions concerning limited segments of the Bible; rather, it focuses on the results of powerful hermeneutic devices that enable the mystic to discover the many hidden meanings latent in the canon (or, I should say, to project his ideas into it). But the natures of these ideas differ: in the case of Abulafia, they are derived from Maimonidean theology and psychology; in that of the theosophical Kabbalists, they relate to the divine structure. Abulafia transforms the letters of biblical words into psychological and physical allegories; the theosophist turns biblical words into symbols of supernal entities.

This activist attitude toward the biblical text became prominent among the Kabbalists during the late 1270s. For former generations, Kabbalah had been the bearer of "the mysterious language of a distant spiritual kingdom, whose marvelous accents resound within us and awaken a higher intensive life."[65] Now the time had come when the Kabbalists had learned the motifs of this mysterious melody and were able to compose novel variations, elaborating upon older motifs and creating new ones. This new work was the *Zohar,* which constituted both the first outpouring and the climax of Kabbalistic symbolic creation.[66] We find only later some interesting uses of symbolism in such literary creations as the poems of Luria; another outstanding symbolic literary creation is the collection of stories of R. Naḥman of Bratslav, whose subtle and allusive symbols contribute substantially to their mysterious atmosphere.[67]

The sociological aspect of the emergence of these novel, relatively free

Kabbalistic interpretations is interesting. Their bearers were R. Joseph Gikatilla, R. Moses de Leon, R. Abraham Abulafia, R. Joseph of Hamadan, and, at least in theory, R. Baḥya ben Asher. Although these men were important figures in the development of Kabbalah, both in their own day and for posterity, as far as we know they never bore communal responsibilities. The intellectual freedom that characterized their activity must have been suspect in the eyes of more conservative minds, who were also the recognized spiritual leaders. The clash between R. Solomon ben Adret and Abraham Abulafia is a case in point. Said the former of the latter: "He accustoms himself to imaginary [issues] and expounds [biblical] verses and the words of the sages by the method of gematria, mixing into them some few true things taken from philosophical works."[68] At stake here was the free application of imagination to classical texts.[69] This controversy closely reflected the recurrent quarrel of authority with charismatic phenomena: "cette longue querelle de la tradition et de l'invention, de l'Ordre et de l'Aventure," as Apollinaire felicitously put it.

Abulafia's doctrine did not succeed in penetrating Spanish Kabbalah, and the same is true of his hermeneutics. In terms of the history of Kabbalah generally, however, they contributed to the renaissance of linguistic speculation in Safedian Kabbalah and Ḥasidism. Nevertheless, the Spanish emphasis upon the unlimited vocalization of the biblical text was never criticized; indeed, as we have seen, even such halakhic masters as R. David ben Zimra were prepared to accept it.[70] This openness to a relatively novel type of hermeneutics is striking when compared to the hermeneutical principle of Johannes Cocceius, a seventeenth-century Dutch theologian, who affirmed that "quod significare potest verbum, id significat" (whatever a word may signify, it [indeed] signifies).[71] This postulate of plurivocality is far more limiting than that of the Kabbalists, as, according to Cocceius, it does not allow a free inventive exegesis; notwithstanding this fact, it stirred a fierce controversy.[72]

The outburst of symbolic thought in the *Zohar* and among Kabbalists contemporary with it left a decisive impression on Kabbalah. Shortly after the work's appearance, various attempts were made to decode the precise symbolic meaning of zoharic discussions; subsequently, a large literature arose containing translation, commentaries, and dictionaries of zoharic terminology and symbolism. The canonization of the *Zohar* generated this body of writings, which enriched Kabbalistic literature and enhanced the book's understanding, but only marginally contributed to the further development of symbolic thought in Kabbalah. Few Kabbalists imitated the zoharic symbolic language, and even fewer added something new to the symbolic structure of the Kabbalah. The *Zohar* thus became a canonic monument, to be explained rather than continued. Innovative Kabbalah, as reflected in the *Zohar,* had a splendid but short life; the conservative factors in Kabbalah, which were now focused on the doctrine of the *Zohar,* began the process of systematization of its fragmentary, ambiguous, and at times contradictory thought.

A major example of this activity appears in the literary work of R. David ben Yehudah he-Ḥasid. At the end of the thirteenth century, he undertook a Hebrew translation of parts of the *Zohar,* in which the translated text was commented upon by means of the addition of letters above the words that alluded to the Sefirot. The greater part of this supercommentary indeed reflects zoharic symbolism, but sometimes a nonzoharic symbolic usage was superimposed upon the text. Moreover, many words that were not intended to function as symbols were interpreted as such, a technique rendering the zoharic text into a gothic agglomeration of symbols wherein the peculiar dynamics of the composition are lost.[73] Paraphrasing Emil Male's words, we can say that true symbolism holds so large a place in the zoharic text, it is unnecessary to seek it where it does not exist.[74] This relatively indiscriminate, mechanical superimposition of symbols indicates that the *Zohar* had become a canonical work, whose words had to be symbolized, as were the words of the Bible. The spirit of zoharic symbolic creation, rather than symbolic interpretation, was lost. To take another example from the works of R. David: this Kabbalist was not only the first translator of the *Zohar* but also its first, or at least one of its earliest, commentators. In his commentary on *Idra Rabba* entitled *Sefer ha-Gevul,* he attempted an extremely complex exegesis of this treatise, illustrated by endless circles and figures that obfuscate, rather than illuminate, the significance of the text.

The works of R. David, together with those of R. Joseph ben Shalom Ashkenazi, hence opened the way for a comprehensive symbolization of every issue, thereby serving as an intricate and complicated intermediary between the subtle symbolism of the *Zohar* and the gothic symbolism of Lurianic Kabbalah. Moses Cordovero and Isaac Luria, the great experts on zoharic literature, succeeded in combining these disparate symbols into relatively comprehensive and coherent conceptual systems, whose influence on Jewish theosophy was tremendous. Jewish symbolism, however, only secondarily benefited from these developments. Symbols rarely maintain their freshness, ambiguity, and allusive characteristics when they become integrated into a more elaborate and detailed structure. The greater the area Kabbalistic mythology conquered for itself, the less vital space for symbolic élan remained. No wonder that Lurianic Kabbalah, the most complicated Jewish theosophy, has produced only marginal discussion on symbolism and practically no significant commentaries on the ten Sefirot. The scholastic structure of Safedian Kabbalah was pernicious for the evolution of symbolism.

The *floruit* of Kabbalistic symbolism stands, therefore, between two stages in the history of Kabbalah; its beginnings and its maturation. The age of youth, so to speak, was a brief period of flowering, whose vigor and enthusiasm gradually faded as the more sophisticated, "mature," and conservative theosophies became prominent.[75]

3. Symbolism and Philosophy

Gershom Scholem proposed the Goethean definition of symbolism as an adequate one for Kabbalistic symbols, although, as far as I know, this fact was not acknowledged by Scholem himself.[76] The gist of this approach is the drawing of the distinction between symbol and allegory; for Scholem, the former is "a form of expression which radically transcends the sphere of allegory."[77] As a result, the philosopher using allegory and the Kabbalist using symbolic expression can metamorphose the same biblical material in order to point to different levels of reality. Again, according to Scholem, philosophical allegory "can be defined as the representation of an expressible something by another expressible something," whereas "the mystical symbol is an expressible representation of something which lies beyond the sphere of expression and communication."[78] This approach presupposes an expressible layer of reality depicted in allegory and another, inexpressible level found in symbolism. It seems to me that this distinction, as interesting as it may be, deals with only part of the relationships between these two modes of expression. In the following discussion, one further facet of this relationship will be explored.

As we have seen above, the difference between ecstatic and theosophical Kabbalah is reflected on the hermeneutical level, in which, respectively, the allegorical and symbolical means of interpretation are applied to the same text.[79] Beyond this pair of concepts looms, as Scholem observed, the opposition between philosophy and Kabbalah. But the unqualified affirmation that philosophical interpretation prefers the medium of allegory and Kabbalistic exegesis is predominantly symbolic is an oversimplification; it underrates the unique contribution of allegory to the expression of psychological processes or the description of the relationship between the human and the Divine. Allegory was not merely an adoption of philosophical forms of thinking but, in some important cases, an inherent need of Kabbalah itself in its primarily mystical rather than theosophical modes. Kabbalists of a more mystical inclination found in philosophy not only the idealization of the union with a higher being, which was germane to their spirit, but also an elaborate nomenclature for discussing it. As we have seen above, the cleaving of thought theme that recurs in several Kabbalistic schools was obviously indebted to philosophical conceptions,[80] nor can allegory, which is one of the main vehicles of medieval philosophy, be considered as marginal to Kabbalistic exegesis. Scholem's view that allegorization was not "the main constituent" of the Kabbalists' "faith and method" has therefore to be corrected, stemming as it does from a unilateral perception of Kabbalah as theosophy.[81] Moreover, even theosophical Kabbalah used allegory in order to express psychological processes; for example, R. 'Ezra of Gerona expressed the state of union or cleaving of the soul to God through the metaphor of a kiss. As we have seen above, this metaphor was previously used by a philosopher,[82] and I would imagine that its use by a Kabbalist did not effect a radical change in its nature. Therefore, when R. 'Ezra used the terms *himshil* or *mashal,* he meant by them what the philosophers do—namely, an allegory for a unitive experience.[83]

One can easily see that those psychological experiences that were the subject of symbolical description in some non-Jewish mystical literature were rendered in Kabbalah by means of allegory, symbolism remaining the patrimony of theosophical processes. The reason for this difference is clear. Non-Jewish mystics regularly described their own experiences, or at least attempted to do so—hence the ambiguous terminology, the feeling of ineffability, the awareness of the failure of their descriptions, and the need to employ symbolic means of expression. The Kabbalist, including the ecstatic, only rarely presented his own experience directly; this is the reason so few mystical diaries were composed by Jewish mystics, and even then the problem of ineffability seems peripheral. It is as if the Kabbalist had the impression both that he was better able to understand his experience than was his Christian counterpart and that he felt his language was adequate to convey his mystical feeling. Given the philosophical education of many of the Kabbalists, including the early ecstatic ones, philosophical allegory was accepted as an important medium of expression.

I therefore propose that the relationship between symbolism and allegory in theosophical Kabbalah be viewed not as a relationship between a central and a peripheral form of Kabbalistic writing but as a functional division: between descriptions of theosophic processes through the means of a large range of symbols, and descriptions of psychological processes achieved mainly by the allegorical method.

Even this distinction, however, must be made cautiously. Are all the references to the Sefirot symbols of one basic type, as Scholem implies? A short survey of the nature of theosophic symbol, as proposed by Scholem himself, will show that the "intrusion" of philosophical terminology raises some problems.

The main sources of Kabbalistic symbolism are the canonic books of Judaism, the Bible and the Talmud, both of which were conceived as reflecting the sefirotic pleroma and were, to varied extents, decoded symbolically. But in addition to these two major sources, there were some other, minor bodies of literature that supplied material for Kabbalistic symbolism. One of these was the philosophical tradition, familiar to the Kabbalists through, especially, the Hebrew translations of Maimonides' *Guide.* Such Aristotelian terms as *matter, form, steresis* or *intellect, intellection,* and *intelligibilia* were understood as symbols for the three highest Sefirot. Although these concepts were transformed into symbols, however, the peculiar nature of this type of symbolism needs to be delineated.

The "natural" sources of symbolism are words referring to tangible objects, which are infused with a symbolic valence that adds to the original meaning of the word without superseding it.[84] Thus, a simple, plain meaning is enriched by the superimposition of one or several symbolic meanings. In principle, then, Kabbalistic symbolism did not destroy the basic structure of a word. On the other hand, philosophical terminology is, by definition, abstract, so that any attempt to add another abstract significance to it becomes complicated. Focused as it is on the abstract, the philosophical term can only peripherally absorb an additional, also abstract meaning. When this happened in Kabbalah, the basic meaning of the speculative concept became obliterated. For example, matter, form, and steresis are abstractions that serve to convey an understanding of the physical processes taking place in the sublunar world; they do not refer to distinct entities that can be separated from each other or contemplated per se.[85] In Aristotelian philosophy, steresis stands for nonbeing, privation; it refers to the entirety of potential forms that can be received by a certain substratum. In the Kabbalah of R. 'Azriel of Gerona, these concepts stand for the highest Sefirot, privation (*efes*),[86] symbolizing the Sefirot of *Keter*.[87] Accordingly, says R. 'Azriel, any change can take place only by the return of the thing to the source, and only after its destruction will a new form be given by this Sefirah—the form that is found in the realm of privation in the Aristotelian system. Despite the similarity of the processes, however, there are obvious discrepancies in the way in which the philosopher and the Kabbalist understand the use of these terms. For the Kabbalist, *efes* is identified with *ayin,* the "nothingness" that signifies the fullness of being that transcends being itself.[88] Privation is thus regarded as its precise opposite: fullness of form and hence of being. Elsewhere in R. 'Azriel, the realm of *efes* is described as the place of *coincidentia oppositorum*—a conception that demolishes the philosophical understanding of privation. In this way, the essential meaning of the Aristotelian concept is obliterated and a new concept is identified with the term.

Viewed from this perspective, the coexistence of two opposing abstract meanings is highly problematic; symbolization of philosophical terms must then be regarded as a change in the meaning of a given word rather than as an addition to the primary meaning, which would remain relatively stable. Thus, this phenomenon may be regarded as allegorization rather than as a symbolic use of philosophical terms.[89] The sensory pole never existed in this case; therefore, the transformation from the philosophical to the Kabbalistic sense occurs solely on the level of the ideological pole, which is "exploded" by the confrontation of two ideologies. To the extent that the philosophical concept takes on a specifically theosophic meaning, its former significance is obliterated. The nature of these concepts is obviously different in philosophy than in Kabbalah. For the mystic, there are three divine hypostases: the three Sefirot, which are interconnected but nevertheless still maintain their peculiar characteristics and existence as separate entities; they are emanated in a certain order, influence each other, form a certain relationship of closeness and separation, and so on. Nothing similar can be attibuted to Aristotle's concepts.

As another example, let us examine the attribution of concepts of intellect, intellection, and intelligibilia to the higher Sefirot. In the moment of intellection, the three aspects of this mental act cannot be separated, whereas beyond the act of intellection their existence is totally separated, except in the case of God, in which they are constantly existing "together." For the Kabbalists, these terms symbolize three hypostases that are neither totally separated nor completely united, so that their particular nature is effaced.[90] The hypostatic character of Kabbalistic thought is a main obstacle to applying these Aristotelian terms to a theosophic system while maintaining their proper meaning.

Let us now turn to the case of the symbolic transformation of Neoplatonic terminology. Given its strong hypostatical bias, this kind of thought was more easily assimilated into theosophical Kabbalah, in both its content and its terminology. In this case, we face a different question; as the Neoplatonic cosmic hierarchy was partially absorbed into Kabbalistic theosophy, the changes in the meaning of the terms that had previously referred to Neoplatonic hypostases were sometimes minimal. Such terms as *will, thought, world of the mind,* and so on, retained their basic significance even when used in reference to the sefirotic realm, as the latter was molded under the Neoplatonic influence of Isaac Israeli, Solomon ibn Gabirol, Moses ibn ʿEzra, and others. To the extent that philosophical concepts passed into Kabbalistic systems together with their referents, there was no particular reason to attenuate their conceptual content except in a marginal way.

We have briefly analyzed some references to the highest stages in the divine structure, which, notwithstanding their "hiddenness" and "inexpressibility," were designated by philosophical terms and were neither regarded as inappropriate means of expressions nor metamorphosed into "classical" theosophic symbols, as defined by Scholem.

4. Symbolism and Dynamism

In the Christian Middle Ages, symbolism was commonly viewed as the way in which the divine harmony was reflected in the material domain. The archetypes of things present in the divine thought were embodied in nature or in art by inspired artists, and these lower manifestations served as a ladder that helped the contemplator reach the higher paradigm. The Platonic conception of reality was no doubt present, in one way or another, in Christian symbolism; as part of this perception, the paradigm was seen as the static essence whose particular nature was to be realized by those who deciphered the symbols. Even when the symbols referred not to an essence but to a certain event, such as a specific detail in the life of Christ, this event became fixed, an entity in itself taking place in the past, although its relevance would extend through the ages. The Passion, for example, was seen as a redemptive action that was closed as a process, although its results still reverberated in the life of each Christian. When such scenes were presented in pictures or sculpture, their static nature was strengthened by the medium of expression—the divine mystery was a fait accompli. As Saint Damian put it, "Mea grammatica Christus est."

For the Kabbalist, this grammar was composed not only of a variety of divine powers but also of a syntax that governed their changing interrelations. For most of the Kabbalists, symbolism was more than the representation of divine manifestations in texts or nature; the individual words of a text—the Bible or the *Zohar*—were understood as pointing to a particular Sefirah. The theosophical Kabbalists, however, were interested in more than tracing a specific word to its corresponding Sefirah or Sefirot. They wished to realize the process taking place between these entities. The dozens of extant commentaries on the ten Sefirot, which classify the various symbols according to the order of the Sefirot, were not intended to teach the ultimate meaning of the Kabbalah. Rather, they were clues to be used by learned persons to fathom the depths of texts, using their hermeneutic acumen. The significant unit of

Kabbalistic exegesis was not the word but the verse, or at times even a cluster of verses. The Kabbalists captured the dynamics of the divine forces by a comprehensive understanding of sequences of words that presented an articulated event rather than merely pointing to the existence of certain divine forces. Interactions, relationships, union, or separation of Sefirot from one another were the syntax of Kabbalistic hermeneutics. The divine manifestations therefore were seen not as ideas existing in frozen perfection within the divine thought but as living entities whose dynamism often attained imperfect states, to be repaired by human activity. A Kabbalistic symbol invited one to act rather than to think.

I suppose that one of the most important features of theosophical symbolism—especially in those theosophies that conceived the Sefirot as the essence of Deity—was its dynamism, far more than its disclosure of an inexpressible realm of existence. Let me exemplify this dynamic symbolism by a comment made by the *Zohar* upon a verse from Psalms:[91]

> "Great is the Lord and highly to be praised, in the city of our God, in the mountain of his holiness."[92] When is the Lord called "great"? When *Knesset Yisrael* is to be found with him, as it is written, "In the city of our God is he great." "In the city of our God" means "with the city of our God" . . . and we learn that a king without a queen is not a [real] king and is neither great nor praised. Thus, so long as the male is without a female, all his excellency is removed from him and he is not in the category of Adam, and moreover he is not worthy of being blessed.

The pattern of this interpretation, similar to many other passages in the Kabbalah, involves a differentiation between the meaning of two divine names: the Tetragrammaton—the Lord—standing for *Tiferet* or the male, and *Elohenu*, referring to *Malkhut* or the female attribute. The novelty here, however, is not to be found in this distinction; the focus of interest is rather on the word *great,* which articulates the relationship between these attributes. Greatness is not an inherent quality of the male but is acquired through his relation to the female; only by the act of intercourse, as hinted by the *Zohar* shortly following the above passage, is the quality of "great" and "praised" made applicable to the male, whereby he becomes "man." The sexualization of the relationship between the attributes is a well-known Kabbalistic exegetical device.[93] But beyond the investment of divine names with sexual qualities, common in the Kabbalah, this passage of the *Zohar* adds something specific: how the greatness and excellence of the male is attained, both in the human and the divine realms. The gist of this exegetical endeavor is the appearance of a quality through the establishment of a certain relationship.

The ultimate message of the *Zohar,* however, is not the mere understanding of the condition for perfection; although its symbolism may indeed invite someone to contemplation, his awareness of certain theosophical and anthropological ideas does not change man. In order to attain his perfection and that of Divinity, he must act appropriately; otherwise, the very purpose of the exegetical process is not fulfilled. The experiential aspect of apprehending the zoharic exegesis is, therefore, only the first step toward the ultimate goal; understanding is, for the Kabbalist, an inescapable invitation to action, as otherwise the male does not reach the status of man and moreover cannot perform the theurgic activity intended to influence the supernal syzygies. The definition of *man* is given in a very peculiar context: how should we understand the occurrence of the term *'Adam* in the verse "If any man of you bring an offering to the Lord . . . ?"[94] Symbolism is therefore to be viewed as part of the deepening of the understanding of human activity, oriented to the higher world, not as a disclosure of the static meaning projected onto certain words, alone. In this specific case, we may therefore distinguish three distinct steps: (1) the understanding of the theosophical and theurgical significance of the verse; (2) the acquisition of the status of man—that is, an ongoing way of life together with his wife, just as two Sefirot are to be together above; and (3) as a perfect man, the inducement of divine harmony through the performance of the commandments. As we shall see below in the parable of the palace of the maiden, according to the *Zohar* even the fathoming of the depths of the biblical text has an experiential aspect; the second step here, becoming a man, is to be seen not as the attainment of a static perfection but as a dynamics to be cultivated in relation to the wife.

To return to the passage above: its plain sense is simple and obvious—that the Lord is great and, as a separate assertion, that his mountain is located in his holy city. The former is a theological assessment, unconditional and absolute; the latter indicates that the sacred mountain is located geographically in the sacred city. The relationship between God's greatness and the sacredness of the mountain is not even alluded to; these two theological statements can easily be understood separately, and so I assume that there is no intention of describing any peculiar dynamics between God and his city. Even though the biblical conception of the holy city as the city of God is explicit, no changing pattern of relationship is implied by this assertion: it is chosen forever. The pattern of relationship is a vertical one; divine holiness is imposed upon a material entity, which is metamorphosed into a sacred center. The *Zohar* radically changes this pattern: the vertical relationship is transposed on the divine plan, where it can now be viewed as horizontal—that of two sexually differentiated entities.

In order to determine the relationship between the two parts of the verse, the Hebrew prefix *be* ("in") is interpreted as meaning "with"; the dynamics that emerge from the sexualization and interrelation of the two divine names create the specific quality of Kabbalistic exegesis in comparison with other types of Jewish exegeses. Kabbalah alone can put into relief divine attributes whose affinity with one another gradually turns at times into semimyths and at other times even into full-fledged myths.

The transformation of the vertical relationship into an intradivine polarity, however, does not obliterate the previous vertical understanding of the relation of God to the city. As we have already noted, the corporeal reality is not ignored by the theosophic Kabbalist but, rather, reinterpreted without detracting from its substantiality. Symbolism in the theosophical vein does not supersede material reality; it only adds a new layer of significance. The real city is holy because it represents a higher entity of female nature in the lower world. We can speak of a "horizontal descending symbolism"[95] that, on the level of corporeal reality, turns into a vertical symbolism, as a Kabbalist would put it; or, as a modern man would put it, the vertical relationship of God and his city is transformed into an ascending symbolism on the horizontal divine level, without attenuating its primary significance.[96]

As we observed above, issues and relations connected to this world were projected by Kabbalistic exegesis onto the divine inner structure in order to portray the dynamism of this realm. Indeed, Kabbalah was characterized by its focus on theosophy and theosophic processes, which its symbolism made transparent. This dynamization of the concept of God, however, was not an idea expressed first in the earliest Kabbalistic documents. The midrashic interest in the various meanings of the divine names represented incipient stages in a direction fully exploited by the Kabbalists. This dynamization in the realm of theology presumably found its expression in the domain of hermeneutics. A fine example of what I would describe as a dynamic perception of a biblical verse appears in the *Mekhilta*'s interpretation of Exodus 24:10:[97]

> "Even that selfsame day it came to pass that all the hosts of the Lord went out from the Land of Egypt." . . . Whenever Israel is enslaved, the *Shekhinah*, as it were, is enslaved with them, as it is said, "And they saw the God of Israel, and under his feet there was," and so on.[98] But after they were redeemed what does it say? "And the likeness of the very heaven for clearness."

The full biblical verse goes as follows: "(a) And they saw the God of Israel (b) and under his feet there was a kind of paved work of sapphire stone (c) and it was as the likeness of the very heaven for clearness." Part (c) expands and explains the content of (b), the subject of both phrases being the same: "a kind of paved work"; (c) merely complements the description of the "work" as "sapphire stone" by adding the attribute of clearness. The Midrash, however, perceives the two parts (b) and (c) as relating to opposite situations. Part (b) is conceived as describing the vision of Moses and the elders of Israel while still enslaved, a reading seemingly substantiated by an intertextual understanding of *livnat ha-sappir*—"paved work of sapphire"—which the ancient exegete regarded as an allusion to *levenim*—bricks[99]—seen as a symbol of Jewish slavery in Egypt.[100]

This pun allows one to attribute the state of slavery to God himself: he, like the children of Israel, had bricks beneath his feet.[101] Once they had been redeemed, however, the vision changed: part (c) describes the new state of God when his feet were apparently "clear." The link between the two motifs is ensured by the recurrence of the noun *'eẓem* both in connection with the Exodus from Egypt and in the context of the vision of God as "clear."[102] We can easily perceive that an entire myth of the passage of Israel from slavery to freedom is here attributed analogically to God himself, described in highly anthropomorphic terms. We witness an explicit case of the Divine participating in the human experience of slavery and liberation; in the words of the sequel in the *Mekhilta,* "in all their afflictions he was afflicted."[103]

This changing perception of history and of the divine attributes can be more adequately qualified, however. In the same Midrash, we learn that God revealed himself under two main attributes: that of mercy and that of judgment.[104] When the Midrash wishes to exemplify the appearance of the attribute of mercy, it quotes, inter alia, part (c) of our verse. On the basis of this view, I conjecture that the attribute of judgment is conceived as hinted at by the name *Elohey Yisrael*, the name *Elohim* usually being the common denominator of this attribute. Thus, our verse was regarded as pointing to a double revelation: of judgment and of mercy.[105] Moreover, even if this assumption proves to be incorrect, we still encounter a dynamization of the biblical verse: according to the *Mekhilta,* it refers to an entire process that occurs simultaneously on the historical and the divine planes. This intimate affinity between the two spheres of existence and their dynamics is forced upon the verse, using current devices of midrashic hermeneutics. What distinguishes this particular interpretation from the more common midrashic ones is the correlation achieved between two processes—not states—that, although ontologically remote, are part of a higher dynamic structure. We are here at the edge of myth, but one indeed of a specific type. As R. 'Akiva went on to say: "Were it not expressly written in scripture, one could not say it. Israel said to God: 'Thou hast redeemed thyself'—as though one could conceive such a thing."[106] The redemption of the *Shekhinah* depends upon the prior salvation of Israel.

Another kind of dynamism is revealed by the structure of the Kabbalistic discourse itself. Examples of this mode of expressing a dynamic perception of reality are to be found mostly in the *Zohar,* one of the few Kabbalistic books whose literary quality is sometimes dominant. The author, using the persona of an old man exposing supreme secrets to the other heroes of the *Zohar*,[107] expounded the mystical meaning of the verse:[108]

> " 'And Moses went into the midst of the cloud and got him up into the mount.' Now, what does the cloud signify?" he asked, and he answered his own question, saying: "There is a reference here to the words 'I set my bow in the cloud,'[109] namely the rainbow, in reference to which we have learnt that it [the rainbow] removed its outer garments, as it were, and gave them to Moses, who went up to the mountain with it [the rainbow] and saw through it all the sights he had seen, and he delighted from all."

This passage, which is meaningless to an outsider, was enthusiastically welcomed by the Kabbalists, who "prostrated themselves before him, wept and said: 'Had we come into the world only in order to hear these words from your mouth it would have been sufficient.' "[110] But the old sage declares that he is not going to restrict himself to this one saying and proceeds to relate one of the finest parables in the *Zohar.*[111] A beautiful damsel secluded in a palace hints to her lover to approach her, and after a sequel of disclosures and discussions, he becomes her husband. This state is seen as tantamount to his possessing the palace and all of its beloved secrets. The significance of the parable is offered by the *Zohar* itself: the damsel is the Torah, which is dressed in four, or perhaps even five, levels of meaning that must be penetrated by the perfect student of the Torah in order to reach its ultimate layer, the Kabbalistic meaning—a state portrayed as having overt sexual overtones.

It seems obvious that Moses' receiving God's garments—the rainbow—and the maiden's progressive removal of her clothes are similar, albeit complementary, actions; on his way to receive the Torah, Moses must identify himself with the attributes of the rainbow, a classical symbol of the male sexual member, that is, the Sefirah of *Yesod.*[112] The Hebrew form *kashti* would therefore signify "the bow of *Tiferet*," which is alluded to in the first-person possessive. Furthermore, Moses' ascent after he has assumed the attributes of the rainbow may symbolize the descent of *Tiferet* to *Yesod* as a preliminary to the union with *Malkhut*, symbolized by the cloud. He enters the cloud, a manifestly female symbol, just as the lover must enter the palace, in order to become the mystical husband of the Torah. Two different directions, however, are juxtaposed here: the Torah reveals itself by a process of undressing, but man can receive it only through a process of dressing. For the Torah, the significance of undressing is its return to a supernal position prior to its descent into the material world. For the human being, dressing is the only way by which he can ascend to higher worlds, as by dressing in its garments he assumes the qualities of these worlds; these garments serve as defensive armor, enabling the Kabbalist to survive the dazzling light of the higher worlds. The revelation of the Torah is indeed described as its emergence from its sheath, a metaphor employed in Jewish classical texts as a tremendous eschatological event, when the sun will shine with an overwhelming light.[113] The apparently contrasting movements, which must be juxtaposed in order to be understood, nevertheless create an organic unity by their dynamic nature. The act of acquiring supernal knowledge involves a change in both the known and the knower; it is presented as an active event, or penetration, in both parts of the old sage's discourse. As we may learn from the parable of the maiden, it is a reciprocal initiative; she beckons to her lover, but he must enter the palace in order to meet her. Similarly, in the Bible, Moses was called to come to the mountain in order to receive the Torah. Finally, this act of encounter seems to be highly charged—as is evinced by the sexual imagery itself.

The major point I want to emphasize, however, is that the hidden meaning of the passage on Moses cannot be properly understood without realizing the sexual implications of the maiden parable. Only thus can the significance of the "delight" of Moses be understood; it is a sexual experience, alluded to as well by the use of the words *go into,* which in Hebrew carry a strong sexual connotation. The hero of the first part, Moses, has no partner; we can assume that the Torah is to be revealed to him, although this is not explicitly stated; in lieu of this, we have the allusion to entering into the cloud. Moreover, Moses is not referred to here as the husband of the Torah, but through comparison with the maiden parable, we can assume that he is the master of the palace. Moses is referred to elsewhere in the *Zohar* as the "husband of the *Shekhinah*," implying that he has mythical intercourse with this divine manifestation.[114] This epitheton is based upon the Hebrew phrase, *Ish ha-Elohim* ("the man of God"), the divine name *Elohim* being interpreted as a symbol of the *Shekhinah*. Indeed, in the context of Moses entering the cloud, we learn that "Moses went up to the mount of God [Elohim]."

This phrase seems to have prompted the author of the *Zohar* to offer a special interpretation of its occurrence, since, shortly before this, Moses' call to ascend in order to receive the Torah is addressed to him by the Tetragrammaton. This discrepancy may have aroused the suspicion that the divine name *Elohim* alludes to a particular manifestation of God, different from that reflected by the Tetragrammaton. All these images conspire to a statement that Moses' ascent to the "Mount of *Elohim*" and his receiving of the Torah are but concealments of, or hints at, a sexual experience with the Divine. This erotic perception of Moses' revelation is corroborated by another understanding of Moses, to whom the *Zohar,* following a midrashic source, attributes a sexual property.[115] The description of the Kabbalist as a person who has a vague vocation for the esoteric meaning of the Torah, and the Torah, in its innermost sense, as a damsel attracting him, points to an invitation to an experiential study of Torah. For the Kabbalist, the understanding of the inner sense of the text or of the tradition is more than simply comprehension of some additional details; it implies a radical change in the perception of the Torah, as well as of the personality and status of the Kabbalist himself. No longer an outsider, he becomes the lord of the palace—*heikhal*—a word alluding to the location of the Torah Scroll in the synagogue; he actualizes his uniqueness by leaving the surrounding ignoramuses in order to become one of the *perfecti*—an overwhelming experience, which goes beyond the passive contemplation of the symbolic sense of a text. More than an interiorization of specific contents, this study entails the establishment of a close relationship.

Let me conclude my analysis of this zoharic parable by noting an interesting reverberation of it in a mystic vision. The famous visionary Emanuel Swedenborg reports:

> There appeared to me a beautiful girl with a fair countenance, advancing quickly towards the right, upwards and hurrying a little. She was in the first bloom of youth—not a child nor a young woman. She was dressed attractively in a black shining dress. So she hastened cheerfully from light to light. I was told that the interior things of the Word are such when they first ascend. The black dress stood for the Word in the letter. Afterward, a young girl flew towards the right cheek, but this was only seen by the interior sight. I was told that those are the things of the internal sense that do not come into the comprehension.[116]

The veiled girl compared to the literary level of the Torah corresponds here to the dressed girl; in both cases, the initiative is taken by the girl, who approaches the man. It is perhaps significant that the second girl's dress is not mentioned; she may correspond there to the woman who discloses her secrets in the zoharic parable. I would therefore suggest that Swedenborg has once again interiorized Kabbalistic material into his visions.[117] Significantly, the most striking difference between Swedenborg's version and that of the *Zohar* lies in the fact that, whereas for the Christian mystic the gist of the parable is to understand something related to the Holy Scripture, for the Kabbalist, its focus is upon experiencing this meaning and becoming the husband of the Torah.

Another interesting example of symbolic dynamics may be seen in one of R. Joseph of Hamadan's books:[118]

> Why is his name Tubal-Cain?[119] Because the *Shekhinah* is sometimes clothed in him, and sometimes he stands alone. When the *Shekhinah* is clothed in him, he is called Tubal-Cain, since at this time he is brought to the king with gladness and joy, and thus he is then called Tubal-Cain. But when he is alone, he is called Cain. This is the reason for the names Cain and Tubal-Cain.

The supermundane entity referred to by the two names is the angel Metatron; being the closest angel to the divine *Shekhinah*, the latter sometimes embodies herself in it in order to approach the king, that is, the Sefirah of *Tiferet*. These processes of embodiment and approach are symbolized in the twofold name Tubal-Cain; this phrase indicates the coexistence of two entities in one, together with the movement of these two beings, *Shekhinah* and Metatron, toward the Sefirah of *Tiferet*. This movement is derived from the form *tuval,* understood as meaning "brought to." Thus, the two names signify two states of one entity: its interrelation with another force or even with two other forces—*Malkhut* (*Shekhinah*) and *Tiferet*—or its separateness from *Shekhinah*. These two types of relationships, closeness and separateness, are described without the use of Kabbalistic terminology: *Shekhinah*, "king," and Metatron are all names used in classical Jewish literature. Symbolism silently enters the story through the structure of the situation: the *Shekhinah* who approaches the king implies a bipolar structure, with the former portrayed as a female who adorns herself before approaching the king—the male. This rendezvous has sexual overtones alluded to in the phrase "gladness and joy." The term *Cain* is also seen as allusive to a certain type of relationship: separateness. These names are not simply denominations for synonyms of Metatron but, in relation to the angel, symbols of situations that can be taught by the names of these two biblical figures. Thus, the biblical narrative reflects two opposite cases of Metatron's position in relation to the *Shekhinah*: Cain, the murderer who fled from God's revenge, symbolizes the separation of the angel from the divine force or, implicitly, its fall; on the other hand, Tubal-Cain reflects the angel's ascent to the infradivine domain. Here, the myth is by and large focused upon the processes concerning an angel rather than a divine power. Thus, we see that Kabbalistic readings of the Torah can reflect through the use of symbolic hermeneutics not only divine processes but also the angelic dynamics. As R. Joseph of Hamadan put it,[120] "The entire Torah is filled with pearls,[121] as it tells the matter of the genealogy of the angels."

Let us examine another level of interpretation of Tubal-Cain; according to the same Kabbalist,[122] Ẓillah, the mother of Tubal-Cain, gave birth to her son "through the aspect of the demonic powers," and therefore "he is the bearer of murder, like Cain and Abel, and he is the evil inclination, and he brings hatred to the world, for men need weapons[123] to fight one another." Thus, Ẓillah, who symbolizes the *Shekhinah*,[124] gave birth to a demonic power that perpetuates struggle in the world. Far from participating in the harmonious union of *Shekhinah* and the king in the supernal world, Tubal-Cain is the agent of violence below; this is the result of the pernicious impregnation of the *Shekhinah*, presented here in relation to demonic forces. This biblical verse can thus be read as symbolizing several levels of supermundane events: demonic, angelic, and divine. This Kabbalist explains how it is that Ẓillah, symbol of the *Shekhinah*, can be envisioned as having something to do with the demonic realm:[125] "Everything in the Torah is to be interpreted according to seventy aspects of uncleanness [that is, demonic] and purity [divine], as it is written, 'God has made the one as well as the other.' "[126]

This is a highly significant hermeneutical postulate; as it applies to the same word (in this case, the name Ẓillah), it means that the biblical text can be interpreted as simultaneouly revealing totally different levels of existence. The fluidity of symbol in relation to the entities symbolized is self-evident; there is no fixed set of symbols disclosing the divine structure, as against another germane to representing its demonic counterpart. Every word in the Bible concomitantly reflects entirely different ontological structures; hence, the assumption that there is an immanent relationship between the symbol and the symbolized becomes difficult—the more polysemous the nature of the symbol, the less organic is its affinity to the symbolized. Moreover, at least implicitly, Tubal-Cain is presented as the counterpart of Cain or, in the Kabbalistic view, as his reincarnation. This use of metempsychosis is one of the main ways in which R. Joseph of Hamadan interprets biblical texts.[127]

One could adduce examples of this dynamic quality to the theosophical symbol *ad libitum;* however, the passages cited above illustrate the point. I would like, however, to elaborate upon certain implications of this presentation of Kabbalistic symbolism. I assume that the main aspect of the sefirotic realm is not its "indescribability" or "inexpressibility," as Scholem conceives it, but rather its dynamism. In our case, symbols are necessary precisely because several aspects of the ever-changing system need to be expressed, not because the revealed facet of divinity is beyond expression in conceptual terms owing to its transcendence.[128] I want to emphasize that Scholem's conception is highly disputable: even according to him, the Sefirot constitute "intermediary states between the first Emanator and all things that exist apart from God."[129] It is bizarre to assume that one of the qualities of the Sefirot qua manifestations is their "hiddenness." This epitheton is perhaps appropriate to the higher Sefirot and to *'Eiyn Sof*, although even in these cases their hiddenness is not total, and lengthy discussion of precisely these higher aspects of the divine world appear in the *Zohar.*[130] As we shall see below,[131] Kabbalists perceived the *Zohar*, and I assume also the Bible, as reflecting the incessantly changing nature of the higher worlds, a fact that renders this book a thesaurus of infinite meanings. If Goethe envisioned symbolism as the revelation of "Dauer im Wechsel," Kabbalists would propose a definition of symbol as the reflection of the "Wechsel" in the "Dauer," in which the text, like Divinity itself, is perceived as such a "Dauer"; the text remains unchanged, yet time and again reflects a higher process.[132] Like a magic ball that remains always the same although refracting varied moving lights, so the text of the Torah or of the *Zohar* enables us to perceive an ever-changing reality.[133]

The Kabbalist is, however, far more than one who has succeeded in understanding a given event in the divine world. As Ricoeur aptly put it, symbols "invite thought." But interesting as this diagnosis of symbolism may be for Christian thought, in mystical Judaism it is still only a preliminary step. Understanding the higher structures and dynamics, the Kabbalist is invited, even compelled, to participate in the divine mystery, not by understanding, faith, and enlightenment, but primarily by an *imitatio* of the dynamics. The transparence of the divine world through symbols is secondary to the pedagogic role of bringing someone to action. The comprehension of the "mystery" is meaningless if not enacted in every commandment, even in every movement one performs. In other words, the main role of Kabbalistic symbolism is the presentation of a reflection of the theosophical structure. This dynamic structure functions as a powerful instrument of ensuring the dynamism of human activity and endowing it with a sublime significance, which is why the "pure contemplation" of Kabbalistic symbolism falls short of penetrating its ultimate nature. In 1942, Scholem wrote in a rather tragic vein:

> Die alten Symbole sind hier expliziert.
> Der Kabbalist war kein Narr.
> Doch was die verwandelte Zeit gebiert
> Bleibt fremd und unsichtbar.
>
> (Vae Victis—oder, der Tod in der Professur)

Even the most profound explanation of symbols cannot help someone cope with his contemporary reality; neither was the explanation of these symbols, in the Middle Ages, intended as a self-sufficient goal. The Kabbalistic symbols strove to induce an active mood or approach to reality rather than to invite contemplation.

Two final remarks on Kabbalistic symbolism seem pertinent here. As we have seen from R. Joseph of Hamadan's passages, the same symbol, "Ẓillah," can point to both the divine and the demonic realms. The entire area of demonic symbolism as an integral part of Kabbalistic symbolism has been neglected in the theoretical treatment of the subject. In fact, a series of important Kabbalists who were contemporaries of R. Joseph of Hamadan, such as R. Joseph ben Shalom Ashkenazi and R. David ben Yehudah he-Ḥasid, expanded the already existing symbols of evil present in some works of R. Isaac ben Jacob ha-Cohen and in the zoharic literature. Although modern scholars were aware of the existence of such a type of symbol, this awareness was not integrated in their discussions of the symbol.[134] For example, Tishby explicitly assumes that the "hidden object" of Kabbalistic symbolism is "God or the divine world."[135] The demonic powers are not only a counterpart of the divine structure; they also attempt to imitate it by their actions—hence the affinity between the processes taking place among the powers of evil and those in the Sefirot.[136] Again, understanding of this type of symbolism encouraged the Kabbalist to act in accordance with the prescriptions of the Torah; if the positive commandments are, according to theosophical Kabbalah, a way of participating in the divine life by influencing it, the negative ones are intended to separate man from the demonic world.

My second remark concerns the possibility of finding a definiton for Kabbalistic symbolism in general. I have so far used texts mainly from the latter part of the thirteenth century; my emphasis upon dynamism and participation as part of the emergence of the Kabbalistic symbol fits, I assume, this important period of Kabbalah. At a later date, they are still present to the extent that the zoharic literature is influential. The attempt to find a comprehensive definition of Kabbalistic symbolism applicable in an unqualified way to Kabbalah in general is indeed a kind of hubris. Hundreds of Kabbalistic texts, written by hundreds of Kabbalists in remote places and various periods of time, cannot agree upon such a basic question as the essence of the symbol. Each Kabbalist, with his idiosyncratic perception of the symbol, contributed to the expansion and diversification of Kabbalistic notions of symbolism: as in literature, where Goethe's view of the symbol differs from that of Schiller, not to mention that of the Symbolist poets, so in Kabbalah. The awareness that symbolic systems must be studied separately before a more general definition can be deduced from particular studies is crucial for a serious approach to the subject. For the time being, I would propose accepting Erwin Goodenough's description of the symbol as "an object or a pattern which, whatever the reason may be, operates upon men, and causes effects in them, beyond mere recognition of what is literally presented in the given form."[137] This general conception of the symbol may serve as a fair description of most of Kabbalistic symbolism.

II. THE PNEUMATIC INTERPRETER AND UNION WITH THE TORAH

I want now to comment upon the history of a singularly neglected approach that guided several important Jewish mystics in their attempts to understand the hidden meaning of the Scripture. In sharp contrast to the attitudes of earlier Jewish interpreters,[138] certain Kabbalists saw divine inspiration as a sine qua non for fathoming the sublime secrets with which the Bible is fraught; the notion that altered states of consciousness were a prerequisite for a more profound understanding of the sacred text attests to a new awareness that, in order to delve into the depths of a text, one must return, or at least attempt to return, to the level of consciousness that characterized the person who received the inspiration or revelation that catalyzed the writing of this text. Mystical interpretation of a text was thus a function not only of its symbolic or esoteric nature but also of the spiritual state of the reader or exegete himself. The clearest formulation of this view is found in the earliest texts dealing with this approach, written by Christian theologians. Abelard viewed the prophetic pneuma as "gratia interpretandi, id est exponandi verba divina."[139] Later on, Joachim di Fiori, the famous abbot of Calabria, is reported to have asserted: "Sed Deus, inquit, Qui olim dedit prophetis spiritum prophetiae, mihi dedit spiritum intelligentiae, ut in Dei spiritu omnia mysteria sacrae Scripturae clarissime intelligam, sicut sancti prophetae intellexerunt qui eam olim in Dei spiritu ediderunt."[140]

Thus, a clear understanding of Holy Scripture is attained by returning to the frame of mind of the ancient prophets who had received the "spiritus."[141] It is worth emphasizing at this point that, like Joachim, although apparently not under his influence, most of the Jewish Kabbalists to be mentioned below perceived their pneumatic interpretations in terms of an eschatological scheme.[142] Abraham Abulafia,[143] the anonymous author of *Sefer ha-Meshiv,*[144] Solomon Molkho,[145] and Ḥayyim Vital[146] were all nourished by eschatological drives, hopes, and aspirations, and they viewed their own era as immediately preceding and in some cases preparing the eschaton. Let us now examine in more detail the Jewish examples:

1. R. Abraham Abulafia created a complex system of seven methods for interpreting the Bible. The last of these is described in one of his works as follows: "The seventh path is a peculiar one, which includes all the others, and it is the holy of holies and is intended solely for prophets . . . and through its attainment, the 'speech' coming from the Agent Intellect to the intellectual faculty is acquired . . . and it is the path of the essence of prophecy."[147] Therefore, prophets alone—namely, mystics using Abulafian techniques—are worthy of utilizing the "highest" hermeneutic method, which consists of atomizing or monadizing the biblical texts.

The process of dividing the continuum of letters into discrete entities is reminiscent of, and closely akin to, Abulafia's mystical technique of attaining prophecy by means of the musical recitation of separate letters.[148] We therefore confront here a comprehensive phenomenon of atomization of the text, or any other linguistic material, into primary elements that are considered absolute monads[149] or, according to *Sefer ha-Yeẓirah,* twenty-two primary letters.[150] This process constitutes a transformation of a "langage classique," to use Roland Barthes's phrase, into a mystical and magical series of sounds that can reasonably be described, again employing Barthes's terms, as a "discontinue du nouveau langage."[151] The disintegration of language into linguistic monads is obviously a regression from the purely social point of view, although it may well constitute the restoration of a hypothetical primary language.[152] In a passage that seemingly reflects Abulafia's instruction to one of his students, the latter is requested to transcend any significant linguistic expression:

> My son, it is not the intention that you come to a halt with some finite or given form, even though it be of the highest order. Much rather is this the "path of the names": the less understandable they are, the higher their order, until you arrive at the activity of a force which is no longer in your control, but rather your reason and your thought is in its control. . . . And he produced books for me made up of [combinations of] letters and names and mystic numbers [gematriot] of which nobody will ever be able to understand anything, for they are not composed in a manner meant to be understood. He said to me: "This is the [undefiled] path of the names."[153]

The mystic was asked to efface the natural and even the spiritual forms by means of the incantation of unintelligible combinations of letters intended to alter his state of consciousness and cause him to reach "prophecy"—a mystical state. For this anonymous Kabbalist, as well as for Abulafia, language is a powerful instrument for understanding natural reality, and even the spiritual world is adequately projected onto the structure of linguistic material.[154] When a man strives for an ultimate mystical experience, however, he must break the structured language, as he needs to efface the forms inscribed in his mind in order to make room there for higher entities to dwell. This practice, as well as other Kabbalistic devices,[155] reminds one of modern surrealistic methods of artistic creation; with André Breton, the ecstatic Kabbalist would say, "Language has been given to man so that he may make Surrealist use of it."[156] The disintegration of social language into meaningless units is considered by Abulafia as the path of transformation of human language into divine names.

As we know from Abulafia's works, his request is neither a utopian condition nor a theoretical desideratum; he perceived himself as a classical prophet[157] and deemed his own period as the beginning of the messianic eon, in which he saw himself playing an eschatological role in relation to Jews and Christians.[158] Moreover, Abulafia produced a commentary on the Pentateuch, named *Sefer ha-Maftehot,* in which he applied his own peculiar hermeneutic techniques.[159] We can therefore conclude that the previously quoted statement on prophecy as a prerequisite for the use of the seventh method is conclusive evidence of the actual impact of mystical states upon a certain aspect of the interpretive experience in Kabbalah.[160] It is worth noting that a prophetic experience is attained as a result of the utilization of this "path," and we presumably encounter a situation wherein prophecy sustains interpretation, and vice versa.[161] According to Abulafia, the *sensus propheticus* of the monadized text is tantamount to knowledge of the divine name or names, which, in turn, is the best method of attaining prophecy.[162] In other words, the atomization of the texts as part of the interpretive method is concomitant to attaining summa perfectio. The less important the crystallized form of the canon, the more important is the spiritual achievement of the interpreter. Apparently under the impact of Abulafia's views, an anonymous Kabbalist of the fourteenth or fifteenth century writes:[163]

> One cannot comprehend the majority of the subjects of the Torah and its secrets and the secrets of the commandments cannot be comprehended but by means of the prophetic holy intellect which was emanated from God onto the prophets. . . . Therefore, it is impossible to comprehend any subject among the secrets of the Torah and the secrets of performing the commandments by means of intellect or wisdom or by *intellectus acquisitus,*[164] but [only] by means of the prophetic intellect . . . by the divine intellect given to the prophets, which is tantamount to the secret of knowledge of the great [divine] name.

Hence, knowledge of the inner aspects of the Torah is conditional upon the attainment of the highest intellectual faculty, the prophetic intellect, which is seen as tantamount to a prophetic experience.[165] It is worthy of note that the understanding of the secrets is a function of blurring the gap between God and man; the latter acquires a divine, holy intellect, which is the sine qua non of penetration into the secrets of the Torah. A text written under the inspiration of the divine spirit can be properly understood only by re-creating an appropriate state of consciousness.

2. In an anonymous Kabbalistic work entitled *Sefer ha-Meshiv* (*The Book of the Answering* [*Angel*]),[166] written during the generation preceding the expulsion from Spain, we encounter a surprising view, worth quoting in extenso, concerning the manner of composition of the Jewish literary tradition:[167]

> You should know that the secret causing the descent of the supernal book is the secret of the descent of the supernal chariot, and when you pronounce the secret of the great name, immediately the force of the "garment"[168] will descend downward, which is the secret of Elijah,[169] who is mentioned in the works of the sages. And by this R. Simeon bar Yoḥai[170] and Jonathan ben Uzziel learned their wisdom, and they were deserving of the secret of the "garment," to be dressed in it. And R. Ḥanina and R. Neḥuniya ben ha-Kaneh and R. 'Akiva and R. Ishmael ben Elisha and our holy rabbi [R. Judah the Prince] and Rashi and many others [learned] likewise.[171] And the secret of the "garment" is the vision of the "garment," which the angel of God is dressed in, with a corporeal eye, and it is he who is speaking to you. . . . And the secret of the garment was given to those who fear God and meditate upon his name; they have seen it, those men who are the men of God were worthy of this state. And they were fasting for forty days[172] continuously, and during their fast they pronounced the Tetragrammaton forty-five times,[173] and on the fortieth day [the "garment"] descended to him and showed him whatever he wished [to know], and it stayed with him until the completion of the [study of the] subject he wanted [to know]; and they [Elijah and the "garment"] were staying with him day and night. Thus was it done in the days of Rashi to his master, and the latter taught him [Rashi] this secret [of the "garment"], and by means of it [the secret] he [Rashi] composed whatever he composed, by the means of his mentor and instructor.[174] Do not believe that he [Rashi] wrote this down from his own reason,[175] for he did it by the secret of the "garment" of the angel and the secret of mnemotechnics, to explain the questions one is asking or to compose a book one wishes to compose, and [thus] were all the sciences copied,[176] one by one. . . . And this happened in the days of the Talmud and in the days of Rashi's master and in the days of Rashi, too, since his master began this [usage], and Rashi ended it, and in their times this science [how to receive revelations] was transmitted by word of mouth, one man to another, and this is the reason all the sages of Israel relied upon

> Rashi, as at that time they knew the secret. Therefore, do not ever believe that he [Rashi] composed his commentary on the Talmud and on the plain meaning of the Bible out of his reason, but by means of this force of the secret of the "garment," and that [force] which dressed it, which is an angel, since by means of it he could know and compose whatever he wished. . . . And those who were able to see it were like prophets, and in the times of the Talmud many used it.

We encounter here an audacious reconstruction of the origin of Jewish techniques of interpretation: great figures of ancient and medieval Jewish literature were considered to have used magical devices, including fasting and the pronunciation of divine names, in order to receive the vision of an angel, which was viewed as the authoritative means of receiving the contents of the book or commentary one intended to write. It is worthy of note that not only are Kabbalistic subjects included in this passage but also the classical popular commentary on the "plain meaning" of the Bible by Rashi.

Our author traces the use of the "garment" technique to the talmudic period, declaring that the persons who used it were like prophets, evidently disregarding the well-known talmudic view according to which prophecy had already ceased in the tannaitic period.[177] Therefore, according to this anonymous Kabbalist, as we have previously seen in Abulafia's work, a prophetic status is a precondition for writing authoritative commentaries—in this case, even when these are not concerned with mystical issues. It seems clear, however, that these initial statements on the manner in which commentaries were written were not only intended as theoretical discussion; they formed part of a larger commentary on the Pentateuch, of which only a goodly fragment of the commentary on Genesis is extant.[178] As I have attempted to demonstrate, this commentary was apparently composed through the use of magical devices, whose affinity to the above-mentioned practice is evident.[179] We can therefore conclude that it is plausible that this work was the result of the de facto application of the techniques attributed by the author to earlier Jewish authorities; by mentioning his illustrious antecedents, this anonymous Kabbalist was evidently attempting to legitimize his own composition in the eyes of the Jewish public. In this work, the gap between God and man is bridged by the descent of spiritual entities, enveloped in corporeal garments, enabling terrestrial beings to receive messages from them concerning the secrets of Torah.

I would like to elaborate upon the metamorphosis of Rashi—R. Solomon Iẓḥaki, the paragon of Jewish "plain" exegesis—into a mystic who learned everything from supernal sources. This was indeed a strange transformation for this figure to undergo: his penetrating expositions of the straightforward meaning of the biblical and talmudic texts could not, according to the anonymous Kabbalist, stem from the human intellect; their authoritative status had, accordingly, to be generated by inspiration or revelation from above. This understanding of Rashi did not remain the patrimony of an isolated Kabbalist; later authors reiterated this mystical perception of the famous exegete, only one of them doing so under the apparent influence of *Sefer ha-Meshiv.*[180] The author of *Gallya Raza* affirmed that "it is well known that Rashi's words are true, since he said them under the inspiration of the divine spirit, and we surely ought to believe that the divine spirit moved in him." The younger contemporaries of the author of this Kabbalistic treatise, R. Simeon ibn Lavi and R. Gedaliah ibn Yaḥya, apparently independently of one another and of the previous texts, portrayed Rashi in similar colors: the former asserted that, whether or not Rashi was a Kabbalist, the divine spirit dwelled upon him;[181] the latter declared that the divine spirit flowed in Rashi's words, in which he interpreted all the written and oral law according to the authentic tradition.[182] Most surprising, however, is a tradition attributed to R. Israel Ba'al Shem Tov, transmitted via R. Ẓevi Hirsch of Zhidachov to his nephew, R. Isaac Yehudah Safrin of Komarno: "Wherever Rashi uses [the phrase], 'the plain meaning of the verse,' he intended [to say] that, when you shall divest yourself of your corporeality and be stripped of any material issue, you will [surely] apprehend the plain meaning of the verse, stripped of any idea [referring] to the hidden secrets."[183] The paradox implied in this passage is astounding: the plain meaning of the Bible can be understood only through a total divestment of corporeality,[184] a kind of spiritualization or "simplification," in Plotinus' jargon. In contrast to the more commonly held perception of secrets as attained by *ascensio mentis,* they are now viewed, as I understand this passage, as pertaining to the world of multiplicity,[185] whereby the plain meaning now becomes the crowning achievement of the mystic. Rashi is thereby portrayed as an exegete who hinted at the need for a mystical experience that had to precede the understanding of the plain meaning. We no doubt witness here an interesting rejection of the theosophical secrets, opening an avenue to a direct and experiential perception of the biblical text.[186] I assume that, according to this tradition, esoteric interpretations were viewed as an obstacle to the understanding of the plain and sublime meaning of the text. No wonder, then, that quotations from Rashi's commentaries were so widespread in Ḥasidic literature.

3. To return to *Sefer ha-Meshiv:* I believe that a striking reflection of its pneumatics may be seen in the activity of R. Solomon Molkho.[187] In a passage discussed above in part,[188] this visionary confessed that:[189]

> Sometimes in these days I see the celestial academy[190] of sages, and the books are open before them and they study the Torah and they discuss [issues concerning Torah], and they comment upon verses and statements of our sages, blessed be their memory; and from their discussions I hear and learn something. And since I did not learn [Hebrew], nor was accustomed to the holy language and [!] I did not comprehend all their discussions. But from what I was taught there in that Holy Academy, I answer people who ask for interpretations of verses and statements, which are seen as difficult to understand to the sages of [our] generation. And whoever wishes may ask me whatever he wants, to comment on recondite verses and statements, [for] with the help of God, I am confident that I may answer everyone who asks me in a satisfactory manner, sublime things which are sufficient for any intelligent person, which are not [written] in books, [but in] which I was instructed from heaven.[191] But I had never learned science from the mouth of a mortal master or colleague. And whatever anyone will ask me, I am allowed to answer, regarding the twenty-four [books of the Jewish biblical canon], except the Book of Daniel.

We find prior evidence here of Molkho's oracular exposition of the canon; he openly acknowledges that his interpretations cannot be the result of previous studies, as he confesses his prior ignorance of Hebrew and apparently also of Jewish matters.[192] Like the preceding Kabbalists, Molkho authored *Sefer ha-Mefo'ar,* a book that, although a collection of homilies, focuses upon important subjects dealt with in the Bible.

4. The nexus between prophecy and comprehension of the secrets of the Torah is clear in the writings of the famous Kabbalist R. Ḥayyim Vital. According to him:

> All the prophets followed him [Moses] by directing the people and by illuminating their eyes regarding the wisdom of the Torah and its secrets, by means of the divine spirit which enwrapped him. [Therefore] we conclude that prophecy and divine spirit must be in existence in the world, and this is an easy thing, provided that worthy men live.[193]

We likewise learn from the introduction to Vital's *'Eẓ Ḥayyim* that "the mysteries of the Torah and its secrets will not be revealed to men through their intellectual hylic faculty, but by means of the divine influx, emanated from the supernal holiness."[194]

We again perceive that human capabilities are insufficient to penetrate the secret meaning of the Torah; hence the paranormal states of consciousness—here the descent of divine forces—are of paramount importance in decoding these secrets. Vital's statements are in full accord with both Abraham Abulafia's view, discussed above in brief, and with that of R. Isaac Luria Ashkenazi, his main master in Kabbalistic matters, who maintains, in a way reminiscent of the stand of *Sefer ha-Meshiv,* that one ought to study only books written as a result of revelation.[195] Luria himself, as we know, was considered to have received a revelation of Elijah.

According to Vital's view in *Sha'arey Kedushah,* we find that prophecy is made possible by virtue of the particular structure of the human being, which includes all the divine and extradivine worlds, and especially because "there is no other light united with the light of the ten Sefirot like the light of the source of the souls."[196] According to another treatise of Vital, when the source of the highest human soul is blessed by the supernal influx, then it expands and draws a "prophetic power" upon its soul so that he will understand and comprehend the secrets of the Torah.[197] The greater this supernal influx, claims Vital, the greater is the human capability to understand the secrets of the Torah as if by the divine spirit. This is an explicit reference to the crucial role of the pneuma for fathoming the Kabbalistic secrets concealed in the Torah.

5. Under the impact of the Kabbalistic views mentioned above, we also find in Ḥasidism unequivocal evidence of the pneumatic experience as anticipating the interpretation of biblical verses. I will deal here with only a few passages attesting to this view, beginning with Solomon Maimon's *Autobiography.* Before I examine the pertinent passages, however, it is worth remarking that the attainment of a state of self-annihilation was a major goal of the masters of early Ḥasidism in general, and not only within the context of interpreting the Torah. They indicated that the true spiritual activity is that performed by the divine presence, which dwells in the body of the perfect man and uses his limbs like a musical instrument.[198] Hence, the role played by the conscious activity of the interpreter is, according to the Ḥasidic masters, virtually nil. Indeed, Maimon's qualification of this major feature of Ḥasidic mysticism is clear:

> Their sermons and moral teachings were not, as these things commonly are, thought over and arranged in an orderly manner beforehand. This method is proper only to the man who regards himself as a being existing and working for himself apart from God. But the superiors of this sect hold that their teachings are divine, and therefore infallible, only when they are the result of self-annihilation before God, that is, when they are suggested to them ex tempore, by the exigence of circumstances, without their contributing anything themselves.[199]

Immediately thereafter, Maimon decribes a peculiar example of this way of expression. He reports that he begged a Ḥasid "to communicate to me some of these divine teachings. He clapped his hand on his brow as if he were waiting for inspiration from the Holy Ghost."[200] After giving the contents of this sermon, which itself dealt with the problem of self-annihilation, Maimon remarks, "Quite charmed with this ingenious method of interpreting the Holy Scripture, I begged the stranger for some more expositions of the same kind. He proceeded therefore in his inspired manner."[201] Once again, Maimon could not restrain his admiration: "I could not help being astonished at the exquisite refinement of these thoughts and charmed with the ingenious exegesis by which they were supported."[202]

It seems that the wheel of history had come full circle: prophecy, which was the main vehicle for the formation of the Holy Scriptures in biblical times, was excluded from the rabbinic type of interpretation; it returned in the Kabbalistic texts, culminating in the Ḥasidic view that the real speaker in the exposition of the Scriptures is the divine spirit, invoked as a precondition to homiletics, according to the method clearly in use among some disciples of R. Israel Ba'al Shem Tov.

I shall give only one significant example: R. Elimelekh of Lyzhansk affirms that "when a Ẓaddik wishes to comment upon a certain concept or biblical verse, before he begins to speak he shakes his [supernal] root, and the interpretation comes down to him from his root."[203] We find here a certain similarity to Vital's view of the supernal source of the soul as the ultimate origin of the secrets of the Law; the Safedian Kabbalist and the Ḥasidic master share a belief that authentic interpretations are generated by a high transpersonal—although individual—entity that inspires the human soul when she quests for a profound understanding of texts.

Later on, R. Naḥman of Bratslav proposed an entire metaphysic of interpretation; it is the universal soul that serves as a channel for all the interpretations that reach our world:

> Know that there is a soul in the world through which all interpretations of the Torah are revealed. . . . All interpreters of Torah receive [their words] from this soul. . . . And when this soul falls from its rung, and its words become cold, it dies. When it dies, the interpretations that had come through it also disappear. Then all the interpreters are unable to find any meaning in the Torah. . . . He who wants to interpret the Torah has to begin by drawing unto himself words as hot as burning coals. Speech comes out of the upper heart. . . . The interpreter [first] has to pour out his words to God in prayer, seeking to arouse his mercies, so that the heart will open. Speech then flows from the heart, and interpretation of the Torah flows from that speech. . . . On this heart are inscribed all the interpretations of the Torah.[204]

The interpreter is therefore nourished by a supernal source, "the heart," that is identical with the universal soul, summoned up by prayers to provide the human exegete with a particular interpretation.

The survey of the above passages has shown that, in Jewish medieval Kabbalistic traditions, as in Ḥasidism, there is clear evidence supporting the conclusion that pneumatic experiences are viewed as a prelude to a particular kind of literary activity—biblical exegesis. It may, therefore, be instructive to examine other medieval commentaries from this perspective, and it is possible that the range of examples will be considerably greater.[205]

As we have seen, the interpreter needs the pneuma in order to penetrate the secrets inherent in sacred texts; the presence of a pneumatic experience as a condition for understanding some secrets can also be regarded as bridging the gap between interpreter and God, before bridging the gap between his plain understanding and the depth of the text. The three main components of the exegetical experience—God qua author of the text, the text itself, and the interpreter—become intimately related to one another. In the quotations above, the distance between these three elements was reduced without becoming completely effaced. The interpreter turns into a pneumatic, activated by the divine spirit; through the same activity of the pneuma, the Torah turns from a book dealing with history and halakhah to a revelation of the life of the intradivine structure, in the theosophical Kabbalah, or alternatively to a path for attaining an experience of the Divine, in the ecstatic Kabbalah. God himself undergoes a certain change; the hermeneutical process reveals its immanent facets both on the level of hermeneutics and on that of Torah. There are also Kabbalistic texts, however, that imply an actual union of these three elements. This radical conception, which is a rare one, is deserving of more detailed analysis.

An important view of the Torah, stemming from philosophical circles, regarded it as identical with the intellectual realm;[206] this idea had already appeared in Philo.[207] According to R. Abraham ibn ʿEzra, it is identical with the world of wisdom;[208] with ibn Latif, it is identical with the world of the separate intellects.[209] R. Barukh Togarmi adds the crucial view that the Torah is, in the previous contexts, also the divine name and therefore facilitates the comprehension of God.[210] Moreover, this Kabbalist seems to have assumed that God himself is part of the spiritual world.[211] R. Abraham Abulafia was acquainted with these views, to which he added a description of the understanding of the Torah as the Aristotelian epistemic act of intellection of the intelligible by the human intellect; the intelligible is, for Abulafia, the Torah, and understanding it is tantamount to an identification of the intellect with the Torah, and thereby with the intellectual world, which presumably includes God.[212]

Abulafia gave a peculiar turn to the saying in *'Avot*, "Turn it and turn it, since everything is in it,"[213] which he understood as implying that the continuous contemplation of the Torah by the practice of letter combination would result in an experience of the mystic being entirely in the Torah, and of the Torah being entirely in the mystic.[214] This identification of the Scripture and the mystic is reminiscent of a similar concept of identity of the Koran and the mystic occurring in the thought of Abu Bakr Muhammad ibn 'Arabi, Abulafia's older contemporary.[215]

The Aristotelian explanation of the identification of man, text, and God via the noetic act is based upon the explicit assumption that these three entities share a common notable feature—they are intelligible or intelligent beings. It is this intellectual substratum that enables the mystical identification with each other. I should now like to deal with another preliminary essential identity that, together with the previous one, had repercussions on the later interrelationship of the elements of the hermeneutical triangle. As I have tried to show elsewhere, the Torah was envisioned in ancient Jewish texts, and even more explicitly in medieval Kabbalah, as identical with God himself.[216] According to the earlier works, the biblical text was inscribed on the divine body, and therefore this book was perceived as having an anthropomorphic configuration.[217] According to these same ancient texts, the intense and disinterested study of Torah for its own sake can be transformed into a visionary experience of the supernal chariot and the *Shi'ur Komah*; thus the Torah becomes the path to a mystical encounter with the Divine. Hence, there is a common structure to God, man, and Scripture: the anthropomorphical feature. The Kabbalistic views added a further element: God qua wisdom is identical with a divine potency, the Sefirah *Ḥokhmah* (wisdom).[218] Moreover, numerous other Kabbalistic passages directly posit the identity of the entire structure of ten Sefirot with the Torah.[219] At the same time, Kabbalah regarded the souls of the people of Israel as of divine origin, and thence as themselves divine.[220] These and other concepts merged into what became a widespread dictum, the precise source of which is not clear, stating that "God, Israel and the Torah are one entity."[221] Basically, this is a statement of the identity of the origin, God, and those entities that emanated therefrom; hence, it is a Neoplatonic type of preliminary identity, which is an ontic one. At times, the Sefirah of *Tiferet* is conceived as the Sefirah that uniquely represents the Divinity and at the same time is identical with the supernal written law and the archetypal Israel. According to some Kabbalists, the study of the

Torah is the way of union with God, given its identity with him. R. Solomon Alkabeẓ, an important Safedian figure, asserts that the Torah "brings us to a state of *devekut* in him, may he be exalted, because when we cleave to her [the Torah], we also cleave to our Creator, since he and his wisdom are one."[222] Therefore, the original affinity of the three factors must be enacted by the Kabbalistic study of the Torah.

At the end of the eighteenth and the early nineteenth centuries some Ḥasidic masters reiterated some of the concepts described above. R. Moses Ḥayyim Ephraim of Sudylkow, the grandson of R. Israel Ba'al Shem Tov, reported that in one of his dreams his father-in-law, R. Naḥman, told him that a person who is righteous is close to the Torah and that the Torah is in him and he is in the Torah.[223] The affinity of this formulation to Abulafia's above-cited view is striking.[224] After quoting the Kabbalistic dictum mentioned above, R. Moses Ḥayyim Ephraim of Sudylkow asserts:[225]

> "Man" is God, as the numerical value of the Tetragrammaton when spelled fully is forty-five, like the value of 'Adam [man], and the Torah is [constituted] of 248 positive commandments and 365 interdictions . . . . And when man studies Torah for its own sake, to keep it and perform it, then he brings all his limbs close to their source whence they originated and were generated, namely, to the Torah, and each of his limbs becomes a substratum of a particular commandment[226] pertinent to this particular limb, and he becomes identical with the Torah in a unification and a complete union, like the unification of man and woman.

The study of the Torah is here regarded as a restoration of the original state of the human body through its purification, culminating in a mystical union with the Torah, which dwells upon the sanctified members; the mystical study of the Torah is instrumental in the achievement of the triune state. Similarly, R. Mordekhai of Chernobyl asserts:[227]

> If a man sanctifies each of his members and cleaves to the Torah, a cleaving of spirit to spirit,[228] and he himself becomes a complete Torah, [then] "this is the Torah of Man,"[229] since the man himself becomes Torah, and "the Torah of God is perfect,"[230] [since] it has no imperfection, and it causes the return of the human soul to her source, and her source is restored in the supernal place.

The perfect man not only becomes a perfect Torah, but this perfect Torah is viewed as the divine Torah, opening the way for the return of the human soul to her source in the divine realm. It is worth remarking that R. Mordekhai differs from R. Moses Ḥayyim Ephraim of Sudylkow on a crucial point: for the former, the human body is restored to its pristine sanctity, which is now brought about by the achievement of religious perfection; for the latter, the return to the source is reported only in the case of the soul. In another passage, R. Mordekhai comments upon the Kabbalistic dictum above, saying: "just as God, blessed be he, is infinite, so also is the Torah infinite, and likewise the worship of Israel is infinite."[231] Here, infinity is seen as the clue to the unity of the three elements. In order to reach this state, however, an activist attitude is necessary; Torah, by its infinite essence, shows the way to an infinite worship that ensures union with the infinite God.

But the most elaborate presentation of the way to achieving mystical union with God by cleaving to the Torah is found in a classic of Jewish mysticism, R. Shneur Zalman of Lyady's *Likkutey 'Amarim*. According to this Ḥasidic master: "The Torah and the Holy one, blessed be he, are one. The meaning of this is that the Torah, which is the wisdom and will of the Holy one, blessed be he, and his glorious essence are one, since he is both the knower and the knowledge."[232] The Aristotelian principle is here applied to explaining the identity of God and Torah.[233] Elsewhere, the same noetic principle is mentioned in reference to the study of the Torah: "the Torah is absorbed by his intellect and is united with it and they become one. This becomes nourishment for the soul and its inner life from the giver of life, the blessed *'Eiyn Sof*, who is clothed in this wisdom and this Torah that are [absorbed] in it [the soul]."[234] The mystical study of the Torah therefore enjoys a special superiority over every other commandment, since thereby, "the intellect is clothed in divine wisdom, and this divine wisdom is also contained in it."[235] According to R. Shneur Zalman, this is also true with regard to the study of Mishnah, Gemara, and Posekim, as they also embody the divine wisdom. The mystical study of the canonic corpus of Judaism culminates with: "a wonderful union, like which there is none other, . . . whereby complete oneness and unity . . . could be attained."[236]

It remained for one of the most popular classics of modern Jewish mysticism to merge Aristotelian psychology with the Neoplatonic views of primordial, essential identity of soul and her source, to formulate an influential mode of experiential study of the Torah.[237] Here, the mystic not only absorbs the Torah as an intelligible but is himself absorbed by the Torah, a formulation reminiscent both of Abulafia and R. Moses Ḥayyim Ephraim of Sudylkow.

At this point, it is pertinent to reflect upon the nature of the relationships among the three factors of hermeneutic processes; the two types of relationships to God—the conditioning of the mystical interpretation by previous contact with the Divine and the cleaving to God through the Torah—share a profound perception of the Author as a living power involved in the interaction between man and the Bible. For the mystic, they cannot be separated, for the text is a representation of the Divine. Thus, the relationship to the Bible never becomes "complete" or "intact," as Ricoeur would put it;[238] the Kabbalist was interested not in the perfected text whose author is dead and can no longer respond but in contact with the living Author for whom the text is an intermediary. Even when the pneuma was needed in order to better understand the Bible, the content of this deeper apprehension was, in many cases, a better insight into divine matters. According to the French philosopher, the death of the author is a condition for finalizing the text and rendering it into a static perfection, allowing for a "complete" relation. This request is based upon a rigid attitude toward the contents, which are to be approached when they can no longer change. It is an axiom of the Kabbalists that the sacred text is in an ongoing process of change, evidently a symptom of its inherent infinity and divinity. For them, Scripture is a way of overcoming the postprophetic eclipse of revelation, an endeavor to recapture the presence of the Author and its nature; the biblical text produces a silent dialogue and eventually even union between Author and reader,[239] as against the "double eclipse" produced by the complete text as envisioned by Ricoeur.[240] The act of "writing" was, in rabbinic thought and especially in Kabbalah, the act of revelation at Sinai, in which there were present not only those Israelites living at the time but the souls of all following generations. Thus, the readers were not at all "absent from the act of writing," nor is God, the Author, "absent from the act of reading," as Ricoeur describes the "double eclipse."[241] The acts of writing and reading are perfect when performed by isolated individuals; for the Kabbalists both acts are shared experiences.

No wonder that the Kabbalists identified Torah with Divinity, a conception rather common in a long series of Kabbalistic texts, in which the encounter is explicit.[242] But even milder Kabbalistic traditions testify to the presence of the Divine in the Torah. According to R. Shema'iah ben Isaac, a late thirteenth-century author:[243] " 'God created man in his own image,'[244] this [image] being the Torah, which is the shadow of God, blesssed be he." Thus, the same matrix of anthropomorphic structure unifies author, reader, and text; their encounter is facilitated by a shared pattern permitting the lower anthropos to reach the higher one, by the intermediacy of a middle anthropos—the text.[245] Far from being the reason for an "eclipse of God," the text is a window by which to contemplate him; Kabbalists were interested not in a *Verfremdung* from the "world of the Author" but in a gradual appropriation of this world as far as possible. "The world of the text," its fixation, is only a primary starting point.[246]

In the eyes of Jewish mystics, the quest for a final or perfect understanding of a text would be a self-imposed and superfluous limitation generated by man's projection of his own limitations upon a living and infinite entity—the Torah. Or, as R. Israel Ba'al Shem Tov once put it, "The book of the *Zohar* has, each and every day, a different meaning."[247] As far-reaching as this statement may be for zoharic exegesis, it is a mitigated formulation of a tradition adduced in the name of R. Isaac Luria, who stated that "each and every moment the [meaning of the] passages of the Holy *Zohar* are changing."[248] This is not merely a theoretical assumption; it was cited in order to justify the composition of R. Isaac Yehudah Yeḥiel Safrin's commentary on the *Zohar,* named *Zohar Ḥai,* shortly after his venerated uncle, R. Ẓevi Hirsch of Zhidachov, had composed his own commentary on the *Zohar, 'Ateret Ẓevi.* Moreover, this statement was reported by R. Eliezer Ẓevi Safrin, the son of R. Isaac Safrin; as we know, R. Eliezer himself composed a voluminous commentary on the *Zohar* entitled *Damesek Eliezer,* a monument to the practical application of the Lurianic dynamic view of the *Zohar*.

I want to discuss briefly the technical explanation of this ever-changing significance of the *Zohar.* R. Isaac Luria compares the different positions of the stars, which change every hour, to the infinite movements in the infinite supernal worlds, which preside over the various understandings of the *Zohar:*

> The worlds change each and every hour, and there is no hour which is similar to another. And whoever contemplates the movement of the planets and stars, and the changes of their position and constellation and how their stand changes in a moment, and whoever is born in this moment will undergo different things from those which happen to one who was born in the preceding moment; hence, one can look and contemplate what is [going on] in the supernal infinite, and numberless worlds . . . and so you will understand the changes of the constellation and the position of the worlds, which are the garments of *'Eiyn Sof*; these changes are taking place at each and every moment, and in accordance with these changes are the aspects of the sayings of the book of the *Zohar* changing, and all are words of the living God.[249]

In *'Eẓ Ḥayyim,* the phrase "infinite worlds" points to the supernal worlds beyond the primeval anthropos. Therefore, the theosophical dynamics of these worlds influence the meaning of the *Zohar.* Thus, even theoretically, the possibility of attaining its "ultimate" significance is nil; each moment brings its own novel understanding. I want to emphasize Vital's interesting comparison between contemplating the celestial bodies and interpreting a text. In principle, this constitutes an application of an older comparison of Kabbalah to astrology, the Kabbalist who reads the Torah being considered as a sort of superastrologer.[250] What is peculiar to our text is the emphasis upon the repercussions of divine dynamics upon the understanding of the *Zohar.* This text cannot be properly interpreted outside of its appropriate context: the divine life. Every commentator therefore comprehends a particular aspect; he momentarily glimpses the infinite possibilities without being able to exhaust them; he can contribute only a very limited part, depending upon the particular angle the configuration of divine powers allows him to disclose. Luria's—or perhaps Vital's—view of the dynamics of changes bore fruit among the Ḥasidic Kabbalists of Komarno, who indeed supplied commentaries on the *Zohar,* generation after generation.

CHAPTER 10

From Jewish Esotericism to European Philosophy: An Intellectual Profile of Kabbalah as a Cultural Factor

In the previous chapters, I have presented the major aspects of Jewish mysticism, focusing upon two crucial subjects: the quest for ecstasy and union, which uses chiefly anomian techniques, and the theurgical interest, which employs nomian ways. I will now address some issues concerning the emergence of Kabbalah on the theater of history, its perception as a cultural phenomenon, and the historiosophical theses of Scholem regarding Kabbalah. Finally I will briefly survey the history of Kabbalah, based upon the interplay of its two main foci, and conclude with a discussion of Kabbalistic anthropology.

I. THE EMERGENCE OF KABBALAH

In principle, mystics endeavor to uncover an "other dimension" of religion, to use Louis Dupré's phrase; the same is true of Jewish mystics. Sometimes this was done by mystical-symbolic interpretations of the Holy Scriptures and rituals, and sometimes as part of a quest for types of spiritual experiences beyond those cultivated within the normative religious structures. Given the vacillation between the use of nomian and anomian mystical techniques and the expressions employed by mystics to describe their experiences—daring unitive phrases versus sharp theurgical understanding of the commandments—the question arises as to how these differing types of mysticism were received by and integrated in Jewish culture in general.

It is a striking fact, which has curiously remained largely unnoticed by Kabbalah scholarship, that the emergence of major Kabbalistic schools did not stir significant controversies in the Jewish milieus in which they arose. The first Kabbalistic documents surfacing in Provence provoked, as far as we know, only a very brief attack by R. Meir ben Simeon of Narbonne.[1] His critique consists of no more than a page, being directed to certain specific aspects of early Kabbalah, mainly its interpretation of prayer, without, however, attacking any of the major personalities who were regarded as Kabbalists, such as R. Abraham ben David (Rabad), R. Jacob of Lunel, R. Yehudah ben Yakar, and R. Isaac the Blind. The target of this critique was either unnamed persons or the anonymous *Sefer ha-Bahir.* The paucity of criticism is surprising when compared to a parallel phenomenon, close both in time and location to the rise of Kabbalah: the attitude toward Maimonides' philosophy. Prima facie, there is something surprising in this controversy: it was directed against a personality who combined an outstanding mastery of Halakhah and, as a philosopher, a precise, careful manner of writing, intended to avoid the very situation in which he and his thought became involved: religious controversy. The fact that such a controversy nevertheless erupted demonstrates that his thought appeared amid delicate circumstances, in which any kind of innovation, even a prudently formulated one, was subject to careful examination and eventually to sharp criticism.

Early thirteenth-century Provence was not only the arena in which the great renaissance of twelfth-century Jewish learning took place but a religiously tense area where both religious heresy—Catharism—and philosophical pantheism were violently attacked. Notwithstanding the circumstances, however—such as the church's scrutiny and suspicion of novel intellectual directions and the fiery attacks upon Maimonides—Kabbalah, which emerged as a historical factor in the late twelfth and early thirteenth centuries in Provence and Catalonia, escaped stirring polemics and banishments (which were to be the lot of Maimonides' works) or excommunication (which was the fate of David de Dinant, Amaury de Bene, and Aristotle).

Two factors seem to have protected the emerging Kabbalah: first, unlike philosophy, it was studied within families and limited groups, making no attempt to disseminate its tenets to larger audiences. Although there were some exceptions that were criticized by the Kabbalists themselves,[2] this mystical lore only gradually surfaced, a process that facilitated its broader recognition a century after the composition of the first historical Kabbalistic documents. Moreover, Maimonides' thought was the achievement of a single extraordinary personality; his reinterpretation of Judaism in Aristotelian terms was unprecedented, no major intellectual Jewish circle backing his stands in his own lifetime. He attempted to change certain prevailing religious concepts, attacking works that were considered part of the ancient spiritual patrimony of Judaism, such as *Shi'ur Komah,* and ignoring others, such as the various interpretations of *Ma'aseh Bereshit* and *Ma'aseh Merkavah* contained in the *Heikhalot* literature and in *Sefer Yeẓirah*. He proposed in their stead his own philosophical interpretation of the ancient Jewish esoteric teachings.[3] Kabbalah, on the other hand, enjoyed the support of powerful personalities, who formed a major segment of the spiritual elite of Provence and Catalonia: Rabad, R. Jacob the Nazirite of Lunel, Naḥmanides, and later R. Solomon ben Adret. To attack Kabbalah was not like entering into conflict with one major Jewish figure living in distant Egypt; rather, a challenger would be confronting a coalition that could be overpowered only with great difficulty. Although during the twelfth and the early thirteenth centuries, Kabbalists belonged to different mystical circles, they were nevertheless aware of each other,[4] so that any criticism of the mystical dimension of Judaism would entail a confrontation with powerful forces in the Jewish establishment.

Moreover, the Maimonideans, such as Samuel ibn Tibbon or David Kimḥi, although remarkable intellectual figures, were nevertheless newcomers in Provence and, more important, lacked the authority invested in some of the early Kabbalists by their vast halakhic erudition. Although ibn Tibbon was the outstanding Provençal expert in matters of Arabic and Jewish philosophy, and Kimḥi in those of the Bible, they could not compete as experts on the mystical implications of oral law or oral traditions. We can assume that some criticism of Kabbalah is no longer extant,[5] but I am nevertheless of the opinion that the great religious authority of some of the early Kabbalists intimidated critics from the beginning or managed to silence them even if they uttered attacks.

The second, and more important, reason for the silent acceptance of Kabbalah in Provence and Spain was its deep affinity with certain rabbinic patterns of thought. As I have dealt with this issue previously, I want here only to point out the difference between the abrupt break represented by Maimonides' rationalistic reinterpretation of the Jewish tradition and the slow and gradual articulation of some aspects of Judaism in the emerging Kabbalah. It seems that it was easier to convince a person immersed in rabbinic studies of the correctness of the mythical-mystical resonance of ancient Jewish texts than of their philosophical overtones.

The crucial question in this context is why Kabbalah emerged at the same time and locale as the Maimonidean controversy.[6] Graetz answered this question by proposing that Kabbalah was an innovation motivated by an interest in counteracting the spread of philosophy, an idea already implied by Modena. Scholem was not happy with such a "reactive" answer and solved the quandary with a purely phenomenological plan: early Kabbalah emerged then and there because "Gnostic" traditions merged with Neoplatonic thought. I suggest a third hypothesis: that Kabbalah emerged in the late twelfth and early thirteenth centuries as a sort of reaction to the dismissal of earlier mystical traditions by Maimonides' audacious reinterpretation of Jewish esotericism and his attempt to replace the mystical traditions with a philosophical understanding. Kabbalah can be viewed as part of a restructuring of those aspects of rabbinic thought that were denied authenticity by Maimonides' system. Far from being a total innovation, historical Kabbalah represented an ongoing effort to systematize existing elements of Jewish theurgy, myth, and mysticism into a full-fledged response to the rationalistic challenge. Indeed, we can consider Kabbalah as part of a silent controversy between the rationalistic and mystical facets of Judaism. It was "silent" in that the main organon of the Kabbalistic response took the form not of open attacks on Maimonides—an extremely rare phenomenon in early Kabbalah—but of an ongoing building of an alternative to his system on the basis of earlier materials. Just as some later Kabbalists, such as R. Shem Tov ibn Shem Tov, R. Meir ibn Gabbay, and R. Ḥayyim Vital considered themselves opponents, critics, or even emenders of Maimonides' unilateral interest in philosophy as against mysticism, so did the anti-Kabbalists, such as R. Elijah del Medigo or R. Yehudah Aryeh of Modena (Leone da Modena), view themselves as defenders of the philosopher's ideas.

II. FROM ESOTERICISM TO EXOTERICISM

Kabbalah is by definition an esoteric body of speculation; whether in its theosophic-theurgical explanation of the rationales for the commandments,[7] or in the ecstatic trend dealing with techniques of using divine names,[8] esotericism is deeply built into this lore. According to R. Isaac the Blind, his predecessors never wrote down Kabbalistic matters,[9] and Abraham Abulafia viewed the path of the names as a higher, and therefore more secret, lore than the path of the Sefirot. Notwithstanding this, both R. Isaac the Blind and Abulafia composed Kabbalistic treatises, the latter even boasting that his literary productivity surpassed that of the former Kabbalists.[10] By the end of the thirteenth century, approximately a hundred years after the appearance of the first Kabbalistic documents, there had already been produced a large body of literature consisting of several thousand folios. This explosion of Kabbalistic creativity was facilitated by the neutralization of those inhibitions that had prevented earlier Kabbalists from expanding upon the esoteric traditions inherited from their teachers. Such scholars as Rabad, Naḥmanides, and R.

Solomon ben Adret (Rashba), although Kabbalists and, in the case of the latter two, even known as teachers of Kabbalah, were faithful to the halakhic interdiction against the public transmission of topics related to the "Account of the Creation" and the "Account of the Chariot," and refrained from dealing with such issues either in writing or in public speech. Furthermore, they seem to have preserved earlier traditions meticulously without attempting to expand on them, to elaborate their details, or to effect a larger speculative synthesis; they saw themselves by and large as the repositories of an esoteric lore, interested in its intact preservation within limited scholarly circles rather than in its transformation into a body of speculations.

Some of the contemporaries of Naḥmanides and of his disciple Rashba, however, envisaged Kabbalah in a very different way; it was seen not only as a collection of fragments of esoteric lore of hoary antiquity but also as an open science to be furthered by experiences of the individual and his ability creatively to interpret the Holy Scriptures or other canonic texts. Kabbalah was regarded no longer as only a single esoteric meaning but as the totality of the mystical-mythical senses that could be extracted or infused into the authoritative texts.[11] It became more a lore that promoted the production of secrets—*nistarot*—than a custodian of secret lore—*Ḥokhmat ha-nistar.* This plurality of equally valid meanings counteracted the esoteric view of there being but one authoritative meaning or tradition. One can easily understand the psychological reasoning whereby a Kabbalist, who was aware of the creative process in himself that produced a certain Kabbalistic explanation, could hardly envisage it as an esoteric topic to be carefully withheld from the vulgus; it is understandable, then, why the systematic and voluminous treatises of such Kabbalists as Abraham Abulafia, Moses de Leon, Joseph Gikatilla, and Joseph of Hamadan were only rarely represented by their authors as esoteric teachings.

As a result of its self-perception as dealing with psychological processes, the Kabbalah was opened to new creativity. As we have seen above,[12] the theosophical system of the Sefirot was interpreted by Abraham Abulafia as referring to human actions and psychological states; thus he neutralized the esoteric aura surrounding the Sefirot viewed as pointing to a mysterious divine structure whose true nature could be realized only by the few who were the recipients of ancient traditions. The theological dangers inherent in the contemplation and activation of a complex system of divine powers were attenuated by the transposition of this system into the human psyche; in principle, the psychologizing of Kabbalah in the ecstatic trend served to bridge the immense gap between it and philosophical psychology, which never emphasized the esoteric nature of this realm of speculation.[13] R. Pinḥas Elijah Horowitz wrote in his *Sefer ha-Berit:* "There are [persons] who are not interested in secrets and say . . . that all these are parables and metaphors for the powers found in man."[14] According to this Kabbalist, secrecy was perceived as an inherent characteristic of the Kabbalistic ontology, related to the "objective" existence of divine powers or configurations symbolically alluded to in canonic texts. Horowitz perceptively remarked that Ḥasidim were not interested in "secrets"; indeed, the exoteric nature of Ḥasidic mysticism was clear in comparison with the previous stages of Jewish mysticism. Some earlier events, however, prepared the way for a more exoteric type of Jewish mysticism. Thus, Abraham Abulafia expounded his particular type of Kabbalah, not only in numerous and voluminous treatises and letters, but also orally, to both Jews and Christians in a number of countries.

Later, Kabbalists who were expelled from Spain elaborated Kabbalistic matters in systematic ways that rendered superfluous, or at least significantly reduced, the need for oral instructions from a Kabbalistic master. Such treatises as R. Meir ibn Gabbay's *Derekh 'Emunah* and *'Avodat ha-Kodesh* and Cordovero's *Pardes Rimmonim* are examples of lucid presentations of a wide range of Kabbalistic topics. I do not intend to imply that these Kabbalists had no esoteric teachings that they excluded from their compendia—it is more than reasonable to assume that there were such—but overall, Kabbalah ceased to be an esoteric lore. Therefore, it is not surprising that Cordovero's students popularized his teachings in ethical treatises that leaned heavily upon classical Kabbalistic texts but were nevertheless explicitly intended for the masses.

The next major development in Kabbalistic theosophy, however—Lurianic Kabbalah—represented a setback from the perspective of exoteric Kabbalah.[15] Luria's immediate predecessors, such as R. David ben Zimra (Radbaz), ibn Gabbay, and Cordovero, presented Kabbalistic teachings as they found them in written texts—hence the plethora of quotations that characterize their writings. Rather than revealing or introducing new Kabbalistic views, they were arranging and classifying older views and eventually counterpoising one against another. Therefore, their writings offered no revelation of recondite theories or of orally taught secrets. Although Cordovero and his students seem to have been immersed in practicing a variety of mystical techniques and were known as the recipients of various revelations, the content of their revelations was not presented as part of their written teachings. Cordovero's *Sefer ha-Gerushim,* Vital's *Sefer ha-Ḥezyonot,* and R. Eleazar Azikri's mystical diary, which include interesting documentation of their mystical lives, are strikingly different from their "classical" works. The Kabbalah revealed by the Safedian masters consists almost exclusively of either theoretical lore—which includes details of mystical techniques—or ethical mysticism, rather than personal confessions.

III. KABBALAH: FROM EXPULSION TO ḤASIDISM

One peculiar feature of Kabbalah, especially that of the theosophical-theurgical school, was its scholastic nature. Kabbalists studied such classics of Kabbalistic literature as *Sefer Yeẓirah, Sefer ha-Bahir,* Naḥmanides' works, and, in particular, the *Zohar* and were profoundly influenced by those works, either absorbing their ideas and elaborating upon them in their own works or writing commentaries upon them. These modes of dealing with sources also explain their hints and allusions: fragmentary passages were related to one another, obscure texts were elucidated, and, in general, broader Kabbalistic systems emerged over the course of time. Particularly following the Expulsion from Spain, the tendency to systematize earlier Kabbalistic ideas and traditions became a major part of the process of reconstructing the shattered socio-intellectual Spanish experience. This development of Kabbalistic writing was, in essence, a gradual passage from esotericism to exotericism.[16]

This process, characteristic of Spanish Kabbalists, was coupled with a similar contemporary phenomenon in the Italian Kabbalah. From the 1480s on, certain Jewish Italian intellectuals, such as R. Yoḥanan Alemanno, R. David Messer Leon, R. Isaac of Pisa, and R. Abraham de Balmes, initiated a notable attempt to interpret Kabbalah in accordance with the philosophical concepts widespread in their intellectual environment. This translation of Kabbalah into a philosophical key also represented implicitly a metamorphosis into a system of ideas that could easily be understood by non-Kabbalists, either Jews or Christians, assuming they were acquainted with the kinds of philosophical thinking used in the writings of Jewish authors.[17] The manner in which Alemanno or de Balmes interpreted Kabbalah seems conspicuously cognate to its decoding by their contemporaries and acquaintances in the Christian camp—for example, Pico della Mirandola or Johannes Reuchlin. Kabbalah was conceived by both Jewish and Christian Renaissance figures as an ancient theology, similar to and, according to the Jews, the source of such later philosophical developments as Platonism, Aristotelianism, Pythagoreanism, and atomism.[18]

The interest in the Kabbalah during the period of the Renaissance was shared by Italian Jews and Christians; although it was a bridge between the two religions, it was nevertheless exploited for Christian missionary activities, as openly acknowledged by Pico della Mirandola.[19] The fact, however, that Kabbalah was interpreted in both camps according to philosophical views signifies not only its adaptation to Neoplatonic-Hermetic speculations prevalent during that period but also the reduction of its esoteric nature. In sharp contrast with the more esoteric conception of Kabbalah found among the Spanish Kabbalists,[20] their Italian contemporaries envisaged it as a speculative and thus exoteric lore. This discrepancy between the two conceptions can be found partly in the different ways it was studied by the Kabbalists. In Spain, and after the Expulsion in Safed also, Kabbalah was taught in talmudic academies—*yeshivot*—and transmitted not only in written form but also orally.[21] In late fifteenth-century Italy, persons interested in studying Kabbalah had to do so exclusively from manuscripts without the guidance of an authoritative mentor and in at least one instance—that of R. David Messer Leon—against the will of his father and teacher.[22] The absence of an oral tradition and the unique focus upon written material contributed to a turn from esotericism to exotericism among the Italian Kabbalists.

This twist in the perception of Kabbalah is highly important for an understanding of the printing of the *Zohar.* As we know, the publication of this Kabbalistic chef d'oeuvre stirred a bitter controversy among some Italian Jewish authorities, many of whom fiercely opposed the publication of Jewish esoteric lore.[23] The printers, R. Isaac de Lattes and R. Meshulam of St. Angelo, presented their activity as part of a messianic effort to spread its secrets, thereby preparing for the coming of the Messiah. Although this messianic pretext has been accepted by modern scholarship as the real motive for the printing of the *Zohar,*[24] these two Kabbalists were not otherwise known as messianic activists nor were their opponents to be accused of antimessianic views. Moreover, both printers were influenced by Yoḥanan Alemanno's exoteric Kabbalah, as we may infer from the fact that both of them copied his voluminous treatises and carefully studied them.[25]

The Kabbalistic writings of Cordovero and of his students, the printing of the *Zohar* in Italy, and the dissemination of Kabbalah among Christians[26] prompted a return to stringent orders for secrecy in the circle of R. Isaac Luria.[27] His teachings were carefully reserved for a few elite Kabbalists and jealously kept from the eyes of curious scholars long after his death. Although some Lurianic treatises made their way to Italy and Greece,[28] the greatest part of the Kabbalistic corpus in the possession of R. Ḥayyim Vital remained unknown to the wider public for several decades. The widespread dissemination of Lurianic Kabbalah in the wake of Sabbatianism, assumed by modern scholarship, has yet to be demonstrated by detailed studies.[29] Insofar as I can tell, Luria's and Vital's texts enjoyed only a very limited circulation among a readership that had access to only a small part of the Lurianic corpus, mainly in the version of R. Israel Sarug. Even his Kabbalistic propaganda was successful solely among the elite, and Lurianic Kabbalah became influential in the written works of R. Menaḥem ʹAzariah da Fano, R. Aaron Berakhiah of Modena, R. Abraham Herrera, and R. Joseph Solomon del Medigo, known as Yashar of Candia. As a result of the complexity of this system, Lurianic Kabbalah remained forever inaccessible to the masses. It was accepted, however, by the European Kabbalists according to their intellectual interests. Philosophically oriented individuals, such as Herrera or del Medigo, interpreted it in accordance with their Neoplatonic or atomistic brands of philosophy, substantially altering the mythical structure of the lore.[30] Other Kabbalists, such as Abraham Yagel or Manasseh ben Israel, were even less interested in mythical Lurianic Kabbalah than were their intellectual contemporaries mentioned above.[31] This type of Kabbalah remained the prerogative of a very limited circle of Kabbalists in Jerusalem, who continued to cultivate it and redact their works in various versions, but they were not active in its propagation to a larger public. Hence the supposed link between the "widespread" Kabbalah during the generation preceding Sabbatianism and the spread of messianism must be carefully examined.[32]

Notwithstanding Scholem's assessments of the preparation for the way to Messiah by Lurianic ideas, then, the facts seem to be different. First, the knowledge of Lurianic Kabbalah was, roughly speaking, limited to the elite; only a few Kabbalists could be considered to have really mastered this complicated type of theosophy. For example, when it was propagated in some limited circles or in confraternities in northern Italy, its influence was exerted mainly in ritual and customs—*minhagim*—and only marginally in a *weltanschauung*. Second, some of those who were sympathetic to it, such as Herrera, del Medigo, and Manasseh, did *not* perceive it as a messianic ideology. These authors, who were among the few Europeans to study Luria's views, even attenuated the mythical, demonical, theurgical, and eschatological facets of Kabbalah to various extents. Therefore, at least in the manner in which they adopted Luria's thought, its spread had nothing to do with heightening messianic expectations or tensions.[33] Third, to the extent that Lurianic Kabbalah had a messianic message, it was not greater than the messianic burden of earlier Kabbalah. The Kabbalah of Abraham Abulafia and that of the *Zohar*[34] had already incorporated some messianic elements, and they were not intensified by the specific formulations of Luria. Given their theurgical tendencies, zoharic and Lurianic Kabbalah perceived human activity to be capable of restoring the primeval harmony to the divine world, but such an activity, although it might carry eschatological overtones, certainly did not constitute messianic activism. Luria, like the *Zohar,* envisioned the achievement of a perfect state in the divine world as a cumulative process requiring collective theurgical activity. As Scholem accurately put it, in Lurianic Kabbalah the advent of the Messiah would be the result of preparatory human actions rather than a sudden eruption of the eschaton in the world.[35] The individual Messiah was emblematic of the attainment of the messianic age rather than its initiation. Sabbatianism, on the other hand, represented a type of messianism focused upon the specific person of the Messiah—Sabbatai Ṣevi. *His* redemptive acts and his special dialectic *fatum*, not those of the people of Israel, would initiate the eschaton. Hence, Lurianism and Sabbatianism displayed opposing versions of messianism, which could not easily be reconciled. No detailed explanation of this quandary has been supplied, so far.

These observations are intended to stimulate a reevaluation of Scholem's thesis concerning the dependence of Sabbatianism upon Lurianic Kabbalah. Although a reevaluation cannot be offered here, it must be mentioned because the postulated "triumph" of this messianic ideology has been assumed to be the result of an alleged spread of Lurianic Kabbalah among the Jewish masses. The attempt to disentangle Lurianism from Sabbatianism is one that ought to be conducted primarily on the sociological level. Rumors of the coming of the Messiah in the person of a specific individual were believed not because they fit into Lurianic messianism but for rather different reasons: indeed, the motivations of the ex-Marranos for eagerly accepting Ṣevi as Messiah must have been different from those of Polish Jewry after the massacre of 1648. Kabbalah, even Lurianic Kabbalah, had little to do with the mass psychologies prevalent in the middle of the seventeenth century.

Notwithstanding this, I want to stress that Sabbatianism indeed benefited from Lurianic Kabbalah, primarily through the adoption of its theosophy and mythology. Although Ṣevi himself was not particularly interested in this type of Kabbalah, his prophet, Nathan of Gaza, can be considered as a Lurianic Kabbalist who employed Lurianic terminology creatively, giving it a special twist that "illuminated" the personal myth of Ṣevi. Moreover, the theological language of Ṣevi's followers was predominantly Lurianic, although again it was used and understood only by the very few. A perusal of Sabbatian documents demonstrates that they were as obscure as the Lurianic texts, far beyond the reach of the understanding of the masses.

The diffusion of Sabbatian texts written in a Lurianic jargon and sometimes even under Luria's name in the aftermath of Ṣevi's career prompted a reaction, and the study of Luria's works from manuscripts or before the age of forty was banned.[36] Although the enactment of these prohibitions seems to have been a failure, the ban against studying Lurianic Kabbalah at a relatively early age lingered on within the consciousness of Jewish masses, from the early decades of the eighteenth century up to individuals now alive. The cumulative effect, however, of what is generally called Kabbalistic Mussar literature and the emergence of Ḥasidism contributed to the dissemination of some Kabbalistic concepts, rituals, and motifs even when their broader theosophical framework remained unknown to the larger public. The belief in transmigration of souls (*gilgul*), demonic possession (*dibbuk*), and homunculus (*golem*), as well as the plethora of Kabbalistic terms that infiltrated ordinary Hebrew[37] and the performance of customs and rituals incorporating Kabbalistic elements, such as the Tikkun of *Shavu'ot* night, are evidence of the penetration of Kabbalah into the non-Kabbalistic Jewish public.

IV. THEOSOPHY AND THEURGY

As a speculative system, Kabbalah was relatively open to alien influences; the theosophical trend mainly integrated these into its discussions of certain aspects of the divine infrastructure, where Neoplatonism and medieval Aristotelianism left their impression. In the realm of practice, I would consider the penetration of the technique of visualization of colors as a major exception, confirming the rule of a hermetical closeness. Ecstatic Kabbalah built most of its theology upon clearly philosophical concepts that were only slightly adapted to accommodate ancient sources, such as the Midrash, the Talmud, and Heikhalot literature. Its mystical techniques seem to have been deeply influenced by Ashkenazic sources and even earlier traditions, such as those of the Heikhalot literature, although the absorption of breathing devices and seclusion point to the infiltration of extraneous elements. We can therefore consider the two Kabbalistic mainstreams as relatively more conservative on the practical than on the speculative level; in other words, whereas actual practice changed only peripherally, the theological superstructures were far more open to the reception of external influences.

Accordingly, we can regard the Kabbalah as being composed of a certain hard core that assumed various expressions from cultural environments throughout the ages. Ecstatic Kabbalah used Maimonidean, Averroësian, Neoplatonic, and eventually Sufic languages to describe the theology and psychology that articulated mystical experiences, but the quest itself remained stable: ecstasy, union, revelation. Theurgy preceded the historical Kabbalah and set the tone for its two major phases: zoharic and Lurianic Kabbalah. Although these two principal theosophies differed in some key concepts, they nevertheless agreed on the necessity of improving the divine structure through human performance of the commandments. This quest characterized the theocentric Kabbalah, just as the quest for paranormal spiritual experiences was the crux of anthropocentrical ecstatic Kabbalah. These speculative systems served as vehicles of expression or fashions of self-understanding of the Kabbalistic practices, rather than as the real foci of Kabbalah.

There were Kabbalists, however, who were attracted more by the speculative than by the experiential realm. These men included the anonymous authors of the Kabbalistic literature written about the same time as *Sefer ha-'Iyyun*,[38] R. Isaac ben Jacob ha-Cohen, R. Moses of Burgos, R. Isaac ibn Latif, the anonymous author of *Ma'arekhet ha-'Elohut*, R. Yehudah Campanton, and others among the Spanish Kabbalists; R. David Messer Leon, R. Berakhiel Kafman, and R. Abraham Yagel in Italy; R. Abraham Herrera and R. Manasseh ben Israel in Holland; and R. Joseph Solomon del Medigo in Poland; among others. Their work provides evidence of the temptation that existed to dissolve the link between practice and speculation in favor of the latter. This movement from a complex structure to one of its components attested by these Kabbalists is an interesting phenomenon that may be significant for at least two reasons. As I pointed out earlier,[39] Gnosticism was conceived by Cornelius Agrippa and Simone Luzzatto, respectively, as influenced by and a distortion of Jewish Kabbalah. It would be worthwhile to ponder these assessments once more. As I have tried to demonstrate, theosophical schemes of seventy-two forms or of anthropos qua decad were shared by Kabbalah and Gnosticism. What sharply divided these two religious phenomena were not so much the details of their schemes as their religious contexts. For the Gnostic, the knowledge of one or another cosmogonic scheme was part of the salvific gnosis that enabled him to escape this world; for the theurgical Kabbalist, the theosophical scheme was a blueprint for his modus operandi. The question that then arises concerns the nature and role of those ancient Jewish theosophies that presumably preceded the Gnostic ones: were their theoretical speculations on the essence of God and cosmos solely quasi-Gnostic constructions, or were they congenial to the Kabbalistic synthesis of the theoretical and the practical, theosophy and theurgy? Any answer to such a question is highly speculative, given the paucity of information available to us; however, on the basis of certain hints in Gnostic texts that mystically interpret Jewish issues connected to ritual, I incline to a positive answer. If this assumption is correct (and, I repeat, for the present it is no more than an assumption), then Gnosticism can be seen as a type of theosophy that severed itself from the ritualistic—eventually theurgic—backgrounds that had sustained and motivated it,[40] one of these backgrounds possibly being a Jewish synthesis of theosophy-theurgy similar to the midrashic-Kabbalistic view of "adding strength above." Theosophy, which liberated itself from the "burden" of compulsory activity related to it, may indeed have flowered in different and, in this case, even wild directions, as did indeed Gnosticism. Rituals, which anchor theology in practice, can therefore be seen as important factors in the institutionalization of speculative religions, and praxis and speculation can be considered as complementary and interpenetrating domains, necessary for a balanced social type of religion. The free-wheeling theosophical speculation that became part of Gnosticism ultimately contributed to a divorce between it and a larger public; bizarre theosophies are commonly the patrimony of elites, who are not interested in a more popular type of spirituality.

The above analysis is also relevant to a certain extent to Heikhalot literature; increasingly focusing on the description of the supernal domains of the *Merkavah* and Godhead, this type of Jewish mysticism ignored the impact of halakhic deeds as a major spiritual vehicle. The anonymous mystics employed anomian techniques that, indeed, were to be used only by persons who had already attained halakhic "perfection,"[41] but their peculiar type of religious mentality transcended the standard—if I may use such an adjective—Jewish view. In this context, the theurgy of augmentation is conspicuous by its absence in Heikhalot treatises, notwithstanding the fact that its authors, too, recurrently use the epitheton *Dynamis* for God. Crucial for these ancient Jewish mystics were knowledge—a certain type of salvific gnosis—and vision, to use Ithamar Gruenwald's terms. In the classical controversy on the priority of activity versus learning, they would certainly have favored "knowledge, for it leads to acts," not vice versa. Heikhalot literature contained a cosmology and a theology unrelated to the halakhic worldview, although not conflicting with it;[42] its importance lay—as in Gnosticism—in its serving as the scheme for the mystical ascent.

A disentanglement of theosophy from theurgy recurred in the Christian version of Kabbalah, which emerged during the Renaissance. One of the crucial differences between the original Kabbalistic texts and their perception by the Christian Kabbalists was the neutralization of the theurgical aspect, so central for the Jewish Kabbalah,[43] with the concomitant acceptance of Kabbalistic theosophy as the ultimate message of Jewish mysticism. It is easy to understand why such a neutralization was necessary before Kabbalah could be accepted into the Platonic-Pythagorean-Hermetic Renaissance synthesis. The working hypothesis of Marsilio Ficino, Pico della Mirandola, and Johannes Reuchlin was that the appraisal and proof of Christian truths could transpire through the variegated garbs of the ancient theologies and philosophies.[44] Since these truths had also to be corroborated by Kabbalah, its uniquely Jewish component, halakhic theurgy, had to be annulled in its Christian version on the ground of the Christian abrogation of the commandments.[45] Thus, R. Menaḥem Recanati, a prominent representative of the theurgical understanding of the commandments[46] and simultaneously one of the pillars of Christian Kabbalah,[47] was quoted selectively by the Christian Kabbalists so as to serve as a mine of theosophical teachings and hermeneutics but not as a theurgical author.[48] Kabbalah was thereby transformed into a gnosis, including esoteric theosophy, comparable to other similar ancient lores. I want to emphasize the importance of this metamorphosis of Kabbalah: some precious tones of this lore were lost in the Christian key.[49] The Renaissance perception of Kabbalah was widely disseminated in European languages—Latin, Italian, French, and English—and it became one of the sources of the incipient studies of Kabbalah, which made full use of it. This is true not only of Franz Molitor's voluminous presentation of Kabbalah, so influential with Scholem, but also of Adolphe Franck who, significantly, began his book with a survey of Christian Kabbalah![50] The speculative presentation of this kind of mysticism, which suppressed its practical side, was consonant with the Reform religious tendencies of the nineteenth-century Jewish Western Europe, so that they conspired, consciously or not, to present Kabbalah in most Western-language studies as a philosophy—an abstract system of thought.

But Jewish Kabbalah not only found its way into the Christian world as a "philosophy"; it was highly appreciated both as a style of speculation and as a repository of extremely important hermeneutics. From the beginning, Christian Kabbalah overemphasized this aspect of Jewish mystical lore. Time and again Christian Kabbalists explained the significance of *gematria*, *notarikon*, and *temurah*, fascinated by the new exegetical avenues opened by Kabbalistic hermeneutics.[51] As Christians, they felt they had finally found the keys, sacrosanct even in the eyes of the Jew, that could unlock the gates of the mysteries of the Scriptures and ultimately demonstrate Christian truths, using Jewish rules. This attempt had already been undertaken by Pico della Mirandola,[52] and it became a leitmotiv of the entire Christian Kabbalah.

Thus, with the passage of Kabbalah into the realm of Christianity, we again witness a separation of two interrelated Kabbalistic matters. As we have seen above, the symbolical interpretation characteristic of theosophical Kabbalah was intended not only to unfold a certain theosophical process but to strengthen the importance of human activity—the performance of the commandments. So also with ecstatic hermeneutics; Abulafia's seventh path of interpretation, for example, culminated in an ecstatic experience. When used by Christian intellectuals, both the symbolic and the combinatory hermeneutics were employed in order to extract speculative religious or philosophical statements from the Scriptures rather than to endorse a theurgical dromenon or an ecstatic experience. Madame Helena Blavatsky, a follower of the Renaissance Christian Kabbalists, aptly formulated their conception of Kabbalah as follows: "The Kabbalist is a student of 'secret science,' one who interprets the hidden meaning of the Scriptures with the help of the symbolical Kabbalah, and explains the real one of these means."[53]

From the late fifteenth until the late nineteenth century, Kabbalistic theosophies, in their classical and Lurianic versions, were sources of inspiration for European thought. English Platonists and scientists such as Newton, and German idealistic thinkers, such as Schelling, paid attention to this body of Jewish thought. Although it never became a major intellectual factor, Kabbalah contributed in a modest way to European philosophy. The influence of Kabbalistic theosophies was far greater on European occultism, however, which drew on various versions of pre-Lurianic, Lurianic, and Sabbatian texts.

V. EXPULSION AND KABBALAH

The commonly accepted presentations of Kabbalah are based upon the historical approach, the most important volume in this genre being Scholem's *Major Trends in Jewish Mysticism.*[54] The implicit assumption seems to be that a given cultural and religious phenomenon is closely intertwined with or dependent upon its immediate historical predecessors. *Historia non facit saltus.* Lurianic Kabbalah therefore logically follows zoharic Kabbalah; Sabbatianism, the Lurianic school; and Ḥasidism, Sabbatianism.[55] This assumption obviously also postulates the influence of one mystical phenomenon on another by way of reaction and controversy; Ḥasidism, for example, is explained as the result not only of Sabbatian influence, but to a certain extent, of a profound restructuring of Lurianic Kabbalah.[56] There are, no doubt, some sound reasons for such an approach; proximity in time certainly induces a particular dynamics that cannot be denied or underestimated. But the historical approach employed by itself, yields incomplete and at times even misleading conclusions.[57] Nathan of Gaza, for example, was a Lurianic Kabbalist, whereas Sabbatai Ṣevi was not interested in this brand of Kabbalah,[58] being closer to the zoharic and ecstatic schools.[59] Polish Kabbalists of the early seventeenth century were as interested in Luria's works as in the hermeneutical techniques of their predecessors living in the twelfth and thirteenth centuries,[60] and the Ḥasidim, who printed an impressive amount of Kabbalistic literature, preferred to publish works originating from the thirteenth through the fifteenth centuries rather than Lurianic works.[61] History therefore is only one possible path scholars may follow in order to describe the evolution of religious movements; another avenue is phenomenology.

Let me briefly describe the historiosophic assumptions underlying Scholem's book and their weaknesses. As he himself remarked, Kabbalah, like other types of mysticism, was not interested in history;[62] it focused rather on the primordial and eschatological processes, in a manner reminiscent of Neoplatonic thought. This sound approach, however, was not followed in Scholem's own historiosophy of Kabbalah; he conceived of at least two historical events as fraught with far-reaching implications for the evolution of Kabbalistic thought. The Expulsion of the Jews from the Iberian Peninsula was seen as structuring Lurianic Kabbalah's particular interest in the questions of exile, messianism, and evil.[63] We see here an obvious absorption of the implications of a historical event into the basic structure of a specific type of Kabbalah. Scholem's proposal for explaining the characteristics of Lurianic Kabbalah was based on the assumption that this type of mystical lore included important conceptual innovations that had to be explained in terms of historical change rather than inner developments; moreover, it implied a neglect of the Kabbalistic material extant in the manuscripts. This approach seems also methodologically problematic; Lurianic texts never mention the Expulsion, nor are their innovative concepts of such magnitude that we must turn for an explanation of their source to issues totally absent in them.

Moreover, there are no psychological reasons that compel us to indulge in such speculative adventures. Luria, Scholem's hero of the Kabbalistic interiorization of the Sephardic exodus, was in fact an Ashkenazic figure,[64] who, while teaching his disciples in a small town in Palestine, could have perceived the arrival of so many Jews in the Promised Land as a striking act of divine providence. I am by no means sure that Luria regarded the Expulsion in positive terms. I suggest only that, given the absence of Lurianic discussion of the Expulsion issue, Scholem's universally accepted theory regarding the interconnection of the two is in fact only one of many options that could easily be advanced; the demonstration of their validity, of course, would be difficult, if not impossible. But Scholem's thesis, or any other like it, places psychology between history and theosophy, and a theory that attempts seriously to connect all three must be carefully proved, not merely stated in an eloquent manner.

To recapitulate, the far-reaching impact of the Expulsion is a cornerstone of Scholem's historiosophy. It was supposed to have inspired the messianic expectations that, according to Scholem, were articulated by Luria's Kabbalah. The latter then was considered to have paved the way for Sabbatianism, and this messianic movement, in turn, was the starting point for processes that generated not only Frankism but also, through the neutralization of the messianic core of Lurianism, Ḥasidism and, in a dialectic way, the Jewish Enlightenment.[65] The conviction that characterizes Scholem's statements and the uncritical way in which they have been accepted by both the larger public and the scholars who deal with Jewish mysticism and history, have had little to do with the historical facts as I know them. No elaborate discussions based upon detailed analysis of all the pertinent material underpin these far-reaching historical visions. Drawn by an extraordinary fascination with the Sabbatian phenomenon, Scholem meticulously collected every fact regarding the biography of Sabbatai Ṣevi, which is brilliantly documented; but the relationships between this messianic movement and its predecessors and later historical phenomena are only briefly stated. The alleged preparation of the ground for the emergence of Sabbatianism by the spread of Lurianic messianism has already been discussed above.[66]

Let me briefly point out the problems involved in another linkage advocated by Scholem: that of Sabbatianism and Ḥasidism. In his *Major Trends,*[67] he not only affirms that Lurianism, Sabbatianism, and Ḥasidism are part of one process of Kabbalistic proselytizing but also explicitly proposes a more organic connection between the Sabbatian Kabbalist R. Heshel Ẓoref's *Sefer ha-Ẓoref,* and the Ba'al Shem Tov.[68] He attempted to identify the works of the legendary R. Adam Ba'al Shem mentioned in *Shiveḥey ha-Besht* with *Sefer ha-Ẓoref.*[69] This identification proved wrong, but it is not this point I want to emphasize.[70] In 1930 Scholem described a manuscript of the rare *Sefer ha-Ẓoref;*[71] in his *Major Trends,* written nine years later, he made no attempt to substantiate his assumption of a possible influence of this work on the Besht, nor has such an attempt been made since then.[72] Therefore, a major thesis of Scholem's historiosophy is primarily based upon a tradition as to the possession of a Sabbatian manuscript by the Besht, but with no attempt to compare its contents to specific Ḥasidic ideas. As in the case of the connection between the Expulsion and Lurianism, or between Lurianism and the emergence of Sabbatianism, Scholem's assertions concerning an alleged Sabbatian-Ḥasidic linkage may be mainly based upon a historical sequence of events rather than on a detailed analysis of the pertinent doctrines. In their favor are his wide acquaintance with the material and his gift for accurate observation. Whether his assertions will prove to be justified remains to be seen.

VI. KABBALISTIC ANTHROPOLOGY

As we have seen above, both ecstatic and theurgical activity required a tremendous spiritual effort on the part of the Kabbalist. The ecstatic of the Heikhalot literature had to undergo an experience in which he transcended the mundane world and penetrated a perilous domain, ruled by dangerous angels who might indeed kill him.[73] This spiritual journey was attributed not only to such tannaitic figures as R. 'Akiva and R. Ishmael but also to Moses, who was portrayed as a Heikhalot mystic ascending on high to receive the Torah.[74] He had to overcome the enmity of seven dreadful angels and to controvert them; only then could he proceed victoriously to receive the Torah.[75] Accordingly, ancient Jewish mysticism encompassed ecstasy and activism: both were necessary for the fulfillment of the highest goal.

The medieval ecstatic Kabbalist hyperactivated his mind by concentrating with great intensity upon the combination of letters, their ongoing permutations, vocalizations, chants, breathing exercises, and head and hand movements. He was chiefly interested in one human faculty, the intellectual, which had to be saved by freeing it from the boundary of the body. Although several details of the ecstatic techniques were connected with the body, the latter was considered to be an obstacle rather than a means for attaining the mystical goal.

The theurgist had to concentrate both on the punctilious performance of the commandments and on their theurgic significance, and, according to some views, he had also to propel his energy, as structured by the acts he exercised, into the divine realm.[76] In contrast to the ecstatic mystic, the theurgical Kabbalist fully activated both the spiritual and the corporeal components of his human existence, his activity thus being more comprehensive. Whereas the ecstatic Kabbalah reduced man to his highest capacity alone, the theurgical one required the cooperation of all the variegated aspects of man in order to attain its goal. The mystic acted on two planes: the corporeal performance of the commandments and the mental activity that accompanied it. Thus, prior to their achievement of religious goals—union, ecstasy, unification of the divine powers above, the ascent into the divine pleroma—the various types of Kabbalists had to invest an extraordinary amount of energy in their mystical pursuits. This vision of human spiritual activity as necessary, possible, and fruitful colored Jewish mysticism with activist implications. Only rarely did quietistic attitudes prevail,[77] mostly in Ḥasidic mysticism;[78] the major tendency was to sanctify activity, whether nomian or anomian.

Let me propose a certain phenomenology of activism: mystical techniques, in all kinds of Jewish mysticism—albeit sometimes less so in Ḥasidism—involved an overactivation of man's spiritual faculties; they were in principle not stilled but agitated. But insofar as the mystical experience itself was concerned, there were major discrepancies among the various approaches. In Heikhalot literature, the mystic maintained his separate personality even during the contemplation of the Godhead and had to continue reciting the same hymns and songs he had recited before.[79] Theurgical Kabbalah required a strong core of personality to generate enough energy or will to have an impact on the divine powers throughout the process of performing the commandments. As David Blumenthal put it,[80] the *Zohar* (and I would extend this to include all Jewish theurgy, including the ancient classical one)[81] assumed two foci: God and man. I propose seeing not only God as the source of energy and man as the "prism" or "recycling agent" but also the opposite: man as the source and the sefirotic system as a prism and recycling agency.[82] Although these two perceptions appear mutually exclusive, they could, as we have seen above, coexist in the frame of Kabbalistic anthropology and theosophy. The theurgical Kabbalah even envisaged *devekut* as a means of acquiring higher powers in order to act after the experience of union. In ecstatic Kabbalah and in Ḥasidism, however, the situation was more complex; the reader encounters descriptions of passivity, of the divine power taking possession of the mystic, and of the mystic's temporary change into an instrument. But notwithstanding this, we must be mindful that Abraham Abulafia and the early Ḥasidic masters were deeply involved in surrounding events and attempted to influence them no less, if not more, than did the theurgical Kabbalists. The existence of passive moments in their mystical paths did not attenuate their activism in their daily lives, as was the case, too, among a great number of non-Jewish mystics. There is a notable difference between the quest for fusion with God in ecstatic Kabbalah and Ḥasidism, and the paramount importance of the human-Divine polarity in the theurgic model; in the latter the distance between the two foci is essential for the theurgical operation, requiring as it does a transfer of power or influence from one realm to another or a structuring of the Divine by human intention.[83]

The emergence of a third approach to human action is easily understandable against this background of emphasis upon activism; no less than had previous types, magical Kabbalah envisaged man as endowed with superior powers that could dominate nature, angels, demons,and even God. I will discuss here only two types of Kabbalistic magic to complete the picture of Kabbalistic anthropology. First, under the influence of Hermetic elements, a conception of the halakhah as a powerful organon by which to attract the supernal powers on man and the Temple was gradually elaborated by Jewish authors, culminating in the thought of Yoḥanan Alemanno.[84] According to this conception, if natural magic is connected with natural sciences, such as agriculture and astronomy, supermagic depends on the knowledge of the supernatural science—Kabbalah.[85] The perfect way to combine this higher gnosis with practice is by the Kabbalistic performance of the precise prescriptions of the halakhah. Man, therefore, does not disrupt the processes of natural causation but transcends it by his consciousness and by the skillful employment of a higher order of causation that depends on the Sefirot.[86] Halakhic man, conscious of the deeper meaning of his deeds, is a Kabbalistic archmagician. This magical interpretation of Jewish ritual was similar to its theurgical conception in its all-comprehensive nature, which envisioned every human act as potentially fraught with occult meanings. Whereas the theurgists were mainly interested in the divine harmony and power, however, Alemanno focused on the human ability to use them for the welfare of the terrestrial world.[87]

Second, while Alemanno's version of Hermetic activism can be understood as a continuation of previous Jewish and non-Jewish concepts, some of them congenial to the contemporary Renaissance thought, a deep interest in a very different kind of magic erupted in the generation preceding the Expulsion from Spain. More interested in demonology and coercive incantations to summon demons, angels, and even God, this brand of magic was connected with certain messianic trends[88] absent in Italian "natural" magic. *Sefer ha-Meshiv,* our main source for the knowledge of this development in magical Kabbalah, is closely connected with the notorious R. Joseph della Reina, the most famous Jewish magician and an interesting predecessor of Faust.[89] According to legend, he attempted to overcome the princes of the demonic realm, Sammael and Ammon of No, in order to hasten the arrival of the redemption. This daring adventure, popularized in several sixteenth-through-eighteenth-century versions,[90] was a foil to Faust's quest; the Jew was interested in magic not only for material gain, as in alchemy, but primarily for a transpersonal aim: redemption. Della Reina never signed a pact with a counterpart of Mephistopheles, but he did attempt to overcome the demonic leaders.[91] The sources of magic were divine, being dictated by God or his highest angels, and the ultimate goal of the magical Kabbalist was not gnosis but its use for both personal and national purposes. Unlike the natural magic of Alemanno and his sources, the fifteenth-century Spanish magical Kabbalah had an obvious particularistic orientation, which was later followed by Lurianic Kabbalah. This stood in contrast to the more universalistic Italian approach, notwithstanding its Hermetic interpretation of the halakhah.

But despite their discrepancies, these two independent views of magic shared an emphasis on human activism. Moreover, this emphasis was strengthened by the ascent of the thirteenth-century "strong theurgy" expressed in the writings of R. Meir ibn Gabbay, as well as by the ideas of R. Menaḥem Recanati and the influence of the *Zohar,* which became dominant in the generations following the Expulsion. Jewish Kabbalah therefore exploited some of its resources in order to reemphasize the impact of human activity on the natural, demonic, and divine realms. This happened during the period in which the new Renaissance image of man, partly influenced by Jewish thought, was emerging in Florence. This is not the place to elaborate upon the possible historical and phenomenological affinities between these two intellectual developments (on the strength of certain manuscript material, I tend, for example, to see an impact of Judeo-Arabic views on man in Pico). But it is important to note here that the natural magic of Alemanno, like his philosophical interpretation of the Kabbalah, reverberated in Italy, and somewhat in Safed, and that the theurgical view of the halakhah was continued with some changes by the Cordoverian and Lurianic Kabbalah. Sabbatianism, particularly in its interpretation by Nathan of Gaza, emphasized the extraordinary theurgical forces of Sabbatai Ṣevi that were part of his struggle with the demonic realm. The theurgical usage, however, was considerably attenuated in Ḥasidism, the ecstatic understanding of the commandments now becoming dominant.

Let me conclude this chapter with a translation of a legend (which Scholem narrates in a different version at the end of his *Major Trends*) that illustrates the decline of theurgy in Ḥasidism:[92]

> Our holy master [R. Israel of Rizhin] told us a story of the Ba'al Shem Tov, blessed be his memory. Once there was a stringent necessity to save an only son, who was a very good person, and so on.[93] He [the Besht] ordered that a candle of wax be made, and he traveled to a forest where he attached this waxen candle to a tree,[94] and [did] some other things and performed some *yiḥudim*, and so on, and he succeeded in saving [the son] with the help of God. Afterward, there was such an incident involving my grandfather, the Holy [Great] Maggid, and he did likewise, as mentioned above, and he said: "The *yiḥudim* and the *kavvanot* performed by the Besht are not known to me,[95] but I shall do this on the basis of the *kavvanah* which

> the Besht intended"; and his [prayer] was also answered. Afterward, a similar thing happened to the holy R. Moshe Leib of Sassov, blessed be his memory, and he said: "We do not even have the power to do that, but I shall only tell the story to God,[96] so that he will help." And so it happened, with God's help.

The magical operation of the Besht—the preparation of the candle—was accompanied by theurgic acts: *kavvanot* and *yiḥudim*. Over the course of time, only the external act was remembered, while the theurgical aspect was forgotten. But by the time of R. Moshe Leib of Sassov, even the external deed could not be accomplished: in lieu of the magical-theurgical behavior characteristic of its founder, later Ḥasidism stressed a personal approach. I want to emphasize that, in this version, the effects of the magical-theurgical acts of the Besht, of the magical act of the Great Maggid, and of R. Moshe of Sassov's telling of the story are identical: all of them achieve their purpose.[97] If there is a decline, it is in the knowledge of theurgy, which is, however, complemented by a direct address to God, characteristic also of another disciple of the Maggid, R. Levi Isaac of Berdichev. The loss of theurgy, still present in the Ba'al Shem Tov, is compensated by the discovery of forms of personal mysticism.

In a still later development, however, even this personal mysticism was lost, leaving man with only the ability to tell the story. Franz Kafka's *Before the Law* is an instructive example of the last remnants of Jewish mysticism operating in a world in which the confidence in man's acts has disintegrated. The "Mann vom Lande," a countryman, or, as M. Robert has noticed, an *'am ha-'areẓ* (ignoramus),[98] is still aware of the mystical facet of the Law, which has reached him as "a radiance that streams immortally from the door of the Law." But his passivity prevents him from daring to attempt to do what Jewish mystics had done in previous generations: overcome their fears, as Moses overcame the dreadful angels, in order to enter another dimension. Kafka's Law, like the maiden in the *Zohar* parable, is intended for everyone who dares, but the loss of self-confidence, faith, and energy leaves man with only the capacity to tell mystical stories about an impersonal, fascinating world that, according to Kafka, is *ex definitio* beyond his reach. All that remains is the awareness that "a radiance streams immortally from the door of the Law." Is not the basic Kabbalistic metaphor for the mystical dimension of the Law, *Zohar*—radiance?[99] Does not the *Zohar* use the metaphor of entering a palace in order to reach the Law itself, not merely viewing its radiance from outside?[100]

Abbreviations

JOURNALS

AHDLMA	*Archives d'histoire doctrinale et littéraire du Moyen Age*
AJSreview	*Association of Jewish Studies Review*
HTR	*Harvard Theological Review*
HUCA	*Hebrew Union College Annual*
JJS	*Journal of Jewish Studies*
JQR	*Jewish Quarterly Review*
MGWJ	*Monatschrift für Geschichte und Wissenschaft des Judentums*
PAAJR	*Proceedings of the American Academy for Jewish Research*
REJ	*Revue des Etudes Juives*

MONOGRAPHS AND ARTICLES

Altmann, *Faces of Judaism:* Alexander Altmann. *Faces of Judaism* (in Hebrew). Edited by A. Shapira. Tel-Aviv, 1983.

Altmann, "The Question of Authorship": Alexander Altmann. "The Question of Authorship of *Sefer Ta'amei ha-Mizvot* Attributed to R. Joseph Gikatilla" (in Hebrew). *Kiryat Sefer* 40 (1965): 256–276, 405–412.

Altmann and Stern, *Isaac Israeli:* Alexander Altmann and S. Stern. *Isaac Israeli: A Neoplatonic Philosopher of the Early Tenth Century.* Oxford, 1958.

Baer, *Israel among the Nations*: Yitzhak F. Baer. *Israel among the Nations* (in Hebrew). Jerusalem, 1955.

Baer, "The Service of Sacrifice": Yitzhak F. Baer. "The Service of Sacrifice in Second Temple Times" (in Hebrew). *Ẓion* 40 (1975): 95–153.

Benayahu, *Sefer Toldot ha-'Ari:* Meir Benayahu. *Sefer Toldot ha-'Ari* (in Hebrew). Jerusalem, 1960.

Biale, *Gershom Scholem, Kabbalah and Counter-History*: David Biale. *Gershom Scholem, Kabbalah and Counter-History.* 2d ed. Cambridge, Mass., 1982.

Buber, *Ḥasidism*: Martin Buber. *Ḥasidism.* New York, 1948.

Buber, *Tales of the Ḥasidim: Early Masters*: Martin Buber. *Tales of the Ḥasidim: Early Masters.* New York, 1964.

Cohen, *The Shi'ur Qomah: Liturgy and Theurgy*: Martin S. Cohen. *The Shi'ur Qomah: Liturgy and Theurgy in Pre-Kabbalistic Jewish Mysticism.* Lanham, Md., 1983.

Cohen, *The Shi'ur Qomah: Texts and Recensions*: Martin S. Cohen. *The Shi'ur Qomah: Texts and Recensions.* Tübingen, 1985.

Dan, *The Esoteric Theology*: Joseph Dan. *The Esoteric Theology of Ashkenazi Ḥasidism* (in Hebrew). Jerusalem, 1968.

Dan, *Studies*: Joseph Dan. *Studies in Ashkenazi-Ḥasidic Literature* (in Hebrew). Givatayim and Ramat Gan, 1975.

Eliade, *Images and Symbols*: Mircea Eliade. *Images and Symbols*. New York, 1969.

Eliade, *The Quest*: Mircea Eliade. *The Quest: History and Meaning in Religion*. Chicago and London, 1971.

Epstein, *Mi-Kadmoniot ha-Yehudim*: Abraham Epstein. *Mi-Kadmoniot ha-Yehudim* (in Hebrew). Jerusalem, 1957.

Fallon, *The Enthronement of Sabaoth*: F. T. Fallon. *The Enthronement of Sabaoth*. Leiden, 1978.

Fine, *Safed Spirituality*: Lawrence Fine. *Safed Spirituality.* New York, Ramsey, and Toronto, 1984.

Fossum, *The Name of God and the Angel of the Lord*: Jarl E. Fossum. *The Name of God and the Angel of the Lord.* Tübingen, 1985.

Franck, *La Kabbale*: Adolphe Franck. *La Kabbale ou la philosophie religieuse des Hébreux.* Paris, 1982.

Ginzberg, *On Jewish Law and Lore*. Louis Ginzberg. *On Jewish Law and Lore*. New York, 1970.

Goetschel, *Meir ibn Gabbay*: Roland Goetschel. *Meir ibn Gabbay: Le discours de la Kabbale Espagnole*. Leuven, 1981.

Goodenough, *By Light, Light*: Erwin Goodenough. *By Light, Light*. New Haven, Conn., 1935.

Gottlieb, *The Kabbalah of R. Baḥya*: Ephraim Gottlieb. *The Kabbalah in the Writings of R. Baḥya ben Asher* (in Hebrew). Jerusalem, 1970.

Gottlieb, *Studies*: Ephraim Gottlieb. *Studies in the Kabbalah Literature* (in Hebrew). Edited by J. Hacker. Tel Aviv, 1976.

Green, *Tormented Master*: Arthur Green. *Tormented Master: A Life of Rabbi Naḥman of Bratslav.* University, Ala., 1979.

Heller-Wilensky, "Isaac ibn Latif, Philosopher or Kabbalist?": S. Heller-Wilensky. "Isaac ibn Latif, Philosopher or Kabbalist?" In *Jewish Medieval and Renaissance Studies,* edited by Alexander Altmann, 185–223. Cambridge, Mass., 1967.

Heschel, *The Circle of the Ba'al Shem Tov:* Abraham J. Heschel. *The Circle of the Ba'al Shem Tov: Studies in Ḥasidism.* Edited by S. H. Dresner. Chicago and London, 1985.

Heschel, *Theology of Ancient Judaism:* Abraham J. Heschel. *The Theology of Ancient Judaism* (in Hebrew). 2 vols. London and New York, 1965.

Idel, "Abraham Abulafia": Moshe Idel. "Abraham Abulafia's Works and Doctrines" (in Hebrew). Ph.D. diss., Hebrew University, 1976.

Idel, "Abraham Abulafia and the Pope": Moshe Idel. "Abraham Abulafia and the Pope: The Meaning and the Metamorphosis of an Abortive Attempt" (in Hebrew). *AJSreview* 7–8 (1982–83): 1–17.

Idel, "Abraham Abulafia and *Unio Mystica*": Moshe Idel. "Abraham Abulafia and *Unio*

Mystica." In *Studies in Medieval Jewish History and Literature,* edited by Isadore Twersky, vol. 3. Forthcoming.

Idel, "Between the Views of Sefirot as Essence and Instruments": Moshe Idel. "Between the Views of Sefirot as Essence and Instruments in the Renaissance Period" (in Hebrew). *Italia* 3 (1982): 89–111.

Idel, "The Concept of the Torah": Moshe Idel. "The Concept of the Torah in Heikhalot Literature and Its Metamorphoses in Kabbalah" (in Hebrew). *Jerusalem Studies in Jewish Thought* 1 (1981): 23–84.

Idel, "Differing Conceptions of Kabbalah": Moshe Idel. "Differing Conceptions of Kabbalah in the Early 17th Century."

Idel, "Enoch Is Metatron": Moshe Idel. "Enoch Is Metatron" (in Hebrew).

Idel, "The Evil Thought of the Deity": Moshe Idel. "The Evil Thought of the Deity" (in Hebrew). *Tarbiẓ* 49 (1980): 356–364.

Idel, "Hermeticism and Judaism": Moshe Idel. "Hermeticism and Judaism." Forthcoming.

Idel, "*Hitbodedut* as Concentration": Moshe Idel. "*Hitbodedut* as Concentration in Ecstatic Kabbalah" (in Hebrew). *Da'at* 14 (1985): 35–82. (A shorter English version was printed in *Jewish Spirituality,* edited by Arthur Green, 405–438. New York, 1986.)

Idel, "The Image of Man": Moshe Idel. "The Image of Man above the Sefirot" (in Hebrew). *Da'at* 4 (1980): 41–55.

Idel, "Infinities of Torah in Kabbalah": Moshe Idel. "Infinities of Torah in Kabbalah." In *Midrash and Literature,* edited by G. Hartman and S. Budick, 141–157. New Haven, Conn., 1986.

Idel, "Inquiries": Moshe Idel. "Inquiries in the Doctrine of *Sefer Ha-Meshiv*" (in Hebrew). *Sefunot,* edited by J. Hacker, vol. 17, 185–266. Jerusalem, 1983.

Idel, "Kabbalah and Ancient Philosophy in R. Isaac and Yehudah Abravanel": Moshe Idel. "Kabbalah and Ancient Philosophy in R. Isaac and Yehudah Abravanel" (in Hebrew). In *The Philosophy of Leone Ebreo,* edited by M. Dorman and Z. Levy, 73–112. Hakibbutz Hameuchad, 1985.

Idel, "Kabbalistic Material": Moshe Idel. "Kabbalistic Material from R. David ben Yehudah he-Ḥasid's School" (in Hebrew). *Jerusalem Studies In Jewish Thought* 2 (1983): 169–207.

Idel, "Kabbalistic Prayer and Colours": Moshe Idel. "Kabbalistic Prayer and Colours." In *Approaches to Medieval Judaism,* edited by D. Blumenthal. Vol. 3. Forthcoming.

Idel, "The Magical and Neoplatonic Interpretations": Moshe Idel. "The Magical and Neoplatonic Interpretations of Kabbalah in the Renaissance." In *Jewish Thought in the Sixteenth Century,* edited by B. D. Cooperman, 186–242. Cambridge, Mass., 1983.

Idel, "The Magical and Theurgical Interpretation": Moshe Idel. "The Magical and Theurgical Interpretation of Music in Jewish Texts: Renaissance to Ḥasidism" (in Hebrew). *Yuval* 4 (1982): 33–63.

Idel, "Maimonides and Kabbalah": Moshe Idel. "Maimonides and Kabbalah." Forthcoming.

Idel, "Métaphores et pratiques sexuelles": Moshe Idel. "Métaphores et pratiques sexuelles dans la Cabbale." In *Lettre sur la sainteté: Le Secret de la relation entre l'homme et la femme dans la Cabbale,* edited and translated by Charles Mopsik, 329–358. Paris, 1986.

Idel, "Music and Prophetic Kabbalah": Moshe Idel. "Music and Prophetic Kabbalah." *Yuval* 4 (1980): 150–169.

Idel, *The Mystical Experience in Abraham Abulafia*: Moshe Idel. *The Mystical Experience in Abraham Abulafia.* Albany, 1987.

Idel, "Perceptions of Kabbalah": Moshe Idel. "Perceptions of Kabbalah in the Second Half of the 18th Century." Forthcoming.

Idel, "Prophetic Kabbalah and the Land of Israel": Moshe Idel. "Prophetic Kabbalah and the Land of Israel." In *Vision and Conflict in the Holy Land,* edited by R. I. Cohen, 102–110. Jerusalem and New York, 1985.

Idel, "R. Joseph of Hamadan's *Commentary on Ten Sefirot*": Moshe Idel. "R. Joseph of Hamadan's *Commentary on Ten Sefirot* and Fragments of His Writings" (in Hebrew). *'Aley Sefer* 6–7 (1979): 74–84.

Idel, "Sefirot above Sefirot": Moshe Idel. "Sefirot above Sefirot" (in Hebrew). *Tarbiẓ* 51 (1982): 239–280.

Idel, "Shelomo Molkho as a Magician": Moshe Idel. "Shelomo Molkho as a Magician" (in Hebrew). *Sefunot,* n.s. 3, no. 18 (1985): 193–219.

Idel, "Types of Redemptive Activities": Moshe Idel. "Types of Redemptive Activities in the Middle Ages" (in Hebrew). In *Messianism and Eschatology,* edited by Z. Baras, 253–279. Jerusalem, 1984.

Idel, "We Have No Kabbalistic Tradition on This": Moshe Idel. "We Have No Kabbalistic Tradition on This." In *Rabbi Moses Naḥmanides (Ramban): Explorations in His Religious and Literary Virtuosity,* edited by Isadore Twersky, 51–73. Cambridge, Mass., 1983.

Idel, "The World of Angels in Human Shape": Moshe Idel. "The World of Angels in Human Shape" (in Hebrew). *Jerusalem Studies In Jewish Thought,* ed. J. Dan and J. Hacker, *Studies In Jewish Mysticism, Philosophy and Ethical Literature Presented to Isaiah Tishby*, 1–66. Jerusalem, 1986.

Jellinek, *Auswahl*: Adolph Jellinek. *Auswahl Kabbalistischer Mystik,* Erstes Helf. Leipzig, 1853.

Jellinek, *BHM*: Adolph Jellinek, ed. *Bet ha-Midrasch.* 6 vols. Vienna, 1877.

Katz, *Halakhah and Kabbalah*: Jacob Katz. *Halakhah and Kabbalah: Studies in the History of Jewish Religion* (in Hebrew). Jerusalem, 1984.

Katz, "Language, Epistemology, and Mysticism": Steven T. Katz. "Language, Epistemology and Mysticism." In *Mysticism and Philosophical Analysis,* edited by S. T. Katz, 22–74. New York, 1978.

Liebermann, *Sheki'in*: Saul Liebermann. *Sheki'in* (in Hebrew). Jerusalem, 1970.

Liebes, "The Messiah of the *Zohar*": Yehuda Liebes. "The Messiah of the *Zohar*." In *The Messianic Idea in Israel* (in Hebrew), 87–234. Jerusalem, 1982.

Liebes, "Sefer Ẓaddik Yesod Olam": Yehuda Liebes. "Sefer Ẓaddik Yesod Olam—A Sabbatian Myth" (in Hebrew). *Da'at* (1978): 73–120.

Matt, *Zohar*: Daniel C. Matt, trans. and intro. *Zohar: The Book of the Enlightenment*, New York, Ramsey, and Toronto, 1983.

Pachter, "The Concept of Devekut": Mordechai Pachter. "The Concept of Devekut in the Homiletical Ethical Writings in Sixteenth-Century Safed." In *Studies in Medieval Jewish History and Literature*, edited by Isadore Twersky, 2: 171–230. Cambridge, Mass. 1984.

Piekarz, *The Beginning of Ḥasidism*: Mendel Piekarz. *The Beginning of Ḥasidism: Ideological Trends in Derush and Musar Literature* (in Hebrew). Jerusalem, 1978.

Ricoeur, *The Conflict of Interpretations*: Paul Ricoeur, *The Conflict of Interpretations*. Evanston, Ill., 1974.

Ricoeur, *The Symbolism of Evil*: Paul Ricoeur. *The Symbolism of Evil*. Boston, 1969.

Schäfer, *Synopse*: Peter Schäfer. *Synopse zur Hekhalot Literature*. Tübingen, 1981.

Schatz-Uffenheimer, *Quietistic Elements*: Rivka Schatz-Uffenheimer. *Quietistic Elements in Eighteenth-Century Ḥasidic Thought* (in Hebrew). Jerusalem, 1968.

Scholem, "The Authentic Commentary on Sefer Yeẓirah of Naḥmanides": Gershom Scholem. "The Authentic Commentary on Sefer Yeẓirah of Naḥmanides" (in Hebrew). *Kiryat Sefer* 6 (1929–30): 385–412.

Scholem, *Bi-'Iqvoth Mashiaḥ*: Gershom Scholem. *Bi-'Iqvoth Mashiaḥ* (in Hebrew). Jerusalem, 1944.

Scholem, *CCCH*: Gershom Scholem. *Catalogus Codicum Cabbalisticorum Hebraicorum* (in Hebrew). Jerusalem, 1930.

Scholem, "The Concept of Kavvanah": Gershom G. Scholem. "The Concept of Kavvanah in the Early Kabbalah." In *Studies In Jewish Thought*, edited by A. Jospe, 162–180. Detroit, 1981.

Scholem, *Elements*: Gershom Scholem. *Elements of the Kabbalah and Its Symbolism* (in Hebrew). Jerusalem, 1976.

Scholem, *Explications and Implications*: Gershom Scholem. *Explications and Implications: Writings on Jewish Heritage and Renaissance* (in Hebrew). Tel Aviv, 1975.

Scholem, *Jewish Gnosticism*: Gershom G. Scholem. *Jewish Gnosticism, Merkabah Mysticism and Talmudic Tradition*. New York, 1960.

Scholem, *Kabbalah*: Gershom G. Scholem. *Kabbalah*. Jerusalem, 1974.

Scholem, *Major Trends*: Gershom G. Scholem. *Major Trends In Jewish Mysticism*. New York, 1961.

Scholem, *Messianic Idea in Judaism*: Gershom G. Scholem. *The Messianic Idea in Judaism, and Other Essays on Jewish Spirituality*. New York, 1971.

Scholem, "New Document": Gershom Scholem. "A New Document for the History of the Beginning of Kabbalah" (in Hebrew). *Sefer Bialik*, 141–162. Tel Aviv, 1934.

Scholem, *On the Kabbalah*: Gershom G. Scholem. *On the Kabbalah and Its Symbolism.* New York, 1969.

Scholem, *Les Origines de la Kabbale:* Gershom G. Scholem. *Les Origines de la Kabbale.* Paris, 1962.

Scholem, *Reshit ha-Kabbalah*: Gershom Scholem. *Reshit ha-Kabbalah (1150–1250)* (in Hebrew). Jerusalem and Tel Aviv, 1948.

Scholem, *Sabbatai Ṣevi*: Gershom Scholem. *Sabbatai Ṣevi: The Mystical Messiah (1626–1676).* Princeton, N.J., 1973.

Scholem, "Seridim": Gershom Scholem. "Seridim Ḥadashim mi-Kitvey R. 'Azriel mi-Gerona." In *Sefer Zikkaron le-Gulak ve-Klein,* 201-222. Jerusalem, 1942.

Scholem, "Two Treatises of R. Moshe de Leon": Gershom Scholem. "Two Treatises of R. Moshe de Leon" (in Hebrew). *Koveẓ al Yad,* n.s. 8 (1976): 325–384.

Stace, *Mysticism and Philosophy*: W. T. Stace. *Mysticism and Philosophy.* London, 1961.

Stroumsa, "Form(s) of God": Gedaliahu G. Stroumsa. "Form(s) of God: Some Notes on Metatron and Christ." *HTR* 76 (1983): 269–288.

Tishby, *The Doctrine of Evil*: Isaiah Tishby. *The Doctrine of Evil and the "Kelippah" in Lurianic Kabbalism* (in Hebrew). Jerusalem, 1984.

Tishby, *Paths of Faith and Heresy*: Isaiah Tishby. *Paths of Faith and Heresy* (in Hebrew). Ramat Gan, 1984.

Tishby *Studies*: Isaiah Tishby. *Studies in Kabbalah and Its Branches* (in Hebrew). Vol. 1. Jerusalem, 1982.

Tishby, *The Wisdom of the Zohar*: Isaiah Tishby. *The Wisdom of the Zohar* (in Hebrew). 2 vols. Jerusalem, 1957, 1961.

Twersky, *Rabad of Posquières*: Isadore Twersky. *Rabad of Posquières, A Twelfth-Century Talmudist.* Cambridge, Mass., 1962.

Urbach, *'Arugat ha-Bosem*: Ephraim E. Urbach, ed. *Sefer 'Arugat ha-Bosem Auctore R. Abraham b. R. 'Azriel* (in Hebrew). 4 vols. Jerusalem, 1939–63.

Urbach, *The Sages*: Ephraim E. Urbach. *The Sages: Their Concepts and Beliefs.* 2 vols. Jerusalem, 1979.

Urbach, "The Traditions about Merkavah Mysticism": E. E. Urbach. "The Traditions about Merkavah Mysticism in the Tannaitic Period" (in Hebrew). In *Studies in Mysticism and Religion Presented to Gershom G. Scholem,* 1–28. Jerusalem, 1967.

Vajda, *Le Commentaire d'Ezra de Gérone*: Georges Vajda. *Le Commentaire d'Ezra de Gérone sur le Cantique des Cantiques.* Paris, 1969.

Vajda, *Recherches*: Georges Vajda. *Recherches sur la philosophie et la Kabbale dans la pensée juive du Moyen Age.* Paris and La Haye, 1962.

Werblowsky, *Karo*: R. J. Zwi Werblowsky. *Joseph Karo, Lawyer and Mystic.* Philadelphia, 1977.

Zaehner, *Hindu and Muslim Mysticism*: R. C. Zaehner. *Hindu and Muslim Mysticism.* London, 1960.

Zaehner, *Mysticism: Sacred and Profane*: R. C. Zaehner, *Mysticism: Sacred and Profane.* Oxford, 1973.

Notes

INTRODUCTION

1. R. Meir ben Solomon ibn Avi Sahulah; cf. Scholem, *Les Origines de la Kabbale*, p. 48.
2. "Ve-Zot li-Yihudah," cf. Jellinek, *Auswahl*, pp. 15, 19.
3. See R. Solomon's *Responsa* I, no. 548.
4. "Ve-Zot li-Yihudah," cf. Jellinek, *Auswahl*, p. 19.
5. Cf. Idel, "Prophetic Kabbalah and the Land of Israel."
6. Cf. Chaps. VII–VIII.
7. See below, Chap. VII, sec. IV.
8. An interesting subject to be traced by Kabbalah scholarship would be the examination of the proportion of space devoted to theosophy by each Kabbalist, in order to determine the issue he emphasized.
9. See Margaliot, par. 109, p. 48; par. 123–124, pp. 54–55; and so on.
10. See Scholem, *Les Origines de la Kabbale*, pp. 273–274.
11. Vajda, *Recherches*, pp. 356–384.
12. Idel, "We Have No Kabbalistic Tradition on This," p. 63.
13. See Gottlieb, *Studies*, pp. 121–128.
14. See Idel, "R. Joseph of Hamadan's *Commentary on Ten Sefirot*," pp. 76–82.
15. Gottlieb, *Studies*, pp. 214–230.
16. See Altmann, "On the Question of Authorship," pp. 256–262.
17. Venice, 1543; heavily influenced by Recanati's similar work.
18. Heavily influenced by R. Joseph of Hamadan.
19. See Idel, "Kabbalistic Prayer and Colours."
20. There are also rabbinical traditions concerning the esoteric nature of the divine names (for example, *Kiddushin* 71a), but their ecstatic implications have yet to be studied in detail.
21. See Ira Chernus, "Individual and Community in the Redaction of the Heikhalot Literature," *HUCA* 52 (1981): 253–274.
22. See Chap. III.
23. Cf. Idel, "Maimonides and Kabbalah."
24. Idel, "On R. Moshe Cordovero and R. Abraham Abulafia—Some Remarks" (in Hebrew), *Da'at* 15 (1985): 119–120.
25. Idel, "Perceptions of Kabbalah."
26. This issue will be dealt with in a separate study.
27. See Goldreich, *Mei'rat 'Eynaim*, pp. 399–400.
28. See Chap. III, n. 152.
29. On this issue, see Scholem, *The Messianic Idea in Judaism*, pp. 176–202, and Isaiah Tishby, "The Messianic Idea and Messianic Tendencies in the Emergence of Ḥasidism" (in Hebrew), *Ẓion* 32 (1967): 1–45.

30. Abulafia, although pretending himself to be a Messiah, referred to individualistic salvation as the highest religious experience, far beyond his marginal discussions of national messianism. R. Isaac of Acre and the anonymous author of the ecstatic *Sha'arey Ẓedek* were even less interested in messianism.
31. Cf. Chap. III, sec. VII.
32. Cf. Chap. VIII, sec. II.

CHAPTER 1

1. I have deliberately omitted the rich literature on Kabbalah by Christians, as this was mainly concerned with missionary interests, or with the relationship between Kabbalah and such philosophers as Spinoza or the idealists, and only rarely with Kabbalah as part of Jewish religion. See Scholem, *Kabbalah*, pp. 196–201, 209–210. Likewise, Orthodox Jewish writings on Kabbalah, interesting as they may be, remain beyond the scope of this survey.
2. See Scholem, *Kabbalah*, pp. 201–203, and the studies he refers to on p. 210; see also the helpful survey of zoharic studies by Tishby, *The Wisdom of the Zohar*, vol. 1, pp. 44–67; and the survey by Cohen, *The Shi'ur Qomah: Liturgy and Theurgy*, pp. 13–42, concerning the various views on *Shi'ur Komah*.
3. This appreciation is based upon a manuscript testimony of R. Avigdor Kara, a fifteenth-century Kabbalist of Prague, who possessed longer critical works on Kabbalah that are apparently lost. This text is published and commented upon in a paper by Frank Talmage and myself, now in preparation.
4. For example, Abraham Abulafia's criticism of the theosophical Kabbalah: see Chap. IX, sec. I.
5. On Messer Leon's philosophical stand, see Abraham Melamed, "Rhetoric and Philosophy in *Nofet Ẓufim* by Yehudah Messer Leon" (in Hebrew), *Italia* 1, no. 2 (1978): 7–38; Robert Bonfil's preface to the facsimile edition of Messer Leon's *Nofet Ẓufim* (in Hebrew) (Jerusalem, 1981), pp. 22–32.
6. Compare the warning of the Kabbalists themselves; Chap. VI, n. 208.
7. Cf. the letter of R. Yehudah printed by Simḥah Assaf in *Minḥah le-David* (Jerusalem, 1935), p. 227; Idel, "The Magical and Neoplatonic Interpretations," p. 218.
8. Cf. A. L. Motzkin's translation in his *A Renaissance Philosophy of Religion: Elia del Medigo's Critique of Religion* (forthcoming). See also his article "Elia del Medigo, Averroës and Averroism," *Italia* 6 (forthcoming).
9. In his Hebrew commentary of Averroës' *De Substantia Orbis*, MS Paris 968, fol. 41b, Idel, "The Magical and Neoplatonic Interpretations," p. 219.
10. See Moshe Idel, "The Journey to Paradise: The Metamorphosis of a Mythological Motif in Judaism" (in Hebrew), *Jerusalem Studies in Jewish Folklore* 2 (1982): 7–16.
11. As his Christian contemporary had, and therefrom also Yoḥanan Alemanno: Idel, "The Magical and Neoplatonic Interpretations," pp. 217–218.
12. Idel, "The Magical and Neoplatonic Interpretations," p. 219.
13. No similar view regarding the *Zohar* is known from the extant writing of the circle of Pico. Alemanno, who was not particularly influenced by the *Zohar* and could copy a statement on the mistakes found in it did not, however, mention such a view of the *Zohar*.
14. Ibn Gabirol's authorship of the philosophical work *Fons Vitae* (*Mekor Ḥayyim*), a classic of

medieval Neoplatonism, was known by del Medigo's contemporary and, I suppose, his acquaintance, Yoḥanan Alemanno, who also quotes from ibn Gabirol's work. See Idel, "The Magical and Neoplatonic Interpretations," p. 216 n. 164; and R. David Messer Leon (in the same article).

15. See D. P. Walker, *The Ancient Theology* (London, 1972), p. 80.
16. See Idel, "Kabbalah and Ancient Philosophy in R. Isaac and Yehudah Abravanel" and "Kabbalah, Platonism and Prisca Theologia—the Case of R. Menashe ben Israel" (forthcoming).
17. David B. Ruderman, *The World of a Renaissance Jew* (Cincinnati, 1981), pp. 52–56.
18. Dr. Jordan S. Penkower has recently detected some evidence of Levita's criticism of the antiquity of the *Zohar*, to be elaborated in a future study.
19. *Ari Nohem*, ed. N. S. Leibovitz (Jerusalem, 1971), p. 52.
20. Ibid., p. 53.
21. Ibid., pp. 4–5.
22. Ibid., p. 4.
23. On Modena's attitude to Plato, see Idel, "Differing Perceptions of the Kabbalah," n. 92.
24. See Tishby, *Studies* 1:177–254; *Ari Nohem*, p. 1.
25. On this issue, see Idel, "Differing Conceptions of the Kabbalah."
26. *Ari Nohem*, pp. 96–97.
27. This document was quoted by R. Joseph del Medigo in his *Maẓref le-Ḥokhmah*, fol. 22a, but this author cannot be seen as an explicit critic of the Kabbalah or of the *Zohar*.
28. *Ari Nohem*, pp. 71–73. For details on this document, see Tishby, *The Wisdom of the Zohar*, 1:28–32, 50–51.
29. See, for example, Franck, *La Kabbale*, p. 256; Munk, *Mélanges*, pp. 275–276 n. 2; S. D. Luzzatto, *Dialogues sur la Kabbale et le Zohar* (in Hebrew) (Gorice, 1852), pp. 112–114.
30. The original Italian text regarding Kabbalah was reprinted with important notes by François Secret, "Un Texte malconnu de Simon Luzzatto sur la Kabbale," *REJ* 118 (1959–1960): 121–128; and in the Hebrew translation of R. B. Baki and M. A. Schulwass, ed. A. Z. Aeshkoli (Jerusalem, 1951), pp. 143–147. As Secret has noticed (p. 121 n. 4), Luzzatto's discussions on Kabbalah were translated into Latin and French in the eighteenth century, and so were widely disseminated in European milieus.
31. Secret, ibid., 123–124; Aeshkoli, ibid., pp. 144–145.
32. Secret, ibid., p. 124; Aeshkoli, ibid., p. 145.
33. Secret, ibid., p. 124; Aeshkoli, ibid., p. 146. Luzzatto's perceptive remark and the entire Kabbalistic tradition concerning this issue were ignored in Lovejoy's famous study on this subject, nor was it discussed in the literature on the "Chain of Being" that followed the publication of Lovejoy's work.
34. Secret, ibid., pp. 126–127; Aeshkoli, ibid., pp. 146–147. This resemblance had already been pointed out by R. Isaac Abravanel in 1498: see Idel, "Kabbalah and Ancient Philosophy in R. Isaac and Yehudah Abravanel," p. 76.
35. On this issue, see E. R. Dodds, *Proclus: The Elements of Theology* (Oxford, 1971), pp. 313–321; on the Renaissance reverberation of this theory, see D. P. Walker, "The Astral Body in Renaissance Medicine," *Journal of the Warburg and Courtauld Institutes* 21 (1958): 119–133.

36. For a survey of Agrippa and Kabbalah, see W. D. Müller-Jahncke in *Kabbalistes Chrétiens*, pp. 197–209.
37. Chap. XLVII: "Ex hoc cabalisticae superstitionis judaico fermento prodierunt (puto) Ophitae, Gnostici, et Valentiniani haeretici, qui ipsi quoque cum discipuli suis graecan cabalam commenti sunt, literas et numeros protrahentes."
38. See Idel, "The World of Angels in Human Shape," p. 63 n. 242.
39. *Adversus Haereses* XIV, 1.
40. *Ta'am Leshed: Nouveaux Dialogues sur la Kabbale* (in Hebrew) (Livourne, 1863), pp. 107ff.
41. Moses Gaster, *Texts and Studies* (London, 1925–28), 3:1350–1353.
42. Scholem, *Elements*, pp. 161–163; Scholem, *Major Trends*, p. 65.
43. Stroumsa, "Form(s) of God," pp. 280–281.
44. Idel, "The World of Angels in Human Shape," pp. 1–2.
45. See Secret, "Un Texte malconnu," p. 125 n. 1. Agrippa, or one of his followers, seems to be the source of J. F. Buddeus, J. L. van Mosheim, and J. A. W. Neander's views of Gnosticism as emerging from earlier Jewish speculations: see Fossum, *The Name of God and the Angel of the Lord*, p. 8.
46. Secret, ibid., p. 125.
47. See Chap. II, nn. 31–34.
48. The scholars of Jewish mysticism who have paid attention to Agrippa's remarks are Franck, *La Kabbale*, pp. 11–12, and Secret, "Un Texte malconnu."
49. Franck, *La Kabbale*, p. 101.
50. See Tishby, *The Wisdom of the Zohar*, 1:53–56.
51. See Idel, "Perceptions of Kabbalah," par. II.
52. *An Autobiography,* trans. I. Clark Murray (London, 1888), pp. 94–95.
53. See Idel, "Perceptions of the Kabbalah," par. II, n. 2.
54. See Franck, *La Kabbale*, pp. 295–304; Joseph Weiss, "*Via passiva* in Early Ḥasidism," *JJS* 11 (1960): 137–155; and so on.
55. Although an "Eastern" Jew, Krochmal's thought was deeply influenced by German idealism.
56. Compare to Leone Modena's view that, although an authentic ancient Jewish esotericism indeed existed, Kabbalah, as a medieval fabrication, was a degeneration of Jewish secrets; see Idel, "Perceptions of Kabbalah," and Maimon, in the discussion above (n. 52).
57. See David Biale, "The Kabbala in Nachman Krochmal's Philosophy of History," *JJS* 32 (1981): 85–97.
58. His findings were published posthumously in a series of short essays in *Literaturblatt des Orients* 6 (1845).
59. See, for example, *Wesen und Form des Pentateuch* (Stuttgart, 1838).
60. *La Kabbale ou la philosophie religieuse des Hébreux* (Paris, 1892), pp. 202–265. Interestingly, Franck begins his discussion of the antiquity of Kabbalah by quoting Christian Renaissance authorities, such as Pico and Reuchlin, as witnesses for Kabbalah being an ancient lore; see ibid., p. 39; see also his preface, where an interesting survey of Renaissance interest in Kabbalah is offered.
61. Ibid., pp. 266–294.
62. "Il est impossible de considerer la Kabbale comme un fait isolé, comme un accident dans le

judaisme; elle en est au contraire la vie et la coeur" (ibid., p. 288); English quoted from A. Franck, *The Kabbalah: The Religious Philosophy of the Hebrews* (New York, 1940), p. 219. Franck rejected Modena's criticism of Kabbalah as an alien lore; he was aware of Modena's views, which were in print three years before the printing of his work, and even refers to him from time to time (see p. 256). Interestingly, Modena, the sharp critic of Kabbalah because of its abuse in Christian Renaissance thought, is criticized by Franck, who is influenced by that same thought (see above, n. 60).

63. Scholem, *Explications and Implications*, p. 66; according to Biale, *Gershom Scholem, Kabbalah and Counter-History*, p. 44, Scholem's source might be Molitor, although this point is not elaborated.
64. Compare David Biale's assessment that the consideration of Jewish mysticism in its own right had to await the historiography of Gershom Scholem in the present century, in "The Kabbala in Nachman Krochmal's Philosophy of History," p. 97.
65. See Salomon Munk, *Mélanges de philosophie juive et arabe* (Paris, 1853), pp. 275–291, 490–494. See his shorter remarks, written in the same vein, in his earlier *Palestine* (Paris, 1845), pp. 509–524.
66. Munk, *Mélanges*, pp. 468–469.
67. Ibid.; compare also Franck, *La Kabbale*, pp. 256–257; and see below Chaps. II and VI.
68. Ibid., p. 492.
69. Ibid., p. 276.
70. Ibid., pp. 285–286, 290–291.
71. Ibid., pp. 276–283.
72. Ibid., p. 276.
73. Franck, *The Kabbalah*, trans. I. Sassmitz (New York, 1940), p. 302 n. 52. Jellinek's agreement with Franck's view of Kabbalah and the *Zohar* as representing an ancient lore gradually changed in his later works, which mainly continued Landauer's historical-philological method; the peak of Jellinek's achievement was his booklet, *Moses ben Schem Tob de Leon und sein Verhaeltnis zum Zohar* (Leipzig, 1851), in which he convincingly shows the similarities between de Leon's Hebrew writings and some passages of the *Zohar*.
74. *Ta'am Leshed* (n. 40 above), dedication to Ascoli. Just as Luzzatto reacted to Franck, ben Amozegh reacted to Luzzatto, his *Ta'am Leshed* being a refutation of the *Dialogue*, entitled *Nouveau Dialogue*, its main aim being to prove the antiquity of the Kabbalah. Ben Amozegh's positive attitude to Kabbalah, motivated by his traditional inclination, may have to do with the influence of Fichte, who is prominent in some of his writings; again, we see a certain affinity between German idealism and the interest in Kabbalah.
75. Ibid.
76. See Scholem, *The Messianic Idea in Judaism*, pp. 307–309.
77. See, for example, Marcus Ehrenpreis, *Die Entwickelung der Emanationslehre in der Kabbala des XIII Jahrhunderts* (Frankfurt A/M, 1895); or later, David Neumark, *Geschichte der Judischen Philosophie des Mittelalters* (Berlin, 1907), Band I, pp. 179–236.
78. *JQR*, n.s. 20 (1908), reprinted in *The Cabbalists* (London, 1922), p. 34.
79. See, for example, Robert Alter, "The Achievement of Gershom Scholem," *Commentary* 55 (1973): 69–73; Biale, *Gershom Scholem, Kabbala and Counter-History;* Yosef ben-Shlomo, "The Spiritual Universe of Gershom Scholem," *Jerusalem Quarterly* 29 (Fall 1983): 127–144; Alexander Altmann, "Gershom Scholem, 1897–1982," *PAAJR* 51 (1984):

1–14; Maurice Kriegel, "Gershom Scholem: Ecriture historique et renaissance nationale au xxe siècle," *Debat* 33 (January 1985): 126–139; and Rotenstreich's article (see Chap. IV n. 4). For scholarly critiques of Scholem's approach, directed mostly to the place and role of Kabbalah in Judaism in general, see Barukh Kurzweil, *Struggling on the Values of Judaism* (in Hebrew) (Jerusalem and Tel Aviv, 1970); and Eliezer Schweid, *Mysticism and Judaism according to Gershom G. Scholem* (in Hebrew), *Jerusalem Studies in Jewish Thought*, Suppl. 2 (Jerusalem, 1983); and the rejoinders of J. Dan. N. Rotenstreich, and H. Lazarus-Jaffe in the same journal, 3, no. 3 (1983–84): 427–492 (in Hebrew), and the review of Tamar Ross, "Scholem, Mysticism and Living Judaism," *Immanuel* 18 (Fall 1984): 106–124. An English version of Schweid's book was published recently: *Judaism and Mysticism according to Gershom Scholem*, trans. D. A. Weiner (Atlanta, Ga., 1985).

80. Exactly as Molitor did a century before Scholem. Scholem was inclined to overemphasize the differences between Kabbalah and philosophy as, for example, his conception of symbol and allegory shows (see below, Chap. IX, sec. I), while also acknowledging the influence of philosophy—mainly Neoplatonism—on Kabbalah. Even when Kabbalah was envisioned as different from philosophy, however, he was inclined to unfold what he considered to be the speculative substratum, "the metaphysics," far more than to approach Kabbalah as primarily an experiential lore.

81. See Scholem's 1937 letter to Zalman Schocken in Biale, *Gershom Scholem, Kabbalah and Counter-History*, p. 31; German original: p. 155.

82. Ibid. See also Scholem, *Major Trends*, p. 350, where, in speaking of the future evolution of Jewish mysticism, he writes: "The story is not ended, it has not yet become history, and the secret life it holds can break out tomorrow, in you or in me." The words *in me* can easily be misunderstood as a general reference to the outbreak of mysticism; against the background of the related material, a more personal interpretation seems more appropriate.

83. Ibid., p. 32, "professional death." See also Scholem's poem, " 'Vae Victis' oder der Tod in der Professur," *Ḥadarim* 4 (1984): 13. The poem was written in 1942.

84. *Mi-Berlin li-Yirushalayim* (Tel Aviv, 1982), p. 161.

85. See Scholem's *Vae Victis* (n. 83), "Ich war zum Sprung auf den Grund bereit. Aber habe ich ihn gemacht?"

86. Ibid. "Die Warheit hat den alten Glanz, doch wie Empfanger sein?"

87. See, for example, Alexander Altmann, "Moses Narboni's Epistle on Shi'ur Qomah," in Altmann, ed., *Jewish Medieval and Renaissance Studies* (Cambridge, Mass., 1967), pp. 225–264; Vajda, *Recherches.*

88. See, for example, Vajda's *L'Amour de Dieu dans la théologie juive du Moyen Age* (Paris, 1957); Altmann's studies on "The Ladder of Ascension" and "The Delphic Maxim in Medieval Islam and Judaism," reprinted in his *Studies in Religious Philosophy and Mysticism* (Ithaca, N.Y., 1969).

89. "Lurianic Kabbalah in a Platonic Key," *HUCA* 53 (1982): 317ff.; or "Lessings Glaube an die Seelenwanderung," *Lessing Yearbook* 8 (1976): 7–41, and so on.

90. See Heller-Wilensky's various studies on R. Isaac ibn Latif and Blumenthal's on R. Ḥoter ben Shelomo.

91. Y. F. Baer, *Israel among the Nations* (in Hebrew) (Jerusalem, 1955), Chap. V; Baer, "On the Problem of Eschatological Doctrine during the Period of the Second Temple" (in Hebrew), *Ẓion* 23–24 (1958–59): 3–34, 141–165.

92. *Israel among the Nations*, p. 91; "On the Problem," p. 32.
93. See Chap. VII.
94. Collected in two volumes: *Kitvey R. Abraham Epstein*, ed. A. M. Habermann (Jerusalem, 1950), and *Mi-Kadmoniot ha-Yehudim*, ed. A. M. Habermann (Jerusalem, 1957).
95. See *Ḥasidim ha-Rishonim* (Waizen, 1917), a biography of R. Samuel ben Yehudah he-Ḥasid and R. Yehudah he-Ḥasid, and the preface to his edition of R. Eleazar of Worms's *Sodey Razaya*.
96. See his two papers printed in *Ẓion* 3 (1937): 1–50, and 32 (1967): 129–136; "On the Doctrine of Providence in *Sefer Ḥasidim*" (in Hebrew), in *Studies in Mysticism and Religion Presented to Gershom Scholem* (Jerusalem, 1967), pp. 47–62.
97. Scholem, *Major Trends*, Chap. 3; "Reste neuplatonischer Spekulation in der Mystik der deutchen Chassidim . . . ," *MGWJ* 75 (1931): 172–191; and several important discussions in *Les Origines de la Kabbale*.
98. *Esoteric Theology*, and the collection of his papers, *Studies in Ashkenazi-Ḥasidic Literature*, as well as the papers cited below in n. 104.
99. "De quelques infiltrations chretiennes dans l'oeuvre d'un auteur anglo-juif du 13e siècle,' *AHDLMA* 28 (1961): 15–34, and in n. 105 below.
100. See his monumental *'Arugat ha-Bosem*, 4 vols. (Jerusalem, 1939–63).
101. "Topics in the *Ḥokhmat ha-Nefesh*," JJS 17 (1967): 65–78; "Three Themes in the *Sefer Ḥasidim*," *AJS Review* 1 (1976): 311–357.
102. *Piety and Society* (Leiden, 1981); "The Organization of the *Haqdamah* and *Hilekhot Ḥasidut* in Eleazar of Worms's *Sefer ha-Rokeaḥ*," *PAAJS* 36 (1968): 85–94; "*Ḥasidei Ashkenaz* Private Penitentials," in J. Dan and F. Talmage, eds., *Studies in Jewish Mysticism* (Cambridge, Mass., 1982), pp. 57–83; "The Politics and Ethics of Pietism in Judaism: The *Ḥasidim* of Medieval Germany," *Journal of Religious Ethics* 8 (1980): 227–258; "The Recensions and Structure of Sefer Ḥasidim," *PAAJR* 45 (1978): 131–153.
103. His researches cover the historical dimensions of Ashkenazi Jewry, serving as a solid basis for the study of the emergence of intellectual phenomena in this region. See *The Early Stages of Ashkenaz* (in Hebrew) (Jerusalem, 1981).
104. I refer to *Sefer ha-Navon*, treatises of the literature designated as *Sifrut ha-Yiḥud*, fragments of *Ḥokhmat ha-'Egoz, Sefer ha-Ḥayyim,* and two important works of R. Elḥanan ben Yakar.
105. "Commentary on Sefer Yeẓirah of R. Elḥanan ben Yakar," *Koveẓ 'al-Yad* 16 (1966): 147–197.
106. See Chap. V.
107. Scholem, *Les Origines de la Kabbale*, pp. 49–51.
108. Ibid., pp. 194–201.
109. Dan, *The Esoteric Theology*, pp. 119–129.
110. Ibid., p. 118.
111. Ibid., p. 129.
112. I hope to elaborate upon this evidence elsewhere; meanwhile, see Chap. VIII, sec. III, near nn. 158, 194.
113. Chap. V, sec. III.
114. See on this school the introduction of Paul Fenton to his edition of *The Treatise of the Pool—Al-Maqala al-Hawdiyya*, by 'Obadyah b. Abraham b. Moses Maimonides (London, 1981), pp. 1–71, who mentions the pertinent bibliography.

115. Idel, "Prophetic Kabbalah and the Land of Israel"; Idel, "The World of Imagination and the Collectanaea of R. Nathan" (in Hebrew), *Eshel Be'er Sheva'* 2 (1980): 165–176; Idel, "*Hitbodedut* as Concentration," pp. 45–58; and Fenton, *Treatise of the Pool,* in his introduction.
116. On a later Kabbalistic treatise, allegedly written under Sufic influence, see Gershom Scholem, "A Note on a Kabbalistical Treatise on Contemplation," in *Mélanges offerts à Henry Corbin* (Tehran, 1977), pp. 665–670. A recent attempt to argue for other Islamic influences on Jewish mysticism was made by David S. Ariel, "The Eastern Dawn of Wisdom: The Problem of the Relationship between Islamic and Jewish Mysticism," *Approaches to Judaism in Medieval Times* 2 (1985): 149–167. Ariel's argument that Jewish Eastern traditions, which reached Germany and Provence, absorbed Sufic influences is, in my opinion, unproven from the material he offers.
117. Shelomo Pines, "Shi'ite Terms and Conceptions in Judah Halevi's *Kuzari*," *Jerusalem Studies in Arabic and Islam* 2 (1980): 243–247; D. R. Blumenthal, "An Example of Ismaili Influence in Post-Maimonidean Yemen," in *Studies in Judaism and Islam Presented to S. D. Goitein* (Jerusalem, 1981), p. 157; Idel, "Sefirot above Sefirot," pp. 270–271.
118. Jacob Katz, *Halakhah and Kabbalah*, and see below, Chap. VII.

CHAPTER 2

1. See the studies of Stace, Zaehner, Staal, Lasky, and so on, who only rarely refer to Kabbalah or Jewish mysticism.
2. Gershom Scholem, "A List of the Commentaries on the Ten Sefirot" (in Hebrew), *Kiryat Sefer* 10 (1933–34): 498–515.
3. See, for example, Scholem's article, "The Meaning of the Torah in Jewish Mysticism," in *On the Kabbalah*, pp. 32–86, where the hermeneutic views of the Kabbalists are discussed, nevertheless ignoring Abulafia's discussions, which are both more detailed than those of his contemporaries and, at times, more illuminating; compare Idel, "Abraham Abulafia," pp. 167–249.
4. For example, this Kabbalist declared that he had composed a book entitled *Sefer ha-Pardes* on the four exegetical methods alluded to in the title of the book; knowledge of this work would contribute in a substantial way to our understanding of a crucial phase in the formation of Kabbalistic hermeneutics. This work is mentioned in de Leon's Kabbalistic responsa edited by Tishby, *Studies*, 1:56.
5. His work *Divrey ha-Yamim* seemingly consisted of hagiographical material related to Jewish mysticism; the only substantial passage that survived, R. Isaac of Acre's story on his quest for the origin of the *Zohar*, is a highly significant text for the history of Kabbalah, repeatedly quoted in many of the studies concerning Kabbalah in general and the *Zohar* in particular. It is probable that this Kabbalist also authored a work on mystical anecdotes in Sufic vein, different from *Divrey ha-Yamim*, which was still extant among the Safedian Kabbalah.
6. He mentions his *Livyat Ḥen* and *Tiferet Adam* as treatises dealing with important Kabbalistic issues; these works are no longer extant.
7. See Idel, "Abraham Abulafia," pp. 13–15.
8. Idel, "Inquiries," pp. 185–192.

9. Werblowsky, *Karo*, pp. 36–37.
10. See Scholem, "New Document," pp. 143–144.
11. See the preface to his commentary on the Pentateuch, and Idel, "We Have No Kabbalistic Tradition on This," pp. 59–61.
12. The comparison of the parallel and almost concomitant disclosure of Kabbalah and Ashkenazic Ḥasidism was noticed by Ginzberg, *On Jewish Law and Lore*, p. 204.
13. See Idel, "Sefirot above Sefirot," pp. 239–240.
14. See M. Idel, "On the History of the Interdiction to Study Kabbalah before the Age of Forty," *AJSreview* 5 (1980) (Hebrew part): 10–11.
15. See Chap. V, sec. IV, on R. David's text on visualization of colors.
16. See Scholem, *Major Trends*, p. 151.
17. For the problematics inherent in the limitations to philology, see Eliade, *The Quest*, pp. 60–61; Raffaele Pettazzoni, *Essays on the History of Religions* (Leiden, 1954), pp. 215–219.
18. I refer, for example, to the study of Provençal and Geronese Kabbalah, which flourishes in both Israeli and foreign universities, but which nevertheless restricts itself to the historical-philological area, despite the fact that all the major texts were printed and analyzed.
19. The conviction that Scholem presented both the "basic facts" and the "principal patterns," within whose overall framework Kabbalah research is looking for answers, was eloquently exposed by Joseph Dan, "The Historical Perceptions of the Late Professor Gershom Scholem" (in Hebrew), *Ẓion* 47 (1982): 167.
20. See Chap. IV.
21. See Chap. V, secs. III–IV. For an outstanding use of psychology to fathom mystical experiences, see Werblowsky's *Karo*.
22. See Urbach, "The Traditions about Merkavah Mysticism."
23. David Halperin, *The Merkabah in Rabbinic Literature* (New Haven, Conn., 1980), and his review of Schäfer's *Synopse*, in *JAOS* 104–03 (1984): 544, 549–551.
24. "Tradition and Redaction in Heikhalot Literature," *Journal for the Study of Judaism* 14 (1984): 172–181.
25. See Dan, *The Esoteric Theology*.
26. See Chap. V, secs. II–III.
27. Kabbalah was considered by Renaissance figures as part of a *prisca theologia* or, according to another formulation, of a *philosophia perennis*, and thus in concordance with Platonic, Neoplatonic, Hermetic, and atomistic concepts that were allegorically or symbolically hinted at in Kabbalistic literature.
28. See Idel, "Perceptions of Kabbalah," sec. I.
29. *Kabbalah*, p. 45; see also Buber, *Ḥasidism*, p. 140.
30. See, for example, *Major Trends*, pp. 74–75.
31. See, however, his remark that Gnosticism, or at least certain of "its basic impulses, was a revolt, partly perhaps of Jewish origin, against anti-mythical Judaism" (*On the Kabbalah*, p. 98).
32. For example, "Der Gnostische Anthropos und die Judische Tradition," *Eranosjahrbuch* 22 (1953): 195–234; "Ezekiel 1:26 in Jewish Mysticism and Gnosis," *Vigiliae Christianae* 34 (1980): 1–13.
33. "The Jewish Background of the Gnostic Sophia Myth," *Novum Testamentum* 12 (1970): 86–101.

34. See, for example, "Jewish Elements in Gnosticism and the Development of Gnostic Self-Definition," in *Jewish and Christian Self-Definition*, ed. E. P. Sanders (London, 1980), 1:151–160, as well as his "Friedländer Revisited: Alexandrian Judaism and Gnostic Origins," *Studia Philonica* 2 (1973): 23–39.
35. *Another Seed: Studies in Gnostic Literature* (Leiden, 1984).
36. *The Name of God and the Angel of the Lord.*
37. For a short survey of the change in the view of modern scholarship from the "Christian" and "Iranian" theories of the origin of Gnosticism to a "Jewish" one, see Simone Pétrement, *Le Dieu séparé: Les Origines de gnosticisme* (Paris, 1984), pp. 9–11. Herself opposing the view that Judaism is the ultimate source of Gnosticism, she wrote on this theory: "Cette hypothèse est celle qui règne actuellement sur presque toute la recherche." See now the thesis of Fossum, who attributes a crucial role to Samaritan thought—considered by him to continue Jewish conceptions—for the emergence of Gnosticism; see his *The Name of God and the Angel of the Lord.*
38. For these studies, see nn. 39–41 below and n. 13 above.
39. Idel, "The World of Angels in Human Shape."
40. Idel, "The Concept of the Torah."
41. Idel, "Enoch Is Metatron." This methodological approach is also used in a forthcoming important article of my colleague Yehudah Liebes.
42. See, especially, Chap. VI.
43. See also Chaps. VII and X.
44. See Chap. X.

CHAPTER 3

1. See, for example, Zaehner's typology of mystical experiences, whose underlying principle is the theological stand that is an a priori category for judging the nature of the mystical union. See his *Hindu and Muslim Mysticism*, pp. 21ff., and *Mysticism: Sacred and Profane*, pp. 153ff.
2. See, for example, Katz, "The 'Conservative' Character of Mystical Experience," in Steven T. Katz, *Mysticism and Religious Traditions* (Oxford, 1983), pp. 3–60.
3. See Scholem, *On the Kabbalah*, p. 8.
4. Katz, "Language, Epistemology, and Mysticism," p. 40.
5. Eliade, *The Quest*, p. 69.
6. Ricoeur, *The Conflict of Interpretations*, p. 482.
7. See, for example, Deut. 4:4; 6:5, 11, 22.
8. See *Sefre, 'Ekev*, paragraph 49, and the discussion and sources in Judah Goldin, "Freedom and Restraint of Haggadah," in *Midrash and Literature*, ed. G. H. Hartman and S. Budick (New Haven and London, 1986), pp. 67, 74–75, n. 69.
9. *Beraita* quoted in *Sanhedrin*, 64a:

"ואתם הדבקים בה' אלהיכם—דבוקים ממש."

See Heschel, *Theology of Ancient Judaism*, 1:154–155. It is important to point out the apparent discrepancy between this and the following talmudic texts in *Sanhedrin*, which stress the possibility of cleaving to God or to the *Shekhinah*, and the prevalent attitude in the Heikhalot literature, where this possibility seems to be unacceptable. Compare, however, the usage of the phrase "mystical communion" in connection with Heikhalot matter in

Cohen, *The Shi'ur Qomah: Liturgy and Theurgy*, pp. 5–6, with no evidence to support such an assertion. However, in a midrashic text that seems to have some connection with the Heikhalot literature, the verb *dvk* is used twice:

א״ר אבין בשם ר׳ יהושע : ״והייתם לי״ למ״ד גדולה מכל האותיות יו״ד קטנה מכל האותיות. נאה לגדול מדבק בקטן. גדול אדוננו ורב כח, כי אתם המעט מכל העמים. נאה לגדול מדבק בקטן בעה״ז היו ישראל דבקים להקב״ה.

Pesikta Rabbati, par. XI, ed. M. Friedman (Vienna, 1880), fol. 86b. *Gadol* or *Lamed* symbolizes God, the Great, which is referred to in the classical verse of the *Shi'ur Komah* description of God, Psalm 7:7, while *Katan* or *yod* refers to Israel; nevertheless, they occur together in the word *li*, thereby testifying to the possibility of cleaving between these two entities.

10. Heschel, *Theology of Ancient Judaism*, 1:153–154.
11. *Sanhedrin*, fol. 64a:

״כשתי תמרות הדבוקות זו בזו״

Compare to the *Seliḥah* of R. Elijah ben Shemaiah, an eleventh-century poet in southern Italy, who described Israel in these words:

דבוקים אחריך כצמידים ותיום

"They are cleaving after Thou as bracelets and as [united] citrus (see Daniel Goldschmidt, *Maḥzor Leyamim ha-Noraim* [Jerusalem, 1970], 2:695). The meaning of the citrus metaphor is identical to that of the two palm dates in the talmudic text; according to Rashi's interpretation of a talmudic text, *Sukkah*, fol. 36a, the word *Tiom* refers to "two citruses cleaving to each other." Therefore, the line quoted above envisions *devekut* of Israel and God as an organic phenomenon, comprising at least a certain point where they are inseparable. Compare, however, to Lev. R. 2:4, and see the theurgical interpretation of this assessment in Menaḥem Recanati's *Commentary on the Pentateuch*, fol. 81b.

12. *Sifrei, Shofetim,* par. 173, ed. M. Friedmann (Vienna, 1864), fol. 107b:

״המדבק בשכינה, דין הוא שתשרה עליו רוח הקודש״

On R. Ḥayyim Vital's elaboration of this view, see Werblowsky, *Karo*, p. 66; see also Heschel, *The Theology of Ancient Judaism*, 1:154 n. 5, for some parallels to R. Eleazar's view attributed to R. 'Akiva. See also below, Chap. VI, n. 333.

13. E. R. Dodds, "Numenius and Ammonius," *Entretiens sur l'antiquité classique—les sources de Plotin* (Vandoeuvres and Geneva, 1960), 5:17–18; Dodds, *Pagan and Christian in an Age of Anxiety* (Cambridge, 1965), 93–96. On Numenius and Plotinus, see Edouard des Places, *Numenius-Fragments* (Paris, 1973), pp. 23–26. On Numenius and the Jews, see Menaḥem Stern, *Greek and Latin Authors on Jews and Judaism* (Jerusalem, 1980), 2:206–216. On Philo and Numenius, see ibid., p. 207 n. 5. Our hypothesis on the possible influence of the ancient Jewish mystical interpretation of *devekut* on Greek thought is comparable to the possibility that a certain pattern of describing the beauty of a woman found in Hellenistic poetry was introduced therein by a poet of Syrian extraction under the influence of a Semitic descriptive schema; cf. Shaye J. D. Cohen, "The Beauty of Flora and the Beauty of Sarai," *Helios* n.s. 8 (1981): 41–53.
14. Ibid., pp. 94–96.
15. See *Legum Allegoriarum*, 2, 56. For another affinity between Philo and Plotinus, apparently via Numenius, see David Winston, *Philo of Alexandria* (New York, 1981), p. 315 n. 103. Winston implicitly accepted a certain relationship between Philo and Plotinus: see his

paper "Was Philo a Mystic?" in *Studies in Jewish Mysticism*, ed. J. Dan and F. Talmage (Cambridge, Mass., 1982), pp. 29, 32.

16. See Stern, *Greek and Latin Authors*, p. 207 and n. 3.
17. See Winston, *Philo*, p. 32.
18. See the perceptive analyses of the mystical implications of Aristotelian epistemology in Philip Merlan, *Monopsychism, Mysticism, Metaconsciousness: Problems of the Soul in the Neoaristotelian and Neoplatonic Traditions* (The Hague, 1963), especially pp. 16ff., 85ff. For an ancient mystical understanding of the Aristotelian epistemic principle of the identity of the knower and the intelligible, see Andrew Louth, *The Origins of the Christian Mystical Tradition* (Oxford, 1981), pp. 108–109, where the author discusses Evagrius of Pontus' views; compare also to the Brahmanic sources cited by Arthur Avalon, *Shakti and Shakta* (New York, 1978), p. 455.
19. For more on the importance of philosophical terminology for a particular type of Kabbalah—the ecstatic—see Idel, "Abraham Abulafia and *Unio Mystica*."
20. See E. R. Dodds, "Theurgy and Its Relationship to Neoplatonism," *Journal of Roman Studies* 38 (1947); Pierre Boyance, "Théurgie et télestique néoplatoniciennes," *Revue d'Histoire des Religions* 74 (1955): 189–209.
21. For a short survey of the history of descending spiritualities in Jewish mysticism, see Idel, "Differing Conceptions of the Kabbalah." I have refrained from elaborating on this point here; see also Idel, "The Magical and Neoplatonic Interpretations," pp. 195–215, and Chap. VII, par. III.
22. See Scholem, *Elements*, p. 194:

    הצדיק מעלה נפשו הזכה והטהורה בנפש העליונה הקדושה ויתאחד עמה ויודעת העתידות. וזאת ענין הנביא ודרכו שאין יצר הרע שולט בו להפרידו מנשמה העליונה. על כן נפש הנביא מתיחדת עם הנשמה העליונה יחוד גמור.

    Although the text is anonymous, in all the manuscripts therein it is extant, Scholem (*Elements*, p. 194) seems to be correct in his attribution of the text to R. 'Ezra.
23. The phrase "**נפש עליונה**" stands for the universal soul, as it does in similar contexts in ibn 'Ezra's writings. See nn. 29 and 31 below.
24. See R. Abraham ibn 'Ezra's *Commentary on Psalms 139:18*, and compare the view of the Great Maggid of Mezerich, expressed in *'Or ha-'Emet*; cf. Schatz-Uffenheimer, *Quietistic Elements*, p. 126.
25. These two helpful terms were proposed by Merlan, *Monopsychism, Mysticism, Metaconsciousness*, pp. 27ff., but I use them in a slightly different manner.
26. In the original, *be-ḥidudah*; this phrase seems to point to a peculiar quality of the soul, as it does in R. Isaac of Acre's description of Naḥmanides, who was, in his youth, "confident of his sharpness," but had forgotten the Kabbalistic traditions he did not write down. See Idel, "We Have No Kabbalistic Tradition on This," pp. 62–63.
27. Commentary on Deut. 13:2:

    הנפש בחדודה הדבק בשכל הנבדל ותתכוין בו והאיש הזה יקרא נביא כי מתנבא הוא.
28. Strangely enough, Naḥmanides accepts here an Aristotelian view of prophecy as the separate intellect being its source; see n. 57 below. Compare also to R. Joseph Gikatilla's *Keẓat Beurey* [!] *me-ha-Moreh* (Venice, 1574), fol. 21c.
29. Scholem, *Elements*, p. 194:

    "כי האדם כלול מכל הדברים ונפשו קשורה בנפש העליונה"

    Compare Chap. VIII, n. 38, the text from *Sefer ha-Ne'elam*.

30. It seems that this phrase is elliptic, its fuller form apparently being "הדברים העליונים" ("the supernal things")—namely, the ten Sefirot. This formula recurs in R. 'Ezra's works; see Scholem, "Two Treatises of R. Moshe de Leon," p. 383 n. 100. It is obvious that the body is referred to as comprising the things, as against the soul, which cleaves to the supernal soul. On the "human body" as comprising "all things," see Chap. VI.

31. *Commentary on Pentateuch*, fol. 37d:
כשהיו החסידים ואנשי המעשה מתבודדים ועוסקים בסודות העליונים היו מדמים בכח ציור מחשבותם, כאלו הדברים ההם חקוקים לפניהם, וכשהיו קושרים נפשם בנפש, העליונה, היו הדברים מתרבים ומתברכים ומתגלים מאליהם . . . כשהיה מדביק נפשו בנפש העליונה היו חקוקים בלבו הדברים הנוראים.

32. In Hebrew, *Mitbodedim*; my interpretation of this verb as pointing to mental concentration is corroborated by Geronese parallels, which will be printed and analyzed in my forthcoming study on *hitbodedut*.

33. Namely, before their eyes.

34. Recanati, *Commentary on Pentateuch*, fol. 38b:
ודע כי כמו שהפרי כשהוא נגמר יפול מן האילן ולא יצטרך עוד לחבורו, כך הוא חבור הנפש עם הגוף כי כשהשיגה מה שביכולתה להשיג יתרבק בנפש העליונה, תפשט מלבוש העפר מעליה ותנתק ממקומה ותרבק בשכינה זהו מיתת נשיקה.
Compare also ibid., fol. 37d:
אין שכינה שורה לא מתוך עצלות וכו' אלא מתוך שמחה. ואולי תתגבר עליו אותה השמחה עד כי יתחדש עליו בכיה רבה ומופלאה ותבקש נשמתו ונפשו להפרד מגופו וזו היא מיתת נשיקה, שמורה חיבור הנושק בדבר האהוב לו כי אז יתחבר נפשו בשכינה.
Ibid., fol. 38b:
כי מרוב הדביקות נדבקה נפשותם בנפש העליונה עד שמתו בנשיקה.
On the philosophical source of this passage—Maimonides' *Guide of the Perplexed* III:51—and other relevant material, see Chaim Wirszubski, *Three Studies in Christian Kabbala* (in Hebrew) (Jerusalem, 1975).

35. Recanati, or his source, is heavily influenced by the fruit metaphor occurring in R. Abraham ibn 'Ezra's *Commentary on Psalm 1*, where the verb *davek* is also employed.

36. Compare below, n. 64, where the attempt to think about issues that transcend the comprehension of human thought causes unnatural death.

37. Recanati qua Kabbalist viewed the ultimate source of the human soul in the infradivine structure; her originating in the universal soul would be, in his eyes, tantamount to accepting Greek psychology. On this issue, see Vajda, *Recherches*, pp. 371–378.

38. *Commentary on Song of Songs*, Chavel, *Kitvey ha-Ramban* 1:480:
והנשיקה משל לדביקות הנשמה . . . אך אחר שהמשיל דביקות הנשמה להנשיקה בפה, הוצרך לומר "פיהו" לקשר המשל בו, כמו שהקדים לכתוב בספרו אחד מחכמי הדור.
See ibid, p. 485.

39. On the problem of allegory and symbolism, see Chap. IX, where I shall again refer to this text.

40. See Scholem, *Les Origines de la Kabbale*, pp. 399–400; Vajda, *Le Commentaire d'Ezra de Gérone*, pp. 145–146.

41. See in R. 'Ezra and R. 'Azriel; cf. the latter's *Commentary on the Talmudic Aggadot*, p. 15.

42. Fol. 98b:

התעלה נפש הצדיק בעודנו חי מעילוי לעילוי עד מקום תענוג כל נפשות הצדיקים אשר הוא דבקות הדעת נישאר הגוף בלא תנועה והוא כענין שנאמר ואתם הדבקים בה' אלקיכם חיים כולכם היום.

On *ta'anug*, see Chap. VI, n. 369.

43. Deut. 4:4. Compare the interpretation of this verse in R. David ben Zimra's *Meẓudat David*, fol. 3c.
44. See Chap. IV and nn. 90ff.
45. See his *Minḥat Yehudah*, printed in the anonymous *Ma'arekhet ha-'Elohut*, fols. 95b–96a.
46. See Wirszubski, *Three Studies*, pp. 14–22.
47. Ibid., p. 15.
48. See Aviezer Ravitsky, "Anthropological Theory of Miracles in Medieval Jewish Philosophy," in *Studies in Medieval Jewish History and Literature*, ed. I. Twersky (Cambridge, Mass., 1984), 2:233–235, and Howard Kreisel, "Miracles in Medieval Jewish Philosophy," *JQR* 75 (1984): 94–133.
49. Ravitsky, "Anthropological Theory," pp. 238–239.
50. See throughout Ravitsky's and Kreisel's articles.
51. See Vajda, *Recherches*, pp. 385ff.; Idel, "Abraham Abulafia," pp. 230–232.
52. Chavel, *Kitvey ha-Ramban*, 2:334:

כי בהיות החסידים מדבקים מחשבתם בעליונים, כל דבר שהיו מחשבים בו ומתכונים עליו, באותה שעה היה מתקיים, אם טוב ואם רע... ומן הענין הזה הוא ענין התפלה והקרבנות, שהוא סוד הדיבוק בעליונים.

Compare to the view of R. Isaac the Blind, quoted below, n. 128.

53. Ibid., p. 335.
54. On the whole subject, see Bezalel Safran's fine remarks in "Rabbi 'Azriel and Naḥmanides: Two Views of the Fall of Man," in I. Twersky, ed., *Rabbi Moses Naḥmanides (Ramban): Explorations in His Religious and Literary Virtuosity* (Cambridge, Mass., 1983), pp. 102–104.
55. Ibid., p. 102 n. 101.
56. *Commentary on Job*, in Chavel, *Kitvey ha-Ramban*, 1:108.
57. *Sermon on Kohelet*, in ibid., p. 192; he mentions the *devekey ha-Shem ha-Meforash*, and shortly before that we learn that

"ובשם המיוחד נעשים אותות ומופתים מפורסמים מחודשים בעולם"

Strangely enough, the righteous who cleave to the Sefirah of *Malkhut*, and the pious who cleave to the Sefirah of *Tiferet* are implicitly superior to the prophets, who are referred to by Naḥmanides as cleaving to the separate intellect, which is ontologically "lower" than the sefirotic realm. See n. 28 above. On cleaving to the divine name, see also the anonymous text, printed by Scholem in *Kiryat Sefer*, 6:414.

"והכל בכח שמו ית' אשר הוא ספר החיים ממש לדבקים"

The use of the form *devekim* (cleavers) sounds as if it were a *terminus technicum* for a specific type of mystic; see also sec. V and nn. 123, 134 below.

58. Sermon *Torat ha-Shem Temimah, Kitvey ha-Ramban*, 1: 168.
59. *Commentary on Talmudic Aggadot*, in *Likkutey Shikheḥah u-feah*, fol. 8a:

בחסידים הראשונים מעלים מחשבתם עד מקום מוצאה והיו מזכירים המצוות והדברים ומתוך ההזכרה והמחשבה הדבקה היו הדברים מתברכים ומתווספים ומתקבלים שפע מאפיסת המחשבה.

60. R. Isaac the Blind had referred to cleaving of the thought: see R. 'Ezra's *Commentary on the Song of Songs*; Chavel, *Kitvey ha-Ramban*, 2:521–522 (n. 128 below).

61. In original, "דברים", which I vocalize as *dibberim*—the Ten Commandments.

62. On the influx stemming from "the annihilation of thought," see R. 'Ezra's *Commentary on the Song of Songs*, Chavel, *Kitvey ha-Ramban* 2:494, 526; see also Pachter, "The Concept of Devekut in the Homiletical Ethical Writings of the 16th Century Safed," *Studies in Medieval Jewish History and Literature*, ed. I. Twersky (Cambridge, Mass., 1984), 2:189.

63. *Commentary on the Talmudic Aggadot*, p. 20.
"אמור לחכמה אחותי את": ר"ל להרביק המחשבה בחכמה להיות היא והוא דבר אחד.
Tishby, ibid., n. 11, did not distinguish between this Neoplatonic view and the Aristotelian epistemic union as it occurs in Maimonides. On the phrase "היא והוא דבר אחד", see Georges Vajda, "En marge du commentaire sur le cantique des cantiques de Joseph ibn Aqnin," *REJ* 124 (1968): 187 n. 1; Vajda, *Recherches*, pp. 26–28, Chap. IV below, and here, n. 112. Abulafia was very fond of using this phrase. See Idel, "Abraham Abulafia and *Unio Mystica*," nn. 29, 38.

64. *Commentary on Talmudic Aggadot*, in *Likkutey Shikhehah u-feah*, fol. 8a:
מרוב כפיית המחשבה להרביקה במה שאינה יכולה להשיג, תעלה נפשו ותנתק ותשוב לשרשה.
Compare R. 'Azriel, *Commentary on Talmudic Aggadot*, p. 39; R. Moshe de Leon in *Shoshan 'Edut*, printed in Scholem, "Two Treatises of R. Moshe de Leon," p. 347, and his *Commentary on ten Sefirot*, ibid., p. 371; Recanati, *Commentary on the Pentateuch*, fol. 37d–38a.

65. See Idel, "Abraham Abulafia and *Unio Mystica*" and Chap. IV below.

66. R. Joseph ben Shalom Ashkenazi's *Kabbalistic Commentary on Genesis Rabbah*, ed. Moshe Hallamish (Jerusalem, 1984), p. 140:
כי אין האדם משכיל מצד גשמו אלא מצד השכל שבו ולכן כשישכיל הצדיק את יוצרו על ידי הכוונה ועשייתו מצוותיו, אזי נרבק בי"י שנ' ואתם הדבקים בי"י אלהים חיים כולכם היום"
Compare also R. David ben Zimra's *Meẓudat David*, fol. 3cd.

67. Deut. 4:4.

68. See Chap. IX, sec. II, in the discussion on the identification of the mystical interpreter with the Torah.

69. MS. München, 22 fol. 187a:
בהזדכך השכל כשהוא בחמר בעודו באותו המשכן, באמת הוא מדרגה גדולה, להרבק בעלת העלות אחר הפרד הנפש מאותו החומר.

70. *'Oẓar Ḥayyim*, MS Moscow-Günzburg 775, fol. 112a:
ראיתי סוד "ובשנה הד' יהיה כל פריו קרש הלולים ליי'," שצונו השם להגביר נפש שכלינו על נפש תאותינו ג' שנים, שירמזו לג' עולמות, למען תרבק נפשנו בסוד השנה הד' הרומזת לסוד האלהות שלמעלה מג' עולמים. ובשנה החמישית רמז לאין סוף, המקיף הכל, ותרבק נפש זו באין סוף ותשוב כל כללי גמור אחר היותה פרטית מצד היכלה בעוד היותה כלואה בו, תשוב כללית בסוד אמיתת סוד מחצבה.

71. Lev. 19:24.

72. Probably referring to ibid., 19:25: "I am the Lord your God."

73. See Chap. IV, n. 69, for another quotation from *'Oẓar Ḥayyim,* where the *makif* refers to the highest divine aspect.

74. See Chap. IV, n. 60, the passage of R. Menaḥem Naḥum of Chernobyl, where cleaving is connected to the transformation of the particular into the universal. R. Isaac is apparently

influenced by ibn 'Ezra (see the text quoted in n. 17, Chap. IV below), either directly or indirectly through Abraham Abulafia. Compare also to the text that was probably written by R. Nathan, probably R. Isaac's master, where the linking of one's soul to God is indicated by the words:

"קשר נפשו בכלל הכל שהוא הש"י... והחלק, חלק ר"ל אשר דבקה נפשו בהבלי העו' הזה".

See M. Steinschneider and A. Neubauer, "Joseph ibn Aknin," *Magazin für die Wissenschaft des Judentums* 14 (1888): 106.

75. *'Or ha-'Emet* (Bnei Berak, 1969), fol. 8a:

"תפילין דמארי עלמא מה כתיב בהו: 'מי כעמך ישראל גוי אחד בארץ.' " דאיתא בכתבי האר"י ז"ל תפילין נקראים מוחין. פ"י מוחין נקרא תענוג והתלהבות מה שאנו דבוקים לו ית' "וראו כל עמי הארץ כי שם ה' נקרא עליך," כביכול אתה נקרא בשם ד' יתברך, שאתה נעשה אחדות עמו ית' והתענוג הזה נקרא תפלין שלנו. והתענוג שלו ית' שנתענג מחמת שאנו דבוקים בו יתברך נקרא תפלין שלו. "ומי כעמך ישראל גוי אחד," כשהם דבוקים לו יתברך נעשה אחדות שבאים למעלה ממספר, והמספר הוא בידם... הזמן בידם לעשות כמו שרוצים שהם למעלה מזמן(!). והוא ית' דבוק בנו רק המניעה מכחינו ע"ד "שובו אלי ואשובה אליכם", שהוא ית' שורה במחשבה. וכשאדם חושב דברי שטות ח"ו דוחה אותיות, "ולא יכול משה לבא אל אוהל מועד," השכל אינו יכול לשרות באדם, "כי שכן עליו הענן," כי החשכות שורה בו.

On the relationship between worship and delight, see Chap. VI, n. 336. An interesting parallel to this understanding of the phylacteries as union is found in a work written under the heavy influence of the Great Maggid: See R. Meshullam Phoebus of the Zbaraz's *Yosher Divrey Emet*, fol. 123a, where R. Isakhar Dov is reported to have said:

תורה ותפילין ר"ל שהדביקות והמחשבה נקרא תורה כנ"ל ונקרא תפילין שנקרא על שם דביקות השכל בהשי"ת ותפילין לשון דביקות.

Note especially the occurrence of the term *devekut ha-sekhel* ("the cleaving of the intellect"), which explains the significance of phylacteries. On phylacteries and *devekut*, see R. Baḥya ben Asher, *Kad ha-Kemaḥ*, paragraph on *Lulav*, in *Kitvey Rabbenu Baḥya*, ed. H. D. Chavel (Jerusalem, 1970), p. 234.

76. *Berakhot*, 6a.
77. I Chron. 17:21.
78. In Hebrew *eḥad*, namely, "one."
79. See *Peri 'Eẓ Ḥayyim*, Gate of Tefillin, passim.
80. Deut. 28:10. This verse is written in the common phylacteries, which are referred to below as "our phylacteries."
81. On God enjoying the union with man, see Chap. IV, my discussion of R. Shneur Zalman of Lyady's view of "swallowing."
82. Zech. 1:3.
83. Exod. 40:35.
84. *'Or ha-'Emet*, fol. 5c:

"כביכול כשאנחנו עושים מעשים הגונים נתרחב עולם השכל ית'."

On the relationship between good deeds and the "expansion" of the divine world, see Chap. VIII.

85. On this problem, see especially Michael E. Marmura and J. M. Rist, "Al Kindi's Discussion of Divine Existence and Oneness," *Medieval Studies* 25 (1963): 338–354; Georges Vajda,

"Le Problème de l'unité de Dieu d'après Dawud ibn Marwan al-Mukammis," in *Jewish Medieval and Renaissance Studies*, ed. A. Altmann (Cambridge, Mass., 1967), pp. 49–73.

86. See, for example, *Ennead*, III, 7.

87. Compare the Great Maggid's view in *Maggid Devarav le-Ya'akov*, p. 11: "as if the Ẓaddikim causes God to be as their mind, since he thinks whatever they think." See also *'Or Torah*, p. 135, and Scholem, *Explications and Implications*, p. 356.

88. *The Messianic Idea in Judaism*, p. 218.

89. Scholem's assertion that Lurianic views of what he calls adhesion, which were transmitted orally, deeply influenced the Ḥasidic view of adhesion seems to me to be doubtful; see *Kabbalah*, p. 372. Another affinity between philosophy and Ḥasidic mysticism is referred to below, Chap. VI, sec. IV.

90. See below, Chap. IV, where we shall see again the reverberations of earlier Kabbalistic metaphors in Ḥasidic discussions of mystical experiences, and Chap. VI, sec. IV. Recently, Isaiah Tishby proposed to see in the works of R. Moses Ḥayyim Luzzato an important source of Ḥasidic views of *devekut*; see his "Les traces de Rabbi Moise Haim Luzzato dans l'enseignement du hassidisme," in *Hommage à Georges Vajda*, ed. G. Nahon and C. Touati (Louvain, 1980), pp. 427 n. 16, 428–439. Tishby's assessments put a heavier emphasis on the importance of Luzzato's teaching for Ḥasidism than it appears from both the available literary and historical documents; nevertheless, his findings open an important avenue, neglected by previous scholarship, for the understanding of Ḥasidic mysticism.

91. Scholem, *The Messianic Idea in Judaism*, p. 208; Joseph Weiss, "*Talmud Torah* in R. Israel the Besht's Thought" (in Hebrew), in *Tiferet Israel: Festschrift to Israel Brody* (London, 1967), Hebrew section, p. 153.

92. *Sefer Me'irat 'Eynaim*, p. 218:
הזוכה לסוד ההתרבקות יזכה לסוד ההשתוות ואם יזכה לסוד ההתבודדות, ומאחר שזכה לסוד ההתבודדות, הרי זה יזכה לרוח הקדש ומזה לנבואה עד שיתנבא ויאמר עתידות.
For a detailed analysis of this passage, as well as R. Isaac's view of *devekut*, see Idel, "*Hitbodedut* as Concentration," pp. 46–47, and the notes accompanying it. For the possible Eastern Ḥasidic and Sufic background of R. Isaac's mysticism, see Idel, "Prophetic Kabbalah and the Land of Israel," pp. 103–110. It should be mentioned that the influence exercised by Sufic teachings on Eastern Kabbalah, especially on aspects of extreme mysticism, is a field of research requiring far more study than I have done in the above articles, but only after a close perusal of the extant Hebrew material, such as the works of Abraham Abulafia.

93. *Me'irat 'Eynaim*, p. 218:
וסבת ההשתוות הוא דבוק המחשבה בשם ית׳ כי דבוק וחבור המחשבה בשם ית׳, הוא מסבב אל האיש ההוא שלא ירגיש בכבוד הבריות לו, ולא בבזיון שעושים לו.

94. MS British Library, Cat. Margoliouth, Nr. 749, fol. 17b; Idel, "*Hitbodedut* as Concentration," p. 49 nn. 77–78.

95. Irrefutable evidence of the influence of this passage of R. Isaac on early Ḥasidism is the view of equanimity as caused by cleaving in *Ẓava'at ha-Ribash:*
כלל גדול השתוות הוא דבוק המחשבה בשם ית׳ כי דבוק וחבור המחשבה בשם ית׳ הוא מסבב אל האיש ההוא שלא ירגיש בכבוד הבריות לו, ולא בבזיון שעושים לו.
כלל גדול השתוות ופ״י שיהיה שוה אצלו אם יחזקוהו לחסרון ידיעה או יודע בכל התורה כולה. ודבר הגורם לזה הוא הדביקות בבורא תדיר.

96. *Me'irat 'Eynaim*, p. 217:

אני יה״ב שנ״ר דעת״ו אומ׳ בין ליחידים בין להמון שהרוצה לידע סוד קשירת נפשו למעלה ודיבוק מחשבתו באל עליון . . . ישים לנגד עיני שכלו ומחשבתו אותיות השם המיוחד.

See Idel, "Abraham Abulafia," pp. 262–263.

97. See also R. Joseph Karo *Maggid Meisharim* Per. Mikeẓ (Jerusalem, 1960), p. 37.

"׳שויתי ה׳ לנגדי תמיד׳ ואם כה תעשה להרבק מחשבותיך תמיד בי."

See Joseph Weiss, "The Beginnings of Ḥasidism" (in Hebrew), *Ẓion* 16 (1951): 60–62, in which he looks for the source of R. Naḥman of Kosov's technique of contemplation of the Tetragrammaton in *Berit Menuḥah*; Piekarz, *The Beginning of Ḥasidism*, pp. 23–24, quoted sources where the verse of Psalm 16 is used, albeit without mentioning *devekut*. Compare also nn. 104, 152 below.

98. Gate of Love, Chap. X:

מי שירצה לשמח את נפשו יתבודד מקצת היום לחשוב בגדולת אותיות ידוד . . . שאמר דהמע״ה "שויתי ה׳ לנגדי תמיד" . . . לכן בחשבו בשם ידוד הנשמה מאירה . . . והיא שמחה . . . וזו היא מעלת הצדיקים הרבקים בשם ה׳ שאפילו במיתתם קרואים חיים, כי מפני התרבקותם בשם ידיד . . .

The impact of de Vidas' view of *devekut* upon early Ḥasidism was briefly discussed by Gedaliah Nigal, "The Sources of Devekut in Early Ḥasidic Literature" (in Hebrew), *Kiryat Sefer* 46 (1970–71): 345–46, without, however, referring to this passage, which was also ignored by Pachter in "The Concept of Devekut," pp. 96–115, and in his article in *Festschrift Y. Tishby* (forthcoming). Compare also below, Chap. IV, n. 92.

99. *Reshit Ḥokhmah*, Gate of Love, Chap. X:

"רננו צדיקים בידוד" . . . שיהיה השם הזה לנגדכם שתייחדו אותו באופן שהרנה כזו היא הרבקות הגמור ואפשר לומר כי הכוונה לומר שסתם רנה גורם דבקות . . .כמה שבחים בשבחו של מקום תקן החסיד ר׳ יהודה הלוי ע״ה, האומרם גורם דבקות נפשו באלהי׳.

100. Psalms 32:1.

101. Cf. Idel, "Music and Prophetic Kabbalah," pp. 150–169. On the praxis of Abulafia's techniques in the entourage of de Vidas, see Idel, "Some Remarks on R. Moses Cordovero and R. Abraham Abulafia" (in Hebrew), *Da'at* 15 (1985): 117–120.

102. Idel, "Music and Prophetic Kabbalah," pp. 168–169.

103. This fact was noted by 'Azriel Shohat, "On Joy in Ḥasidism" (in Hebrew), *Ẓion* 16 (1961): 32–33, who explored the Kabbalistic sources of the Ḥasidic view of joy.

104. I hope to elaborate upon the mystical interpretation of *Shiviti* in a separate study.

105. *Sefer ha-Berit* (Warsaw, 1897), p. 167.

106. See Scholem, *The Messianic Idea in Judaism*. p. 210.

107. See Piekarz, *The Beginning of Ḥasidism*, pp. 119–126, 133–134. See also several passages of R. Nathan Neta of Sienawa, *Siddur 'Olat Tamid* (Premislany, 1896), fol. 38b, 53b, 59a, 68b, and Piekarz, *The Beginning of Ḥasidism*, pp. 23–24.

108. Fol. 186a:

"ובעודו מתבודד שיהי׳ שם הויה של ד׳ אותיות נגד פניו."

109. *Commentary on the Sacrifice*, MS Oxford, Christ Church, 198, fol. 12b:

וכאשר מקריב הכהן הקרבן הוא מרביק נפשו למזבח ומתעלה הנשמה למעלה . . . ע״כ בהרביקו נפשו למעלה בתחלה מתעלה רוחו של אדם . . . ושבה לשרשה מאשר לוקחה . . . ואחרי כן מתעלה למעלה עד מקום שרשה מעילוי לעילוי כמו המים שעולים עד המדרגה שממנה יוצאים וזהו ברכת כהנים . . . מרבקים נפשם למעלה ומברכים את העם.

Compare R. Isaac the Blind's concise formulation (n. 128 below), where the relationship between sacrifice and *devekut* is stated explicitly. Interestingly, this conception of the early Kabbalists was echoed in the sixteenth century in R. Meir ibn Gabbay's *Tola'at Ya'akov*, fol. 4b:

וזהו סוד הברכות כי המברך מרביק מחשבתו בצורות הקרושוה ובאמצעות תפלתו ודבוקו כי הוא משלים במושכל במורגש במוטבע בא השפע לכח המנהיגים התחתונים וממנו לכל התחתונים.

We can easily see here the combination of the terminology of R. 'Azriel—*Muskal, murgash, mutba'*—with that of *Sefer ha-Bahir*—*Ẓurot kedoshot, manhigim.*

110. See the texts referred to in n. 64 above.

111. Chavel, *Kitvey ha-Ramban*, 2:333:

ידוע לבעלי הקבלה שמחשבת האדם היא ממקום הנפש השכלית הנמשכת מהעליונים ויש כח במחשבה להתפשט ולהעלות ולהגיע עד מקום מוצאה. ואז תהיה נרבקת בסור העליון שנמשכת משם ונעשין היא והוא דבר אחד . . . הוצרכו חז"ל לומר כי בהתחבר האדם עם אשתו ומחשבתו נדבקת בעליונים, הרי אותה המחשבה מושכת האור העליון למטה והיא שורה על אותה הטפה שהוא מתכוון אליה ומהרהר בה . . . ונמצא אותה טיפה נקשרת לעולם באור הבהיר. לפי שהמחשבה בה נקשרת בעליונים והיא מושכת האור הבהיר למטה.

112. See n. 63 above.

113. Compare R. Jonah Gerondi's *Sha'arey ha-'Avodah* (Bnei Berak, 1967), p. 58:

והמשכיל בהם [במצוות] תתעלה נפשו בעולם הרוחני ותדבק בעליונים משרתי עליון להרבק אליהם, לעבוד בורא עולם בקצה העליון שבעבודה.

Therefore, the ultimate goal is not the cleaving, but the perfect worship, attained only after the cleaving. Compare also Gerondi, ibid., pp. 41–44, 60.

114. On the *Ẓaddik* as channel, see R. Nathan Shapira of Jerusalem's introduction to R. Ḥayyim Vital's *Peri 'Eẓ Ḥayyim*, ed. J. Ashlag (Tel Aviv, 1966), p. 2, and Samuel H. Dresner, *The Ẓaddik* (New York, 1974), pp. 277 n. 33, 378 n. 34.

115. *Zohar*, I, fol. 43a:

"ומשיך ברכאן על עלמא"

116. Ibid., III, fol. 68a.

117. MS Berlin, Or. Qu. 833, fol. 98c; ibn Gabbay, *'Avodat ha-Kodesh*, II, 6 fol. 28a.

אם יחרבו הסדרים נשאר להם לישראל השם הגדול במקום הקרבנות להידבק בו במקומות מוקדשים, והצדיקים והחסידים והאנשים המתבודדים ומייחדים את השם הגדול ומאחזין את האש במדורת המוקד בלבותם, ואז במחשבתו הטהורה יתייחדו כל הספירות ויתקשרו זה בזה עד הימשכם עד מעיין השלהבת שאין סוף לרוממותו וזהו הסוד שכל ישראל דבקים בה' יתברך: "להגיד בבקר חסדך ואמונתך בלילות," זהו סוד היחוד של האדם שבתפילה בבוקר ובערב בהעלאת כל הספירות באגודה אחת ובאחודן ואזי הוא דבק בשם הגדול.

On this passage, see Scholem, *Les Origines de la Kabbale*, p. 324; Scholem, "The Concept of Kavvanah," p. 168. I have recently identified a third version of this passage in MS Sassoon, 919 p. 171, whose varia did not differ drastically from the preceding quotation.

118. I assume that R. 'Ezra refers to ritually pure sites; compare to the story related to R. Isaac the Blind, who avoided passing beside impure sites, as his thought was constantly united with God; cf. Scholem, *Les Origines de la Kabbale*, p. 321 n. 188.

119. Compare R. 'Ezra's view of the suffering in the exile as a substitute for living in the Land of Israel; there, the "atoning altar" of suffering is mentioned. See Scholem, "A New

Document," pp. 161–162, and Idel, "Some Opposing Conceptions of the Land of Israel in Medieval Jewish Thought" (forthcoming).

120. In *'Avodat ha-Kodesh*, the version is a longer one:

"בשם ית' מתוך דבוק המחשבה בעשר הספירות"

that is, " . . . to God, out of the cleaving of the thought to the ten Sefirot." Therefore, according to this version, there is a sequel of cleavings: to the letters of the great name, to the Sefirot and the God, by the intermediacy of his ten manifestations.

121. Psalms 92:2.

122. *iḥudan;* in *'Avodat ha-Kodesh* the version is *kayamot temidot*, namely, "everlasting and continuing," which fits the phrase *temidy nimraẓ* in the passage from ibn Gabbay quoted below.

123. Cleaving to the Tetragrammaton is mentioned by R. Abraham ibn 'Ezra in his *Commentary to Exod. 3:15*; he also attributes wondrous features to this cleaving. On cleaving to the Tetragrammaton, see n. 57 above, n. 134 below.

124. Compare to R. 'Ezra's statement:

"לפי שיודע לייחד שם המיוחד הוא כאלו בונה פלטין של מעלה ושל מטה"

Commentary on the Song of Songs; Chavel, *Kitvey ha-Ramban*, 2:521; and see also ibid., p. 523. On p. 526, the Kabbalist explicitly compares the divine name to the house, presumably the intent being to the Temple:

". . . אם תרע לייחד שם המיוחד . . . שמצינו שנקרא שמו של הקב"ה בית, שנאמר
"ה' בחכמה יבנה בית, לביתך נאוה קודש."

Compare also to R. 'Azriel in Scholem, "Seridim," p. 219. See also Chap. VIII, the quotation from *Sefer Yesod 'Olam* of R. Abraham of Eskira on building and theurgy, and R. Meir ibn Gabbay, *Tola'at Ya'akov*, fol. 4a.

125. As the Kabbalists stressed time and again, the sacrifices were dedicated solely to the Tetragrammaton, but not to the divine name Elohim. See Vajda, *Le Commentaire d'Ezra de Gérone*, pp. 382–385.

126. Ibid., pp. 395ff.

127. Compare the aforecited text of R. 'Azriel on the cleaving of the priest's soul before the performance of the act of sacrifice.

128. See the *Commentary on the Song of Songs*, pp. 521–522:

ולשון עבודה הו' לכבוש המחשבה הטהורה בעסקי העולם הבא ולהביא בשעבוד הכוונה. . . ואמת רבינו החסיד ז"ל עיקר עבודת המשכילים וחושבי שמו ובו תדבקון וזה כלל גדול שבתורה, לתפלה ולברכות, להסכם מחשבתו באמונתו כאלו דבקה למעלה, לחבר את השם באותיותיו ולכלול בו עשר ספירות כשלהבת קשורה בגחלת, בפיו יזכרנו בכינויו, ובלבבו יחברנו בבנינו ובכתבו.

See also R. 'Azriel's *Commentary on the Talmudic Aggadot*, p. 16, and Gabrielle Sed-Rajna, *Commentaire sur la liturgie quotidienne de R. Azriel de Gérone* (Leiden, 1974), pp. 10–11.

129. In the original, *maskilim.*

130. Mal. 3:16.

131. Namely the Sefirot; the relationship between the letters of the Tetragrammaton and the ten Sefirot was evident already in one of the earliest Kabbalistic texts: the "Kabbalah" of R. Jacob ha-Nazir of Lunel. See Scholem, *Reshit ha-Kabbalah*, pp. 73–74.

132. *Kevushah*, namely, dedicated to matters of the supernal world: see R. Isaac's text, n. 128 above.

133. This metaphor occurs several times in Kabbalistic and Ḥasidic descriptions of mystical experience, where it assumes a positive significance; see, for example, the Abulafian text extant in MS Sassoon, 56, p. 33:

"שישוב כל ענף לשרשו וידבק בו וכל רוחני לנפשו ויקשר עמו והיה המשכן אחד"

See also Chap. IV, n. 85.

134. *'Avodat ha-Kodesh*, II, 6 fol. 29a, immediately before the anonymous text quoted above:

... ועל זה הדרך שרמז הרב החסיד ז"ל... באמרו עיקר עבודת המשכילים וחושבי שמו ובו הדבקון אשר הכוונה באמרו ז"ל וחושבי שמו לרמוז על הכוונה הראויה בעבודה והוא שהעבודה צריך לחשוב ולכוין בעבודתו ליחד את השם הגדול ולחברו באותיות ולכללן בו כל המעלה וליחדם במחשבתו עד אין סוף. ואמרו: "ובו תדבקון" לרמוז על המחשבה שתהיה פנויה טהרה מכל דבר כבושה, דבקה למעלה דבוק תמידי נמרץ ליחד הענפים בשרש בלי שום פירוד ובזה מיחד דבק השם הגדול.

On "cleaving to the great name" compare nn. 57 and 123 above; compare also Goetschel, *Meir ibn Gabbay*, pp. 310–311.

135. Idel, "Sefirot above Sefirot," pp. 278–280.

136. Ibid, p. 280.

137. In Hebrew, *middah* implies "measure" and hence limitation.

138. Compare above, the mentioning of morning and evening in the anonymous text.

139. In Hebrew *'aleph* represents also "unity."

140. In Hebrew, it stands for "eight."

141. See n. 123 above.

142. Compare the references cited in Idel, "Sefirot above Sefirot," pp. 278–280.

143. See Altmann, *Faces of Judaism*, pp. 87–88.

144. *Shoshan 'Edut*, printed by Scholem, "Two Treatises of R. Moshe de Leon," p. 354:

צריך האדם להיותו ברוגמא של מעלה כענין אמרו "ובו תדבק" וכתיב "והלכת בדרכיו" באותו דוגמא ממש.

145. Deut. 10:20.

146. Deut. 28:9.

147. See especially *Shoshan 'Edut* (n. 144 above), p. 355:

ואתה צריך להיות בדוגמא אחת כמותו והואיל והדבר כך צריך האדם להתדמות אליו בכל אשר יפנה, ישכיל היאך יתקרב קורבתו לנגדו ויתדמה.

148. See Liebes, "The Messiah of the *Zohar*," pp. 175–181. See also above, Chap. III, par. V, on "Devekut qua Mediation."

149. See Idel, "Types of Redemptive Activities," pp. 269–273.

150. *Meẓudat David*, fol. 2b:

כשהאדם מיחד בלב שלם ובכוונה שלימה אז נקשרת ונדבקת נפשו באהבת הקב"ה כד"א שויתי ה' לנגדי תמיד כי מימינו בל אמוט, כמו שאיני שוכח ימיני כך איני שוכח אהבתו, כי לעולם הוא נגדי. ודע כי האוהב את ד' אהבה שלימה גורם אהבה למעלה, והמידות פניהם איש אל אחיו בתשוקה ואהבה.

Compare, however, ibid., fol. 3c–d, where the *devekut* experienced is not connected to any theurgical activity.

151. Presumably an allusion to the *Shekhinah*.

152. Psalms 16:8. This verse was fully exploited by Jewish mystics (see, for example, Chap. V, n. 244) and is a subject deserving of a separate monograph. See above, n. 97.

153. Previously on this page, the phrase refers to the two cherubim, or to the "great love"—the

bridegroom or *Tiferet*—and the "love of the world"—the bride or *Malkhut*; see immedately below.

154. Fol. 2b:

"דע כי המקשר נפשו באהבת יוצרו מקשר אהבת עולם באהבה רבה."

155. Vital, *Sha'ar ha-Mizvot*, per. *Va-'etḥanan*, p. 78, and Luria's *Hanhagot*; cf. Fine, *Safed Spirituality*, p. 68; Jacob Ẓemaḥ's *Nagid u-Meẓaveh* (Lemberg, 1863), fol. 19b–20a. Compare also to R. Ẓevi Hirsch of Zhidachov, *'Ateret Ẓevi*, II, fol. 17c, where the oscillation between the ideal of mystical union and theurgical activity is obvious. See also *'Eẓ Ḥayyim, Sha'ar ha-Kelalim*, Chap. I, where the goal of the creation of the world is to create creatures that will know God and become as a "chariot" to him in order to cleave to him. However, I doubt if Vital refers here to *unio mystica*; I assume that he implies that the Divinity will dwell in the mystic. See also Tishby, *The Doctrine of Evil*, pp. 112–134, who describes at length the goal of human activity in Lurianic Kabbalah as theurgical operation, without mentioning—correctly, in my opinion—the ideal of *devekut*, and R. Nathan Shapira's discussion referred to in n. 114 above.

156. Scholem, *Be 'Iqvoth Mashiaḥ*, p. 104:

נשמת המלך המשיח באתדבק באילנא דחי, דשליט בכל גנזי אבוי עביד תקונים בכל בחינות ומציאות . . . והכל תיקון לגביה מכח התקשרותו באילנא דחיי.

On the context of this quotation, see Scholem *Sabbatai Ṣevi*, pp. 809–810.

157. Ibid, p. 811.

158. On the son who is the master of the treasures of the father as a description of a high mystical state, see Yehudah Liebes, "R. Naḥman of Bratslav's *Hatikkun Hakkelali* and His Attitude toward Sabbatianism" (in Hebrew), *Ẓion* 44 (1980): 213–214.

159. On *unio mystica*, see Chap. IV; on *devekut* as a prerequisite for the achievement of various revelatory phenomena, see Vital's *Sha'arey Kedushah*, Introduction.

160. Quoted by his disciple R. Meshulam Phoebus of Zbaraz, *Yosher Divrey Emet*, fol. 122a:

שנסתר נקרא דבר שאין אדם יכול להבינו לחבירו כמו הטעם של המאכל אי אפשר לספר האדם שלא טעם זה מעולם, ואי אפשר לפרש לו בדיבור איך ומה ונקרא זה דבר סתר, כך ענין אהבת הבורא ויראתו ית' אי אפשר לפרש לחבירו איך היא האהבה בלב וזה נקרא נסתר. אבל מה שהם קוראים נסתר חכמת הקבלה, האיך הוא נסתר, הלא כל מי שרוצה ללמוד הספר לפניו ואם אינו מבין הוא עם הארץ, ולפני איש כזה גמרא ותוספות גם כן נקרא נסתר, אלא ענין הנסתרות שבכל הזוהר וכתבי האר"י ז"ל הכל בנויים על פי דביקות הבורא למי שזוכה להדבק ולהיות צופה במרכבה העליונה כמו האר"י זלה"ה. דהוי נהירין ליה שבילין דרקיע והיה מהלך בהם תמיד בעיני שכלו, כמו הארבעה חכמים שנכנסו לפרדס.

See a slightly different version in *Likkutey Keter Shem Tov*, printed in *Shivḥey ha-Besht*, ed. B. Mintz (Jerusalem, 1969), pp. 208–209.

161. This term signifies regularly "hidden," "concealed," "esoteric," and is part of the phrase *ḥokhmat ha-nistar*: "esoteric lore" or Kabbalah. I left it untranslated, since R. Menaḥem Mendel gave it a peculiar turn.

162. The comparison of a mystical experience to the ineffable savior is common mainly among the Sufis. In Jewish thought, it occurs in R. Yehudah ha-Levi's *Kuzari*, and in R. Yoḥanan Alemanno's writings.

163. *"Devekut ha-Bore'"*; in *Likkutey Keter Shem Tov, "devekut ha-'Elohut."* Compare the quotation from R. Menaḥem of Lonzano, cited by R. Simḥah Bunim of Przysucha, *Torat Simḥah*, in

Simḥat Yisrael (Pieterkov, 1910), fol. 62b:
שכל שאינו מופשט מגשמיות אינו מבין אפי' נקודה אחת מזוה"ק ונדמה להם שיורעים.
Compare to the tradition quoted in the name of the Besht, Chap. III, n. 182.

164. Cf. *Berakhot* 58b. On the connection between one of the four sages who ascended to *Pardes* and familiarity with the paths of the firmament, see Schäfer, *Synopse*, par. 873, p. 287.

165. On the spiritualization of the ascent to *Pardes*, see Chap. V, sec. II.

166. This view, characteristic of the ecstatic Kabbalah and of Ḥasidism, was expanded by Scholem to the Kabbalah in general, underrating thereby the importance of theurgical activity in the theurgical-theosophical Kabbalah; see *Sabbatai Ṣevi*, p. 15. In this discussion, Scholem uses the phrase "total *debequth*" as one of the two aims of "contemplative Kabbalism," thereby implying *unio mystica* as a paramount goal of the Kabbalah! See, however, his rejection of *unio mystica* as compatible to Kabbalah in the following chapter.

CHAPTER 4

1. *The Evolution of Theology in the Greek Philosophers* (Glasgow, 1904), 2:214.
2. Ibid.
3. *Major Trends*, pp. 122–123. Compare also his *The Messianic Idea*, p. 227; *Kabbalah*, p. 176. See, however, Scholem's views referred to in Chap. III, n. 158, above.
4. See, for example, N. Rotenstreich, "Symbolism and Transcendence: On Some Philosophical Aspects of Gershom Scholem's Opus," *Review of Metaphysics* 31 (1977–78): 610–614; R. J. Zwi Werblowsky, "Some Psychological Aspects of Kabbalah," *Harvest* 3 (1956): 78; J. Ben-Shlomo, in *Gershom Scholem—The Man and His Opus* (in Hebrew) (Jerusalem, 1983) p. 21; or Fine, *Safed Spirituality*, p. 21.
5. Stace, *Mysticism and Philosophy*, pp. 106–107, 228–229; R. C. Zaehner, *At Sundry Times* (London, 1958), p. 171; Zaehner, *Hindu and Muslim Mysticism*, p. 2; Katz, "Language, Epistemology, and Mysticism," pp. 34–35; Geoffrey Parrinder, *Mysticism in the World's Religions* (London, 1976), p. 119.
6. *Mysticism and Philosophy*, p. 158. See his entire discussion there on Buber's nonunitive self-interpretation of a mystical experience as inadequate, because of the "pressure of the Jewish tradition against the concept of union" (p. 157). Stace's ingenuous interpretation notwithstanding, in Buber's case we witness a shift from his previous ecstatic period, when he underwent the experience of union, to the dialogical phase, when his interpretation was committed to writing.
7. *A Social and Religious History of the Jews* (New York, 1958), 8:112–113.
8. Tishby, *The Wisdom of the Zohar*, 2:288–290; Gottlieb, *Studies*, pp. 237–238; Pachter, "The Concept of Devekut," pp. 224–225; Louis Jacobs, "The Doctrine of the 'Divine Spark' in Man in Jewish Sources," in *Rationalism, Judaism, Universalism, In Memory of Leon Roth* (New York, 1966), pp. 80–89.
9. See *Les Origines de la Kabbale*, p. 320 n. 184; see also Katz, "Language, Epistemology and Mysticism," p. 69 n. 31a.
10. Scholem, "Mysticism and Society," *Diogenes* 58 (1967): 16: *Devekut*, he asserts, "means literally 'cleaving' or 'adhering' to God. . . . The necessity to compromise with medieval Jewish theology dictated this terminology, not the act itself, which may or may not

include a state of mystical union." See also Katz, "Language, Epistemology, and Mysticism," pp. 35–36.

11. See Idel, "Abraham Abulafia and *Unio Mystica*," n. 11; Israel Efros, "Some Aspects of Yehuda Halevi's Mysticism," *Studies in Medieval Jewish Philosophy* (New York and London, 1974), pp. 146–148.
12. This is obviously the situation in the case of Abulafia; see Idel, ibid.
13. See Idel, "Enoch Is Metatron."
14. See Duncan B. Macdonald, *The Religious Attitude and Life in Islam* (Chicago, 1909), p. 187; Geoffrey Parrinder, *Worship in the World's Religions* (Totowa, N.J., 1974), p. 181; and especially Falaturi in his essay, "How Can a Muslim Experience God Given Islam's Radical Monotheism?" in A. Schimmel and A. Falaturi, eds., *We Believe in One God: The Experience of God in Christianity and Islam* (New York, 1979), p. 85: "Unio mystica . . . can occur precisely because of Islam's radical monotheism."
15. *Sitrey Torah*, MS Paris BN 774, fol. 140a and fol. 171b.
16. On the philosophical sources of this phrase, see Idel, "Abraham Abulafia and *Unio Mystica*," nn. 19–23.
17. MS Paris BN 774, fol. 155a.
18. See above (Chap. III, n. 74) for the text of R. Isaac of Acre's *'Oẓar Ḥayyim*, where a similar expression is to be found, and n. 61 below.
19. On immortality as deification, see W. R. Inge, *Christian Mysticism* (London, 1925), pp. 357–358; Abulafia's stand would confirm Inge's category of deification through transformation (see ibid., p. 365 and W. R. Inge's *Mysticism in Religion* [Chicago, 1948], p. 46).
20. See *The Messianic Idea in Judaism*, pp. 203–227; *Kabbalah*, pp. 174–176.
21. See *Major Trends*, pp. 140–141, where Scholem has translated a crucial passage wherein Abulafia asserts that "he is so intimately adhering to Him that he cannot by any means be separated from Him, for he is He." Scholem, after quoting this text, maintains that "complete identification is neither achieved nor intended." Indeeed, I cannot but wonder at Scholem's self-confidence that permitted him to indicate that Abulafia was not interested in mystical identification. I confine my analysis to the textual evidence, which, even in Scholem's rendering is sufficient to refute this interpretation. Interestingly enough, Stace, *Mysticism and Philosophy*, p. 116, explicitly indicates the unitive nature of the text, notwithstanding his statement, ibid., p. 158, referred to in n. 6 above.
22. *Guide* II, p. 40.
23. See Idel, "Abraham Abulafia and *Unio Mystica*," nn. 46, 72.
24. MS Jerusalem 8° 148 fol. 56a:

    הנה הוא יוד בעולם הזה אשר קבל כח מהכל וכולל הכל, כדמות היוד בספירות, הנה אם כן אין בין זו היו״ד ובין זו היו״ד אלא כמלא הנימא כלומ׳ ענין דק קטן מאד מצד הרוחניות והוא מלוי יוד אחרת . . . וזהו סוד ובו תדבקו דבוק יוד עם יוד להשלים הגלגל.

    Compare to Abulafia's view in his *Sitrey Torah* MS Paris BN 774, fol. 172a, where two decades are also referred to in connection with the structure of man. This view is ancient: see Idel, "The Image of Man," pp. 46–47, and the midrashic interpretations of Gen. 2:7 on the two "iods" of "wa-yiẓer." See, for example, "Alphabet of R. 'Akiva," Wertheimer, ed., *Batey Midrashot*, 2:412; this Midrash was used also by Abraham Abulafia in his own commentary on his *Sefer ha-Ḥayyim*, MS München 285, fol. 23b, where two *iods* are referred to as necessary for the perfection of man; see also Abulafia's "Vezot li-Yihudah"; Jellinek, *Auswahl*, p. 20; and Chap. VI.

25. Jer. 23:5.
26. MS Jerusalem 8° 148, fol. 55a:

כי יוד אשר היא חצי גלגל... וזהו ענין האדם התחתון יתעלה ונעשה עליון אדם שעל הכסא וזה שמו אשר יקראו י״י צדקנו.

See also ibid., 39a:

וזהו ענין האדם התחתון שנתעלה ונעשה אדם שעל הכסא בכח הש׳.

On yod as a semicircle, see also ibid., fol. 35a:

כי היוד... מצטיירת כצורת חצי גלגל בתחתוני׳ עד היותו גלגל שלם בעליונים.

and fol. 35b. Compare also to Abulafia's view, n. 28 below. On the perfect man as sitting on the throne, see Abraham Abulafia's *'Imrey Shefer*, MS Paris 777, p. 48.

27. See R. Abraham ibn 'Ezra, *Sefer ha-Shem*, Chap. III, and so on.
28. See also MS Jerusalem 8° 148, fol. 57a, where the soul is described as ascending and reaching the degree of *ha-Shem Ẓeva'ot*:

והנה בהיותו נדבק בו... ואז תהיה הנפש בדמות מראה... ותעלה אל מעלת השם צבאות.

Compare to Abulafia's *'Or ha-Sekhel*, MS Vatican 233, fol. 115a, where the *unio mystica* between the human intellectual and divine intellectual loves is portrayed as the union of *'EḤAD* = 1, whose numerical value is 13, with *'EḤAD*, thus 26, which is equivalent to the numerical value of the Tetragrammaton. Therefore, the "human existence" is included in the divine name; see also n. 26 above.

29. MS Oxford 1649, fol. 206a:

בני אתה אני היום ילדתיך. וכן ראו עתה כי אני אני הוא והסוד הוא דבוק הכח הוא הכח האלהי העליון הנקרא גלגל הנבואה, עם הכח האנושי וכן אמרו אנכי אנכי.

Compare to Abu Yazid al-Bistami's formulation, discussed by Zaehner, *Hindu and Muslim Mysticism*, pp. 113–114; Idel, "Abraham Abulafia and *Unio Mystica*"; and cf. Annemarie Schimmel, *As through a Veil: Mystical Poetry in Islam* (New York, 1982), p. 219 n. 42.

30. Psalms 2:7. The use of this verse, so crucial to Christian theology and mysticism, may have something to do with Christian influence.
31. Deut. 32:39.
32. Jer. 43:11.
33. MS Jerusalem 8° 148, fol. 54a:

כי נפש הכל נפש אחת היא ונחלקה מצד חילוק החומר לשנים

34. Compare ibn Rushd's view: "the soul is closely similar to light; light is divided by the division of illuminated bodies, and is unified when the bodies are annihilated, and the same relation holds between soul and bodies" (*Tahafut al-Tahafut*, trans. S. Van der Berg [London, 1954], 1:16). See also n. 62 below.
35. It seems that the identification of the soul of the highest sphere with the universal soul was not so obvious to the anonymous Kabbalist; see also the previous note.

שכל הנפשות הטבעיות באות מנפש גלגל ערבות והיא הרוחנית והדקה מכל נפשות העולם... אם כן אפשר לצייר בשום דרך שנפש האדם תתעלה ותפעל אפי׳ בנפש ערבות לשנות הטבעיות...

שנפש העולם העליון הגלגלי בשורש, ר״ל בערבות... וכמדומה לי שקורין לה הפילוסופי׳ נפש הכל.

36. *Symposium*, 189a.

37. See Hunain ibn Isaac's *Musarey ha-Philosophim*, ed. A. Loewental (Frankfurt, 1896), pp. 38–39.

38. See Sa'adia's *Emunot we-Deot*, vol. 10, Chap. 7. On the penetration of this view into early Kabbalah, see Idel, "Sefirot above Sefirot," p. 268 n. 150; Ze'ev Gries, "From Mythos to Ethos—Contributions to the Thought of R. Abraham of Kalisk," *Nation and History*, ed. S. Ettinger (in Hebrew) (Jerusalem, 1984), 2: 120–123.

39. *Sefer Sha'arey Ẓedek* was explicitly mentioned by de Vidas's master, Cordovero; see Idel, "*Hitbodedut* as Concentration," p. 69 and n. 214.

40. *Reshit Ḥokhmah*, Gate of Love, Chap. 3:
פלגא דגופא״... ובהתייחד חלק הנשמה התחתונה עמ׳ ב׳ החלקים נתייחדו ונעשו א׳.

41. See Schatz-Uffenheimer, *Maggid Devarav Le-Ya'akov*, pp. 38–39:
עשה לך שתי חצוצרות כסף פ׳ שתי חצי צורות ע״ד על הכסא דמות כמראה אדם עליו ממעלה כי האדם הוא רק דל״ת מ״ם והדיבור שורה בו וכשמתדבק בהקב״ה שהוא אלופו של עולם נעשה אדם... ואדם צריך לפרוש א״ע מכל גשמיות כ״כ עד שיעלה דרך כל העולמות ויהא אחדות עם הקב״ה עד שיבוטל ממציאות ואז יקרא אדם.
For parallels to this text in Ḥasidic literature, see Schatz-Uffenheimer, *Quietistic Elements*, p. 128 n. 29. See also Scholem, *The Messianic Idea in Judaism*, pp. 226–227; Tishby, *The Wisdom of the Zohar*, 2:290 n. 70, who proposes seeing the source of this interpretation in R. Elijah de Vidas's text analyzed above.

42. Num. 10:2.

43. Ezek. 1:26. It is important to emphasize that his verse was understood by a distinguished disciple of the Great Maggid as symbolizing the deep affinity between the human and the Divine; according to R. Abraham Joshua Heschel of Apt, the man on the chariot is identical with the plene spelling of the Tetragrammaton and, at the same time, stems from the lower man, who generates or makes God by his performance of the commandments. This interpretation ostensibly reduces, or even obliterates, the distance between God and man.
דע מה למעלה ממך: מה בגימ׳ אדם, היינו שלמעלה על הכסא-הוא ממך, ר״ל ע״י קיום התורה ומצותיה אנו עושין כביכול להבורא.
Quoted by R. Ẓevi Hirsch of Zhidachov, *'Aṭeret Ẓevi* part III, fol. 25a, peris. *'Aḥarey Mot;* cf. also Chap. VIII.

44. Shortly beforehand the Maggid referred to the descending contractions that permitted a union of God to man. Here, man returns to his origin, ascending the *scala contemplationis*, which implies gradual obliterations of contractions, culminating in annihilation of the human existence. See also n. 43 above.

45. *Dibbur*; I prefer the version found in *'Or ha-Torah*, p. 73: *dibbur Malkhut*, namely, "speech" and "Malkhut," which obviously stands for the letters *D* and *M* that form parts of the word *'ADaM*. Thence, it seems that "speech" may represent here the Sefirah of *Tiferet*; compare, however, Schatz-Uffenheimer's remark in her edition of *Maggid Devarav Le-Ya'akov.* My interpretation turns *'ADaM* into a symbol for three aspects in Godhead: the *'A*—master of the universe, that is, the transcendent aspect, and two immanent aspects—*Malkhut* and *Tiferet*.

46. *DaM* in Hebrew is "blood."

47. The Maggid uses a pun: *'Aluf* is both master and champion but also close to *'Aleph*, the principle of the world. Compare also to R. Levi Isaac of Berdichev's discussion in *Kedushat*

ha-Levi, fol. 64b–c, where the reference to *'Aleph* is explicit. The source is apparently *Ḥagigah* 16a.

48. See *Sod Bat Sheva*, MS München 131, fol. 11a:

לפי שאין עושים מלמעלה חצי צורה לעולם אלא צורה שלמה... צורת זכר וצורת נקבה בראם.

This text was printed in *Likkutey Shikhehah u-feah* (Ferrara, 1556), which could have influenced the Great Maggid's interpretation of *ḥaẓoẓerot* directly or indirectly.

49. They stand respectively for the *Shekhinah* and for God himself—presumably *Tiferet*—as he points out shortly before.

50. *Eḥad el eḥad*—literally "one to one," an expression reminiscent of Plotinus' famous "monos pro monon."

51. *Degel Maḥaneh Ephraim*, p. 194:

בחצוצרות היינו בחצי צורות, היינו צער השכינה כביכול שיש פירוד למעלה והם שני חצי צורות שם ושמים המתגעגעים להתקרב ולהתייחד אחד אל אחד אזי בודאי אם כה תעשו באמת אזי ונזכרתם לפני ה' אלקיכם ונושעתם.

For a theosophical interpretation of the two trumpets as symbolizing the Sefirot *Tiferet* (or *Yesod*) and *Malkhut*, see the text of R. Joseph of Hamadan, quoted in Altmann, "The Question of Authorship," p. 410.

52. I doubt whether Tishby's hypothesis (n. 41 above) on the influence of de Vidas's *Reshit Ḥokhmah* passage discussed above on the Great Maggid is plausible, as the Safedian Kabbalist did not mention the phrase "two halves of forms" which occurs in Gikatilla. See n. 48 above.

53. *The Messianic Idea in Judaism*, pp. 226–227.

54. See below my discussion of R. Levi Isaac of Berdichev's interpretation of mystical poverty and spiritual death.

55. Compare below, n. 84, the text of R. Yeḥiel Mikhael of Zloczow. Commonly, self-annihilation follows union, as *fana'* precedes *baqa'* in Sufic texts. Compare also to R. Levi Isaac of Berdichev, *Kedushat ha-Levi*, fol. 60a:

זה האדם כשהוא במדריגה זו שיש לו עזר ה' להסתכל על האין, אז השכל שלו בטל במציאות.

On self-annihilation in early Ḥasidism and its sources in Kabbalah, see Bezalel Safran, "On Considering One's Self as Nothing: Towards the History of a Ḥasidic Term," an unpublished paper presented at a symposium of eighteenth-century Jewish thought at Harvard University, 1984.

56. *Rosh ha-Shanah* 31a, *Sanhedrin* 97a.

57. *'Or ha-'Emet*, fol. 6b:

וחד חרוב-כשבא הכל לאחדות, חרוב ונתבטל העולם ממציאות.

See also R. Isaac Yehudah Yeḥiel of Komarno, *Noẓer Ḥesed* (Jerusalem, 1982), p. 112.

58. *'Or ha-Torah*, p. 73:

כשיתדבקו יחד נעשה צורה שלמה... וכ"א [וכל אחד] בעצמו אינו בשלימות ואינו רק חצי צורה ושניהם ביחד הוי צורה שלימה.

59. Compare, however, R. Shmuel Shmelke of Nikelsburg's *Divrey Shmuel* (Jerusalem, 1974), pp. 90–91. There, the cleaving of two Yods stands for the cleaving of the human soul to her supernal source; the author was a disciple of the Great Maggid.

60. *Me'or 'Eynaim*, p. 11:

לקרב את עצמו, עם חלק אלוהות ששוכן בתוכו, לשורש הכל, בו ית', ונעשה דבוק בדביקות אלוהותו ית' ע"י שנתאחד החלק בהכל, שהוא א"ס. ונמצא שאור קדושתו של א"ס מופיע בתוכו מאחר שהחלק דבוק לשורשו . . .

61. On the transformation of the part in all, see above note 18. This type of expression occurs also in R. Ẓadok ha-Cohen of Lublin, *Siḥat Mal'akhey ha-Sharet* (Lublin, 1927), fol. 24d: הרגשת התאחדות הגמור ודביקות החלק בהכל וכל הכחות נכללים במקורם ומתייחדים בו. Compare also ibid., fol. 24bc.

62. For the return of the soul to her root and her union with it, see a passage of R. Moses Narboni, a mystically biased philosopher of the fourteenth century, who indicated that "when our soul departs, it returns to its root and becomes united with it": *The Epistle on the Possibility of Conjunction with the Active Intellect by ibn Rushd with the Commentary of Moses Narboni*, ed. Kalman P. Bland (New York, 1982/5742), p. 23 (Hebrew part, p. 3). It may be significant that, shortly before, Narboni quoted a pseudo-Platonic view on the nature of the soul, which becomes undifferentiated after the removal of the bodies. See Bland, p. 113 n. 4. The Hebrew source of Narboni uses the terms *hit'aḥed* and *shoresh*, like the Ḥasidic text. See also R. Yehudah Albotini's *Sullam ha-'Aliyah*, printed by Scholem, *CCCH*, p. 228.

63. *Hindu and Muslim Mysticism*, p. 46. See also pp. 51–52, 102. See also Paul Deussen, *The System of the Vedanta* (New York, 1973), pp. 434–435; Stace, *Mysticism and Philosophy*, pp. 313–315.

64. See Annemarie Schimmel, *Mystical Dimensions of Islam* (Chapel Hill, N.C., 1978), p. 284; Farid ud-Din Attar, *The Conference of the Birds* (Shambhala, Colo., 1971), p. 43; and the elaborate discussion of Robert E. Lerner, "The Image of Mixed Liquids in Late Medieval Mystical Thought," *Church History* 40 (1971): 397–411. For the Aristotelian source of this image, see Jean Pepin, "Stilla aqvae modica multo infusa vino . . . " in *Divinitas*, vol. 2, *Miscellania André Combés* (Rome, 1967), pp. 331–375. Interestingly, here an additional Aristotelian issue served as an expression of mystical union.

65. *'Oẓar Ḥayyim*, MS Moscow-Günzburg 775, fol. 111a: תרבק בשכל האלוהית והוא ידבק בה . . . ונעשית היא והשכל דבר אחד כשופך כד מים במעין נובע שנעשה הכל אחד וזהו סוד כוונת רז"ל באומרם חנוך הוא מטטרון הרי זה סוד אש אוכלת אש.

66. I follow Gottlieb's interpretation of this text as referring to soul and divine intellect, the latter signifying God himself. See *Studies*, p. 237 n. 11.

67. See ibid, p. 237 n. 13. See Idel, "Abraham Abulafia and *Unio Mystica*," n. 54.

68. The motif of sinking recurs in writings written by Jewish Oriental authors or persons who arrived there. I suppose it to be of Sufic origin; see Idel, "Prophetic Kabbala and the Land of Israel," pp. 105, 108 n. 23, and below Chap. V, n. 35.

69. *'Oẓar Ḥayyim*, MS Moscow-Günzburg 775, fol. 161b: כאשר אמ' מרע"ה: הראני נא את כבודך, את המות בקש, למען ישלול נפשו מחיצת היכלה, המבדיל בינה ובין האור האלוהי המופלא, אשר היתה מתעוררת לראות ומפני היות עדיין ישראל צריכין לו לא רצה הקב"ה שתצא נפשו מן היכלה למען תשיג את אורו זה . . . ועתה אתה בני השתדל לראו' אור עליון כי ודאי הכנסתיך בים אוקיינוס המקיף את העולם והשמר לך ושמור נפשך מאד מהביט ולבך מהרהר, פן תטבע, וההשתדלות לראות ולהנצל מהטביעה . . . תראה נפשך אור אלוהי' ודאי תדבק בו והיא יושבת בהיכלה.

70. Exod. 33:18.

71. A recurrent image for the body. Compare to the different usages of related terms, like *castellum*, in Christian mysticism in order to refer to the innermost spiritual element of the soul; cf. R. C. Petry, ed., *Late Medieval Mysticism* (Philadelphia, 1957), p. 173 n. 4.

72. *Yam ha-'Okiyanos;* see especially *'Oẓar Ḥayyim*, MS Moscow-Günzburg 775, fol. 170a–b, where the exclamation *Mayyim Mayyim*, namely "Water, Water," which R. 'Akiva warns his companions not to exclaim on the moment of their arrival to the supernal realm, is interpreted by R. Isaac of Acre as referring to the "secret of Godhead." For the recurrence of the metaphor of ocean for God, to whom all returns, see ibn 'Arabi's material cited by Schimmel, *As through a Veil*, pp. 61–62, 231. It is pertinent to recall the fact that R. Isaac of Acre had studied in the vicinity of the most important center of ibn 'Arabi's thought—Damascus. See Idel, "Prophetic Kabbalah and the Land of Israel," pp. 104–106.

73. An overt allusion to the highest aspect of the Godhead: see R. Isaac's passage quoted above from *'Oẓar Ḥayyim*, MS Moscow-Günzburg 775, fol. 233b.

74. *Le-hishtake'a* recurs in *'Oẓar Ḥayyim* as a term for focusing one's interest upon a peculiar subject, be it material or intellectual. See, for example, fol. 2b–3a.

75. Compare *'Oẓar Ḥayyim*, MS Moscow-Günzburg 775, fol. 16a, where Moses describes his will to leave the material world as connected to the feature of his soul "to sink (*le-hishtake'a*) and ardently desire your secret." Shortly before, Moses also requests the cleaving to God as well as his own death (see fol. 15b–16a).

76. See Gottlieb, *Studies*, pp. 242–243.

77. On ecstatic death, see Idel, "Music and Prophetic Kabbalah," p. 163 and n. 50. See also *'Oẓar Ḥayyim*, MS Moscow-Günzburg 775, fol. 87a.

78. Cf. the translation of Scholem, *Major Trends*, p. 151. This passage is a perfect example of what Lasky called "intensity ecstasies": cf. *Ecstasy* (New York, 1968), pp. 19, 47–56. Compare the description of "dhikr" by the Sufi Najm Kobra, as quoted by Henry Corbin, *The Man of Light in Iranian Sufism* (London, 1978), p. 76: "When the dhikr is immersed in the heart, the heart is then sensed as though it were itself a well and the dhikr a pail lowered into it to draw up water."

79. The addition within the brackets is Scholem's.

80. See, however, Katz, "Language, Epistemology, and Mysticism," p. 41.

81. The milder form, that of the drop of wine and water, which does not convey a final fusion, is older in the pagan and Christian sources; see Lerner, "Image of Mixed Liquids," pp. 397–398, and Pepin, "Stilla aqvae," passim.

82. Lerner, "Image of Mixed Liquids," pp. 399–406.

83. On this Ḥasidic master, see Heschel, *The Circle of the Ba'al Shem Tov*, pp. 174–178.

84. See *Mayyim Rabbim*, fol. 15a:

הם מרבקים כל כוחותם במחשבתם בבורא ית"ש כמקדם. נמצא הם גדולים מאד כי הענף בא לשרשו והוא אחדות א' עם השורש. והשורש־א"ס. א"כ הענף גם כן אין סוף כי נתבטל במציאות כמשל טיפה אחת שנפלה לים הגדול ובאתה(!) לשרשה וא"כ היא אחת עם מי הים וא"א להכירה בפני עצמה כלל.

85. The terms *shoresh* and *'anaf* for *'Eiyn Sof* and soul often recur in the Great Maggid's teachings: see *Maggid Devarav le-Ya'akov*, pp. 125–26, 136, 198, and the passage from R. Naḥum of Chernobyl quoted above, n. 60. Interestingly, the image of the return of the branch to its roots was seen in a very negative way in the theosophical Kabbalah, where it

symbolized incestuous relationships. See also Chap. III, n. 113, and R. Reuven Horovitz's *Dudaim ha-Sadeh*, for example, fol. 52b.

86. See the discussion in n. 55 above on the passage of the Great Maggid, where annihilation is preceded by cleaving; compare also R. Menaḥem Mendel of Vitebsk, *Peri ha-'Areẓ*, fol. 19a.

87. Compare the image of drop and sea occurring in another work of the Great Maggid's milieu, *'Or ha-'Emet*, fol. 39c:

החשוב שנשמתו היא אבר מהשכינה כביכול כטפה מן הים.

" . . . one may consider his soul to be as if a limb of the *Shekhinah*, as a drop of the sea."

88. See below, n. 117, the quotation from R. Shneur Zalman of Lyady for the expression:

"ליחשב לדבר בפ"ע כלל"

Compare also the extreme unitive phrase used by another student of the great Maggid, R. Menaḥem Mendel of Vitebsk, *Peri ha-'Areẓ*, fol. 24b:

"הדביקות הגמור שהוא נכלל בא"ס ב"ה"

R. Menaḥem Mendel's view of *unio mystica* will be discussed elsewhere.

89. We know, however, also about R. Yeḥiel's own assiduous quest for worship of God with *devekut* in a state of complete isolation: cf. Heschel, *The Circle of the Ba'al Shem Tov*, p. 175.

90. *Nedarim* 64b.

91. *Tamid* 32a; for the Platonic background of this dictum, see Altmann and Stern, *Isaac Israeli*, pp. 201–202.

92. *Zikkaron Zot*, Peris. *Beha'alotekha* (Brooklyn, N.Y., 1981), fol. 29c:

א' הרוצה לחיות ימית עצמו. שמעתי מהרב מפינצק שיחי' שפי': הרוצה לחיות לא יחשוב עניני גופו כ"א תהיה מחשבתו בהבורא ב"ה דבוקה. וזה ימית עצמו, יסתלק מעצמו ממילא הוא חי כי הוא דבוק בחי החיים... מי שהוא עני עי"ד שהוא דבוק בהבורא ב"ה, הוא ודאי חשוב... כמת ונפטר ממיתה והי בהם.

Compare also de Vidas's quotation cited in Chap. III, n. 98.

93. The withdrawal from the influences of the body as a prerequisite for cleaving has Neoplatonic sources: see Altmann and Stern, *Isaac Israeli*, pp. 190–191, 214. See also Abraham Abulafia's text referred to by Scholem, *Major Trends*, p. 131, and Stace, *Mysticism and Philosophy*, pp. 116–117.

94. This phrase occurs also in R. Levi Isaac's *Kedushat ha-Levi*, fol. 64c, and in quotations from R. David of Mikhalaieff, a contemporary of R. Israel Ba'al Shem Tov, cited in the anonymous *Likkutey 'Amarim* printed in *Sefarim Kedoshim Meha-Ar"i ha-Kadosh* (New York, 1983), fol. 4a–4d. Interestingly, R. David also offers a parable for cleaving, wherein the poor person cleaves to "the life of lifes," although the unitive motif is not so radical as in R. Levi's. Several other references to this phrase occur in fragments of R. David printed at the end of *Ḥesed le-'Abraham* by R. Abraham ha-Mal'akh, and in R. Menaḥem Mendel of Vitebsk, *Peri ha-'Areẓ*, fol. 25b. The origin of the phrase seems to be the book *Shi'ur Komah;* see Cohen, *The Shi'ur Qomah: Texts and Recensions*, p. 165:

"חי החיים הראשון והאחרון"

95. In Hebrew *yistalek* may signify both dying and departure.

96. Compare Abulafia's view in *'Or ha-Sekhel* that the vitality disparate throughout the world will return to its source through dying for this world but being born for the next one: see Idel, "Abraham Abulafia and *Unio Mystica*," n. 38.

97. See also the view of R. Isaac Yehudah Safrin of Komarno that an uninterrupted drive of enthusiasm and cleaving may end with annihilation:

כי כל דבור ודבור חושק ומתלהב לחזור לשורשו להתדבק שם, לכך הנשמה מתלהבת תמיד להתדבק בשורשה למעלה, ע"י חשק ואור בתורת השם ועבודה. ואם היה מתלהב תמיד לאור עליון היה בטל ממציאותו כמו קודם עולם התיקון כטעם כי שם קברו את העם המתאוים

Netiv Miẓvotekha (New York, 1970), p. 22. The annihilative stage is here the effect, not the cause, of enthusiasm and cleaving.

98. See Altmann and Stern, *Isaac Israeli*, pp. 201–202.

99. *Tamid* 32a.

100. See also R. Shem Tov ibn Gaon's, R. Ḥayyim Vital's, and R. Eleazar Azikri's views in Idel, "*Hitbodedut* as Concentration," pp. 58, 80–81.

101. Compare the story on R. Dov Baer cited by R. Isaac Yehudah Safrin of Komarno, *Netiv Miẓvotekha*, p. 79, where the Great Maggid manifestly contrasts richness to wisdom, the latter being identified by him with *Ayn*—"annihilation."

102. Compare R. Benjamin of Zalozitch, *Torey Zahav* (Mohilev, 1816), fol. 56d:

כי אם מת הוא, כפגר מובס, רק הכל הוא מית' שמו.

103. On the problem of poverty as a precondition to, not as a culmination of, the mystical path, see Tishby, *The Wisdom of the Zohar*, 2:692–698.

104. Compare, however, the view of R. 'Akiva, that the imperative of "Live by them" refers to the world to come: cf. Heschel, *The Theology of Ancient Judaism*, 1:127–128.

105. *Regnum Deum Amantium*, Chap. 22; cf. Underhill, *Mysticism*, p. 425. See also below, n. 118. On "eating" mysticism in Christianity, see C. W. Bynum, "Fast, Feast and Flesh: The Religious Significance of Food to Medieval Women," *Representations* 11 (1985): 1–25.

106. Katz, "Language, Epistemology and Mysticism," p. 41.

107. Compare, however, ibid.

108. The view that the mystic has to delight God is pervasive in several Ḥasidic texts: see, for example, Chap. III, n. 81.

109. *'Oẓar Ḥayyim*, MS Moscow-Günzburg 775, fol. 111a:

אש אוכלת אש... וענין אכילה זו הוא הדבר הנבלע בחבירו ודבק באשתו לבשר אחד, כאשר החסיד המשכיל נותן לנפשו התעלות להדבק דיבוק נכון הסוד האלוהי אשר דבקה בו בולע אותה וזהו סוד ולא יבאו לראות כבאה"ו [כבלע את הקדש ומתו]...

110. For the verb *bl'* used in the sense of sexual union, see R. Isaac's *Mei'rat 'Eynaim*, p. 189; however, there the union is between the two cherubim, which symbolize the Sefirot *Tiferet* and *Malkhut*, not between the individual mystic and the Divinity. Therefore, we witness in *'Oẓar Ḥayyim* a psychologization of a theosophical process. Compare above, near n. 51 and below, Chap. VI, par. IV, 4.

111. See *'Oẓar Ḥayyim*, MS Moscow-Günzburg 775, fol 111a, where R. Isaac indicates that if the soul is not consumed by Divinity, she is consumed by hell: see also ibid., fol. 110ab. Therefore, although mystical death is not recommended as an end in itself, it still represents the better possibility for the mystic.

112. See also ibid., 111a:

וסוד אכילה זו הוא הדבקות הנכונה

Compare, however, the theurgical understanding of eating in R. Moses Cordovero's *'Or Yakar* (Jerusalem, 1983), 12:28:

"להיותו במעשה המצוה והתורה והכשרון, מזון ומאכל לשכינה."

113. Num. 4:20.

114. In Hebrew, *ke-bala'* may also be understood as "are swallowed."

115. See Gottlieb, *Studies*, p. 237.

116. *Seder ha-Tefillah* (Warsaw, 1866), part I, fol. 26a. Thanks are due to Professor M. Hallamish, who has drawn this passage to my attention.

117. Ibid:

כמו שאנו רואים כאשר ידבק האדם בה' והיה ערב לו תכלית הערבות והמתיקות עד שיבלע בתוך לבבו כל' כבליעת החיך הגשמי, והוא הרבקות האמיתית מאחר שנעשה עצם א' עם אלקות שנבלע בתוכו בלתי יפרד ליחשב לדבר בפ"ע כלל. וזהו ובו תרבקון ממש.

I will elaborate elsewhere on other expressions of *unio mystica* in R. Shneur Zalman of Lyady. For the appearance of *unio mystica* descriptions in the works of followers of this master, see Ra'hel Elior, *The Theory of Divinity of Ḥasidut Ḥabad: Second Generation* (in Hebrew) (Jerusalem, 1982), pp. 304–310.

118. Compare to Ruysbroeck's other description: "We feel that he has surrendered and given himself to our free desires, for us to savor him in every way that we could wish; and then we learn, in the truth of his vision, that all we savor, compared with what we still lack, is as a drop of water compared to the sea." Cf. Lerner, "Image of Mixed Liquids," p. 407. Therefore here the mystic savors God not as does the Ḥasidic master, where the situation is opposite; see also my discussion in Chap. III, n. 75, on the Great Maggid's view of the phylacteries. However, compare Ruysbroeck's discussion in *The Sparkling Stone*, Chap. III, in which God is described in an active way as a consuming fire; see P. C. Petry, ed., *Late Medieval Mysticism* (Philadelphia, 1957), pp. 295–296.

119. The Hebrew may also allow the passive rendering: "he [the man] will be consumed into his heart."

120. Compare above, n. 84, the text of R. Yeḥiel Mikhael of Zloczow, which certainly preceded R. Shneur Zalman's wording.

121. Deut. 15:5. In Hebrew the form *u-vo tidbakun* may also be understood as implying "into him you shall cleave."

122. See Louis Jacobs, "Eating as an Act of Worship in Ḥasidic Thought," in *Studies in Jewish Religious and Intellectual History Presented to Alexander Altmann* (University, Ala., 1979), pp. 157–166; Shlomo Pines, "Shi-ite Terms and Conceptions" in Judah Halevi's *Kuzari*," *Jerusalem Studies in Arabic and Islam* 2 (1980): 245–246.

123. *Kedushat ha-Levi*, fol. 102b:

שהצדיק מדבק עצמו בהאי"ן והוא בטל במציאות אז יעבוד את הבורא בבחי' כל הצדיקים כיון ששם אינו נראה כלל ח"ו שום חלוקות המדות... כי יש צדיק אשר הוא מדבק עצמו בהאי"ן ואעפ"כ חוזר לעצמותו אח"כ, אבל מרע"ה היה תמיד בטל במציאות מחמת כי מרע"ה הסתכל תמיד בגדלות הבורא יתברך ולא חזר לעצמותו כלל כידוע כי מרע"ה היה תמיד דבוק באי"ן ובבחינה הזאת היה בטל במציאות... כי כאשר מסתכל בהבורא ב"ה אז אין בו שום עצמותו (!) מחמת שהוא בטל במציאות... יסתכל באי"ן ויהיה בטל במציאות... ומשה היה תמיד דבוק באי"ן.

124. *Ben Beiti* (Przemislany, 1900), fol. 109d:

הרי בכל הגלות אין לי אלא מעט אוכל היינו לפרקים ידועים כשיארע איזה יחוד עם הצדיק הנקרא מעט, ואכילה היא יחוד הקדוש כנודע, וזהו מעט אוכל.

Compare also R. Reuven Horovitz's *Dudaim ba-Sadeh*, fol. 47a:

והנה אכילה הוא לשון זיווג והתקשרות... תאכלו ר"ל שתראה לזווג ולקשר מדריגה זאת שהיא הנפש בעשי' במדריגת חי שהיא מדריגת אצי'.

On "me'at" and *devekut*, see the midrashic source quoted in Chap. III, n. 10.

125. Cf. Mircea Eliade, *Rites and Symbols of Initiation* (New York, 1958).
126. Ibid., pp. 35–37, 62–64.
127. Compare, however, to John of the Cross's description of swallowing in his *Ascent of Mount Carmel;* cf. Rudolf Otto, *The Idea of the Holy* (London, 1959), p. 122. There, a dreadful experience is discussed, some of whose details are reminiscent of the initiatory encounter with a monster, although there the object of the experience is God. It seems, however, that this awful experience belongs to the "dark night of the soul," which precedes the actual experience of union.
128. On fascination and mysticism, see Otto, *The Idea of the Holy*, pp. 45–55.

CHAPTER 5

1. Exceptions are Werblowsky's important discussion in *Karo*, pp. 38–83, and Lawrence Fine, "Maggidic Revelation in the Teachings of Isaac Luria," in *Mystics, Philosophers and Politicians: Essays in Jewish Intellectual History in Honor of Alexander Altmann*, ed. J. Reinharz and D. Swetschinski (Durham, N.C., 1982), pp. 141–152; Fine, "Recitation of *Mishnah* as a Vehicle for Mystical Inspiration: A Contemplative Technique Taught by Ḥayyim Vital," *REJ* 116 (1982): 183–199; Louis Jacobs, *On Ecstasy: A Tract by Dobh Baer of Lubavitch* (New York, 1963).
2. Among these figures we may include Abraham Abulafia, Isaac of Acre, Cordovero, Luria, and Vital, as well as some Ḥasidic masters.
3. See Idel, "Inquiries," pp. 201–226.
4. I hope to discuss this practice in a separate study.
5. Idel, "*Hitbodedut* as Concentration."
6. For letter combinations, see Idel, *The Mystical Experience in Abraham Abulafia*, Chap. 1.
7. An elaborate study of this mystical technique is in progress.
8. See Peter Kuhn, *Gottes Trauer und Klage in der rabbinischen Überlieferung* (Leiden, 1981); Melvin Glatt, "God the Mourner—Israel's Companion in Tragedy," *Judaism* 28 (1979): 79–80.
9. I do not refer to any instances of weeping as the result of ecstatic experiences, as these are not part of specific technique; on this type of weeping, see Schatz-Uffenheimer, *Quietistic Elements*, pp. 42–43; Z. Gries, "Hasidic Conduct (Hanhagot) Literature as an Expression of Ethics" (in Hebrew) (Ph.D. diss., Hebrew University, 1979), pp. 165–167.
10. Version A, in the translation of F. I. Anderson, in J. H. Charlesworth, ed., *The Old Testament Pseudepigrapha* (New York, 1983), p. 107. In the parallel version, J, ibid., p. 106, Enoch is reported to have wept in the dream preceding the revelation.
11. Translation of B. M. Metzger, in ibid., p. 532.
12. Ibid.
13. Ibid., p. 535.
14. Translation of A. F. J. Klijn, in ibid., p. 623.
15. *Ecclesiastes Rabbah* 10:10.
16. According to S. Lowy, "The Motivation of Fasting in Talmudic Literature," *JJS* 9 (1958): 34, R. Simeon appeared in a dream to his former disciple.
17. On the opposition to visiting cemeteries for occult purposes, see ibid., pp. 33–34.

18. On this Midrash, see Samuel T. Lachs, "Midrash Hallel and Merkabah Mysticism," *Graetz College Anniversary Volume* (Philadelphia, 1971), pp. 193–203, esp. p. 199.
19. Cf. Jellinek, *BHM*, V, p. 97:

"ההופכי הצור אגם מים" מלמד שהיו ר' עקיבא ובן עזאי טרשים כצור הזה ועל ידי שצערו עצמן על תלמוד תורה פתח להם הקב"ה פתח לתורה, ודברים שבית שמאי ובית הלל לא היו יכולים לעמוד בהם... ודברים שהיו סתומים בעולם, עמד ר"ע ופירשם שנא' מבכי נהרות חבש ותעלומה יוצא אור; מלמד שראתה עינו של ר"ע כדרך שראתה עינו של יחזקאל הנביא, לכך נאמר: "ההופכי הצור אגם מים."

An interrelation between *ẓa'ar* and secrets is also implied in a Merkavah text; see Scholem, *Jewish Gnosticism*, p. 113.
20. On the ancient Jewish view of wells of wisdom, see David Flusser and Shmuel Safrai, "The Essene Doctrine of Hypostasis and R. Meir," *Immanuel* 14 (1982): 45–57. In our text, the mythical well became the human being himself; the whole problem will be the subject of a future study.
21. Psalms 114:8.
22. Job 28:11. The same verse is quoted in a similar context in *'Avot de-R. Nathan*, Version A, Chap. 6. See Urbach, "The Traditions about Merkavah Mysticism," p. 11, and compare to his *The Halakhah: Its Sources and Evolution* (in Hebrew) (Givataim, 1984), p. 186.
23. Compare Job 28:10: "and his eye sees every precious thing."
24. Compare R. Joshua Falk's commentary, *Binyan Yehoshu'a*, on *'Avot de-R. Nathan*, Chap. 6.
25. Although the vision of the *Merkavah* and the disclosure of secrets can certainly be regarded as two separate topics, there does seem to be a close affinity between them. Urbach has noted the similarity between two passages—one appearing in *Midrash Shir ha-Shirim*, ed. Grünhut (Jerusalem, 1897), p. 8:

"הביאני המלך חדריו" — הדברים שהיו מסותרים מן הבריות מששת ימי בראשית גלה הקב"ה לישראל.

—and one in R. Moshe ibn Tibbon's *Commentary on Shir ha-Shirim* (Lyck, 1874), fol. 9a, cited as a quotation from *Genesis Rabbah:*

"'הביאני המלך חדריו' — אלו חדרי מרכבה שגלה הקב"ה לישראל."

Cf. E. E. Urbach, "Sermons of Our Sages, the Commentary of Origen to Song of Songs and the Jewish-Christian Polemics" (in Hebrew), *Tarbiẓ* 30 (1961): 150 n. 7. Thus, the parallelism between "the hidden things" and "the chambers of the *Merkavah*" seems to be significant. On the secrets of Torah and the *Merkavah* in early Kabbalah, see Idel, "Maimonides and Kabbalah," sec. II. Compare also Urbach's treatment of *'Avot de-R. Nathan*, the passage referred to in n. 22 above.
26. I Kings 18:42.
27. *Berakhot* 34b.
28. *'Avodah Zarah* 17a. On the repentance and cathartic function of weeping in Orthodox Christian asceticism, see Ignace Briantchaninov, *Introduction à la tradition ascétique de l'Eglise d'Orient* (Saint-Vincent-sur-Jabron, 1978), esp. pp. 270–276; and also n. 84 below.
29. The acquisition of the world to come in a moment is mentioned in relation to R. Ḥanina ben Teradyon, a hero of ancient Jewish mysticism, *'Avodah Zarah* 18a.
30. *Heikhalot Zutarti*, Schäfer, *Synopse*, no. 424, and the responsum of R. Hai Gaon in *'Oẓar ha-Geonim*, vol. 4 on *Ḥagigah* (Jerusalem, 1931), pp. 13–15, and sec. II below.
31. See Scholem, *Major Trends*, p. 49.

32. MS New York, JTS 1786, fol. 26a:
אמר ר' ישמעאל נתתי לבי לדרוש בחכמה ולחשוב מועדים ורגעים וקיצים ועידין [! כצ"ל עתים] עידנין ושמתי פני לקודש עליון בתפילה ובתחנונים בצום ובכי וכך הייתי אמ' ה' אלהים צבאות אלהי ישראל עד מתי אנו זנוחין . . .
This text is the opening of an eschatological treatise entitled "'Aggadat R. Ishmael," printed in Yehudah Even Shemuel's *Midreshey 'Aggadah* (Jerusalem and Tel Aviv, 1954), p. 148. However, the printed version, which includes some better readings of the above quotation, does not mention the weeping motif.

33. *Zohar* III: 166b. The affinity between weeping and the disclosure of secrets of the Torah reappears several times in the *Zohar*, always in connection with R. Simeon; see *Zohar* I: 1b, 7b, 11a, 113a; II: 9a, and so on. Compare R. Menaḥem Recanati's *Commentary on the Pentateuch*, fol. 37d, in which he indicates that R. Simeon's weeping is the result of the ecstatic disclosure of secrets, and not a "technical" weeping. However, this understanding is a reading of the Geronese view of ecstasy into the *Zohar*. Compare Chap. III, above.

34. It is noteworthy that, although Ezekiel's prophecies open with a vision of the *Merkavah*, they conclude with a vision of the Temple. See also the sixteenth-century practice of Elijah's posture in order to attain vision of supernal lights; cf. R. Joseph ibn Sayaḥ's *'Even ha-Shoham* adduced in Scholem, *CCCH*, p. 90. This practice was also used by the Sufis. See Ernst Bannerth, "Dhikr et Khalwa d'après ibn 'Ata' Allah," *Institut Dominicain d'Etudes Orientales du Caire, Mélanges* 12 (1974): 69.

35. *De Beatitudine: Capita Duo R. Mosi ben Maimon Adscripta*, ed. H. S. Davidowitz and D. H Baneth (Jerusalem, 1939), p. 7. There are several discrepancies between the Arabic original and the Hebrew translation, although these are inconsequential for our subject. On music and ecstatic experience, see Idel, "Music and Prophetic Kabbalah," p. 156 n. 27. The term translated here as "ecstatic experience" also has the connotation of "drowning" or "being overwhelmed"; cf. above, Chap. IV, n. 68. On the question of the author of this treatise, see Idel, "Prophetic Kabbalah and the Land of Israel," p. 108 n. 18. Prayer and weeping are indeed also related in medieval texts (cf., for example, *Sefer Ḥasidim*, ed. Jehudah Wistinetzki [Frankfurt, 1924], par. XI, p. 9; par. 415, p. 123; and R. Eleazar of Worms, *Sefer ha-Rokeaḥ* [Jerusalem, 1960], p 30; references provided by Professor I. Marcus). The mystical impact of this act, however, is not easily perceptible in these texts.

36. MS Oxford 1706, fol. 494b:
כתב הר"ר אברהם הלוי להשגת החכמה. . . התנאי הב' בכל התפלות וב"ש בלמוד במקום שתתקשה ולא תוכל להבין ולהשיג החכמה הלימודי' או איזה סוד, תעורר בכי המארים (!) עד שיזלגו עיניך דמעות וכל מה שתוכל להרבה — תרבה. ותגדלו בכי כי שערי דמעות לא ננעלו ויפתחו לך שערי העליונים.
Compare to *Hanhagot ha-'Ari*; cf. Benayahu, *Sefer Toldot ha-'Ari*, p. 319:
גם א"ל הר"א הלוי יצ"ו שא"ל מורי ז"ל עצה לענין ההשגה והיא זו שלא ישיח שיחה בטילה ושיקום בחצי הלילה ויבכה על חסרון הידיעה ושילמוד בזוהר דרך בקיאות בלבד.
See also R. Jacob Ẓemaḥ's *Nagid u-Meẓaveh* (Lemberg, 1863), fol. 22a:
. . . גם דברי תורה שלא תבינם, תבכה עליו כל שתוכל, גם עליית הנשמה בלילה לעולם העליון ולא תשוט בהבלי העולם תלוי שתישן בבכיה.
(quoted in the name of Vital's *Collectanaea*). On ascent of the soul in Luria, see below, near n. 123. Compare also R. Isaac Safrin's *Zohar Ḥai*, vol III, fol. 130a, on Luria:
שהיה טורח שבוע אחד על מאמר אחד מטריח מאד בבכייה בכמה לילות עד שהשיג באמת את חלקו בתורה.
On R. Abraham Berukhim and his *hanhagot*, see Fine, *Safed Spirituality*, pp. 47–53.

37. בקבלת התענית התפללתי לפני הקב״ה בבכיה גדולה על שאיני זוכר שום דבר ממה שלומדים עמי בחלום.

Cf. G. Scholem, *The Dreams of the Sabbatean R. Mordecai Ashkenazi* (in Hebrew) (Jerusalem, 1938), p. 17.

38. *Shivehey ha-'Ari;* cf. Benayahu *Sefer Toldot ha-'Ari*, pp. 231–232. See also Safrin, *Netiv Mizvotekha*, pp. 86–87.

39. See below, Safrin's vision of the back of the *Shekhinah*.

40. Cf. *Pesikta Rabbati*, ed. Friedmann (Vienna, 1880), fol. 130b; *Yalkut Shim'oni*, Jeremy, no. 293.

41. The version in *Yalkut Shim'oni* here is "Woe to me for your sake, Mother Zion." Compare below Vital's dream, where the phrase "Mother, Mother" occurs in a similar context.

42. *Sefer ha-Ḥezyonot*, ed. A. Z. Aeshcoli (Jerusalem, 1954), p. 42:

שנת שכ״ו, ליל שבת ח׳ לטבת, אמרתי קדוש ואשב על השלחן לאכול והיו עיני זולגות דמעה נאנח ונעצב... וקשרו אתי בכשפים... גם בכיתי על בטול עסק התורה בשתי שנים ההם... ומרוב דאגתי לא אכלתי כלל ואשכב במטתי על פני בוכה, עד שנרדמתי מרוב הבכיה ואחלום חלום נפלא.

43. Tying is a well-known device connected to causing sexual impotence in the bridegroom, as is clear from our context. See Saul Lieberman, *Greek and Hellenism in Jewish Palestine* (in Hebrew) (Jerusalem, 1962), p. 83 and n. 124.

44. See Aeshcoli's footnote, ibid., p. 43 n. 67.

45. I have here translated a combined version of this segment of the vision, based both upon Aeshcoli's edition, p. 44, and, especially, upon a quotation from *Sefer ha-Ḥezyonot* found in R. Isaac Yehudah Yeḥiel Safrin of Komarno, *Netiv Mizvotekha*, p. 87; R. Isaac's version states:

וכן מה שמבואר בספר החזיונות למרן הרח״ו והנה אשה חשובה והיא יפה כשמש נצב לנגדי ותאמר: מה לך פה בני חיים בוכה ואני שמעתי דמעתך ובאתי לעזרתך ואקרא אל האשה אמי אמי עזרני (!) ואראה את השם יתברך יושב על כסא, עתיק יומין וזקנו לבנה כשלג מהודר עד אין תכלית.

46. See above, n. 41.

47. Isa. 6:1.

48. Dan. 7: 9.

49. Scholem, *Sabbatai Ṣevi*, pp. 204–205. Compare this passage to the passages cited above from the apocalyptic literature, where the apparitions of angels precede the fast and weepings—which they apparently prescribe—and are then followed by the main vision or revelation.

50. Another vision of the *Merkavah* is reported later on. See Scholem, *Sabbatai Ṣevi*, p. 206.

51. Ibid.

52. D. Ben-Amos and J. R. Mintz, eds., *In Praise of the Ba'al Shem Tov* (Bloomington, Ind., and London, 1972), pp. 53–54.

53. See the preface of R. Elijah's grandson to his commentary to *Sifra' de-Ẓeni'uta* (Vilna, 1891):

סיפר לי הגאון הגדול מהו׳ חיים נ״י אב״ד דוואלאזין כמה פעמים אירע שרא׳ פני רבו אא״ז הגאון זצ״ל והנה נהפך פניו לירקון ונפשו מרה לו, לחם לא אכל ושינ׳ בעיניו לא ראה יום או יומיים ובכה בכה רב, על אשר העלים ה׳ מאתו איזה סוד מסתרי׳ התורה וכאשר נתגלה לו הרז מיד צהלו פניו ותארנה עיניו.

54. Ed. Naftali ben Menaḥem, Jerusalem, 1944, p. 19. This editor has already noted the

affinity between the passage in *Megillat Setarim* and the one in *Netiv Miẓvotekha* (p. 19 n. 53), but was misled by Safrin's practice of using the third-person form in some of his books even when relating his own experiences. Hence, ben Menaḥem understood that in the latter work the passage is cited in connection with R. Levi Isaac of Berdichev, who is mentioned shortly before this. However, there is no sound reason to accept this supposition. In *Megillat Setarim*, the author uses the first-person form throughout the account. A number of late nineteenth-century collections of Ḥasidic hagiography gave our story in the name of R. Levi Isaac of Berdichev, apparently being misled by the peculiar form by which it was referred to in *Netiv Miẓvotekha*; see Buber, *Tales of the Ḥasidim, Early Masters*, p. 204.

55. P. 87. In this version, the author uses the third-person form; I have changed this for the first person in those instances that are missing in the *Megillat Setarim* version. In *Netiv Miẓvotekha*, the date given is the twentieth.

56. See on this concept Norman Cohen, "Shekhinta Ba-Galuta: A Midrashic Response to Destruction and Persecution," *Journal for the Study of Judaism* 13 (1982): 147–159.

57. This phrase, as well as the context, stems from the *Zohar* III: 115b.

58. The vision of a shining young woman is also hinted at in Safrin's version of *Sefer ha-Ḥezyonot*, cited above. On the "virgin of light" as a denotation for the *Shekhinah*, see also M. Idel, "The Attitude to Christianity in *Sefer ha-Meshiv*" (in Hebrew), *Ẓion* 46 (1981): 89–90, and in R. Asher Lemlein's vision, on which see Ephraim Kupfer, "The Visions of R. Asher ben R. Meir Lemlein Reutlingen" (in Hebrew), *Kovez̤ 'al-Yad* 8 (18) (Jerusalem, 1976), 402–403; compare p. 398, where a woman dressed in dark clothes is the object of his vision.

59. The young woman is mentioned only in *Megillat Setarim*, where the author uses the first-person form; in *Netiv Miẓvotekha*, he wrote: "etc."

60. On these ornaments, see Liebes, "The Messiah of the *Zohar*," p. 214 n. 33.

61. Compare R. Abraham Berukhim's vision above.

62. Exod. 33:20.

63. *Netiv Miẓvotekha*, p. 87. Compare the view of repentance and weeping in R. Elimelekh of Lyzhansk's *No'am 'Elimelekh* (Jerusalem, 1960), fol. 29b:
הכרח לחלק אלהי להתלבש בלבושים על גבי לבושים לסבול הצער הגדול על העבירה וזהו סוד גלות השכינה ואח"כ כשאדם חוזר בתשוב' ובוכה על עונותיו זה הוא שבוכה על גלות השכינה, ועל ידי זה הוא משבר את הלבושים שהוכרח החלק האלהי להתלבש בהם ותגלה בתיקונו כשמתקן עונו.

64. See Werblowsky, *Karo*, pp. 109–111. Compare also the experience of Nathan of Gaza discussed by Scholem, *Sabbatai Ṣevi*, pp. 217–218. On the ecstatic nature of *Shavu'ot*, see Liebes, "The Messiah of the *Zohar*," pp. 208–215.

65. *Netiv Miẓvotekha*, pp. 18–21.

66. Ibid., p. 86.
גילוי שכינה ע"י ואחרי הצער שמצערין אותו ומרגיש בצער השכינה ומה שהגלוי הוא בציור ובדמות, זהו מחמת שהוא בגוף.

67. Compare the relevant account of R. Isaac Safrin on the occasion of the visit to his master, R. Abraham Joshua Heschel of Apt: "Once I was in his presence and he was speaking with a widow and I understood that his words to her were of profound wisdom, concerning the exile of the Shekhinah, who was like a widow, and I began to weep and he wept too" (*Zohar Ḥai* II: 395a). A slightly different version was related by Safrin's cousin, R. Isaac Eisik of

Zhidachov, which was briefly analyzed by Erich Neumann, "Mystical Man," in *The Mystic Vision*, ed. J. Campbell (Princeton, N.J., 1982), p. 411. We may easily see how the very mention of the exile of the *Shekhinah* was sufficient to trigger weeping.

68. It is important to note that for Safrin, the experience of *Shekhinah* without ornaments is higher than that which includes the *Shekhinah* in its ornaments. Compare the parable of the maiden in *Zohar* II, 99a, below, Chap. IX.

69. The need to participate in the exile of the *Shekhinah* was already formulated in the *Zohar* and in Safedian Kabbalah. See Berakhah Zack, "The Galut of Israel and the Galut of the Shekhinah in R. Moshe Cordovero's book *'Or Yakar*" (in Hebrew), *Jerusalem Studies in Jewish Thought* 1, no. 4 (1982): 176–178. However, the weeping and the visible revelation of the *Shekhinah* seem to be absent there. Safrin highly appreciated this practice, as we learn from *Nozer Ḥesed*, p. 65.

70. *Heikhal ha-Berakhah* I, fol. 219c:
וכלב נשבר בוכה... פתאום יבוא האדון ויאיר לך מאורו... וממש נבראת בריה חדשה ממש ממש.
Interestingly, at the end of the first introduction to his *'Ozar Ḥayyim* and *Heikhal ha-Berakhah* R. Isaac Safrin confesses that, after a hard period, God made him a new creature:
מאיר עלי מאורו ומזיוו... עד שנעשיתי ממש ממש בריה חדשה ואין לי שום הרגשה עוד משום ענין.
Therefore we can assume that the first quotation may reflect a personal mystical transformation, associated with weeping.

On weeping and self-abasement at midnight, see the account of the seer of Lublin, a disciple of R. Jacob Isaac ha-Levi Horowitz, regarding his master, quoted by Safrin in *Heikhal ha-Berakhah* II, fol. 276c,d. It is plausible that the custom of weeping came to Safrin via the intermediary of his uncle, R. Zevi Hirsch of Zhidachov, a student of the visionary of Lublin. On the latter's weeping, see also *'Eser Meorot* in *Sefarim Kedoshim mi-kol Talmidei ha-Besht* (Brooklyn, N.Y., 1981), vol. 2, fol. 45a, 52a.

71. *Zohar Ḥai* II, 426ab.

72. See n. 70 above on the relationship between divine light and weeping in Safrin's work, and below in the quotation from *Zohar Ḥai* II, 455d.

73. Compare Moses' weeping request for heaven and earth to pray for him, in order that he escape death. Cf., for example, *The Sermon on Moses' Death* in Eisenstein, *'Ozar ha-Midrashim*, p. 380. The same phrase recurs in Safrin's description of his own supplication, in *Zohar Ḥai* II, fol. 456a.

74. Compare below the quotation from *Zohar Ḥai* II, 455d.

75. *Zohar Ḥai* II, 455d.

76. Prov. 18:4. The numerical value of this part of the verse is 629, corresponding to the year 1869, the time when Safrin completed the composition of the first part of *Zohar Ḥai*.

77. *Damesek 'Eli'ezer* (Przemyslani, 1902), vol. 1, fol. 5b–6a (Preface).

78. The content of the dream was analyzed by R. Isaac Safrin, whose son asked him to interpret its meaning.

79. Namely R. Ibba, one of the heroes of the *Zohar*.

80. *'Avot* 6:1. Interestingly, these secrets were regarded as *Ma'aseh Bereshit, Ma'aseh Merkavah*, and *Sefer Yezirah*. See *Maḥzor Vitri*, ed. S. Horwitz (Jerusalem, 1963), p. 555; and also Idel, "The Concept of Torah," p. 36 n. 38. Compare Safrin's statement (*Megillat Setarim*, p. 14)

that, by the means of studying Talmud, one attains an experience of "great light" connected with the indwelling of the *Shekhinah*.

81. *Midrash Tehilim* on Psalms 105:1; Idel, "The Concept of Torah," pp. 36–37 n. 39.
82. See n. 80 above, where Safrin, who used the mystical anomian technique, asserted that he also received a mystical experience by means of a nomian technique. As we know, the statement of *'Avot* 6:1 was the motto of mystical study of Torah in Ḥasidism.
83. *Shabbat* 30a.
84. See mainly the issue of "the gift of tears"; cf. Jean Leclercq, *The Love of Learning and the Desire for God* (New York, 1982), pp. 58–59 and n. 28 above, and some material referred to by Margaret Smith, *The Way of the Mystics* (New York, 1978); see also George A. Maloney, *Inward Stillness* (Denville, N.J., 1975), pp. 105–120.
85. See Smith, *The Way of the Mystics*, pp. 155–157, especially p. 157; "O brethren, will ye not weep in desire for God? Shall he who weeps in longing for his Lord be denied the Vision of Him?" A Sufic group of ascetics was called *bakka'un*—weepers; see ibid., p. 155; Annemarie Schimmel, *Mystical Dimensions of Islam* (Chapel Hill, N.C., 1978), p. 31; and n. 84 above.
86. Compare my discussion in Chap. VI on the preservation of ancient Jewish views in Gnostic texts and their revitalization in medieval Kabbalah.
87. *Ecstasy* (New York, 1968), pp. 168–170.
88. Therefore, types of mental ascent such as those of Bonaventura in Christian mysticism or the ascent of mystical intention—*kavvanah*—in Jewish mysticism are outside the framework of this discussion. These types of ascent were mainly a spiritual journey of one of the faculties of the soul, commonly the rational one, and rarely of the imagination. The Neoplatonic introvertive journey of the soul to the divine inherent in her is also different from the category we are dealing with. On the influence of the latter view in Jewish mysticism, see Idel, "Types of Redemptive Activity," pp. 256–257 n. 20. On the continuity of the practice of "ascent of the soul" from the Heikhalot tradition through R. Israel Ba'al Shem Tov, see also the forthcoming study of Tali Loewenthal, *Communicating the Infinite: The Emergence of the Ḥabad School*.
89. The eschatological ascent of the soul at the time of death is thus excluded from this discussion. On this issue, see Alexander Altmann, "The Ladder of Ascension," in *Studies in Mysticism and Religion Presented to Gershom G. Scholem* (Jerusalem, 1967), pp. 1–29.
90. I shall mention here only two recent studies dealing with ascent of the soul: Allan Segal, "Heavenly Ascent in Hellenic Judaism, Early Christianity, and Their Environment," *Aufstieg und Niedergang der romischen Welt*, II, Principat, vol. 23, 2 (Berlin, 1980), pp. 1333–1394, especially pp. 1388–1394 which contain a selected bibliography; Ioan Petru Culianu, *Psychanodia, I—A Survey of the Evidence concerning the Ascension of the Soul and Its Relevance* (Leiden, 1983). See also the references in n. 91 below.
91. Morton Smith, "Ascent to the Heavens and the Beginnings of Christianity," *Eranosjahrbuch* 50 (1981):403–429; Smith, *Clement of Alexandria and a Secret Gospel of Mark* (Cambridge, Mass., 1973), pp. 237–249; Smith, *Jesus the Magician* (New York, 1981), pp. 124–125.
92. "Ascent," p. 415.
93. Ibid., pp. 426–428.
94. II Cor. 12:3. On this text, see Peter Schäfer's recent article, "New Testament and Hekhalot Literature: The Journey into Heaven in Paul and in Merkavah Mysticism," *JJS* 35 (1984):

19–35. Schäfer did not consider Smith's, or his predecessors', reading of Paul's statements as possibly related to Jesus himself.

95. See Scholem, *Jewish Gnosticism*, p. 18; and Itamar Gruenwald, "Knowledge and Vision," *Israel Oriental Studies* 3 (1973): 106, who points out the occurrence of the phrase in *Odes of Solomon* 35:7.

96. *Genesis Rabbah* 14:9, pp. 133–134. The nightly ascent of the soul is in no way eschatological, nor does it point to a mystical experience. In this context it may be pertinent to mention R. Shimeon bar Yoḥai's statement:

"ראיתי בני עליה והן מועטין"

(*Sukkah* 45a), which implies that bar Yoḥai's vision of the few elect in the upper world was the result of a mystical journey. On this statement, see A. Kaminka, "Die Mystischen Ideen des R. Simon b. Joḥai," *HUCA* 10 (1935): 165, and the parallels adduced by the author.

97. "Heikhalot Rabbati," Chap. XX, in Wertheimer, *Batey Midrashot* 1:97–99, Schäfer, *Synopse*, no. 225–228. On this passage, see Lawrence H. Shiffman, "The Recall of Rabbi Nehuniah ben Ha-Qanah from Ecstasy in *Heikhalot Rabbati*," *AJSreview* 1 (1976): 269–281; Saul Lieberman in Gruenwald, *Apocalyptic and Merkavah Mysticism* (Leiden, 1980), Appendix, pp. 241ff.

98. *Heikhalot Rabbati*, ibid.

99. See also a peculiar version of the discussion concerning mystical study of *Ma'aseh Merkavah*, preserved in R. 'Azriel's *Commentary on the Talmudic Aggadot*, p. 40, where ben 'Azzai is approached by R. 'Akiva, who says to him: "I heard that you sit down and study, and flames surround you. I said [to myself], 'You have descended to the chambers of the Chariot.' " The standard version of this statement in *Leviticus Rabbah* 16:4 and *Song of Songs Rabbah* on paragraph I, 10 (p. 42) states that "perhaps you deal with the chambers of the Chariot." This discrepancy is crucial; the first version assumes that, while ben 'Azzai has descended (that is, ascended) to the supernal world, the fire surrounded his body here below; according to the second version, the very study of this esoteric subject was sufficient to cause the appearance of the fire. Scholem, *CCCH*, p. 197 n. 4, notices this difference between the versions and infers that the occurrence of the "descending" motif is later; although this may indeed be the case, it cannot be ascertained. If R. 'Azriel's version indeed reflects an older concept, it constitutes an interesting parallel to R. Neḥuniya's description in *Heikhalot Rabbati*. Significantly, R. 'Azriel interprets this text as referring to the ascent of human thought to the higher Sefirot and its cleaving there.

100. *'Oẓar ha-Geonim*, ed. Levin, on *Ḥagigah* (Jerusalem, 1932), *Teshuvot*, pp. 14–15:

כי הרבה מן החכמים היו סוברים כי מי שהוא הגון בכמה מדות זכורות ומבוארות כשמבקש לצפות במרכבה ולהציץ בהיכלות של מלאכי מרום, יש לו דרכים לעשות שישב בתענית ימים ידועים ומניח ראשו בין ברכיו ולוחש לארץ שירות ותשבחות הרבה שהן מפורשות ובכן מציץ בפנימיו' ובחדריו כמי שהוא רואה בעיניו היכלות שבעה וצופה כאילו הוא נכנס מהיכל להיכל ורואה מה שיש בו. ויש שתי משניות שהתנאים שונין אותן בדבר זה, ונקראות היכלות רבתי והיכלות זוטרתי, ודבר זה מפורסם וידוע. ועל אותן הצפיות שנה תנא זה ארבעה נכנסו לפרדס, המשיל את ההיכלות הללו לפרדס והעלה להם השם הזה... כי הקב"ה... מראה אותן בפנימיות מראות היכליו ומעמד מלאכיו.

I have partially followed the translation of the first half of the quotation given in Scholem, *Major Trends*, p. 49.

101. That is, the posture of Elijah: see above, sec. III.

102. Scholem's rendering of this as "the interiors and the chambers" (*Major Trends*, p. 49) implies that the phrase refers to external entities, presumably parts of the palaces. However, this understanding seems rather difficult; the form *ba-penimi uva-ḥedri* suggests the subject of the verb, *maniaḥ rosho*, thereby referring to the mystic himself. See also Cohen, *The Shi'ur Qomah: Liturgy and Theurgy*, p. 5, who more adequately translates: "he gazes within himself." However, his general interpretation (pp. 5–6) is erroneous: R. Hai did not imply "a mystic communion with God," nor does his passage "have the ring of truth, as well as the support of the gaon's unimpeachable authority." See my view below that this passage is a reinterpretation—or misinterpretation—of the practices of the Heikhalot mystics. The spiritual understanding of Hai's view of the ancient mystics was first proposed by Adolph Jellinek, *Beiträge zur Geschichte der Kabbala* (Leipzig, 1852), Zweites Heft, pp. 15–16 n. 22, where he affirms that R. Hai was influenced by Sufi mysticism. Our passage has recently been discussed by David Y. Halperin, "A New Edition of the Heikhalot Literature," *Journal of the American Oriental Society* 104, no. 3 (1984): 544, 547, 550–551. However, on p. 544, he translates our phrase, "He thus peers into the inner rooms and chambers," without referring to the possessive form of these nouns; thus Halperin's opinion is that R. Hai's passage reflects a heavenly ascension. See also Halperin, *The Merkabah in Rabbinic Literature* (New Haven, Conn., 1980), pp. 3, 89, 177.

103. Or, "two *mishnayot* taught by the tannaim."

104. See Scholem's view, *Major Trends*, pp. 49–50, in which he claims that R. Hai Gaon is describing a "mystical ascent." Halperin, "A New Edition," pp. 544, 551, accepts Scholem's understanding of this passage, although he disagrees with his assumption that the passage reflects a view occurring in *Heikhalot Zutarti*; he denies the presence of reference to a celestial journey in this treatise and argues that R. Hai misunderstood the earlier source. It is my opinion that the gaon misinterpreted the ancient experiences by transforming an ecstatic experience into an introvertive one.

105. *'Arukh ha-Shalem*, ed. A. Kohut, 1:14, sub voce: *'avney shayish ṭahor:*
ולא שהן עולין למרום אלא בחדרי לבן רואים וצופין כאדם הרואה וצופה בעיניו דבר ברור ושומעין ואומרין ומדברין בעין הסוכה ברוח הקודש, זה פי' ר' האי גאון.

106. *'eyn ha-sukkah;* compare *Leviticus Rabbah* I:
"נביאים שסוכים ברוח הקודש."

107. See Urbach, *'Arugat ha-Bosem*, 1:198 n. 2, 199–200. See also on p. 202 the phrase *ha-sekhel libam*, "the intellect of their heart"; see also David Halperin, "Origen, Ezekiel's Merkavah, and the Ascension of Moses," *Church History* 50 (1981): 263, 273–274. The occurrence of the phrases "cordis oculis" in Origen or *binat levavkhem* in Hebrew texts may evidence a psychologistic interpretation of the vision of the *Merkavah* in ancient Jewish sources; see also Halperin, *Merkabah*, pp. 174–175.

108. See Scholem, *Major Trends*, p. 29, where he refers to Macarius the Egyptian, who in the fourth century interpreted the vision of Ezekiel as the vision of "the secret of the soul." See also n. 107 above.

109. See, for example, R. Hai Gaon's assertion that the mystic may attain visions of palaces and angels, intentionally ignoring the vision of God. For his father's reaction to the book

Shi'ur Komah, see *'Oḥar ha-Geonim*, ed. B. Levin, *Ḥagigah teshuvot*, pp. 11–12. R. Sherira refuses to endorse an anthropomorphic conception of Godhead.

110. See also R. Hai's reservations concerning mystical and magical practices connected with the divine names: Levin, ibid., pp. 16–24; and Colette Sirat, *Les théories des visions surnaturelles dans la pensée juive du Moyen Age* (Leiden, 1862), pp. 33–35.

111. See especially his view (R. Hai, ibid., p. 15) that inner visions are miraculous events granted by God to the righteous. This attitude is an obvious attempt to discredit the efficacy of the mystical techniques.

112. See Scholem, *Les Origines de la Kabbale*, p. 254. Strangely, he regarded the techniques of Heikhalot literature as degenerating into "mere literature" (see *Major Trends*, p. 51), a curious view in light of reports of the ascents of souls throughout the nineteenth century, as we shall see below.

113. Ibid, pp. 254–255.

114. See R. Abraham of Torrutiel's supplements to *Sefer ha-Kabbalah* of R. Abraham ben David, reprinted in *Two Chronicles from the Generation of the Spanish Exile* (in Hebrew), introduction by A. David (Jerusalem, 1979), p. 28:

והר' מיכאל המלאך שעשה שאלות ועלתה נשמתו לשמים לשאול ספקותיו כי נסגר בחדר שלשה ימים וצוה לבלתי יפתחו החדר. ויציצו אנשי ביתו בין השערים והנה הושלך גופו כאבן דומם. וישכב כן שלשה ימים מוסגר כמת מוטל על מטתו ולא זע ולא נד. ולאחר שלשה ימים ויהי, ויקם על רגליו ויקראו אותו על ככה רבי מיכאל המלאך.

115. See Gershom Scholem, "On the Prophecy of R. Ezra of Moncontour" (in Hebrew), *Tarbiẓ* 2 (1931): 244.

116. This poem, consisting of three verses, was printed by Naftali Fried, *Tarbiẓ* 2 (1931):514 (in Hebrew).

117. See R. Naftali Ẓevi Hirsch Treves's *Commentary on the Siddur* (Thiengen, 1560), fol. 40, Ib:

אל ברוך גדול דעה מיוסד בא"ב במדרש ר' אליעזר קליר: כשרצה לייסד הפיוט עלה לרקיע על ידי השם ושאל למיכאל היאך מלאכים משוררים והיאך שירתם מיוסדת. וא"ל בא"ב. והנהיג הוא ג"כ לעשות כל שבחיו בא"ב.

118. On *Ḥagigah* 15b:

"עלו לרקיע על ידי שם"

119. *Shibboley ha-Leket*, ed. Samuel K. Mirsky (New York, 1966), vol. 1, paragraph 28, p. 46, and *Maḥzor Vitri*, ed. S. Hurwitz (Nuremberg, 1923), p. 364. Compare also to *Shibboley ha-Leket*, p. 176.

120. Printed in Daniel Goldschmidt's *Maḥzor to Rosh ha-Shanah* (Jerusalem, 1970), p. 216. The content of this poem is, significantly, closely related to Ezekiel's vision.

121. See Urbach, "The Traditions about Merkavah Mysticism," pp. 4–10.

122. R. Moshe of Taku's *Ketav Tammim*, in *'Oẓar Neḥmad* IV (1863), p. 85.

123. Benayahu, *Sefer Toldot ha-'Ari*, p. 155. Compare also above, n. 36, where the spiritual ascent is attained by intentional weeping.

124. Ibid., pp. 154–155.

125. *Baddei ha-'Aron*, MS Paris, BN 840, fol. 45a:

כי הם חייו לעלות מישיבה תחתונה לישיבה עליונה להתפרנס מזיו השכינה ולא יחוש על בניו ובני ביתו מרוב דביקותו.

126. In a prior sentence, R. Shem Tov speaks about the cleaving to "a pure and clean splendor": ibid., fol. 45a:

"וידבק בזיו הזך והטהור".

127. Ibid, fol. 45a, 45b–46a; see Idel,"*Hitbodedut* as Concentration," par. VI. See also n. 77, where I noted the similarity of this inner perception of the *Merkavah* to R. Hai's interpretation discussed above.

128. See Idel, "Shelomo Molkho as Magician," pp. 204–205, especially n. 78 there. See also below, Chap. IX, sec. II (3), for my discussion of the pneumatic interpreter.

129. *Sefer ha-Ḥezyonot*, p. 112:

...שיום אחד נתעלפתי עילוף גדול, כמו שעה אחת ובאו אנשים זקנים לאין קץ ונשים רבות לראות אותי ותמלא (!) הבית לגמרי. והיו מצטערים כולם עלי. ואחר כך הוסר העילוף ופתחתי עיני ואמרתי להם: דעו כי עתה עלתה נפשי עד כסא הכבוד וחזרו ושלחו את נפשי בעולם הזה, כדי שאדרוש לכם ואדריך אתכם בתשובה ובענייני צדקה.

On the "purely imaginative ascent" of the soul to its root in Vital's *Sha'arey Kedushah*, see Werblowsky, *Karo*, pp. 69–75.

130. We may assume a certain link between the entire situation here and the midrashic dictum that the greatness of repentance is that it reaches the seat of glory. See *Pesikta Rabbati* and Victor Aptowitzer, "Untersuchungen zur Gaonäischen Literatur," *HUCA* 8–9 (1931): 397.

131. See above, sec. I, for the quotation from *Sefer ha-Ḥezyonot*, pp. 42ff. For another interesting discussion of the ascent of the soul, see ibid., pp. 47–49; the precise meaning, however, is elusive.

132. See *Shiveḥey ha-Besht*, ed. J. Mondshine, pp. 235–236, Koretz version.

133. The column linking the lower Paradise to other levels of reality is well known from earlier Kabbalistic sources; see, for example, *Seder Gan 'Eden* in Eisenstein, *'Oẓar ha-Midrashim*, pp. 85–86. The motif of the pillar climbed by shaman or dead souls recurs in various traditions. According to a legend, the last subject discussed by the Besht was the pillar of the souls, see Buber, *Tales of the Ḥasidim: Early Masters*, p. 84.

134. Apparently Aḥijah the Shilonite; on this prophet as a mystical mentor, see Liebes, "The Messiah of the *Zohar*," p. 113 n. 114.

135. On this question, see Scholem, *Explications and Implications*, pp. 309–310; Liebes, "The Messiah of the *Zohar*," pp. 113–114.

136. *Shiveḥey ha-Besht*, ed. Mondshine, p. 235; see also R. Isaac Safrin's *Zohar Ḥai* III, fol. 76b.

137. Interestingly enough, ecstatic practices in which the soul leaves the body for several hours during which oracular dreams are experienced were known in Moldavian Carpats: see Mircea Eliade, *Zalmoxis: The Vanishing God* (Chicago and London, 1970), pp. 191–194.

138. Ibid., p. 237.

139. See the texts collected by Mondshine, *Sheveḥey ha-Besht*, p. 251 and n. 45.

140. See *Mayyim Rabbim* (Brooklyn, N.Y., 1979), p. 140:

ר' יחיאל מיכאל זלאטשוב הי' ישן לא' משני פנים...או בעת אשר רצונו הי' לעלות לרקיע.

Compare also the contemporary descriptions of R. Elijah of Vilna in R. Ḥayyim of Volozhin's preface to R. Elijah's commentary to *Sifra' de-Ẓeni'uta* (Vilna, 1891), where the master is portrayed as a recipient of a secret by means of the ascent of the soul, although he did not appreciate this pattern as a very high one.

141. *Noẓer Ḥesed*, p. 131.

142. See *Heikhal ha-Berakhah*, vol. I, fol. 31a.

143. *Zohar Ḥai* III, fol. 129d:
שהיה הגוף מוטל במעט חיות בענן כמו שעושין כל בעלי עליות נשמה מרן הריב״ש וכיוצא. והרי הגוף מוטל כאבן אבל אינו אלא שעה קטנה ושתי שעות ולא יותר. וגוף של משה רבינו מונח ארבעים יום וחזר בתוכו אחרי ארבעים יום.

144. Cf. Exod. 24:18. Compare the Lurianic view of Moses' ascent adduced by Scholem, *Sabbatai Ṣevi*, p. 53.

145. See Philo's allegorization of Moses as the soul ascending to heaven; cf. Segal (n. 1 above), p. 1358.

146. *Megillat Setarim*, pp. 15–16:
וייחדתי יחוד והתקשרתי בנפש מרן האלקי האר״י ומהדביקות הזו נפלה עלי תרדמה וראיתי כמה נשמות עד שנפל עלי אימה ופחד ורעש כדרכי, והנראה מהם מעניין שאעלה לגדולה. ועליתי עוד וראיתי את ר׳ יהושע־העשיל ... והקיצותי.

147. Compare another dream of R. Isaac Safrin, *Megillat Setarim*, p. 23, where he learned from a certain event that he would "rise to greatness, satisfaction and joy."

148. This is the date of this experience.

149. On the relationship between ben 'Atar and Ḥasidism, see Dan Manor, "Rabbi Haim ben 'Atar in Ḥasidic Writings" (in Hebrew), *Pe'amim* 20 (1984): 88–110. Manor mentions neither the Besht's epistle referred to above nor the question of soul ascent in ben 'Atar.

150. See M. Idel, "On the Metamorphosis of an Ancient Technique of Prophetic Vision in the Middle Ages" (in Hebrew), *Sinai* 86 (1980): 1–7.

151. Irenée Hausherr, "La Méthode d'oraison hesychaste," *Orientalia Christiana* 9 (1927): 68–69.

152. G. C. Anawati and L. Gardet, *Mystique musulmane: Aspects et tendances, expériences et techniques* (Paris, 1976), pp. 187–234.

153. See, for example, Mircea Eliade, *Yoga: Immortality and Freedom* (Princeton, N.J., 1971), pp. 200ff., esp. pp. 216–219, where the similarities between the Sufic "dhikr" and parallel Hindu phenomena are noted.

154. D. T. Suzuki, *Essais sur le Bouddhisme Zen* (Paris, 1943), 2:141–151, and passim.

155. See, for example, Eliade, *Yoga*, pp. 47–52.

156. See Anawati and Gardet, *Mystique musulmane*, pp. 189–190.

157. For a detailed description of these components of Kabbalistic mystical techniques, see Idel, *The Mystical Experience in Abraham Abulafia*, Chap. I.

158. On the influence of Ashkenazic theology on Spanish Kabbalah, see Joseph Dan, "The Vicissitudes of the Esotericism of the German Ḥasidim" (in Hebrew), in *Studies in Mysticism and Religion Presented to Gershom G. Scholem* (Jerusalem, 1967), pp. 91–99. Dan, however, does not discuss the influence of R. Eleazar's mystical technique.

159. See, for example, "Ve-Zot li-Yihudah," in Jellinek, *Auswahl*, p. 25.

160. See Matt, *The Book of the Mirrors*, p. 1.

161. See the quotation from R. Eleazar's *Sefer ha-Ḥokhmah* in n. 167 below.

162. See Idel, *The Mystical Experience in Abraham Abulafia*, Chap. I.

163. See Sec. II above.

164. On this treatise, see Dan, *The Esoteric Theology*, pp. 143ff.

165. MS Cambridge, Add. 643, fol. 19a; MS Oxford 1574, fol 34b; MS Vatican 431, fol. 39a:

אבל הוא מזכיר שמות הקדושים או שמות המלאכים כדי להראות לו רצונו או להודיעו דבר סתר, ואז רוח הקודש נגלה עליו והבשר... נפעמת... מעוז רוח הקדש.

166. *'Oẓar Neḥmad* III (1860), p. 84:

חסרי דעת, המינים. לעשות עצמם נביאים, מרגילים עצמם בהזכרת שמות הקדושים ופעמים יכוונו בקריאתן והנשמה מתבהלת... כשמסתלק ממנו כח השם שהזכיר, חוזר לכמות שהיה בדעת מבוהלת.

See also Scholem, *Major Trends*, pp. 102–103.

167. *Sefer ha-Ḥokhmah* MS Oxford 1812, fol. 55b:

"ומן הדין לא היה לכתוב הכל ולא לנקבו בו פן ישתמשו חסרי הדעת".

On this treatise, see Joseph Dan, "The Ashkenazi Ḥasidic *Gates of Wisdom,*" in *Hommage à Georges Vajda*, ed. G. Nahon and C. Tonati (Louvain, 1980), pp. 183–189; Dan, *The Esoteric Theology*, pp. 44–57.

168. Ibid, fol. 55b:

"נגלה לנו קצת ענייני עתידות ורוחו', במדות על פי הזכרות עומקי השמות לידע רוח החכמות."

169. "מידות" ; the significance is uncertain.

170. The phrase "עומקי השמות" is reminiscent of certain phrases occurring in Abraham Abulafia's works as referring to the highest Kabbalistic path. See Idel, "Maimonides and Kabbalah," nn. 83, 84, 93, 99, and Gikatilla's phrase, n. 105.

171. Compare also R. Eleazar's description of the transmission of the Tetragrammaton to a disciple, which seems to reflect not only an ancient practice but also an extant praxis. Cf. Dan, *The Esoteric Theology*, pp. 74–76; Dan's assertion (p. 75) that the ceremony of transmission of the name has only theological, not magical, overtones must apparently be modified in the direction of more experiential implications of the knowledge gained by the reception of the name.

172. See Idel, "The World of Angels in Human Shape," pp. 1–15.

173. On this issue, see Idel, "The Concept of the Torah," p. 28.

174. See Idel, "The World of Angels in Human Shape," p. 13 n. 52, and Idel, *The Mystical Experience in Abraham Abulafia*, Chap. I; there I deal as well with passages from R. Isaac ibn Latif and R. Moses of Burgos.

175. See, for example, *'Oẓar 'Eden Ganuz*, MS Oxford 1580, fol. 149b, where he mentions the "Chapters of Heikhalot," "The Book of Bahir," and "The Alphabet of R. 'Akiva."

176. MS München 43, fol. 219a. This is a short section from the larger *Sefer ha-Shem*, entitled *'Eser Havvayot*, circulating in some manuscripts. This table was copied from this compendium by R. Yehudah Ḥayyat in his commentary on *Ma'arekhet ha-'Elohut*, fol. 197b, and subsequently in R. Moses Cordovero's *Pardes Rimmonim*, fol. 97c-d. The latter knew of two versions of this table; on the second of these, see n. 192 below.

177. The vowels clearly occur in order to facilitate the pronunciation of the consonants; however, I assume that the mystical and magical feature of the vowels, known from ancient Hellenistic magic, may also have been known in Jewish circles. On vowel mysticism in Abulafia's circle, see also R. J. Zwi Werblowsky, "Kabbalistische Buchstabenmystik und der Traum," *Zeitschrift für Religions und Geistesgeschichte* 8 (1956): 164–169.

178. *Commentary on Sefer Yeẓirah* (Premizlany, 1883), fol. 15d.

"ויתגלגלו בתחלת א"ב ואח"כ יגלגל בהברת א א א א א א ולעולם את השם עמהם אי וכל הא"ב וכו'."

On the penetration of this text into Renaissance literature and praxis, see M. Idel, "Hermeticism and Judaism," par. V.

179. Scholem, *On the Kabbalah*, p. 187.
180. See Matt, *The Book of the Mirrors*, p. 95; *'Or Zaru'a*, MS British Library 771, fol. 92b. It was copied from the latter text by R. Moses Cordovero in *Pardes Rimmonim*, fol 98a. R. Menaḥem Recanati was also acquainted with this peculiar theory of thirty-six combinations of letters and vowels, although he did not copy the table; see his *Commentary on the Pentateuch*, fol. 49b. Nevertheless, the commentator on this text, R. Mordecai Jaffe, obviously perceived the original source of Recanati and gives the detailed combinations.
181. See Moshe Hallamish, ed., *Kabbalistic Commentary of Rabbi Joseph ben Shalom Ashkenazi on Genesis Rabbah* (Jerusalem, 1984), p. 256. Here, as in his unidentified text (see n. 182 below), the recitation of the combinations are related to the creation of the golem.
182. MS Sasson 290, pp. 198–200; this text will be printed and analyzed elsewhere. The identification is provisional, as this text is also close to R. David ben Yehudah he-Ḥasid's thought.
183. Ibid., p 199.
184. Idel, "Kabbalistic Material," p. 198.
185. For further details, see Idel, *The Mystical Experience in Abraham Abulafia*, Chap. I.
186. *'Or ha-Sekhel*, MS Vatican 233, fol. 97b, MS Fulda 4, fol. 32b:

ומפני שיש בהזכרה ענינים גדולים, ואם לא יזהר בה אדם מאד יסתכן בהם, הסתירוה הראשונים ואמנם עתה בזמן הזה כבר נתגלה הנסתר מפני שהגיעה השכחה אל התכלית האחרונה וסוף השכחה הוא ראש ההזכרה.

187. See Idel, "Abraham Abulafia and *Unio Mystica*."
188. Idel, *Abraham Abulafia*, pp. 54–55 n. 161.
189. See Gershom Scholem, "Chapters from *Sefer Sullam ha-'Aliyah* of R. Yehudah Albotini" (in Hebrew), *Kiryat Sefer* 22 (1945): 168; David Blumenthal, *Understanding Jewish Mysticism* (New York, 1982), 2:65–66.
190. *Pardes Rimmonim*, fol. 97a-b.
191. Cordovero does not mention Abulafia's name because, at the time he composed *Pardes Rimmonim*, he mistook this for a work of Gikatilla, *Sha'ar ha-Nikkud*. However, in another, later work, he refers correctly to both author and book.
192. See n. 176 above.
193. See M. Idel, "Some Remarks on R. Abraham Abulafia and R. Moses Cordovero" (in Hebrew), *Da'at* 15 (1985): 117–120.
194. *Pardes Rimmonim*, fol. 97b:

"ודבריו דברי קבלה מפה אל פה או דברי מגיד"

195. See Idel, "Some Remarks," p. 120.
196. *Pardes Rimmonim*, fol 97a:

וכשבאה דעתך להדבק בדעתו הנותנת בך דעת, צריכה דעתך להסיר מעליה כל הדעות הזרות זולת דעתו המשותפת בינך ובינו.

197. Ibid, fol. 97b.: "ומושך כח העליון להדבקו בך"
198. See Chap. III above.
199. For more on this development, see Idel, "Perceptions of Kabbalah" and Chap. VII below.

200. The use of the combinatory techniques of *Sefer Yeẓirah* for mystical purposes is a highly interesting issue, which cannot be presented here. For the time being, see Nicolas Sed, "Le *Sefer Ha-Razim* et la méthode de 'combinaison des lettres,' " *REJ* 130 (1971): 295–303.
201. See Idel, "Egidio da Viterbo and R. Abraham Abulafia's Books" (in Hebrew), *Italia* 2, nos. 1–2 (1981): 48.
202. See Idel, *The Mystical Experience in Abraham Abulafia*, Chap. III.
203. Cf. ibid.
204. See on this topic Gershom Scholem, "The Concept of Kavvanah in the Early Kabbalah," in *Studies in Jewish Thought*, ed. Alfred Jospe (Detroit, 1981), pp. 162–180.
205. See Scholem, *Les Origines de la Kabbale*, pp. 316–319, 437–446.
206. See Gottlieb, *Studies*, pp. 38–55.
207. See above, Chap. III, on the possibility that a certain Geronese text implies interiorization of the ten Sefirot and their unification.
208. See on this issue Arthur J. Deikman, "Deautomatization and the Mystic Experience," in *Altered States of Consciousness*, ed. C. Tart (New York, 1972), pp. 25–46.
209. Some of the historical details concerning this issue were dealt with in Idel, "Kabbalistic Prayer and Colours."
210. On the problem of color in Jewish mysticism, see Gershom Scholem, "Colours and Their Symbolism in Jewish Tradition and Mysticism," *Diogenes* 108 (1979): 84–111; 109 (1980): 64–77. Scholem, despite his lengthy discussions on color, never refers to their visualization within the context of Kabbalistic prayer!
211. I hope to deal with this attribution in a separate study, in which Kabbalistic commentaries on this small treatise will be printed.
212. See Scholem, "The Concept of Kavvanah," pp. 171–174.
213. The treatise attributed to R. 'Azriel deals exclusively with lights connected to prayer, not with colors; later Kabbalists have nevertheless interpreted these lights as colors.
214. MS Cambridge, Add. 505, fol. 8a:
אמ"ר דוד: אין לנו רשות לצייר הי' ספירות אלא בראשי פרקים הבאים לידך כגון מגן אברהם לחסד וכגון חונן הדעת לתפ'. לכן תצייר לעולם באותו צבע של ראשי פרקים, שהוא החשמל של הספירה, כי החשמל הוא מלבוש הספירה בעצמה סביב סביב ואח"כ תמשוך השפע בציורך מעומק הנהר אל העולמות עד אלינו וזהו הנכון המקובל מפה אל פה.
215. The identification of this R. David with R. David ben Yehudah he-Ḥasid has been proven in Idel, "Kabbalistic Prayers and Colours."
216. The Hebrew phrases stem from the *Amidah* prayer, and constitute strong evidence that visualization is connected with prayer. The sequel of our citation mentions *kavvanah* in prayer.
217. *Ḥashmal* and *Malbush* are numerically equivalent: 378.
218. See Idel, "The World of Angels in Human Shape," p. 58 n. 217, and R. Joseph Ashkenazi's *Commentary to Sefer Yeẓirah*, fol. 27a, and so on.
219. For more on these processes, see Chap. VIII below.
220. On this Kabbalist, see Moshe Hallamish's preface to *Kabbalistic Commentary*, pp. 11–27; Georges Vajda, "Un Chapitre de l'histoire du conflit entre la Kabbale et la philosophie: La Polémique anti-intellectualiste de Joseph ben Shalom Ashkenazi de Catalogne," *Archives d'histoire doctrinale et littéraire du moyen age* 23 (1956): 45–144.

221. See Gershom Scholem, "The Real Author of the *Commentary on Sefer Yeẓirah* Attributed to R. Abraham ben David and His Works" (in Hebrew), *Kiryat Sefer* 4 (1927–28): 294–295.

222. Hallamish, *Kabbalistic Commentary*, p. 223:

וכבר כתבו חכמי הפילוסופים בענין הנבואה אמרו דבר וזה לשונם: אינו רחוק שימצא איש מן האנשים שיתדמו לו ענינים בהקיץ כערך שיתדמה לחולם בחלומו, וכל זה בבטול ההרגשות והוא עומד בהקיץ, אחרי שאותיות השם המפורש לנגד עיניו במראות הצובאות. פעמים ישמע קול ורוח ודבר ורעם ורעש בכל כלי חוש השמע, וכן יראה ברמיונו בכל כלי הראות וכן יריח בכל כלי הריח וכן יטעם בכל כלי הטעם וכן ימשש בכל כלי המישוש וכן יהלך ויפרח וכל זה בעוד שאותיות הקדש לנגד עיניו וצבעיו מלובשים בו וזה תרדמת הנבואה.

223. This seems to suggest the technique of contemplating the letters of the divine name—a practice to be analyzed in detail elsewhere—connected to Psalms 16:8. See also n. 244 below.

224. The Hebrew phrase is the biblical "מראות הצובאות"; however, it can be demonstrated that "מראות" is understood here as color, a common medieval meaning of this term. R. Joseph himself writes in his *Commentary on Sefer Yeẓirah*, fol. 27a:

"מראיהן ר"ל צבעיהן"

"צובאות" seems to be parallel to "מלובשים" below, and evidently signifies the occurrence of the colors around the divine name. See also n. 227 below.

225. Cf. *Sefer Yeẓirah* I, 9.

226. "ויפרח"—literally, "he will fly."

227. "מלובשים בו"; compare R. David's text, previously quoted, where the colors surround the Sefirot; here, they cover the letters of the divine name.

228. *Genesis Rabbah* 17:5, p. 156.

229. See R. Joseph Ashkenazi's *Commentary on Sefer Yeẓirah*, fol. 9d, 18b, 30b, and so on.

230. Ibid, fol. 27a:

כשבא הנביא או המייחד להסתכל באורות הקדושות האלו ידע כי פעמים ינוצצו אליו עד שידמה לו כאלו הוא המראה הבזק ומיד יתעלמו ועוד יתנוצצו ועוד יתעלמו.

Compare also Chap. VI, n. 230.

231. MS Paris, Rabbinic Seminary, 108, fol. 95a:

ה' בנקוד דברך: תצייר במחשבתך אותיות ידוד המיוחד לפני עיניך בגלגל צבע אדום כאש ומחשבתך פועלת הרבה מפי הרב תנחום.

232. The vocalization of the word "דברך" in Psalms 119:89 was sometimes seen as one of the ways in which the Tetragrammaton was pronounced; see, for example, an early Kabbalistic fragment preserved in MS Oxford 2240, fol. 248b.

233. The verb "צייר" which occurs here is the same verb as in R. David's aforecited text.

234. MS Milano-Ambrosiana 62, fol. 4a. This circle should be compared with R. Joseph Ashkenazi's circles and the accompanying discussions in his *Commentary on Sefer Yeẓirah*, fol. 18ab, which I hope to do elsewhere.

235. Idel, "Kabbalistic Material," pp. 193–197.

236. See M. Idel, "Again on R. David ben Yehudah he-Ḥasid and R. Isaac Luria" (in Hebrew), *Da'at* 7 (1981): 69–71. The conception of *Ze'ir 'Anpin* as an entity encompassing the Sefirot from Ḥokhmah downward was one embraced by R. Moses Cordovero.

237. For these characteristics of the mandala, see Giuseppe Tucci, *The Theory and Practice of the Mandala* (London, 1961), p. vii.

238. MS New York, JTS 2430, fol. 81a:
ולא יהגה מלת ישראל עד שיצייר השם המפורש שהוא ידוד בניקודו ובצבעו וגם יצייר כאלו מקיפו האות האחרונ׳ של השם, שהיא ההא, כמו גלגל השמים שהוא מקיף כל העולם הן מלמעלה והן מלמטה.

239. Ibid.: "ידוד לבינה בצבע ירוקה כמראה הקשת השם כולו."

240. The identical phrase occurs several times in other texts on visualization in prayer, always as a symbol for the third Sefirah.

241. On the Kabbalistic responsa, from which I am quoting the responsum on prayer, see Gershom Scholem, "The Responsa Attributed to R. Joseph Gikatilla," in *Jacob Freimann Festschrift* (Berlin, 1937), pp. 163–170. Strangely, Scholem decided not to publish the responsum on prayer, although all the other responsa, which were certainly less interesting than this, were printed there. Although Scholem indicated he intended to print it elsewhere, it is not even mentioned in his monograph on colors (n. 210 above). I intend to print this responsum from manuscripts in my research on color mysticism.

242. MS New York, JTS 255, fol. 60a:
בשעה שזוכר ומוציא מפיו דבר שמורה על הכתר יכוין ויצייר שם ידוד בין עיניו בזה הניקוד שהוא נקוד כולו קמץ בציור לבן מאוד כשלג ויכוין שהאותיות הם מתנועעים ופורחים באויר והסוד כולו רמוז בזה הפסוק "שויתי ה׳ לנגדי תמיד."

243. In the diagram, the color of Keter is described as "white as snow"! See also below, in the text quoted from R. Ḥayyim Vital's *Sha'arey Kedushah*, n. 253.

244. Psalms 16:8; see n. 223 above.

245. See also MS New York, JTS 255, fol. 59b:
"דע שהאותיות של התורה הם אותיות חיים ומתנועעים ופורחים באויר עד המרכבה העליונה."

246. MS Milano-Ambrosiana, 62, fol 4:
"כל אלו הרמזים צריכין קבלה מפה אל פה"

247. MS New York, JTS 255, fol. 60a:
"דעו לכם שזו הקבלה המסורה לכם, שאנו כותבי׳ אותה, אסור לגלותה ולמסור אותה לכל אדם אלא ליראי ה׳ ולחושבי שמו ית׳ החרדים על דברו."

248. Mal. 3:16.

249. Isa. 66:2.

250. Idel, "Kabbalistic Prayer and Colours."

251. See Idel, "Kabbalistic Material," pp. 169, 201–206.

252. This manuscript handbook will be published and analyzed in my forthcoming monograph on colors.

253. Gate XXXII, Chap. 2:
ומה טוב ומה נעים אם רצה לצייר הויות האלה בגוונם כי אז ודאיי תפלתו מועילה יותר ויותר ובתנאי שיהיה בכוונתו שאין בעולם הזה דבר שיוכל להמשיל פעולות המדה ההיא אלא בגוון ידוע שהוא פלוני. ומפני שרבו הגוונים אלינו בשער הגוונים לא נבאר הנה הגוונים, אלא כאשר ירצה לכוין הנה השער ההוא לפני המעיין.

254. MS British Library, Margoliouth 749, fol. 16a:
ויצייר שעל רקיע ערבות יש יריעה אחת לבנה גדולה מאד בה מצוייר בציור לבן כשלג הויה בכתב אשורית בגוון ידוע.

255. See n. 243 above.

256. MS British Library, 749, fol. 14b, 18a.

257. See Idel, "The World of Imagination and R. Nathan's *Collectanaea*," pp. 165–167.
258. See Idel, "*Hitbodedut* as Concentration," pp. 46–50.

CHAPTER 6

1. On the entire problem, see John Day, *God's Conflict with the Dragon and the Sea* (Cambridge, 1985), in which an extensive bibliography is provided.
2. See Ricoeur, *The Conflict of Interpretations*, p. 486.
3. See Paul Tillich, "The Religious Symbol," in *Symbolism in Religion and Literature*, ed. Rollo May (New York, 1960), pp. 84–85; Werner Jaeger, *The Theology of the Early Greek Philosophers* (Oxford, 1964), pp. 16–17; Michael Fishbane, "Israel and the 'Mothers,' " in *The Other Side of God*, ed. Peter Berger (New York, 1981), pp. 28–47; and Chap. VII, end of sec. II.
4. Day, *God's Conflict*, p. 187; see also Tillich, "The Religious Symbol," pp. 84–85.
5. *Ḥagigah* 2:1 (*The Talmud*, 8:59).
6. The interdiction refers to extramundane matters; thus, "what is before" refers to precosmogonic events. Interestingly, the very sequence of the Mishnah indicates that "whosoever takes no thought for the honor of his Master, it were a mercy had he not come into the world." Is this warning related to speculation on theogonic processes, which may involve as a repercussion the belittlement of God's honor? For the talmudic interpretation, see *Ḥagigah* 16a.
7. *Pesaḥim* 54a, *Pirkey de-Rabbi Eliezer*, Chap. III.
8. See Urbach, *The Sages*, pp. 198–200.
9. *Ḥagigah* 12a. Interestingly, this list of creative things is introduced in a thirteenth-century treatise by the phrase "ten attributes" (*be-Y' middot*): cf. R. Benjamin ben Abraham min ha-'Anavim's *Perush Alfabetin*, ed. M. H. Schmelzer, in H. Z. Dimitrovsky, *Texts and Studies: Analecta Judaica* (New York, 1977), 1:225.
10. See Scholem, *Major Trends*, p. 74; Scholem, *Les Origines de la Kabbale*, pp. 92–93; who envisages these ten things as traces of "Gnostical speculation and related semi-mythological thought." Why these motifs are to be regarded as Gnostical is not elaborated by Scholem, and I wonder if there is any solid evidence to substantiate this assertion; on this, see Urbach, *The Sages*, pp. 196–197.
11. *Refutation of All Heresies*, Book VIII, Chap. 5, trans. J. H. Macmahon, in *Ante-Nicene Christian Library* (Edinburgh, 1968), 6:320.
12. The phrase "tittle of iota" seems to reflect the Jewish expression, "tittle of yod"; see *Menaḥot* 34a. The authority who uses this phrase, Rav, adduces the following statement in another discussion in connection with R. 'Akiva: "A man will come after several generations whose name is R. 'Akiva ben Joseph, who is destined to comment upon each and every tittle [of the letters] [extracting] heaps of halakhot" (*Menaḥot* 29b). According to my interpretation of "tittles," these point to divine secrets, as the tittle of iota does in Monoimos; see Idel, "The Concept of the Torah," pp. 45–46; Moses Gaster, *The Tittled Bible* (London, 1929), pp. 15, 30–31. See also Carl Jung, *Mysterium Coniunctionis* (Princeton, N.J., 1980), p. 44 n. 26, who pointed out the resemblance between the Gnostic and Kabbalistic understanding of the tittle of iota.

13. The description of supernal beings, such as angels, possessing innumerable eyes is known in Jewish sources; see *'Avodah Zarah* 2b.
14. MS Jerusalem, 4° 19, fol. 195a:
וזה האדם קדמון נרמז בקוצו של יוד משם הויה, כי הוא בחינת כתר של כללות כל העולמות
See also Vital's *'Ez Ḥayyim*, I, III, fol. 1
"וזה האדם נרמז בקוצו של יוד"
15. For yod as Keter, see, for example, the *Commentary on Ma'arekhet ha-'Elohut* by R. Reuven Ẓarfati, printed as *Paz* in *Ma'arekhet ha-'Elohut*, fol. 49b; or in *Sefer ha-Shem*, printed in *Heikhal ḥa-Shem* (Venice, 1601), fol. 7a. The interpretation of the tittle of yod as Keter is a commonplace of Kabbalistic literature.
16. See, for example, R. Moses of Burgos, "An Inquiry in the Kabbalah of R. Isaac ben Jacob Hacohen," in Scholem, *Tarbiẓ* 5 (1934): 188; Liebes, *Sections of the Zohar Lexicon*, p. 39 n. 59.
17. *Refutation of All Heresies* VIII, 6, p. 318: "The monad [that is] the one tittle is therefore, he says, also a decad."
18. See Idel, "The Image of Man above the Sefirot," passim.
19. *Refutation of All Heresies* VIII, 7, p. 320.
20. Ibid., p. 320.
21. *Pesikta Rabbati*, ed. Meir Friedman (Tel Aviv, 1963), fol. 608a-b; *Midrash Tadshe*, in Epstein, *Mi-Kadmoniot ha-Yehudim*, pp. 147–148, 155; Urbach, *'Arugat ha-Bosem* I, p. 219 n. 10.
22. *Refutation of All Heresies* VIII, 6, p. 319: "And it [tittle] comprises in itself whatever things the man also possesses [who is] the Father of the Son of Man." Hence the tittle, which is the Son, contains whatever is found in his source, which is also the source of his decadic nature.
23. *A Coptic Gnostic Treatise*, ed. C. A. Baynes (Cambridge, 1933), p. 17.
24. Ibid., p. 18.
25. See Scholem, *Major Trends*, p. 365 n. 89; Idel, "The Image of Man above the Sefirot," pp. 46–47.
26. *Epistle to the Colossians* I:15–17, 19. See S. J. Grasowski, "God 'Contains' the Universe: A Study in Patristic Theology," *Revue de l'Université de Ottawa* 26 (1950).
27. *The Refutation of All Heresies* VIII, 6, p. 319.
28. *A Coptic Gnostic Treatise*, p. 8 n. 3.
29. Stroumsa, "Form(s) of God," pp. 269–288.
30. Ibid., p. 282.
31. Ibid., p. 283.
32. P. 3; compare also p. 39, "He in [himself] these universes knows, the universes in himself he contemplates. Uncontainable is he himself, whilst the universes he contains possessing them in him"; p. 40. "This is he in whom the universes move to and fro; he giveth form to them within himself." Compare this statement to Acts 17:28: "For in him we live, and have our being."
33. Ibid., p. 12.
34. Note the plural form, which also occurs in the previous quotation. It appears that the "image" enclosing the universes is to be identified with "man." See also ibid., p. 22, where the "hair of his body"—namely, the man's body—was created "after the pattern of the

worlds of the pleroma." See also the view of the Ptolemaic Gnostic school quoted by Irenaeus, *The Refutation of All Heresies* I, VI, 3: " . . . man, and that this is the great and abstruse mystery, namely that the power which is above all others and contains the wholes in his embrace is termed man."

35. *The Refutation of All Heresies* VIII, 5, p. 318.

36. Ibid., p. 317.

37. Preserved in *Yalkut Shim'oni*, Genesis, par. 34. Cf. the translation offered in Scholem, *On the Kabbalah*, p. 163, who was primarily interested in the status of the primeval anthropos as golem. Scholem did not quote the last sentence. The parallels to this passage in talmudic-midrashic literature have been pointed out by A. Marmorstein in his article on *Midrash 'Avkir: Devir* (1923), 1:140; cf. Victor Aptowitzer, "Zur Erklärung einiger Merkwurdiger Agadoth uber die Schopfung des Menschen," *Festschrift . . . of Professor David Simonsens* (Kobenhaver, 1923), pp. 115–117, and his footnotes. However the phrase on the "concentration" of the world in this "golem" is unparalleled in ancient Jewish sources. See, however, *Bahir*, par. 26, where the letter shin "כולל כל העולם" whereas the Torah, ibid., par. 118, "כוללת כל העולמות". On the meanings of the root *kll* in the Palestinian *Piyyut*, see M. Zulai, "Linguistic Remarks on Yannai Piyyutim" (in Hebrew), *Studies of the Research Institute for Hebrew Poetry in Jerusalem* 6 (1945): 199–201, 233. An important significance of this verb in this body of poetic literature is "to accomplish" or "to finish," a meaning that may be reflected also in our passage, as Zulai argues on pp. 200–201. Such an understanding of the verb would drastically change the way in which we have to understand the text and therefore render superfluous the whole interpretation offered in the following pages. I would consequently like to elaborate upon the probability of my reading of the text in the proposed manner. First, the peculiar sense of this verb as accomplishing or ending is an idiosyncrasy of the language of the Palestinian *Piyyut*, a language that has specific linguistic features not to be found elsewhere. Second, my interpretation is reinforced by the existence of the view of man as microcosmos (which is found in the ancient Jewish texts, *as' Avot De-R. Nathan*) or the recurrent conception of Adam as comprising the entire world (according to both talmudic and midrashic sources; cf. Niditch's article, n. 43 below). Therefore the proposed view is not a novelty in Jewish thought but, rather, reiterates an already existing view in both Jewish and non-Jewish sources. Moreover, the author who is presented as the source of the conception of the gigantic size of man is no other than R. Berakhiah, in whose name *Midrash 'Avkir* adduces the above quotation; this fact cannot be considered a mere coincidence. Third, the later interpretation, confirmed by the Kabbalists, strengthens my reading, a fact whose significance is, however, limited. Fourth, the occurrence of the verse asserting that "man is become like one of us" is meaningless in a context that describes man as the first and last creation; if, however, man is conceived as an all-comprehensive entity, it may refer to a unique nature of man that may resemble God, described in ancient Jewish texts as the place of the world, and be comparable to the parallel view in the Gnostic sources. Fifth, the primordial man is portrayed as comprising, in one way or another, all of human history, a view that is partially similar to the view of his nature as concentrating the entire world. These observations notwithstanding, the sense of "accomplishing" for *kll* is not to be overlooked, and I assume that R. Berakhiah may have played on both meanings of this verb.

38. He is a fourth-century amora, whose interest in the special nature of man is also evident

from other traditions; see, for example, *Lamentations Rabbati Petiḥta*, par. 31, where he is the transmitter of a tradition that the righteous are greater than the angels, or *Genesis Rabbah* 8:3, p. 59, and so on.

39. Compare *Sanhedrin* 38b, where the "heretics" (*minim*) were mentioned as potentially ready to say, regarding the Creation of man on the first day, "The Holy One, blessed be he, had a partner in his work of Creation." This passage is considered by Gilles Quispel, "Ezekiel 1:26 in Jewish Mysticism and Gnosis," *Vigiliae Christianae* 34 (1980): 6, as definitive proof "that the Gnostic Anthropos is derived from heterodox Jewish circles, which are older than Philo." Compare especially to the Magharian account of the creating angel: H. A. Wolfson, "The Pre-Existent Angel of the Magharians and Al-Nahawandi," *JQR* n.s. 51 (1960–61): 86–106, Norman Golb, "Who Were the Mougaria?" *JAOS* 80 (1960): 347–359.

40. Psalms 139: 5; for a slightly different interpetation of this verse on the Creation on the first day, see *Tanḥuma, Tazri'a*, par. 2; *Genesis Rabbah* 8:1, p. 56, and so on. In these sources, the Creation of man on the first day involves his spirit or soul, not his body, as in *Midrash 'Avkir;* thus, the concentration of the world in his body becomes impossible.

41. Gen. 3:22.

42. Compare *Zohar* III, 5a, where man is portrayed as sacrificing "when God created the world": "כדברא קב"ה עלמא", a phrase that may be interpreted as pointing to a sacrifice taking place simultaneously with the Creation. If so, and this seems to be the only reasonable way to understand the passage in the *Zohar*, then this classic of Jewish mysticism preserves a tradition opposed by both the classical Midrash (see n. 40 above) and by *Midrash 'Avkir*—namely, that Adam preceded the Creation as a full-fledged person who acted in a ritualistic way, presumably in order to help God in the process of Creation. On sacrifice and Creation, see below, Chap. VII, sec. IV.

43. See the texts of *Genesis Rabbah* 24:2, p. 230, 14:8, p. 132, cited by Scholem, *On the Kabbalah*, p. 163; Susan Niditch, "The Cosmic Adam: Man as Mediator in Rabbinic Literature," *JJS* 34 (1983): 137–146. This scholar explicitly indicates, in contrast to commonly held views, that "their [the rabbis'] Adam owes nothing to that of the gnostics and, more importantly, that descriptions of him have great relevance for understanding the Rabbinic world-view, quite apart from any anti-gnostic polemic" (pp. 138–139). See also Idel, "Enoch Is Metatron"; and Fossum, *The Name of God and the Angel of the Lord*, pp. 272–273.

44. See, for example, Altmann, *Faces of Judaism*, pp. 31–43, and Aptowitzer, "Zur Erklärung."

45. *Commentary on the Song of Songs*, in Chavel, ed., *Kitvey ha-Ramban* II:

"האדם כלול מכל הדברים הרוחניים"

See also p. 510, where Adam is portrayed as:

"כלול ומוכתר ומעוטר מיו"ד ספירות"

It would seem that the triple description of Adam is influenced by similar forms in the *Bahir*, par. 146, 190, 196. It may be that the form *Kalal* in R. 'Ezra, or *Mukhlal* in the *Bahir*, when it occurs together with *Mukhtar*, signifies "embellished." In R. 'Ezra's *Commentary on Talmudic Aggadot*, printed in *Likkutey Shikheḥah u-Feah*, fol. 18a, man is again:

"כלול מהדבר הרוחני"

and in fol. 16b:

״שהוא כלול מעשרה דברים“

See Tishby, ed., R. 'Azriel's *Commentary on Talmudic Aggadot*, p. 5 n. 7. It is worth mentioning also the recurrent usage of the form *kelulah* in connection with the last Sefirah, Malkhut, sometimes in order to point out that she comprises all the higher Sefirot. See, for example, the works of R. Joseph of Hamadan, which abound in the term *kelulah*. The same form also occurs in connection with the evil side: see for example, R. Nathan Shapira of Jerusalem's *Maḥberet ha-Kodesh* (Koretz, 1783), fol. 56a:

״שהיה כלול הנחש יו״ד מדרגות הטומאה“

See also n. 301 below, and the "Secret of Murderer" from *Sefer ha-Ne'elam*, discussed in Chap. VIII.

46. See Chap. III, n. 29.
47. MS British Library 759, fol. 7a:

״כי האדם כלול מכל הדברים הרוחניים שהוא נברא בצלם ודמות“

See also below, n. 56.

48. Compare R. Moses de Leon, in Scholem, "Two Treatises," p. 383, where the Sefirah *Malkhut* is understood as receiving from "all the spiritual things."
49. *Commentary on the Torah*, fol. 51b; this passage will be dealt with more fully in Chap. VII.
50. *Zohar* III, 141b (Idra Rabba):

בגין דדיוקנא דאדם הוי דיוקנא דעלאין ותתאין דאתכללו ביה ובגין דהאי דיוקנא כליל עלאין ותתאין, אתקין עתיקא קדישא תקונוי ותקונא דזעיר אפין בהאי דיוקנא ותיקונא.

The continuation of this quotation is analyzed below in par. 3 on *du-parẓufim*. See also ibid., III: 135ab.

51. Compare also *Zohar* III, 117a, 135a (quoted below in n. 60).
52. The human form is, accordingly, the pattern of the divine one; for more on this issue, see Chap VIII, sec. I.
53. It is nevertheless possible that the *Zohar* assumes that the form of lower and higher men is constituted by ten entities, since immediately afterward it mentions the creation of man by two yods, which may well be an allusion to a decad, thus reflecting the view found also in R. 'Ezra; see n. 45 above.
54. *Sefer ha-Nefesh ha-Ḥakhamah*, col. C, 2, 3–4; this view is also paralleled by the *Zohar* II, 259a.
55. *Pardes Rimmonim* IV, fol. 23c:

כי האדם כולל בבריאתו כל הנמצאות כלם מן הנקודה הראשונה עד תכלית הבריאה והיצירה והעשייה כדכתב בראתיו יצרתיו אף עשיתיו.

56. Isa. 43:7; compare R. Moses de Leon's discussion in *Sefer ha-Rimmon*, MS British Library, 759, fol. 9b:

הוא עשה אותו דוגמא עליוני׳ . . . על עניין סוד בריאה, עשייה, יצירה שנתהוו שלושתן באדם, להיות דוגמת הדברים הרוחניים למעלה והכל בה להכיר בוראו.

Compare *'Avot de-Rabbi Nathan*, Chap. 41, version A, p. 134, and n. 60 below.

57. Vital, *Sha'arey Kedushah* III, 1, pp. 84–85; III, 2, pp. 91–92, and so on.
58. *'Eẓ Ḥayyim* I, I, 2, fol. 12d:

״ובזה האדם נכללין כל העולמות“

See also Vital, *Sha'arey Kedushah* III, 2, pp. 91–92.

59. This is the exact verb used by *Midrash 'Avkir.*

60. See *Zohar* III, 135a (Idra Rabba):
תקוני דזעיר אפין... כדמות אדם עליו מלמעלה כמראה אדם דכליל כל דיוקנין... כמראה אדם דביה סתימין כל עלמין עלאין ותתאין.
Setimin here means "hidden," but it seems, by comparing with the aforecited sources, that it alludes also to the concentration of these worlds in the human shape. See also n. 56 above.
61. Idel, "The Image of Man above the Sefirot," pp. 48–54.
62. See also below, n. 69, for the existence of phrases of "comprising worlds" in the Torah.
63. *The Refutation of All Heresies* VIII, 6, pp. 318–319; compare also above, the passage referred to in n. 11. In this context, a highly interesting passage, stemming from the Nag Hammadi corpus, is to be adduced as relevant to both Gnostic and Kabbalistic views. In the *Tripartite Tractate*, we learn: "The aeon of the truth, being a unity and multiplicity, is honored with little and great names according to the power of each to grasp it—by way of analogy, like a spring which is what it is, yet flows into rivers and lakes and canals and branches, or like a root which extends into trees with branches and fruit, or like a human body which is partitioned in an indivisible way into members of members, primary members and secondary, great [and] small" (Robinson, *The Nag Hammadi Library*, p. 66).
64. *A Coptic Gnostic Treatise*, pp. 12, 17, 138, 140.
65. Ibid., p. 17.
66. Ibid., p. 15; see also p. 9.
67. On this issue, see Idel, "Sefirot above Sefirot," pp. 278–280. The material referred to by Israel Weinstock, *Studies in Jewish Philosophy and Mysticism* (in Hebrew) (Jerusalem, 1969), pp. 111–112 n. 19, as allegedly referring to the Kabbalistic mystery of one and ten is irrelevant, as it includes a regular philosophical formulation, wherein the unity despite the existence of the decad is neither explicit nor implicit.
68. Quoted by R. Menaḥem Recanati, *Commentary on the Pentateuch*, fol. 82b:
והחסיד ר' יצחק בן הרב ז"ל פי' הח' מחכמה עד היסוד הסוף נמצא שהכל כלול במלת אחד.
See also Gottlieb, *The Kabbalah of R. Baḥya*, pp. 86–87.
69. The verb is *kll*, the same root referred to above, nn. 37, 39, 45, 47. Significantly, in *Sefer ha-Bahir*, ed. Margaliot, par. 118 (p. 53), the ten ma'amarot are evidently identical with the "Torah of truth," and "comprise all the worlds":
"כוללת כל העולמים"
Idem, par. 138 (pp. 60–61):
ומאי ניהו תורת אמת, דבר שמורה על אמיתות העולמים... והוא מעמיד עשרה מאמרות שבהם עומד העולם.
Compare also Tishby, "R. 'Azriel's *Commentary on Talmudic Aggadot,*" p. 3. See also the anonymous *Sha'arey Ẓedek*, MS Gaster 954, British Library Or. 10809, fol. 21b:
"...סתרי התורה אשר היא כלולה מכל הצורות התחתונות והעליונות."
See also the fourteenth-century *Sefer ha-Temunah*, fol. 30a; and ibn Gabbay, *'Avodat ha-Kodesh*, fol. 20c,d.
70. Commentary on *Kriat Shema'*, printed in Scholem, "Seridim," p. 222.
וליחד הכל במלה אחת שהאלף של אחד רמז למה שאין המחשבה יכולה להתפשט בה, והחית רמז לח' ספירות והדלת היא גדולה, רמז לספירה העשירית.
71. See n. 45 above.
72. "Ve-Zot li-Yihudah," in Jellinek, *Auswahl*, p. 19:

"בעלי הקבלה הספיריית... אומרים כי האלוהים עשר ספירות והעשרה הם אחד."

See also above, Chap. III, sec. VII, near n. 136. The same text, in a phrase not cited there, states that the Kabbalist must "direct [his thought] so that all the Sefirot are one."

73. Chap. 31, version A, pp. 90–91. I shall return to the analysis of this text in Chap. VII.

74. Chap. 31, 3:

"ויצר באדם כל מה שברא בעולמו"

Ibid.:

"כל מה שברא הקב"ה בעולמו ברא באדם"

75. Chap. 31, 2:

"שאדם אחד שקול כנגד מעשה בראשית כולו"

76. R. Nathanael ben al-Fayyumi's *Bustan Al-'Ukul*, ed. Joseph Kappaḥ (Jerusalem, 1954); on this author, see S. Pines, "Nathanael ben Al-Fayyumi et la théologie ismaelienne," *Revue de l'histoire juive en Egypte* 1 (1947): 5–22.

77. Ibid., pp. 4–5. On ten things in man, see *Nedarim*, 31a, *Ecclesiastes Rabbah*, 5:13, 7:38, and so on. Compare the view found in *Corpus Hermeticum, Asclepius*, no. 8: "dei, cuius imagines duae mundus et homo." There is at least a certain resemblance between "mundus" and "homo," as both of them are images of God.

78. See n. 29 above.

79. Ibid., p. 273.

80. Ibid., p. 272 n. 14.

81. Ibid., p. 280; *On the Origin of the World*, par. 104–105; cf. Robinson, *The Nag Hammadi Library*, p. 166.

82. Ibid., p. 280 n. 59.

83. *Eugnostos*, 83; Foerster, *Gnosis*, 2:32.

84. Margaliot, par. 94, p. 40; Scholem, *Bahir*, p. 64:

שנים עשר אבנים הם ע"ב כנגד ע"ב שמות של הקב"ה ומאי טעמא התחיל השתים עשרה, ללמדך שי"ב מנהיגים יש לו להקב"ה, ובכל אחד ואחד ששה כוחות.

85. *Manhigim*: cf. *Sefer Yeẓirah* V, 2.

86. Compare the *Coptic Gnostic Treatise*, p. 83, where three aspects of the twelve fathers form the number thirty-six, just as in *Bahir*, the six powers of the twelve leaders form the number seventy-two. If the sentence, "And those that are exterior to them received character from them . . . " refers to the aspects and not to the fathers, then we may assume that this is a hint to seventy-two.

87. Cf. n. 81 above. Compare also *The Hypostasis of the Archons*, 95; cf. Robinson, *The Nag Hammadi Library*, p. 158. On the seventy-two faces of the creatures sustaining the chariot, see R. Joseph of Hamadan's *Sefer Tashak*, p. 401; this early fourteenth-century commentary on the *Merkavah* is seemingly the only Jewish text that preserved a tradition concerning the figure seventy-two and the divine chariot. See also Fossum, *The Name of God and the Angel of the Lord*, p. 303, who sensitively wrote on the above-mentioned Gnostic texts that they "palpably draw upon Jewish tradition" without, however, pinpointing specific Jewish texts.

88. For a parallel to the distinction between "throne" and "chariot," see below, R. Yehudah ha-Levi's *Kuzari* IV, 3.

89. This is a Jewish view: see Fallon, *The Enthronement of Sabaoth*, p. 100 n. 30.

90. The regular Jewish view assumes the existence of seventy languages or nations. The Gnostic

and Kabbalistic figure is exceptional and paralleled by Pseudo-Clementinus, *Recognitiones*, 2, 42, as Fallon, *The Enthronement of Sabaoth*, pp. 103–104, has remarked. See also the *Hebrew Enoch*, Schäfer, *Synopse*, p. 13, par. 23:

"שבעים ושנים שרי מלכויות"

91. The continuous praise of God by the angels is a commonplace in Heikhalot literature: see K. E. Grözinger, *Musik und Gesang in der Theologie der fruhen Judischen Literatur* (Tübingen, 1982), pp. 281–315.

92. Margaliot, par. 98, p. 43:

"וכל הצורות הקדושות ממונות על כל האומות"

See also par. 167, p. 72.

93. *Bahir*, Margaliot, no. 95, p. 42; Scholem, *Bahir*, p. 65.

וכלם אינם יותר מל"ו צורות וכלם נשלמו בל"ב, מסור לל"ב ל"ב—ונשארו ארבעה— והם ס"ד צורות. ומנלן דנמסר ל"ב לל"ב דכתיב כי גבוה מעל גבוה שומר וא"כ היינו ס"ד. חסר שמונה לע"ב שמותיו של הקב"ה והיינו דכתיב וגבוהים עליהם. והם ז' ימי השבוע, וחסר א היינו דכתיב ויתרון ארץ בכל.

94. "מסור": on this verb, see Scholem, *Bahir*, p. 73 n. 1.

95. Eccles. 5:7.

96. Ibid.

97. Compare the Gnostic figure 360, which is viewed in *Eugnostos* as connected with the days of the year (Foerster, *Gnosis*, 2:32), thus, the reference to the days of the week is a further affinity to the ancient source; see my analysis below.

98. Eccles. 5:8. I understand the usage of this verse as proof of the excellence of the "earth"—that is, the seat of glory (see n. 106 below) in comparison with the seventy-one entities. Furthermore, on the ground of the *Bahir* (Margaliot, par. 130, p. 57; par. 146, p. 64) the "earth" points to the Sefirah of Ḥokhmah. Compare, however, a very different interpretation of the meaning of the verse of Ecclesiastes in Scholem, *Les Origines de la Kabbale*, pp. 145–146 n. 136.

99. On Ezek. 1:6, and see also Rashi *ad loc.*

100. Cf. Scholem, *Explications and Implications*, pp. 270–283.

101. Cf. Scholem, *Bahir*, pp. 66–67.

102. *Seder Gan 'Eden*, quoted by Scholem, ibid., p. 66 n. 7.

והאילן הזה הוא שרשיו בלבנון שהם כסא הכבוד ית' והוא לבנון כנגד הלבנון העליון ושרשיו שבעים ושתים שרשים.

103. For the symbolism of "Lebanon" as one of the highest Sefirot, that is, Ḥokhmah, see Chap. VIII below.

104. *Hilkhot Yesodey ha-Torah*, 7:1:

דעתו פנויה תמיד למעלה קשורה תחת כסא להבין באותן הצורות הקדושות הטהורות.

The Hebrew phrase "holy forms" is identical with that of the *Bahir*, as pointed out by Scholem, *Les Origines de la Kabbale*, p. 64 n. 10. In Maimonides, the forms are, presumably, the separate intellects, namely "angels," although the latter term differs radically from the rabbinic understanding of this subject. It would seem that Maimonides inherited a tradition according to which the angels connected to the divine throne are designated as forms. The meaning of the "throne" seems to be the "convexity of the diurnal sphere"; see Warren Z. Harvey, "A Third Approach to Maimonides' Cosmology-Prophetology Puzzle,"

HTR 74 (1981): 297 n. 37–38. However, the way in which this meaning of the divine throne fits its connection to the forms qua separate intellects is still to be elaborated.

105. Ibid.: "כשיכנס בפרדס"

106. *Bahir*, Margaliot, par. 96, p. 42; Scholem, *Bahir*, p. 69:
"מאי ניהו ארץ שנחצבה ממנו שמים, והוא כסאו של הקב"ה."

107. *Kuzari* IV:3.

108. It is possible, however, that this distinction has something to do with the Islamic *'arsh* and *Kursi*, which mean "Seat," but this cannot be ascertained with certainty, since ha-Levi preserved his Hebrew terminology in the Arabic text.

109. Most of these forms recur in the same paragraph of *Kuzari* IV:3; see also ibid., II:4, IV:5, 11, 25; and Wolfson, *Studies* II, pp. 86–95, who nevertheless does not elaborate upon the meaning of the forms; see Wolfson, p. 10 n. 4.

110. *Bahir*, Margaliot, par. 98–99, pp. 43–44; Scholem, *Bahir*, p. 71:
בכל נתיב מהן צורה שומרת דכתיב לשמור את דרך עץ החיים; ומאי ניהו צורות? דכתיב (שם) וישכן מקדם לגן עדן את הכרובים ואת להט החרב המתהפכת לשמור את דרך עץ החיים.

111. Gen. 3:24.

112. Ibid.

113. Par. 94–95; Robinson, *The Nag Hammadi Library*, p. 158.

114. Compare to the *Untitled Document*, col. 250, ed. H. M. Schenke, where the phrase "seven dynameis, of the seven heavens of Chaos" refers to Yaldabaoth; thus, seven powers and children are different designations of the same entities.

115. Margaliot, par. 171, p. 74; Scholem, *Bahir*, p. 123:
למלך שהיו לו שבעה בנים ושם כל אחד ואחד ממקומו ואמר להם שבו זה ע"ג זה.
Compare also par. 128–129 discussed below.

116. Margaliot, par. 172, p. 74; Scholem *Bahir*, p. 123:
"וכבר אמרתי לכם ששבע צורות קדושות יש לו לקב"ה."

117. Margaliot, par. 119, p. 53:
ומאי הוי אילן דאמרת? א"ל כוחותיו של הקב"ה זה על גב זה והן דומין לאילן.

118. Margaliot, par. 105, p. 46:
ומאי ואת הבנים תקח לך ר' רחומאי אמר אותם בנים שגדלה. ומאי ניהו: שבעת ימי בראשית.

119. Deut. 22:7.

120. Margaliot, par. 81, p. 36:
"ימי השבוע, ללמדך שכל יום יש לו כח."
Compare also par. 82, p. 36:
"כי בכל יום ויום יש לו כחו"

121. See n. 84 above.

122. Compare *Origen Contra Celsum*, VI, 31–32; Irenaeus, *The Refutation of All Heresies* I, xxviii, 3, where the sons of the Ogdoads are related to the seven planets.

123. Margaliot, par. 128–129, p. 56; Scholem, *Bahir*, pp. 96–97:
ומאי הוי קדוש קדוש אחר כך ה' צבאות מלא כל הארץ כבודו; אלא קדוש כתר עליון, קדוש שורש האילן, קדוש דבק ומיוחד בכלם, ה' צבאות מלא כל הארץ כבודו. ומאי ניהו קדוש שהוא דבק ומיוחד, אלא למה"ד למלך שהיו בנים ולבנים בנים, בזמן שבניהם עושים רצונו נכנס ביניהם ומעמיד הכל.

124. Isa. 6:3.

125. On the possible significance of this term and its source, see Joseph Dan, *The First Kabbalistic Circles* (in Hebrew) (Jerusalem, 1977), pp. 92–96.
126. Compare the text of *Bahir*, par. 171, adduced above, n. 115.
127. Margaliot, par. 133, p. 57:

"וכי אין כבוד ה' זה אחת מצבאותיו לא גרע."

128. "Jaldabaoth Reconsidered," *Mélanges d'histoire des religions offerts à Henri-Charles Puech* (Paris, 1974), pp. 420–421. For a criticism of Scholem's etymology, see Fallon, *The Enthronement of Sabaoth*, pp. 32–34.
129. Strangely, Scholem did not mention the preceding texts of the *Bahir* in his article, although he did remark there on "the transition from the Hebrew word for troops, *ḥayalot*, to forces and archons" (p. 421 n. 3) in the *Bahir*, which is described there as using "sources deriving from Jewish Gnostic circles in the Near East."
130. See especially Scholem's remark, ibid., p. 420, that *Ẓevaot* had already been translated as the "Lord of dynameis" in ancient times.
131. See Fallon, *The Enthronement of Sabaoth*, pp. 90–91.
132. Margaliot, par. 172, p. 74:

שבע צורות קדושות יש לו לקב"ה וכולם כנגדן באדם שנאמר כי בצלם אלהים עשה את האדם.

Compare also par. 143 (quoted below), par. 172, and par. 119, pp. 53, 63, 74–75.
133. Gen. 9:6.
134. See Idel, "The World of Angels in Human Shape."
135. *Songs of the Sabbath Sacrifice: A Critical Edition* (Atlanta, Ga., 1985), pp. 293, 332.
136. Margaliot, par. 143, p. 63:

"חצב הקב"ה כל אותיות התורה וחקקו ברוח ועשה בו צורותיו."

137. *Adversus Haereses*, I, 14, 1; for the Jewish background of this text, see Idel, "The World of Angels in Human Shape," pp. 2–15, where I pointed out several Jewish texts identifying angels with letters. See also below, the phrase "forms of truth."
138. See Idel, ibid., p. 3 n. 7.
139. *Sefer Kerovot*, ed. Wolf Heidensheim (Hannover, 1838), p. 141:

...ומתחתיהם שלושים מעלות...זו למעלה מזו עולות—ועד כסא הכבוד מסות ועולות—בשיח נעימות שיר המעלות.

According to the version in *Sifre*, quoted in *Yalkut Shim'oni, 'Ekev*, no. 872, these thirty degrees seem to be the righteous men. It would seem that this figure is connected to the fifteen "Songs of Degrees" of the Psalms. For material on the thirty degrees in poetical sources, see Ezra Fleischer, "Solving the Qiliri Riddle" (in Hebrew), *Tarbiẓ* 54 (1985): 394–395.
140. For *Ma'alot* approximating the concept of angels, see Maimonides, *Hilkhot Yisodey ha-Torah* 2:5.
141. Psalms 121:1.
142. MS Oxford, Christ Church 198, fol. 73b; MS Moscow 131, fol. 187a:

והיא התחלת הצורות הנוראות המושגות במראות הנבואות ומהם נבראו כסא הכבוד ואופנים ושרפים וחיות הקדש ומלאכי השרת.

143. Hence, the lower Sefirot are portrayed as visible or at least directly apprehensible in the prophetic experience, a view that contradicts the common conception of the Sefirot as perceptible only through the decoding of their symbols.

144. Compare the list of *Sefer Yeẓirah* I, 12.
145. See M. Friedlander, *Essays in the Writings of Abraham ibn Ezra* (London, 1943), Hebrew sec., pp. 23–24; Dan, *Esoteric Theology*, p. 232. The term *Ẓurah* has various meanings in *Sefer ha-Ḥayyim*, ranging from astrological to angelic significance; this issue is deserving of a more detailed examination than can be done here. The Ashkenazic Ḥasidic masters' usage of the term *Ẓurah* was also influenced by R. Sa'adyah Gaon's description of the *Shekhinah* as a *Ẓurah* or created entity; see Dan, *Esoteric Theology*, pp. 104ff., although I assume that these authors probably also have other sources. Sa'adyah's use of the term *Ẓurah* is to be analyzed against the background of the mystical significance of the same term in ancient Jewish texts. If this suggestion is verified, then we can easily understand why the Ashkenazic masters integrated Sa'adyah's view in their theology. See also Stroumsa, "Form(s) of God," p. 272 n. 14.
146. Scholem, *Elements*, p. 294.
147. Some aspects of this question were analyzed in Idel, "Métaphores et pratiques sexuelles," pp. 337–342.
148. Published by Scholem, *Reshit ha-Kabbalah*, p. 79; see also Scholem, *Les Origines de la Kabbale*, pp. 232–233; Twersky, *Rabad of Posquières*, p. 291 n. 20. I hope to elaborate on the profound influence of this early piece of Kabbalistic speculation on later Kabbalah in a separate study on *du-parẓufim*.
149. Cf. *Genesis Rabbah* 8:1, p. 55, *'Erubin* 18a.
150. On the Greek sources of the loan words *du-parẓufim* and *androgynos*, which occur in the Midrash in connection with the Creation of man, see Wayne A. Meeks, "The Image of the Androgyne: Some Uses of a Symbol in Earliest Christianity," in *History of Religions* 13 (1974); 186 n. 90.
151. This phrase stems from the blessing of the moon and refers to the sun and moon, here symbolically alluding to masculine and feminine divine powers.
152. Cf. Exod. 36:13.
153. Gen. 19:24.
154. Such a theory existed in a relatively explicit text, which may be dated from the end of the thirteenth century: see Idel, "Kabbalistic Material," pp. 193–197.
155. Printed in Epstein, *Mi-Kadmoniot ha-Yehudim*, p. 144:
שני כרובים על ארון העדות כנגד שני שמות הקדושים ה' אלהים.
See also Raphael Patai, *The Hebrew Goddess* (New York, 1978), p. 82, who noted the affinity between Philo and *Midrash Tadshe*.
156. See *Yoma*, 54a.
157. *Babba Batra*, 99a.
158. See *Sefer ha-Rokeaḥ* (Jerusalem, 1960), p. 22.
159. *Sodei Razaya*, p. 58.
160. II Sam. 2:6.
161. (Jerusalem, 1965), pp. 242–243:
"שני כרובים נגד ה' אלהים דהיינו מה"ד והרחמים."
162. On I, 3; cf. *Sefer Yeẓirah*, p. 41:
"כמעור איש ולוות שהיה בבית המקדש להרבות פריין ורביין של ישראל." "שהיה"
In the Premyzlany edition of the Commentary, fol. 3b, the sentence from *she-hayah* onward

is missing. See in his commentary, ibid., fol. 22b, where R. Eleazar again adduces the correspondence between the cherubim and the divine names.

163. I Kings 7:30.

164. Cf. *Tanḥuma*, ed. Buber, Numbers, fol. 17a. See also Idel, "Métaphores et pratiques sexuelles," p. 340 n. 35.

165. *Baddei ha-'Aron*, MS Paris BN 840, fol. 6a:
נברא אדם וחוה—בגזירה שוה—דו־פרצופין—זה בזה מעורין—רמוזים בצורת הכרובים.

166. The talmudic description of the cherubim as intertwined may easily be understood as referring to an androgynous entity.

167. See his *Commentary on Song of Songs*, in *Kitvey ha-Ramban*, 2:493, 496; Tishby's remark in R. 'Azriel's *Commentary on the Talmudic Aggadot*, p. 11 n. 1 and p. 71; R. Abraham of Cologne's *Keter Shem Tov*, printed in Jellinek, *Auswahl*, pp. 42–43; Recanati, *The Commentary on the Pentateuch*, fol. 49b (below I shall deal also with another view reflected in Recanati's work).

168. See Idel, "Jerusalem in Medieval Jewish Thought."

169. *Questiones et Solutiones in Exodus* II, 66, quoted in Goodenough, *By Light, Light*, pp. 25–26. Compare also to the pair of entities existing before the Creation in Pseudo-Philo, *Liber Antiquitatum Biblicarum* 60, 2, which is considered to be a syzygy of powers, which precedes and probably influenced their Gnostic counterparts. Cf. Marc Philonenko, "Essenisme et Gnose chez le Pseudo-Philon," in *Le Origini dello Gnosticismo* (Leiden, 1967), pp. 409–410.

170. According to Goodenough, *By Light, Light*, p. 25, Philo refers here to the divine names "Kyrios" and "theos."

171. *Jewish Symbols in the Greco-Roman Period* (Princeton, N.J., 1954), 4:132.

172. He adduced the passages from *Yoma* 54a-b, see above n. 156.

173. *Jewish Symbols*, p. 132.

174. Ibid., p. 132.

175. Elsewhere, in his *By Light, Light*, pp. 359–369, Goodenough discussed the affinities between some Philonic views of the divine powers and the Kabbalistic perception of Sefirot, albeit with no reference to the above-mentioned passage of Philo or to Rabad's text. On Philo and the Kabbalah on the problem of divine attributes, see the remarks of Patai, *The Hebrew Goddess*, pp. 76, 119–120. This author conceived the Philonic attributes as corresponding to masculine and feminine categories, an issue neither explicit in Philo nor discussed in Richard A. Baer's monograph *Philo's Use of Categories Male and Female* (Leiden, 1970). Were Patai correct, the affinity between Philo and Rabad would be even greater.

176. See below, n. 186.

177. See Gedaliahu G. Stroumsa, "Le Couple de l'ange et de l'esprit—traditions juives et chrétiennes," *Revue Biblique* 88 (1981): 42, 46–47, 53–55.

178. Ibid., p. 46.

179. *Shoḥer Tov*, on Psalm 27:
אמר ר׳ הושעיא דו פרצופין היו פרצוף של אור לישראל ופרצוף של חושך למצרים
In *Midrash Tehilim* on the same psalm, the version is:

"שני פרצופין"

180. See, for example, the phrases:

"שאני מביא אור לישראל וחשך לאומות"

כבר הראה הקב"ה דוגמא בעולם הזה, שנאמר ויהי חשך אפלה בכל ארץ מצרים . . .

181. Compare the use of the word *parsopa* by the Syrian theologian John the Solitary. According to A. de Halleux, this term "applique a la manière d'être et d'agir du Saveur": see his "Jean le Solitaire," *Le Museon* 94 (1981): 10.

182. See *Leviticus Rabbah*, ed. M. Margaliot (Jerusalem, 1972), p. 26; *Midrash Exodus Rabbah*, ed. A. Shinan (Jerusalem and Tel Aviv, 1984), p. 160. In these texts, the term *du-parẓufim* relates to the twofold action of the divine voice; cf. Ze'ev Gries, "From Myth to Ethos" (in Hebrew), in *Nation and History*, ed. S. Ettinger (Jerusalem, 1984) 3:121–122.

183. See *Mi-Kadmoniyot ha-Yehudim*, pp. 139–140.

184. See Twersky, *Rabad of Posquières*, p. 34.

185. See the hypothesis of Isaac Baer, "The Service of the Sacrifice," pp. 101–104, who has already adumbrated the possibility that ancient concepts of the cherubim and the divine attributes influenced early Kabbalah; however, he did not analyze either R. Abraham's view or that of *Midrash Tadshe*. Moreover, Baer's views seem to have been largely ignored by the scholars of Kabbalah.

186. *Pesikta de-R. Kahana*, ed. Buber, fol. 162a:

ואע"פ שהדין והרחמים נראין רחוקין זה מזה, שניהם ארוקין זה בזה, כי לפעמים יפעל אדם בדין והדין ההוא שב למידת הרחמים ופעמים הרחמים שב למידת הדין.

See A. Marmorstein, *The Old Rabbinic Doctrine of God* (Oxford, 1927), 1:44; and the passage we quoted above from Philo; and N. A. Dahl and A. F. Segal, "Philo and the Rabbis on the Names of God," *Journal for the Study of Judaism* 9 (1978): 1–28. Compare also the words of Rabad's grandson, R. Asher ben David, *Commentary of Thirteen Attributes*, p. 18:

כי הנה ה' יוצא ממקומו יוצא ממדה למדה, ממדת הדין למדת הרחמים.

See also the Ashkenazic Ḥasidic text printed by Dan, *Esoteric Theology*, p. 122.

187. See Isa. 26:21; the verse continues, "to punish the inhabitants of the earth."

188. *Commentary on the Pentateuch*, fol. 49b:

יש מפרשין כי הכרובים רומזים לדו פרצופין וכן נראה דעת הרמב"ן ז"ל ולזה נוטה מאמר חז"ל שאמרו ב' כרובים כנגד יי אלהים.

The sages cited by Recanati seem to be *Midrash Tadshe;* see n. 155 above. Compare also *Sha'arey Ẓedek* from Abulafia's school, MS Jerusalem, 8° 148, fol. 50a:

ותהפך מדת הדין למדת הרחמי' בסוד להט החרב המתהפכת את הכרובים, כרובים זכר ונקבה.

189. See Altmann, "The Question of Authorship," p. 410.

190. Ibid., pp. 274–275, 410.

191. *Sukkah* 5b: "אפי זוטרתי" "אפי רברבי" See Liebes, "The Messiah of the *Zohar*," p. 130.

192. Ibid.:

"פנים של מעלה" "פני אלהים"

193. Gerhard Scholem, *Einige Kabbalistische Handschriften im Britischen Museum* (Jerusalem, 1932), pp. 19–21; Altmann, "The Question of Authorship," pp. 274, 410.

194. Tishby, *The Wisdom of the Zohar*, 1:110–111, 157.

195. Ibid., p. 111.

196. A third possibility would be that there were two distinct traditions already existing in the thirteenth century, and they were used by various Kabbalists with no need to reinterpret either one of them. This alternative seems as reasonable as the other two.

197. *Zohar* III, 141b:

וייצר—תרין יודין למה—רזא דעתיקא קדישא ורזא דזעיר אפין.

198. Gen. 2:7.

199. It may be that the yod also points to "ten," that is, the decad that presumably composes the divine structures; see n. 53 above.

200. *Batey Midrashot*, Wertheimer, II, p. 412:

"אחת כנגד פרצוף פניו ואחת כנגד פרצוף אחריו."

See also R. Yehudah Hadassi, *Eshkol ha-Kofer*, fol. 36c; Chap. IV, n. 24 above.

201. *Zohar* III, 141b.

כלא הוא במתקלא חדא אבל מכאן אתפרשין אחרוי אתפשטן רחמי ומכאן אשתכח דינא.

Compare *Zohar* III, 117a, where the motif of *du-parẓufim* is obvious, but is treated in a classical rabbinic way.

202. R. Simeon ibn Lavi, *Ketem Paz*, fol. 27c; on "the depths of nothingness," see below, Chap. VIII.

203. Scholem, *Kabbalah*, pp. 96–116; Gottlieb, *Studies*, pp. 223–31, 404–411; Tishby, *The Wisdom of the Zohar*, 1:95–117, 131–161; Hava Tirosh-Rothschild, "Sefirot as the Essence of God in the Writings of David Messer Leon," *AJSreview* 7–8 (1982–83): 409–425; Idel, "Between the Views of Sefirot as Essence and Instruments"; Ben Shlomo, *The Mystical Theology of R. Moses Cordovero;* Rachel Elior, *The Theory of Divinity of Hasidut Habad* (in Hebrew), pp. 78–118.

204. See Idel, "Sefirot above Sefirot," p. 239.

205. The anthropological conception of the Sefirot, which will be treated at the end of this chapter, is characteristic of the ecstatic Kabbalah, and seems to have been a product of the last quarter of the thirteenth century.

206. *Commentary on Sefer Yeẓirah*, p. 6:

"סופן בתחלתן": שהרבה חוטין הם נמשכים מן הגחלת שהיא אחת, שהשלהבת אין יכולה לעמוד בעצמה אלא ע"י דבר אחד בלבד, כי כל הדברים וכל המדות שהן נראות שהם נפרדות אין בהם פירוד שהכל אחד, כמו ההתחלה שהוא מיחד הכל במלה יחיד.

207. Ibid., pp. 8–9, and the quotation in the name of "the Ḥasid," that is, R. Isaac, in MS Paris 353, fol. 30b–31a. See Scholem, "An Inquiry in the Kabbalah of R. Isaac ben Jacob Hacohen," *Tarbiẓ* 2 (1931): 419; 3 (1932): 37, 42.

208. *Keter Shem Tov*, in *Ma'or va-Shemesh*, fol. 25a; this text was quoted by a long series of Kabbalists.

209. "שכל מושכל". I assume that R. Shem Tov's intention is to again refer to the relationship between two strata in Godhead, just as he does immediately thereafter when he mentions the "burning coal"—*'Eiyn Sof*—and the "flame"—the Sefirot. However, the elaboration on Godhead as intellect in *Ma'arekhet ha-'Elohut*, Chap. 2, does not refer to the "intelligible."

210. On the connection between these works, see Gottlieb, *The Kabbalah of R. Baḥya*, pp. 249–259.

211. *Ma'arekhet ha-'Elohut*, fol. 28a, 49a:

"הן האלוהות"

212. Ibid., fol. 6b:

"מצד המקבלים"

213. Compare R. Joseph ibn Ẓaddik, *'Olam Katan* II:2; R. Yehudah ha-Levi, *Kuzari* IV:3.

214. Scholem, "The Authentic Commentary on Sefer Yeẓirah of Naḥmanides," p. 418:

שכשם שלא נודע עצמו של הב"ה, כך לא נודע עצתו, אבל מתוך הקבלה למדנו ששמו וצלמו ועצמו, הכל ההוא הוא, כי שמו הוא ציון הגדול להכיר גודל מעלתו ותפארתו ית' וצלמו ועצמו עשר ספירות ... עשר ספירות בלימה הם עצם הבורא וצלמו.

215. Ibid., p.418 n. 3; p. 419 n. 1.

216. Printed in Scholem, *CCCH*, pp. 205–206:

... הספירות, שהם עצמו של הקב"ה כביכול, כמן יסודות האדם באדם, והבן זה כי על כן אמר יחזקאל כמראה אדם עליו מלמעלה, דמות כבוד כלו... שכל אלו הספירות הם כחות נבדלות, פשוטות בתכלית הפשטות, והם כלם כבוד א' בלי שום חילוק ופירוד אלא מצד הפעולות המגיעות אלינו מהם, וכל אלו הספי' בראם האל ית' שמו לכבודו, מהם כלם נעשה אחדות שווה ונקראו כולם נשמה והקב"ה נשמה לכל הנשמות.

217. Ezek. 1:26.

218. Compare n. 213 above.

219. Naḥmanides several times uses the phrase *'eẓem ha-kavod*, referring to each of the Sefirot. See Scholem, "The Authentic Commentary on Sefer Yeẓirah of Naḥmanides,' pp. 402–404; see also R. 'Ezra's *Commentary on Song of Songs* in Chavel, *Kitvey ha-Ramban* II, p. 478.

220. *Ta'amey ha-Miẓvot*, quoted by R. Yehudah Ḥayyat in *Ma'arekhet ha-'Elohut*, fol. 30a:

"כשהעשר ספירו' הם הבורא ית' בעצמותו"

Ibid.:

"אין לשים חלק בעצמות"

Ibid.:

"כי אין הספירות עצמות הבורא"

See also Recanati's *Commentary on Prayer*, MS New York, JTS 1887, fol. 137b. Recanati also rejects the formula:

"הם הבורא ממש"

See ibid., fol. 30a, 31a, 35a.

221. Ibid., fol. 30a, 35b.

222. Recanati uses terms characteristic of the *'Iyyun* circle, such as "Soul of Souls," and even quotes the *Book of 'Iyyun*.

223. See Idel, "Between the Views of Sefirot as Essence and Instruments," pp. 104–105.

224. See below, par. IV, sec. 3.

225. *Ma'arekhet ha-'Elohut*, fol. 5b–7a:

ושלילת השנוי היא כוללת ב' ענייני' שנוי מחשב' ושנוי פעולה.

226. Ibid., fol. 36b.

227. (London, 1911), p. 113.

228. Cf. Ezek. 1:14.

229. On contemplation in water, see M. Idel, "The Metamorphosis of an Ancient Technique of Prophetic Vision in the Middle Ages" (in Hebrew), *Sinai* 86 (1980): 1–7.

230. This work was identified by Gershom Scholem, "Eine unbekannte mystische Schrift des Mose de Leon," *MWGJ* 71 (1927): 109–123; the text translated above is printed at pp. 118–119 n. 5. Scholem has already adduced most of the parallel texts from the *Zohar* and

Shekel ha-Kodesh; we may add to his list de Leon's *Commentary on the Merkavah* (printed in Idel, "Metamorphosis of an Ancient Technique," p. 5), and an interesting parallel in ibn Gabbay's *'Avodat ha-Kodesh* IV, 19, fol. 128b. See also Chap. V, n. 230, above.

231. See *Zohar* I, 41b; *Zohar Ḥadash* 39d.

232. *Shekel ha-Kodesh*, p. 123. Interestingly, ibn Gabbay has already adduced these two types of mystical contemplation together: see n. 230 above.

233. *Zohar* I, 42a, 97a-b; II, 23b.

234. Compare Gershom Scholem, "Das Ringen zwischen dem Biblishen Gott und dem Gott Plotins in der Alten Kabbala," *Eranosjahrbuch* 33 (1964): 47–48.

235. See Chap. IX, sec. IV; on sefirotic dynamism, see also Chap. VIII, sec. II. On the emphasis on dynamism in Jewish theology generally, as opposed to Christian theology, see Jaroslav Pelikan, *The Christian Tradition* (Chicago and London, 1971), 1:22.

236. Gottlieb, *Studies*, pp. 293–315, 404–411; Tishby, *The Wisdom of the Zohar*, 1:95–117, 131–161.

237. Margaliot, par. 57, p. 26:

וכן קבלתי מדכתיב כי ששת ימים עשה ה', כמה דאת אמר: ששה כלים נאים עשה הקב"ה, ומאי הם: את השמים ואת הארץ.

238. Exod. 31:7.

239. Cf. *Berakhot* 57a: *kelim na'im*. Compare, however, Scholem, *Les Origines de la Kabbale*, p. 93, where he adduces a Gnostic parallel from the Valentinian school: "vas pretiosum." As the Hebrew phrase of the *Bahir* is identical to the expression used in this talmudic passage, I doubt that the Kabbalistic treatise draws upon the Gnostic source.

240. Margaliot, par. 158, p. 68:

שכל יום ויום יש לו מאמר שהוא ארון לו, לא מפני שהוא נברא בו אלא מפני שהוא פועל בו הפעולה המסורה בידו.

241. Compare Margaliot, par. 81–82, p. 36:

שכל יום יש לו כח . . . כי ששת ימים עשה ה' את השמים ואת הארץ ולא אמר בששת, מלמד כי כל יום ויום יש לו כח.

The relationship between the six days of Creation and the six Sefirot was crucial for the later emergence of the doctrine of *shemitot*, each ruled by a Sefirah, which were dominant for seven thousand years, each of which was considered as a "day." See the interesting discussion of R. 'Ezra of Gerona, *Commentary on Song of Songs*, in Chavel, *Kitvey ha-Ramban* II, p. 511.

242. *Commentary on Song of Songs*, Chavel, *Kitvey ha-Ramban* II, p. 482:

"ועשה מדות וכלים שיש להם הקר וגבול."

See also p. 511.

243. *The Commentary on the Tetragrammaton*, p. 8:

המדות שבו קצות הם ככלי לרוח הפנימי הם הם נטיעותיו, הם הם מידותיו והוא הפועל בהם.

244. Namely, the divine influx either operating or operating through the six extremities—Ḥesed, Gevurah, Neẓaḥ, Hod, Yesod, Malkhut—after it descended through the "medial line," that is, Tiferet.

245. *Commentary on Talmudic Aggadah*, MS Vatican 294, fol. 37b:

"ויכולו השמים והארץ"—נעשו כלים . . . וזהו שש קצוות הנקרא שמים וארץ שנשתוקק הב"ה לבראותו.

246. Gen. 2:1.

247. Obviously a pun upon *va-yekhulu—kelim*. I assume that the "desire" to create is also derived from *va-yekhulu*—understood as "he longed for."
248. See n. 247 above.
249. The six extremities were connected to the sixth day, when the Creation was completed: see, for example, R. Baḥya ben Asher, *Commentary on the Pentateuch*, ed. Chavel, I, p. 52.
250. See also the commentary on the *Bahir, 'Or ha-Ganuz*, probably written by R. Joseph Ashkenazi, on par. 57, where he explicitly identifies *kelim* with the six extremities viewed as vessels.
251. Margaliot, par. 159, p. 69:

למלך שהיה לו שבעה גנות, ובגן האמצעי מעין נובע ממקור חיים, ג׳ מימינו וג׳ משמאלו, ומיד שפועל פעולה זו או מתמלא, שמחים כולם כי אמרו לצרכינו הוא מתמלא.

252. Compare also to Margaliot, par. 23, pp. 11–12.
253. Compare to Margaliot, par. 178, p. 78, where a related type of symbolism occurs, based upon Song of Songs 4:15: "A fountain of gardens, a well of living waters."
254. *Commentary on Tetragrammaton*, p. 8:

וכל הפעולה שפועל הקו האמצעי, שהוא מדת רחמים, פועל בכח הפנימי הפועל בו . . . והוא ככלי לרוח. ודוגמתו היה הנביא כלי לרוח הקדש שבו, כשהיה הדבור עמו ואפילו על כרחו . . . הרוח מדבר בו והנביא לו ככלי ועל אחת כמה וכמה שקו האמצעי הזה שהוא ככלי לרוח הפנימי המתפשט בו.

This comparison of the seven Sefirot and the inner spirit to the prophet and the divine spirit could be influenced by the *Bahir*, Margaliot, par. 174, p. 76, where man is described as possessing six extremities and an additional entity, that is, seven. See also R. Asher's observation in his *Commentary on the Thirteen Attributes*, p. 13:

שלוחי(ו) של הב״ה, נביאיו ועבדיו נקראים בשמו . . . לפי הדברות שהם דבקים בו . . . בודאי ראויים הם להקרא מדותיו של הב״ה.

See also below Chap. 7, n. 51.

255. On this motif, see Idel, "Music and Prophetic Kabbalah," p. 155 nn. 18–24.
256. *Commentary on Song of Songs*, in Chavel, *Kitvey ha-Ramban* II, pp. 507, 513.
257. *Bahir*, Margaliot, par. 174, p. 76:

"כנגד שש קצוות שבאדם"

See also ibid., par. 82, p. 36:

"אינו אלא שש קצוות . . . וכנגדן כוחותם בשמים"

On the connection between the extremities and man, see *Sanhedrin* 38b, using the verse in Deut. 4:32.

258. This metaphor was employed by most of the Kabbalists, who considered the Sefirot as instruments.
259. *Commentary on the Tetragrammaton*, p. 1; see also *Ma'arekhet ha-'Elohut*, fol. 74a, where this metaphor is employed as part of an "essential" view.
260. *Commentary on Song of Songs*, in Chavel, *Kitvey ha-Ramban* II, pp. 488, 513.
261. See also R. Joshu'a ben Naḥmias's *Migdol Yeshu'ot*, MS Mussaiof 122, fol. 30a:

"כי בשביעי נשלמו המדות ונעשו כלים נאים אשר הם כלים מכלים שונים."

262. See Recanati, in his *Ta'amey ha-Miẓvot*, quoted by R. Yehudah Ḥayyat in *Ma'arekhet ha-'Elohut*, fol. 34a:

כי הפעולה באה מהמדות שהם כלי הפעולה, אם כן העולם צריך לשבעה קצוות שנקרא עמודי׳ . . . והם שבעה ימי בראשית.

Compare also to *'Avot de R. Nathan* (Schechter's edition), version I, Chap. 38, p. 111.

263. Ibid., fol. 34b:

"אבל השלשה הראשונות הם שכליות ולא נקראו מדות."

See also the Naḥmanidean tradition that the three higher Sefirot are not referred to by the term *day*, which is limited to the seven lower ones. Cf., for example, R. Isaac of Acre, *Mei'rat 'Eynaim*, p 14:

"הראשונו' שהם הכתר והחכמה והתשו' אין שם היום נתפש בהם"

See also ibid., p. 12:

כי היא (בינה) נשמה לכל הבנין כנשמה בגוף... כי העולם רומז לשבע ספירות... ואמ' לאדונינו ורב כח תדע שעור קומה.

Compare the view of the *Shi'ur Komah* as the seven lower Sefirot to the view of man in connection with the seven extremities, n. 257 above.

264. For the present, no "instrumental" role of the Sefirot can be found in the extant material of R. Isaac the Blind, the teacher of both R. 'Ezra and R. Asher. We may therefore assume that this conception of the Sefirot is a later development in Provençal and Catalan Kabbalah, induced by the appearance of the *Bahir.* R. Isaac, for example, does not use the simile of the bunch found in the works of two of his followers.

265. See Idel, "We Have No Kabbalistic Tradition on This," pp. 56ff.

266. MS Vatican 431, fol. 4b:

ואמנם האומרים כי הם הם מדות האל ית', הם הולכים בדרך בעלי התארים מן הישמעאלים, אלא שהישמעאלים הספיק להם שלשה חכמה וגבורה ורצון, ואלו ביותר מזה.

267. See Frank Talmage, ed., *The Polemical Writings of Profiat Duran* (in Hebrew) (Jerusalem, 1981), p. 12.

268. Ibid., pp. 12–13.

269. *Ta'amey ha-Miẓvot*, quoted by R. Yehudah Ḥayyat, in *Ma'arekhet ha-'Elohut*, fol. 35ab; this is analyzed in M. Idel, "Attributes and Sefirot in Kabbalistic Theology" (forthcoming).

270. Scholem, *Major Trends*, p. 143; on Abulafia's view of Sefirot, see below, sec. 4d; see also *Sha'arey Ẓedek*, from Abulafia's school, MS Jerusalem 8° 148, fol. 44b:

אשר קוראים להם הפילוסופים צורות נבדלות והמקובלים קורי' להם מדות וספירות.

See also in ibn Latif; cf. Heller-Wilensky, "Isaac ibn Latif—Philosopher or Kabbalist?" p. 214.

271. Alexander Altmann, "Moses Narboni's 'Epistle on Shi'ur Qomah' " in *Jewish Medieval and Renaissance Studies* (Cambridge, Mass., 1967), p. 245.

272. *Sefer ha-'Ikkarim* II, Chap. 11.

273. Herbert A. Davidson, *The Philosophy of Abraham Shalom* (Berkeley and Los Angeles, 1964), p. 12.

274. See H. A. Wolfson, "Extradeical and Intradeical Interpretations of Platonic Ideas," in *Religious Philosophy* (Cambridge, Mass., 1965), p. 37.

275. Giuseppe Sermoneta, "Jehudah ben Moseh ben Daniel Romano, Traducteur de Saint Thomas," in *Hommage à Georges Vajda*, ed. G. Nahon and C. Touati (Louvain, 1980), p. 246. Romano was no doubt influenced by Aquinas' discussions of intradivine ideas.

276. *Responsa of Abravanel to R. Saul ha-Cohen* (Venice, 1574), fol. 12d. In another work, *Mif'alot 'Elohim* (Lemberg, 1863), fol. 61–62, Abravanel considers the Sefirot identical with Godhead, sharing the same essence.

277. See Tirosh-Rothschild, "Sefirot as the Essence of God," pp. 422–424, and see n. 275 above.

278. Idel, "The Magical and Neoplatonic Interpretations," pp. 227, 242 n. 234.

279. Ibid., p. 227.

280. Ibid., pp. 225–226.

281. *Sefer ha-Shem*, quoted and analyzed in Dan, *Esoteric Theology*, p. 95:

כשתחשוב בלבבך על בורא עולם, היאך הוא חניתו—למעלה למעלה עד אין קץ, וכן לפנים ולאחור, לאחורי מזרח ומערב, צפון ודרום, למעלה ומטה עד אין קץ בכל מקום ... ותתן לבבך כי הוא יצר הכל ואין זולתו הוא בכל ומושל בכל.

Compare also below, Chap VII, n. 128, where *Midrash Tadshe*—a work quoted by R. Eleazar of Worms (see n. 158 above)—envisions the Sefirot as entities sustaining the world, not as instruments of creation.

282. *Ḥanyyato*—a term borrowed from Heikhalot literature.

283. See Dan, *Esoteric Theology*, p. 97.

284. Ibid., p. 97; Idel, "Sefirot above Sefirot," p. 278.

285. MS Oxford Christ Church 198, fol. 73b; MS Moscow 131, fol. 186b:

בי' מאמרות נברא העולם, והיצורים כולם, והם נמצאים בכל, כאשר ימצא התירוש באשכול, והם הם י"ס (עשר ספירות) ארדוקות זו בזו.

286. The metaphor of the juice and the clusters is used by a contemporary of R. Barzilai, R. Asher ben David, in order to describe the relationship between the divine influx and the Sefirot qua vessels; see Gottlieb, *Studies*, pp. 311–312.

287. *Ẓurat ha-'Olam*, ed. Z. Stern (Vienna, 1860), p. 5:

היה הוה ויהיה המורים... ומציירים צורת העולם ותכונתו ושיעור קומתו ועשר ספירותיו.

Compare the texts of R. Eleazar of Worms, cited by Dan, *Esoteric Theology*, p. 97; Idel, "Sefirot above Sefirot," pp. 261 n. 110, 278–279.

288. Ibid., p. 25:

"עשר ספירות שהם שיעור קומת העולם"

289. Ibid., p. 29:

כי העשר הספירות כלל עשר מעלות שהם בנין העולם וצורתו ושיעור קומתו.

See also p. 18.

290. MS Vatican 441, fol. 112a:

"הכחות הכלליות אשר בכל המציאות הם העשר ספירו'"

On this treatise, see Idel, "Sefirot above Sefirot," pp. 260–262.

291. On the question of the authorship of this treatise, see Idel, "Abraham Abulafia," pp. 72–74.

292. MS München 10, fol. 155b–156a:

שהשם בכל העולם ובתוך העולם וחוץ לעולם עד אין סוף והוא מנהיג הכל ובו מתקיים הכל.

293. Ibid., fol. 156a:

כי השם הוא הם והם הוא אלא שהשם האציל כחותיהם על הברואים ושמם בהם.

294. Ibid., fol. 156a:

מדותיו הם שפעים ואצילות והויות רוחניות נמצאו במציאות העולם ונתגלו לא שהיו איכויות בו בכח ויצאו לפעול בצאת העולם לפעל, אבל עצמו השפיעם עם העולם, כי הם דברים צריכים לעולם... כי הן עשר מדות ונחלקות בעולם ובשנה ובנפש.

295. On the "Sefirot of the soul," see ibid., fol. 130a and paragraph 4d.

296. Heller-Wilensky, "Isaac ibn Latif—Philosopher or Kabbalist?" pp. 202–203.

297. See *Mafteaḥ ha-Re'ayon*, MS Oxford 1658, fol. 61a; *Sefer ha-Ḥeshek*, MS New York, JTS 1801, fol. 10a.

298. *Commentary on the Guide of the Perplexed*, fol. 30c; *Ginnat 'Egoz*, fol. 52d, 54b, 66cd, 67c. Some hints of the immanence of the Sefirot in the world occur in *Ginat 'Egoz*, fol. 52d, 53b.

299. MS München 10, fol. 156a.

300. On Sefirot in man, see the short remark of R. Eleazar of Worms, *Sefer ha-Shem*, MS New York, JTS fol. 3b:

והארם שהוא כ״ב ספירות והשנה שהוא כ״ב ספירות כולן תלויין ביחיד מושל עולם.

"And man, who consists of twenty-two Sefirot, and the year, which consists of twenty-two Sefirot, all of them depend upon the Unique One, the governor of the world."

301. MS Paris BN 774, fol. 172a:

עשר המרים מכלל מה שאתו במציאותו. גופו מהתחתונים וכן עוד נתן לו מכלל מה שאנו עשרה דברים ממציאות נפשו מן העליונים כי בעשרה מאמרות נברא העולם ובנה הגוף והנפש נחקקו ביו״ד.

Compare also to Abulafia's *'Imrey Shefer*, MS Paris 777, p. 56:

"הארם שהוא בצורת י׳ כלומ׳ עולם קטן כולל הכל"

Note: Abulafia uses the same verb, *kolel*, as used by Kabbalists since R. 'Ezra: see n. 45 above. I tend to assume that Abulafia reflects a mystical tradition independent from that of R. 'Ezra.

302. Yod—I suppose that Abulafia hints here to two decads, the spiritual and corporeal, since the spelling out of yod in full, in lieu of Y, suggests the numerical value of twenty. Compare Abulafia's *Mafteaḥ ha-Sefirot*, MS Milano-Ambrosiana 53, fol 156b:

"כי סוד אנכי אני כ כלומר אני יוד"

As is evident from the context, the *'anokhi* of the first commandment is seen as referring to both God and man, the latter being described as "an inverted tree." See also Chap. IV, near nn. 24–27.

303. MS Paris BN 774, fol. 172a:

"כי הנפש כוללת י׳ הויות עליונים(!) מן השמימיים"

See also *Sha'arey Ẓedek*, MS Jerusalem 8° 148, fol. 37b:

נקראו הספירות העליון(!) האלהיות ארם עליון השם הגדול, והתחתונות, ארם התחתון, ארם קטן.

Thus, the ten lower Sefirot are the microanthropos, as against the divine macroanthropos.

304. Ibid., p. 48b; see Idel, "Sefirot above Sefirot," pp. 260–261.

305. Jellinek, *Auswahl*, p. 20:

כי המורכב האחרון שהוא הארם, הכולל כל הספירות אשר שכלו הוא השכל הפועל, כשתתיר קשריו תמצא עמו הייחוד הוא המיוחד, ואפילו האצילות הראשונה שהוא המחשבה.

306. On this phrase—its source and occurrence in Abulafia—see Idel, "Abraham Abulafia and *Unio Mystica*," nn. 45–47.

307. On this view of the active intellect as an entity existing in the human spirit, not only in cosmic spirituality, see Abulafia's *'Or ha-Sekhel*, MS Vatican 233, fol. 119a. This understanding of the concept of active intellect is probably the result of the influence of the scholastic Christian concept of active intellect.

308. Namely, the knots of the "compound entity"—that is, man; see also below, n. 347.

309. See "Ve-Zot li-Yihudah," Jellinek, *Auswahl*, pp. 20–21:
כי הכחות הפנימיות והרוחות הנעלמות האנושיות הם תוך הגופים בחלקים, ובעצם אמיתת כל כח וכח וכל רוח ורוח, כשיותרו מקשריהם, ירוצו אל מקורם הראשון שהוא אחד בלתי שום שניות וכולל ריבוי עד א"ס (אין סוף) וההתרה מגעת עד למעלה ויושב בראש הכתר העליון והמחשבה שואבת משם ברכה.
See also ibid., p. 27.

310. Ibid., pp. 16–17, corrected according to MS New York, JTS 1887:
בעלי הספירות יקרא להם שמות ויאמר כי הספירה הראשונה שמה מחשבה ויוסיף לה שם, לבאר ענינה ויקראוה כתר עליון מצד היות הכתר דבר מונח בראשי המלכים ... ויוסיף לה שם ביאור ויקראנה עוד אויר קדמון ... ככה יעשה לכל ספירה וספירה מעשר ספירות בלימה, ובעל השמות כוונתו כונה אחרת מעולה מזאת מאד מאד ואינה ועמקת דרך זו של שמות היא עמקה שאין בכל עמקי מחשבות האדם עמוקה ומעולה ממנה, והיא לבדה משתתפת המחשבה האנושית עם האלוהית לפי יכולת האנושית ולפי מה שהאדם מוטבע עליו. וידוע שמחשבת האדם היא סבת חכמתו וחכמתו היא סבת בינתו ובינתו סבת חסדו וחסדו סבת יראת קונו, ופחדו סבת תפארתו ותפארתו סבת נצחונו ונצחונו סבת הודו והודו סבת עצמו הנק' חתן, ועצמו סבת מלכותו הנקרא כלתו.

311. On this concept see George Margoliouth, "The Doctrine of the Ether in the Kabbalah," *JQR* o.s. 20 (1908): 825–861. Particularly interesting is the fact that the relatively rare phrase, *'Avir Kadmon*, also occurs in an anonymous Kabbalistic commentary on prayer that is closely related to Abulafia's ecstatic Kabbalah: see ibid., p. 834; and also *Gan Na'ul*, MS München 58, fol. 336a.

312. On the symbolic tendency of theosophical Kabbalah as evaluated by Abulafia, see Chap. IX, n. 4.

313. See also "Ve zot li-Yihudah," Jellinek, *Auswahl*, p. 16:
אם יאמר אומר כי הספירות בעלי שמות שבהם נבדלות זו מזו—כי זה אינה כוונת בעלי השמות וארוני החכמות.
Thus, Abulafia again asserts that, as a Kabbalist focusing on the divine names, he does not understand the names of the Sefirot as the theosophical Kabbalah does.

314. *'Omek*. On the occurrence of this noun in connection with divine names, see Chap. V, nn. 168, 170.

315. This description of ecstatic Kabbalah is very characteristic of Abulafia; compare, for example, to *'Or ha-Sekhel*, MS Vatican 233, fol. 115a:
ומפני שבין שני אוהבים שני חלקי אהבה, שהיא שבה דבר אחד ... והם שתוף אהבה אלהית שכלית עם אהבה אנושית שכלית והיא אחת ... מכח השם.
Or ibid.:
"דעתו המשתפת בינך ובינו על פי שמו הנכבד"
See Idel, "Abraham Abulafia and *Unio Mystica*," n. 38, and Chap. IX, n. 16.

316. Abulafia uses two terms—*yir'ah*, or reverence, and *paḥad*, or fear—in order to refer to the Sefirot of *Gevurah*. Both terms are common symbols of this Sefirot.

317. The seventh Sefirah is regularly referred to as *Neẓaḥ*, but Abulafia uses the form *Niẓaḥon*, which is quite unusual, in order to relate this quality to human action. *Neẓaḥ* would be improper, since its literal meaning, "eternity," is difficult to integrate into his "anthropoic" scheme; see, however, his usage of *Neẓaḥ* in *Mafteaḥ ha-Sefirot*, quoted below, n. 322.

318. *'Azmo;* I prefer the rendering as "his essence," although the meaning is not clear. According to the Sefirotic scheme, this term refers to the Sefirah of Yesod, although I have never found such a symbolic interpretation for *'ezem*. In several symbolic systems, *'Ezem ha-Shamayim* designates the Sefirot Neẓaḥ and Hod.

319. I added this phrase from MS New York, JTS 1887; Yesod is an explicitly male-functioning divine power, but is only rarely referred to as bridegroom, a common symbol of Tiferet. Nevertheless, in the writings of Abulafia's contemporary, R. Joseph of Hamadan, *ḥatan* recurs several times as a major symbol of Yesod.

320. In print "בלתו", which is meaningless; see the text quoted in n. 370 below.

321. See *'Or ha-Sekhel*, MS Vatican 233, fol. 15a, where the human intellectual and divine intellectual loves (cf. n. 315 above) and the human and divine existences are referred to respectively as bride and bridegroom. See also Chap. IX, n. 16, where God and Knesset Israel—that is, the perfect man—are allegorically alluded to by the Song of Songs. See also the text printed in n. 333 below.

322. MS Milano-Ambrosiana 53, fol. 155b–156a:

שזה השפע שנשפע מהסופר, נכלל ועובר מא׳ לי׳ כלום׳ מן הראשונ׳ שבספירות אל העשירית לה, פי׳ מן המחשבה עד צדק, ובהן תהיה מחשבת האדם צדקת(!) כלום׳ כשתולד מהמחשבה חכמה, וממחשבת החכמה תוליד בינה וממחשבת החכמה והבינה גדולה שהיא מידת החסד, ויתגדל החושב בם. ומכולן גבורה ויגבר כח החושב, שהוא החושב שהוא הסופר הספירות ותולד מהן האמת. מיד התפארת מתגלה בחזקה ומביאה את האיש המשיגה להתפאר בה ולהתפאר בנבואה על פי האמת, אלא שהנבואה היא מדרגות השגה בעצמה ועל כן המשיג באמת דומה ליעקב אבינו שנא׳ תתן אמת ליעקב... יתחייב היות תולדת הנצח מהאמת וזה שיודע האמת הוא מנצח אפי׳ מערכת המזלות והככבים ואז הוא מתברך משם אל שדי. והנצח יולד הוד ממנו וזהו עניין ונתת(!) מהודך עליו... והספירה התשיעית... קראה כל נשמה יסוד ביה... ומשם מקור השפע והברכה... הספירה העשירית שהיא השכינה ושמה צדק... ומזה געניין הנרמז בספירות לפי ההשגה בם ולפי קבלת האיש כח מהם, לפי הידיעה באמת השמות, יתעלה ויתגדל כח נביא אחד על כח נביא אחר.

323. "סופר הספירות" was previously used by Abulafia as a name for God, or *'Eiyn Sof*. It seems that in this phrase, Sefirot stands for "numbers," as it does regularly in Abulafia's works.

324. A pun upon "justice" and "right," which, in Hebrew, are expressed by the same root.

325. Gedulah, interpreted immediately afterward as human thought.

326. See n. 323 above; the similarity between man and God is an important issue in a relatively long discussion, which I eliminated from this quotation and will deal with elsewhere.

327. Tiferet: Abulafia plays on various symbols of this Sefirot, such as *Ya'akov* and *'Emet*, but interprets Tiferet as human boasting, again a pun on the Hebrew root *pe'er*, which can also denote splendor.

328. Compare Abulafia's description of himself in "Ve-zot li-Yihudah," Jellinek, *Auswahl*, pp. 18–19 (corrected according to MS New York, JTS 1887):

לפי דעתי השמות והחותמות, לא הביאני אל תפארת הנבואה... אבל בהגיעי אל השמות ובהתירי קשרי החותמות, נגלה אלי אדון הכל וגלה לי את סודו... ואז הכריחני להתפאר בנבואה.

See also below, near n. 389.

329. Micah 7:20.

330. In a passage I omitted, Abulafia described Jacob as standing above the twelve constellations, MS Milano-Ambrosiana 53, fol. 155b:

"נמצאו י"ב מזלות מתנהגים תחתיו"

On the subduing of the planets, see also *Gan Na'ul*, MS München 58, fol. 335b.

331. Num. 27:20.

332. Perhaps connected to the verse Psalms 150:6:

"כל הנשמה תהלל יה"

333. MS Sassoon 56, fol. 33a:

שכל ספירה וספירה אפשר לאדם להדבק בה מצד מהות השפע השופע מאצילותה על ספירותיו שהם עשר מדותיו . . . וצריך להתבודד אל ההשגה עד שישיג מהם המשכיל המקובל, שפע ניכר אצלו, וזה כי מאחר שהאותיות הנכתבות הם גויות, והנבטאות הם רוחניות והנחשבות הן שכליות, והנאצלות הן אלוהיות . . . ועם ההתבודדות להכין כח הכלה לקבל שפע מכח החתן יניעו האלוהיות את השכליות ועם התמדת ההתבודדות ורבויו, וחזקו ורוב חשקו ואומץ כספו ותוקף תשוקתו להשיג הדבקות והנשיקה יהיה כח הכלה ושמה ועצמה נזכרים לטובה ונשמרים לנצח, כי זכו בדינם והתחברו הנפרדי' ונפרדו המחוברים והתהפך המציאות ויחייב מזה שישוב כל ענף לשרשו וידבק בו וכל רוחני לנפשו ויקשר עמו והיה המשכן אחד והיה ידוה אחד ושמו אחד. ואם ככה יעשה בסדר הספירות ובמערכת כ"ב אותיות וקרב אותם אחד אל אחד לך לעץ אחד והיה לאחדים בידך.

Compare Abulafia's statement that man ought to cleave to every Sefirah to the similar view of an obscure Kabbalist, R. Joseph ben Ḥayyim, who is reported to have maintained that:

וכל אשר צונו הבורא ית' שמו לידבק בו שנא' ובו תדבק וכי אפשר לידבק בו אלא לידבק במידותיו . . . ע"כ אפרש י' ספירות כלליות אלוהיות על פי הקבלה כדי לידבק בהם . . . ובהדבקו בהם יכנס רוח הקדש אלהי בקרבו בכל הרגשותיו ותנועותיו.

"All that the Creator, blessed be his name, commanded to us to cleave to him, . . . Therefore, I shall explain the [meaning of] the ten Sefirot, the universal and divine ones, according to the Kabbalah, in order that [you] will cleave to them . . . and by his cleaving to them, the divine and holy spirit will enter him, also into his senses and movements" (MS New York, JTS 1885, fol. 74b–75a). Remarkably, after this text, the same Kabbalist also discusses the ten Sefirot as human activities, in the vein of the passage from Abulafia's "Ve-Zot li-Yihudah," ibid., fol. 75a-b. On the relationship between cleaving and the divine spirit, see Chap. III, n. 12.

334. See Abulafia's *Gan Na'ul*, MS British Library, OR. 13136, fol. 4b:

ועתה אבאר לך איך תתנהג בהשגת השם, בכח הספירות הנזכרות, בקבלך שפעם בכלל מהותך.

In the version copied in *Sefer ha-Peliah* I, fol. 73c is slightly corrupted: *mahutam*.

335. See ibid.:

יש באדם שלושה עניינים שבהם הוא משיג כל השגותיו בכח השנים מהם בו כוללים י' ספירות לבד, והם חצי י' השניים פנימיים תלויים בשכל ובנפש.

The version in MS München 58, fol. 320b, is slightly different.

336. Compare to Abulafia's *Gan Na'ul*, MS British Library, OR. 13136, fol 3a:

וצריך שישתדל המקבל שמקבל שמות הספירות תחלה לקבל שפע אלהי מהם בעצמם לפי מדותיו וידבק בכל ספירה וספירה מהם לבדה, ויכלול דביקותו עם הספירות כלן יחד ולא יקצץ.

Therefore, the focus of Kabbalistic activity is not the Sefirot, but their names, which enable the Kabbalist to attain *devekut*. Moreover, as in the epistle, the human attributes are mentioned as the means of receiving the divine emanations. This text was copied anonymously in *Sefer ha-Peliah*, I, fol. 72a, with slight variations.

337. *Lehitboded:* On the meaning of this verb as "to concentrate" in Abulafia's works, see Idel, "*Hitbodedut* as Concentration," pp. 41–45, esp. p. 44 n. 51.
338. The awareness of the source of revelation or inspiration is important in Abulafia: see the text translated in Scholem, *Major Trends*, p. 140.
339. These three levels of the letter are also explicitly connected to Abulafia's mystical technique in his other works; see Idel, *The Mystical Experience in Abraham Abulafia*, Chap. I.
340. The meaning of these letters is not entirely clear; I assume that they stand for the forms emanated onto the lower world.
341. The Hebrew text seems to be corrupted here, as in other parts of this epistle.
342. On the kiss as an allegory of union, see above, Chap. III, sec. III.
343. See n. 319 above.
344. *'Aẓmah*; see n. 318 above.
345. *Nizkarim le-tovah*; probably by the bridegroom, namely the active intellect or God.
346. Namely, the human and separate spiritual forces that, prior to *devekut*, were divided.
347. I suppose this refers to the human spiritual forces from the corporeal forces; see the text referred to in nn. 308, 328 above.
348. An obvious reference to the transmutation of the human into the Divine. Abulafia's type of mysticism, which presupposes the possibility of a radical change of the human into the Divine, is also evident in other texts: see, for example, Chap. IV, nn. 19, 21, 29. Cf. the relevant description of the "Great Work" mysticism in Underhill's *Mysticism*, pp. 128–129, group C, which indeed approximates the Abulafian experience.
349. On this metaphor, see Chap. III, n. 85; Chap. IV, nn. 62, 85.
350. *Nafsho*, an Arabism introduced by Tibbonian translations.
351. Exod. 26:6.
352. Zech. 14:9.
353. Abulafia viewed the future perfect state when the excellency of the Tetragrammaton would be recognized: see Idel, "Abraham Abulafia and the Pope," pp. 12–14.
354. Ezek. 37:17.
355. Compare *Gan Na'ul*, MS München 58, fol. 335b:
דרך ההשגה הנבואית עם האותיות, אלה ראשית דרכיו להמציא ממנו כל הלשונות וכל החכמות, באמצעות מדות הספירות והחותמות ולהוריד בהם הכחות העליונות האלהיות ולהשכינם בארץ.
356. This motif recurs in Abulafia's writings; see, for example, *Ḥayye ha-Nefesh*, MS München 408, fol. 70a, which will be elaborated elsewhere; see also below, Chap. IX, near n. 26.
357. See, for example, the emphasis on this view in Cordovero's *Pardes Rimmonim*, I, 5; xxxi, 1. Even his conception of the necessity to imitate the qualities of the Sefirot in human acts, as he presents them in *Tomer Devorah*, is an application of the theosophical structure to man's behavior. For Abulafia, however, the understanding of the names of Sefirot as primarily pointing to human activities, ignoring their theosophical meanings, is presented as the higher understanding of them.
358. Compare Abulafia's "Ve-Zot li-Yihudah," Jellinek, *Auswahl*, p. 27, to MS München 10, fol. 130a, 156a. See also *Sefer 'Even Sappir*, written under the influence of Abulafian

Kabbalah, by R. Elnathan ben Moshe Kalkish, MS Paris, BN 727, fol. 158a–158b; Idel, *The Mystical Experience in Abraham Abulafia*, pp. 94–95.

359. *Commentary on Sefer Yeẓirah*, fol. 22c-d, 24c–25a.

360. See Idel,"Between the Views of Sefirot as Essence and Instruments," pp. 106–111.

361. See Liebes, "Ẓaddik Yesod 'Olam," pp. 81 nn. 53–55, 85 n. 85, remarks that there are some psychological and epistemological terms in Nathan of Gaza's presentation of his theosophical system. However, no psychologization of theosophy is to be found there, since the processes dealt with by Nathan take place in Godhead, not in man's consciousness or activity.

362. See Idel, "Perceptions of the Kabbalah," par. I.

363. On the psychological turn in Ḥasidism, see Scholem, *Explications and Implications*, pp. 357–358.

364. See Idel, "Perceptions of Kabbalah," where another instance of Abulafian influence on Ḥasidism was noted, concerning the peculiar concept of language.

365. See, however, Liebes's opinion, in "Ẓaddik Yesod 'Olam," p. 81, that the Ḥasidic interest in psychological terms represents a broadening of a Sabbatian phenomenon.

366. *Toldot Ya'akov Yoseph*, fol. 86a:

קבלתי ממורי כי יש עשר ספירות באדם הנקרא עולם קטן כי המחשבה נק' אבא ואחר הצמצום להחליט נקרא אמא וכו' עד והאמנה נק' תרי ירכי קשוט, ותענוג בעבודת הש"י נק' יסוד, צדיק, ברית מילה וכו'.

Compare also to his *Ẓafnat Pa'aneaḥ*, fol. 31a:

ובאמת, כששופע על הצדיק הרוחניות בתפילתו ובתורתו, אין לך תענוג גדול מזה.

Compare also Louis Jacobs, *Ḥasidic Prayer* (New York, 1928), pp. 75–77, and see Chap. III, n. 75, where "delight" is connected to worship, and Chap. VIII, n. 227.

According to a remarkable passage in the writings of R. Levi Isaac of Berdichev, the study of the Torah brings the mind of the scholars into the "world of delight"—*'olam ha-Ta'anug*—which is identical with the Sefirah of Binah; cf. *Kedushat ha-Levi*, fol. 123 cd. This master confines the perception of delight only to the realm of worship, as any unholy activity can prevent man from enjoying the delight descending from the Divine.

367. Namely, the divine configuration corresponding to the Sefirah of Ḥokhmah; the reference to Ḥokhmah as "thought" or as the "world of thought" is characteristic of some Ḥasidic mystics.

368. Cf. *Tikkuney Zohar* 19, fol. 38a.

369. I did not find a symbolic usage of the term *ta'anug* in theosophical Kabbalah. According to *Sefer ha-Bahir*, Margaliot, par. 71, p. 31, it stands for an emotional event, but not as a symbol. Compare also Chap. III, n. 42.

370. MS München 408, fol. 65b:

"הדבקות כל הדעת בשם בפעלה בסוד תענוג החתן והכלה."

371. החתן והכלה = 529 = תענוג See also Abulafia's *'Or ha-Sekhel*, MS Vatican 233, fol. 115a; see also Idel, *The Mystical Experience in Abraham Abulafia*, Chap. IV.

372. See n. 319 above.

373. *'Or ha-'Emet*, fol. 36c-d:

פעם אחת היה הרב מוכיח לאחד על מה שדרש קבלה ברבים והשיב לו האיש, מפני מה דרש ג״כ קבלה ברבים? והשיב לו הרבי אני לומד את העולם שיבינו שבעוה״ז ובאדם ג״כ כל הדברים הנאמרים בס׳ עץ החיים, ולא שאני נותן להבין את הרוחני כמו שכתוב בע״ח; אבל מר דורש כל הדברים ככתבן בע״ח א״כ אתה עושה מרוחניות גשמיות, שאין הפה יכול לדבר למעלה, בעולם הרוחני.

Compare also Dov Baer's disciple, R. Levi Isaac of Berdichev, *Kedushat ha-Levi*, fol. 109b, and the quotation in the name of R. Abraham ha-Mal'akh, R. Dov Baer's son, adduced by R. Abraham Ḥayyim in *Peri Ḥayyim* (Safed, n.d.), fol. 2c:

שמעתי מהרב בוצינא קדישא מו״ה אברהם ז״ל בהה״ק בוצינא קדישא מו״ה דוב בער זללה״ה פי׳ ע״ז משום שהאדם צריך להכניע שבע מידותיו שיש בו כגון אהבה ויראה והתפארות וניצוח וכו׳ תחת יראת ה׳ כמ״ש לך ה׳ הגדולה והגבורה והתפארת והנצח וההוד וכו׳.

See also R. Reuven Horowitz's *Dudaim ba-Sadeh*, fol. 3a:

כי נודע שעיקר התכלית לעבודת הבורא ב״ה לתקן האדם שבע מדותיו שכל אהבות ויראות והתפארות וניצוח והודי׳ והתקשרות וממלכו׳ יהי׳ הכל רק להבורא ב״ה.

374. Printed in Mordecai Wilensky, *Ḥasidim and Mitnaggedim* (in Hebrew) (Jerusalem, 1970), 2:164.
375. *Nikhlal ba-'Adam*; this phrase recurs in Lurianic sources. See above, n. 58, and Wilensky, ibid., p. 160.
376. *'Attika Kaddisha*, the first configuration.
377. *'Arikh 'Anpin*: the second configuration.
378. See above, n. 194.
379. In the Lurianic system Jacob does not stand for a configuration, distinct from *Ze'ir 'Anpin*.
380. Each of them is a configuration: the fifth and third ones, respectively.
381. *Middat ha-'adam ve-koḥotav*; this phrase seems a *terminus technicum*. The phrase *middat ha-'adam* occurs alone several times in R. David's work; see Wilensky, *Ḥasidim and Mitnaggedim*, pp. 165, 167.
382. Wilensky, ibid., p. 167.
383. Compare the interesting essay of R. J. Zwi Werblowsky, "Some Psychological Aspects of Kabbalah," *Harvest* 3 (1956): 77–96; cf. the opinions of F. C. Burkitt, *Church and Gnosis* (Cambridge, 1932), pp. 41–42, and E. R. Dodds, *Pagan and Christian in an Age of Anxiety* (New York and London, 1970), pp. 18–20, who regard the Gnostic mythologies as hypostatization of the Gnostics' inner experiences.
384. Wilensky, *Ḥasidim and Mitnaggedim*, pp. 167–168.
385. Ibid., p. 160.
386. See Idel, "Abraham Abulafia," pp. 185–191. Abulafia may be considered by all standards to be an extreme allegorist, even in comparison with those most criticized as such among the philosophers.
387. See Chap. III, n. 152.
388. Pp. 45–46. On the first part of this passage, see Chap. X.
389. Compare above, n. 328.
390. *Ḥakor u-vahon bahen*; cf. *Sefer Yeẓirah* I, 4, on the ten Sefirot.
391. See Chap. IX, sec. II (5).
392. This issue will be treated in detail elsewhere.

393. On the experiential aspect of Kabbalistic symbolism, see Chap. IX. See also, especially, the emphasis on this matter in Eliade's studies in general—for example, his "Methodological Remarks on the Study of Religious Symbolism," in *The History of Religions—Essays in Methodology* (Chicago, 1959), pp. 102–103, and n. 383 above.
394. See below, Chaps. VII–VIII.
395. See Scholem, *Kabbalah*, pp. 144–152; Joseph ben Shelomo, "The Problem of Pantheism in the Theistic Mysticism of R. Moses Cordovero and Meister Eckhardt" (in Hebrew), in *Revelation, Faith, Reason* (Ramat Gan, 1976), pp. 71–86.
396. See above, par. 4.
397. See Schatz-Uffenheimer, *Quietistic Elements*, Chap. 8; Buber, *Ḥasidism*, pp. 134–135.
398. See Idel, "Types of Redemptive Activities," pp. 254–263.
399. See Scholem, *Sabbatai Ṣevi*, pp. 303—304.
400. See Scholem, *Messianic Idea in Judaism*, p. 34; Scholem, *Major Trends*, p. 20; Idel, "Types of Redemptive Activities," p. 273 n. 85. Scholem, however, attributed special importance to the trauma of the Expulsion from Spain for the formation of Lurianic Kabbalah; see *Major Trends*, pp. 248–250. See M. Idel, "Particularism and Universalism in Kabbalah: 1480–1650," presented at a symposium on the sixteenth and seventeeth centuries held at the Van Leer Institute in Jerusalem, January 1986, and Chap. X below.
401. Weinstock, *Studies in Jewish Philosophy and Mysticism*, pp. 153–241.
402. This view is obviously connected to the above-mentioned view of the seven lower Sefirot as appointed on the Creation of the world.
403. See Scholem, *Sabbatai Ṣevi*, pp. 811–814.

CHAPTER 7

1. Scholem, *On the Kabbalah*, pp. 132–133; the emphasis is in the original. Compare also ibid., pp. 94, 98, and below, sec. IV; see also Scholem, *Major Trends*, pp. 29–30.
2. Compare, however, Scholem, *Major Trends*, p. 31. There he affirms that Aggadah includes mythical elements; on p. 35, he asserts that there were no mythical elements in the inner experience of ancient Jewish mystics; see also Scholem, *On the Kabbalah*, pp. 98, 120–121.
3. Scholem, *Major Trends*, p. 34, and Tishby, *The Doctrine of Evil*, pp. 60–61. Recently, a rather extreme description of the nature of Jewish mysticism has been articulated by Joseph Dan, *Jewish Mysticism and Jewish Ethics* (Seattle and London, 1986), p. 2. Kabbalah allegedly includes "many extreme, radical and even seemingly heretical schools of thought," which, according to him, were integrated—enigmatically—"into a constructive, traditional ethics." This characterization seems to be a radicalization of Scholem's views, going far beyond the facts.
4. Scholem, *Major Trends*, p. 35, and Scholem, *Les Origines de la Kabbale*, p. 211. See also Katz, *Halakhah and Kabbalah*, p. 12, where he even sees an essential contradiction between these two domains.
5. Chap. VI, sec. I.
6. Compare to Dan's theory that the theosophical system emerged in order to solve the contradiction between the philosophical and traditional concepts of God. However, as we have seen in Chap. VI, it is doubtful whether the twelfth- and thirteenth-century

Kabbalists were the first to introduce innovations in theosophy; cf. J. Dan, "The Emergence of Mystical Prayer," in *Studies in Jewish Mysticism*, ed. J. Dan and F. Talmage (Cambridge, Mass., 1982), pp. 102ff.; see also Idel, "Maimonides and the Kabbalah," par. 1.

7. Compare Baer, *Israel among the Nations*, pp. 103–104, who emphasized mythical aspects of the halakhah; and Jacob Neusner, *A History of the Mishnaic Law of Purities* (Leiden, 1976), pp. 220–231, in which the author proposes a peculiar understanding of Mishnaic ritual as incorporating mythical elements. See also Isadore Twersky, "The Shulhan 'Arukh," *Judaism* 16 (1967): 156 nn. 38, 41, who regards halakhah as the medium for discovering God's glory.
8. A tacit assumption of Katz, *Halakhah and Kabbalah*, is the existence from the beginning, of two different domains, halakhah versus Kabbalah, which sometimes were competing. Although such a competition indeed arose in later texts, I suppose that it is part of the independent development of Kabbalah, which gradually became less and less dependent on both halakhah and Aggadah.
9. Compare, however, Katz, *Halakhah and Kabbalah*, p. 12, who asserts that the ultimate goal of Kabbalah had no affinity to halakhah, emphasizing its autonomy. On the problem of the interrelationship between theosophy and theurgy, see also below, Chap. X.
10. Compare also the understanding of the Christian sacraments qua theurgical in Pseudo-Dionysios, where they facilitate the relationship between man and the Divine: cf. Andrew Louth, *The Origins of the Christian Mystical Tradition* (Oxford, 1981), pp. 163–164; for Pseudo-Dionysios, the theurgical nature of the sacraments is a matter of institution rather than of an "occult sympathy between the material elements used and the constitution of the divine." This understanding of the Christian ritual is partially similar to the nature of the Jewish commandments; in both cases, human activity, not only certain material, is important for establishing a connection between man and the Divine. For a more mystical conception of theurgy, see A. J. Festugière, "Contemplation philosophique et art theurgique chez Proclus," in *Etudes de philosophie grecque* (Paris, 1971), pp. 585–596.
11. See, for example, E. R. Dodds, "Theurgy and Its Relationship to Neoplatonism," *Journal of Roman Studies* 38 (1947): 61–62. Curiously, Buber, *Ḥasidism*, pp. 142–144, fails to distinguish between magic and Kabbalistic theurgy, envisioning Kabbalah, in general, and the Kabbalistic kavvanot, in particular, as transforming mystery into magic. Compare also below, Chap. IX, n. 75.
12. See Cohen, *The Shi'ur Qomah: Liturgy and Theurgy*, pp. 110, 116–118.
13. See, for example, Deut. 10:17, Psalms 147:5.
14. Urbach, *The Sages*, pp. 80–86; Baer, "The Service of Sacrifice," pp. 148–149. It is worth remarking that, although the name *Gevurah* recurs also in Heikhalot literature, there it is never part of a theurgical view, as happens in the midrashic literature. Compare, for example, *Ma'aseh Merkavah*, printed by Scholem in *Jewish Gnosticism*, p. 113, where the phrase appears:

"כח גבורה של אביך שבשמים."

—namely, "the power of the Dynamis who is your father in heaven." In the midrashic literature, man adds power to the supernal *Dynamis*; here, it is referred to as independent of man, which seems to remain constant forever; cf. p. 115:

"כי גבורתך לנצח נצחי נצחים"

Compare, on the same page

"מלאכי השרת . . . מגדלין גבורתך"

"the attendant angels . . . are praising your Dynamis." However, the verb *megaddelim*, rendered here as "are praising," may also be understood as "are aggrandizing," though this sense is less appropriate in the specific context.

15. The bibliography on this important subject is astonishingly poor: see Urbach, *The Sages*, pp. 95–96, and compare n. 48 below.
16. Sec. 26, ed Mandelbaum, pp. 379–380; compare *'Eikhah Rabbati* 1, 35.
17. Job 17.9.
18. Deut. 33:21.
19. Num. 14:7. Compare also the use of this verse in *Shabbat* 89a.
20. The omitted passage will be discussed below.
21. Deut. 32:18.
22. Psalms 60:14.
23. *Na'asah*, like the form *'oseh* above (n. 18) is understood, according to the context, as actually creating the power or justice of God, or in God. For the use of this verb in Kabbalah, see Chap. VIII on 'asa 'o or 'asa 'ani, nn. 85, 100.
24. *Kivyakhol;* see A. Marmorstein, *The Old Rabbinic Doctrine of God* (London, 1937), 2:131.
25. Lam. 1:6.
26. On divine will as commandments, see the *Targum* to Song of Songs 1:15, where *Ra'ayati* is translated as:

    "עבדא רעותי ועסיקא באורייתא"

    In *Midrash Rabbah* it stands for commandments. *Ra'ayati* is understood as "my will," an interesting hermeneutical tour de force, given the conspicuous affinity between the roots *r'h* and *rẓh*.
27. Lev. 23–12. Compare also *Numbers Rabbah* 9.
28. Deut. 32:18.
29. This is a pun on
30. Cf. *Berakhot* 60a.
31. I, 10; cf. also *Yalkut Makiri*, ed. Buber, on Psalms 60:27, p. 310.
32. According to another version (see Marmorstein, *Old Rabbinic Doctrine*, p. 131 n. 63), it is written: "when the righteous are worthy."
33. Psalms 60:14.
34. Lam. 1:6.
35. Fol. 11a. See Recanati, *Commentary on the Torah*, fol. 51b, where he adduces the passage from *Megillah* beside the midrashic view of the diminution of divine power.
36. See *Corpus Hermeticum* XIII, 18–19, 21; compare also X, 2. On other possible Jewish influences on another Hermetic treatise, see B. A. Pearson, "Jewish Elements in *Corpus Hermeticum* I (Poimandres)," in *Studies in Gnosticism and Hellenistic Religion Presented to G. Quispel*, ed. R. van den Broeck and M. J. Vermaseren (Leiden, 1981), pp. 336–348; see also Urbach, *The Sages*, pp. 86–87, and below, Chap. VIII, n. 147). On "Dynamis" as a possible Jewish influence on Hermeticism, see the view of C. H. Dodds, *The Bible and the Greeks* (London, 1935), pp. 17, 110; and the more moderate attitude of R. P. Festugière, La

Révélation d'Hermes Trismegiste (Paris, 1953), 3:141 and 148ff., and Scholem, *Jewish Gnosticism*, p. 23 n. 6.

37. MS Paris 772, fol. 110a:
כשישראל מברכין שם כבודו, הכבוד מתברכת, כדכתיב, "וחסידיך יברכוך (!) כבוד מלכותך יאמרו וגבורותיך יגידו."

38. Psalms 145:10-11.

39. Scholem, *Jewish Gnosticism*, pp. 67–68.

40. Commentary on *Ha-'Aderet veha-'Emunah*, printed in *The Siddur of R. Naftali Herz̡ Treves* (Thiengen, 1560), fol. BH, 2, b:
כשישראל מברכין להק׳ אז הכבוד מתגאה ומרומם למעלה למעלה ומתרומם כמו שנ׳ רוממו יי׳ ומי יכול לרוממו, אלא הכבוד מתרומם לפי הברכה והשבח ועל זה אמר וחסידיך יברכוכה ואח״כ כבוד מלכותך יאמרו וגבורתך ידברו... כשמברכין לו אז מתגאה ומתגדל... בשביל הברכות והשבחו׳ שמשבחים לו ישראל כמו אדם שמשבחין לו אז מתגדל לבו, כך הוא.

On the relationship between R. Eleazar's *Commentary on Prayers* and this commentary, see Joseph Dan, "Commentaries on *ha-'Aderet veha-'Emunah* authored by Ashkenazi Ḥasidim" (in Hebrew), *Tarbiz̡* 50 (1981): 339—340.

41. Compare R. Menaḥem Recanati's view, in his *Commentary on the Pentateuch*, fol. 71d–72a, that the glory ascends toward the Tetragrammaton. Even more important seems to be Recanati's discussion, fol. 43c, where "the supernal glory" is presented as longing to ascend to the supernal light, in the context of the meaning of the recitation of *'Alenu Le-shabeaḥ*. Interestingly, on the same page R. Eleazar of Worms is quoted twice, as is R. Yehudah he-Ḥasid. The Ashkenazic presentation of the glory is an issue of great importance, as it may evidence a dynamism of the glory preceding the Kabbalistic dynamics of the Sefirot, which served as one of the starting points for the intradivine Kabbalistic processes. See also below, Chap. VIII, sec. III.

42. Psalms 99:5.

43. Urbach, *'Arugat ha-Bosem* II, p. 116 and n. 9. On the wide interest in the "Will of God" in *Sefer Ḥasidim*, see Ḥaym Soloveitchik, "Three Themes in the *Sefer Ḥasidim*," *AJSreview* 1 (1976): 311–325.

44. See Scholem, *On the Kabbalah*, p. 130; Daniel C. Matt, "The Mystic and the Miz̡wot," in *Jewish Spirituality*, ed. A. Green (New York, 1986), 1:367–404. An interesting presentation of the importance of human acts, both for the universe and for the redemption of God, which assumes the affinity between exoteric and esoteric layers of Judaism, can be found in Elie Benamozegh, *Israel et l'Humanité* (Paris, 1961), pp. 227–229, where, however, the author ignores augmentation theurgy. See also the vague remarks of Buber, *Ḥasidism*, p. 63.

45. Tishby, *The Wisdom of the Zohar*, 2:10, stated that these Aggadic views are "exceptional and few," and the Kabbalists could use them as a "pretext" for "their faith." Scholem, *Les Origines de la Kabbale*, p. 90, considered it as "scabreuse"! See also Morris M. Faierstein's Scholemian treatment of the issue of Kabbalah and the rabbinic view of the commandments in *Conservative Judaism* 36 (1982): 45–59, and Shaḥar's article referred to below, n. 48.

46. *Ari Nohem*, pp. 94–95. Modena's answer to the Kabbalistic theurgical interpretation of the commandments is borrowed from Pseudo-Dionysios, without, understandably, mentioning his name; see Idel, "Differing Conceptions of Kabbalah," par. II.

47. *On Jewish Law and Lore*, pp. 190–191.

48. Margaliot, par. 129, p. 56:
למלך שהיו לו בנים ולבנים—בנים. בזמן שבניהם עושים רצונו, נכנס ביניהם ומעמיד הכל, ומשביע לכל ומשפיע להם טובה, כדי שישבעו האבות והבנים. וכשאין הבנים עושים רצונו, משביע להם האבות כדי צרכם.

Compare, however, the opinion of Shulamit Shaḥar, "Catharism and the Beginnings of the Kabbalah in Languedoc" (in Hebrew), *Tarbiẓ* 40 (1971): 503–507, who attempts to relate the bahiric theurgy to Catharic sources, without dwelling upon the Jewish or classical texts!

49. Margaliot, par. 113, p. 51:
ואם לא יזכו הבנים ולא יעשו דברים הגונים לפני, הרי הצנורות...אתן להם מים על מנת שלא יתנו לבניהם דבר, אחרי שאינם עושים רצונו.

On the channels, see also in a cognate text of R. Joseph Gikatilla, quoted below, Chap. VIII, n. 68.

50. On Exod. 20:1, *Commentary on the Torah*, ed. Chavel, II, p. 183; the text was borrowed by ibn Gabbay, *'Avodat ha-Kodesh* II, 2, fol. 26b.

51. This stands for the divine influx which activates the seven lower Sefirot, according to R. Asher ben David's Kabbalistic theory; see above, Chap. VI, n. 254.

52. Deut. 32:18.

53. Psalms 60:14.

54. *Commentary on the Torah*, p. 184.

55. See ibid., pp. 183–184, where a lengthy explanation on the meaning of the "Trisagion" and blessing is provided within the context of the cited passages.

56. *Commentary on the Torah* 111, p. 89. The terminology of this text is emblematic to R. Asher ben David and, although the precise source of the latter's works cannot be detected, it is probable that R. Baḥya preserved an earlier discussion. Compare also ibid., p. 492, and R. Baḥya's commentary to Deut. 33:26.

57. Deut. 33:26; in the original, *be-'ezrekha* means "to thy help." See also *Bahir*, par. 185, p. 83.

58. On "heaven" as Sefirot, see Gottlieb, *The Kabbalah of R. Baḥya*, p. 65.

59. Psalms 60:14.

60. Compare the ascents or retreats of the *Shekhinah* from this lower world, sec. III below.

61. Deut. 33:26. Compare also Baḥya's commentary on this verse.

62. Ibid., 32:18

63. Recanati quotes from *Sefer ha-Yiḥud* without mentioning its source; a part of this passage will be analyzed below, Chap. VIII, n. 77. This work also emphasized the importance of augmentation theurgy; see MS Milano-Ambrosiana 62, fol. 113a, quoted below, Chap. VIII, n. 82.

64. *Commentary on the Pentateuch*, fol. 51b.

65. For more on this concept, see below, Chap. VIII, sec. II. Compare also to Recanati, ibid., fol. 69c, where the multiplication or diminution of the channels of mercy or judgment is a function of human deeds.

66. "ויתרבי חילא ותיסק עד רישא"

Compare Yehudah Liebes, "Songs for the Shabbat Meals Written by R. Isaac Luria" (in Hebrew), *Molad* 23 (February 1972): 551.

67. Ed Mandelbaum, p. 379; compare also *Numbers Rabbah* 16:14; *Mekhilta de-Rashbi*, ed. M. Friedmann, fol. 39a.

68. On R. Ya'akov bar Aḥa as related to another conception of the extraordinary power of human activity, see below, n. 125. Consequently, it seems that the first important traces of rabbinic theurgy are to be dated no later than the beginning of the fourth century in Palestine.

69. Num. 14:17.

70. *Berakhot* 7a; this text is an exact repetition of the prayer of God himself, mentioned shortly before. On the bibliography referring to this passage, see Baer, "The Service of Sacrifice," pp. 134–135. Compare also R. Benjamin ben Abraham min ha-'Anavim's *Perush Alfabetin* (cf. above, Chap. VI, n. 9), p. 231:

"התפלל יצחק... כשם שאני כובש את יצרי להישחט לפניך כך יכבשו רחמיך את כעסך."

Here, human self-sacrifice is viewed, as is human prayer above, as a way to mitigate the pernicious influence of divine anger.

71. *Babba Batra* 99a. See Idel, "Métaphores et pratiques sexuelles," pp. 337–338, and R. Abraham ben Eliezer ha-Levi's assessment:

כל זמן שישראל עושין רצונו של הב"ה, המלך מזדווג לכלה ומתאהב אצלה לפי שישראל בן בכור לש"י... וכל זמן שישראל אינם עושים רצונו אז מתרחק ממה.

"As long as Israel does the divine will, [that is, the king who is the Sefirah of Tiferet] has intercourse with the bride [Malkhut] and falls in love with her, since Israel is God's firstborn . . . and so long as Israel does not do his will, he [the king] departs from her" (*Sefer Masoret ha-Ḥokhmah*, printed by G. Scholem in *Kiryat Sefer* 7 [1930]: 451). It is obvious that this Kabbalist interprets the talmudic dictum in *Babba Batra*.

72. See also *Sotah* 14a, and Moshe Idel, "Notes in Wake of the Medieval Jewish-Christian Polemic," *Immanuel* 18 (1984): 56–60.

73. Margaliot, par. 34, pp. 16–17.

74. *Canticles Rabbah* I:9:

"רעיתי"—אמר רבי יוחנן: מפרנסתי.

Compare to the material collected by Baer, "The Service of Sacrifice," pp. 142–145.

75. See *Bahir*, Margaliot, par. 97, p. 43; R. 'Ezra of Gerona, *Commentary on Talmudic Aggadot*, MS Vatican 441, fol. 27ab; *Commentary on Song of Songs*, in Chavel, *Kitvey ha-Ramban* II, pp. 498–499. R. Shneur Zalman of Lyady, *Sefer TKSḤ* (New York, 1976), pp. 17–18.

76. H. Frankfort, H. A. Frankfort, J. A. Wilson, T. Jacobsen, and W. A. Irwin, *The Intellectual Adventure of Ancient Man* (Chicago and London, 1977), pp. 369–370. See also Chap. VI, n. 3.

77. 19:7, p. 176.

78. See *Hebrew Enoch*, ed. and trans. Hugo Odeberg (New York, 1973), pp. 15–16; Hebrew text, pp. ix–x. Odeberg collected several ancient Jewish sources concerning the removal of the *Shekhinah* because of idolatry: p. 18 n. 13. See also Phillip Alexander, "The Historical Setting of the Hebrew Book of Enoch," *JJS* 28–29 (1977–78): 175 n. 38; Arnold M. Goldberg, *Untersuchungen über die Vorstellung von der Schekhinah* (Berlin, 1969), pp. 125–159.

79. *Hebrew Enoch*, p 16; Hebrew text, p. x.

80. Compare Song of Songs 2:8, and *Midrash Rabbah*, on this verse as referring to idolatry.

81. Compare to *Alphabet of R. 'Akiba*, in Wertheimer, *Batey Midrashot* II, p. 375.

82. I Kings 22:19.

83. Compare to *Tanḥuma*, Genesis 12, where the form *ro'im* is to be corrected to *moridim* in connection with the sun and moon; cf. Louis Ginzberg, *The Legends of the Jews*, 5:152 n. 56.
84. See also Saul Liebermann, *Hellenism in Jewish Palestine* (New York, 1950), p. 121 n. 33.
85. *Babba Batra* 99a.
86. Compare *Yoma* 54b, and the quotation from R. Yom Tov Ashvili in R. Shemuel Edeles, *Novellae ad locum*.
87. *Sotah* 17a; see Idel, "Métaphores et pratiques sexuelles," pp. 336ff.
88. See his commentary on Exodus 29:46, where he implies that the literal sense of the dwelling as fulfilling a human need must be interpreted otherwise, given expressions where God wishes to dwell in the temple. After the end of the thirteenth century, the formula indicating "the dwelling of the Shekhinah below [or, amidst Israel] is a necessity for the most high" became widespread. See, for example, Gottlieb, *Studies*, p. 32; Vajda, *Recherches*, pp. 191–192; Scholem, "New Contributions to the Biography of Rabbi Joseph Ashkenazi of Safed," *Tarbiz* 28 (1959): 88.
89. See Peter Schäfer, "Die Beschwörung des *Sar ha-Panim*," *Frankfurter Judaistische Beiträge* 6 (1978): 115:

במה משביעים את שר הפנים לירד לארץ לגלות לאדם רזי מעלה ומטה ומחקרי יסודי מעלה ויסודי מטה ותעלומות חכמה.

Schäfer offered a German translation on p. 114; compare also p. 131.

90. Ibid., p. 115:

"לפי ששכינה עמו בכל מקום."

91. A description of this work can be found in Joseph Dan, *Three Types of Ancient Jewish Mysticism* (Cincinnati, 1984), pp. 24–31; D. Blumenthal, *Understanding Jewish Mysticism* (New York, 1978) 1:97–98; Ithamar Grünwald, *Apocalyptic and Merkabah Mysticism* (Leiden, 1980), pp. 169–173. Dan, following Urbach, advocates a rather late date for this opus—the seventh or eighth century; Scholem, *Jewish Gnosticism*, pp. 12–13, prefers a much earlier one, on the grounds of an Aggadic reference to Yophiel, the prince of Torah, and of the similarity of this practice to the magical papyruses of the fourth century—two points that passed unnoticed by those scholars who advocate a later date of composition. The affinity to Hermeticism, discussed above, seems to strengthen Scholem's dating.
92. Schäfer, *Synopse*, par. 297. *En passant*: Dan's remark, ibid., p. 26, that the term *razim* occurring in *Sar ha-Torah* has nothing to do with a "mystical esoteric meaning of the Torah" is bizarre, given the parallel to *Sar ha-Panim* quoted above, where *razim* occurs precisely in connection with esoteric lore; see also *Ma'aseh Merkavah*, printed by Scholem in *Jewish Gnosticism*, p. 103.
93. See Pierre Boyance, "Théurgie et télestique néoplatoniciennes," *Revue d'histoire des religions* 74 (1955): 194–209.
94. See Idel, "Hermeticism and Judaism"; Idel, "Magical and Neoplatonic Interpretations," pp. 198–208. See also below, Chap. IX, sec. I, the text of Alemanno.
95. See below, Chap. VIII, n. 155, and n. 87 in this chapter, as well as the famous dictum "the forefathers are the chariot" in *Genesis Rabbah* 69, 3.
96. Cf. *Yebamot* 64a; see also below, n. 113.
97. Idel, "Métaphores et pratiques sexuelles," pp. 338–342.
98. *Shekel ha-Kodesh*, p. 70:

כי עיקר המצוות והמעשים טובים (!) אשר האדם עושה בעולם הזה הוא לכונן את נפשו ולתקון עניינים גדולים וטובים למעלה להמשיך עליו המשכת אור שפע של מעלה.

99. On the same page, de Leon also mentions another formulation of this issue:

"לתקן נפשו לאור באור החיים"

100. Ibid.:

הכונה בהיות האדם בעולם הזה יסוד וכסא לניח עליו הכסא המתנשא.

101. *Sha'arey 'Orah*, ed. Joseph ben Shelomo, 1:49–50.

102. *Zohar* II, 117b.

103. *Tikkuney Zohar*, par. 70, fol. 132a.

104. See Matt, "The Mystic and the *Miẓwot*" (n. 44 above), pp. 390, 394.

105. *Ma'amar Sod ha-Yiḥud*, MS Jerusalem 4° 537, fol. 145a.

106. This issue will be dealt with in a separate study.

107. See above, Chap. V, end of sec. III.

108. Printed in Scholem, *Reshit ha-Kabbalah*, p. 222:

כי כל מי שיודעו ומתפלל בו השכינה שורה עליו ומתנבא כמו הנביאים הראשונים.

109. Ibid., p. 226.

110. *'Or ha-Sekhel*, MS Vatican 233, fol. 110b.

נגן בחריק הנמשך למטה ומושך כח עליון להרביקו בך.

111. On the entire question, see Idel, "Perceptions of the Kabbalah," and Chap. VI, sec. IV.

112. *Pardes Rimmonim* 30, 3. For another type of drawing-down practice, see below, Chap. IX, the passage of *Sefer ha-Meshiv* quoted near n. 167.

113. On the prophet as vessel, see also Chap. VI, sec. II. Compare also to A. D. Nock, *Essays: On Religion and the Ancient World*, ed. Zeph Steward (Cambridge, Mass., 1972), pp. 191–192, where the descent of God upon the magician is connected to "union."

114. MS Oxford 2234, fol. 164r; see Idel, "Magical and Neoplatonic Interpretations," pp. 198–199.

115. Exod. 19:15.

116. Scholem, *On the Kabbalah*, p. 94.

117. Ibid., p. 95. Compare also Tishby, *The Wisdom of the Zohar* II, p. 196, who reiterates Scholem's view.

118. Scholem, *On the Kabbalah*, p. 95. Compare, however, with p. 165, where Scholem correctly points out the ancient Jewish sources of a certain motif that recurs in Gnostic sources.

119. Scholem, *Explications and Implications*, p. 66.

120. It is superfluous to point out that Judaism managed also to survive in circles that did not adopt Kabbalah long after its emergence. On the Bible and myth, see above, Chap. VII.

121. I borrowed the phrase *universe-maintaining* from P. L. Berger and T. Luckman, *The Social Construction of Reality* (New York, 1967), pp. 104ff.

122. *'Avodah Zarah* 3a.

123. That is, the creatures.

124. *Pesikta de Rav Kahana*, Buber, fol. 140b; see Baer, "The Service of Sacrifices," p. 149.

125. *Ta'anit* 27b; *Megillah* 31b. See Saul Liebermann, *Tosefta Ki-Peshuta* (New York, 1962), 5:1103; Baer, "The Service of Sacrifices," p. 149.

126. *Midrash Shir ha-Shirim*, ed. E. Greenhut, fol. 17ab.
127. *'Avot* 5, 1; *Midrash 'Avkir*, printed in *Devir* 1 (1923): 120.
128. "בעשרה מאמרות נברא העולם ועל עשרה דברות יעמוד העולם."

See Paul Kraus, "Hebräische und syrische Zitate in ismäilitischen Schriften," *Der Islam* 19 (1930): 260. Salomon Pines, "Shi'ite Terms and Conceptions in Juda Halevi's *Kuzari*," *Jerusalem Studies in Arabic and Islam* 2 (1980): 243–244. No doubt the quotation found in the Ismaili source and its parallel in the Jewish Ismaili work reflects an older Jewish view; this sentence is paralleled by two short statements occurring in *Midrash Tadshe*, a later Midrash that evidently includes earlier material as well, as some scholars have recognized. According to one statement:

שהעולם עומד בזכות לומדים ועושים י' דברות, ובי' מאמרות נבראו וספירותיו עשרה.

"The world is maintained by the merit of those who study [the Torah] and perform the Decalogue; and the world was created by ten logoi [*ma'amarot*], and its Sefirot are [also] ten."

Shortly thereafter, the Midrash asserts:

". . . אלו עשר ספירות בלימה שעליהם העולם עומד."

"The world is maintained by the ten Sefirot of Belimah."

Cf. *Midrash Tadshe* in Epstein, *Mi-Kadmoniot ha-Yehudim*, p. 145. This Midrash implicitly identifies the ten Sefirot with the Decalogue; compare below, Chap. VIII, n. 108. It is important to emphasize the fact that the view expressed in this Midrash conspicuously contradicts that of *Sefer Yeẓirah*, where the Sefirot, rather than the *ma'amarot*, are the instruments by which the world was created. See above, Chap. VI, sec. II.

129. Kasher, *Torah Shelemah, Va-'Era'*, p. 43.
130. Margaliot, par. 138, pp. 60–61; Scholem *Bahir*, p. 101, to be compared to the *Bahir*. Margaliot, par. 135, pp. 58–59; Idel, "Sefirot above Sefirot," pp. 269–276.
131. Gottlieb, *The Kabbalah of R. Baḥya*, pp. 99–101; R. Isaac Todros' *Commentary on the Maḥzor*, MS Paris BN 839, fol. 195a, and the text printed in R. Moses de Leon's *Sefer ha-Nefesh ha-Ḥakhamah*, col. P, 3–4; *Zohar* III, 11b–12a; Wertheimer, *Batey Midrashot* II, pp. 97–99; MS Cambridge Add. 123, fol. 1–9b; MS Berlin, Or. 942, fol. 42b–43a, and in a rather different form in *Bahir*, Margaliot, par. 124, p. 55.
132. Chap. VIII, sec. II. We must also take into consideration the possibility, which I cannot prove, that diminution or augmentation of divine power may have a direct impact on the universe, and therefore the universe maintenance may have some theurgic implications. The nexus of theurgy with "universe maintenance" is already obvious when comparing, for example, the two bahiric passages referred to in n. 130 above.
133. *Commentary on the Pentateuch*, fol. 51b:

יש לו לאדם להתבונן במצות התורה כמה עולמות מקיים בעשייתן וכמה עולמות מחריב בביטולן.

CHAPTER 8

1. H. G. Enelow, "Midrash Hashkem Quotations in Alnaqua's Menorat ha-Maor," *HUCA* 4 (1927): 319:

אמר הקב"ה למשה: לך אמור להם לישראל: שמי אהיה אשר אהיה, כלומר כשם שאתה הווה עמי כך אני הווה עמך.

See also *Midrash-Hizhir*, ed. Meir Freimann (1873), fol. 43, where a similar formulation is to be found; the quotation of Naḥmanides from *Midrash Aggadah* in his *Commentary on the Pentateuch* to Exodus 3:14; and the significant remark of M. Kasher, *Torah Shelemah* (New York, 1944), 8:153 n. 188. On the early Kabbalistic discussions on the significance of *'Ehyeh 'asher 'Ehyeh*, see Nicolas Sed, "L'Interprétation Kabbalistique d'Exode 3, 14 selon les documents du XIIIe siècle," in *Celui qui est: Interprétations juives et chrétiennes d'Exode 3,14*, ed. Alain de Libra and Emilie Zum Brunn (Paris, 1986), pp. 25–46.

2. Anonymous, *Sefer ha-Malmad*, MS Oxford 1649, fol. 205b:
וכן פרשו החכמים זה הסוד בשם אהיה אשר אהיה שאמר הקב"ה למשה: משה היה עמי ואהיה עמך. והביאו ראיה מן הכתוב ה' צלך על יד ימינך כמו שמפורש במדרש השכם.
3. Psalms 121:5.
4. See Chap. IV, near n. 29, where the expression of mystical union, which follows from our quotation, is analyzed; cf. Idel, "Abraham Abulafia and *Unio Mystica*," where additional materials from fol. 205b–206a are quoted and discussed.
5. MS Paris, BN 774, fol. 32b:
הנה שניהם האדם השפל כמו ששניהם באדם הנכבד וידוע שהאדם הנכבד לא יפעל דבר זולתי כפי מעשי האדם השפל לגמול או לעונש. נמצאת אומ' שאם האדם השפל פועל פעולות נכבדות, יש לאדם הנכבד להמשך אחרי פעולותיו.
6. Constantinople, 1560, fol. 4a:
ובמדרש, אמר לו הקב"ה למשה לך אמור להם לישראל כי שמי אהיה אשר אהיה, מהו אהיה אשר אהיה, כשם שאתה הווה עמי כך אני הווה עמך, וכן אמר דוד יי' צלך על יד ימינך, מהו יי' צלך, כצלך: מה צלך אם אתה משחק לו הוא משחק לך, אם אתה בוכה לו הוא בוכה כנגדך, ואם אתה מראה לו פנים זעומות או מסבירות אף הוא נותן לך כך, אף הקב"ה ה' צלך, כשם שאתה הווה עמו הוא הווה עמך ע"כ.
7. Compare to *Yalkut Shim'oni*, Exodus, par. 286:
אני ה' אלהיך: אמר רבי חנינא בר פפא, נראה להם הקב"ה פנים זועפות פנים מסבירות פנים בינוניות פנים שוחקות: . . . אמר להם הקב"ה אע"פ שאתם רואים כל הדמויות הללו אנכי ה' אלהיך.
See also Yochanan Muffs, "Joy and Love as Metaphorical Expressions of Willingness and Spontaneity in Cuneiform, Ancient Hebrew and Related Literatures," in *Christianity, Judaism and Other Greco-Roman Cults: Studies for Morton Smith at Sixty*, ed. Jacob Neusner (Leiden, 1975), 3:10–11 n. 21.
8. On divine weeping, see below, sec. IV.
9. The opposite tendency in Kabbalah, which regards the "real" in Platonic rather than in theurgic terms, as it does here, obviously views the human hand as the "shadow." See Scholem, *Major Trends*, p. 208.
10. *Tola'at Ya'akov*, fol. 4a:
העליונים אצל התחתונים דוגמת הצל אצל הצורה, כפי מה שהצורה מעוררת צל מעורר.
11. Namely, the Sefirot cause the emanation from *'Eiyn Sof* to descend from above.
12. Chap. VI, sec. II.
13. See Goetschel, *Meir ibn Gabbay*, pp. 165–174.
14. For more on this issue, see below, Chap. X.
15. See above, Chap. VI, the passage from *Zohar* III, 141b.
16. See Chap. IX, sec. II.
17. On other religious nuclei of interest that reduce the role of symbolism, see Chap. IX, sec. I.
18. *Tola'at Ya'akov*, fol. 4a:

וכשהמאור העליון משקיף על בני האדם ורואה מעשיהם הטובים המתוקנים, כפי מה שמעוררים הם למטה, מעוררים למעלה ופותח את אוצרו הטוב ומוריד השמן הטוב על הראש ומשם לשאר מדותיו.

19. This phrase seems to be influenced by *Sefer Berit Menuḥah*, where it signifies the highest divine layer.
20. Cf. II Kings 9:6; Isa. 39:2. The oil symbolizes the supernal influx that descends upon the Sefirah of Keter.
21. Fol. 34d—36b.
22. See Recanati's similar view of demut, below, n. 113.
23. On ibn Gabbay's view of the Torah as an intermediary "man," see Idel, "The Concept of the Torah," p. 75, and below, n. 122.
24. Fol. 36d: "... המצות והוא האמצעי המעורר הדמות העליון לקראת התחתון"
25. Ibid.:

התורה והמצות הם האמצעי המחבר הדמות התחתון עם העליון מצד היחס אשר לו עם שניהם.

26. On the history of the metaphor of the two violins in Jewish theology and theosophy, see Idel, "The Magical and Theurgical Interpretation," passim.
27. MS Paris, BN 858, fol. 98a:

וכמו שהיתה המלחמה למטה היתה למעלה והכל בעון ישראל, שכשהם צדיקים, מוסיפים כח וגבורה בפמליא של מעלה... וכשהם בהפך, כביכול מתישים כח של מעלה... כי התחתונים כדמות שורש ואופן לעליונים.

28. That is, angels.
29. *Ophan:* I translated this as "modus," although this contradicts the perception of the lower entities as "root."
30. Compare R. Ḥayyim of Volozhin's interpretation of the Midrash in classical Kabbalistic terms in *Nefesh ha-Ḥayyim* (Vilna, 1874), fol. 12a-b, and *L'Ame de la vie*, ed. and trans. Benjamin Gross (Paris, 1986), p. 27.
31. Quoted by R. Levi Isaac of Berdichev, *Kedushat ha-Levi* (Jerusalem, 1972), fol. 39c; the Besht and R. Levi Isaac were fond of this verse, which they repeatedly interpret.
32. In Hebrew, *yashir* can be understood both as "he will sing" and "he will cause [someone else] to sing."
33. Num. 21:17.
34. *Cherubinischer Wandersmann* V, 259: "Gott wird, was ich itz bin, nimmt meine Menschheit an; Weil ich von Er gewest, drum hat er es getan." Compare also III, 20.
35. See also below, Chap. IX, my discussion on *Zohar* III, 5a.
36. On this work, see Asi Farber, "On the Sources of Rabbi Moses de Leon's Early Kabbalistic System" (in Hebrew), in *Studies in Jewish Mysticism Presented to Isaiah Tishby*, ed. J. Dan and J. R. Hacker (Jerusalem, 1984), pp. 67–96.
37. MS Paris, BN 817, fol. 73b:

סוד הרוצח: האדם הוא כלול מכל הדברים הרוחניים והוא שלם מכל המדות ונברא בחכמה גדולה... כי הוא כלול מכל סתרי המרכבה ונשמתו שם היא נקשרת אעפ"י שהאדם בעולם הזה. ותדע שאלמלא שהוא שלם מכל כוחותיו של הב"ה, לא היה יכול לעשו' כמותו. ואמרי רבא ברא גברא ואיבעו צדיקי' ברו' עולמו'. להודיעך שיש בבני אדם כח גדול של מעלה, שאין אדם יכול לספרו ובהיות באדם שלימות גדול כזה, אינו דין להפסיד צורתו מן העולם ונשמתו משם. וההורג את הנפש מה הפסד הוא עושה? הוא שופך דמו של זה ומעט הצורה כלו' מיעט כח הספירו'.

38. See R. 'Ezra and R. Moses de Leon's formulas adduced above, Chap. VI, sec. I.
39. Man comprises all the secrets according to the *Zohar*, although the *Merkavah* is not mentioned there; see *Idra Rabba*, in III, 135a:

"כמראה אדם דכליל כל רזין"

40. Compare R. 'Ezra's view, cited in Chap. III, n. 29.
41. This formulation seems to reflect the Plotinian psychology of the connection of the human soul to the universal soul even during its sojourn in this world.
42. *Sanhedrin* 65b; on the context of this passage and its significance, see Scholem, *On the Kabbalah*, pp. 165–166.
43. See n. 113 below.
44. See Chap. VI, n. 73; Chap. VII, n. 128.
45. Cf. Ricoeur, *The Symbolism of Evil*, p. 194.
46. Professor Thorkild Jacobsen has kindly informed me, in an oral conversation, that this proverb can also be understood as pointing to the protection of God on the king-man, and of the latter on men. The Assyrian *ẓilu*, like its Hebrew counterpart *ẓel*, may be interpreted as both "shadow" and "protection."
47. Robinson, *The Nag Hammadi Library*, p. 365.
48. Thorkild Jacobsen, *The Intellectual Adventure of Ancient Man* (Chicago and London, 1977), p. 138.
49. *Commentary on Song of Songs*, in Chavel, *Kitvey ha-Ramban* II, p. 504.
50. Ibid., p. 504:

וקראו רז"ל כמו כן אצילות ההויות וגלויה—עקירה, כדאיתא בב"ר יוטע ה' אלהים גן בעדן, הה"ד ישבעו עצי ה' ארזי הלבנון אשר נטע; אמר ר' חנינא: כקרני חגבים היו, ועקרן הקב"ה ושתלן בתוך גן עדן.

See also below, n. 55.
51. 15, 1, p. 135.
52. Gen. 2:8.
53. Psalms 104:17. For the view of God as planting a cosmic tree, see Scholem, *Les Origines de la Kabbale*, pp. 81–83, esp. p. 83 n. 36, where he points to an interesting parallel to *Sefer ha-Bahir* in a fragment attributed to Simeon Magus; cf Hippolytus, *Elenchos* Vl, 9. See also Isaac Baer, "The Early Ḥasidim in Philo's Writings and in the Hebrew Tradition" (in Hebrew), *Ẓion* 18 (1953): 104, and Urbach's critique thereof in *The Sages*, p. 791 nn. 67–69. It seems however, that the passage of *Genesis Rabbah* supplies an interesting hint of the importance of mythic and cosmic trees in ancient Judaism.
54. Compare Naḥmanides' critique of the view that the planted trees were brought from another place, in his *Commentary* on Genesis 2:8. The difference between him and R. 'Ezra seems to me significant, and I do not even exclude the possibility that Naḥmanides was critical of the manner in which R. 'Ezra understood this matter. See also above, Chap. IV, par. 1–2, on the difference between the essentialist view of Sefirot in Naḥmanides' Kabbalistic school and the instrumentalist view of R. 'Ezra.
55. Printed in Scholem, "New Document," p. 158:

עוטה אור כשלמה ר"ל זיו החכמה ועל זה נקרא חכמה לבנון והאמת כי ההויות היו אבל האצילות מחודש ולא היה כי אם גלוי הדברים.

On this text, see Alexander Altmann, "A Note on the Rabbinic Doctrine of Creation," *JJS* 6–7 (1955–56): 204–206.
56. Psalms 104:2.

57. On this view of emanation qua revelation of hidden entities, see Idel, "Sefirot above Sefirot," pp. 241–243.
58. Compare R. 'Ezra's *Commentary on the Talmudic Aggadot*, MS Vatican 294, fol. 38a:
ישבעו עצי יי׳ ארזי לבנון. א״ר חנינ׳ כקרני חגבים היו ועקרן הב״ה ושתלן בגן עדן. ויטע יי׳, מי שנוטע צרי׳ נטיעות לכך דמה ר׳ חני׳ אצילות ההויות הדקות שהיו בחכמה לעקירה, ובריאתן וגדילתן לנטיעה.
Lebanon as a symbol of Hokhmah is found in *Sefer ha-Bahir*, Margaliot, par. 178. There seems to be no precedent for this symbolism for Lebanon in rabbinic sources: see Geza Vermes, *Scripture and Tradition in Judaism* (Leiden, 1973), pp. 26–39; H. F. D. Sparks, "The Symbolical Interpretation of *Levanon* in the Fathers," *Journal of Theological Studies*, n.s. 10 (1959): 264–279.
59. *Commentary on Song of Songs*, in Chavel, *Kitvey ha-Ramban* II, p. 504:
והדברים הרוחניים מתעלים ונמשכים אל מקום יניקתם וכן הוא אומר כי מפני הרעה נאסף הצדיק ולכן צריך להשתדל ולהאציל ולהמשיך אל האבות את הברכה, להיות לבנים המשכה.
60. Isa. 57:1. Compare the different usage of the same verse in R. Isaac the Blind's *Commentary on Sefer Yeẓirah*, p. 17, where the disappearance of the righteous is viewed in a positive way, as an escape from a future evil.
61. I assume that the righteous man stands for each of the seven lower Sefirot, as it seems to be associated with the idea of cedar; cf. Psalms 92:13: "The righteous man flourishes like the palm tree, he grows like a cedar in Lebanon."
62. On this symbolism, see above, Chap. VII, sec. II, near nn. 48–49.
63. *Commentary on Song of Songs*, p. 486:
כי תכלית חפצם וכוונתם להתדבק ולהעלות למקום יניקתם ולכן תקנו חכמינו הברכה והקדושה והיחוד, להאציל ולהמשיך מקור החיים אל שאר הספירות, האבות, להסתפק לבניהם אחריהם.
See also below, n. 266.
64. Compare R. 'Ezra's formulation in his *Commentary on Song of Songs*, p. 504:
אין הפרש בדבר הסובב בין מעלה ומטה והירידה היא עליה והעליה היא ירידה.
The view of the emanational process as descent must have a counterpart, here designated as ascent; this countermovement is the natural tendency to return.
65. See Chap. VII above, sec. IV.
66. Two of Abulafia's works describing mystical techniques and experiences include in their titles either the word *'Eden—'Oẓar 'Eden Ganuz*—or *Gan—Gan Na'ul.*
67. This is Eliade's explanation of the "easy way" to realize this nostalgia: *Images and Symbols*, p. 55. The phrase is underlined in the original; see also "the desire of man to find himself at the center *without any effort.*"
68. Ed. Ben Shelomo, 1:100; compare also to p. 99.
69. The verse Isaiah 57:1 occurs in ibid., p. 100.
70. Ibid., p. 99. Compare to *Bahir*, ed. Margaliot, par. 113, p. 51, analyzed above, Chap. VII.
71. Contraction or return is mentioned previously on the same page.
72. On the relationship between good deeds and the expansion of the divine world, see also Chap. III, n. 84.
73. R. David ben Abraham ha-Lavan, *Sefer Masoret ha-Berit*, ed. G. Scholem, *Koveẓ 'al-Yad, Minora Manuscripta Judaica*, n.s. 1 (1936): 39:

"אדם החוטא מחזיר המדות לאין, לעולם הקדמון, לישות הראשון ואינם משפיעים טובות למטה בעולם השפל."

On this work, see Gershom G. Scholem, "David ben Abraham ha-labhan-ein unbekannter judischer Mystiker," in *Occident and Orient . . . Gaster Anniversary Volume*, ed. B. Schindler and A. Marmorstein (London, 1936), pp. 505–508.

74. On "nothingness" in R. David, see Scholem, *Kabbalah*, p. 95.

75. Ibid., p. 31:

ואם יחזרו כל הכחות לאין, יעמוד הקדמון, שהוא עילה לכל, ביחודו בעמקי האין, באחדות השווה.

See also p. 41.

76. Namely, the divine attributes.

77. MS Milano-Ambrosiana 62, fol. 112b:

כי בהיות האדם התחתון פוגם אחד מאיבריו הרי בהיות אותו האבר פגום מלמטה, כביכול הוא מקצץ אותו האבר למעלה, וענין הקצוץ הוא שיתקצץ אותו האבר והולך ומתקבץ ונכנס אל עמקי ההויה הנקראת אין וכאלו אותו האבר חסר למעלה, וכאשר היתה צורת האדם השלימה למטה, גורמת שלימות למעלה, כך טומאת האבר למטה גורמת אסיפת דוגמא אותו האבר של מעלה אל עמקי האין, עד שמטיל פגם בצורה העליונה הה"ד כי מפני הרעה נאסף הצדיק,—נאסף ממש.

On this work, see Idel, "R. Joseph of Hamadan's *Commentary on Ten Sefirot*," pp. 82–84. This passage was copied anonymously by R. Menaḥem Recanati, *Commentary on the Pentateuch*, fol. 51b, and thereby disseminated through the printed edition of this work.

78. Isa. 57:1. See also *Sefer ha-Yiḥud*, fol. 115a.

79. MS Milano-Ambrosiana 62, fol. 113a:

. . . אדם שלם והיינו דאמרי האבות הם הם המרכבה, המרכבה ממש, דוק ותשכח, אבר מחזיק אבר . . . כי האבר המוכן המחזיק האבר שהוא בדיוקנו.

80. *Genesis Rabbah* 82:6, p. 983, etc.

81. See Yehudah Avida', "'Ever Maḥazik 'Ever," *Sinai* 29 (1957): 401–402; Altmann, "On the Question of Authorship," pp. 275, 411; Moshe Hallamish, "Leket Pilgamim," *Sinai* 80 (1977): 277; Sheraga Abramson, *Issues in Gaonic Literature* (in Hebrew) (Jerusalem, 1974), pp. 128–129 n. 9.

82. MS Milano-Ambrosiana 62, fol. 113a:

החסידים ואנשי מעשה יודעי' לכוון אל הכחות. ומאי אנשי מעשה, אלא כההוא דאמרי: כל המקיים מצותי מעלה אני עליו כאלו עשאם. הה"ד עת לעשות ליי'—ממש, כביכול כל הפוגם למטה פוגם למעלה וכל המטהר עצמו למטה, מוסיף כח . . . .

This text was copied with some variations by R. Menaḥem Recanati, *Commentary on the Pentateuch*, fol. 51c; in ibn Gabbay's *'Avodat ha-Kodesh* I, 2, fol. 26c; and his *Tola'at Ya'akov*, fol. 7bc. See also his allusion in *Derekh 'Emunah*, fol. 15d.

83. In ancient Jewish literature, this term refers to holy wonder-workers. See G. Ben-Ami Sarfati, "Ḥasidim and Men of Deeds, and the Early Prophets" (in Hebrew), *Tarbiẓ* 26 (1957): 142–148; Baruch M. Bokser, "Wonder-Working and the Rabbinic Tradition: The Case of Ḥanina ben Dosa," *Journal for the Study of Judaism* 16 (1985): 42–92.

84. Namely, the Sefirot.

85. In the Milanese manuscript the version is "**עשאם**", "he made them," that is, the commandments. However, all other manuscripts of this work I have checked have the reading "**עשני**" or "**עשאני**" —namely, "he made me"; so also the literal quotation from

Sefer ha-Yiḥud by Recanati, who is probably the first author to have quoted this book. The manuscripts checked were, for example, MS Cambridge, Add. 644; Cambridge, Add. 1833; MS Paris 799, and so on.

86. Psalms 119:126; I translated the verse in the way the author intended it to be understood. Strangely, the second half of the verse states: "They have made void thy Torah." The nexus between this verse and "making God" is peculiar to *Sefer ha-Yiḥud* and to those Kabbalists who copied from it, but it is missing in the *Zohar*, where this verse is interpreted in other ways. See Liebes, "The Messiah of the *Zohar*," pp. 146, 166–167, 169–170.
87. R. Abraham ben Ḥananel of Eskira, *Sefer Yesod 'Olam*, MS Moscow-Günzburg 607, fol. 69b:
כי אין האיש בביתו הב״מ [הלך בדרך מרחוק], שישוב בעמק ההויה ונשאר בעיר שמה ושאיה, כל הפוגם למטה גורם ענין זה חרבן באמת . . . והמטהר בונה . . . ומדרשם כל המקיים מצותי מעלה אני עליו כאלו עשאני.
88. Prov. 7:19.
89. Compare the same phrase above, in the text cited in n. 77.
90. Isa. 24:12.
91. On building as a result of theurgical activity, see also Chap. III, n. 124.
92. See *Zohar* III, 113a; Tishby, *The Wisdom of the Zohar*, 2:434–435 n. 50; and Chap. VII above.
93. This statement can easily be proved by several Kabbalistic texts written during the first hundred years following the expulsion from Spain. I hope to print the pertinent texts and analyze them in a more detailed study on *The Theosophy of Depths of Nothingness*.
94. Cf. Liebes, "Sefer Ẓaddik Yesod 'Olam," p. 85.
95. Scholem, *Sabbatai Ṣevi*, p. 301.
96. Liebes, "Sefer Ẓaddik Yesod 'Olam," pp. 85–86, 95 n. 114.
97. See Idel, "The Evil Thought of the Deity," pp. 360–362.
98. *Zohar* III, fol. 113a:
ועשיתם אותם: מאי ועשיתם אותם כיון דאמר תלכו ותשמרו, אמאי ועשיתם אלא מאן דעביד פקודי אורייתא ואזיל באורחוי, כביכול כאלו עביד ליה לעיל. אמר קב״ה: כאלו עשאני. ואוקמוה: וע״ד ועשיתם אותם: ועשיתם אתם כתיב ודאי והואיל ומתערי עלייהו לאתחברא דא בדא לאשתכחא שמא קדישא כדקא יאות ועשיתם אתם ודאי.
99. Lev. 26:3.
100. Cf. *Leviticus Rabbah* 35:6 and, in another context, *Sanhedrin* 99b:
כאלו עשאו לעצמו, שנאמר ועשיתם אותם אל תקרי אותם אלא אתם.
There, the form *'asa'o*, close to *'asa'ani*, occurs in the same context as the verse in Leviticus 26:3. Compare n. 111 below. See also the phrase, "עושים בהן את התורה", which means "Israelites are 'doing' the Torah by means of the secrets revealed to them by Moses"; see *Ma'aseh Merkavah*, printed in Scholem, *Jewish Gnosticism*, p. 103.
101. "ומתערי עלייהו" The printed version "עלייכו" is problematic; I preferred that appearing in Cordovero, cf. *'Or ha-Ḥamah* (Benei Berak, 1973), III, fol. 91a.
102. *Zohar* III, 113a, n. 12.
103. *The Wisdom of the Zohar*, 2:475 n. 50; Matt, "The Mystic and the Miẓwot," p. 39 n. 49.
104. *Ta'amey ha-Miẓvot*, fol. 65a; *Commentary on the Pentateuch*, fol. 51c:
ואמרו רז״ל כל המקיים מצותי מעלה עליו הכתוב כאילו עשאני הה״ד עת לעשות לה'
105. Compare the midrashic view which indicates that "if you will perform my command-

ments, you are like me":

"אם תעשה מצותי הרי אתה כיוצא בי".

Cf. Liebermann, *Sheki'in*, p. 14; Heschel, *The Theology of Ancient Judaism* 1:155.

106. 33:7:

"הקב"ה נתן תורה לישראל ואומר להם: כביכול לי אתם לוקחים."

107. *Zohar* II, 60a.

108. MS Milano-Ambrosiana 62, fol. 114a. Compare also in R. 'Azriel's *Commentary on the Talmudic Aggadot*, p. 38:

"כל המצוות הם כבוד"

This identification of the commandments with the sefirotic realm is reminiscent of the implicit identification of the ten Sefirot with the Decalogue; see above, Chap. VII, n. 128.

109. The following phrases stem from MS Milano-Ambrosiana, 62, fol. 113b, and were printed and discussed in Idel, "The Concept of the Torah," pp. 62–64.

110. On forms and letters, see above, Chap. VI, nn. 136–138.

111. "ורזא סתימאה, עשאו לש"י". Compare n. 100 above.

112. See above Chap. VII.

113. *Ta'amey ha-Mizvot*, fol. 65a:

כאלו עשאני, הה"ד עת לעשות לה', כביכול כל הפוגם למטה כפוגם למעלה ועל זה אמר: ממעט הדמות.

See also above, near nn. 22, 24, 25, 43.

114. Compare above, n. 37, to the "secret of the murderer" in the anonymous *Sefer ha-Ne'elam*, MS Paris, BN 817, fol. 73b:

"... וממעט הצורה כלו' מיעט כח הספירו' ".

On the question of supernal Demut in ancient Jewish texts, see Heschel, *Theology of Ancient Judaism*, 1:155, 220–223.

115. Introduction to Recanati's *Ta'amey ha-Mizvot*, fol. 13c:

כל המקיים מצוה א', הנה הוא משפיע כח לאותה המצוה למעלה, מאפיסת המחשבה, והרי הוא כאילו קיים חלק א' כביכול מהקב"ה ממש.

See also Scholem, *On the Kabbalah*, pp. 124–125, who was, however, unaware of the sources of Recanati.

116. *Ta'amey ha-Mizvot*, fol. 18a:

כי המצוות אינן עולות ומתאחדות אלא עד מקום המדות, כי המצות והמדות הם דבר א'.

117. Ibid., fol. 13c:

מאחר שהאדם נעשה כדוגמא העליונה א"כ כשתעלה ותרומם כל מצוה ומצוה עד שתגיע המצוה ההיא לה' ית'.

See also ibid., fol. 14a, where Recanati explains how to direct someone's performance of the commandments in order to reach God. See also ibid., 14d, and especially fol. 18b:

"מצות התורה הם תרי"ג מצוות והם עולות ומתאחדות בשבע קצוות עליונות".

See also ibid., fol. 18c, and see on the ascent of the letters of the prayer to the supernal world according to the text discussed in Chap. V, near n. 245; Cordovero, *Pardes Rimmonim*, Gate 27, Chap. 2; *Shivḥey ha-Ba'al Shem Tov*, pp. 235–236; R. Ḥayyim of Volozhin, *Nefesh ha-Ḥayyim*, fol. 25c. The entire subject requires detailed analysis.

118. *'Avodat ha-Kodesh* II, 1 fol. 25d:

כי בעשית המצות למטה יעשום למעלה ויעוררו דוגמתם לתקן במעשיהם הכבוד העליון ומעלין על העושה כאלו עשאו ממש, . . . על זה הדרך הוא עשיית השם הנאמר בדוד ויעש דוד שם והוא תקון הכבוד סוד השם הנכבד שהיה מתקן ומיחד בעסק התורה ובקיום מצותיה ובעבודתו שהיה עובד תמיד באין הפסק שכל זה גורם עשיית השם אשר הוא הרצון והחפץ העליון והכוונה בבריאה.

Compare the statement of R. Abraham Joshua Heschel of Apt:

"ע"י קיום התורה ומצותיה אנו עושין כביכול להבורא."

"By means of our performance of the Torah and her commandments, it is as if we make God"; quoted by R. Abraham's disciple, R. Ẓevi Hirsch of Zhidachov, in *'Ateret Ẓevi*, part III, peris. *'Aḥarey Mot*, fol. 25a.

119. II Sam. 8:13; see also *Zohar* III, 113ab.

120. On name as sefirotic pleroma, see *'Avodat ha-Kodesh* I, 15, fol. 16c–17b.

121. Printed and analyzed in Idel, "The Concept of the Torah," p. 63. See also Idel, "Infinities of Torah in Kabbalah," pp. 145, 154 n. 10. Although *Sefer ha-Yiḥud* remained in manuscript, this peculiar passage was quoted in Recanati's *Commentary on the Pentateuch*, fol. 23c-d, with slight variations, and from there in R. David ben Zimra's *Meẓudat David*, fol. 20c. The reproduction of this quotation in well-known Kabbalistic texts contributed to the spread of its ideas. See MS Milano-Ambrosiana 62, fol. 113b:

כל אותיות התורה בצורותיהן בחיבורם ובפרודם ובאותיות לפופות, עקומות ועקושות ויתרות וחסרות וקטנות וגדולות ומנוזרות וכתב האותיות ופרשיות סתומות ופתוחות וסדורות הן הן צורות הש"י וית'.

On the context of this quotation, wherein the Torah is referred to as the picture of God, see Idel, "Infinities of Torah in Kabbalah," pp. 144–145; Idel, "The Concept of the Torah," pp. 62–63.

122. *Ta'amey ha-Miẓvot*, MS Jerusalem 8° 3925, fol. 110b, discussed in Idel, "The Concept of the Torah," p. 65. The passage reads:

אשרו ואשרי חלקו ומי יודע לכוון אבר כנגד אבר וצורה כנגד צורה בשלשלת הקדושה והטהורה ית' שמו לפי שהתורה הוא צורתו ית' צונו ללמוד תורה כדי לידע דוגמתו של צורה העליונה כמו שאמרו קצת המקובלים ארור אשר לא יקים את דברי התורה הזה (!). וכי יש תורה נופלת אלא אזהרה לחזן שיראה כתיבת ספר תורה לקהל כדי שיראו דוגמא של צורה העליונה, כל שכן ללמוד תורה שרואה סודות עליונות ורואה כבודו של הקב"ה ממש.

Compare this view of the Torah as an intermediary between man, or the community, and God to the conception of the rite as a mesocosmos in Joseph Campbell, *The Mark of God: Primitive Mythology* (New York, 1970), pp. 148–150, esp. p. 150, where he asserts: "The myth and rites constitute a mesocosm—a mediating, middle cosmos, through which the microcosm of the individual is brought into relation to the macrocosm of all. And this mesocosmos is the entire context of the body social, which is thus a kind of living poem, hymn or icon of mud and seeds." Compare the passage of *Sefer ha-Yiḥud* previously quoted, and ibn Gabbay's view cited in n. 24 above.

123. Compare above, the theory of "a limb supports a limb."

124. This term means the ten Sefirot; see also Idel, "The Concept of the Torah," p. 67.

125. Another term meaning the sefirotic pleroma; see also Idel, "The Concept of the Torah," p. 67, and below, n. 216.

126. According to Altmann, "On the Question of Authorship," p. 267 n. 28, R. Joseph refers to Naḥmanides, Deut. 27:26.

127. Deut. 27:26.

128. Literally, "does not maintain."

129. *Legatio ad Gaium*, par. 210–211; cf. David Winston, *Philo of Alexandria* (New York, 1981), p. 292.

130. Compare to *De Decalogo* 10–12.

131. Compare also the Neoplatonic view that the laws imitate the ideas or laws of nature: cf. Goodenough, *By Light, Light*, pp. 88–89.

132. *Ta'amey ha-Mizvot*, fol. 2a–3a; Idel, "The Concept of the Torah," p. 68.

133. On this interdependence, see Chap. VII above.

134. On Recanati's sources for this view of identity, see Idel, "The Concept of the Torah," pp. 68–69. See especially *Zohar* II, 162b, and Tishby, *The Wisdom of the Zohar*, 1:145.

135. Chap. VI, sec. II.

136. Idel, "The Concept of the Torah," nn. 136, 137.

137. Compare also to *Bahir*, ed. Margaliot, par. 184, p. 80:

"שחי העולמים כלולים בו כל המצוות כולן".

and par. 196, p. 90.

138. *Commentary on the Pentateuch*, fol. 23b-c; discussed in Idel, "The Concept of the Torah," pp. 68–70. Compare Recanati, fol. 43c, where this Kabbalist, following the *Bahir* (Margaliot, par. 184, p. 80), asserts that "all the commandments are comprised in God."

139. *'Osot*, just as in the phrase *'asa'o;* Recanati mentions the latter form at the end of the passage.

140. See Liebes, "The Messiah of the *Zohar*," pp. 219–220.

141. On the problem of preservation of older authentic midrashic material in works of the High Middle Ages, some of them nonrabbinic, see Liebermann, *Sheki'in*, passim.

142. See n. 143 below and *Midrash Tehilim* on Psalms 19.

143. *Hagigah* 13b; *Pesikta Rabbati*, fol. 97a; the *Aggadah on Shema' Israel* in *'Ozar ha-Midrashim*, p. 550; *Midrash Tehilim*, on Psalms 88. See also Karl E. Grözinger, *Musik und Gesang in der Theologie der fruhen judischen Literatur* (Tübingen, 1982), pp. 90–92; Liebermann, *Sheki'in*, p. 13; and R. Joseph of Hamadan, *Sefer Tashak*, pp. 389–390.

144. *Midrash Konen*, in *'Ozar ha-Midrashim*, p. 254:

אופן אחד בארץ אצל החיות וסנדלפון שמו, שקושר כתרים לבעל הכבוד, מקדושות וברוך הוא ואמן יהא שמיה רבא שעונין בני ישראל בבתי כנסיות, ומשביע הכתר, בשם המפורש, והולך ועולה לו בראש האדון; מכאן אמרו החכמים כל המבטל קדוש וברכו ואמן יהא שמיה רבא, גורם למעט העטרה.

145. Ezek. 1:15.

146. Interestingly, the etymology of this name, which is obscure, may include the Greek form *syn*—"together"—thus alluding to the intermediary role of this angel. Equally probable is the relationship between *syn* and its bounding the prayers.

147. The status of the *Kavod* here needs to be discussed elsewhere. Meanwhile, compare to the phrase *doxokrator*, "the Lord of Glory," occurring in the *Coptic Gnostic Treatise*, p. 151, and Irenaeus' report of Marcus the Gnostic's view: "And these powers being all simultaneously clasped in each other's embrace, do sound out the glory of him by whom they were produced; and the glory of that sound is transmuted upward to the Propator" —*Against Heresies* I, XIV, 7, p. 338. The transmission of sound of the powers is reminiscent of the

adding power in the *Dynamis*, surveyed in the preceding chapter. The powers referred to by Marcos are seven angelic beings, corresponding to the seven Greek vowels.

148. In the original, *Kaddish*, but I corrected this on the grounds of the preceding enumeration of parts of prayer.

149. Ed. Solomon Schechter (Cambridge, 1896), p. 34. Compare *Pesikta de-Rav Kahana*, ed. Mandelbaum, p. 7; and Baer, *Israel among the Nations*, p. 92. In *'Aggadath Shir ha-Shirim* (p. 35), it seems that the 'Atarah may be understood as identical with the *Shekhinah*:

"עטרה שעיטרה לו אמו ביום חתונתו, שירדה שכינה לבית המקדש"

The *Shekhinah* may refer here both to 'Atarah and the mother.

150. That is, God, who is referred to as the Possessor of Peace, on the basis of a pun on the name *Shelomo—Shalom*.

151. *A Coptic Gnostic Treatise*, p. 138; see also p. 102.

152. See the same term in *Midrash Konen*; see also pp. 42, 116, where the crown is described as standing upon the head of the Father. See also pp. 89, 91, 101–102, 110, 157.

153. Compare to the relationship between the crown and the divine name in *Midrash Konen*; see also Idel, "The Concept of the Torah," pp. 30–31. R. Ẓadok warns against the use of the words of Torah in order to glorify oneself, using the phrase:

אל תעשם עטרה להתגדל בהם.

The occurrence of the 'Atarah is coupled by the dictum of Hillel: "Whoever uses the crown (*taga'*) dies." Now, *taga'* stands for both Keter, or here 'Atarah, and the divine name; see Scholem, *Jewish Gnosticism*, pp. 54–55. Therefore, we can again see here a combined discussion of the divine name, 'Atarah or crown, and a religious activity—study of words of Torah—that parallels the formation of the 'Atarah from the words of prayer.

154. *Yebamot* 64a.

155. See Arnold M. Goldberg, *Untersuchungen über die Vorstellung von der Schekhinah* (Berlin, 1969), pp. 357–359, 508–509.

156. Cohen, *The Shi'ur Qomah: Texts and Recensions*, p. 128:

"עטרה שבראשו ששים רבבות כלפי ששים רבבו' אלפ' ישראל".

The same figure recurs in the other recensions of this text; see Cohen's footnote there. However, on p. 187, he printed a medieval text including *Shi'ur Komah* traditions, without being aware of its conceptual background (see Idel, "The World of Angels in Human Shape," pp. 20–23) where the size of the crown is mistakenly indicated as 100 (ק) rather than (ס) as in the manuscript (see Idel, "World of Angels," p. 20). According to *Canticles Rabbah*, ed. Dunski, p. 103, 600,000 crowns (*'atarot*) were given at Sinai to the children of Israel.

157. On the magical aspect of this work, see Idel, "The Concept of the Torah," pp. 39–40, 37 n. 39; and Cohen, *The Shi'ur Qomah: Liturgy and Theurgy*, passim, who was, seemingly, not acquainted with the above-mentioned article. I should like to stress here the theurgic implication of the 'Atarah, which has nothing to do with magic.

158. MS New York, JTS 1786, fol. 43a; MS Oxford 1812, fol. 101b–102a:

הוה ג' ביט וכן ג' אהיה לפי שהוא שם השכינה שנ' ואהיה אצלו אמון והיא צלותא, וקול התפילה העולה למעלה כמו שפרש"י ויה' קול מעל הרקיע אשר על ראשם בעמדם תרפינה כנפיהם פי' ויהי קול תפילתם של ישראל כי התפילה הולכת למעלה על הרקיע אשר על ראשם והולכת ויושבת בראשו של הקב"ה ונעשית לו עטרה... כי התפילה יושבת כעטרה... כי כשהצלותא והתפילה עולה למעלה אז מתלחשים ומלחשים החשמל כנגד התפילה שלנו... והעטרה של הקב"ה ס' רבבות אלף פרסאות כנגד ס'

ריבאות של ישראל ושמה של העטרה שריאל (אותיות ישראל) והוא גימ' תפילה אב אחד. לפי שאב אחד מסדר מן התפילות עטרה ובעלית הכתר רצים משתחווים וממהרים להניח כתריהם בערבות, ונותני' לו המלוכה. וממעל לרקיע אשר על ראשו כמראה אבן ספיר דמות כסא ועל דמות כסא מראה דמות אדם. וכן התפילות העטרות העולות על הכסא, דומות לכסא והכסא מתוקן מאבן ספיר.

159. HWHH = 21 = BYṬ = EHYH.

160. Prov. 8:30.

161. צלותא is related to the form אצלו in the verse from Proverbs.

162. Ezek. 1:25.

163. I did not find this explanation in Rashi.

164. The missing phrase will be dealt with below, n. 194.

165. The angels who oppose the ascent of the prayer.

166. The ḥashmal—electrum—as a dangerous entity occurs also in the Talmud, *Ḥagigah* 13a.

167. Cf. Cohen, *The Shi'ur Qomah: Texts and Recensions*.

168. Apparently a version of the rabbinic view that the word *Israel* is inscribed on the Tefillin of God: see *Berakhot* 6a and, above, Chap. III, n. 75. See also the view of *Midrash Tanḥuma, Ki Tisa'*, 8: "R. Yehudah bar Simon said: 'A parable; this is comparable to one who made an 'Atarah. Another person passed, saw it and said [to him]: "With whatever you can adorn it, precious stones and jewels, do so and put [them] in it, since it is intended to be on the head of the King. So God said to Moses: "With whatever you can praise Israel to me, and embellish them, do so, for by them I boast, as it is said [Isa. 49:3] 'Israel, in whom I will be glorified.'"'" Here, the identity of the 'Atarah with Israel is explicit.

169. "תפילה אב אחד" = 541 = "ישראל"

170. The text until the word *kingship* is cited as a direct quotation from "*Heikhaley Kodesh* and *Midrash Abba Gurion*," in *Sefer ha-Navon*, ed. Dan, *Studies*, p. 129. See *Alphabet of R. 'Akiva, Batey Midrashot* II, 379–380.

171. See the *Hebrew Enoch*, Schäfer, *Synopse*, pp. 13–14, par. 23–27.

172. Compare the quotation from *'Aggadat Shir ha-Shirim*, quoted near n. 139 above.

173. Ezek. 1:26.

174. See Dan, *Studies*, pp. 112–114; Cohen, *The Shi'ur Qomah: Texts and Recensions*, pp. 220–225, who copied the passages stemming from the *Shi'ur Komah* tradition from *Sefer ha-Navon*.

175. Dan, *Studies*, p. 128.

176. Num. 10:36.

177. I suppose that the correct version is *Sariel*, as seen above, since the phrase immediately afterward, *'otiyot Yisrael*, is identical to that found in the other Ashkenazi text.

178. Dan, *Studies*, pp. 128–129.

179. On Metatron, rather than Sandalfon, as the binder of prayers, see Liebermann, *Sheki'in*, pp. 13–14.

180. In the original, *rosham*—"their head"—which seems to be a mistake.

181. "גנוז ונגנז"—a pun on *GNZ*.

182. Dan, *Studies*, p. 130.

183. See Scholem, *Jewish Gnosticism*, pp. 61, 64, 132; and Idel, "The Evil Thought of the Deity," p. 358 n. 7. An important subject that cannot be dealt with here is the theurgical aspect of *Merkavah* traditions, found also in the Piyyut literature, concerning the rela-

tionship between divine garments and the songs sung by men and angels, as well as the theological—and in my opinion also theurgical—significance of the ongoing song of the angels.

184. On this work, see above, Chap. V, n. 167.

185. Scholem, *Les Origines de la Kabbale*, pp. 197–200; Dan, *Esoteric Theology*, pp. 118–129; Dan, "The Emergence of Mystical Prayer," in *Studies in Jewish Mysticism*, ed. J. Dan and F. Talmage (Cambridge, Mass., 1982), pp. 112–115.

186. On this divine name, see Lawrence H. Schiffman, "A Forty-two-Letter Divine Name in the Aramaic Magic Bowls," *Bulletin of the Institute of Jewish Studies* 1 (1973): 97–102; see also the text of R. Eleazar printed in Dan, *The Esoteric Theology*, p. 124.

187. This figure stems from another version of *Shi'ur Komah* found in *Sefer Raziel*; see Cohen, *The Shi'ur Qomah: Texts and Recensions*, pp. 96–97, where it is also connected to Israel; see also p. 79 in the varia.

188. Psalms 91:1.

189. בצל שדי יתלונן is anagrammed as בצלות שדי נתלונן.

190. "צלות"

191. Probably a reference to Proverbs 8:30. It is worth remarking that the *Shekhinah* was regarded as an 'Atarah on the head of Israel in a thirteenth-century text: see R. Benjamin ben Abraham min ha-'Anavim (above, Chap. VI, n. 9), p. 199.

"ועטרת תפארת בראשך—זו שכינ'."

192. On the problem connected to this translation, see Scholem, *Les Origines de la Kabbale*, p. 199 n. 201.

193. That is, "his daughter," in Aramaic.

194. MS New York, JTS 1786, fol. 43b:

ונעשית לו עטרה שנ' יושב בסתר עליון. בסתר גי' אכתריאל, כי התפילה יושבת כעטרה כדכתיב והיה כתר לראש אכתריאל יי' אלהי ישראל.

It is worth remarking the recurrence of the terms *moshav, yoshevet* in connection with the fitting of the 'Atarah on the head of God, since they parallel the phrase *moshav yeqareh* found in Heikhalot literature; hence, the 'Atarah is reminiscent of God's glory. Compare R. Eleazar's *Comentary on Song of Songs*, on 3:11:

"עטרה זו היא התפילה שהיא עטרה לקב"ה"

Interestingly, in another treatise of R. Eleazar, *Hilkhot Tefillah*, he indicates that the 'Atarah is tantamount to the divine phylacteries; cf. MS New York, JTS 1885, fol. 19b:

"והעטרה—על התפילין דקרושא (!) ברוך הוא."

Compare also to n. 209 below.

195. Psalms 91:1.

196. *Ba-Seter* = 662 = '*Akatriel*. On 'Akatriel as the secret name of the divine crown—Keter, see Scholem, *Jewish Gnosticism*, p. 54.

197. See Scholem, *Major Trends*, p. 363 n. 57.

198. Compare also the motif of God's residence in a place named "secretness"; cf. *Ḥagigah* 5b, which is attributed to the *Shekhinah* in the *Alphabet of R. 'Akivah, Batey Midrashot* II, pp. 360, 428.

199. See n. 149 above.

200. See n. 151 above.

201. Cf. also R. Eleazar in MS Oxford, 1568, fol. 24b from *Sefer ha-Ḥokhmah*: see Scholem, *Les Origines de la Kabbale*, p. 109.

202. See *Seder Rabbah de-Bereshit*, Schäfer, *Synopse*, par. 745.

203. Margaliot, par. 171, p. 74.

204. *Commentary on Song of Songs*, in Chavel, *Kitvey ha-Ramban* II, p. 494:
"שכל הבנין ידבק ומתיחד ומתעלה עד אין סוף"
Compare also to *Zohar* III, 5a, where the crowning of the holy name symbolizes a state of harmony.

205. That is, the lower seven Sefirot which are afterward referred to also as *Da'at* (ibid., p. 495).

206. Ibid., p. 494:
"הברכה והקרושה והיחור הנמשכים מאפיסת המחשבה הנקראים עטרת וכתר".
See also above, n. 63.

207. *Midrash Tehilim* on Psalm 19, quoted in extenso, in ibid., pp. 494–495; see also R. 'Ezra's *Commentary on Talmudic Aggadot*, MS Vatican 441, fol. 34a-b, where the whole discussion in his *Commentary on Song of Songs* is repeated with slight changes.

208. See his *Commentary on Talmudic Aggadot, Likkutey Shikhehah u-Feah*, fol. 2a; Tishby, R. 'Azriel's *Commentary on Talmudic Aggadot*, pp. 6–7.

209. Compare also Chap. III, nn. 117, 128, 134. Compare also to *Sefer ha-Yiḥud*, MS Milano-Ambrosiana 62, fol. 114b, where the commandment of phylacteries is described as crowning the king with an 'Atarah; see also n. 168 above.

210. See the *Commentary on a Kabbalistic Song*, printed in Koriat's *Ma'or va-Shemesh*, fol. 3a:
ואע"פ שהיא למטה, לפעמים תתעלה עד אין סוף ותעשה עטרה על ראשם ולזה הסוד נקראת עטרה.
Although this commentary is a late work, it also includes early Kabbalistic material: see Idel, "Kabbalistic Material," pp. 170–173.

211. See above, Chap. VI, n. 29.

212. MS Vatican 441, fol. 114a:
התחיל בעטרת להודיעך שאף הוא הכתר אם תהפוך הספירות, אז המלכות ראשונה . . .
שאין להם לא ראש ולא סוף תחלת המחשבה הוא סוף המעשה.
See also ibid., 114b, where 'Ateret is twice referred to as the "cornerstone"—*rosh pinnah*.

213. This dictum emphasizes the fact that Malkhut, the last divine Sefirah, was the first to emerge in the divine thought. On the sources of this dictum, see S. M. Stern, "'The First in Thought Is the Last in Action': The History of a Saying Attributed to Aristotle," *Journal of Semitic Studies* 7 (1962): 234–252.

214. Jerusalem, 1983, fol. 9d:
מפני מה שערי דמעה לא ננעלו. והענין כי האדם התחתון דוגמת צורה עליונה והיו
פיו כפה העליון ועיניו כעיני העליון וכאשר יתעוררו למטה יתעוררו למעלה.

215. *Berakhot* 32b.

216. This phrase refers to the divine pleroma and is typical of R. Joseph of Hamadan's style; see n. 125 above.

217. *Zohar ha-Rakia'*, fol. 9d–10a.

218. Ibid., fol. 10ab.

219. *'Eẓ ha-Da'at Tov*, part II (Jerusalem, 1982), fol. 5b.

220. Ibid.:

והנה בהיות האדם בוכה ומוריד דמעות על אדם כשר גורם גם למעלה הורדת דמעות וכמו שמצי׳ כביכול בו ית׳ ויקרא ה׳ אלקים לבכי ולמספד וכו׳ במסתרים תבכה נפשי וכו׳ וכמ״ש מי נתן ראשי מים וכו׳ יר׳ הנני מתאוה אל מעלה התחתונים שבהיותן בוכים למטה הם גורמים ליתן ראשי מים ובעיני דמעה מי יתן זה להם וע״י כך ואבכה גם אני את חללי.

221. Isa. 22:12.
222. Jer. 13:17.
223. Ibid., 8:23.
224. *'Ez̩ ha-Da'at Tov*, fol. 5b.
225. Ibid.
226. See ibid., fol. 6a, for the anthropopathic description of shedding of tears as a catharsis of the stern and rude elements in both the human and the divine psyches, causing the emergence of mercy and clemency.
227. Compare, for example, the emphasis placed in Ḥasidic literature on the causing of divine "delight"—**עונג**—by human activity. See Chap. IV, near n. 117, and R. Abraham Joshua Heschel of Apt's *Torat 'Emet* (Lemberg, 1854), fol. 23a, 31ab, 34b, and so on. As we have seen above (Chap. VI, sec. IV), "delight" is also referred to in connection with worship.

CHAPTER 9

1. *Explications and Implications*, p. 226. See also *Major Trends*, p. 26; extremely representative is this: "Of such symbols the world of the Kabbalist is full, nay the whole world is to the Kabbalist such a *corpus symbolicum*" pp. 27–28.
2. *Paths of Faith and Heresy*, p. 11. Strangely, Tishby did not refer at all to Scholem's similar appreciations of symbolism (n. 1). Recently, Scholem's and Tishby's conception of Kabbalistic symbolism has been repeated by Joseph Dan in his introduction to *Early Kabbalah* (New York, 1986), pp. 9–12.
3. See below for further discussion of their definition of Kabbalistic symbolism.
4. Printed by Jellinek in *Philosophie und Kabbalah* (Leipzig, 1854), 1:37–38: והם אומרים שקבלו מן הנביאים ומן החכמים שיש שם עשר ספירות... וקראו לכל ספירה וספירה שמות מהם משותפים ומהם מיוחדים, וכששאלום לא ידעו היודעם מהם אלה הספירות, על איזה דבר יפלו שמותיהם... והשמות ידועים מספריהם והם נבוכים בהם מאד.
5. That is, the same symbols refer to two or more Sefirot, whereas the particular names refer to one Sefirah alone.
6. Cf. the translation of Scholem, *Major Trends*, p. 149; see also below, near n. 153.
7. The affinity between the negative attitude of ecstatic Kabbalah toward symbols and its interest in experience and words, on the one hand, and the deep interest of theosophical Kabbalah in hierarchies and sacraments, on the other, is reminiscent of the distinction between, respectively, the Augustinian notion of sign and Pseudo-Dionysios' conception of symbol; see M. D. Chenu, *Nature, Man and Society in the Twelfth Century* (Chicago and London, 1968), pp. 119–128.
8. Nathan Rotenstreich, "Symbolism and Transcendence: On Some Philosophical Aspects of Gershom Scholem's Opus," *Review of Metaphysics* 31 (1977–78), p. 605. Rotenstreich, however, accepted Scholem's denial of *unio mystica*, which implicitly reinforces the role of

symbolism. No wonder that Abulafia's nonsymbolic thought focused on the direct mystical experience. On the nonsymbolic conception of God as a superior way of knowledge, see Paul Tillich, "The Religious Symbol," in *Symbolism in Religion and Literature*, ed. Rollo May (New York, 1960), pp. 96–97.

9. On this author, see Chap. VIII, n. 73.
10. See Chap. VI.
11. See Chap. VI.
12. MS Oxford 2234, fol. 8b; see Idel, "Magical and Neoplatonic Interpretations," p. 203.
13. John E. Smith, *Experience and God* (Oxford, 1968), p. 159.
14. Ibid., p. 158.
15. *Major Trends*, p. 226.
16. *Gan Na'ul*, MS München 58, fol. 323a, discussed in Idel, "Métaphores et pratiques sexuelles," p. 333. Cf. *'Oẓar 'Eden Ganuz*, MS Oxford 1580, fol. 131b–132a, and *Sefer Mafteaḥ ha-Sefirot*, MS Milano-Ambrosiana 53, fol. 170b–171a, translated and discussed in Idel, *The Mystical Experience in Abraham Abulafia*, Chap. IV.
17. *'Imrey Shefer*, MS Paris 777, p. 57; Idel, "Métaphores et pratiques sexuelles," pp. 333–334.
18. On the perfect man as an allegory for the perfect intellect, see Warren Z. Harvey, "Hasdai Crescas' Critique of the Theory of the Acquired Intellect" (Ph.D. diss., Columbia University, 1973), pp. 205–212. For Abulafia, the word *Israel* is presumably understood here as composed of the letter yod, pointing to the tenth Sefirah—Malkhut; sar—prince, conspicuously denoting Metatron, the prince of the world, an entity commonly identified with the tenth separate intellect; and El—God. In other words, Israel points to the active intellect which is at the same time the perfect man, as apparently understood by Maimonides. The same identification of Israel with *Sekhel ha-Po'el*, the active intellect, recurs in Abulafia's works, strengthened by the fact that the two have the same numerical value, 541.
19. See Idel, "Perceptions of Kabbalah," par. I.
20. Cf. Chap. IV.
21. In this context, the generally negative attitude to symbolism in Judaism, expressed by Abraham Joshua Heschel, is easily understandable; see his "Symbolism and Jewish Faith," in *Religious Symbolism*, ed. F. E. Johnson (New York, 1954), pp. 53–79, esp. pp. 76–77, where Heschel emphasizes the inherent contradiction between symbolism and immediacy.
22. See Fritz A. Rothschild, ed., *Between God and Man: An Interpretation of Judaism* (New York and London, 1965), pp. 19–20, 114–115.
23. See Idel, *The Mystical Experience in Abraham Abulafia*, Chap. III.
24. Alexander Altmann, "The Delphic Maxim in Medieval Islam and Judaism," in *Biblical and Other Studies*, ed. A. Altmann (Cambridge, Mass., 1963), pp. 198, 208; Tishby, *Paths of Faith and Heresy*, pp. 14–17, who overemphasizes the chasm between body and soul in theosophical Kabbalah; Idel, "*Hitbodedut* as Concentration," p. 73. To a certain extent, ecstatic Kabbalah reflects philosophical conceptions of the dichotomy between body and soul. On the emphasis on the bodily performance of the *mizvah* of *sukkah* in Kabbalah, in comparison to the abstract allegories of philosophy, see Frank Talmage, "*Apples of Gold*: The Inner Meaning of Sacred Texts in Medieval Judaism," in *Jewish Spirituality*, ed. Arthur Green (New York, 1986), 1:338–340.
25. MS Oxford 2047, fol. 69a:

"וקללת הנגלה הוא ברכת הנסתר וקללת הנסתר הוא ברכת הנגלה."

Compare to R. Joseph Gikatilla's *Ginnat 'Egoz* (Hanau, 1615), fol. 3b:

"שכל—יסוד הכל אשר ישכון בלב תורה והיא אצלו אחוזת קבר"

Compare also to *Tikkuney Zohar, Zohar* I, fol. 27b–28a, where the plain sense of the Mishnah is regarded as the grave of the esoteric sense. The relation of the tension between plain and esoteric meanings in Abulafia's circle to the *Tikkuney Zohar* and *Ra'ya Meheimna*, on the one hand, and to *Sefer ha-Peliah*, on the other, is an issue that still needs to be studied in detail.

26. *Sefer ha-Ẓeruf*, MS Paris 774, fol. 4b–5a:

ויתמעטו כחות הקשות שבשמאלי והוא הנקרא יצר הרע ושמואל וסמאל ושטן ומלאך המות ונחש וכולם יושלכו מעליך וכל כחותיהם האבניות כמו שאמ׳ והסירותי את לב האבן מבשרכם וישובו כוחותם נכנעות לפני כחות השכליות כמו שאמ׳ ונתתי לכם לב בשר ותהיינה עיניך פקוחות באילו העניינים האלהיים התוכים והאמצעיים, לא הקלפיים, וכשתגיע למעלה, אז תטהר מכל החלאות הגופניות והמחשבות ההרגשיות ולא יתערב כח השכלי עם ההרגש לא מעט ולא הרבה זולתי שיהיה ההרגש כלי לקבל מה שבתוכו.

On this work, see Idel, "Abraham Abulafia," pp. 69–71. An elaborate analysis of the background of this passage will be presented in an article by S. Pines and myself.

27. *Babba Batra* 16a.
28. Ezek. 36:26.
29. Ibid.
30. *Sefer ha-Ẓeruf*, MS Paris 774, fol. 5a:

משל ומליצה ר״ל דבר האמצעית כמו שאמ׳ כי המליץ בינותם כלומ׳ שהיא מתהפכת לדבר שיהפכנוה אם להרגש אם לשכל והיא היא המליץ בין השכל וההרגש ר״ל משלי התורה.

See also fol. 6a.

31. Chap. VIII, sec. I.
32. See the plural form of the talmudic statements cited in Chap. III, nn. 10, 11; however, see also n. 12 there.
33. As far as erotic motifs connected to the Temple are extant in ancient Jewish sources—as opposed to Gnostic ones—they refer to the cherubim, not to the experience of the high priest; see below, n. 114.
34. Idel, "Métaphores et pratiques sexuelles," pp. 332–336.
35. See Idel, "Abraham Abulafia and *Unio Mystica*."
36. Tishby, *The Wisdom of the Zohar*, 1:149, speaks about "the transition from pure symbolism to the path of myth."
37. R. Solomon ben Adret; cf. the anonymous commentary on the ten Sefirot, MS British Library 755, fol. 93b; MS Berlin 122 (MS Or. 8° 538), fol. 96a; and the source cited in the next footnote. On the symbolism of "Ẓion," see Idel, "Jerusalem in Medieval Jewish Thought."
38. R. Isaac Todros, cf. R. Shem Tov ibn Gaon, *Keter Shem Tov*, in R. Judah Koriat, *Ma'or va-Shemesh*, fol. 26b.
39. See Idel, "The World of Angels in Human Shape," pp. 39–40; the relationship between the four, and perhaps five, commentaries of this author will be discussed in detail elsewhere.
40. See Gershom Scholem, "Two Treatises of R. Moses de Leon," pp. 371–384, where two versions of one commentary were printed; this issue is also dealt with in de Leon's *Shoshan*

'Edut, ibid., pp. 333ff., and in his *Shekel ha-Kodesh*. Furthermore, I believe that a fragment of an unknown commentary of de Leon is extant anonymously in a mutilated manuscript, to be printed and analyzed elsewhere.

41. See Idel, "R. Joseph of Hamadan's *Commentary on Ten Sefirot*," pp. 74–76.
42. A similar phenomenon occurs in the *Zohar*'s various redactions of what finally became the *Idra Rabba;* see Liebes, "The Messiah of the *Zohar*," p. 101 and n. 53.
43. Idel, "Maimonides and Kabbalah."
44. I presume that Abulafia was not the main channel for the transfer of this peculiar type of Kabbalah to Castile, as it seems to have been intensively cultivated at the period he visited Castile; this issue will be analyzed in detail elsewhere.
45. See R. Solomon ben Adret's *Responsa* I, vol. 548.
46. See Goldreich, *Me'irat 'Eynaim*, pp. 361—364.
47. See Mark N. Verman, "Sifrei ha-'Iyyun" (Ph.D. diss., Harvard University, 1984), pp. 173–178.
48. Abraham Abulafia, a nonsymbolic Kabbalist, definitely belongs to the school of creative Kabbalah, albeit most of his literary activity took place outside Spain.
49. Idel, "We Have No Kabbalistic Tradition on This," pp. 71–73; on the problem of innovation in the Christian Middle Ages, see Preus's article, n. 141 below.
50. See Idel, "Infinities of Torah in Kabbalah," p. 146.
51. Ibid, p. 154 n. 18.
52. See Gottlieb, *Studies*, pp. 112, 129–130.
53. Idel, R. Joseph of Hamadan's *Commentary on Ten Sefirot*," pp. 75–76.
54. *Commentary on the Pentateuch*, fol. 40b.
55. Idel, "Infinities of Torah in Kabbalah," p. 147.
56. On the influence of the later Gikatilla and the *Zohar* on R. Baḥya, see Gottlieb, *The Kabbalah of R. Baḥya*, pp. 148–193; see also pp. 194–213, where the impact on Baḥya of another text, influenced by the *Zohar*, is demonstrated.
57. *Commentary on the Pentateuch* (on Num. 11:15), ed. C. D. Chavel, III, p. 62:
כי בספר תורה שאינו מנוקד יוכל האדם לקרוא... כי האותיות כשאינן מנוקדות סובלות כמה כוונות ומתחלקות לכמה ניצוצות ומפני זה נצטוינו שלא לנקוד ספר תורה כי משמעות כל מלה ומלה לפי הנקוד ואין משמעותה עם הנקוד כי אם ענין אחד ובלתי נקוד יוכל האדם להבין בה כמה ענינים נפלאים רבים ונכבדים.
Compare also the *Commentary* on Gen. 18:3 and Deut. 7:2.
58. In Hebrew, *niẓoẓot;* this term is used in contemporary Kabbalistic literature to refer also to parts of the human soul; cf. the thirteenth-century text printed by Scholem in *Tarbiẓ* 16 (1965): 143. Is there any affinity between the view that each word contains numerous sparks—meanings—and the view that the soul contains several sparks? On the spark as a metaphor for the soul in its deepest aspect, see Michel Tardieu's important article in *Revue des études Augustiniennes* 21 (1975): 225–255; regarding Jewish discussions of this metaphor, see Louis Jacobs, "The Doctrine of the 'Divine Spark' in Man in Jewish Sources," in *Rationalism, Judaism, Universalism: In Memory of Leon Roth* (New York, 1966), pp. 87–144. Interestingly, the vowels that fix the specific meaning of a given combination of consonants are described as their souls in a Kabbalistic passage dealing with vocalizations and meaning; see Idel, "Infinities of Torah in Kabbalah," p. 146; Idel, "R. Joseph of Hamadan's *Commentary on Ten Sefirot*," pp. 76–77.

59. Idel, "Infinities of Torah in Kabbalah," p. 146.
60. See Scholem, "The Authentic Commentary on Sefer Yeẓirah of Naḥmanides," p. 414:
דע כי מפני שהניקוד הוא צורה ונשמה לאותיות לפי' לא נעשה ספר תורה נקוד לפי שהוא כולל כל הפנים וכל הדרכים העמוקים והחיצונים וכולם נדרשים בכל אות ואות פנים לפנים ותעלומה מפנים מתעמולה ואין גבול ידוע אצלינו כאומרו תהום אמר לא בי הוא.
Scholem attributed this text to Naḥmanides, an attribution that was rightly questioned by Gottlieb, *Studies*, pp. 128–131, who cited important evidence to prove the authorship of this short treatise. Notwithstanding this proof, the question of its authorship is still open, and the affinities between this text and those of R. Joseph of Hamadan are equally relevant, as are those between the anonymous text and Gikatilla's views. Our text also appears anonymously in one of R. David ben Zimra's *Responsa* (vol. III, no. 643), and I took its variants into consideration in my translation. Compare also J. Faur, *Golden Doves with Silver Dots* (Bloomington, Ind., 1986), pp. 136–137.
61. Job 28:14.
62. Scholem, "The Authentic Commentary on Sefer Yeẓirah of Naḥmanides," p. 414.
63. *'Oẓar 'Eden Ganuz*, MS Oxford 1580, fol. 171a:
"דרך השבת האותיות לחמרם הראשון ותת בהם צורה"
See Idel, "Abraham Abulafia," pp. 226–227, where additional material is discussed.
64. Cf. Idel, ibid., pp. 226–227; compare also below (n. 204) to the view of R. Naḥman of Bratslav, who perceives the inspired interpreter to be identical with the universal soul.
65. This is E. T. A. Hoffman's description of music, as quoted in W. P. Lehmann, "The Stony Idiom of the Brain," in *Literary Symbolism: A Symposium*, ed. Helmut Rehder (Austin and London, 1967), p. 15.
66. This view of the *Zohar* as the zenith of a certain process taking place over the two decades of 1270 to 1290 is not, however, identical with the view that this work is the exclusive composition of R. Moses de Leon, as assumed by Scholem or Tishby. I believe that older elements, including theosophical views and symbols and perhaps also shorter compositions, were merged into this Kabbalistic work, which heavily benefited from the nascent free symbolism.
67. On the place of symbolism in R. Naḥman, see Joseph Dan, *The Ḥasidic Story: Its History and Development* (in Hebrew) (Jerusalem, 1975), pp. 132–188; Yoav Elstein, *Ma'aseh Ḥoshev: Studies in Ḥasidic Tales* (in Hebrew) (Tel Aviv, 1983); Yoav Elstein, *In the Footsteps of a Lost Princess* (in Hebrew) (Ramat Gan, 1984).
68. *Responsa* I, no. 548.
69. See J. L. Teicher, "The Mediaeval Mind," *JJS* 4 (1955): 1–13.
70. See n. 60 above. See also Dov Hercenberg, "Deux modèles d'écriture: Essai sur le rapport entre ordre et liberté," *Revue Philosophique* 16 (1982): 483–486, where the affinity between RaDBaZ' text or vocalization and Umberto Eco's treatment of the open work is discussed.
71. Cf. Leszek Kolakowski, *Chrétiens sans église* (Paris, 1969), pp. 305, 343 n. 21.
72. Ibid., pp. 305–307. On Cocceius and his study of Jewish material, see Aaron L. Katchen, *Christian Hebraists and Dutch Rabbis* (Cambridge, Mass., 1985).
73. On this issue, see M. Idel, "R. David ben Yehudah he-Ḥasid's Translation of the Zohar" (in Hebrew), *'Aley Sefer* 8 (1980): 72–73.
74. Emil Male, *The Gothic Image* (New York, 1958), p. 51.

75. Buber, *Ḥasidism*, pp. 69, 141, aptly describes the tendency of "the Kabbalah" to schematize the mystery; however, this evaluation is especially true of Safedian Kabbalah, far more than of earlier phases of Kabbalah; by and large, for Buber "Kabbalah" is the Lurianic school. See also Chap. VII, n. 10. On the analogous phenomenon in Western Christian culture, compare Johan Huizinga, *The Waning of the Middle Ages* (New York, 1954), Chap. XV.
76. See n. 1 above, and Biale, *Gershom Scholem, Kabbalah and Counter-History*, p. 138 and n. 108, where he refers to Goethe's *Ursprung des deutschen Trauerspiels*, 176; a more articulate discussion of Goethe, more cognate to that of Scholem, occurs in *Spruche in Prosa*, 742–743. For the reverberations of Goethe's definitions of allegory and symbols in scholarly literature, see Talmage, *"Apples of Gold"* (n. 24 above), nn. 124, 128, 137.
77. Scholem, *Major Trends*, p. 27.
78. Ibid., p. 27.
79. See near n. 16 above.
80. Chap. III, sec. IV.
81. Scholem, *Major Trends*, p. 27.
82. Chap. III, n. 40.
83. Ibid., n. 38.
84. Scholem, *Major Trends*, p. 27.
85. Cf. David Ross, *Aristotle* (London and New York, 1964), p. 66.
86. This term for steresis occurs, as observed by Scholem in references in n. 87 below, in Abraham bar Ḥiyya's *Megillat ha-Megalleh*, p. 5. 'Efes qua symbol for Keter occurs also in R. David ben Yehudah he-Ḥasid: see D. C. Matt, *Sefer Mar'ot ha-Zove'ot* (*The Book of Mirrors*) (Chico, Calif., 1982), p. 21.
87. See the text printed by Scholem, "Seridim," p. 215, and his discussion in *Les Origines de la Kabbale*, pp. 443–445.
88. Scholem, *Les Origines de la Kabbale*, pp. 445–448; see also Donald F. Duclow, "Divine Nothingness and Self-Creation in John Scotus Erigena," *Journal of Religion* 57 (1977): 109–123. The transformation of philosophical terms into allegories, and nonphilosophical terms into symbols, evidence the postreflective nature of Kabbalistic language in general and of its symbolic language in particular. Compare, however, Eliade's emphasis on the prereflective quality of symbolism, which originates from his limiting himself to the study of primitive or archaic mentalities; see his "Methodological Remarks on the Study of Religious Symbolism," in *The History of Religion: Essays in Methodology*, ed. M. Eliade and J. M. Kitagawa (Chicago, 1959), pp. 98–100.
89. Scholem, *Major Trends*, p. 27, states that "the thing which becomes a symbol retains its original form and its original content." See also Victor Turner's distinction between the "sensory pole" of the symbol and its "ideological pole": V. Turner and E. Turner, *Image and Pilgrimage in Christian Culture* (New York, 1978), p. 247.
90. The three highest Sefirot: see, for example, R. Joseph ben Shalom Ashkenazi, *Commentary on Sefer Yeẓirah*, fol. 17b; MS Paris, BN 776, fol. 189b; *Ma'arekhet ha-'Elohut*, fol. 50a.
91. *Zohar* III, fol. 5a. It is important to note that a conspicuous case of non-Kabbalistic dynamization of the quasi-divine realm of the divine name is to be found in the Ashkenazi *Sefer ha-Navon*; see Dan, *Studies*, pp. 119–120. The entire question of dynamization of supernal entities in the pre-Kabbalistic period is worthy of a detailed study that may

eventually clarify some issues connected to the dynamic dimension of the Sefirot in early Kabbalah.

92. Psalms 48:2.
93. See above, Chap. VI, sec. III, for my discussion of Rabad's passage.
94. Lev. 1:2.
95. On the significance of "ascending" versus "descending" symbolism, see Erich Kahler, "The Nature of the Symbol," in *Symbolism in Religion and Literature*, ed. Rollo May (New York, 1960), pp. 50–75; and Idel, "Métaphores et pratiques sexuelles," pp. 329–331.
96. See also above, n. 89, for my discussion on the relation between the symbolic value of a word and its "sensory pole."
97. See *Mekhilta de-Rabbi Ishmael*, ed. and trans J. Z. Lauterbach, in Max Kadushin, *A Conceptual Approach to the Mekilta* (New York, 1969), pt. II, p. 113; see also *Yalkut Shim'oni* on Num. 10:31, par. 730. For the background of the Exodus verse, see G. H. Skipwith, "The Lord of Heaven," *JQR* o.s. 19(1902): 693.
98. Kadushin, ibid., pt. 1, p. 185, corrects "All the time. . . . "
99. Exod. 1:14.
100. Interestingly, the noun *sapphire* was also understood as hinting at slavery; in *TJ, Sukkah IV*, 3, it is related to Ezekiel 1.26, "אבן ספיר" ("stone of sapphire"), concluding that the Babylonian Diaspora is harder than the Egyptian one: stone in comparison to brick.
101. See Kadushin, *Conceptual Approach*, pt. 1, p. 186; see especially the tradition adduced in the name of *Midrash 'Avkir* by R. Eleazar ha-Dashan, in his *Sefer ha-Gematriyot*, printed by Abraham Epstein, *Ha-'Eshkol* 6 (1909): 207:

    כמעשה לבנת הספיר—רמז כשם שישראל היו דורסין ברגליהן בחומר לעשות לבנים, כך כאילו למעלה בכל צרתם לא צר.

    "a kind of paved work of sapphire stone: it reflects the status of Israel, when they were treading the mortar with their feet; as though one could conceive it was above: in all their affliction he was afflicted."
102. See Kadushin, ibid., pt. 1, pp. 186–187.
103. Isa. 63:10.
104. *Mekhilta de-Rabbi Ishmael, Masekhet de-Shirta*, vol.4, ed. M. Friedmann (Vienna, 1870), fol. 37b.
105. See *Tanḥuma*, perisc. *Ha'azinu*, 4, where a series of contradicting descriptions of God is adduced in relation to our verse.
106. *Mekhilta*, p. 114.
107. *Zohar* II, fol. 99a; the translation is that of H. Sperling, M. Simon, and P. Levertoff, *Zohar* (London and New York, 1933), 3:301, which I have corrected in some details; see also Matt, *Zohar*, pp. 123–126, and his notes on pp. 251–253.
108. Exod. 24:18.
109. Gen. 9:13.
110. *Zohar* 3:301, fol. 99a.
111. Ibid., pp. 301–302. Compare also G. Scholem, *Zohar: The Book of Splendor* (New York, 1970), pp. 88–91; however, Scholem did not include in his translation the first discussion of the old man! See also Scholem, *On the Kabbalah*, pp. 55–56; on pp. 45–46, Scholem points to the Philonic view of the Torah as a living organism; see Franck, *The Kabbalah* (New York, 1940), pp. 262–263.

112. See, for example, Scholem, "Two Treatises of R. Moses de Leon," pp. 363–364. However, Tishby, *The Wisdom of the Zohar*, 1:64, considers the rainbow to be a symbol of Malkhut, the female divine attribute; see also Matt, *Zohar*, p. 252.

113. See *'Avodah Zarah* 3b; *Zohar* III, fol. 17a, and compare here to Moses' entering the cloud.

114. See Tishby, *The Wisdom of the Zohar*, 2:190–191; Liebes, "The Messiah of the *Zohar*," p. 122; Idel, "*Hitbodedut* as Concentration," p. 56; Idel, "Métaphores et pratiques sexuelles," pp. 344–345. It is noteworthy that Moses' entering the cloud is compared in *Zohar* II, fol. 229a, to the entrance of the high priest for at least two reasons: (1) the most sublime passage of the *Zohar*, the end of the *Idra Zuta* (*Zohar* III, fol. 296a-b), portrays the entry of the high priest into the Holy of Holies in terms of the intercourse between the attribute of mercy and that of judgment; and (2) the term *heikhal*, used in the parable for "palace," is parallel to the word used by Spanish Jews for the ark of the Torah, but can also allude to the Temple! See also n. 33 above, and see *Zohar* III, fol. 300a, where Moses is described as *Marey de-Beita*—the "master of the house"—referring to the *'ohel mo'ed*—the tent of meeting; and see *Zohar* III, fol. 4b. On the mythical conception of Moses in ancient sources, wherein he was understood as a divine person by his investment as king and god, inter alia by his receiving "a robe of light," see Wayne A. Meeks, "Moses as God and King," in *Religions in Antiquity: Essays in Memory of E. R. Goodenough*, ed. J. Neusner (Leiden, 1968), pp. 354–371. Moses' reception of the garments of the rainbow may therefore reflect his installation according to the ancient texts. See also Fossum, *The Name of God and the Angel of the Lord*, pp. 87–106.

115. Cf. Menaḥem M. Kasher, "The Zohar," *Sinai: Jubilee Volume* (in Hebrew) (Jerusalem, 1958), pp. 47–48. On the sexual perception of the Kabbalist's relation to the Torah, see, for example, R. Moses de Leon in Tishby, *Studies*, p. 43; R. Meir ibn Gabbay, *'Avodat ha-Kodesh*, fol. 3c, and R. Jacob Joseph of Polonnoye, *Toldot Ya'akov Yoseph*, fol. 133c; R. Dov Baer of Mezherich, *Maggid Devarav le-Ya'akov*, p. 87.

116. *Arcana Caelestia*, par. 1872, trans. in *Internal Sense of the Word* (London, 1974), p. 41.

117. For other examples of the influence of the Kabbalah on Swedenborg, see Idel, "Infinities of Torah in Kabbalah," p. 150; Idel, "The World of Angels in Human Shape," pp. 64–65.

118. Printed anonymously by Jacob Toledano in *Sefer ha-Malkhut* (Casablanca, 1930), fol. 110b:

ומפני מה נקרא שמו תובל קין? מפני שלפעמים מתלבשת בו שכינה ולפעמים יושב בפני עצמו. וכשמתלבשת בו שכינה נקרא תובל קין, מפני שהוא מובל למלך בשמחות וגיל, ולפי׳ באותו זמן נקרא תובל קין. וכשהוא בפני עצמו נקרא קין ולפי׳ נקרא שמו קין ותובל.

The authorship of this work was established by Gottlieb, *Studies*, pp. 254–255. According to another passage of R. Joseph, the *Matronita*, that is, the Sefirah of Malkhut, is androgynous, sometimes being called "male" and other times, "female"; *Sefer Tashak*, p. 436:

מטרוניתא דאיהי רזא דאנדרוגינוס דכר ונוקבא: לזמנים קרא לה דכר ולזמנים קרא לה נוקבא.

Compare also to Recanati's *Commentary on the Pentateuch*, fol. 43b:

כשהשכינה פועלת בכח ה׳ ספירות אחרונות נקראת יד וכשפועלת לבדה נקראת אצבע.

119. Cf. Gen. 3:22.

120. MS Paris, BN 841, fol. 268a:

"שהתורה כולה מרגליות שמספר עניין תולדות המלאכים."

121. This term stands for secrets hidden in the biblical text, as in Maimonides' *Guide of the Perplexed*; see Idel, "The Concept of the Torah," p. 66 and n. 162.

122. MS Paris, BN 841, fol. 267a:
וצלה גם היא ילדה מצד כחות הטומא' את תובל קין, שמוביל רצחנות כמו קין והבל
והוא יצר הרע והוא המביא שטנה לעולם, שצריכין בני אדם כלי זין להלחם אלו עם אלו.

123. Cf. Gen. 3:22, where Tubal-Cain is described as "forger of every sharp instrument in brass and iron."

124. MS Paris, BN 841, fol. 267a:

"שצלה היא השכינה"

125. MS Paris, BN 841, fol. 267b:
שצלה היא שכינה והיאך אמ' שמדבר כנגד כחות הטומא', הכל נדרש בתורה לשבעים
פנים טומאה וטהרה כדכתי' גם את זה לעומת זה עשה האלהים.

See R. 'Ezra of Gerona's *Commentary on Song of Songs*, in Chavel, *Kitvey ha-Ramban* II, p. 478.

126. Eccles. 7:14; this verse is a *locus probans* for the Kabbalistic view of the creation of evil by God.

127. See *Sefer ha-Malkhut* (n. 118 above), fol. 109a:

"על דרך הקבלה אמ' בדרך גלגול הנשמה"

and fol. 73d, 74a (*Sefer Toldot 'Adam*)"

"ועל דרך גלגול הנשמות"

128. Scholem, *Major Trends*, p. 27: "The Kabbalist . . . discovers . . . a reflection of the true transcendence," or his view that the symbolized realm is "a hidden and inexpressible reality." See also p. 28.

129. Scholem, *Kabbalah*, pp. 99, 105–106.

130. See the anthropomorphical descriptions of the *'Eiyn Sof* in Idel, "The Image of Man," pp. 41–55, esp. p. 55.

131. See the discussion on R. Isaac Luria and the school of Komarno, below, n. 249.

132. See Tishby, *Paths of Faith and Heresy*, p. 13, who briefly notes that a symbol can also stand for a "process."

133. Scholem's and Tishby's assertions (ibid., p. 13) that the reality symbolized by a symbol cannot be perceived otherwise is based upon the tacit assumption that union with the divine world is marginal in Kabbalah. But an experience of cleaving or union is a way to directly perceive the divine world; symbolism is therefore an alternative, not a unique way to experience divinity. Tishby (ibid., pp. 17, 20) regards symbols as ways to attain cleaving to God, a view that contradicts his assumption on p. 13; as we have seen above (Chap. III, secs. VI–VII) *devekut* to God must precede the performance of the commandments, or it can be achieved by anomian techniques.

134. See, for example, Tishby, *The Wisdom of the Zohar*, 1:288–307.

135. Tishby, *Paths of Faith and Heresy*, p. 13.

136. See, for example, R. J. Zwi Werblowsky, "Ape and Essence," in *Ex Orbe Religionum* (Leiden, 1972), pp. 322–324.

137. *Jewish Symbols in the Greco-Roman Period* (Princeton, N.J., 1954), 4:28.

138. On the older attitudes to interpreter, text, and God, see Idel, "Infinities of Torah in Kabbalah," pp. 141–144; and Fishbane, *Biblical Interpretation in Ancient Israel* (Oxford, 1985), pp. 108–109, 245, where the author perceptively demonstrates the retreat of the

ancient Jewish exegetes from "inquiry of God" to inquiry of the Torah. The medieval texts quoted below evince an opposite direction; after a long period, the Torah was perceived as an indispensable intermediary between God and interpreter, divine inspiration becoming an indispensable prerequisite for mystical interpretation. Compare to D. Weiss-Halivni's description of the Midrash as representing "distance from God" or "a substitute for direct intervention, through either revelation or prophecy," in his *Midrash, Mishnah and Gemara* (Cambridge, Mass., and London, 1986), p. 16. The possibility of understanding the term *prophet* (as applied to certain twelfth- and thirteenth-century Ashkenazic authors) as referring to "an ability to derive exegetically the esoteric divine will" was proposed by Ivan Marcus, *Piety and Society* (Leiden, 1981), p. 163 n. 59. I leave aside the important parallel to the medieval phenomena discussed below, found in Qumran-inspired exegeses, as its influence on later rabbinic or Kabbalistic literature was negligible; see Naftali Wieder, *The Judean Scrolls and Karaism* (London, 1962), pp. 62–67. On ancient Christian views of pneumatic interpretation, see David E. Aune, *Prophecy in Early Christianity and the Ancient Mediterranean World* (Grand Rapids, Mich., 1983), pp. 339–346; E. E. Elli, *Prophecy and Hermeneutic in Early Christianity* (Grand Rapids, Mich., 1978); Colette Estin, "Saint Jerome, de la traduction inspirée à la traduction relativiste," *Revue Biblique* 88 (1981): 199–215.

139. In his *Commentary on the Epistle of Paul to the Romans*, Book 4, *Patrologia Latina*, vol. 178 c. 939C. On this phenomenon, see Phillip Alphandery, "La Glossolalie dans la prophetisme médiéval Latin, "*Revue d'histoire des religions* 52 (1931): 419.

140. Cf. Marjorie Reeves, *The Influence of Prophecy in the Later Middle Ages* (Oxford, 1969), p. 13 (compare also p. 474); Bernard McGinn, *Apocalyptic Spirituality* (New York, Ramsey, and Toronto, 1979), pp. 99–102.

141. On Joachim's "Intelligentia Spiritualis," see Reeves, ibid., pp. 16–17, 71–72, and Bernard McGinn, *The Calabrian Abbot: Joachim of Fiore in the History of Western Thought* (New York and London, 1985), pp. 125–138; and compare similar stands in Christian medieval movements; cf. James S. Preus, "Theological Legitimation for Innovation in the Middle Ages," *Viator* 3 (1972): 20.

142. See Joachim's observation that he may witness the reign of the Antichrist; cf. Reeves, ibid., p. 13.

143. See n. 158 below.

144. See Idel, "Types of Redemptive Activities," pp. 275–278.

145. Aaron Z. Aescoly, *Jewish Messianic Movements* (in Hebrew) (Jerusalem, 1956), pp. 365–405.

146. See David Tamar, "Ha-Ari and he-Raḥu [Vital] as Messiah ben Joseph" (in Hebrew), in *Studies in the History of the Jewish People* (Jerusalem, 1972), pp. 115–123.

147. Idel, "Abraham Abulafia," p. 230.

148. See Idel, "Music and Prophetic Kabbalah," pp. 163–169. Compare Steiner's statement: "the musical sounds . . . are beginning to hold a place in literate society once firmly held by the word." See George Steiner, "The Retreat of the Word," in *Language and Silence* (New York, 1977), p. 30.

149. Idel, "Abraham Abulafia," pp. 255–260.

150. On Abulafia's notion of primary letters, see Idel, "Abraham Abulafia," pp. 143–144. On

his monadic perception of letters, its sources and influences, see Idel, "Perceptions of Kabbalah," sec. IV.

151. Barthes's description of the shift from classical language into modern poetical language may indeed be viewed as a tendency toward a more "primitive" and magical perception of the nature of language. Abulafia's atomization of the text anticipates the process of destruction of classical language as it was proposed by Barthes, but in a more extreme way: the language turns not into separate words but into letters. Cf. Roland Barthes, *Le Degré zéro et l'écriture* (Paris, 1964), pp. 45–46: "La poésie moderne détruisait les rapports du langage et ramenant le discours à des stations de mots." Highly instructive is his remark on p. 46: "Il n'y a pas d'humanisme poétique de la modernité: ce discours debout est un discours plein de terreur, c'est-à-dire qu'il met l'homme en liaison non pas avec les autres hommes, mais avec les images les plus inhumaines de la nature; le ciel, l'enfer, le sacré." Compare Abulafia's warning that the process of letter combination may be disturbed by demonic apparitions, which are in his view pure imaginary conceits (M. Idel, "Was Abraham Abulafia Influenced by Catharism?" [in Hebrew], *'Iyyun* 30 [1981]: 138 n. 30).

152. Compare also the interesting diagnosis of Allen Tate on the symbolists' view of language: ". . . that idolatrous dissolution of language from the grammar of a possible world, which results from the belief that language itself can be reality, or by incantation can create a reality" ("The Angelic Imagination," in *The Man of Letters in the Modern World* [New York, 1955], p. 117). See also the fascinating essay of Steiner, "The Retreat of the Word," pp. 12–35; and, from another perspective, Jacques Derrida, *L'Écriture et la différence* (Paris, 1967), pp. 23–24.

153. The author is an anonymous late thirteenth-century Kabbalist, whose ecstatic experiences are described in his *Sefer Sha'arey Ẓedek*, from which I quote here Scholem's translation in *Major Trends*, pp. 149–150. On this passage, see also my discussion in n. 6 above.

154. On Abulafia's positive attitude toward Hebrew as a domain of contemplation of the natural world, see Idel, "Abraham Abulafia," pp. 148–155.

155. See the oneiric practices employed in order to compose Kabbalistic works in Idel, "Inquiries," pp. 201ff.

156. *Manifesto of Surrealism* (1924), trans. R. Seaver and H. R. Lane, in *André Breton Manifestoes of Surrealism* (Ann Arbor, Mich., 1969).

157. Abulafia composed a series of prophetic books, one of which was intended to be read in synagogues as *haftarah*; see Idel, "Abraham Abulafia," pp. 14–15.

158. See Idel, ibid., pp. 395–433; Idel, "Abraham Abulafia and the Pope," pp. 1–17; Idel, "Abulafia on the Jewish Messiah and Jesus," *Immanuel* 11 (1980): 64–80. According to Abulafia, the science of the divine name or names is the true Judaism (cf. Idel, ibid., pp. 13–14), which he apparently attempted to discuss with the pope.

159. For a bibliographical description of the material belonging to this commentary, see Idel, "Abraham Abulafia," pp. 20–21.

160. It is evident that a special spiritual attitude was instrumental in the composition of Abulafia's *Commentary on the Pentateuch*. He acknowledges two reasons for his divulgence of the secrets of the Torah in his commentary: (1) a divine reason, that is, the immediacy of the eschaton, which allows the dissemination of secrets; and (2) a "human" reason, that he was the only Kabbalist in his period! (cf. his introduction to the commentary, MS Parma 141, fol. 1a) The first reason must be connected with the revelation of the date for the

beginning of the messianic era; compare Abulafia's acknowledgment that God revealed himself to him, and that he revealed his secret to him and announced to him the time of the end of the Dispersion and of the beginning of the Salvation: cf. the epistle, written during the same period that he composed his *Commentary on the Pentateuch* and printed by Jellinek, *Auswahl*, p. 18, amended according to manuscripts. Therefore, the divine reason is closely connected to a revelatory experience, which apparently prompted the writing of the *Commentary*.

161. Compare also a passage written by one of Abulafia's disciples, the anonymous author of *Sefer Sha'arey Ẓedek*, who deals in an ambiguous manner with the relationship between the understanding of the secrets of the Torah, the *Mele'khet ha-Torah*, presumably the labor involved in the understanding of the Torah, and the emergence of the "new spirit" (*ruaḥ ḥadashah*) or the spirit of the living God. Cf. British Library, MS Or. 10809 (Olim, Gaster 954), fol. 21b–22a. Compare also the passage from Gikatilla's *Sha'ar ha-Nikkud*, quoted in Idel, "Infinities of Torah in Kabbalah," p. 148; see also the view of John Cassien, discussed by Henri de Lubac, *L'Écriture dans la tradition* (Aubier and Montaigne, 1966), pp. 281–282.

162. Idel, "Abraham Abulafia," pp. 228–232.

163. See MS New York, JTS 1805, fol. 6a; this text will be analyzed in detail in a future study on the relationship between philosophy and Kabbalah as it is expressed in the differentiation between *intellectus acquisitus* and *intellectus propheticus*.

164. On the significance of the terms "prophetic holy intellect" or *intellectus acquisitus*, see the Avicenian theory of prophecy analyzed by Fazlur Rahman, *Prophecy in Islam* (London, 1958), pp. 14–20.

165. See the citation from *Sefer Sha'arey Ẓedek*, cited above, n. 161.

166. On this book, see M. Idel, "The Attitude to Christianity in *Sefer ha-Meshiv*," *Immanuel* 12 (1981): 77–95; Idel, "Inquiries," pp. 185–266, and Scholem's paper, cited in n. 178 below.

167. MS Oxford, Bodleiana 1597, fol. 38a–39b; on the problems related to this passage, see Idel, "Inquiries," pp. 194–195, 240–241. The preceding quotation is an interesting example of a peculiar type of drawing-down theurgy, tainted with magical implications.

168. In Hebrew: *Malbush*, that is, the garment every spiritual entity has to wear when it descends to the nether worlds in order to reveal itself to men.

169. Elijahu was considered in most Kabbalistic sources to be an angel, and therefore, according to the doctrine of *Sefer ha-Meshiv*, he must use a garment when he descends into our world.

170. These are two famous "mystical" sages of ancient Judaism; the former is the principal hero of the *Zohar*, which was spuriously attributed to him. The second was the author of an Aramaic translation of the Bible. It is possible that the author of *Sefer ha-Meshiv* mentions them together because both of them "interpreted" the Torah, the *Zohar* being a homiletic commentary on the Bible and several scrolls.

171. With the exception of R. Yehudah ha-Nasi, the compiler of the Mishnah, all the names are those of ancient tanaitic masters who were heroes of ancient Jewish mystical literature.

172. Fasting for forty days is mentioned in the Heikhalot literature in connection with the attempt to acquire mystical knowledge; interestingly, fasting was related to prophecy. See, for example, Rudolf Arbesmann, "Fasting and Prophecy in Pagan and Christian Antiq-

uity," *Traditio* 7 (1949): 1–71. Prophecy is mentioned at the end of our quotation from *Sefer ha-Meshiv*. I shall deal with this problem in a detailed study.

173. This number returns in similar contexts: see Idel, "Inquiries," pp. 213–215.

174. In Hebrew, *rabbo ve-'alufo*—alluding to angelic guidance.

175. Literally, "his own head."

176. In Hebrew the root "עתק" is used. However, it points to transmission of the sciences from their celestial source to our world by means of copying divine books; see Idel, "Inquiries," p. 261 n. 81.

177. *Megillah*, 17v; see E. E. Urbach, "When Did Prophecy Cease?" (in Hebrew), *Tarbiẓ* 17 (1945–46): 1–11; N. N. Glatzer, "A Study of the Talmudic Interpretation of Prophecy," *Review of Religion* 10 (1945): 115–137; B. J. Bamberger, "Revelations of Torah after Sinai," *HUCA* 16 (1941): 97–113.

178. See Gershom Scholem, "The Revelations Attributed to the Maggid (Angelic Messenger) of Rabbi Joseph Taytaczack" (in Hebrew), *Sefunot* 11 (1971–78): 73–74.

179. Idel, "Inquiries," pp. 201–206.

180. (Mohilev, 1812), fol. 19a, and Idel, "Inquiries," p. 240 n. 289.

181. *Ketem Paz* (Djerba, 1940), vol. 1, fol. 152b:
"כן שהיה מקובל הן לא רוח ה' נוססה בו"

182. *Shalshelet ha-Kabbalah* (Jerusalem, 1962), p. 110:
"שרוח הקודש נושבת בדברי רש"י להיות מפרש כפי הקבלה האותיות כל תורה שבכתב ושבע"פ"

183. *Zohar Ḥai* II, fol. 17d:
שבכל מקום שרש"י אומר פשוטו של מקרא כוונתו כשיהיה לך התפשטות הגשמיות ותהיה נפשט מכל עניני חומר, תשיג הפשטות של המקרא מופשט מכל רעיון בסודות נעלמות.

184. The text is based upon an obvious pun on the root *P-Sh-T*, which signifies both "plain" and "strip" or "divest." Compare also the discussion of R. Simḥah Bunim of Przysucha, who recommended to his disciple that he accept as his teacher a person who would be able to explain to him the plain meaning (*peshat*) of half a page of the *Zohar*. The student understood this recommendation as connected with R. Menaḥem of Lonzano's view that the *Zohar* can be understood only by those who have achieved a state of divestment of corporeality—*hitpashtut*—another occurrence of the root *PShT;* cf. Chap. III, n. 160.

185. Note the plural form: "בסודות נעלמות"

186. See also Idel, "Perceptions of Kabbalah," sec. I.

187. On this figure, see Roland Goetschel, "Kabbale et Apocalyptique dans le Sefer ha-Mefo'ar de Salomon Molkho," in *Proceedings of the Eighth World Congress of Jewish Studies: Division C* (Jerusalem, 1982), pp. 87–92, and the discussions of Rivka Schatz and Yoram Jacobson in their respective articles in *Da'at* 11 (1983): 53–89.

188. Idel, "Shelomo Molkho as Magician," pp. 204–205, where the quotation that follows in the text is printed for the first time. The Hebrew version seems deficient in several instances, its general meaning being nevertheless clear and corroborated, at least in part, by other texts connected with Molkho. See above, Chap. V, sec. II.

189. On the view of his Christian contemporary, Luther, that the understanding of Scripture depends upon the Holy Spirit and cannot be known before the revelation of the spirit, cf. J. S. Preus, *From Shadow to Promise* (Cambridge, Mass., 1969), p. 148.

190. The terms *academy* here and *Holy Academy* below stand for the "celestial academy," namely, the collectivity of the souls of the righteous, angels, Messiah, and God himself, who study Torah in the next world. The phrase "celestial academy," in relation to revealing secrets from above, occurs several times in the introduction to *Sefer ha-Kaneh*, which influenced Molkho's visions. See A. Z. Aeshkoli, "Notes on the History of Messianic Movements" (in Hebrew), *Sinai* 12 (1943): 84–89, and see also Idel, "Inquiries," p. 237. It is pertinent to remark that both *Sefer ha-Kaneh* and *Sefer ha-Peliah* were written as partial revelations from above. For our discussion, the latter work is important for at least two reasons: (1) that it is a commentary on the first chapters of Genesis and therefore fits within the peculiar genre of interpretations dealt with here—pneumatic exegesis; and (2) that it has been profoundly influenced by Abulafian Kabbalah.

191. On instruction from heaven, see Twersky, *Rabad of Posquières*, pp. 296–297.

192. Compare a testimony in the same vein written by a Kabbalist at the end of the sixteenth century; he compares Molkho's ignorance and visionary experiences with those of Jeanne d'Arc; printed in Idel, "Shelomo Molkho as Magician," pp. 202–203.

193. *Sha'arey Kedushah* III, 3, p. 97.

194. See Idel, "Inquiries," p. 241.

195. Ibid., p. 242.

196. II, 2, immediately before the above-mentioned passage on prophecy and the secrets of Torah.

197. *'Eẓ ha-Da'at Tov*, on Prov. 5, (ed. Jerusalem, 1982), vol. II, fol. 91a:
כאשר יהי' מקור נשמתו העליונה מבורכת משפע עליון רוחני, אז יתפשט וימשך כח נבואיי בנשמתו אשר למטה בעה"ז ויבין וישכיל רזי תורה... כי כפי הברכה הנתוספת למעלה במקור נשמתו כך יהיה בו כח להבין ולהתחכם ברזי תורה בבחינת רוח הקדש.

198. See Joseph G. Weiss, "*Via Passiva* in Early Ḥasidism," *JJS* 9 (1960): 137–155; Schatz-Uffenheimer, *Quietistic Elements*, p. 117.

199. Salomon Maimon, *An Autobiography*, trans. J. Clark Murray (London, Montreal, and Boston, 1888), pp. 164–165. See also Weiss, *Via Passiva*, p. 151.

200. Maimon, *Autobiography*, p. 165, and compare also p. 168; Weiss, "*Via Passiva*," pp. 151–152.

201. Maimon, *Autobiography*, pp. 165–166. This passage was analyzed by Weiss, "*Via Passiva*," pp. 140–141.

202. Maimon, *Autobiography*, p. 167.

203. *No'am Elimelekh*, per. *Terumah*, fol. 47d.

204. Cf. the translation of Green, *Tormented Master*, pp. 200–201; see also his "The *Ẓaddik* as *Axis Mundi* in Later Judaism," *Journal of the American Academy of Religion* 45 (1977): 341. Cf. also above, n. 64. The passage from R. Naḥman seems to be a mystical interpretation of the medieval statement that words that come from the heart, that is, sincere words, enter the heart of one who hears them.

205. I should like to mention here some major works whose manner of composition is obscure. First, the *Zohar* is a large homiletic commentary on the Bible; see the discussion by Matt, *Zohar*, pp. 27–30, who elaborates upon the hypothesis that the *Zohar* was composed through automatic writing. R. Moses de Leon, the Kabbalist viewed by modern scholarship as the author of the *Zohar*, was in contact with the Kabbalistic group from which

Abulafia's prophetic Kabbalah stemmed. Second, the Kabbalistic work of R. Joseph Karo, *Maggid Meisharim*, is a collection of homilies, arranged by later editors, following the order of the biblical pericopes. They were pronounced as the result of a kind of *oratio infusa*, and deal with the interpretation of biblical verses. Cf. Werblowsky, *Karo*, pp. 36–37, 257–286; Idel, "Inquiries," pp. 224–226; and see also R. Moses Ḥayyim Luzzato's confessions that he composed lengthy commentaries upon various texts inspired, or even dictated, by his Maggid. Cf. *R. Moshe Ḥayyim Luzzato and His Contemporaries: A Collection of Epistles and Documents* (in Hebrew), ed. S. Ginzburg (Tel Aviv, 1937), p. 31.

206. On the perception of the Torah as the intellectual world, see Idel, "Abraham Abulafia," pp. 167–172. The discussion that follows is a short survey of some texts analyzed there in detail.

207. See H. A. Wolfson, *Philo* (Cambridge, Mass., 1947), 1:258 n. 42.

208. M. Friedlander, *Essays on the Writings of Abraham ibn Ezra* (London, 1877), Hebrew Appendix, p. 4.

209. *Sha'ar ha-Shamayim*, long version, I, 7, MS Vatican 335, fol. 20b–21a; short version in *Kerem Ḥemed*, vol. 4 (1839), p. 7.

210. See Scholem, *The Kabbalah of Sefer ha-Temunah* (in Hebrew) (Jerusalem, 1969), pp. 238, 243.

211. Idel, "Abraham Abulafia," pp. 168–169.

212. See especially *Sitrey Torah*, MS Paris, BN 774, fol. 137b, printed and analyzed, together with other pertinent material; Idel, "Abraham Abulafia," pp. 169–170.

213. On the peculiar version of *'Avot* used by Abulafia, see Charles Taylor, *Sayings of the Jewish Fathers* (Cambridge, 1897), pp. 60, 69.

214. See *Mafteaḥ ha-Sefirot*, MS Milano-Ambrosiana 53, fol. 164b:

"וכולה בך וכלך בה"

The entire context was printed and analyzed in Idel, "Abraham Abulafia," pp. 194–196. See also below, near n. 223.

215. See Henri Corbin, *Creative Imagination in the Sufism of Ibn Arabi* (London, 1970), pp. 211–212, 227–228.

216. Idel, "The Concept of the Torah," pp. 23–84.

217. Ibid., pp. 43–46.

218. Idel, "Infinities of Torah in Kabbalah," pp. 147–148, and see also below, near n. 222.

219. Idel, "The Concept of the Torah," pp. 62-84. At times the Torah is described as identical only with the seven lower Sefirot; in both versions, the Sefirot, whether seven or ten, are explicitly envisaged as the divine anthropos.

220. See, for example, Moshe Ḥallamish, "On the Origin of a Dictum in the Kabbalistic Literature, 'Whoever blows does so from his Inner Essence'" (in Hebrew), *Bar Ilan Annual* 13 (1976): 211–223: Tishby, *The Wisdom of the Zohar*, 2:3ff., 69ff.

221. See the lengthy article by Isaiah Tishby, "Kudsha Berikh Hu, Orayyta and Israel, All [the Three] Are One—The Source of the Dictum in R. Moshe Ḥayyim Luzzato's Commentary on Idra Rabba" (in Hebrew), *Kiryat Sefer* 50 (1975): 480–492, 668–674; Berakha Sack, "More on the Metamorphosis of the Dictum: Kudsha Berikh Hu, Orayyta and Israel, All [the Three] Are One" (in Hebrew), *Kiryat Sefer* 57 (1982): 179–184.

222. See Pachter, "The Concept of Devekut," pp. 178, 189; Sack, "More on the Metamorphosis," pp. 180–181.

223. *Degel Maḥaneh Ephraim*, p. 284:

”האדם כשהוא צדיק הוא מקורב אל התורה והתורה בו והוא בה“

224. See n. 214 above.

225. Ibid., p. 175:

כי האדם הוא הקב"ה בחינת שם הוי"ה ב"ה במילוי מ"ה מספר אדם ואורייתא היא ברמ"ח מצות עשה ושס"ה מצות ל"ת... וכשאדם עוסק בתורה לשמה לשמור ולעשות אזי מקריב כל אבריו לשורשם מהיכן שנמשכו ונתהוו היינו אל התורה ונעשה כל אבר שלו מרכבה למצותה פרטי המתייחסת לאותו אבר ונעשה הוא והתורה אחד ביחוד ואחדות גמור כמו יחוד איש ואשה.

On the author's recurring use of this formula, see Tishby, "Kudsha Berikh Hu," pp. 482–484. Compare also to the view of R. Ḥayyim of Volozhin in his preface to R. Elijah of Vilna's *Commentary on Sifra' de-Zeni'uta:*

”כל העוסק בתורה... הוא הדבוק בו ית"ש כי קב"ה ואורייתא חד.“

226. On this view, see above, Chap. VIII, sec. III.

227. *Likkutey Torah* (Bnai Berak, 1983), fol. 36a-b:

שאם אדם מקדש עצמו בכל פרטי אבריו ונתדבק בתורה בדביקות רוחא ברוחא ונעשה בעצמו תורת האדם, שאדם עצמו נעשה תורה, תורת ה' תמימה—אשר אין בה מום—משיבת נפש לשורשה וניתקן שורשה במקור העליון.

Compare with R. Leib Sarah's statement; cf. Buber, *Tales of the Ḥasidim: Early Masters*, p. 169

228. This is the phrase for mystical communion recurring in the *Zohar*.

229. II Sam. 24:19. Interestingly, the words following the quoted phrase are two divine names, "Lord God." This may be an allusion to the transition from the Torah of man to a divine status, as implied by the peculiar interpretation of the verse in Psalm 19. See n. 230 below.

230. Psalm 19:8. For the interpretation of this verse as referring to the return of the soul to her source, here into Godhead, see Idel, "Types of Redemptive Activities," pp. 264–265 n. 46.

231. *Likkutey Torah*, fol. 14d–15a:

”כמו שהקדוש ברוך הוא א"ס כך התורה א"ס וכך עבודת ישראל א"ס.“

Compare also his father's discussion of a related question, which does not mention the identification of man with Torah: R. Menaḥem Naḥum of Chernobyl, *Me'or 'Eynaim*, peris. *Teẓaveh*, fol. 117a–118a.

232. Chap. 4. I used an anonymous English translation printed in 1973. Compare Abraham Abulafia's *Sefer Mafteaḥ ha-Sefirot*, MS Milano-Ambrosiana 53, fol. 171a, translated and discussed in Idel, *The Mystical Experience in Abraham Abulafia*, Chap. IV.

233. The author explicitly mentions the identification of knower, knowledge, and known in the same chapter (4), as it appears in Maimonides.

234. *Likkutey 'Amarim*, Chap. 5.

235. Ibid.

236. Ibid.

237. On the emanation, or descent, of Torah into the world in a clearly Neoplatonic vein, see Chap. 4.

238. See Paul Ricoeur, *Hermeneutics and the Human Sciences*, ed. and trans. John B. Thompson (Cambridge, London, and Paris, 1982), p. 147.

239. Ibid., p. 146: "The book divides the act of writing and the act of reading into two sides, between which there is no communication."

240. Ibid., p. 147.

241. Ibid., pp. 146–147.

242. Idel, "The Concept of the Torah," pp. 58–75; Idel, "Infinities of Torah in Kabbalah," pp. 144–145, and above, Chap. VIII, sec. II.

243. *Sefer Ẓeror ha-Ḥayyim*, MS Leiden 24, fol. 198a:

"ויברא אלהי' את האדם בצלמו זהו התורה שהיא צל הש"י."

See also Idel, "The Concept of the Torah," p. 67.

244. Gen. 1:27. On Torah as the matrix of man, see Idel, ibid., pp. 58–59.

245. Compare R. Meir ibn Gabbay's view of the Torah, as described in Idel, "The Magic and Theurgical Interpretation," pp. 46–49.

246. Ricoeur, *Hermeneutics*, p. 139. Compare R. Naḥman of Bratslav's view that union with God is, mutatis mutandis, union of the mystic's Torah with that of God. Interestingly, this union is acquired by expansion of the act of knowledge. See Arthur Green, "Ḥassidism, Discovery and Retreat," in *The Other Side of God*, ed. Peter Berger (New York, 1981), pp. 120-121.

247. Quoted in *Degel Maḥaneh Ephraim*, p. 98:

"וכמו ששמעתי מאא"ז זלל"ה שספר הזוהר יש לו בכל יום פ' אחר"

Compare this highly reliable testimony to a related sentence adduced in the name of the Besht; R. Eliezer Ẓevi Safrin cites his father, reporting that:

"כבל יום ויום לומדים במתיבתא דרקיעא זהר הקרוש בפירוש חדש"

"In each and every day, the Zohar is studied in the celestial academy, according to a novel interpretation" (introduction to *Zohar Ḥai*, vol. 1, unnumbered, first folio). It is possible that the name of the collection of zoharic material printed under the title of *Zohar Ḥadash*—the new *Zohar*—may have influenced the emergence of the new interpretations of the *Zohar*, as formulated by R. Isaac Safrin.

248. Ibid., preface, fol. 3a:

"כתב האר"י זלה"ה בע"ח שבכל רגע ורגע משתנים מאמרי זהר הקרוש"

On the Lurianic source of this view, see next footnote.

249. R. Ḥayyim Vital, *'Eẓ Ḥayyim* I, I, 5, fol. 15a; quoted with slight changes in R. Eliezer Ẓevi Safrin's preface to *Zohar Ḥai*, fol. 1b:

שבכל שעה ושעה משתנים העולמות ואין שעה זו דומה לשעה זו ומי שמסתכל בענין הילוך המזלות וכוכבים ושינוי מצבן ומעמדן ואיך ברגע אחר הם באופן אחר והנולד בו יקרה לו מאורעות שונות מהנולד ברגע שקדם לזה. ומזה יסתכל ויבין בעולמות העליונים שאין להם קץ ומספר . . . ובזה תבין איך משתנה מעמד ומצב העולמות, שהם הלבושים של א"ס לכמה שינויין בכל עת ורגע וכפי השינויין ההם כך נשתנו בחי' המאמרים של ס"ה [ספר הזהר] דברי אלהים חיים.

The continuous process of theosophical and cosmic change is a characteristic of Lurianic Kabbalah: see Tishby, *The Doctrine of Evil*, pp. 18–19. See also the unique impact of each prayer, which causes the emergence of novel influxes; cf. Vital, *Peri 'Eẓ Ḥayyim* (Tel Aviv, 1966), pp. 31–32.

250. See Idel, "The Magical and Neoplatonic Interpretations," pp. 201–202. As we know, Vital was deeply interested in astronomy, and even composed astronomical and astrol-

ogical treatises; see his *Sefer ha-Tekhunah* (Jerusalem, 1866) and Bernard Goldstein, "The Hebrew Astronomical Tradition: New Sources," *Isis* 72 (1981): 245, 248.

CHAPTER 10

1. Scholem, *Les Origines de la Kabbale*, pp.420–425.
2. Scholem, "New Document," pp. 143–144, 151.
3. On Maimonides' restructuring of ancient Jewish esotericism, see Idel, *"Sitre 'Arayot* in Maimonides' Thought," in *Maimonides and Philosophy*, ed. S. Pines and Y. Yovel (Dordrecht, Boston, and Lancaster, 1986), 79–91, and Idel, "Maimonides and Kabbalah."
4. R. Isaac the Blind wrote a letter to Naḥmanides and R. Jonah Gerondi on Kabbalistic matters; R. 'Azriel of Gerona composed an opusculum sent to Burgos; Naḥmanides was addressed by a student of a presumably Castilian Kabbalist named R. Joseph ibn Mazaḥ; and so on.
5. See above, Chap. I, n. 3.
6. On this entire question, see more details in Idel, "Maimonides and Kabbalah."
7. See R. Isaac's statement in *Sanhedrin* 21b.
8. See Abraham Abulafia's "Ve-Zot li-Yihudah," Jellinek, *Auswahl*, p. 15: "כי הקבלה הזאת הנעלמת מהמון הרבנים"
9. Cf. Scholem, *Les Origines de la Kabbale*, p. 216.
10. "Ve-Zot li-Yihudah," Jellinek, *Auswahl*, p. 17. Abulafia himself asserts that his works are the more explicit: *Mevo'arim*.
11. See above, Chap. IX, sec. 1.
12. Chap. VI, sec. IV.
13. See ibid.
14. Ibid., n. 388.
15. For a totally different view, see Scholem, *Major Trends*, p. 327, who proposes a three-phase sequence of popularization of Kabbalah, Lurianism—Sabbatianism—Ḥasidism, as part of his attempt to link Ḥasidism to the two preceding mystical stages. He does not mention Cordoverean treatises, the most important attempt to disseminate Kabbalistic views; see also n. 29 below. For an extreme elaboration upon Scholem's view, overemphasizing the importance of the Lurianic "Musar" literature, see Joseph Dan, *Jewish Mysticism and Jewish Ethics* (Seattle and London, 1986), pp. 76–103.
16. Notwithstanding this assessment, it is highly reasonable to assume that, in addition to the written or exoteric Kabbalah, there were Kabbalistic matters in the sixteenth century that were not committed to writing, owing to their esoteric nature.
17. Idel, "Particularism and Universalism in Kabbalah: 1480–1650," par. II (forthcoming).
18. On these issues, see in detail Idel, "Kabbalah and Ancient Philosophy in R. Isaac and Yehudah Abravanel" (in Hebrew), in *The Philosophy of Leone Ebreo*, ed. M. Dorman and Z. Levi (Tel Aviv, 1985), pp. 73–112.
19. See *Opera* (Basel, 1572) 1:108.
20. See n. 17 above.
21. See Joseph R. Hacker, "On the Intellectual Character and Self-Perception of Spanish Jewry

in the Late Fifteenth Century" (in Hebrew), *Sefunot* n.s. 2 (17), ed. J. Hacker (Jerusalem, 1983), pp. 52–56.

22. Cf. Salomon Schechter, "Notes sur Messer David Leon," *REJ* 24 (1892): 121.
23. See Tishby, *Studies*, pp. 79–130.
24. Ibid., pp. 127–130.
25. See Idel, "Major Currents in Italian Kabbalah," in *Italia Judaica*, ed. J. Sermonetta and S. Simonsohn (Rome, 1986), vol. 2.
26. It is extremely interesting that the first to print Kabbalistic material were the Christian Kabbalists—Pico, Reuchlin, Egidio da Viterbo, and so on—who preceded the first printing of Jewish Kabbalah. See Idel, "Particularism and Universalism in Kabbalah: 1480–1650" (forthcoming).
27. See Gershom Scholem, "A Document by the Disciples of Isaac Luria" (in Hebrew), *Ẓion* 5 (1940): 133–160.
28. See Joseph Avivi, "The Writings of Rabbi Isaac Luria in Italy before 1620" (in Hebrew), *'Aley Sefer* 11 (1984): 91–130.
29. See the opinion of Scholem, *Sabbatai Ṣevi*, pp. 68–80. The nature of Scholem's proofs for his views on the spread of Lurianic Kabbalah cannot be discussed here in detail, but will be the subject of a future study.
30. These nevertheless appear in Scholem's discussion of the influence of mythical Lurianism, which opened the way to messianism; see ibid., p. 68. Nothing was stranger to them than a mythical messianism, which Scholem would implicitly have us believe to have been spread by their writings.
31. See Joseph Dan, "The Concept of Evil and Demonology in R. Manasseh ben Israel's book *Nishmat Ḥayyim*" (in Hebrew), in *Studies in Aggadah and Jewish Folklore*, ed. I. Ben-Ami and J. Dan (Jerusalem, 1983), pp. 263–264; Idel, "Major Trends in Italian Kabbalah"; Idel, "Kabbalah, Platonism and *Prisca Theologia*—The Case of R. Menasseh ben Israel" (forthcoming).
32. The nature and extent of messianism in Lurianism is a matter that still needs to be analyzed in detail
33. Scholem, *Sabbatai Ṣevi*, p. 67: "Wherever Lurianism came, it produced messianic tensions"!
34. See Liebes, "The Messiah of the *Zohar*," passim.
35. Scholem, *Sabbatai Ṣevi*, pp. 44–50.
36. See Idel, "The Interdiction to Study Kabbalah before the Age of Forty" (in Hebrew), *AJSreview* 5 (1980): 14–15.
37. See Menaḥem Z. Kadari, *The Medieval Heritage of Modern Hebrew Usage* (in Hebrew) (Tel Aviv, 1970), pp. 57–144.
38. On their theories, see Scholem, *Les Origines de la Kabbale*, pp. 327–385.
39. Chap. I, nn. 30, 37.
40. Gnostic rituals retain some allegorized forms of Jewish elements, as evinced by the *Gospel of Phillipos*. The ritual of union between the soul and the supernal entities in the bridal chamber is conspicuously based upon the sexual perception of the Holy of Holies; see Idel, "Métaphores et pratiques sexuelles," esp. pp. 339–340 nn. 34–35.
41. Scholem, *Jewish Gnosticism*, p. 10.
42. Ibid., pp. 9–13.
43. Although not of their magic aspects, which are largely anomian. Time and again Christian

Kabbalists refer to Kabbalah as a sort of magic, even a superior magic. See Frances A. Yates, *Giordano Bruno and the Hermetic Tradition* (Chicago and London, 1964), pp. 87–106.

44. See Charles Schmitt, "Perennial Philosophy from Agostino Stenco to Leibniz," *Journal of the History of Ideas* 27 (1966): 505–532; "Prisca theologia e philosophia perennis: Due temi del rinascimento italiano e la loro fortuna," *Il pensiero italiano del rinascimento e il tempo nostro* (Florence, 1970): 211–236.

45. It may well be that in antiquity, as in the period of the Renaissance, among the most active agents of the transition of Jewish esotericism to alien culture were the apostates, who served as cultural bridges, thereby enriching some non-Jewish theosophies by providing easily acceptable pieces of esoteric thought.

46. See above, Chaps. VII and VIII, passim.

47. See Chaim Wirszubski, *A Christian Kabbalist Reads the Law* (in Hebrew) (Jerusalem, 1977), p. 30.

48. See Chap. IX, n. 55.

49. As I have noted above, a similar phenomenon occurred also among Jewish speculative Kabbalists, although not to the same extent.

50. See above, Chap. I, n. 60.

51. See above, Chap. IX, nn. 59, 70, and Joseph L. Blau, *The Christian Interpretation of the Cabala in the Renaissance* (New York, 1944), pp. 8, 12, 32, 57.

52. Chaim Wirszubski, *Three Studies in Christian Kabbalah* (in Hebrew) (Jerusalem, 1975), pp. 26–27.

53. H. P. Blavatsky, *Isis Unveiled* (Pasadena, Calif., 1972), p. xxiv.

54. See, for example, Ernst Müller, *History of Jewish Mysticism* (New York, 1946); Ben-Zion Bokser, *The Jewish Mystical Traditions* (New York, 1981); Alfonso M. di Nola, *Cabbala e mistica giudaica* (Rome, 1984).

55. See, for example, Scholem, *Major Trends*, p. 327.

56. Ibid., pp. 326–334.

57. See, for example, Scholem's proposal to identify the legendary R. Adam Ba'al Shem with R. Heshel Zoref, a Sabbatian Kabbalist, in connection with his attempt to find Sabbatian sources for Ḥasidism (ibid., pp. 331–333); this proposal was shown to be baseless by Chone Shmeruk, *Yiddish Literature in Poland* (in Hebrew) (Jerusalem, 1981), pp. 119–146, and n. 70 below.

58. See Yehuda Liebes, "Shabbetai Zevi's Attitude toward His Own Conversion" (in Hebrew), *Sefunot* n.s. 2 (17), ed. J. Hacker (Jerusalem, 1983), pp. 290–293.

59. Ibid., pp. 286–290; I want to elaborate upon this issue elsewhere.

60. See, for example, the works of R. Samson of Ostropol or of R. Nathan Shapira of Cracow; cf. Scholem, *Sabbatai Ṣevi*, pp. 80–95; Yehudah Liebes, "Mysticism and Reality—Toward a Portrait of the Martyr and Kabbalist R. Samson Ostropoler" (in Hebrew), *Tarbiẓ* 52 (1983): 83–103.

61. See, for example, *Sefer ha-Peliah, Sefer ha-Temunah.*

62. Scholem, *Major Trends*, pp. 19–20.

63. Ibid., pp. 248–250; Joseph Dan, "The Historical Perceptions of the Late Professor Gershom Scholem" (in Hebrew), *Ẓion* 47 (1982): 169.

64. And as such, like the Italian Jews, he was practically uninterested in the "catastrophe" of

Spanish Jewry as a paramount event. See Idel, "Particularism and Universalism in Kabbalah: 1480–1650."

65. See Jacob Katz, "On the Question of the Connection between Sabbatianism, the Enlightenment and the Reform" (in Hebrew), in *Studies in Jewish Religious and Intellectual History Presented to Alexander Altmann*, ed. S. Stein and R. Loewe (University, Ala., 1979), pp. 83–100.
66. Sec. III.
67. P. 327.
68. Ibid., pp. 331–333.
69. Ibid., p. 333.
70. See n. 57 above and Mondshine's introduction to *Shiveḥey ha-Besht*, pp. 58–65.
71. *CCCH*, pp. 157–158.
72. See Mondshine, ibid., p. 62. Scholem himself seems to have silently abandoned his linkage between the contents of *Sefer ha-Ẓoref* and the Besht, in his article, "The Sabbatian Movement in Poland" (in Hebrew), in *Beit Israel in Poland* (Jerusalem, 1954) 2:52.
73. See Peter Schäfer, *Rivalität Zwischen Engeln und Menschen* (Berlin and New York, 1975); Idel, "The Concept of the Torah," pp. 24–32.
74. Idel, ibid., pp. 25–29.
75. See the introduction to *Shimmushey Torah*, printed as *Ma'ayan Hokhmah* in Jellinek, *BHM* 1, pp. 58–59; Schäfer, *Rivalität*, pp. 131–135.
76. Theurgical Kabbalah may be fruitfully compared to some types of Tibetan Yoga, as described by Govinda, where the importance of the concentrated energy is also paramount; see L. A. Govinda, *Foundations of Tibetan Mysticism* (London, 1973), pp. 173ff. and above, Chap. V, sec. IV.
77. Idel, "Inquiries," pp. 220–222.
78. Compare Schatz-Uffenheimer, *Quietistic Elements*, passim.
79. Scholem, *Jewish Gnosticism*, pp. 20–30.
80. D. Blumenthal, *Understanding Jewish Mysticism* (New York, 1978), 1:154–157, 159.
81. Compare ibid., p. 154, where he limits the influence of Jewish ritual to the universe-maintenance role, viewing even what I called soft theurgy as a zoharic or Kabbalistic "heresy" (p. 156), being "very strange" to the "traditional rabbinic Jew" (p. 155). This is true from the perspective of modern scholarship's understanding of the nature of rabbinism. Compare Jellinek's remark on Franck's view above, Chap. I, n. 73.
82. Compare above, Chap. VIII, secs. I–II. The "making God" view is, in my opinion, the strongest theurgical conception, unsurpassed even by the Lurianic theurgy. Compare Blumenthal, ibid., p. 157.
83. Compare the similar distinction between two types of religion in Paul Tillich, *A History of Christian Thought* (New York, 1968), p. 467, where he proposes two main possibilities: the principle of identity—that is, essentially, mysticism—and the principle of estrangement, for which I have substituted here the principle of polarity.
84. Idel, "The Magical and Neoplatonic Interpretations," pp. 195–215.
85. See above, Chap. VII, sec. III and n. 114.
86. See above, Chap. IX, n. 250.
87. See Idel, "The Magical and Neoplatonic Interpretations," pp. 203–204.
88. See Idel, "Inquiries" and "Particularism and Universalism in Kabbalah: 1480–1650."

89. On this figure, see G. Scholem, "On the Legend of Rabbi Joseph Della Reina" (in Hebrew), in *Studies in Jewish Religious and Intellectual History*, pp. 101–108; Idel, "Inquiries," pp. 226–232, 244–250.

90. See Joseph Dan, "The Story of Rabbi Joseph de la Reina" (in Hebrew), *Safed Volume*, ed. I. Ben-Zvi and M. Benayahu (Jerusalem, 1962), 1:311–326; Mikhal Oron, "Waiting for Salvation—History and Literature in the Metamorphosis of the Legend of R. Joseph della Reina" (in Hebrew), *Between History and Literature* (Tel Aviv, 1983), pp. 79–90.

91. Harold Fisch, "The Pact with the Devil," *Yale Review* 69 (1980): 520–532.

92. R. Israel of Ruzhin, *Knesset Israel* (Warsaw, 1906), fol. 12a:

מרן הקדוש סיפר מעשה הבעש"ט זלה"ה כי פ"א [פעם אחת] הי' ענין פקוח נפש גדול שהיה איזה בן יחיד וטוב מאד וכו'. וצוה לעשות נר של שעוה ונסע ליער ודבק את הנר לאילן ועוד איזה ענינים ויחד יחודים וכו' ופעל ישועה בעזהי"ת. ואח"כ היה מעשה כזו אצל זקינו המגיד הק' ועשה ג"כ כנ"ל ואמר: היחודים והכוונת (!) שכיוון הבעש"ט איני יודע, רק אעשה על סמך הכוונה שכיון הבעש"ט ונתקבל ג"כ. ואח"כ הי' מעשה כזו אצל הה"ק ר' משה ליב מסאסוב ז"ל ואמר אני אין לנו כח אפילו לעשות כך, רק אספר המעשה להשי"ת יעזור וכן הי' בעזהי"ת.

Another version of this legend was told by S. Y. Agnon to Scholem, *Major Trends*, pp. 349–350. However, the gist of Agnon's version as well as Scholem's interpretation differs from the above and from the interpretation proposed here. See also Elie Wiesel, *Célébration ḥassidique* (Paris, 1972), p. 172; Geoffrey Hartmann, *The Fate of Reading and Other Essays* (Chicago and London, 1974), pp. 273–274; and n. 96 below.

93. In Agnon's version, as transmitted by Scholem, the nature of this need is rather vague, as is its magical implication; in Wiesel's version, it is the necessity to save the Jewish people from an imminent catastrophe.

94. I presume that the candle is a substitute for the soul of the son, according to the verse: "The spirit of man is the candle of God" (Prov. 20:27). The tree presumably stands for the tree of souls, while the link between the candle and the tree is accordingly an act of sympathetic magic, intended to strenghten the affinity between the son and his family. On the "tree of souls" in Kabbalah, see Scholem, *Elements*, pp. 219, 221–222. It should be noticed that our version does not mention the lighting of the candle, as in Agnon's story, where the fire in the woods is hardly understandable. It may well be that the motif of the fire is the result of a misunderstanding of the role of the candle in our version.

95. On the decline of the importance of Lurianic kavvanot in Ḥasidism, see Idel, "Perceptions of Kabbalah," par. III.

96. In the Hebrew version of R. Israel of Ruzhin, the word להשי"ת may be a mistake, as noted by Mendel Piekarz, *Studies in Braslav Ḥasidism* (in Hebrew) (Jerusalem, 1972), p. 103, the correct version being והשי"ת, namely, "and [then] God helps." However, even if this correction is acceptable, the common interpretation that the storytelling is mainly directed toward man, thereby causing a certain result through the help of God, is not self-evident. Even according to the proposed correction, God may be the principal aim of the narration, preserving the theurgical nature of this activity.

97. On the important religious role of storytelling in Ḥasidism, see Piekarz, ibid., pp. 83–113, esp. pp. 102–103, where our story is referred to.

98. Marthe Robert, *As Lonely as Franz Kafka* (New York and London, 1982), p. 119; Ritchie Robertson, *Kafka: Judaism, Politics, and Literature* (Oxford, 1985), p. 126.

99. As has been recently suggested by Robertson, ibid., p. 126.

100. See Chap. IX above.

Sources

'Avodat ha-Kodesh. R. Meir ibn Gabbay's classic exposition of theosophical Kabbalah (Jerusalem, 1963).

Bahir or *Sefer ha-Bahir*. Includes important annotations and a commentary on the *Bahir*, entitled *'Or ha-Ganuz*, ed. Reuven Margaliot (Jerusalem, 1978).

Commentary on the Pentateuch. R. Menaḥem Recanati (Jerusalem, 1961).

Degel Maḥaneh Ephraim. R. Moses Ḥayyim Ephraim of Sudylkov's homiletic commentary on the Pentateuch (Jerusalem, 1963).

Dudaim ba-Sadeh. R. Reuven ha-Levi Hurwitz's nineteenth-century homiletic commentary on the Pentateuch (Lemberg, 1859).

'Eẓ Ḥayyim. R. Ḥayyim Vital's most important version of Lurianic theosophy (Warsaw, 1891).

Ginnat 'Egoz. R. Joseph Gikatilla's treatise on linguistic Kabbalah (Hanau, 1615).

Heikhal ha-Berakhah. R. Isaac Yehudah Yeḥiel Safrin of Komarno's commentary on the Pentateuch (Lernberg, 1869, five volumes).

Kitvey ha-Ramban. A collection of Naḥmanides' speculative treatises compiled by H. D. Chavel (Jerusalem, 1964, two volumes). Includes also spurious works, for example, the *Commentary on the Song of Songs* by R. 'Ezra of Gerona and the anonymous epistle on sexual union.

Ma'arèkhet ha-'Elohut. An anonymous classic of early fourteenth-century Kabbalah (Mantua, 1558).

Maggid Devarav le-Ya'akov. A collection of teachings by R. Dov Baer of Mezherich, ed. Rivka Schatz-Uffenheimer (Jerusalem, 1976).

Ma'or Va-Shemesh. R. Yehudah Kuriat's collection of Kabbalistic treatises (Livorno, 1799).

Me'irat 'Eynaim. R. Isaac ben Samuel of Acre's commentary on the Pentateuch, ed. Amos Goldreich (Jerusalem, 1981).

Ha-Nefesh ha-Ḥakhamah. R. Moses de Leon's work on Kabbalistic psychology and eschatology (Basel, 1608).

'Or ha-'Emet. A collection of the mystical teachings of R. Dov Baer of Mezherich (Benei Berak, 1967).

Pardes Rimmonim. R. Moses Cordovero's summa of Kabbalah (Jerusalem, 1962).

Sha'arey Kedushah. R. Ḥayyim Vital's exposition of the path to mystical experiences (Benei Berak edition, 1973).

Sha'arey 'Orah. R. Joseph Gikatilla's classic explanation of the designations of the ten Sefirot, ed. Joseph ben Shelomo (Jerusalem, 1970, two volumes).

Shekel ha-Kodesh. R. Moses de Leon, ed. A. W. Greenup (London, 1911).

Tashak. R. Joseph of Hamadan's *Sefer Tashaq*, ed. Jeremy Zwelling (Ph.D. diss., Brandeis University, 1974).

Ha-Temunah or *Sefer ha-Temunah*. An important, anonymous Kabbalistic interpretation of the significance of the Hebrew alphabet (Lemberg, 1892).

The Nag Hammadi Library. Ed. James M. Robinson (San Francisco, Calif., 1977).

Tola'at Ya'akov. R. Meir ibn Gabbay (Jerusalem, 1967).

Yeẓirah or *Sefer Yeẓirah*. An ancient classic of mystical cosmological and cosmogonical speculations, attributed to Abraham or to R. 'Akiva (edition of Jerusalem, 1965). Includes several important commentaries, among which is that of R. Joseph ben Shalom Ashkenazi, attributed in print to Rabad.

Zohar. The most important corpus of Jewish mysticism; Reuven Margaliot's edition, which consists of five volumes: three on the Pentateuch, one containing *Tikkuney Zohar* and one entitled *Zohar Ḥadash* (Jerusalem, 1978).

Zohar Ḥai. A commentary on the *Zohar* by R. Isaac Yehudah Yeḥiel Safrin of Komarno (Lemberg, 1869, five volumes).

Index of Manuscripts (by order of reference)

Index of Sources

MYSTICAL

NON-JEWISH

GNOSTIC

CHRISTIAN

OTHER NON-JEWISH

Index of Persons

General Index

Temple Israel

Minneapolis, Minnesota

IN MEMORY OF FATHER
SIDNEY RIVKIN
BY
JAMES & MARGARET R. HUNEGS